22만 6천 편입합격생의 선택

김영편입 영어

논리

워크북 **2** 단계

22만 6천 편입합격생의 선택

김영편입 영어
논리

워크북 **2**단계

PREFACE

당신이 탑을 높이 쌓고 있다고 상상해 보시길 바랍니다. 무턱대고 탑을 쌓다보면 탑은 얼마 안 되어 금방 무너져 버릴 것입니다. "무엇이 잘못되었을까요?" 탑을 받치는 아랫부분이 넓고 튼튼했어야 했는데, 그러지 못해서 탑을 위로 높이 쌓아 올릴 수 없었던 것입니다.

지금 이 책을 보는 편입 수험생의 경우도 마찬가지입니다. 목표는 저 위에 있어서 실력을 쌓으려고 하는데, 자신의 실력이 어느 정도인지, 내가 무엇을 잘하고 무엇을 못하는지 알지 못한 채 무턱대고 책상에 앉아 공부만 한다면, 우리가 상상해봤던 탑처럼, 금방 무너져 버려 중도하차해 버리고 싶은 마음이 들 수도 있습니다.

그래서 공부는 탑을 쌓는 마음으로 해야 합니다. 탑을 쌓을 때처럼 기초 실력이 탄탄하다면, 그 실력을 바탕으로 더 높이 목표에 도달할 수 있을 것입니다.

바로 이것이 "워크북 2단계"가 나오게 된 이유입니다. "기출 2단계"에서 어려운 기출문제를 풀면서 고급 문제를 내 것으로 소화했다면, "워크북 2단계"에서는 이미 학습한 기출문제의 출제 포인트를 기출문제를 토대로 출제한 예상문제로 다시 한 번 숙지하고 반복학습을 해서 실력을 한층 더 강화하는 데 목표를 두었습니다.

"김영편입 워크북 시리즈"는 "김영편입 기출 시리즈"와 동일한 구성으로 단계별 학습이 가능하도록 만든 책입니다. 따라서 "기출 2단계"를 풀고 나서 "기출문제 해설집"으로 바로 넘어가도 좋지만, "기출문제 해설집"으로 가기에는 실력이 아직 부족하다면, "기출 2단계"와 동일한 난이도의 "워크북 2단계"로 실력을 보강한 다음 "기출문제 해설집"을 학습하시기 바랍니다.

"워크북 2단계"는 편입시험의 대표 유형인 문법, 논리, 독해의 3종으로 구성되어 있습니다. 문법과 논리의 경우, 기출 1단계와 워크북 1단계에서 핵심 이론을 학습하고 이론을 문제에 적용하는 연습을 했다면, 워크북 2단계에서는 기출 2단계와 마찬가지로 다양한 유형의 문제를 학습하여 응용력을 심화시킬 수 있도록 했습니다. 그리고 독해의 경우, 기출 1단계와 워크북 1단계에서 유형별 학습을 하는 데 초점을 맞췄다면, 워크북 2단계에서는 기출 2단계와 마찬가지로 분야별 학습을 하는 데 중점을 두어 다양한 주제의 지문으로 실전 문제풀이 능력을 향상시킬 수 있도록 구성했습니다.

문제는 많이 풀수록 나의 실력이 됩니다. '스스로 학습할 수 있도록 제작된 책'이라는 워크북(workbook)의 사전적 의미처럼, "워크북 2단계"를 통해 어떤 어려운 문제라도 자신 있게 풀어낼 수 있는 능력을 만들 수 있기를 기원합니다.

김영편입 컨텐츠평가연구소

HOW TO STUDY

출제자의 관점으로 문제를 바라보자!

한번쯤은 출제자의 입장이 되어 볼 필요가 있습니다. '이 문제에서는 무엇을 물어볼까?', '여기쯤에 함정을 파놓으면 어떨까?' 이렇게 출제자의 관점에서 문제를 바라보면, 모든 문제가 완전히 새롭게 보일 수 있습니다.

문제의 난이도를 몸으로 익혀보자!

강물의 깊이를 알면 더 빠르고 안전하게 건널 수 있듯이, 문제의 난이도가 어느 정도인지 파악하게 되면, 문제를 더 노련하게 접근해 풀 수 있습니다. 그리고 난이도를 몸으로 익힐 수 있는 지름길은 없습니다. 다양한 난이도의 문제를 가능한 많이 풀어보는 것이 유일한 방법입니다.

제한시간을 설정하자!

실전에 대비할 수 있는 가장 좋은 방법은 실전과 똑같은 환경에서 훈련하는 것입니다. 문제를 풀 때는 반드시 제한시간을 설정하여 학습하시길 바랍니다. 실전에서와 같은 압박감과 긴장감을 조성하기에 가장 좋은 방법입니다.

오답에서 배우자!

편입시험은 정답만 기억하면 되는 OX 퀴즈가 아닙니다. 문제를 풀고 난 후엔 맞힌 문제보다 틀린 문제에 주목해야 합니다. 어째서 정답을 맞히지 못했는지 일련의 사고 과정을 면밀히 되짚어봐야만 틀린 문제를 다시 틀리지 않을 수 있습니다.

문법, 논리, 독해는 원래 한 몸이다!

본 시리즈는 문법, 논리, 독해라는 세 가지 영역을 나눠서 각각을 한 권의 책으로 구성했지만, 영역 구분에 지나치게 신경 쓰며 학습하는 것은 좋지 않습니다. 오히려 독해문제에서 중요 어휘와 문법구문을 정리하는 방식처럼 서로 영역을 통합해 학습하게 되면 더 큰 시너지를 일으킬 수 있습니다.

실전 문제 TEST

- 최신 기출문제를 토대로 출제된 중·고급 난이도의 예상문제를 총 32회분, 800문제를 수록하였습니다.

- 다양한 유형과 난이도의 문제를 골고루 섞어 실제 시험에 매우 가깝게 구성하여 실전 대비 학습을 할 수 있도록 구성했습니다.

정답과 해설 ANSWERS & TRANSLATION

- 시험에 자주 출제되는 5가지 논리 문제 유형을 바탕으로 논리적으로 빈칸을 추론하는 방법을 상세히 수록하였습니다.

- 논리 문제는 보기의 모든 어휘가 시험에 출제될 수 있습니다. 따라서 문제에 제시된 주요 어휘들의 뜻을 상세히 수록하여 어휘와 논리완성에 대비할 수 있도록 했습니다.

CONTENTS

해설편

 교재의 내용에 오류가 있나요?

www.**kimyoung**.co.kr ➡ 온라인 서점 ➡ 정오표 게시판

정오표에 반영되지 않은 새로운 오류가 있을 때에는 교재 오류신고 게시판에 글을 남겨주세요. 정성껏 답변해 드리겠습니다.

22만 6천 편입합격생의 선택

**김영편입 영어
논리**

워크북 **2**단계

TEST

01-32

❚ Choose the one that best completes the sentence(s).

▶ ▶ ▶ ANSWERS P.214

01   He worked for six months at that company before they discovered he was _____: he had lied on his application about his credentials and education.

① agonizing   ② conceding
③ dithering   ④ dissembling

02   Genetic evidence has been used to _____ Darwin's theory of evolution, proving its veracity beyond a reasonable doubt.

① corroborate   ② capitulate
③ enunciate   ④ abrogate

03   That is effective especially for violent offenders and sex offenders who might _____ their way into working with children.

① parry   ② wheedle
③ dither   ④ tether

04   Normally, transparency is hard to measure, since it tends to improve only gradually, but the shift this time is unusually _____.

① fickle   ② stark
③ vague   ④ rash

05   Initially, doctors thought it could be malignant, but the tumor turned out to be _____.

① benign   ② infectious
③ lethal   ④ fetid

06   The country's economy remains _____, with jobs for high-paid engineers and low-paid baristas but not enough in between.

① lopsided   ② divested
③ bifurcated   ④ decentralized

07   He is still as addicted to _____ as he was two decades ago, and still as obsessed with the notion that everything he touches is unparalleled in its greatness.

① personification   ② foresight
③ hyperbole   ④ euphemism

08   In some cases, it's an argument of etiquette: some say voice mail is _____, while others believe it's rude not to leave one. It's actually neither.

① obnoxious   ② clandestine
③ deferential   ④ salutary

09   Using straightforward terms instead of _____ buzzwords will help you to make your point and will also help you stand out from the crowd.

① ambiguous   ② authentic
③ reliable   ④ downbeat

10   _____ traditional third-person omniscient narration, they preferred to represent characters through their shifting thoughts, memories and sensations.

① Rejuvenating   ② Repudiating
③ Endorsing   ④ Upholding

11   Although sugar was one of the world's most valuable commodities for millennia, modern geology, technology, and food processing have made it cheap and _____.

① ubiquitous   ② abstemious
③ dormant   ④ weighted

12   The biggest disease today is not cancer but the feeling of being unwanted and uncared for by everybody. This _____ toward one's neighbors is the greatest evil.

    ① imposture   ② acrimony

    ③ nonchalance   ④ dysfunction

13   Amid mounting frustration over taxation and banking problems, small but growing numbers of Americans are taking the weighty step of _____ their citizenship.

    ① renouncing   ② affirming

    ③ considering   ④ imbibing

14   Two years after John's bankruptcy, his young daughter fell ill with fever, or typhoid, doubtlessly contracted from the _____ conditions in which the family was living.

    ① well-to-do   ② impoverished

    ③ sanitary   ④ pastoral

15   Dropping into a _____ state allows animals to use their body's energy reserves at a slower rate than they would if they were maintaining themselves at their typical basal metabolic rate.

    ① vigorous   ② robust

    ③ turbulent   ④ torpid

16   Parents are advised to use the opportunity provided by summer vacations to teach their children not to litter, not to disturb others with their _____ games and generally to follow society's rules.

    ① querulous   ② subdued

    ③ lugubrious   ④ raucous

17   When revolutions succeed, they constitute true historical leaps: an immense area of humanity, which up to then lay _____, is suddenly opened to the creative activity of human beings.

① rancid   ② vestal
③ fallow   ④ suave

18   The US government tightened _____ on Cuba. It restricted educational and cultural travel and banned American citizens from visiting 180 hotels and businesses with alleged financial links to the Cuban armed forces.

① verdicts   ② appropriations
③ sanctions   ④ embarkments

19   The newspaper pointed out that the local militants' denial of the bombing attack is a common tactic used to _____ the origins of their attacks and to extend the myth that the bombings are the work of foreign elements.

① inquire   ② excruciate
③ obscure   ④ interpret

20   Unlike the carefully weighed and _____ compositions of Dante, Goethe's writings have always the sense of _____ and enthusiasm.

① inspired — vigor   ② planned — immediacy
③ laborious — endeavor   ④ developed — construction

21   Tullock's insight was that expenditures on lobbying for privileges are costly and that these expenditures, therefore, _____ some of the gains for beneficiaries and cause inefficiency.

① channel   ② dissipate
③ subdue   ④ distend

22   He has changed from a _____ character incognizant of the activities in his surroundings to a person conscious of everything, so enlightened by the new world he is exposed to.

① dainty   ② scintillating
③ stolid   ④ congenial

23   People are _____ with anti-Japan sentiment. But the government should retain its composure. The National Security Council is scheduled to issue Seoul's doctrine today over Tokyo's attempt to distort history and harm Korea's territorial integrity.

① bickering   ② imposing
③ simmering   ④ fighting
⑤ sustaining

24   To say that information technology is transforming business enterprises is simple. But what this transformation will require of companies and top managements is much harder to _____.

① reinforce   ② decipher
③ encode   ④ eschew

25   _____. Don't be a workplace whiner. If your workmates want to wallow in misery, leave them to it and hang out with the happy gang instead. It will lift your mood and make time fly.

① Build relationships   ② Say no to negativity
③ Don't procrastinate   ④ Up the energy factor

▌ Choose the one that best completes the sentence(s).

▶ ▶ ▶ ANSWERS P.218

01 When the little boy lost his toy, his _____ was so great that I, too, became sad.

① deception   ② bliss

③ dejection   ④ animation

02 Researchers whose goal is to prove a theory's validity are likely to view discovery of a(n) _____ as failure.

① anomaly   ② concordance

③ viability   ④ cohesion

03 I pray more people will support this meaningful mission which can surely help _____ the pain of our less fortunate brothers and sisters.

① assay   ② alleviate

③ allude   ④ allure

04 I don't have enough time to read through this book carefully, so I'll just _____ it quickly.

① skim   ② gaze

③ span   ④ flap

05 The use of torture _____ that which most distinguishes us from our enemies: our belief that all people, even our enemies, possess basic human rights.

① entails   ② validates

③ incites   ④ compromises

06   Even though all of the guests at the dinner party were _____, the food was so poorly prepared that no one ate more than a small portion.

① surly   ② invited
③ ravenous   ④ forewarned

07   Although his speech was _____ and delivered on the spur of the moment, it was one of the most sincere and passionate I have ever heard.

① wordy   ② cynical
③ violent   ④ impromptu

08   Although the two men work together very well, they couldn't be more different: Bob is relaxed and _____, whereas Will is tense and silent most of the time.

① anxious   ② calm
③ loquacious   ④ bleary

09   Milton Hershey certainly didn't invent chocolate, but his innovations to the recipe and manufacture turned a luxury for the _____ into an affordable treat for all.

① gourmet   ② majority
③ affluent   ④ frugal

10   We all know that Simon Cowell is not a man to beat around the bush or _____ his words, especially when it comes to contestants on his show.

① cleave   ② mince
③ pierce   ④ sickle

11   Many other states give insurers much more _____ in deciding whom and what they must cover, how much they can charge and even, in some cases, when they must pay claims.

① verve   ② nuisance
③ leeway   ④ indictment

12 La Familia, a cultish bible-thumping drug cartel that forbids its members from consuming drugs and alcohol, is _____ in that it pays the widows of drug violence victims a monthly stipend.

① tractable   ② eccentric

③ philanthropic   ④ impeccable

13 My reflexes are cat-like, I have the eyes of an eagle, and I can run like the wind and jump higher and farther than most men. Calling me beast is a compliment, not a _____.

① confession   ② grapevine

③ bombast   ④ pejorative

14 The head of the local government in Delhi, India's capital, _____ the city to a gas chamber. Schools and many offices were closed as smoke from farmers burning stubble in adjacent states caused air quality to _____.

① adapted — plunge   ② reduced — ameliorate

③ likened — plummet   ④ confronted — ascend

15 The CEO was a master pitchman for Apple's new products, captivating audiences with introductions that seemed _____ but were always meticulously rehearsed.

① in a bind   ② off the cuff

③ on pins and needles   ④ on an even keel

16 The supposed facts and figures are the glossy product of substantial _____ in the academic field, a stealthy aiming at granting the conclusions _____ credence.

① investigation — merited   ② doctrines — clandestine

③ tenets — specious   ④ artistry — ostensible

17 Really successful people often have the ability to completely _____ their mental dispositions. In many fields, it pays to be rigid and _____ at first but then flexible and playful as you get better.

① flip — disciplined   ② juggle — plastic
③ undo — organized   ④ brace — slack

18 Although a few proponents are convinced that hormone supplements can _____ alter the aging process and have advocated their widespread use, the scientific evidence supporting this premise is, for the most part, _____.

① favorably — scanty   ② artificially — warranted
③ expeditely — conclusive   ④ discreetly — reminiscent

19 English writers judge their fellow craftsmen; one they will tell you is pretty good, another they will say is no great shakes, but their _____ for the former seldom reaches fever-heat, and their disesteem for the latter is manifested rather by indifference than by _____.

① affection — panegyric   ② antipathy — innuendo
③ enthusiasm — detraction   ④ idolatry — disinterest

20 Fur coats were a major trend that served as both fashion and function with the _____ Bay Area weather dropping to uncomfortably chilly temperatures at night. Both men and women co-opted fur and faux-fur statement jackets to stay warm while looking _____.

① moderate — innocuous   ② mercurial — chic
③ sizzling — rustic   ④ brisk — pale

21 U.S. negotiators have leverage in negotiating agreements with suppliers such as Brazil and Spain, which are vulnerable to unfair trade actions. These suppliers cannot realistically choose to reject an agreement in favor of countervailing duties and antidumping duties because those duties would be _____.

① prohibitive   ② emulative
③ indiscreet   ④ dulcet

22 Nothing was ever created by two men. There are no good collaborations, whether in music, in art, in poetry, in mathematics, in philosophy. Once the miracle of creation has taken place, the group can build and extend it, but the group never invents anything. The preciousness lies in _____.

① the interaction of art and science
② the high quality of civilizations
③ the individual mind of a man
④ the collective activities of a society

23 I don't mind Obama having his opinions. But the fact that he cannot disagree without distorting the views and condemning the motives of his opponents tells you everything you need to know about him, not to mention the indefensibility of his _____ arguments.

① tenable   ② robust
③ brittle   ④ coherent

24 Walking on eggshells signifies taking great care not to upset someone. It is thought to have originated in politics when diplomats were described as having the remarkable ability to _____, it was as though they were walking on eggshells.

① listen to the voice of rank and file
② elicit potential to solve diplomatic disputes
③ adapt to whatever job they take on
④ tread so lightly around difficult situations

25 Western commentators _____ any form of government other than their pure Western-style democracy, but throughout Asia and Africa, the least successful and often most corrupt administrations are those _____ democracy when their reality demonstrates the very opposite.

① embrace — eschewing   ② disdain — undermining
③ enshrine — touting   ④ demean — proclaiming

❚ Choose the one that best completes the sentence(s). ▶ ▶ ▶ **ANSWERS** P.223

01   Susie and Tom overcame their deep _____ and became friends again.

① rancor   ② comity
③ amity   ④ rapport

02   Employees and representatives agree to keep all such information confidential and not to _____ it to anyone.

① referee   ② arrogate
③ divulge   ④ rectify

03   Inflation has _____ to its lowest level for nearly 40 years, taking even the experts by surprise.

① soared   ② plunged
③ balanced   ④ buckled

04   Since she knew in advance whom she would choose for each role, the so-called "try-outs" for the play were no more than a(n) _____.

① audition   ② travesty
③ mishap   ④ prop

05   There is something wrong in distribution with a world where there is so much _____ while poverty and hunger continue to prevail.

① frugality   ② tribulation
③ pacifism   ④ squandering

06 Those who accumulated wealth tend to be more frugal and live less _____ lifestyles than their peers even though they can afford affluent way of life.

① vigorous   ② opulent

③ incognito   ④ destitute

07 A serious illness doesn't have to _____ your travel plans. With a little advance planning, you can enjoy a safe and satisfying holiday despite physical unfitness.

① antedate   ② endorse

③ propel   ④ sideline

08 The urban roofscape is a little like hell — a lifeless place of bituminous surfaces, violent temperature contrasts, bitter winds, and a(n) _____ to water.

① solution   ② antipathy

③ approach   ④ convergence

09 During imperial times, the Roman Senate was little more than a collection of _____ yes men, intent on preserving their own lives by gratifying the Emperor's every whim.

① flippant   ② reprehensible

③ pedantic   ④ obsequious

10 A state which _____ its men in order that they may be more docile instruments in its hands will find that with small men no great thing can really be accomplished.

① shadows   ② mobilizes

③ courts   ④ balloons

⑤ dwarfs

11 Mr. Fifi Kwetey, Minister of Agriculture, has given the assurance that government would provide the _____ to ignite and link up the value-chain in the production of rice and cassava.

① liability   ② compaction
③ leverage   ④ certification

12 When you feel thankful for things you've received or something that's happened, that's gratitude. It's impossible to feel it _____; others are always responsible, whether they're loved ones, strangers or higher powers.

① en masse   ② en route
③ in moderation   ④ in a vacuum

13 U.S. multinational firms would _____ cash stashed overseas and invest domestically, and it would discourage a flight of capital to offshore destinations, ultimately benefiting workers in America.

① divert   ② repatriate
③ freeze   ④ waive
⑤ allot

14 The system that would allow the city to make fair and objective performance-based layoffs is clearly not yet in place, and also we are _____ that the city will be able to produce one in the next few weeks.

① astonished   ② committed
③ skeptical   ④ adamant

15 Under the Child Protection Act a person can be _____ approved as a foster carer or kinship carer, allowing them to care for a child while their application to be a foster carer or kinship carer is decided.

① presumptuously   ② permanently
③ provisionally   ④ phlegmatically

16 The political system is _____. Whoever you vote for, the same people win, because where power claims to be is not where power is.

    ① on the blink   ② on the house

    ③ on the level   ④ on the ball

17 McGwire admitted _____ what baseball fans have long suspected — that he used performance enhancing drugs before, during and after the 1998 season when he broke Roger Maris' storied single-season record, hitting 70 home runs.

    ① contritely   ② tediously

    ③ infuriately   ④ illicitly

18 However, other environmentalists argue that the Senator's _____ will serve him well at the Department of the Interior, where he'll need to balance protection of the land and species with legitimate development of the country's natural resources.

    ① liberalism   ② character

    ③ centrism   ④ fidelity

19 Performance over time is an important aspect of writing. The written word can remain the same not only over days or months, but from one generation to the next and even over centuries or millennia. In this way it can serve as what has been termed a kind of "_____."

    ① historical remains   ② transpersonal memory

    ③ personal character   ④ written words

20 Alphabets are necessarily incomplete because it is not practical to assign a separate symbol to every possible sound of human speech. Consequently, the same symbol frequently has to _____.

    ① be changed when written

    ② be omitted in final practice

    ③ be translated into different languages

    ④ do duty for two or more sounds

21   Putin and those who make common cause with him repeatedly label so-called enemies as fascists. In Russia, however, basic human rights are frequently ignored, the media are effectively controlled, and _____ and corrupt activities are rampant. Perhaps it would be appropriate to _____ the appellation "fascist" at Putin's Russia.

① nepotism — recant   ② pluralism — backbite
③ cronyism — redirect   ④ legalism — convert

22   When faced with a trade-off between doing and buying, many people opt for the material good. In one sense that's correct: The material good lasts while the experience is _____. But psychologically it's the reverse. We quickly adapt to the material good, but the experience _____ in the memories we cherish.

① passing — vanishes   ② incessant — languishes
③ imperative — persists   ④ fleeting — endures

23   Usually an articulate speaker, as he had given many public addresses over the years, the doctor, however, _____ the keynote speech at the oncology convention. It was clear from their expressions that the audience members were overcome with _____ by the end.

① expatiated — rapture   ② outlined — repulsion
③ lauded — vertigo   ④ flubbed — bewilderment

24   Kurt Cobain felt bored and old. Teenage angst had paid off well, as the line in the Nirvana song "Serve the Servants" put it, but the fame that came with being the frontman of the _____ grunge band that brought punk to the mainstream was taking a toll.

① erstwhile   ② derivative
③ recalcitrant   ④ seminal

25 Spending just the right amount of time caring for grandchildren can keep the mind sharp and lower the risk of developing _____ diseases. The grandmothers who help with child-care one day per week score higher on the IQ tests than the women who spend five or more days a week with their grandkids. This is because feeling overextended _____ the mood of those grandmothers.

① cognitive — dampens   ② mental — ameliorates

③ genetic — overshadows   ④ insidious — enlivens

❚ Choose the one that best completes the sentence(s).   ▶▶▶ **ANSWERS** P.227

01   Before we spend a lot of money on this project, I would like to see _____, rather than theoretical, evidence that it is effective.

① empirical   ② hypothetical

③ cursory   ④ deficient

02   Unlike his calmer, more easy-going colleagues, the senator was _____, ready to quarrel at the slightest provocation.

① whimsical   ② irascible

③ gregarious   ④ ineffectual

03   Made up of immigrants, the population of the United States is far more _____ than that of Japan.

① artificial   ② ingenious

③ heterogeneous   ④ immense

04   Memory-chip makers have been _____ this year caused by a combination of lackluster demand and severe oversupply.

① staggering   ② mushrooming

③ flourishing   ④ germinal

05   Savings can be made by minimizing luxury items, avoiding _____ purchases and curtailing unnecessary spending.

① impulse   ② deliberate

③ stringent   ④ contemplative

06   The public health authorities are combating the claims of _____ who maintain fraudulently that they have cures for many major ailments.

① salesmen   ② pharmacists
③ anthropologist   ④ charlatans

07   Admittedly, the tradition of being _____ in hospitality is now under severe strain from war refugees in countries whose resources are already stretched.

① profuse   ② indiscriminate
③ parsimonious   ④ square

08   The previous group leader encouraged independent thought; unfortunately, the current leader tries to _____ all signs of it.

① suppress   ② elucidate
③ animate   ④ epitomize

09   The article 'Four Ways to Stop Technology Addiction' in the current issue of the magazine is timely. Our gadget-craving society certainly needs this _____ reminder.

① sober   ② somber
③ stolid   ④ sordid

10   The program of _____ imposed by the Prime Minister in order to keep the value of the pound annoyed those who favored a program of government spending.

① laissez faire   ② liberalism
③ austerity   ④ benevolence

11   The passage of time is inherently _____. The shiny promise of youth grows tarnished, and the disappointments mount. The future no longer yawns with infinite possibilities.

① traumatic   ② nostalgic
③ hypocritical   ④ lackadaisical

12 There is a reason why many tell their children fairy tales of heroic princes. Only through early _____ can anyone reach adulthood and believe a monarchy has any place in a modern democratic society.

① indoctrination   ② endorsement

③ secularization   ④ enlightenment

13 This drama depicts the bleak plight of a small army of Portuguese immigrants, _____ eking out an existence in Paris, a bustling metropolis, most of them headquartered in a muddy shantytown in the suburbs.

① naively   ② furtively

③ menially   ④ glossily

14 Protesting students have been dispersed and the prosecution is ready to take legal action with a view to _____ the radical student federation but it will not be easy to remove the root elements of the student struggle.

① dissolving   ② coalescing

③ unfettering   ④ suspending

15 Israel's prime minister, Binyamin Netanyahu, faced a challenge to his leadership after being charged with bribery, fraud and breach of trust in three corruption cases. Mr Netanyahu called the _____ an attempted coup.

① indictment   ② treachery

③ misdeed   ④ demurrer

⑤ clampdown

16 Because the University is committed to free and open inquiry in all matters, it guarantees all members of the University community the broadest possible _____ to speak, write, listen, challenge, and learn.

① latitude   ② discipline

③ rhombus   ④ inception

⑤ retraction

17   On August 16th Lebanon abolished a law that let rapists dodge punishment if they married their victims. Jordan did the same this month, and closed a separate _____ that allowed lighter sentences for "honour killings". Tunisia scrapped its "marry your rapist" law in July.

① loophole   ② atrocity
③ shamble   ④ impunity

18   The Republican presidential candidate cultivates their support by criticising the free trade agreements that have _____ the decline of former strongholds of US manufacturing industry, and brought loss of status, bitterness and despair to the working class.

① deterred   ② precipitated
③ mobilized   ④ subdued
⑤ adulterated

19   South Korea accounts for only 2 percent of camera sales worldwide, but Canon and Nikon say that consumers in the nation are by far the most _____. The number of online reviews, viewers and comments is at least 10 times as high as the number on similar blogs in the United States.

① slovenly   ② arbitrary
③ vivacious   ④ insidious

20   My approach to medication treatments in psychiatry is to be as _____ as possible to use medications as sparingly as possible, ie. at the lowest effective dose. People are constantly _____ by pharmaceutical advertising and this has led to a culture of misinformation as well as exaggerated expectations.

① prodigal — hypnotized   ② recuperative — interrogated
③ esoteric — admonished   ④ parsimonious — bombarded

21 The doorman of the department store would welcome people in, with a caution not to rush. With a thumping heart and starry eyes, they walked briskly, looking at all the beautiful things and not knowing what to buy. Somehow each of them ended up with something at an unbelievable bargain. There was _____ in the air.

① cynicism   ② ataraxia

③ mesmerism   ④ euphoria

22 To say that we live in an age of science is a commonplace, but it is _____. From the point of view of our predecessors, if they could view our society, we should, no doubt, appear to be very scientific, but from the point of view of our successors it is probable that the exact opposite would seem to be the case.

① a paradox as well   ② only partially true

③ all too groundless   ④ equivalent to a whole truth

23 Debilitating as unemployment is, factory work is a _____ improvement to her. It may provide income and a sense of dignity, but these are purchased at an enormous cost. Every day she douses herself in deodorant and scrubs herself raw to _____ the smell of her workplace.

① tangible — circumvent   ② marginal — expunge

③ cardinal — embalm   ④ negligible — camouflage

24 The architects of U.S. foreign policy and strategy are faced with a dilemma regarding how to combat the Islamic State. What is obvious is that a _____ approach to such a threat is likely to create more chaos than _____ the rise of extreme Islam. It is time for a more pragmatic approach to foreign policy.

① doctrinaire — neutralizing   ② utilitarian — forestalling

③ formulated — expediting   ④ makeshift — endorsing

25 Although oncology researchers seek to describe the significance of clinical trial outcomes with scientific rigor, the terminology used to communicate those findings in the peer-reviewed literature sometimes falls short in conveying the impact that a given therapy may have on patients in a real-world scenario. The quest for more precise language is an ongoing struggle, both for oncology specialists and for generalists seeking to _____.

① maintain in-person contact with physicians
② help cancer patients participate in clinical trials
③ translate clinical data into meaningful information
④ integrate an experimental drug into their medical practices

01　Julia _____ the decision for a few years before she finally made up the mind.

① presided over　　　　　② deliberated over

③ counteracted　　　　　④ nullified

02　Forget benchmarking. It only reveals what others do, which rarely is enough to satisfy, much less _____, today's clients.

① gladden　　　　　② disturb

③ flatter　　　　　④ coax

03　The clock striking in *Julius Caesar* is a good example of an _____, as there were no clocks in Caesar's Rome.

① amphibian　　　　　② anachronism

③ apocalypse　　　　　④ apprehension

04　The recently found history book, written in 1880, was tremendously _____, unfairly blaming the South for the Civil War.

① biased　　　　　② objective

③ unfaltering　　　　　④ unfeigned

05　A certain amount of _____ is good, but don't spend so much time trying to understand yourself that you don't have time to actually do something.

① volition　　　　　② introspection

③ inspiration　　　　　④ inspection

06   Just as American producers say it's impossible to predict a smash on Broadway, the global marketplace can be _____.

① burgeoning   ② methodical
③ foreseeable   ④ fickle

07   All I knew was that in my grandmother's house, uttering a negative word about Democrats was like _____ the name of Jesus or disrespecting the memory of the Rev. Martin Luther King Jr.

① chanting   ② blaspheming
③ propagating   ④ endorsing
⑤ manifesting

08   While southern China is relatively wet, the north, home to about half of China's population, is an immense, _____ region that now threatens to become the world's biggest desert.

① desiccated   ② soggy
③ tropical   ④ temperate

09   The scale of the massacre happening in Darfur is very alarming and suggests that the strongest deterrent message must be sent to those who are inclined to _____ the cycle of violence that has shattered the region for long.

① cease   ② bypass
③ countervail   ④ perpetuate

10   The amendments to the Highway Traffic Act will give the court the discretion to incarcerate a person with a history of _____ in the payment of fines when that person has the ability to pay the fine but chooses not to do so.

① defaulting   ② redeeming
③ conniving   ④ oscillating

11 Unlike a lot of common people who believed that adding seasoning helps preserve food, most experts found that many marketed spices were _____ bacteria, moulds and yeasts.

① bereft of   ② teeming with
③ bolstered up by   ④ maimed by

12 Like many other reformers, Alice Paul, author of *the Equal Rights Amendment* introduced in Congress in 1923, received little honor in her lifetime but has gained considerable fame _____.

① anonymously   ② previously
③ odiously   ④ posthumously

13 Some customs travel well; often, however, behavior that is considered the epitome of _____ at home is perceived as impossibly rude or, at least, harmlessly bizarre abroad.

① urbanities   ② eccentricities
③ coarseness   ④ novelties

14 The helium provides lift for the airship to go up, and when the helium is compressed, the craft loses its _____ and can land. Control and propulsion are provided by propeller-engines powered by aviation fuel.

① contractility   ② resilience
③ buoyancy   ④ combustibility

15 People of the Old Stone Age fought a stern battle against a hostile environment. Those who survived were _____ in their early forties. Few lived beyond their fiftieth year.

① discrepant   ② disparate
③ decrepit   ④ robust

16 Modernization has brought with it technology and progress, but it has also given birth to tools that can be used by those who see freedom as a _____ to their power. Freedom is the dog, and Big Brother has the leash.

① route ② menace
③ tribute ④ prey

17 The government has made two moves to shore up our confidence in the immigration system; it has moved to revoke the citizenship of 1,800 people who obtained it _____ and has released a most-wanted list of 30 suspected war criminals.

① fraudulently ② provocatively
③ blamelessly ④ unquestioningly

18 Individuals who have acquired considerable information about the research methods do not necessarily know how to undertake the task of planning their own investigations. The two capacities are far from _____.

① congruous ② dormant
③ incompatible ④ disparate

19 According to the reigning hypothesis, about 4.5 billion years ago, shortly after Earth had _____ into a sphere from its little slub of circumsolar material, another newborn planet, still shaky on its feet, slammed obliquely into Earth with terrifying force.

① flustered ② abridged
③ bungled ④ accreted

20 It's been discovered that a(n) _____ method that is used by many websites to protect users' sensitive data, including passwords, bank accounts, and Social Security numbers, has a significant bug that makes this information _____.

① differentiation — barricaded ② counterfeit — impregnable
③ safeguard — anonymous ④ encryption — vulnerable
⑤ quarantine — concealed

21 Cheaper oil should act like _____ to global growth. A $40 price cut shifts some $1.3 trillion from producers to consumers. The typical American motorist, who spent $3,000 in 2013 at the pumps, might be $800 a year better off — equivalent to a 2% pay rise.

① a cornerstone   ② a threshold
③ a shot of adrenalin   ④ a barometer
⑤ a bird in the hand

22 Our relatives share more than just a physical DNA. We also share a spiritual DNA with the deceased, the thousands and thousands of moments when our father's soul expressed itself in our presence, _____.

① a wearied, languorous feeling creeping over us
② scatterbrained to every minute detail
③ redolent of his love before us
④ showing sullen and truculent response to his soul

23 Toilets, shopping carts, washing machines and other assorted junk have been dumped into the sea to create habitats for marine organisms and the fish that feed upon them. But making reefs from refuse is now _____. Alabama, for example, banned fishermen from sinking vehicles in the Gulf of Mexico in 1996, even when drained of potentially harmful fluids.

① endorsed   ② subscribed to
③ favored   ④ frowned upon
⑤ shored up

24 I've often wondered how the media would respond when eco-apocalypse struck. I pictured the news programmes producing brief, sensational reports, while failing to explain why it was happening or how it might be stopped. Then they would ask their financial correspondents how the disaster affected share prices, before turning to the sport. As you can probably tell, _____ in the industry for which I work.

① I have a very strong affection

② I can see limitless potentials

③ I have an implicit faith

④ I don't have an ocean of faith

⑤ I don't sense the spirit of disbelief

25 Adults often assume that the emotional lives of children are radically different from those of adults, while their thinking is basically the same though less accurate and skillful. In fact, psychologists who have studied children carefully know that _____: children's feelings are much like those of adults, but their ways of reasoning are often very different.

① it is the other way around

② the one is true, but the other is not

③ it can be neither confirmed nor denied

④ both can be understood in the same context

06

❙ Choose the one that best completes the sentence(s).

▶▶▶ ANSWERS P.236

01　While most New York schools were strikebound, classes went on _____ in Ocean Hill.

　　① embarrassed　　　　　　② uninterrupted

　　③ frozen　　　　　　　　　④ unduly

02　During the team's recent seven-game losing streak, the coach was _____ by many local sportswriters.

　　① denounced　　　　　　② enrolled

　　③ vindicate　　　　　　　④ affiliated

03　Torn between loving her parents one minute and hating them the next, Maria was confused by the _____ of her feelings.

　　① conjecture　　　　　　② delusion

　　③ tranquility　　　　　　④ ambivalence

04　As soon as the newspapers carried a _____, an exclusive news, of his connection with the criminals, his friends began to ostracize him.

　　① largesse　　　　　　　② cynosure

　　③ scoop　　　　　　　　④ sleuth

05　Evaluating the impact of advertising is a devilishly tricky business, especially when it involves promoting something as _____ as a corporate or national reputation.

　　① palpable　　　　　　　② subversive

　　③ repercussive　　　　　④ amorphous

06   While many of those companies have been in the e-commerce market for more than a decade, others — especially a few of the larger companies — are _____ whose entry came from recent acquisitions.

    ① faddists   ② connoisseurs

    ③ neophytes   ④ hypocrites

07   The universe is vast and men are but tiny specks on an insignificant planet. But the more we realize our _____ and our impotence in the face of cosmic forces, the more astonishing becomes what human beings have achieved.

    ① cupidity   ② grandeur

    ③ minuteness   ④ significance

08   Cyberspace has not so much of a(n) _____ atmosphere as the government worry, because most Web sites require a person's ID and real-name for the first register and IP addresses can be tracked even when not logged on.

    ① specious   ② anonymous

    ③ serene   ④ cutthroat

09   As if fired by his own words, he took a sort of leap at the ledges of the rock above him, and scaled them with a sudden agility in startling contrast to his general _____.

    ① temperance   ② petulance

    ③ verbosity   ④ lassitude

10   High-tech enables consumers to know exactly where and how their food was produced; shoppers use smartphones to access the information about the exact _____ of each product.

    ① provenance   ② dispensation

    ③ hallmark   ④ inventory

11 Prison reformers in the United States are disturbed by the high rate of _____; the number of men serving second and third terms in prison indicates the failure of the prisons to rehabilitate the inmates.

① penitence   ② self-surrender
③ accomplice   ④ recidivism

12 The individual who fancies he has made his own professional career or the inventor who believes he has the sole right to his invention is ignorant of his debts. Like Bounderby, whom Dickens portrayed in *Hard Times*, he is a monster of _____.

① timidity   ② probity
③ autism   ④ ingratitude

13 Agricultural interest groups prevailed on the state House to weaken the initial version of the bill passed by the Senate. The House measure _____ the penalties against violators of the manure and fertilizer ban so much as to make them effectively meaningless.

① watered down   ② chewed out
③ kept the tab on   ④ pumped up

14 Overall, Dada artworks present an intriguing _____ in that they seek to demystify artwork in the populist sense but nevertheless remain cryptic enough to allow the viewer to interpret works in a variety of ways.

① paradox   ② stereotype
③ dogma   ④ pragmatism

15 The financial rewards of authorship are so small that there is so much eagerness or _____ to win the prizes awarded every year to certain books which not only set an honorable _____ on a career but increase an author's market value.

① scheming — seal   ② hesitating — target
③ concocting — scratch   ④ threatening — cachet
⑤ neglecting — stamp

16 The remarkable fact that many inventions had their birth as toys suggests that people philosophize more freely when they know that their _____ leads to no _____ results.

① persistence — grave   ② consideration — satisfactory
③ speculation — weighty   ④ supposition — trivial

17 Despite the country's dominant ideology of 'one country, one language, one people', the French have long shrugged off a national myth of uniformity and headed for areas where _____.

① provincialism yields to the new centralism
② national traits contribute to national integration
③ other ideologies come to naught in the end
④ regional flavors and customs remain vibrant

18 Just as the measles outbreak in the U.S. shows what can happen when the public gets too complacent about a disease thought to be safely a thing of the past, so might the British public be _____ too soon regarding an even more devastating illness: mad cow disease's human incarnation.

① followed by correct information
② immune to infectious diseases
③ letting down its guard
④ preventing it from spreading

19 Many policies are made by politicians and intellectuals with claims to superior insights. These claims are mostly _____. Every human being knows his own world better than any outsider or expert. Policies must be left to the people who live in the world that is going to be affected by them.

① spurious   ② agnostic
③ congenial   ④ brusque

20 I would certainly sooner live in a monotonous community than in a world of universal war, but I would sooner be dead than live in either of them. My heart is in the world of today, with its varieties and contrasts, its blue and green faces, and my hope is that, through courageous _____, the world of today may be preserved.

① inebriety
② resignation
③ justification
④ magnanimity

21 If the rich really cared about the environment, they'd be taking the bus and living in tents. But that's nonsense. You cannot demand that the wealthy live like monks in order to be environmentally responsible, because that would mean _____ the rewards of capitalism. The rich consume more. That is the nature of rich.

① poising
② cementing
③ repealing
④ catalyzing

22 As always in history, all the elements of the new social system had already developed in the older order which the new one had _____. But while it is important to see how many modern elements existed in the late Middle Ages and how many medieval elements continue to exist in modern society, it blocks any theoretical understanding of the historical process if by emphasizing continuity one tries to _____ the fundamental differences between medieval and modern society.

① supplicated — overlook
② supplanted — accentuate
③ superseded — downplay
④ supervised — endorse

23 History has provided _____. In ancient times, both the Romans in Europe and the Chinese in Asia viewed foreigners as barbarians. In modern times, the German dictator Adolf Hitler argued that the Germans belonged to a superior race whose duty was to destroy "lesser races."

① a cover for genocide and ethnic cleansing
② a rich mythology and many folk tales
③ insights into an increasing variety of policy concerns
④ examples of the destructive effects of ethnocentrism

24 Vacation destinations are unique in that they must try to accommodate a large number of tourists without disturbing the setting to which the tourists are attracted. Places as varied as Yellowstone National Park and the Great Wall of China must contend with this dilemma — allowing as many people as possible to experience the sights without _____.

① the expense incurred of a private tour
② disturbing habitat or desecrating ancient architecture
③ having to worry about where to start or how to get there
④ losing out on all the beauty that surrounds them

25 Even the most gay-friendly societies are rife with discrimination, abuse and hate crimes. Moreover, the remarkable achievements of the past 50 years are no guarantee for the future. History rarely moves in a straight line. There is no reason to think that LGBT liberation will inevitably spread around the world, eventually reaching Saudi Arabia and Brunei. _____, violent homophobic backlashes are possible, even in the most liberal countries. Just last week the Guardian revealed shocking statistics that showed homophobic and transphobic hate crimes have doubled in the UK over the past five years.

① Thus   ② Indeed
③ Otherwise   ④ However
⑤ Instead

01   It is not easy to come across a youth with a vision that is so _____ and incomparable to that of many others who seem to have lost their way.

① knavish   ② stereotyped
③ variable   ④ unprecedented

02   Domestic consumption in Korea remains _____ because people are worried and don't spend.

① amnesiac   ② anemic
③ annihilable   ④ amendable

03   Although he was theoretically an extremely _____ individual, his testimony at the trial revealed that he had been very _____.

① intrepid — prow   ② loyal — hypocritical
③ shrewd — erudite   ④ loathsome — hateful

04   Melodramas, which presented stark oppositions between innocence and criminality, virtue and corruption, good and devil, were popular precisely because they offered the audience a world _____ of _____.

① composed — adversity   ② full — circumstantiality
③ relieved — polarity   ④ devoid — neutrality

05   Kant wrote wisely, "The notion of happiness is so _____ that although every man wishes to attain it, yet he can never convey accurately and distinctly what it is that he really wishes and wills."

① garish   ② nebulous
③ palpable   ④ perfunctory

06   The absence of a functioning government in Libya has meant that the smuggling gangs operate largely _____ as they load increasing numbers of migrants into boats not fit for the crossing.

    ① unmolested   ② encumbered

    ③ unrequited   ④ incapacitated

07   Time talks. It speaks more plainly than words. The message it conveys comes through loud and clear. Because it is manipulated less consciously, it is subject to less _____ than spoken language. It can shout the truth where words lie.

    ① acquisition   ② perversion

    ③ synchronism   ④ hush

08   If you're going to get on your high horse every time I disagree, I don't want to work with you. I respect your years of study and experience, but I can't accept your _____ manner.

    ① complaisant   ② supercilious

    ③ puerile   ④ provident

09   The city has always seemed to be a _____ place. Throughout history, it has made its money from invisible industries such as banking and insurance. It is not a place where people flaunt their talents.

    ① pinched   ② furtive

    ③ wanton   ④ bucolic

10   The Minister of Culture had tried to suppress the novel on grounds of blasphemy, but it ended up by boosting the sales of the book enormously. The writer greatly profited from the _____ on the part of the Government.

    ① piracy   ② imbecility

    ③ acumen   ④ ignominy

11 India's stock market, rocked earlier this year by corruption scandals, has been further _____ by a move to ban selling and buying in the flagship fund of the country's largest mutual fund group.

① writhed   ② roiled
③ hoodwinked   ④ revolved

12 Throughout his career, Reagan's opponents consistently underestimated him, _____ him as a good actor, a _____ who could only read scripts written for him by others.

① eulogizing — deity   ② disregarding — hermit
③ complimenting — puppet   ④ disdaining — simpleton

13 My own conviction is that every leader should have enough _____ to accept, publicly, the responsibility for the mistakes of the subordinates he has himself selected and, _____, to give them credit, publicly, for the triumphs.

① self-sacrifice — otherwise ② bounty — paradoxically
③ humility — likewise   ④ fairness — accordingly

14 A trusted but _____ colleague could improve your creativity. People who are able to understand sarcasm are more creative and better able to solve problems. But to avoid conflict, sarcasm is best used between people who trust each other.

① feverish   ② caustic
③ brazen   ④ quirky

15 We have a whole kingdom where we rule alone, can do what we choose, be it wise or ridiculous, harsh or easy, conventional or odd. But directly we step out of that kingdom our personal liberty of action becomes _____ by other people's liberty.

① loosened   ② satiated
③ qualified   ④ lubricated

16   In order to overcome insomnia, millions of Americans turn to drugs — both over-the-counter drugs and prescription drugs. "No pill will produce normal sleep," says Dr, James Minrad. "You reach no proper levels of sleep through a pill; you're merely _____."

① sedated   ② sober
③ adulterated   ④ somber

17   It is commonly believed that the poor are happier than the rich. They are not. They just bear discomforts and troubles and sorrows more bravely than the rich, because these things are a part of their normal lives. And one more blow means little to the man who have been _____ by many blows.

① dulled   ② demurred
③ stirred   ④ deluded

18   Miike's _____ is evident from the very first scene, an elegantly staged suicide sequence. The director doesn't show the sword enter the man's stomach, the resulting wounds, or any internal organs tumbling out. The suicidal noble just sinks quietly into a smear of blood, viewed coolly from above.

① suspense   ② restraint
③ ribaldry   ④ solecism

19   While first impressions are sometimes altered as we accumulate additional information about a person over a period of time, we can no more _____ the formation and rapid growth of these _____ judgements than we can avoid perceiving a given visual object or hearing a melody.

① accept — inchoate   ② forestall — ultimate
③ prevent — initial   ④ ensconce — succulent

20 Thinking is as unnatural and laborious an activity for human beings as walking on two legs is for monkeys. Since this human _____ to the labour of thought is no less manifest in the public life than it is in private affairs, mankind does not do very much of its historical thinking in easy and prosperous times.

① aversion   ② propriety

③ empathy   ④ fondness

21 The best professors never tell their students what to write. They strive instead to establish an intellectually critical environment _____ to thorough and creative scholarship, because training a student through _____ is never as effective as encouraging a student to develop his faculties independently.

① crucial — autonomy   ② contributive — fulmination

③ baneful — enlightenment   ④ conducive — indoctrination

22 Happy is the man that loves flowers. It is a matter of gratitude that this gift of Providence is the most profusely given. Flowers cannot be _____. The poor can have them as much as the rich. It does not require such an education to love and appreciate them as it would to admire a picture of Turner's or a statue of Michelangelo's.

① monopolized   ② touted

③ jettisoned   ④ festooned

23 The importance of the relationship between art and society will be denied, or at least minimized, by those who see art as a completely _____ or playful activity, those who consider it the manifestation of the most radical individuality, and those who regard it as an absolutely _____ sphere which escapes all conditioning.

① quintessential — pragmatic   ② purposeful — uncontrolled

③ ideological — restricted   ④ gratuitous — autonomous

24 Reprisals and threats of reprisals against converts were common. Members of religious minorities were subject to violence and harassment, and police at times refused to prevent such actions or to charge persons who committed them, which _____ for acts of violence against religious minorities.

① offered a clue to the final punishment
② restricted their activity within narrow limits
③ introduced a bill protecting the minorities
④ contributed to a climate of impunity

25 I have always wondered at the passion people have to meet the celebrated. The prestige you acquire by being able to tell your friends that you know famous men proves only that you are yourself of small account. The celebrated develop a technique to deal with the persons they come across. They show the world a mask, often an impressive one, but take care to conceal their real selves. They play the part that is expected from them and with practice learn to play it very well, but you are stupid if you think that this public performance of theirs _____.

① corresponds with the man within
② is not real
③ is not inborn but acquired
④ is of much importance

01   At the end of the service, the general's wife gave an impromptu _____, which truly venerated his memory and profoundly moved many attendees.

① valediction   ② convocation
③ homage   ④ epiphany

02   Accepting illegal campaign contributions is a serious, and all too common, _____ of ethics among candidates for public office.

① breach   ② plot
③ obedience   ④ accolade

03   In fact, more than 90% of infection occurs in the nostril. _____ problems, such as congestion, can lead to ear and respiratory infection.

① Dermal   ② Tactile
③ Feral   ④ Nasal

04   The two young lovers planned a(n) _____ meeting at a deserted island where anyone could not see them.

① adulterous   ② clandestine
③ diurnal   ④ lascivious

05   Please use a coaster or saucer under your glass in order to avoid _____ the wood furniture.

① felling   ② propping
③ polishing   ④ marring

06 When the three universities to which she had applied accepted her, she was in a(n) _____ as to which one she should attend.

① alacrity   ② quandary
③ bachelor   ④ honor student

07 After an adolescence immersed in his father's creed of utilitarianism, Mill realized, to his father's great _____, that its promise of happiness was chimerical.

① euphoria   ② frowziness
③ chagrin   ④ temerity

08 In the nineteenth century, many women writers used _____ because they were afraid of being labeled "unladylike" and didn't want their real names to be known.

① pseudonyms   ② terminology
③ metaphor   ④ quills

09 Addiction psychiatrists have long recognized the false _____ between the physiological and psychological aspects of addiction, and treat both simultaneously.

① dichotomy   ② diagnosis
③ prognosis   ④ logomachy

10 Even though he is a leading expert on international relations, Andrew Ashworth is a _____ Oxford Professor whose lectures on even the interesting international current affairs cause students to nod and drift away.

① lackluster   ② self-confident
③ conspicuous   ④ meticulous

11 He was generally recognized as a great writer in his own country, but almost unknown outside it. Now he is suddenly discovered and taken up by Western literary establishments after so many years _____.

① in the wilderness ② of efforts by his translators
③ of public negligence ④ in the limelight

12 "Provincial" has always been a term of _____ especially in a highly centralized country such as Britain or France, where a Londoner or Parisian tends to believe that nothing interesting can possibly happen in a small town such as Sheffield or Lyon.

① esteem ② affection
③ nostalgia ④ contempt

13 My mournful cries for help echoed across the cliffs of the canyon's peak. At that moment my family was still probably all asleep in their nice warm beds, unaware that I was even missing, let alone _____ to where I was and the danger that was taking my life away.

① oblivious ② belligerent
③ captious ④ heedful

14 This is not a naked parable and the fact that we get an impression of a real village and real people gives the sense of grim terror. The fictional form thus justifies itself by making _____ and forceful what would otherwise have to be given _____ and undramatically.

① rosy — graphically ② pensive — epically
③ laconic — verbosely ④ vivid — prosaically

15 People tend to think, quite erroneously, that beauty has little to do with the efficient functioning of a city. But very often the biggest headache for the police is likely to coincide with the ugliest part of a city. In the urban design, what is of a great social significance is, among other things, _____ of the streets being designed.

① the economy　　　　　　　② the security
③ the aesthetics　　　　　　 ④ the logistics

16 The most common form of diversion is reading. In that vast and varied field, millions find their mental comfort. But reading suffers from one serious defect: books are too nearly _____ the ordinary daily round of the brainworker to give that element of change essential to real life.

① indifferent to　　　　　　 ② different from
③ wholly in the power of　　 ④ akin to

17 In ordinary life, perceptual recognition claims are open to challenge and should be treated with _____ when they transcend what can reasonably be expected to be known on their basis or when they themselves are based on _____ sense modalities.

① optimism — immature　　　② cynicism — certified
③ pragmatism — routine　　　④ skepticism — untried

18 Time is valuable; people are busy. We all know we need to _____ the news because we're living through a period of historic change, with events that have enormous impact that we can't escape and can't ignore.

① look askance at　　　　　　② stay on top of
③ turn a deaf ear to　　　　　④ put a new face on

19 The inaccuracy of the testimony of eyewitnesses is well known in legal psychology, but the _____ is not _____ — it follows naturally from the particular recoding that the witness used, and the particular recoding he used depends upon his whole life history.

① falsehood — exhaustive

② credibility — mandatory

③ distortion — random

④ confidentiality — persuasive

20 He handled the little girl's innocence like a piece of _____ china. He strove to preserve all that is good — faith, love, beauty and kindness — for as long as he could. He was careful not to break this beautiful realm of childlike wonder, for doing so would _____ out the purity and curiosity which is the essence of childhood.

① antique — sort

② glazed — spell

③ delicate — snuff

④ chipped — scrape

21 If children were let alone, they could be no more afraid in the dark than in broad sunshine; they would as much welcome the one for sleep as the other to play in. There should be _____ to them by any story of more danger or terrible things in the one than the other.

① more limitation put

② no illumination added

③ more attention given

④ no distinction made

22 When we talk about intelligence, we do not mean the ability to get a good score on a certain kind of test, or even the ability to do well in school; these are at best only indicators of something larger, deeper, and far more important. By intelligence we mean a style of life, a way of behaving in various situations. The true test of intelligence is not how much we know how to do, but _____.

① how much more we can do than others

② what we should do to improve ourselves

③ how much we can do without efforts

④ how we behave when we don't know what to do

23   Even though tea contains some jitter-causing caffeine, there are certainly times when it seems to calm rather than _____ the nerves. Turning to the ritual of making and drinking tea has become an almost conditioned response during times of stress. But the calming effects may have nothing to do with chemistry. It is the tea ritual itself, with its associated social aspects, that makes a cup of tea a natural _____.

① toughen — stimulant   ② cushion — sedative
③ jangle — tranquilizer   ④ enervate — panacea

24   In times of deflation, creditors and fixed income receivers tend to gain at the expense of debtors and profit receivers. If prices fall between the time that a creditor lends money and the time it is repaired, then he gets back more purchasing power than he lent. The school teacher who keeps his job and whose pay is not cut, finds that _____.

① his real income has decreased
② his actual income has increased
③ he has less purchasing power
④ his real income has been cut

25   The more I become acquainted with various philosophies, the more I marvel at the power of the human mind to make of them whatever suits its particular motivations. My feeling is that no matter what the dominant philosophy of China had been, the manipulators of public opinion would have _____. I think it is not too hard to present Confucian ideas as paving the way for the teachings of Mao Tse-tung.

① been able to make the dissenters live at their will
② stuck to the very philosophy of their country
③ been able to introduce foreign philosophy
④ been able to engineer consent to their ideology

▌Choose the one that best completes the sentence(s).

▶▶▶ ANSWERS P.251

01   In thinking about cuckoo clocks, one might conjure images of elaborate wood timepieces inside _____ cabins in forests or sleepy chalets on mountainsides.

① bucolic   ② gaudy

③ sumptuous   ④ dilapidated

02   We feel enslaved by conditions that should have no power to bind us, and powerless before forces over which we have been given _____.

① dominion   ② qualm

③ obeisance   ④ patronage

03   Prince Charles can be charming, though royal watchers say that he's also _____, occasionally brusque with his aides and over-serious.

① winsome   ② jocund

③ plucky   ④ cantankerous

04   In George Orwell's famous novel *1984*, "Big Brother" is a(n) _____ political leader, so all-knowing that privacy simply doesn't exist in the world he controls.

① dissident   ② omniscient

③ interim   ④ unctuous

05   Science itself is not only morally neutral, that is, _____ to the value of the ends for which the means are used; it is also totally unable to give any moral direction.

① differential   ② indifferent

③ intertwined   ④ officious

06   Podcasting is a _____ technology that has caused some in the radio business to reconsider some of the established practices and preconceptions about audiences, consumption, production and distribution.

① conventional   ② declining
③ precarious   ④ disruptive

07   Written in an amiable style, the book provides a comprehensive overview of European wines that should prove inviting to both the virtual _____ and the experienced connoisseur.

① novice   ② miser
③ zealot   ④ glutton

08   The artist was famous for making art out of everyday junk he found on the street. His way of seeing were _____ and now many other artists see the whole world as a source of a work of art.

① blunt   ② obdurate
③ protean   ④ contagious

09   We are a long, long way from understanding the complexities of human personality. We don't really know, for example, why from earliest years some individuals seem _____, while others are tossed about by events like the bird in a badminton game.

① corpulent   ② fastidious
③ indomitable   ④ munificent

10   The photos taken by him profoundly impress me. They are breathtaking without _____ the posthumous dignity of the dead. These _____ pictures of aircraft crash scenes are better and deeper than any other analysis.

① upholding — bleak   ② offending — flippant
③ ensuring — luminous   ④ insulting — somber
⑤ harming — methodical

11   What attracted you to your house the moment you saw it? Was it the sunny yard, charming verandah, or original wooden floors? Once you live there, it's natural to focus on what needs improving, but remember to _____ that drew you in, too.

① shrug off the magnets
② dwell on the drawbacks
③ revel in the highlights
④ grope for the hidden blots

12   The Chief of the New York Police Department said his organization was concerned about the increasing number of police officers who were armed while on duty. "Of course the police want to protect themselves, but the reality is that this is _____. Criminals who expect to encounter armed police are more likely themselves to carry arms."

① a sliver lining
② a vicious circle
③ a rule of thumb
④ a pat on the back

13   "If I ever get rich, you shan't have to work any more, mom," said Harry. His mother smiled faintly. She was not hopeful, and thought it probable that before Harry became rich, both she and her husband would be resting from their labor in the village churchyard. But she would not _____ Harry's youthful enthusiasm by the utterance of such a thought.

① uplift
② ignite
③ dampen
④ enliven

14   The protest was about whether the prosecutor performed his role well or woefully inadequately in pursuit of an indictment. Why did he take this course of action? Why didn't he aggressively question Wilson when Wilson presented testimony before the grand jury? Why did he sound eerily _____ when announcing the results?

① like a defense attorney
② biased toward a victim
③ opposed to the jury
④ unlike a suspect
⑤ like a fighter for justice

15 The argument is an interesting one, and one that psychologists have pondered for years. Who is the authentic self — the rude or bigoted person who may come out when we're drunk or enraged or exhausted? Or the person we are the other 99% of time, when _____ allows us to tamp down our unsavory impulses?

① insistency ② sobriety
③ convulsion ④ snit

16 Tanzania's ruling party won 99% of the seats it contested in local elections that were boycotted by the opposition, which accused the government of manipulation. The local poll is a worrying _____ to national elections next year. The government has locked up members of the opposition and journalists.

① prelude ② replica
③ profile ④ attestation
⑤ epitome

17 Democracy only works well with an enlightened electorate free of ingrained _____. As it is, consumerism has drowned people's capacity for independent judgment. As a result, democracy is in _____ not only in the U.S. and Australia but also in Japan and Europe.

① ignorance — cradles ② prejudice — shambles
③ insolence — fetters ④ temperance — shreds

18 A recent proposal to _____ the taxi industry illustrates just how resistant Italy can be to reform. Angry cabbies brought Rome to a halt, blockading the streets. Parliamentarians eventually _____ the most important part of the proposal, which would have enabled the creation of taxi fleets rather than restricting the business to owner-drivers.

① privatize — skipped ② boost — buttressed
③ liberalize — dumped ④ demarcate — reinstated

19 The fungi work by _____ cell walls in Norway spruce — the only wood used to make a violin's top plates — so that sound can move more freely. Less weight means louder and more resonant tones. The fungi also double the _____ function of the wood, taking away too-high, irritating sounds.

① softening — amplifying　　　　② thickening — stifling
③ hardening — buoying　　　　　④ thinning — dampening

20 We should never _____ the influential effect of comparing people with their fellows. An energy company placed monthly hangers on office doors so that employees could compare how much energy each one used — and the process reduced overall usage by 3.5%. Evolutionarily, it is _____ to do what those around us in similar situations have done.

① undermine — fatuous　　　　② overleap — canny
③ underrate — chancy　　　　　④ overblow — impeccable

21 We sometimes misrepresent competition by disguising the impulse to compete as a simple need to survive. Long ago, Bertrand Russell pointed out that what is often meant by "the struggle for life is really the competitive struggle for success. What people fear when they engage in the struggle is not that they will fail to get their breakfast next morning, but that they will fail to _____ their neighbors."

① taunt　　　　　② dismiss
③ outshine　　　　④ spare

22 Cristina Chipurici taught herself to read when she was four years old. As her newfound passion took hold, she devoured every single book in her parents' house. But then something happened. "Once I started primary school and reading became mandatory, I developed a _____ towards the activity, caused by the language teacher we had, and it made me not want to read a book ever again," she says.

① capitulation　　　② penchant
③ repulsion　　　　④ deferment
⑤ relish

23 One of the pleasures or dangers of foreign travel is that you lose your class-consciousness. At home you can never, with the best will in the world, forget it. Habit has rendered your own people as immediately plain and clear as your own language. _____. But in foreign countries your fellows are unreadable. The less obvious products of upbringing escape your notice. The accent, the vocabulary, the inflection of voice, and the gestures, tell you nothing.

① Clothes do not make the man
② A word and a gesture are sufficient
③ Little learning is a dangerous thing
④ Words have wings, and cannot be recalled

24 Colors are created by the various wavelengths of light. When light falls on an object, some of the wavelengths are absorbed by the object. The rest are reflected to our eyes as a particular color. In the air, all the wavelengths are combined into white light. When light passes through a glass prism, it is separated into its different wavelengths, and the multitude of colors that make up white light are revealed. All this talk about wavelengths can be confusing if you think of color as an intrinsic quality of a given object. Objects _____.

① reflect only white light   ② let all light pass through
③ do not, in themselves, contain color   ④ absorb all the wavelengths of light
⑤ can reflect their own particular colors

25 Some people argue against capital punishment because there used to be so much racial prejudice against blacks, and it was mostly blacks who were executed. There is no doubt that capital punishment was used unjustly in many cases, but today racial prejudice is not as great. Capital punishment could be given to all those who deserve such a sentence. Only 17 out of 47 men executed since 1947 were blacks. As a black American, I do not think _____.

① the racial prejudice is more serious than it used to be
② the racial prejudice argument is valid any more
③ the racial prejudice argument is ethical
④ the racial prejudice argument is trivial any more

❚ Choose the one that best completes the sentence(s).

▶▶▶ **ANSWERS** P.256

01 Hamlet's constant _____ often left him immobilized by indecision.

① revenge
② fortitude
③ equivocation
④ catharsis

02 His snobbishness is obvious to all who witness his _____ when he talks to those whom he considers his social inferiors.

① hauteur
② benignity
③ perspicacity
④ epistle

03 The magazine was denied to the country's readers by censors who adjudged the reproduction of the paintings by Egyptian artist Weaam El-Masry to be too _____.

① hermetic
② garish
③ fusty
④ salacious

04 Credit buying is like being drunk — the initial buzz gives you a lift but there is a(n) _____ next day.

① delight
② hangover
③ reinforcement
④ exhortation

05 Greeks are very temperamental and _____. In the cafes, there is a non-stop din as well as yelling out of greetings.

① vociferous
② courteous
③ lethargic
④ puritanical

06 After the police used pepper spray to subdue an out-of-control kid aged eight, his mother said they should have just _____ with him, but I think pepper spray was the minimum force necessary.

① conferred   ② argued

③ reasoned   ④ sided

07 Fuel costs not only take a huge chunk out of an airline's revenue, but they are notoriously _____. From month to month, airlines never know exactly how much fuel is going to cost.

① volatile   ② spurious

③ inexpensive   ④ stagnant

08 While some scientists and inventors are reluctant about reporting an accidental discovery, others openly admit its role; in fact _____ is a major component of scientific discoveries and inventions.

① rapture   ② coinage

③ serendipity   ④ sagacity

09 There was a time when air travel was _____ with luxury: Pan American's first air clippers offered catered meals from Maxim's of Paris, and in the early days of the 747 you could find a piano and a wet bar if you ventured upstairs.

① synonymous   ② reserved

③ itinerant   ④ premature

10 When Abraham Lincoln accepted the nomination to be Illinois's Republican candidate for U.S. Senate in 1858, he used Jesus' words in his speech without _____, knowing his audience would understand whom he was quoting.

① authorization   ② rendition

③ attribution   ④ premeditation

11　Michigan has adopted tough new laws to punish _____ parents. The so-called "Home Alone Laws" carry a 90-day mandatory jail sentence for anyone who willfully neglects the safety of a child by leaving him unattended for long periods of time.

① derelict   ② solicitous

③ mercenary   ④ pedantic

12　Patients tend to feel indignant and insulted if the physician tell them he can find no organic cause for the pain. They tend to interpret the term "_____" to mean that they are complaining of nonexistent symptoms. They need to be educated about the fact that many forms of pain have no underlying physical cause.

① psychogenic   ② morbid

③ invalid   ④ amnesic

13　MTV had been previously dominated by rock music videos and had denied airtime to famous black artists like Rick James, but once it recognized the popularity of Michael Jackson's songs and videos, it oriented itself more toward pop and R&B, which in turn _____ future black artists like Whitney Houston and Prince to gain exposure.

① wreaked havoc on   ② paved the way for

③ kept close tabs on   ④ took the place of

14　In American political discourse, terrorism is a label often _____ for followers of a violent interpretation of Islam, whereas people who commit violence in the name of extremist far-right ideology based on race are sometimes portrayed as troubled young men, or criminals.

① abandoned   ② provoked

③ reserved   ④ mollified

15 Although there is no necessary conflict between linguistics and humanistic goal or stylistic refinements, many American linguists have in fact urged their public to "Leave your language alone" and expressed _____ any linguistic style more elaborate than that of simple oral communication by simple people.

① unusual interest in   ② hostility toward
③ predilection for   ④ great inequity about

16 Given India's more than 800 million _____ voters and the country's great diversity, there's no one _____ of the nation. In one state, a Maoist insurgency may be foremost on voters' minds; in another, it may be subsidies for farmers.

① learned — perk   ② illegible — bent
③ eligible — pulse   ④ illiterate — foible
⑤ registered — margin

17 The doctor, when left alone, was not quite satisfied with what he said in the interview. He had spoken from _____ rather than from judgement, and, as is generally the case with men who do so speak, he had afterwards to acknowledge to himself that he had been _____.

① fusillade — enamored   ② urge — vicious
③ prudence — rash   ④ compulsion — imprudent

18 If you applaud a man's speech at the moment when he sits down, he will take your compliment as _____ by the demands of common civility; but if you let some space intervene and then _____ him for the merits of his speech, he will remember your compliment for a very long time.

① exacted — commend   ② slashed — venerate
③ upgraded — eulogize   ④ induced — denounce
⑤ promoted — remind

19 British author and poet Rudyard Kipling believes working too hard is just as bad as drinking too much. In 1907 Kipling became the youngest winner of the Nobel Prize in Literature and the first Englishman to do so. After his death was incorrectly reported in a magazine, he _____ replied, "I've just read that I am dead. Don't forget to delete me from your list of _____."

① haphazardly — publishers ② vigorously — defectors
③ sarcastically — subscribers ④ imminently — correspondents

20 How many times have you heard or read that 50 percent of US marriages end in divorce? It's not true. Yes, the number of divorces each year is about half the number of marriages that same year. But that's like computing the death rate by comparing the number of people who die with the number of people who are born. That ignores those who neither were born nor died during that 12-month period. The 50-percent divorce figure ignores the number of _____.

① old singles ② intact marriages
③ broken engagements ④ temporary separations

21 Happiness is not, like a large and beautiful gem, so uncommon and rare that all search for it is _____, all efforts to obtain it hopeless; but it consists of smaller and commoner gems, grouped and set together, forming a pleasing and graceful whole. Happiness consists in the enjoyment of little pleasures scattered along the common path of life, which, in the eager search for some great and exciting joy, we are apt to _____.

① futile — overemphasize ② quixotic — stymie
③ uncanny — neglect ④ vain — overlook

22 Drama requires, for its maximum fulfillment, a high degree of social cohesion with regard to values, symbols and myths. Drama must be predicated upon certain understanding of life and its processes held in common by the audience. Above all other arts, drama is the art of shared response. In a theatre, one's feeling of _____ with the audience is the prerequisite of his becoming involved with what happens on the stage. Without the former, the latter can not be very great.

① hegira ② seclusion
③ solidarity ④ decorum

23 Welcome to the lowball culture. In a world of sluggish growth, excess capacity, and depressed expectations, buyers of goods and services — labor, houses, and restaurant meals, among others — have come to believe that desperate sellers should take any offer they make. But that kind of bargain hunting _____: employers short-change workers, workers buy fewer goods — and the overall economy suffers.

① helps lift the price of goods to new high
② becomes the industry norm
③ can create a dangerous spiral
④ induces customers to buy

24 The Iraqi government's underreporting of executions _____. Hangings are conducted in secret, at a heavily fortified locations in Baghdad. Only a few officials are notified beforehand, and the vast majority of the names of those executed are never made public. Human Rights Watch is concerned about the ability of defendants in Iraq to get a fair trial and access to a thorough appeals process.

① causes Human Rights Watch to crack down on its brutality
② leads to an increase in the number of those executed
③ reflects a general lack of transparency in the process
④ conveys the incompetence of the authority dealing with the process

25 It is clearly not enough to tell a fearful man that if he _____, he would fear less. In an age when leprosy was feared much more than it is today, a rich and spoiled young man, impelled by some sudden and irresistible emotion, got down from his gaily caparisoned horse and embraced a leper in the road. From that day, he feared nothing. Yet few of us are visited by such irresistible emotion. How can one help ordinary men and women, if not to eliminate fear, at least to keep it within bounds, so that reason, not fear, may play a stronger role in the affairs of men and nations? This is the most important question that confronts the human race.

① would want less   ② made more friends
③ were less sensitive   ④ would love more

11

01 A tourist was _____ in Norway with only enough money in his pocket to pay his passage back to England.

① validated ② engrossed
③ shunned ④ stranded

02 To criticize one's country is to pay it a compliment; it is a compliment because it _____ a belief that the country can do better than it is doing.

① disproves ② expunges
③ defies ④ evidences

03 In frog anatomy, the major muscles of the shoulder extend from the _____ area, across the shoulder joint, and into the arms.

① faunal ② endocrine
③ osmotic ④ dorsal

04 The mayor is usually a(n) _____ when speaking to local business owners, but on rare occasion she abandons the flattery and speaks her true opinions.

① pediatrician ② adulator
③ prig ④ apprentice

05 In addition, Catalonia's president, Carles Puigdemont, and four of his advisers, face _____ demands after they fled to Brussels to escape arrest.

① naturalization ② enfranchisement
③ extradition ④ amnesty

06   _____ are those who acquire power through their orations by directing them at the people to arouse their passions, prejudices, and emotions.

① Demagogues   ② Autocrats
③ Conspirators   ④ Kingpins

07   The integral unity of a poem means a unity which results from the successful resolution in the work of art of the conflicts of abstraction and _____, of general and particular, of denotation and connotation.

① practicality   ② consequence
③ amalgam   ④ concreteness

08   Psychological examinations have indicated that the correlation between intelligence and ethical standards is quite high, due to the method of testing which relies on the subject's _____ in evaluating the situations portrayed.

① glossary   ② defalcation
③ ratiocination   ④ subjectivity

09   The school district's _____ policy says, "No employee may be assigned to a work location and position in which the employee would report to or be under the immediate supervision of another family member."

① meritocratism   ② provincialism
③ nepotism   ④ bureaucratism

10   Despite strong beliefs to the contrary, there is little in the scientific literature to indicate that adolescents see themselves as _____ to harm. If anything, they appear to overestimate many of the risks around them.

① impious   ② immutable
③ infirm   ④ invulnerable

11   In Victorian times, unmarried mothers and those whose children were abnormal were habitually persuaded that it was in their children's best interests to _____ the disgrace of their birth by giving them away.

① bolster   ② expunge

③ requite   ④ outface

12   Television's contribution to family life has been an equivocal one. For while it has, indeed, kept the members of the family from _____, it has not served to bring them together.

① scathing each other   ② converging

③ dispersing   ④ reuniting one another

13   President's condemnation of the opposition party as an anti-reform force goes contrary to the public official's obligation to remain neutral in election campaigns and infringes upon the article that bans the _____ of rival parties under the Election Law.

① adjuration   ② extollment

③ archenemy   ④ aspersion

14   This is one of the reasons why I have been asking you to look at history in terms of civilizations, not in terms of states, and to think of states as rather subordinate and _____ political phenomena in the lives of the civilizations in whose bosoms they appear and disappear.

① perpetual   ② ephemeral

③ terrestrial   ④ tantalizing

15   The older we get, the more we understand the destiny that rules all things, with now a gentle push with the elbow, with now a leading finger, with now a blow over the heart, and what we think at twenty-five was _____, at seventy-five we know to have been the enormous gesture of God.

① a calling that God gave   ② the niggardly pittance

③ a trifling accident   ④ a horrendous experience

16   The system of _____ is built into almost every product we buy. It brings to mind our washing machine that broke down soon after the warranty ran out. We were told it was outmoded and couldn't be fixed. It was less than three years old. This wasteful practice no doubt contradicts the effort to conserve resources.

① fault detection   ② attrition prevention
③ planned obsolescence   ④ renewed guarantee

17   Thus it seems that the right of a person to choose permanent relief from suffering or a meaningless existence is a basic right; also it seems that parents or other guardians should not only have the right but be encouraged to accept the responsibility of requesting that persons entrusted to their care be _____ useless suffering or a tragic existence.

① denigrated   ② spared
③ exacerbated   ④ added

18   Accusing Russia of committing an "act of aggression" against Georgia by firing a guided missile into its territory, Tbilisi said the EU should not _____ Moscow, but send a "strong and clear-cut" message of _____.

① aggravate — regret   ② pardon — pretext
③ appease — condemnation   ④ excoriate — blame

19   His region faces a seemingly insurmountable economic _____, soaring unemployment, and a political crisis that has exacerbated _____ in the continent rather than spur greater cooperation.

① quagmire — divisions   ② dilemma — elation
③ union — impasse   ④ heyday — disunion

20   Found in the rain-forests of Central and South America, the morpho butterfly is famous for its iridescent blue wings. Grind up these wings, however, and you'll get a drab powder. The butterfly's hue is _____ called structural color. That is, the gorgeous color is created by the way light hits the wings — some light waves get reflected, others absorbed.

① a partial metamorphosis   ② an optical illusion
③ a gene mutation   ④ an insect breeding

21   A man will throw away or part with a useless watch which does not keep time, but he will often be _____ with his mind although it be so sick that it cannot distinguish error from truth, though it has grown almost useless in its _____, and perhaps has never told him what he himself is.

① dissatisfied — vainglory   ② livid — casuistry
③ satisfied — denouement   ④ content — vanity

22   It's enough to live on but not enough to save much. Now there's been no work for four weeks, and housewives are _____. Jennifer says she worries about money a lot, although there's no real hunger yet. So her family has changed its eating habits, no more meat or chicken and more of whatever is cheap and available — rice, eggplants, bananas.

① feeling the pinch   ② calling the shots
③ going against the grain   ④ taking fortune at the tide

23   There is one basic, fundamental reason that President Obama has a good chance at re-election — the same reason that Mitt Romney faces a basic, fundamental challenge. Obama is a(n) _____. Since George Washington took the first oath of office in 1789, a total of 31 sitting presidents have participated in national elections — and 21 have won.

① incumbent   ② minority
③ infidel   ④ influential

24   A man's work reveals him. In social intercourse he gives you the surface that he wishes the world to accept, and you can only gain a true knowledge of him by inferences from little actions, of which he is unconscious. Sometimes people carry to such perfection the mask they have assumed that in due course they actually become the person they seem. But in his book or his picture the real man delivers himself defenceless. His _____ will only expose his vacuity.

① dotage   ② recrimination
③ faultiness   ④ pretentiousness

25   The Scientific Revolution contributed to a belief system known as deism, which became popular in the 1700s. The deists believed in a powerful god who created and presided over an orderly realm but who did not interfere in its workings. The deists viewed God as watchmaker, one who set up the world, gave it natural laws by which to operate, and then _____ (under natural laws that could be proved mathematically). Such a theory had little place in organized religion.

① intervened in mortals' affairs
② followed the laws of nature
③ let it run by itself
④ performed miracles to prove himself

❚ Choose the one that best completes the sentence(s). ▶▶▶ **ANSWERS** P.266

01 Before I left the house, my brother told me to "break a leg" at the auditions. His rare _____ really lifted my confidence.

① invective   ② admonishment
③ malediction   ④ encouragement

02 Authorities say they found counterfeit money in his car and soon learned he was wanted on _____ charges.

① forgery   ② bribery
③ assault   ④ misdemeanor

03 You must exercise caution when intentionally using humor, since it is almost guaranteed that someone will be offended, no matter how _____ you think your humor may be.

① pestering   ② innocuous
③ hackneyed   ④ factual

04 Within a few weeks, I began to notice the lower-back pain that had been sapping the joy from my golf game was gradually _____. Soon I tossed the painkillers out of my golf bag.

① looming   ② sprouting
③ ascending   ④ subsiding

05 Plans for the relocation and expansion of Vacaville's homeless shelter have hit a snag, but it looks like a little gumption and the city's support could keep the project from _____.

① unraveling   ② disentangling
③ derailing   ④ hastening

06   When a video strikes users as cool or interesting, it takes on a life of its own and turns "_____" as it is spread and shared from friend to friend to friend, ad infinitum.

    ① prolific   ② migratory

    ③ picayune   ④ viral

07   Obama came into office determined to relaunch a peace process that had been effectively _____ since Israel's Prime Minister Ariel Sharon assumed office early in 2001.

    ① conflated   ② aligned

    ③ stalled   ④ interlocked

08   There are many patients with a cold who do not respond to the usual treatments. In this case, the danger is of the cold morphing into something more _____, such as sinusitis or asthma.

    ① fugitive   ② sinister

    ③ insipid   ④ contagious

09   Private economic chiefs said Congress must quickly approve some version of the problem-solving measure to start loans flowing and _____ a potential national economic disaster.

    ① stave off   ② lay off

    ③ palm off   ④ call off

10   When apparent altruism is not between kin, it may be based on _____. A monkey will present its back to another monkey, who will pick out parasites; after a time the roles will be reversed.

    ① animosity   ② jingoism

    ③ reciprocity   ④ fealty

11 Money is our biggest source of worry. Households globally have an estimated total debt of US$ 44 trillion. Personal _____ issues are also cited as the top cause of stress for almost half of the world's citizens.

① marital   ② somatic
③ vocational   ④ pecuniary

12 Most British-American literature courses which have not reflected the cultural diversity _____ the intellectual openness essential in our multicultural characteristics.

① insinuated   ② exhilarated
③ stifled   ④ fomented

13 Young people hoping to get a boost in their credit scores by piggybacking on Mom or Dad's credit card accounts may find the move could _____ on them and actually have the opposite effect than they intended.

① backfire   ② reckon
③ infringe   ④ spur

14 In a stunning generational shift, millions of young French _____ the Socialist and conservative parties that had governed the country for generations, voting instead for insurgents like Macron.

① resurrected   ② ditched
③ underpinned   ④ marred

15 Big media organizations pull out the stops for game-changing stories, but they may be bleeding themselves to death in the process. The lumbering old news dinosaurs have _____ their staffs and watched online rivals eat their lunch as ratings and circulation inexorably slide downward.

① replenished   ② pampered
③ slashed   ④ hallowed

16 The actions of men were said to be governed by the faculty of reason, those of animals by the faculty of instinct; and this attribution of the actions of animals to instinct seems to have _____ from most of those who used the word the need for further study or explanation of them.

① necessitated   ② beleaguered
③ disguised   ④ articulated

17 Participants at an Institute of Economic Affairs (IEA) forum marking this year's World Democracy Day have all admitted that the politics of insults, character assassination and the use of intemperate language is fast destroying the country's fledgling democracy and must be _____ without delay.

① nonplussed   ② stemmed
③ upheld   ④ cloistered

18 The way in which many Americans now confuse Islam and al-Qaida is a grave mistake. One of four people on this planet is Muslim. But the way they practice their faith is not _____. As with other global faiths, Islamic traditions vary widely from one place to another, and are often influenced by local cultures.

① whopping   ② monolithic
③ antiquated   ④ sciolistic

19 As we grow older we discover that what seemed at the time an absorbing interest was in reality an appetite or passion which has swept over us and passed on, until at last we come to see that our life has no more _____ than a pool in the rocks filled by the tide with foam and then emptied.

① opprobrium   ② quibble
③ continuity   ④ quintessence

20 Europeans may be in the habit of viewing every Big Mac as a terrifying sign of American cultural imperialism, but Chinese have mostly welcomed the invasion — indeed they have _____ it. In one recent survey, nearly half of all Chinese children under 12 identified McDonald's as a _____ brand.

① internalized — domestic
② excommunicated — multi-national
③ domesticated — world-best
④ vanquished — proxy

21 The most enduring quality of the broader economic recovery has been the gap between _____. While growth and jobs are up, only about 1 in 4 Americans believes the economy is getting stronger. The reason is clear: personal incomes aren't rising, except at the very top.

① reality and perception   ② theory and practice
③ government and citizen   ④ conservatism and liberalism

22 In my experience of university life, it is the middle-class youth who was not interested in studying on a scholarship. Many of them had little reason to care about their studies, having parents who can _____ for them after they graduate. Working-class students, on the other hand, must have a great deal of motivation to attempt a degree.

① be in red   ② pull strings
③ toe the line   ④ go over the top

23 Operating rides, selling souvenirs and the like typically bring only a few dollars over minimum wage. But little-known benefits — free passes, early access to new attractions — have become a huge part of the compensation package for theme park employees. Employers offer _____ for more than just altruistic reasons: Such extras keep workers loyal, which helps reduce _____ and leads to lower costs for hiring and training new workers.

① audits — reward   ② facilities — boredom
③ subsidies — acquisition   ④ perks — turnover

24 More than 160 of the prisoners released or transferred from the Guantanamo detention camp under Presidents Bush and Obama had previously been judged as "likely to pose a threat to the U.S." The decision to release or transfer these detainees, despite their former classification as "high risk," contradicted the Pentagon's own recommendation that _____.

① detainees be transferred or freed despite high risk
② the president should not intervene in the affairs of another country
③ prisoners in this category should remain in detention
④ U.S. ultimately determine whether detainees were truly dangerous

25 "Imagine a sustainable world, driven by clean and renewable energy. And imagine large space sailboats driven by solar radiation, production of biofuels via nanotechnology, the advent of photosynthetic humans. Welcome to the bright green world of solarpunk." A mix of green technology, economic ideology, sociology, science fiction, architecture, and even fashion, solarpunk remains more of an aspirational mindset and lifestyle than a cultural movement, but the popularity of the term speaks to a hunger for an alternative to the _____.

① utopia   ② apocalypse
③ paradise   ④ felicity
⑤ fairyland

01 Many of the subscribers think that the editorials in this periodical are _____ rather than truth-seeking.

① square   ② veracious
③ brusque   ④ tendentious

02 In recent appearances, Bush has shown he's more comfortable and effective when communicating _____ than when reading from a prepared text.

① off-the-cuff   ② topsy-turvy
③ in a nutshell   ④ for a lark

03 The racial tension exploded into _____, triggering angry blacks to burn, loot and rob businesses owned by Koreans in Koreatown.

① dedication   ② nonentity
③ mayhem   ④ armistice

04 I want you to make a _____ of our headquarters building which we can display in the lobby. Inform me of the estimated cost as soon as possible.

① repose   ② remnant
③ recluse   ④ replica

05 Painters wants to see the world afresh, and to discard all the accepted notions and _____ about flesh being pink and apples being yellow or red.

① preambles   ② prejudices
③ hyperboles   ④ apothegms

06 Born in Texas, where Jones still lives outside San Antonio, the _____ actor always has played his cards close to the vest, but he did offer The Hollywood Reporter a few, sometimes curt, words about his new film.

① laconic   ② versatile

③ flamboyant   ④ seclusive

07 Moreover, to parallel the global era, Korea's national structure will be _____ into a more open construction, focusing developments for borderline regions such as eastern, western and southern coasts and inland metropolitan areas.

① retroverted   ② withered

③ revamped   ④ postulated

08 I have a problem finishing my drink to the bottom of a cup, especially if it's an _____ container. The reason for this strange behavior stems from being paranoid about what may be lurking at the bottom of the cup.

① exotic   ② irregular

③ opaque   ④ elliptical

09 With the advent of farming, the Neolithic population grew so rapidly that people no longer knew all the members of their village communities. The resulting _____ produced social disorder.

① strangulation   ② estrangement

③ martyrdom   ④ expulsion

10 To set out on a road that has no end, with no expectation of finding all the answers, has always been more eye-opening than travelling to a fixed destination, because it leaves freedom to stray into by-ways that may prove more rewarding than _____ goals.

① overriding   ② preordained

③ impassable   ④ foretold

11 In the last few years, articles have feared the _____ of the profession, noting a large percentage of librarians that would soon be retiring. But worries about a mass exodus now appear to be unnecessary.

① professionalizing   ② masculinizing
③ graying   ④ feminizing

12 He _____ that veterans are troubled time bombs or robots who can't think for themselves by recognizing that they have gained important leadership and social skills from their military training and deployments.

① confirms the hearsay   ② blemishes the acclaim
③ spreads the myth   ④ breaks the stereotype

13 There is a class of persons who think it enough if a person assents undoubtingly to what they think true, though he has no knowledge whatever of the grounds of the opinion and cannot _____ of it against the most superficial objections.

① make a practical use   ② make a tenable defense
③ offer a critical view   ④ offer a plausible solution

14 More than 1.3 million Americans lost federal unemployment benefits on Dec. 28 as an emergency measure passed during the depths of the recession expired. The government condemned Congress's failure to _____ that measure.

① devise   ② enforce
③ abolish   ④ renew

15 When my family transferred to a house three years ago, the former occupants had two preschoolers who had left crayon marks on some doors and walls. Since then, visitors have often commented on how good an artist my four-year-old is, thinking he is the _____.

① layman   ② outcast
③ culprit   ④ witness

16 To find the beginning of trial by jury, we must go back to the days of Henry the Second. The _____ from which it grew was in existence before his time, but he was the first to establish it in such a way that it could grow into its modern form.

① progeny   ② germ

③ consummation   ④ microbe

17 Both teams, gathered near midfield to shake hands, began scuffling in front of the Station Camp bench, a skirmish that required members of both coaching staffs and police to put a stop to. "I couldn't see how the _____ started," Station Camp coach Shaun Hollinsworth said.

① consternation   ② ramification

③ altercation   ④ contusion

18 A few months' _____ from the office is nothing to stress over. But recruiters will generally start asking questions if they see a void in your employment of six months or longer. Once you realize you have a resume gap, you need to do some damage control to prevent that gap from jeopardizing your prospects.

① disquisition   ② hiatus

③ espionage   ④ arrogation

19 Marco Perduca, a Senator who has been _____ of parliamentary perks, _____ that it's a travesty that a one-term parliamentarian is entitled to a pension for which other people would have had to work for 40 years.

① supportive — argues   ② critical — acknowledges

③ expectant — prophesies   ④ censorious — negates

20 Although the enemies of our prehistoric past, such as animal predators or bands of human marauders, are no longer a threat to our everyday existence, we are _____ by the legacy from our ancestors, who were exposed to and feared these dangers. We unwittingly construct a phantom world composed of individuals who are poised to dominate, deceive, and exploit us. We may misconceive trivial or innocuous events or mild challenges as serious offenses.

① indemnified   ② sublimed

③ regenerated   ④ encumbered

21 DNA, we thought, was a(n) _____ code that we and our children and their children had to live by. Now with new epigenetics evidence suggesting that powerful environmental conditions can influence our genetic code in a single generation, we can imagine a world in which we can tinker with DNA, bend it to our will.

① labile   ② heterodox

③ longwinded   ④ ironclad

22 An acquaintance of Bill Clinton's has said that Clinton felt frustrated that Sept. 11 did not happen on his watch. That is understandable because the best chance any President has for greatness is _____. Apart from the founders, the only great President that Americans have had in good times is Theodore Roosevelt.

① to wage more wars than his predecessors

② to offer his people the longest good times possible

③ to give national defense the highest priority

④ to be in power during war or disaster

23   _____ has characterized human societies throughout history. The ancient Egyptians distinguished between themselves, "men," and others, who were presumably something a little less than human. The ancient Persians held people in progressively _____ the farther those people were from Persia. People everywhere tend to think of themselves and of their ways as somehow better than or superior to other people and their ways.

① Anachronism — rapt attention
② Xenophobia — stronger bondage
③ Nationalism — less contempt
④ Ethnocentrism — lower esteem

24   Darwin formulated his *Origin of Species* with the sense that he was making a completely _____ discovery. But before he was finished, the similar hypothesis of another young naturalist, Wallace, was brought to his attention: it turned out that they had both got their clue from Malthus's *Essay on Population*. By the time Darwin published his second edition, he had at last become aware of a whole line of predecessors.

① pungent   ② putative
③ unique   ④ autochthonous

25   _____. One of the tragedies of the arts is the spectacle of the vast number of persons who have been misled by this passing fertility to devote their lives to the effort of creation. Their invention deserts them as they grow older, and they are faced with the long years before them in which, unfitted by now for a more humdrum calling, they harass their wearied brain to beat out material it is incapable of giving them. They are lucky when, with what bitterness we know, they can make a living in ways, like journalism or teaching, that are allied to the arts.

① An ill workman always quarrels with his tools
② Men talk of killing time, while time quietly kills them
③ Frequent job changes lead you to poverty
④ Youth is inspiration

❙ Choose the one that best completes the sentence(s).   ▶ ▶ ▶ ANSWERS P.276

01   Although we could not understand the words of the song, we got the impression from the _____ tones of the singer that it was a lament of some kind.

① minatory   ② platonic

③ plangent   ④ somnolent

02   I think that your _____ remarks definitely prove that you have not given this problem any serious consideration.

① asinine   ② truculent

③ scintillating   ④ piercing

03   When the design was submitted for approval, it was said to be _____ because it was quite unlike any cricket trophy previously created.

① earthbound   ② thoroughgoing

③ hard-boiled   ④ ground-breaking

04   Courage allowed him not to _____ when his radical economic policies initially caused the worst recession since the Great Depression.

① stint   ② flinch

③ rant   ④ aspire

05   A new study has revealed that the powerful beetle can pull 1141 times its own body weight, the _____ of a 70kg person lifting 80 tons.

① equivalent   ② balance

③ contour   ④ disparity

06 The driver of the car accidentally became a(n) _____ accomplice to murder when his passenger shot a rival gang member.

① berserk   ② jaded
③ unwitting   ④ dishonest

07 The Battle of Lexington was not, as most of us have been taught, a(n) _____ rising of individual farmers, but was instead a tightly organized, well-planned event.

① premeditated   ② emeritus
③ spontaneous   ④ vehement

08 The literary artist, concerned solely with the creation of a book or story as close to perfection as his powers will permit, is generally quite individual, contemplative and _____.

① amiable   ② retiring
③ amorphous   ④ bestial

09 College is really different these days. Fifty years ago we had roughly 15 percent of all high school graduates going to college. We have now up to 70 percent of all high school graduates. So it has become a rite of _____.

① passage   ② trends
③ reconciliation   ④ lifelong commitment

10 In the year 2000, the Internet did not _____ the influence of newspapers, radio or television. However, cyberspace had an advantage over the older news sources: the Internet is an interactive medium.

① dodge   ② inflate
③ portend   ④ eclipse

11 All concerned tried hard to make a good result. But negotiations between the union and the employers have reached a _____; neither side is willing to budge from previously stated positions.

① consensus   ② context
③ cession   ④ stalemate

12 Bulls are color-blind. Thus, a fighting bull is likely enraged by the cape's quick movement instead of its color. So why the bold hue? Some say it helps mask one of the more _____ aspects of a bullfight: splatters of the animal's blood.

① gruesome   ② auspicious
③ mellow   ④ impregnable

13 Every year thousands of books are published, but many of them attract just _____ attention only to disappear gradually from _____ and the minds of readers.

① instant — pandemonium   ② transitory — the world
③ itinerary — the start   ④ momentary — the shelves

14 Many of these thousands of smart youngsters who emigrate for better education remain abroad after graduation, get a job and live as immigrants for the rest of their lives. The _____ phenomenon has been developing in Romania especially since the country joined the European Union.

① brain drain   ② mammonism
③ cultural lag   ④ human alienation

15 Below are a number of plans that we can build for you to a price. Although it is very difficult to give a fixed price quote, we are able to give you a _____ figure. Please send us some details of what you are looking at and we will get an indicative price back to you.

① ball-park   ② low
③ strict   ④ pecuniary

16 Even my leanest salads are only moderately _____. The goal may be to consume lots of vegetables and fruit, but that doesn't _____ garnishes of the salty, meaty and cheesy variety. After all, the better my salads taste, the more likely I am to gobble them up.

① meticulous — ornament   ② abstemious — preclude

③ cosmopolitan — season   ④ extravagant — avert

17 There have been increased debates on Zambia as an investment decision since the change of government last year with some analysts arguing that the lack of policy consistency by the current government will cause investor _____ while the government has tried to _____ the concerns.

① uncertainty — allay   ② confidence — soothe

③ dither — intensify   ④ stipend — surmise

18 The king conducted the rites of praying for rain at the altars of the guardian gods of the state. These gods were also thought of as the _____ spirits of the earth and the grain it produced; in other words, they were the protectors of agriculture and were thus a prime focus of the rainmaking effort.

① sycophantic   ② tutelary

③ cantankerous   ④ waggish

19 A new phrase, reflecting a new mood, was crossing Europe last week: _____. As cold war means sustained hostility short of World War III, it means a sustained truce without a settlement. The mood, which was latent and unexpressed, suddenly popped into the open and is now, reported the London Observer, "the main topic of informed political conversation all over Europe."

① Hot War   ② Trenched War

③ Cold Peace   ④ Hot Peace

20   In some minds, though, the possibility looms of enemy action on the part of something larger than a virus. Since the advent of genetic engineering in the 1970s, conspiracy theorists have pointed to pretty much every new infectious disease, from AIDS to Ebola to MERS to Lyme disease to SARS to Zika, as being a result of human _____.

① trial and error
② tinkering or malevolence
③ contact and contamination
④ confession or exposure
⑤ deployment and operation

21   When I hear people say they have not found the world and life so agreeable or interesting as to be in love with it, or that they look with _____ to its ends, I am apt to think they have never been properly alive nor seen with clear vision the world they think so _____ of, or anything in it — not a blade of grass.

① equanimity — meanly
② apathy — highly
③ provocation — much
④ enmity — badly

22   I find it _____ to be alone the greater part of the time. To be in company, even with the best, is soon wearisome and dissipating. I love to be alone. I never found the companion that was so companionable as _____. We are for the most part more lonely when we go abroad among men than when we stay in our chambers.

① inscrutable — privacy
② wholesome — solitude
③ foolhardy — gregariousness
④ salutary — homage

23   American attitudes towards Chinese tech have passed through several stages of denial in the past 20 years. First it was an irrelevance, then Chinese firms were sometimes seen as copycats or as industrial spies, and more recently China has been viewed as a tech Galapagos, where unique species grow that would never make it beyond its shores. Now a fourth stage has begun, marked by fear that China is reaching _____. American tech's age of "imperial arrogance" is ending, says one Silicon Valley figure.

① parity
② divergence
③ convergence
④ singularity
⑤ promptness

24 Calvinism was never Christianity. It was _____ Christianity that aggrandized the rich, by making visible wealth on earth the signifier of God's love. Calvin's core tenet is that all who will go to heaven were chosen at the beginning of time, as were all who weren't. "The reprobate are damned because they were always meant to be damned." Needless to say, the wealthy citizens of Geneva embraced this.

① a violent resistance to   ② a silent obedience to

③ a reluctant practice of   ④ an active distortion of

25 It's hard to attribute anything but _____ to the fact that Cuban President Raúl Castro issued a major immigration reform on Tuesday, Oct. 16, which was the 50th anniversary of the start of the Cold War's most harrowing moment, the Cuban Missile Crisis. But the two things are nonetheless related. Castro's reform — eliminating the onerous exit visa requirement for Cubans who want to travel outside the communist island — is a reminder of how the missile crisis prompted both Washington and Havana to shut down movement into and out of Cuba for the past half century.

① bedlam   ② rule of thumb

③ furor   ④ coincidence

❚ Choose the one that best completes the sentence(s).   ▶▶▶ **ANSWERS** P.281

01   Islamophobic groups _____ spurious accusations about Islamic jihad threatening America's security.

① disseminate   ② dissimulate
③ encumber   ④ intercept

02   Indeed, Warwick is now called Warwick University PLC and most university vice-chancellors would see that _____ as a compliment, not a criticism.

① appellation   ② varsity
③ disparity   ④ infamy

03   Madonna showed her _____ for motherhood by saying, "Even if I'm the worst mother in the world, I'm better than death!"

① strong zest   ② artistic finesse
③ low benchmark   ④ close grid

04   The newspaper was forced to _____ a published article when it found that many of the sources had been falsified.

① improvise   ② fumble
③ consolidate   ④ recant

05   Darwin showed that, far from being bountiful, nature was so _____ that every species faced mass death and extinction.

① inexplicable   ② fugacious
③ therapeutic   ④ parsimonious

06 Usually, the anxious participant will be faster in responding to probes replacing _____ stimuli than those replacing neutral stimuli.

① auditory   ② viable

③ tactile   ④ salient

07 My parents have to work 12 hours every day, seven days a week, just to earn enough to send me to school. Yet sometimes, I'm not as good as they hope I'd be. From now on, I want to do more to _____ their love.

① retrieve   ② retrocede

③ remit   ④ reciprocate

08 All airlines have been under pressure to reduce their cost base. But rather than relying on _____ amenities, as many airlines have done, Cathay Pacific has focused on increasing the productivity of its personnel.

① muttering   ② recouping

③ juxtaposing   ④ trimming

09 An Englishman has always been attached to his home, not so much owing to his affection for his family as to his _____ of interference from outsiders and to his love of being alone and minding his own business.

① licentiousness   ② sophism

③ detestation   ④ hype

10 Today, people are using religion to hide their own _____ and greed by inciting the masses to commit _____ acts in the name of a peaceful religion.

① leniency — atrocious   ② bigotry — heinous

③ obscenity — philanthropic   ④ euphoria — malicious

11   In an effort to prevent a repeat of that disaster, rescue workers and engineers are trying to finish the protective _____ before the arrival of rain, which experts fear will put irresistible pressure on the reservoir.

① hydrology   ② dike

③ paddock   ④ corral

12   It is easy in the world to live after the world's opinion; it is easy in isolation to live after our own; but the great man is he who in the midst of the crowd keeps with perfect sweetness the _____.

① dependence of singularity   ② independence of solitude

③ dependence of multitude   ④ independence of communality

13   Despite your imagined freedom, you are chained always by the laws of cause and effect. You may be free to leap from a skyscraper or to refrain from eating for a week, but you are not free to _____.

① commit murder   ② perform these actions twice

③ escape the consequences   ④ compel others to do likewise

14   Offensive toponyms have become rarer still in recent decades. Cartographers not only reject _____ place-names as they make new maps but systematically remove them as they revise and update old ones.

① outmoded   ② derogatory

③ hackneyed   ④ enigmatic

15   In November last year, the cabinet took a decision to allow up to 51 per cent foreign direct investment in multi-brand retail. But the move has been kept in _____ due to protests from not only opposition but also some of the allies of the ruling United Progressive Alliance government.

① continuance   ② momentum

③ abeyance   ④ tedium

16   Americans can be excused for thinking that terrorism is largely behind them. Ten-plus years after the attacks, Al Qaeda has yet to strike the US again. Airport screening seems more relaxed, and anxieties over employment, mortgages have _____ worries about anthrax and suicide bombers.

① coaxed   ② intimidated
③ proliferated   ④ supplanted

17   In the past rappers like Snoop Dogg and Ice Cube have cleaned up their acts when their careers were _____. But today's rappers, aware that more _____ images are ultimately better for business, are making a conscious effort to clean up their acts while still on top.

① flagging — palatable   ② high — docile
③ ebbing — aggressive   ④ culminating — pugnacious

18   If you follow the news about health research, you risk whiplash. Garlic lowers bad cholesterol, then — after more study — it doesn't. Eating a big breakfast cuts your total daily calories, or not — as a study released last week finds. Biomedical research can be a _____ here and now.

① valuable resource   ② rigorous methodology
③ fickle guide   ④ costly endeavor

19   If we examine ourselves and those around us, we have to admit that everyone, to some extent, is odd. The terms "normal" and "abnormal" are subjective words whose interpretations can be as varied as the people who speak them. So when we worry about our kids' strange behavior, it may be because they _____ of what life should be like for "well-adjusted" kids.

① put academic achievement ahead
② conform to our society's view
③ are too young to be aware
④ deviate from our own expectations

20 Virtually no one connected to the _____ escaped the nightly melees without paying some sort of price. Local parents scrambled to arrange child care and meals when public-school classes were canceled. Neighborhood workers paid in lost salary because their employers closed early every night. For Americans watching from a distance, the price was _____: another crisis in which leaders offered more angst than answers.

① tumult — psychic ② feast — intangible
③ distress — monetary ④ venture — ethereal

21 It is true that the work of the peasant who cultivates his own land is varied; he ploughs, he sows, he reaps. But he is at the mercy of the _____, and is very conscious of his _____, whereas the man who works a modern mechanism is conscious of power, and acquires the sense that man is the master, not the slave, of natural forces.

① climate — aplomb ② stigma — nemesis
③ elements — dependence ④ paranormal — omnipotence

22 Now, I recognize that we've never been a country of angels guided by a presidium of saints. Early America was _____. One in five people in the new nation was enslaved. Justice for the poor meant stocks and stockades. Women suffered virtual peonage. Heretics were driven into exile, or worse. Native people — the Indians — would be forcibly removed from their land, their fate a "trail of tears" and broken treaties.

① an earthly paradise ② a civilized society
③ a moral morass ④ a gray zone
⑤ a plutocratic country

23 If we tweak John Lennon's words and "imagine there's no paper," how do we then imagine imaginative literature? Right now, the Internet does not appear overly hospitable to originally published literary works: most writers are still happier to see their words first published on paper than on a screen, even if those words originally appeared on a computer screen and were transmitted to a publisher electronically. Paper still carries _____.

① circulation ② servility
③ prestige ④ epithet

24   I can't tell you how many times I've been asked: "So, what's your favorite restaurant?" There's no one-size-fits-all restaurant for me. I'm a fan of dozens of dining rooms. The process of _____ more than 100 potential loves down to a highly personal Top 40 takes months. The next time someone asks me, I'll point him in one of 40 directions.

① modifying   ② imparting
③ tarrying   ④ winnowing

25   When you hear that so-and-so has said something horrid about you, you remember the ninety-nine times when you have refrained from uttering the most just and well-deserved criticism of him, and forget the hundredth time when in an unguarded moment you have declared what you believe to be the truth about him. Is this the reward, you feel, for all your long _____? Yet from his point of view your conduct appears exactly what his appears to you; he never knows of the times when you have not spoken, he knows only of the hundredth time when you did speak.

① escapade   ② quirk
③ tirade   ④ forbearance

16

❙ Choose the one that best completes the sentence(s).　　▶▶▶ ANSWERS P.286

01　I think that it is not too difficult to make a selection from the box, since the contents are _____.

① heterogeneous　　　　　　② standoffish

③ sylvan　　　　　　　　　　④ homogeneous

02　IATA says African airports are among the costliest in the world, and offer _____ service. Nairobi has iffy security and few comforts.

① fiduciary　　　　　　　　② shoddy

③ sophisticated　　　　　　④ prodigal

03　An action intended to cause harm but that _____ causes good results would be judged equal to the result from an action done with good intentions.

① inadvertently　　　　　　② recklessly

③ discursively　　　　　　　④ emphatically

04　The outspoken man has dismissed global warming as a(n) _____, citing cold weather snaps as evidence.

① canard　　　　　　　　　② incubus

③ jeopardy　　　　　　　　④ juggernaut

05　Intuitively, in a _____ argument, if you knew that the premises were true, then it would be reasonable for you to believe the conclusion.

① discordant　　　　　　　② farfetched

③ cogent　　　　　　　　　④ queasy

06 Since Socrates proclaimed the virtue of the examined life, the task of philosophy has been to give a _____ account of human existence, to clarify and illuminate human life.

① gruesome   ② quaint

③ reflective   ④ secondhand

07 Pop art aimed to employ images of popular as opposed to elitist culture in art, emphasizing the _____ elements of any given culture, most often through the use of irony.

① sophisticated   ② piquant

③ banal   ④ squeamish

08 It's hard to believe, but even the world's most brazen comedians and powerful leaders cop to being _____ when they're not performing or giving speeches.

① bashful   ② indolent

③ garrulous   ④ jovial

09 Relations between China and India have long been plagued by tensions over trade, border disputes, and _____ due to China's political and military support for India's rival, Pakistan.

① preference   ② intimacy

③ privation   ④ friction

10 A good deal of research has examined the relationship between learning style and culture. Even though no clear-cut _____ links have been identified, there are some perspectives worth examining.

① caustic   ② casual

③ causal   ④ carping

11 Investment banker Rob Garrus, a deeply _____ man when it comes to routine household chores, has been watching the spring/summer ready-to-wear collections like a hawk, hoping fashionistas declare unironed clothes to be in this season.

① crafty   ② meticulous
③ penniless   ④ sluggish

12 _____ is an act of homage to the majesty of appetite. So I think we should arrange to give up our pleasures regularly — our food, our friends, our lovers — in order to preserve their intensity, and the moment of coming back to them.

① Euphuism   ② Attrition
③ Anorexia   ④ Fasting

13 International observers took notice of Draghi's commitment to do "whatever it takes" to save the euro. But eurozone leaders' inability to _____ doubt about their commitment to the euro after two and a half years of crisis suggests that the problem is deeply rooted.

① inflate   ② betoken
③ cogitate   ④ assuage

14 Grieving parents have become such a movie staple that the theme is now a demonstrable _____. Such grief isn't new in movies, but the preponderance of these stories suggests that filmmakers believe that there's something compelling about the agony of others.

① chagrin   ② cliché
③ fiasco   ④ plagiarism

15 Gift exchanges are so inefficient. Unless everyone's picked out presents via gift registry, there's a decent chance someone will receive an unwanted gift. And if everyone's picked out their own gifts in advance, and there's not much surprise or thought involved, the idea of a gift exchange is something of a(n) _____.

① hallucination   ② annuity
③ charade   ④ vicissitude

16 The banking industry and the economy are now locked in a kind of negative _____, where bad news in one induces pain in the other. Defaults cause bankers to _____ the availability of credit, which causes more defaults.

① symbiosis — restrict   ② antagonism — dwindle
③ synergy — ordain   ④ metabolism — stabilize

17 Humanity is in short supply at many workplaces, where it's been pushed out by automation and a culture of overwork. Adam Waytz writes about a surprising way to restore humanity: Giving people the time and encouragement to _____ completely from their jobs.

① unveil   ② amend
③ unplug   ④ reward

18 Modern man looks eagerly back into the twilight out of which he has come, in the hope that its faint beams will illuminate the obscurity into which he is going; _____ his aspirations and anxieties about the path which lies before him sharpen his insight into what lies behind.

① hopefully   ② conversely
③ inevitably   ④ rapidly

19   The arrest of a 21-year-old Bangladeshi national accused in a _____ bomb plot this week offers the latest evidence that terrorists are determined to strike the U.S. He couldn't achieved his aspirational goal. But, for New York, the incident represents a chilling reminder that the city remains at the top of the hit list.

① roseate   ② lopsided
③ foiled   ④ ravaged

20   Rather than using the rise of China as a strategic _____ to American primacy, most countries in Asia seem to be quietly _____ with the United States. At the same time, many Asian nations are making deals with each other to create a balance against China.

① counterweight — bandwagoning   ② countercoup — coping
③ counterblast — grappling   ④ counterfeit — siding

21   Every man is his own best critic. Whatever the learned say about a book, however _____ they are in their praise of it, unless it interests you it is no business of yours. Don't forget that critics often make mistakes, the history of criticism is full of blunders the most eminent of them have made, and you who read are the final _____ of the value to you of the book you are reading.

① split — bench   ② precarious — judiciary
③ zealous — felon   ④ unanimous — judge

22   Dorothy Dix, who had never missed a deadline, showed no sign of being winded. _____ who never read her column thought of her as an arch sentimentalist who ladled out advice to the not quite bright. However, a professor of mental therapy advised women tortured by doubts and fears to read Dorothy Dix daily. In recognition of her _____ qualities, the Medical Women's National Association made her an honorary member.

① Sceptics — tonic   ② Champions — electric
③ Detractors — downbeat   ④ Antagonists — enervating
⑤ Proponents — exhilarating

23   In fact, the eighteenth and nineteenth centuries, the period of colonial expansion, were an era of economic botany, when the _____ of new plants to the national economy was prominent in the mind of all but the purest taxonomists. But then, the patronage that the explorers enjoyed was such that the Government of British India brought the Sikkim King, who arrested J.D. Hooker for trespassing into his territory hunting for plants, to his knees, and took away the Darjeeling area as a punitive fine for his _____.

① worth — espionage   ② peculiarity — fastidiousness
③ location — vagary   ④ usefulness — temerity

24   Whenever linguists discuss the etymology of words and phrases, folk etymology inevitably arises. Sometimes speakers of English make a mistake so often that _____. For example, the word "apron" came from a common mishearing of the Middle English "a napron". Additionally, the onomatopoeic word "hiccup" was so often mistakenly associated with coughing, that now "hiccough" is an accepted alternative spelling.

① the language could be easily distorted
② they are habituated to slip their tongues
③ it becomes part of the language
④ people ruin the language handed down for generations

25   The publishers will tell you that the average life of a novel is ninety days. It is hard to reconcile yourself to the fact that a book into which you have put, besides your whole self, several months of anxious toil, should be read in three or four hours and after so short a period forgotten. Though it will do him no good, there is no author so small-minded as not to have a secret hope that some part at least of his work will _____. The belief in posthumous fame is a harmless vanity which often reconciles the artists to the disappointments and failures of his life.

① score a success in his lifetime
② reconcile him with his harsh critics
③ be published in many languages
④ survive him for a generation or two

01   The two boxers battled toe-to-toe until the final round, when the longtime champion of the ring was finally _____ by his young opponent's stamina.

①   decimated   ②   galvanized
③   stymied   ④   ostracized

02   I tell every soldier I see about the short-term _____ and things like chronic traumatic encephalopathy.

①   requirements   ②   liabilities
③   ramifications   ④   surges

03   Madonna first started wearing the Kabbalah signature red string on her wrist in 1998, prompting a flurry of stars to _____ suit.

①   wear   ②   order
③   take   ④   follow

04   The status quo is our _____. We are constantly looking for ways that we can take the traditional model and make it better.

①   reminiscence   ②   epiphany
③   improvisation   ④   nemesis

05   Sherlock Holmes was fed up with the way he had been misrepresented by careless critics, and so he attempted to _____ his reputation by solving his last cold case.

①   tarnish   ②   cement
③   relish   ④   redeem

06 Forgiveness is a rare thing these days. Usually when something bad happens, we become angry and often _____ comes to mind.

① vengeance   ② dismay

③ bootleg   ④ cringe

07 Polymer hairs prevent water and oil molecules from being able to latch onto the fibers, so that a wine, coffee or ketchup spill can be _____ as if it were liquid lint.

① brushed off   ② written off

③ locked up   ④ soaked up

08 Being "papped" by the paparazzi is an honour no longer just for the famous. A New York-based business, Methodlzaz, has cottoned on to the public's craving for _____ shots and now takes requests from ordinary folk.

① diagonal   ② unposed

③ dazzling   ④ penny-wise

09 American support for president Pervez Musharraf has always come with a cover story to _____ over the awkward fact that one of the U.S.'s most important allies happens to be a military dictator.

① mull   ② take

③ turn   ④ gloss

10 Rapid physical, emotional, cognitive, and social changes are the _____ of adolescence. During this time, children evolve into mature and independent young adults.

① hallmark   ② obverse

③ maelstrom   ④ coterie

11 What defines borderline personality disorder — and makes it so explosive — is the sufferers' inability to _____ their feelings and behavior. When faced with an event that makes them depressed or angry, they often become inconsolable or enraged.

① preclude   ② calibrate
③ conjecture   ④ procrastinate

12 There are rules of _____ in our society though they can change over time. To avoid stressful and tense situations with those close to us, it is sometimes best to ignore unpleasant incidents. If you cannot do this, then you should talk it out with the person, but not resort to emotional blackmail.

① surmise   ② inference
③ decorum   ④ audacity

13 A vague desire for liberty possessed the French in the 18th century. And yet, curiously, neither the philosophers nor the people wanted to get rid of the king. The idea of a republic was not a _____ one then, and people still hoped that they might have an ideal prince.

① sham   ② neoteric
③ savvy   ④ regnant

14 Because a play has to hold the excited interest of an audience, or fail in production, the drama is the most social of all the arts, necessarily speaking to large groups of people and saying something to grip their minds and feelings. It cannot be a _____ meditation, but must move; nor just an argument, but must act.

① mobile   ② bibulous
③ mendacious   ④ static

15   Of all forms of pain, none is more important for the individual to understand than the "threshold" variety. Almost everyone has a(n) _____ ache that is triggered whenever tension or fatigue reaches a certain point. It can take the form of a migraine-type headache.

① suppositious   ② delusive
③ omnibus   ④ tell-tale

16   The relation of politicians to scientists is like that of a magician in the Arabian Nights to a genie who obeys his orders. The genie does astounding things which the magician could not do without his help, but he does them only because he is told to do them, not because of any _____.

① prodigy of his own   ② coercion by his master
③ impulse in himself   ④ scheme of his master

17   Liechtenstein is a treat for many reasons. One is to see a fine private art collection. Another is a chance to use an otherwise unusable German word. As the only German-speaking feudal country in the world, Liechtenstein is the last _____ of that language's traditional forms of aristocratic address.

① scourge   ② labyrinth
③ refuge   ④ abattoir

18   Having made his name along the trading routes of the British empire, Johnnie Walker might be expected to support the Eurosceptics' contention that Britain would be better off _____ itself from an ailing EU to seek its fortune on the global stage. After all, the best hope of finding new Scotch-drinkers lies with newly affluent Indians and Chinese.

① dissuading   ② unshackling
③ galvanizing   ④ resurrecting

19 Describing the current economy as a recovery that is simply not progressing fast enough is a fundamental mistake. In reality, a minority of the U.S. population — typically the oldest and most affluent part — has been in a moderate recovery for almost three years, while the majority remains thoroughly mired in _____.

① flush   ② recession
③ tenure   ④ gibberish

20 Lee puts a white stone near the very center of the board. It effectively cuts AlphaGo's defenses in half. And the machine _____. Not literally, of course. But its next move is _____. Lee shoots a pointed stare at Huang, the AlphaGo programmer who acts as its human avatar and places its stones on the board, as if his opponent is Huang rather than a billion _____.

① gouges — extemporaneous — bungles
② blinks — horrendous — circuits
③ debilitates — terrific — nerves
④ glimpses — jaded — episodes

21 Assad has failed to learn some lessons from the other dictators removed by the Arab Spring, most of whom were likely out of touch with the facts on the ground beyond the bubble of their inner circles. To many cornered tyrants, _____ by years of total control, it might still be hard to comprehend — even after 1½ years of brutal fighting — that the status quo they wrought over decades can _____ in a flash of smoke.

① accustomed — vaunt   ② wreaked — decay
③ inured — disappear   ④ stultified — rejoice

22 Though living on the street is prohibited, the local police obviously turn a blind eye to the practice, as long as the _____ don't cause any trouble. I reckon their presence actually makes the neighborhood more _____, as their eyes are most certainly on the street.

① footpads — secluded   ② vagabond — vibrant
③ vagrants — secure   ④ scavengers — livable

23 The life history of the individual is first and foremost a(n) _____ to the patterns and standards traditionally handed down in his community. From the moment of his birth the customs into which he is born shape his experience and behavior. By the time he is grown and able to take part in activities, his culture's habits are his habits, its beliefs his beliefs, and its impossibilities his impossibilities.

① accommodation   ② cacophony

③ flivver   ④ upheaval

24 Joseph Heller coined the term "*Catch 22*" in his 1961 novel Catch-22, which describes absurd bureaucratic constraints on soldiers in World War II. The term is introduced by the character Doc Daneeka, an army psychiatrist who invokes "Catch 22" to explain why any pilot requesting mental evaluation for insanity — hoping to be found not sane enough to fly and thereby escape dangerous missions — demonstrates his _____ in making the request and thus cannot be declared insane. This phrase also means a dilemma or difficult circumstance from which there is no escape because of mutually conflicting or dependent conditions.

① own insanity   ② own sanity

③ own dependence   ④ own independence

⑤ own absurdity

25 Because man is a social being, he cares for the judgment of his fellows. To possess a good reputation with family, neighbors, friends, to avoid social condemnation is undoubtedly a motive for good conduct. Pliny stated the case with substantial truth, when he said, "How few there are who preserve the same delicacy of conduct in secret as when exposed to the view of the world!" The truth is, the generality of mankind stand in awe of public opinion, while conscience is feared only by the few. A saying of the Arabs puts the point with cynical brevity: "_____."

① Do unto others as you would have them do unto you

② Actions speak louder than words

③ Lean liberty is better than fat slavery

④ In a town where you know no one do whatever you like

❙ Choose the one that best completes the sentence(s).

▶ ▶ ▶ **ANSWERS** P.296

01 The company's troubleshooter was called upon to _____ in the dispute that had hurt relations between the company and the town.

① turn   ② give
③ chide   ④ intercede

02 It has pleased me very often to show how much of goodness there is, ironically, in persons who by common standards would be _____ condemned.

① leniently   ② contingently
③ tepidly   ④ relentlessly

03 Although he was usually gluttonous and _____, his illness blunted both his appetite and his temper.

① reticent   ② reflective
③ lukewarm   ④ contentious

04 Though they came from _____ social back-grounds, the newly married couple shared numerous interests and feeling.

① desultory   ② jocund
③ lugubrious   ④ disparate

05 Jin-ah must be from a very affluent home. I don't think she has ever suffered from any _____ in her life.

① symmetry   ② malady
③ imputation   ④ deprivation

06 Neanderthals have long been portrayed as _____, but archaeological evidence the British scientists unearthed suggests that they were capable of symbolic thinking.

① miscreant   ② gargantuan
③ imbecile   ④ sanguine

07 The Norwegian Nobel Committee invites nominators from among national assemblies, university deans and professors, and others. Nominators are secret for 50 years unless leaked by insiders _____ to that knowledge.

① prim   ② privy
③ primordial   ④ punitive

08 Every impressionistic picture is the deposit of a moment in the perpetuum mobile of existence, the representation of a(n) _____, unstable balance in the play of contending forces.

① adamant   ② callous
③ detrimental   ④ precarious

09 Many people are still ignorant about AIDS. I think more can be done to educate people so that families of AIDS patients will not be shunned and treated as _____ of society.

① harbinger   ② pariah
③ trencherman   ④ equestrian

10 It is the same thing as the _____ of the artist. That is to say, it is direct knowledge of the world as it is and direct acquaintance with things in the world, and this is the primary knowledge of the artist.

① genius   ② intuition
③ syllogism   ④ dilettantism

11 At present it is out of my power to reward you for your service, but in a month or two I shall come into my inheritance, with the control of my income, and then at least you shall not find me _____.

① lanky   ② unappreciative
③ lavish   ④ mournful

12 It was a landmark achievement on all fronts, _____ one of the most divisive debates in modern medicine and religion. It was lauded by scientists, ethicists and religious groups.

① fermenting   ② inveigling
③ defusing   ④ downplaying

13 Krakatoa became a naturalist's paradise, and the Dutch made it a nature reserve and allowed no one but _____ scientists to set foot on the island. They worked out a complete inventory of life on Krakatoa.

① accredited   ② unaffiliated
③ mesmerized   ④ retired

14 Just as our criticism of a work of art begins only when we have ceased to experience it, so our criticism of our friends begins only when we have ceased to experience them, when our minds can no longer remain _____.

① in artistic inspiration   ② full of critical spirit
③ appreciative of solitude   ④ at the height of intimacy

15 Russia is stepping up its gold sales in the West. Bullion dealers in Zurich report an influx of nearly $200 million worth of gold into Switzerland in October. Analysts speculate that Russia sales are aimed at _____ foreign deposit which dropped $2.5 billion since the end of last year.

① embezzling   ② peculating
③ liquidating   ④ procuring

16 Beethoven wrote fragment of themes in note books which he kept beside him, working on and developing them over years. Often his first ideas were of a(n) _____ which make scholars marvel how he could, at the end, have developed from them such miraculous results.

① virtuoso 　　　　　　　　　② adroitness
③ contraband 　　　　　　　　④ clumsiness

17 Criticism must always profess an end in view. The critic's task, therefore, appears to be quite clearly cut out for him: and it is comparatively easy to decide whether he performs it satisfactorily, and, in general what kinds of criticisms are useful and what _____.

① profane 　　　　　　　　　② otiose
③ chivalrous 　　　　　　　　④ variegated

18 Extreme weather across the globe this year, from drought conditions in Russia and Ukraine to flooding in Pakistan and Canada, is lighting a fire under commodity prices. Wheat prices have _____ since June, while corn rallied to a 23-month high, coffee reached a 13-year peak, and cotton advanced to its most expensive levels since 1995.

① settled 　　　　　　　　　② bungled
③ spiked 　　　　　　　　　　④ jaywalked

19 Couples who have too much independence don't connect or rely on each other enough. If the link is broken, both sides are fine on their own. On the other end of the spectrum, if that link is broken, both sides _____. Ideal is the relationship in which each side needs the other but they are also _____ enough to stand on their own.

① falter — subordinate 　　　　② scramble — adjunctive
③ withstand — detached 　　　　④ tumble — autonomous

20 The great source of both the misery and disorders of human life seems to arise from over-rating the difference between one permanent situation and another. _____ over-rates the difference between poverty and riches; ambition, that between a private and a public station; _____, that between obscurity and extensive reputation.

① Wrath — sloth
② Gluttony — envy
③ Lust — wrath
④ Envy — prudence
⑤ Avarice — vainglory

21 Privacy is something that everyone in this country likes to feel they have a right to. To have that right so easily _____ by the electronic data-collection apparatus, which allows anyone to easily obtain our enlisted telephone numbers, for example, is just _____ to everything this democracy stands for.

① averted — fallow
② guaranteed — hypercritical
③ usurped — counter
④ seized — apposite

22 All too often there exists _____ between what man aims for and what he gets. He sprays pesticides to get rid of insects and weeds, but he thereby kills birds, fishes, and flowering trees. He drives long distances to find unspoiled nature, but he poisons the air and gets killed on the way. He builds machines to escape from physical work, but he becomes their slave and suffers boredom.

① a merciful providence
② a doleful misnomer
③ a painful discrepancy
④ an opportune ambiguity

23 Through defective presentation the Government has allowed the wages pause to be interpreted as involving a substantial sacrifice by all concerned, and especially by those least able to afford it. The very reverse is true. In fact, substantial benefits would _____ to everybody by maintaining existing wage levels, because if this were done for a reasonable time, real earnings, or purchasing power, would improve.

① canvass
② accrue
③ macerate
④ slacken

24 There's a saying in China that _____. The premise of the aphorism — it's better to be over-qualified than under-qualified relative to one's surroundings — is so widely accepted that similar versions of it exist across cultures. Americans and Brits often declare that it's better to be a big frog (or fish) in a small pond than a little frog in a big pond.

① danger foreseen is half avoided
② if the wind will not serve, take to the oars
③ a friend to all is a friend to none
④ honey catches more flies than vinegar
⑤ it's better to be the head of a chicken than the tail of a phoenix

25 The most serious threat to a person's progress arises from his efforts to keep safe in his job, to see to it that he doesn't make mistakes. Sometimes when we adopt "safe" attitudes we tell ourselves that we don't disagree with the boss because we are loyal to him and the organization. Far be it from me to belittle loyalty, but I would rather have a little disagreement. I'd rather have someone give me an argument. Let us remember that two men in an organization think exactly alike, we can _____.

① achieve our goal more easily
② get along without one of them
③ dispense with other organization's help
④ keep our jobs more safe

❚ Choose the one that best completes the sentence(s). ▶▶▶ **ANSWERS** P.301

01 The artist captured the sadness of childhood in his portrait of the boy with the _____ countenance, though other people couldn't notice all about that.

① sadistic   ② rueful

③ salient   ④ gorgeous

02 Casual acquaintances were deceived by his _____ of sophistication and couldn't recognize his fundamental shallowness.

① pinnacle   ② revulsion

③ asperity   ④ veneer

03 Unfortunately, his stubborn refusal to abase himself in the eyes of his followers more irritated the conqueror, who wanted to _____ him.

① humiliate   ② incarcerate

③ manacle   ④ commandeer

04 As soon as the news of his _____ spread throughout Wall Street the next day, all his fellow brokers dropped by to congratulate him.

① coup   ② down-fall

③ trepidation   ④ tribulation

05 The driving force behind the country's new green economy is almost entirely _____. But people of color have much more directly at stake in the greening of America.

① bankrupt   ② white

③ hectic   ④ ethnic

06 He had a terrible habit of boasting so much about his smallest accomplishments that his _____ became renowned throughout the small college campus.

① bluff   ② rectitude
③ diffidence   ④ tempestuousness

07 We have to earn silence, to work for it and to make it not an absence but a presence, that is, not emptiness but _____.

① repast   ② reconnaissance
③ repletion   ④ repulsion

08 The judge asked them to control their usual _____ and to present just simple unvarnished facts.

① vagary   ② understatement
③ axiom   ④ embellishment

09 An ophthalmologist and his sister sprinkled flour in a Connecticut Ikea parking lot. An ensuing bioterrorism scare forced hundreds to _____. The two now face felony charges.

① evacuate   ② converge
③ consort   ④ disport

10 A judge has ruled Paris Hilton will be "in" custody this season, sentencing her to 45 days in county jail. "Paris is known for her variety of looks," he said. "This season it'll be _____."

① green   ② stripes
③ gray   ④ short

11 These days, the safest way to appear intelligent is to be _____ by default. We seem sophisticated when we say we don't believe and disingenuous when we say we do.

① creative   ② equivocal

③ lukewarm   ④ skeptical

12 _____ demand from Chinese automakers and shipbuilders helped push up steel prices last year, promoting POSCO to raise prices of its benchmark hot-rolled coil steel by 52 percent to around $510 per metric ton.

① Voracious   ② Malodorous

③ Judicious   ④ Unpretentious

13 Every 25 minutes in the United States, a baby is born addicted to opioids. That heartbreaking statistic is but one symptom of an epidemic that shows no sign of _____. The 33,000 overdose deaths from opioids last year were a 16 percent rise over the previous year, which also set a record.

① abating   ② persisting

③ surging   ④ budding

⑤ gnawing

14 Hummingbirds aren't the fastest birds in the animal kingdom, but these diminutive aerial acrobats can beat their wings up to 200 times per second, faster than any other bird. This skill combined with the rest of their anatomy enables them to _____ in mid-air like a helicopter and even fly backwards.

① soar   ② haunt

③ overhang   ④ grovel

⑤ hover

15   As the 42nd President of the United States, he was _____, even by his allies, as a Big Mac-scarfing saxophone-blowing sly Southern lawyer. At the same time, even his _____ acknowledged his charm, intelligence and political acumen.

① lampooned — adversaries   ② rhapsodized — opponents

③ discrowned — buddies   ④ lionized — confidants

16   What would American sports look like if all the major sports associations required athletes to prove that they are _____ in English? That is essentially what the LPGA has mandated with a new rule that will require all golfers who have been on tour for two years to pass a test of their spoken English.

① inarticulate   ② garrulous

③ conversant   ④ ethereal

17   To say that he who is old enough to fight his country's battles is old enough to vote is to draw an utterly _____ parallel. The ability to evaluate on the basis of facts is a prerequisite to good voting age. The thing called for in a soldier is _____ obedience, and that is not what you want in a voter.

① fallacious — uncritical   ② convincing — unflinching

③ asinine — vacillating   ④ intriguing — evanescent

18   The ire of their colleagues has not prevented a small, loosely organized band of academic psychologists from rooting out and publicly _____ mental health practices that they view as faddish, _____ or in some cases potentially harmful.

① debunking — unproved

② inveighing against — ingenuous

③ garnering — state-of-the-art

④ pondering — malignant

19 Buffett's detachment was a secret of his success. In 1969, after a fabulous run as a hedge-fund manager, he decided that Wall Street was _____ opportunities and returned his investors' money. This was unselfish as well as _____. The market crashed.

① exempt from — bureaucratic   ② lacking in — fatuous

③ barren of — prescient   ④ fervent to — clairvoyant

20 Tens of thousands of Greek protesters clashed in the streets as European leaders met in Brussels to consider German plans for tighter fiscal unity that would give the European Union power to veto budgets of debtor nations if they don't cut spending enough. "We're protesting against the harsh inhumane _____ measures," said Ira Diamantidi, a teacher in Athens.

① panache   ② impeachment

③ retrenchment   ④ comity

21 In problems of conduct the child is soon aware of his own _____ on some of his acts. He is puzzled by the recrudescence of acts he has forbidden himself. To the psychologist this is the development the super-ego which is result of the relationship established between the child and his social environment. But to the religious educationist this is the sign of a developing _____.

① continence — nirvana   ② objurgation — brawl

③ buffoonery — turpitude   ④ censorship — conscience

22 There is a(n) _____ relationship between the difficulty and expense of communication and the quality of what is communicated. When telegraph operators were paid by the word, and there was always the risk of garbled transmissions, messages were _____ and to the point. When neither length nor complexity affects the cost of a message, however, the field is open for irrelevant and unnecessary communication.

① inverse — concise   ② direct — dilapidated

③ designated — condensed   ④ converse — rambling

23 Take any successful person you know who can do something better than anybody else and try to distract his _____ from it while he is doing it. The late George Grey Barnard, widely regarded as a great sculptor, used to bewilder his friends by literally failing to see them when they dropped into his studio while he was at work. Unless you permit yourself to become thus _____ in the thing that you want to do, there is little chance of your doing that thing exceptionally well.

① intentness — immersed　　　② intransigeance — maladroit
③ concentration — gauche　　　④ foible — absorbed

24 Nor do I _____ "the people." When I began reporting on the state legislature while a student at the University of Texas, a wily old state senator offered to acquaint me with how the place worked. We stood at the back of the Senate floor as he pointed to his colleagues spread out around the chamber — playing cards, napping, winking at pretty young visitors in the gallery — and he said to me, "If you think these guys are bad, you should see the people who sent them there."

① demonize　　　② underestimate
③ romanticize　　　④ deify
⑤ supercede

25 In America, the few security guards working at soft targets often are unarmed, untrained and unmotivated. Camera surveillance systems (when they are in place at all) tend to be monitored only irregularly, and when the cameras are monitored, the security guards usually focus more on potential thieves and troublemakers than on potential terrorists. Absent an attack on a soft target in this country, the American people simply won't _____ the draconian countermeasures that Israelis accept without complaint. The upshot is a deadly double irony. The very fact that there hasn't been an attack on a soft target in the United States increases the danger of one. And, the harder we harden hard targets, the more likely an attack on a soft target becomes.

① tolerate　　　② disdain
③ jeopardize　　　④ censor
⑤ depreciate

20

❚ Choose the one that best completes the sentence(s). ▶▶▶ **ANSWERS** P.307

01 A surprising number of animal species maintain a _____ relationship as the male and the female mate for life.

① bilateral   ② monogamous
③ flimsy   ④ promiscuous

02 Later, she claimed that her ex-husband was a total _____ and wondered why she had ever married him. But all was too late.

① convert   ② mogul
③ cipher   ④ veterinarian

03 Although he is not as yet a _____ and senile old man, his ideas and opinions no longer can merit the respect we gave him years ago.

① touchy   ② doddering
③ naive   ④ nubile

04 The founder of the Children's Defense Fund, Marian Wright Edelman, strongly _____ the lack of financial and moral support for children in America today.

① decries   ② dissimulates
③ simulates   ④ ruminates

05 Although he pretended their encounter was _____, he had actually been hanging around her usual haunts for the past two weeks, hoping she would turn up.

① predestined   ② insipid
③ vapid   ④ fortuitous

06 Ryan's comments on the subject came not from any direct statement but from a(n) _____ story that continued to go the rounds.

① apocryphal   ② gingerbread
③ explicit   ④ voyeuristic

07 The 32-year-old stewardess, on holiday in the Philippines, was glad for the chance to _____ the beaten path, though the grimy shantytown she was visiting for the first time was not a safe neighborhood.

① stray off   ② step on to
③ sweep over   ④ secure against

08 A woman and her 10-year-old child sued police officers for engaging in a body search in violation of their constitutional rights. The court allowed the case to go forward. Alito dissented, arguing that the police had qualified _____.

① immunity   ② consent
③ repatriation   ④ prosecution
⑤ acceptance

09 Hard-liners of Islam who bomb and kill innocent people _____ the image of my beloved country, Indonesia. They use religion to try and justify their destructive actions.

① buttress   ② tarnish
③ denote   ④ brandish

10 The kinds of information that we are willing to share these days not just with our friends and acquaintances but, via social media, with complete strangers is astonishing. No intimate moment is too personal to _____.

① divulge   ② savor
③ lavish   ④ reminisce

11 Roosevelt's nauseating flattery of Stalin is easily matched by Churchill's. Just like Roosevelt, Churchill heaped _____ praise on the Communist murderer, and was anxious for Stalin's personal friendship.

① pernicious   ② titular
③ grisly   ④ fulsome

12 The intense feeling widespread among the satellite country citizens that their country should be freer to run its own affairs is _____ by the reality that it cannot survive without the parton country's blessings.

① deviated   ② vilified
③ adumbrated   ④ tempered

13 Formulating a good working definition of annoyance is a persistent challenge for researchers. One calls it the weakest form of anger, simply _____. Others cite overtones of disgust, dislike and even panic.

① instinctive desire   ② diluted rage
③ intrusive memory   ④ sheer delight

14 Germany's decision to _____ nuclear power after the Fukushima catastrophe in Japan could lead to some of the country's major companies relocating elsewhere in search of cheaper energy.

① stick to   ② capitalize on
③ phase out   ④ trigger off

15 People have tried to say what music is, and what it means to them. The _____ provides a definition. But throughout the ages, poets, philosophers, writers, musicians have found a dictionary definition unsatisfactory to characterize this art.

① bibliographer   ② lexicographer
③ maestro   ④ bigwig

16 The Jewish tradition has shunned the _____ propensities of our Abrahamic cousins, Christianity and Islam, but in doing so, it has seemed, to some, to embrace an ethos of exclusion.

① terrestrial ② proselytizing
③ belligerent ④ sanctifying
⑤ sacrificing

17 If you're overweight and have diabetes, you probably have a fatty liver. But there are ways to _____ the fat. Researchers at Johns Hopkins University found that moderate biking, walking or running three times a week cut the fat in people's livers by as much as 40 percent.

① dilate ② douse
③ prune ④ forge

18 If you are low in calcium, increasing your calcium intake may help _____ weight. It's believed that the brain detects when there is a lack of calcium and compensates by spurring food intake. Sufficient calcium intake seems to _____ the desire to eat more.

① replicate — excrete ② bloat — curb
③ shed — stifle ④ dilate — suture

19 Criticism makes or breaks relationships. The best predictor of relapse for married adults with depression is their response to the question "How critical is your spouse of you?" Patients who relapsed rated their spouses as significantly more critical than did patients who remained well. It's crucial to criticize without _____.

① disparaging or humiliating ② bemoaning or deploring
③ entertaining or flattering ④ venerating or commending

20 On most of us the effect of our general education has been such that we have tended to believe rather _____, first that liberty is a good thing, and secondly that the possession of it is likely to increase our happiness. But a moment's consideration will show us that neither of these propositions is _____.

① giddily — manifest
② considerately — tentative
③ unconditionally — falsified
④ uncritically — self-evident

21 We do not perceive ourselves as part of a social context, as the daughter of so-and-so, as a member of this family or the other; we are _____ individuals. This becomes evident whenever something criminal or immoral is done. In the old days, such an action would bring shame upon the entire family; today, only the individual is considered _____.

① crotchety — draconian
② autonomous — blameworthy
③ self-governing — gung-ho
④ pigheaded — reproachable

22 The country's last revolution took a staggering toll, including an estimated one million people dead. But it also started the country's public dreaming of democracy. What they got instead was a cruel _____ by a political system that _____ a revolutionary name and kept up the old dictatorial ways. The government used repressive tactics to stamp out much of the people's will to fight. It did not, however, extinguish their dream.

① swindle — mitigated
② convalescence — affected
③ extremity — ameliorated
④ hoax — feigned

23 The use of hot language is symptomatic of a certain malaise affecting people, which leads them to believe that life must at all times be exciting, vital, dazzling, full of "fabulous" experiences. This is nonsense, obviously. Everyone spends a great deal of his time doing routine, ordinary things. Thus, the use of hot language makes us _____ our lives, since we take a rather absurd conception of what is normal, measure our lives against this false norm and find ourselves wanting.

① devaluate
② descry
③ habituate
④ inculcate

24   The chief attraction slang has for people is novelty. It is fun to hear an idea phrased in a new, unusual way. But after hundreds of repetition, the novelty wears off; the slang loses its freshness and sparkle. The history of most slang expressions is that they are born — they are overused — they become stale — and they die an early death. That is one reason why slang is often ineffective in speech and inappropriate in writing _____.

① that is intended to be read by literate people
② that is too different from the speech
③ that is too recondite to be understood
④ that is meant to last for some time

25   The next game-changing scientific discovery is as likely to come from an armchair amateur as it is from a researcher toiling away in the pristine chambers of a professional laboratory. These days, thousands of citizen scientists are already readily answering the call of crowdsourcing sites to do the grunt work, brainwork and even funding of applied scientific research. And, instead of _____ of noncredentialed, unschooled wannabes playing in their sandboxes, bona fide scientists are inviting them to jump in, sift through their data and even join in their games, some of which solve significant problems.

① pondering over the merits
② accepting a proposal without reserve
③ bristling at the prospect
④ framing a hypothesis

▌Choose the one that best completes the sentence(s).

▶ ▶ ▶ ANSWERS P.312

01 In that country, the captured knights could escape death only if they agreed to _____ Christianity and embrace Islam as the one true faith.

① hail
② baptize
③ forswear
④ refurbish

02 We tell ourselves that we cherish efficiency, yet we have created a transport system whose design principle is _____.

① frugality
② chagrin
③ presumption
④ profligacy

03 Cate Blanchett hinted Friday that her acting career may _____ to her new role as the artistic director of a leading Sydney theater company.

① come to heels
② play truant
③ come in handy
④ take a back seat

04 He was afraid to call a spade a spade and just resorted to _____ to avoid direct reference to his subject.

① circumlocutions
② lullaby
③ lexicons
④ valediction

05 I do think that you cannot keep your _____ in this affair secret very long; you would be wise to admit your involvement immediately to your superiors.

① corollary
② complicity
③ throe
④ schism

06   After all of us vividly saw his earlier rudeness, we were much delighted to see him get his _____.

① reincarnation   ② paean
③ comeuppance   ④ eclat

07   In the end, all forgivers do the same thing; they restore self-worth to the offender; they cancel a debt; they experience such peace that they lose the urge to _____.

① relegate   ② rejuvenate
③ retaliate   ④ revoke

08   There was nothing tentative or provisional in Moore's early critical pronouncements. She dealt _____ with what were then radical new developments in poetry.

① confidently   ② remissly
③ perversely   ④ surreptitiously

09   So _____ did Jean Lafitte manage this clandestine and lawless trade that, though his brothers were often brought within the clutches of the law, he always escaped.

① overtly   ② adroitly
③ gauntly   ④ waywardly

10   Some people consider desecration of the American flag to be treasonous or even an act of terrorism, but others refuse to treat what they consider a mere symbol as _____.

① seminal   ② sacrosanct
③ obsequious   ④ dubitable

11 The many hours spent surfing the internet have proved _____. Whilst most items of equipment were generally less expensive to purchase in the US, some were purchased on eBay very cheaply.

① providential ② raucous
③ scathing ④ irascible

12 Contracts signed under _____ are voidable and, you cannot be convicted of a crime if you can prove that you were forced or threatened into committing the crime, although this defence may not be available for serious crimes.

① duress ② menopause
③ parturition ④ stupor

13 By winning your point in a quarrel, you only prove that your spouse is not _____. A man and wife who really want to have a happy life together will do well to bear in mind the old saying that love has eye-lids as well as eyes.

① spotless ② heedless
③ restless ④ dauntless

14 By turning a personal tragedy into a force for good, she has changed the thinking of thousands of people. It's too bad that the media doesn't carry more stories like this to _____ the usual gloom and doom we seem to hear daily.

① solidify ② offset
③ concatenate ④ cull

15 A law making it illegal for people to give their pets human names was recently proposed in Brazil after psychologists suggested some children felt depressed because they shared their first name with someone's pet. If the law is _____, pet owners who break the law will be forced to pay fines or do community service.

① fabricated ② abrogated
③ ratified ④ prognosticated

16 Competition over promotions in the workplace is often a source of racially charged conflict in the United States. African-Americans are beginning to vie for positions in greater numbers, and there is _____ from people who do not want more competition for the limited number of jobs.

① fiat   ② concurrence
③ blandishment   ④ backlash

17 Iran's oil revenues are falling and could drop much lower as the _____ on Iranian oil expands and investment in Iran's oil sector dries up. Economic _____ also are inflicting increasing damage on Iran's long-term oil-production potential.

① check — nomenclature   ② clout — anarchy
③ demand — peril   ④ embargo — sanctions

18 Physiologically, we are rhythmical. We must eat, sleep, breathe, and play regularly to maintain good health. Emotionally we are rhythmical, too, for psychologists say that all of us feel _____ periods of relative depression and exhilaration. Intellectually we are also rhythmical, for we must have periods of _____ following periods of concentration.

① alternate — relaxation   ② verdant — recess
③ rotating — centralization   ④ immutable — respite

19 If you think the government is watching your every move, that's crazy — but if you think the government is too good or too honest to try it, that's naive. Whether in the name of fighting crime, communism, terrorism, anarchy, military enemies, or just in the name of patriotism, our government has watched us before and will watch us again. As technology improves, our privacy will inevitably evaporate; the best we can hope for is the power to _____.

① communize the government   ② privatize the private area
③ enlighten naive people   ④ watch the watchers

20　While he declined to mention Spotify by name, Cook told that Apple worries about streaming music losing the human touch, alluding to Spotify's more algorithmic approach to highlighting content. Cook's words embody Apple's longstanding _____ of Spotify, which is that its algorithms are _____ music's spiritual role in our lives. Cook says, "We worry about the humanity being drained out of music."

① reproach — evading　　　　② critique — eroding
③ condescension — evacuating　④ hurrah — exhorting
⑤ depreciation — eavesdropping

21　In European culture, we _____ the sphere of business from that of friendship. The former insists on the rightness of obtaining the best bargain possible, while the latter refuses to treat in terms of bargains at all. Yet there is a(n) _____ sphere. Business has its social morality. Things are done 'as a favour,' and there are concepts of 'fair' prices. Friendship does not necessarily ignore the material aspects. 'One good turn deserves another' epitomizes regard for reciprocity which underlies many friendly actions.

① classify — superlative　　　② synthesize — intermediary
③ demarcate — intermediate　　④ differentiate — extramural

22　Most people think that professional underwater photographers are lucky to get to swim about, shooting scenes of breathtaking marine life. But their art is also a business. Meeting deadlines can require a great deal of knowledge and creativity, mainly because underwater visibility is _____. Rough seas cause reduced visibility for several reasons. One is that the rough surface reflects more sunlight, so that less light penetrates underwater. Another is that wave surges can stir up the silt and sand on the sea bottom, so that the water becomes _____.

① compromised — murky　　　② impounded — shrouded
③ disconnected — cantorial　　④ flared — effulgent
⑤ shrunk — reinstated

23 There's been a lot of talk recently that social media has a negative impact on our mental health, and you might be looking at the beginning of the new year as an opportunity for _____. The early studies suggest that, as well as making us more connected than ever before and giving us exhilarating hits of dopamine, social media usage is associated with symptoms of depression, anxiety and loneliness in some people.

① executable New Year's resolution ② digital detoxing

③ becoming a digital nerd ④ pursuing a return to nature

24 In any matter of which the public has imperfect knowledge, public opinion is as likely to be erroneous as is the opinion of an individual equally uninformed. To hold otherwise is to hold that wisdom can be got by combining many ignorances. A man who knows nothing of algebra cannot be assisted in the solution of an algebraic problem by calling in a neighbor who knows no more than himself, and the solution approved by the unanimous vote of a million such men would _____ against that of a competent mathematicians.

① count for nothing ② be considered serious

③ be infallible ④ be taken for granted

25 Despite Obama's promises to clean up Wall Street, there has not been a single criminal charge filed by the federal government against any top executive of the financial institutions. Why is that? In a word: _____. Take Goldman Sachs, for example. In 2008, Goldman Sachs employees were among Barack Obama's top campaign contributors. Furthermore, when the Senate Permanent Subcommittee issued a report detailing Goldman's suspicious Abacus deal, several Goldman executives began flooding Obama campaign coffers with donations.

① jingoism ② cronyism

③ elitism ④ capitalism

▌Choose the one that best completes the sentence(s).   ▶▶▶ ANSWERS P.317

01   The _____ qualities of his poetry overshadow its literary qualities; the lesson he teaches in his work is more memorable than the lines themselves.

① scathing   ② didactic

③ acerbic   ④ oblique

02   Nobody minded when Professor Renoir's lectures wandered away from their official theme; his _____ were always more fascinating than the topic of the day.

① apologues   ② victuals

③ homilies   ④ digressions

03   People were shocked and dismayed when they learned of their patron's _____ in this affair, for he had always seemed honest and straightforward to them.

① verity   ② fray

③ duplicity   ④ hypnosis

04   The financial picture has grown so _____ at the American Folk Art Museum that its trustees are considering shutting it down and donating all its collections to another institution.

① bleak   ② promising

③ ostentatious   ④ sturdy

05   For decades, Cuba's great resource has been its people, whose unquenchable _____ has somehow sustained them even as everything seems to collapse around them. There's still a Saturday-night vitality to the place.

① edacity   ② verve

③ torpor   ④ qualm

06   It is not only the minority who are in danger of censorship; mainstream, even majority arguments and things formerly considered to be common sense or harmless jokes are increasingly causing their proponents to be _____.

① muzzled   ② safeguarded
③ substantiated   ④ convinced

07   Adriana was outstanding as the moderator; she handled the intensely heated debate with great _____, diplomatically and tactfully keeping the conversation fair and on track.

① haggle   ② finesse
③ prowess   ④ succor

08   I think they were once a great football powerhouse in this country, but their play is _____ these days. I guess too many easy victories caused them to lose their fire — that is to say, their desire to win.

① incorrigible   ② effete
③ effusive   ④ exuberant

09   In China offline retailing is fragmented and underdeveloped except in big cities near the east coast. Thus, online companies are more likely to _____ in China whereas they often disrupted existing industries in the Western countries.

① face a deadlock   ② suffer a loss
③ fill a void   ④ take another leap

10   The 500,000 won she will earn monthly may look _____ compared to Korean wages, but with the low living costs there, the five-hour work days, accommodation and transport fully provided by the employer, it is not bad, she said.

① paltry   ② hefty
③ prodigious   ④ excessive

11 In general, the slave-soldiers adhered to a strict code of conduct, in which obedience and manners were paramount and any violation resulted in harsh punishment. In addition, they were expected to lead a _____ life, never marrying.

① promiscuous   ② pragmatic
③ celibate   ④ diaphanous

12 When the family of a wife send her a message to the effect that she has to return to them because an installment of the purchase money has not been paid up to time, she agrees _____, even if she loves her husband and finds it hard to leave him.

① to pay dowry soon   ② in a fit of spleen
③ to elope with money   ④ without further ado

13 Secondhand smoke is a mixture of the smoke given off by the burning end of a cigarette, pipe or cigar and the smoke exhaled from the lungs of smokers. It is involuntarily inhaled by nonsmokers, can cause or exacerbate a wide range of _____ health effects, including cancer, respiratory infections, and asthma.

① viable   ② listless
③ deranged   ④ adverse

14 Religion is ubiquitous but it is not universal. That is a _____ for people trying to explain it. Religious types, noting the ubiquity, argue that this proves religion is a real reflection of the underlying nature of things. Sceptics wonder why, if that is the case, it comes in such a variety of flavors, from the Holy Catholic and Apostolic Church to the cargo cults of Papua New Guinea.

① rationale   ② pathos
③ mirth   ④ conundrum

15   In theory, prostate cancer cells can spread anywhere in the body. In practice, though, most cases of prostate cancer _____ occur in the lymph nodes and the bones. The spread occurs when cells break away from the tumor in the prostate. The cancer cells can travel through the lymphatic system or the bloodstream to other areas of the body.

① metastasis   ② carcinogen

③ occlusion   ④ incision

16   When you have to remember several series of facts, start by _____. If you have to name the bones of a skeleton, it would be more efficient to start with the bones of the skull, then the neck and back, then the arms and so on, rather than memorizing them haphazardly.

① assessing importances   ② establishing groups

③ identifying features   ④ figuring out cases in point

17   Property owners can get very touchy when a new neighbor comes in and plans on putting up a three story house that completely _____ views from surrounding homes' front porches, back decks, bedroom windows, etc. So, homeowners often have mutual agreements not to build any structures that obstruct existing views.

① supplements   ② antedates

③ obliterates   ④ ornaments

18   When North Korea announced that it was aiming rockets at South Korea, Hawaii, and the U.S. territory of Guam, the Pentagon described this as "bellicose rhetoric." Another Washington Defense official used a perfect synonym for bellicose when describing North Korea's announcement: "We have no indications at this point that it's anything more than _____ rhetoric."

① tumescent   ② warmongering

③ red-tape   ④ felicitous

19 Western democracies have turned into nothing less than insidious and perfidious plutocracies, their economies in _____. We hope a new generation of _____ politicians in the U.S. and Europe will try to find the way to run a country without messing up its economy.

① updrafts — versatile
② moiety — principled
③ shambles — upright
④ straits — crooked

20 _____ on a ship at sea is called mutiny. Special laws impose penalties on a sailor who recalcitrantly acts against the captain or any of his officers. However, a sailor can prove that his disobedience was warranted by some _____ circumstances, such as an illegal order or mentally ill officer.

① Defiance — dilatory
② Camouflage — swarthy
③ Cajolery — palliative
④ Insubordination — extenuating

21 Back in 1999, at the euro's launch, hopes were high that Europe would cleanse itself of its warring past as efficiently as it _____ with historic currencies like the peseta, franc, guilder, and deutsche mark. If anything, the opposite is occurring. The euro coin has become a _____ to many member countries and forced togetherness is reviving prejudices between nations.

① was besieged — nostrum
② dispensed — millstone
③ broke up — gimmick
④ was infatuated — whirlpool

22 Junk turns the user into a plant. Plants do not feel pain since pain has no function in a _____ organism. A plant has no libido in the human or animal sense. Junk replaces the sex drive. Perhaps the intense discomfort of _____ is the transition from plant back to animal, from a painless, sexless, timeless state back to sex and pain and time, from death back to life."

① stationary — withdrawal
② motionless — fanaticism
③ down-to-earth — cold turkey
④ botanical — quarantine

23 Leaders in many organizations mistakenly think that project managers are solely responsible for implementation success or failure. On the surface, such _____ views may appear true — if lots of tasks are late and over-budget, then of course the overall project will follow suit. However, looking more closely it becomes clear that project management is only one dimension among many required for implementation success.

① myopic   ② burlesque

③ auspicious   ④ polemic

24 In primitive ceremonies an individual blessed with the arrival of a baby shared his fortune with the community, to avoid the envy of both his fellows and the gods. The smoke of a proud papa's pipe drifting toward the heavens was a sort of appeasement to the heavenly powers. Today's father's distribution of cigars to celebrate the arrival of a baby may be regarded as a modern _____ of this ritual.

① springboard   ② drawback

③ variant   ④ taboo

25 Whenever someone speaks with prejudice against a group — Catholics, Jews, Italians, Negroes — someone else usually comes up with a classic line of defence: "Look at Einstein!" "Look at Carver!" "Look at Toscanini!" They mean well, these defenders. But their approach is wrong. It is even bad. What a minority group wants is not the right to have geniuses among them but the right to have fools and scoundrels _____.

① without being condemned as a group

② without regard to their mischiefs

③ with all others' bias

④ in its own country

❚ Choose the one that best completes the sentence(s). ▶▶▶ **ANSWERS** P.323

01 Instead of telling Jill directly what he disliked, Jack made a few _____ comments and tried to change the subject.

① pithy   ② terse
③ mealy-mouthed   ④ compendious

02 Your use of _____ expressions such as the one you usually use in your daily conversation in a formal essay spoils the effect you hope to achieve.

① recondite   ② colloquial
③ blasphemous   ④ pusillanimous

03 The judge was especially severe in his sentencing because he felt that the criminal had shown no _____ for his heinous crime.

① sedition   ② tithe
③ iniquity   ④ compunction

04 As it were, he was the kind of individual who would _____ his friends in a cheap card game but remain eminently ethical in all his business dealings.

① mollycoddle   ② cozen
③ betroth   ④ endorse

05 I was unprepared for the state of _____ in which I had found my old friend. To me, he seemed to have aged twenty years in six months.

① zephyr   ② canard
③ decrepitude   ④ muddle

06 Jobs is a classic iconoclast, one who aggressively seeks out, attacks and overthrows conventional ideas. And iconoclasts, especially successful ones, have a(n) _____ for new experiences.

① affinity   ② contretemps
③ rebuff   ④ drudgery

07 _____ attempts at indoor waste disposal have been discovered as far back as 2,500 B.C. It wasn't until Sir John Harrington created an inspired water closet design in the 16th century that indoor plumbing became a practical reality.

① Aborted   ② Medieval
③ Impeccable   ④ Trenchant

08 Explaining the death in simple terms that they can understand is very important in helping children to cope. _____ only add to confusion. Be clear and direct with your explanations.

① Condolences   ② Obituaries
③ Euphonies   ④ Euphemisms

09 Interestingly, Columbia University was not immediately _____ to the proposal by Pulitzer inasmuch as Pulitzer's papers were more known for their sensationalization of the news than for the high quality of the journalism.

① amenable   ② garish
③ dire   ④ venial

10 What happened to the days when publishers had a moral standard? Does the garbage which they print today reflect a decline in social values or is it the _____ of their own making?

① decadence   ② connivance
③ deference   ④ ennui

11 Jin-ah is dead set on crossing the Pacific on her hand-made boat. Her _____ determination has won her the help of a naval officer who willingly trained her in navigation and partially financed her.

① impecunious   ② intemperate

③ irresolute   ④ inexorable

12 Dream Rail is a(n) _____ rail carrier whose _____ is rural areas larger railroads long ago gave up servicing for several reasons. Dream Rail's stock is now performing exceptionally well for an upstart small company.

① newborn — residue   ② conglomerate — realm

③ nascent — niche   ④ old–line — sphere

13 A young Washington confessed to cutting down a cherry tree by proclaiming, "I cannot tell a lie." The story is testament to how much respect Americans have for honesty. But for many, deceit holds the key to money, fame, revenge or power, and these prove all too tempting. In history, this has often resulted in elaborate hoaxes, _____, and forgeries that had enormous ripple effects.

① perjuries   ② professions

③ augury   ④ oblation

14 In 1972, *Science Ninja Team Gatchaman* premiered on Japanese television. Featuring graphic violence, extensive profanity and a transgendered villain, it was one of the most popular animated series of its time. Sandy Frank Entertainment acquired the series in 1978 but deemed it too graphic and shocking for domestic audiences. So, they totally _____ some episodes.

① bowdlerized   ② annealed

③ impugned   ④ annexed

15 An eventful life exhausts rather than stimulates. Milton, who in 1640 was a poet of great promise, spent twenty _____ years in the eventful atmosphere of the Puritan revolution. Cellini's exciting life kept him from becoming the great artist he could have been. It is legitimate to doubt whether Machiavelli would have written his great books had he been allowed to continue in the diplomatic service.

① sterile   ② skittish
③ fecund   ④ muggy

16 Commuting is the act of reducing a sentence. A president has the ability to commute a sentence before it's even begun. A full pardon can do the same thing — it can also reduce a sentence. But more commonly a pardon is granted after a person serves his prison sentence. And unlike a commutation, a pardon can _____ the person of his status as a convicted criminal and restore his civil abilities.

① upbraid   ② absolve
③ stigmatize   ④ capsize

17 The pagan religion of the ancient Greeks may no longer be the established faith of the Aegean peninsula, but references to the legends of its gods and heroes continue to pervade our own culture. Common expressions such as "Pandora's box," "harpy" and "Herculean" are among the many modern-day references to ancient Greek mythology. Its influence can also be detected in a more oblique way; for instance, a number of commentators have observed that modern comic book superheroes _____.

① bear the stamp of Greek myth
② impose their will to change the world
③ fit the archetype of divine beliefs
④ follow a moral code of conduct

18 Our leaders and the media are _____ about the death of Osama bin Laden, with ever more details about the raid being released. Why identify SEAL Team 6, enabling terrorists to seek out team members and their families for retaliation? We are at war. "Loose lips sink ships" is a _____ slogan we have heard so many times but a lesson we need to relearn.

① hush-hushing — foolproof   ② grand-standing — dated
③ ballyhooing — browbeaten   ④ dillydallying — trite

19 For Brazil, India and South Africa, the principle of nonintervention is the _____ of any multilateral foreign policy. They have explicitly opposed the very notion of intervention by the international community to protect civilians and remove dictators, for humanitarian considerations are _____ to defending national sovereignty from foreign interference.

① moniker — auxiliary   ② crux — preferable
③ bedrock — subordinate   ④ touchstone — tantamount

20 The truth is what is the case or what the actual state of affairs in the world is. Some people say that there are no objective truths but only subjective beliefs. Paradoxically, however, this assertion presumes that what they are saying is false. They are asserting that their claim is actually objectively true; it is objectively true that there are no objective truths. _____.

① Absolutism about truth is self-fulfilling
② Relativism about truth is self-fulfilling
③ Absolutism about truth is self-contradictory
④ Relativism about truth is self-contradictory

21 In the recent burst of highly visible hate crimes the emerging pattern seems to be less about specific hates than frenzied _____ staged by a string of losers with a common goal to grab headlines. The reason they are doing this is for their moment of glory, when they feel the whole world is stopping to take notice of them. Society appears to be obliged to pay madmen the _____ they crave.

① habiliment — nuisance   ② qualms — curiosity
③ tantrums — attention   ④ grudge — remission

22 The swimming sky of oceanic expanse in Van Gogh's *The Starry Night*, the human figure born of marble by the careful hands of Rodin, and the graceful, ethereal figure of Degas's ballerina all communicate both emotion and essence in a world where aesthetic reigns supreme. Art has forever been humankind's tool for _____, a form of communication when words fail or are wholly inadequate.

① substantializing ultimate beauty
② flaunting high culture
③ expressing the ineffable
④ assuaging discord

23 Tours with mysterious, eerie, and downright scary themes are popular in New Orleans, and many tour companies have popped up to take visitors through the city's bewitching old cemeteries and haunted buildings. These tours may be too _____ for younger kids, but some adults adore the spine-chilling opportunity to explore the shadowy streets and buildings and creepy cemeteries while listening to fascinating tales of New Orleans history.

① benighted   ② invidious
③ spooky   ④ restive

24 The theory of _____ is the epistemological thesis that individuals are born without built-in mental content and that their knowledge comes from experience and perception. The phrase was made famous by John Locke, who used it to describe his belief that the mind comes into life blank or empty, and is written on by experience. It has been used in education and to argue the nature vs. nurture issue.

① Magnum opus   ② Non sequitur
③ Terra incognita   ④ Tabula rasa

25 Living in a dorm increases the chances that other people will have access to your computer. So, it's wise to take precautions to safeguard private information. The same _____ is needed if your computer is hooked up to a campus network. The school protects individual file storage space by requiring users to register their computers and to create passwords. Users have a(n) _____ responsibility: to change passwords, to log out when ending a session, and to take care where they save their data.

① pilferage — incidental
② alertness — verbatim
③ anathema — accessory
④ vigilance — concomitant

24

▌ Choose the one that best completes the sentence(s). ▶▶▶ ANSWERS P.329

01 The US is not perfect but until recently it has always moved, _____, if slowly and fitfully, in the general direction of justice and greatness.

① fortuitously   ② inexorably
③ expeditiously   ④ waywardly

02 Even though the harsh truth has been obvious from the official data, the related politicians and pundits keep _____. Some of them even say it is irrelevant.

① succumbing   ② prevaricating
③ persevering   ④ receding

03 Before the ground offensive, the UN forces used high-altitude bombers to soften up the enemy forces. The air attacks day in and day out sapped the strength of their ground forces, leaving them _____ when the UN forces advanced.

① invigorated   ② debauched
③ enervated   ④ defiled

04 The Polo family also had to contend with the elements: Rain, snow and other _____ weather caused the trip from Venice to China to be a three-and-a-half- year-trek. Another factor in this delay is that Marco was very sick along the way for nearly a year.

① iridescent   ② libelous
③ inclement   ④ hirsute

05 Political leaders' unwarranted pride is lethal. Absolute rulers' self-conceit tends to corrode their ability to distinguish what is right from wrong or genuine from sham. And sometimes the _____ which tyranny begets digs the grave for such tyrants.

① caprice   ② parochialism
③ hubris   ④ pulchritude

06 C4 is one variety of plastic explosive. The basic idea of plastic explosives is to combine explosive chemicals with a plastic binder material. The binder has an important job. It makes the explosive material highly _____. You can mold it into different shapes to change the direction of the explosion.

① fluorescent ② malleable

③ feculent ④ rancid

07 In the 1976 election, President Gerald Ford made a _____ in a debate with Jimmy Carter, claiming that the Soviet Union did not occupy Eastern Europe. While a majority of viewers thought Ford won the debate, after newscasts focused on the mistake, support for Ford dipped.

① squabble ② slander

③ doublespeak ④ gaffe

08 Of his three daughters, Lear thinks that Cordelia, the youngest, is a(n) _____. In reality, Goneril and Regan, who drive Lear out of their palaces and make him homeless and hungry in rags on a cold stormy night, are ungrateful ones. Lear realizes Cordelia's genuine love too late at their too brief reunion.

① neophyte ② ingrate

③ raconteur ④ virago

09 Richard Lawrence was the first man to be charged for the assassination attempt on an American president, Andrew Jackson. Lawrence was found to have delusional thinking, including the belief he was the king of England and that Jackson had killed his father. He was _____ by reason of insanity and committed to a mental asylum.

① imprisoned ② acquitted

③ edified ④ castigated

10 It probably won't come as much of a shock that pepperoni is the No. 1 pizza topping in America. Other perennial favorites are extra cheese, sausage, mushrooms, green peppers and onions. Anchovies consistently maintain their place as the least popular pizza topping, although they are very popular in some countries. In fact, the world has decidedly _____ taste in toppings.

① dainty   ② eclectic
③ platitudinous   ④ tawdry

11 Old World cities offer meandering streets and broad boulevards that are ideal for walking. Some countries also have walking traditions that can be a joy to discover on a walking vacation. One example is Switzerland, where the hills and mountains are criss-crossed with hiking trails. Another lovely walking tradition is the evening _____ in Spain; whole families converge on central squares to stroll and greet one another.

① masquerade   ② promenade
③ vista   ④ thoroughfare

12 An immuno-therapy drug that turns a patient's own blood cells into cancer killers is on the fast track to USFDA approval. In an ongoing clinical trial, the treatment was administered to advanced lymphoma patients who had not responded to standard treatments or continued to relapse. At three months, 83 percent of patients were in complete _____. As trials progress, scientists hope the therapy could be the next big step forward in cancer treatment.

① digression   ② absolution
③ remission   ④ prostration

13 In a study, a group of acne patients underwent irradiation from blue and red light, using an LED device from Ceragem Medisys, for 2.5 minutes twice daily for four weeks. The _____, meanwhile, was exposed to a placebo device. After 12 weeks, the treatment group saw both inflammatory and non-inflammatory acne lesions decrease by 77 percent and 54 percent, while there wasn't a significant difference in the other group.

① volunteer group   ② response group
③ control group   ④ subsequence group

14 Michael Jackson made his debut in 1964 with The Jackson Brothers, that raised the fame from the '70s until mid-'80s, when Jackson left the group. In 1979, Michael Jackson released his fifth studio album, *Off the Wall*, that topped the Australian chart and went in top 5 in several countries, including United States and United Kingdom. The album went platinum very quickly and _____ the fame of his brothers.

① dismembered   ② disabused
③ eclipsed   ④ acclimated

15 Although we are susceptible to brownnosing, we aren't always fooled. It's easy for a brownnoser to go too far. When the boss finally does recognize that a brownnoser is sucking up for personal gain, the jig is up. The effective brownnoser is careful not to cross the line and make his plans obvious. Psychologists call this problem the _____. It refers to a brownnoser's attempt to get on someone's good side without overdoing it or making his scheme obvious.

① Beginner's Luck   ② Ingratiator's Dilemma
③ Prisoner's Dilemma   ④ All or Nothing

16 We must recall that the economic development dictum is that growth must take place to increase distribution and the _____ order has not worked. One-sided injection of free welfare programs without due strategies on new growth caused a complete economic _____ in Greece recently and in Argentina under Peronism, decades ago.

① depraved — catastrophe   ② adventitious — desuetude
③ reverse — debacle   ④ ignoble — appropriation

17 Women are said to be single-minded. But that which is ordinarily a fault may, on occasion of extraordinary stress, become the most _____ and the most admirable of virtues. I think of this last war and of the share our women and the women of other lands have played in it. No one _____ nor complained at the one-ideaness of womankind while the world was in a welter of woe and slaughter.

① bogus — plodded   ② heinous — mesmerized
③ wistful — balked   ④ transcendent — caviled
⑤ stout — garnered

18 Chavez declared himself cancer-free on Thursday, four months after surgery to remove a malignant tumor. "I am free of illness," Chavez, said in an address. Despite the _____ socialist's declaration, doctors say it is impossible for a cancer patient to be considered out of danger until at least two years after treatment has finished. "His assertion of being cancer-free is overly _____ at this point." said a cancer expert.

① effervescent — gloomy
② despondent — complacent
③ disquieting — ripe
④ ebullient — rosy

19 Whether death means terror or is accepted in quiet resignation, it seems difficult to accept the end of life as the end of being. All the great religions provided beliefs that _____ to this most existential of concerns. It is safe to say that in no known society are members left to face death _____. Rather, it is a mark of human culture that persons are provided with beliefs and rituals that ensure proper passage to a realm beyond death.

① pandered — uninitiated
② catered — embalmed
③ buckled — undaunted
④ succumbed — shielded
⑤ accrued — unprimed

20 Under the postwar plan, Germany was given full responsibility for the payment of reparations. Later, however, the Great Depression hit Germany. In 1931, President Hoover proposed a year's _____ on all intergovernmental debts. So, in June, 1932, an international conference met at Lausanne, and canceled all German reparations until world economic conditions improved. The Treaty of Lausanne marked the end of Germany's payments, for after Hitler's rise to power in 1933 Germany _____ all reparations.

① moratorium — repudiated
② fallout — disapproved
③ reprieve — defrayed
④ decoy — salvaged

21   Now let's take a good look at the fighting armies on both sides fervently praying to God for victory. The army that is victorious thanks God for the victory. The army that is defeated, however, continues to pray to God for _____. Thus, as soon as war is over, we lay the _____ of another. Indeed, there has yet to be a war to end all wars — the war against poverty — especially poverty of the worst kind: — poverty of the human mind and the poverty of the human heart.

① reprisal — foundation　　　　② amity — basis

③ infelicity — swagger　　　　④ retribution — cessation

22   Last week, Hyundai Motor started a two-week test run of its new shift system aimed at abolishing the graveyard shift and cutting working hours. Long work hours are a legacy of the past and ultimately do harm to employers and employees. The company plans to introduce the new shift pattern in March. Hyundai's example needs to be _____ by other companies.

① emulated　　　　② discontinued

③ remanded　　　　④ retarded

23   Most people assume that accounting rules are fairly rigid, and that auditors therefore don't have too much _____ in interpreting results. In fact, there's actually much ambiguity. Even apparently obvious questions like What is an expense? and What is an investment? are open to interpretation. For example, asked by Money magazine to estimate what a fictitious family owed in income taxes, the accountants' answers ranged from about $37,000 to $68,000! That range means that auditors' biases can distort the results.

① peroration　　　　② referendum

③ leeway　　　　④ paradigm

24   Most of the actions of other people which give us annoyance spring from causes that have nothing to do with the motives we assign to them. Othello smothers Desdemona through a misunderstanding about a handkerchief that five minutes' quiet talk would have cleared up. It is an excellent rule to distrust our reading of facts, still more our reading of other people's motives in relation to them. I can hardly recall a case in which my first conclusion as to why So-and-So did this or that has not, on fuller knowledge, turned out to be _____.

① absolutely true
② much annoying
③ beyond my understanding
④ absurdly wide of the mark

25   A modern society that outlaws the death penalty does not send a message of reverence for life, but a message of moral confusion. When we outlaw the death penalty, we tell the murderer that, no matter what he may do to innocent people in our custody and care, women, children, old people, his most treasured possession, his life, is secure. We guarantee it in advance. Just as a nation that declares that _____ finds itself at the mercy of warlike regimes, so a society that will not put the worst of its criminals to death will find itself at the mercy of criminals who have no qualms about putting innocent people to death.

① we don't wage a war unless we are attacked first
② we outlaw the death penalty
③ nothing will make it go to war
④ war is a necessary evil

25

I Choose the one that best completes the sentence(s). ▶▶▶ ANSWERS P.335

01 The _____ purpose of this expedition is to discover new lands, but we are really interested in finding new markets for our products.

① ostensible   ② uncouth
③ fawning   ④ gruesome

02 In spite of all the _____ before the meeting, the delegates were able to conduct serious negotiations when they sat down at the conference table in the next moment.

① palaver   ② petition
③ paucity   ④ parley

03 The Circuit Court of Appeals this spring ruled that Georgia can override a doctor's decision about how much care will be necessary for a handicapped child because the state is "the final _____" of medical decisions.

① bogeyman   ② arbiter
③ entourage   ④ mortician

04 I think I have encroached on your authority while working on this project. So, I offer you the honored first position on the list of names of researchers. I hope that it is enough to _____ my offenses.

① exhilarate   ② expatiate
③ expiate   ④ expurgate

05 The first chops, to the forehead, did not go through the bone and are perhaps evidence of _____ about the task. The next sets, after the body was rolled over, were more effective. One cut split the skull all the way to the base.

① drollery   ② hesitancy
③ simplicity   ④ audacity

06 That _____ occurred during the colony's "starving time" was never in much doubt. At least a half-dozen accounts include reports of corpses being exhumed and eaten, a husband killing his wife and salting her flesh.

① chauvinism ② famine
③ cremation ④ cannibalism

07 We prefer the richer sound that vinyl records make, but our love for vinyl records goes beyond the sound. LP records are tangible reminders of our younger selves and album covers are _____ visual additions to the musical experience.

① friable ② evocative
③ pastoral ④ insurgent

08 The mayor of Ferguson _____ insisted that his city is racially harmonious, paying no attention to the data clearly showing that a mostly white police force has targeted blacks for a disproportionate number of stops and searches.

① blithely ② dejectedly
③ wrathfully ④ judiciously

09 Religion was not a major factor at the start of the uprising against al-Assad in Syria. When Syrian protesters took to the streets in March 2011, they were seeking the implementation of democratic ideals and an end of pervasive _____.

① blasphemy ② secularization
③ heresy ④ depravation

10 She had spoken to her brother just once in 20 years. They lived less than 30 minutes' drive apart, but the dispute that drove a _____ between them after the death of their father seemed _____, the emotions hardened like concrete.

① hedge — indispensable ② linkage — irreversible
③ wedge — unresolvable ④ leverage — impalpable

11   For the rebel brigades and exiled opposition leaders, the involvement of extremist groups was an unfortunate _____ on an otherwise pure uprising against tyranny. To the regime, it was proof of a foreign-funded scheme to _____ the country.

① misstep — bolster   ② blemish — revamp

③ feat — debilitate   ④ stain — perturb

12   Some investors like IPOs because they provide a chance to "get in on the ground floor" and to make a substantial profit. Some scammers, though, spread the word about an upcoming IPO for companies that never intend to go public or that don't exist. Then, they _____ with investors' money.

① abscond   ② grieve

③ wail   ④ preponderate

13   If people hear a cliché that they have heard over and over again, their attention will no longer be on you but instead, something else. Over-used clichés make conversations _____ and disinteresting. To really get their attention, use word, phrase or idea that is creative.

① condescending   ② outlandish

③ threadbare   ④ halcyon

14   Western governments quarrel among themselves over the best approach. Should they offer the candy of inducement or the spank of sanctions? Although _____ punishment is no longer in vogue for the most part in Western countries, physically punishing North Korea is still a third option.

① corporal   ② refulgent

③ colossal   ④ pedagogic

15 Romney has been quite _____ on his views on gun control. In 2004, he passed one of the tightest bans on assault weapons in Massachusetts. But, later on, Romney bought a lifetime membership to the National Rifle Association and hopes to endorse the NRA.

① lackadaisical   ② rule-of-reason
③ henpecked   ④ wishy-washy

16 Declaring sanctions and then not providing us with military force to back them up will only make renegade states view our resolution with _____. They will not take us seriously. Our request for several state-of-the-art naval vessels is the bare minimum we need to show them we mean business.

① whimper   ② verbiage
③ paroxysm   ④ levity

17 At-home moms might take _____ at the suggestion that their domestic responsibilities are less time-consuming and they are without merit. When mothers elect to stay at home with dads bringing home the bacon, women devote 53 hours per week to child-care and household management, whereas the working dads only clock two hours.

① bashfulness   ② umbrage
③ sanctimony   ④ viand

18 Sometimes a poet might want to make you imagine you're hearing something. This is part of a concept called auditory imagery. One common way to create auditory imagery is through the use of _____. Think about words that describe a sound — words like buzz, clap or meow. When you say them aloud, they kind of sound like what they are describing. For example, the "zz" in the word buzz kind of sounds like the noise a bee makes.

① onomatopoeia   ② allonym
③ synecdoche   ④ litotes

19 In general, if you have a healthy vehicle, you should not need gas additives to enjoy the performance, emissions, and fuel savings. There is no _____ that is designed to make your engine magically become more efficient and powerful. About the only time these additives may work is if you are not using the right octane rating fuel as your vehicle requires.

① opus
② elixir
③ nebbish
④ placebo

20 A child is judged academically by how he fits the bed of the common core curriculum measured in standardized tests. Children who fall short are _____, sometimes severely, to attempt to fit them to the Procrustean Bed. Children who exceed the standards do not have their legs hewn off. Instead, they are often _____, prevented from using their academic legs fully. This isn't fair or beneficial to either group.

① stretched — hobbled
② deterred — sprained
③ chastised — praised
④ stomped — reinforced

21 If you found coal in your stocking this morning, don't kid yourself: it ain't clean. No matter what the president-elect might think, "clean coal" is a contradiction in terms. Greenpeace says: 'Clean coal' is the industry's attempt to 'clean up' its dirty image — the industry's _____ buzzword. The Washington Post sez: "Clean coal: Never was there a(n) _____ more insidious, or more dangerous to our public health."

① eco-friendly — incongruity
② greenwash — oxymoron
③ double-faced — tautology
④ sugar-coated — metonymy

22 Each quatrain written by Nostradamus is full of esoteric metaphor and _____; they include few dates or specific geographical references and are not arranged in chronological order. According to preface, the verses were intended to be mystifying. Nostradamus said he was afraid his work would be destroyed if authorities in his time fully know his predictions. According to him, his _____ prophecies would be better understood by enlightened people in the future.

① anthems — occult
② anagrams — cryptic
③ grumbles — forlorn
④ enigmas — antediluvian

23 Psychological theories can also shed light on why people sometimes consume in unpredictable, even seemingly irrational ways. It is no secret that sex is used to sell everything from cars to magazines or that soft drink ads appeal more to a desire for a sense of belonging and self-esteem than to a desire to relieve thirst. People know, at a conscious level, that the tie between such advertising campaigns and what they actually will get by buying the product is _____ at best. But that doesn't stop such campaigns from being successful!

① interactive ② tenuous
③ in direct proportion ④ compelling

24 This is a global problem — an estimated 294 billion e-mails were sent daily in 2010, and the figure continues to increase. As technology advances, it has become more and more difficult to escape it. No longer is e-mail confined to a desktop computer at the office; the advent of smart phones has allowed people to check their e-mail wherever they are. It is almost enough to have one longing again for the day when information was a scarce resource and one had to go out to find it. Now so much information is so readily available that the challenge is _____.

① to make do with an old mail ② to take up time
③ to ask for the moon ④ to sift the wheat from the chaff

25 Aristotle's basic approach to philosophy is best grasped initially by way of contrast. Whereas Descartes seeks to place philosophy and science on firm foundations by subjecting all knowledge claims to a searing methodological doubt, Aristotle begins with the conviction that our perceptual and cognitive faculties are basically dependable, and that we need not dally with _____ before engaging in substantive philosophy. Accordingly, he proceeds in all areas of inquiry in the manner of a modern-day natural scientist. When he goes to work, Aristotle begins by considering how the world appears, reflecting on the puzzles those appearances throw up, and reviewing what has been said about those puzzles to date.

① affirmative postures ② sceptical postures
③ neutral postures ④ unbiased postures

01 Because the country was in a state of anarchy and lacked a leader immediately after the consecutive wars, it was described as a(n) _____ monstrosity.

① acephalous ② grandiose
③ disheveled ④ well-heeled

02 His most popular album, 1973's *Black Byrd*, was _____ by critics, who shuddered at its intermingling of jazz and pop. He shot back, "I'm creative. I'm not recreative. I don't follow what everybody else does."

① hammered ② reclaimed
③ condoned ④ ballyhooed

03 When they find a suspected terrorist, they have three options: kill him, leave him in the field, or work with the local government to detain him. It seems human rights are out, and _____ in. This is more than sad, it's appalling.

① diachronism ② paternalism
③ evangelism ④ vigilantism

04 Even drivers who _____ maintain oil levels and monitor tire pressure should have a mechanic check battery strength, tire treads, and antifreeze levels to make sure the car can withstand another winter of wear and tear.

① fitfully ② fastidiously
③ perfunctorily ④ unwittingly

05 The innkeeper was _____ about a new influx of mainlanders: Chinese tourists, whom he found arrogant and politically incorrect. He refused to host any, even though that cost him business. The Chinese, he said, were trouble.

① apoplectic ② self-possessed
③ perky ④ blithesome

06   Despite her age and great success, Dame Judi Dench is not afraid to portray challenging roles and continue to _____ her talent. She's definitely a good example for young actresses today.

① grill   ② hone

③ pop   ④ smear

07   "_____" is not an obvious word to use about America, a country built on revolution, restless expansion and the unabashed pursuit of profit. Yet the lovely-restored Georgian streets of Colonial Williamsburg look strikingly archaic.

① Wavering   ② Quaint

③ Anemic   ④ Latent

08   Often we read how Beethoven's harmonic language was regarded as adventurous, even _____, by the listeners of his time. Utterly familiar today, his compositions seem anything but grotesque.

① freakish   ② bromidic

③ stiff-necked   ④ verboten

09   It's sad to see that a renowned writer like him has taken the liberty to generalize men as anti-Jane Austen. What _____ me more than his cheesy jokes or his _____ manner against Austen readers is that he doesn't seem to understand the era in which the books were written.

① gratifies — discerning   ② regales — harassing

③ frustrates — approving   ④ baffles — patronizing

10   To give an answer to the question "What is real?", we have to go through the _____ and tiring business of pointing out the various things that the word "real" can mean by contrasting them with what, in that specific context, is not called real.

① winsome   ② gruesome

③ cuddlesome   ④ cumbersome

11 People who have lived through near-fatal physical dangers often recall that in the midst of their ordeal they experienced extraordinarily rich _____ in response to such simple events as hearing the song of a bird in the forest, completing a hard task, or sharing a crust of bread with a friend.

① epiphanies ② increments
③ paroxysms ④ anathemas

12 When children come down with a cold, many parents head straight for the drugstore for a bottle of children's cold medicine. Don't bother. Research has repeatedly shown that cold medicines hardly work for children younger than 6, and they provide only a(n) _____ benefit for children 6 to 12.

① unflinching ② exiguous
③ stupendous ④ nifty

13 Don't let Judge Sutton's rhetoric fool you. Behind the _____ of reasonable-sounding respect for the dignity of gay persons lies the same odious discrimination we have been hearing from the rump of the radical right still apoplectic that two men or two women can marry.

① philia ② insecurity
③ phobia ④ gloss

14 The discrepancy between what we acknowledge women can do and what we let them do — women are still only 19% of the House of Representatives and 5% of Fortune 500 CEOs — reveals a lingering _____: women have to go above and beyond the standards to which men are held to demonstrate their competence; they have to try extra hard.

① dissonance ② redundancy
③ vantage ④ validity

15 University students study abroad for many reasons, including the need to prepare oneself for a global career. Worldwide, the number of migrants with _____ has more than doubled since 2000. And the number of foreign students at universities in America has risen by 40% over the past decade.

① mortar boards   ② green cards

③ walking papers   ④ red carpets

16 The argument today has moved on — to the growing inequality that is a side-effect of new technology and globalisation; to the nature of employment, pensions and benefits in an Uberising labour market of self-employed workers; and to the need for efficient government and welfare systems. Fresh thinking on all this would be welcome — indeed it should be natural territory for the progressive left. But Mr Corbyn is _____ in the past. His "new politics" has nothing to offer but the exhausted, _____ formulas which his predecessors abandoned.

① compromised — salient   ② denounced — refined

③ stuck — hollow   ④ revamped — conducive

17 Robert Boyle would not have approved. The famously _____ seventeenth-century natural philosopher and pioneer of the scientific method argued that technical communication demands detail, not brevity. But there is no room for Boyle-like excess within the confines of the social-networking site Twitter, where users converse in 140-character posts, or 'tweets'. Researchers are now using the site's _____ messages to discuss papers in journal clubs and to share data in real time.

① contemplative — affirmative   ② strenuous — emphatic

③ verbose — abbreviated   ④ garrulous — proliferative

18 Nothing goes by luck in composition. It allows of no tricks. The best you can write will be the best you are. Every sentence is the result of a long probation. The author's character is read from title-page to end. We read it as the essential character of a handwriting without regard to the _____. And so of the rest of our actions; it runs as straight as a ruled line through them all, no matter how many curvets about it. Our whole life is _____ for the least thing well done; it is its net result. How we eat, drink, sleep, and use our desultory hours, now in these indifferent days, with no eye to observe and no occasion to excite us, determines our authority and capacity for the time to come.

① flourishes — taxed   ② majesties — harried
③ virtues — belittled   ④ benefits — stretched

19 There' a real stigma with anal cancer that doesn't exist with other cancers. Attaching societal stigma to those suffering certain cancers is nothing new. Breast cancer, now celebrated loudly with all things pink, _____ — it was considered revolutionary in 1974 when then — first lady Betty Ford openly discussed her diagnosis and radical mastectomy. People with testicular cancers faced similar social shame, until Lance Armstrong went public with his fight.

① was paid attention to by conventional medicine
② brought on a change of perception to lethal diseases
③ could be detected in its early stage by self-diagnosis
④ was once only spoken of in hushed tones

20 Munchausen syndrome is the recurrent faking of catastrophic illnesses. It is a psychological disorder in which the individual keeps coming back for treatment for an acute and often serious illness which does not exist or has been _____ induced — patients recurrently pretend they are seriously ill and ask for treatment. Munchausen syndrome should be spelled with a double "H", as in Munchhausen. However, the misspelling with just one "H" has become so common that it is probably no longer considered as a spelling mistake, and most likely many people, including a significant number of health care professionals, may even see the correct spelling as a _____.

① involuntarily — jargon   ② capriciously — tactic
③ deliberately — typo   ④ judiciously — criterion
⑤ chivalrously — congruity

21 Beethoven is thought to have suffered from a severe depression, which may have led him to turn to alcohol. Less known is the fact his impressive creativity was triggered by a drive and an energy that is actually more consistent with someone afflicted by bipolar disorder rather than by depression alone. At times, the composer was _____, at others he was hypomanic — in a state of complete _____, he could compose several different works simultaneously.

① languid — equilibrium   ② prodigal — felicity
③ suicidal — euphoria   ④ clairvoyant — contentment

22 It is more usual for each member of civilization to take flight from its consequences by protesting that others have failed him. Those whose education and perhaps tastes have confined them to the humanities protest that _____, for plainly no mandarin ever made a bomb or an industry. The scientists say, with equal contempt, that the Greek scholars and the earnest explorers of cave paintings do well to wash their hands of blame; but what in fact are they doing to help direct the society whose ills grow more often from inaction than from error?

① history proves the opposite
② no education or culture works
③ the scientists alone are to blame
④ human civilization is in decline

23 For centuries, we have been told that without religion we are no more than egotistic animals fighting for our share, our only morality that of a pack of wolves; only religion, it is said, can elevate us to a higher spiritual level. Today, when religion is emerging as the wellspring of murderous violence around the world, assurances that only Christian or Muslim or Hindu fundamentalists are abusing and perverting the noble spiritual messages of their creeds _____. What about restoring the dignity of atheism, one of Europe's greatest legacies and perhaps our only chance for peace?

① readily gain momentum   ② are independent of fiasco
③ ring increasingly hollow   ④ put the wire on atheists

24 The concept of using music as a tool for healing purposes is ancient — in fact, it can be traced back to at least the written works of Plato and his student, Aristotle. It emerged as a formal profession after World War I and World War II when the influence of community musicians at hospitals was realized as a positive influence for the veterans suffering from both physical and emotional trauma. In this medical practice, the therapeutic use of music is used to address the numerous needs of individuals. This form of therapy is best when it is _____ to an individual's requirements — the qualified music therapist provides the decided treatment including composing, singing, moving to, or listening to music.

① ruined   ② tailored

③ decreased   ④ unrelated

⑤ amused

25 The 2011 Occupy Wall Street movement was built around an idea and a slogan: 'We are the 99% that will no longer tolerate the greed and corruption of the 1%.' Studies just before it happened showed that almost all of the gains from an economic upturn had gone to the US's wealthiest 1%. This wasn't a historical aberration or a national exception. Almost everywhere a similar outcome has consistently been encouraged by government policy. In France, the tax plans of President Macron will largely benefit 'the richest 280,000 households whose assets are mainly in the form of financial investments and business shares.' Does that mean that everyone else has so much in common that they could overthrow the established order by pooling their energies? I don't think so. That 1% of people command the majority of the world's wealth does not mean that the 99% are a _____ social group, still less a political force at boiling point.

① dispersed   ② salient

③ cohesive   ④ reticent

⑤ garrulous

27

Choose the one that best completes the sentence(s). ▶▶▶ ANSWERS P.346

01 The war in Syria, which began as a civil uprising, now looks more like an international conflict where patron states are replacing their _____.

① wirepullers ② antagonists
③ proxies ④ magnates

02 An earlier pluralist societies, individuals were _____: institutions did not depend on them and individuals, whether peasants or workers, had no bargaining power.

① expendable ② wayward
③ indispensable ④ dominant

03 They aren't usually stressed about the learning process because they aren't going to be graded on their performance. This often means that they can take a more _____ approach to their studies and learn for the pure sake of learning.

① headlong ② down-to-earth
③ bare-faced ④ laid-back

04 The nurse beckoned to one of a group of _____ fathers at the hospital and announced, "You have a fine son." Another man immediately rushed up and complained, "What's the idea? I was here before he was!"

① expectant ② gifted
③ intolerant ④ auspicious

05 He has suffered _____, in spite of a long and honorable career, for the sole crime of wishing to save young people from the misfortunes that they incur as a result of their elders' _____.

① obloquy — bigotry ② vituperation — acumen
③ accolades — rancor ④ plaudits — perspicacity

06 A genetic explanation isn't the only possible answer to the regional disparity of development. Another one invokes the supposed stimulatory effects of cold climates and the _____ effects of hot, humid, tropical climates on human creativity and energy.

① marginal   ② inhibitory
③ provocative   ④ aggregate

07 The argument that migration is the answer to what is largely a question of distribution brings to mind the parable in John Steinbeck's "The Grapes of Wrath". The migration of the Joad family from the dust bowls of Oklahoma to the unfulfilled promise of abundance in California is a cautionary tale of _____ inequality.

① inherited   ② transplanted
③ disguised   ④ stigmatized

08 The sensational press has surrounded her with so much misrepresentation and slander, it would seem almost a miracle that, in spite of this web of _____, the truth breaks through and a better appreciation of this much maligned idealist begins to manifest itself.

① plaudit   ② decorum
③ fracas   ④ calumny

09 The pivotal moment in the biography is Mill's crisis of faith at the age of 20. After an adolescence immersed in his father's creed of utilitarianism, Mill realised, to his father's great chagrin, that its promise of happiness was _____. Under the influence of the Romantic poets, he turned away from a life based on calculation.

① euphoriant   ② a priori
③ feasible   ④ chimerical

10   The city lacks _____ palaces, temples, or monuments. There's no obvious central seat of government or evidence of a king or queen. Modesty, order, and cleanliness were apparently preferred. Pottery and tools of copper and stone were standardized. Seals and weights suggest a system of tightly controlled trade.

① ostentatious   ② callous

③ exuberant   ④ wistful

11   An author's greatness these days is measured by his or her ability to edify and liberate. Such interpretative agendas are more problematic when imposed on much older works. For the sake of creative freedom and intellectual honesty, authors as well as scholars deserve more _____ from the zeitgeist.

① naturalization   ② dependence

③ distraction   ④ pillar

⑤ autonomy

12   Chelsea have their first win under Frank Lampard, managing to squeeze out a 3-2 win over Norwich. It was no thanks to the referee, however, with Martin Atkinson making himself extremely unpopular with some truly odd calls. He awarded us a tight offside, and then ignored a bad stamp from Ben Godfrey. As you can imagine, fans on social media went increasingly _____.

① committed   ② aloof

③ disinterested   ④ ballistic

⑤ disoriented

13   "A blind person has a better sense of feeling, of taste, of touch," he writes, and speaks of these as "the gifts of the blind." And all of these, Lusseyran feels, blend into a single fundamental sense, a deep attentiveness, a slow, almost prehensile attention, a sensuous, intimate being at one with the world which sight, with its quick, flicking, facile quality, continually _____ us from.

① distracts   ② encapsulates

③ crystallizes   ④ calculates

14   The common people in danger of becoming orphans in their own homeland are struggling to prove they are Indians with authentic documents. Prime Minister Narendra Modi is praised for introducing the National Register of Citizens, but it is one of the most horrible things he could do for his own people. It is time for the international community to step in and save the lives of these aggrieved people who are facing a state of _____.

① deception   ② corruption
③ treason   ④ exclusion

15   Many doctors still believe that a yellow or greenish nasal discharge suggests that bacteria are present. But the science has shown this isn't always true. The tinted mucus is a normal by-product of the healing process. To fight an infection, white blood cells release enzymes to kill invaders. Some enzymes contain iron, which has a greenish color. Cloudy mucus _____.

① implies bacteria has destroyed our immune system
② helps white blood cells kill bacteria in our body
③ doesn't automatically signify a bacterial infection
④ doesn't guarantee we will be more healthy than before

16   A(n) _____ is a newer name for an existing thing that differentiates the original form or version from a more recent one. It is thus a word created to differentiate between two types, whereas previously (before there were two types) no clarification was required. Advances in technology are often responsible for the coinage of them. For example, the term "acoustic guitar" was coined at the advent of electric guitars and analog watches were thus renamed to distinguish them from digital watches once the latter were invented.

① etymology   ② semantics
③ retronym   ④ acronym

17   The principle of private property stands in contradiction to the social function of art, which must be based on an extensive interconnection between the artist and the public, that is, on the effective possibility that aesthetic enjoyment can cease to be the exclusive property of a minority and become instead an increasingly profound and human enjoyment. This enjoyment is not _____; it is essential for artistic creation inasmuch as it fully realizes itself in that enjoyment, and it is essential for the consumer inasmuch as art is one of the most rewarding means which human beings, not just artists, possess to deepen their humanity.

① prosaic   ② jocund
③ ethereal   ④ fortuitous

18   The right is changing what it means to belong. In Hungary and Poland the right exults in blood-and-soil nationalism, which excludes and discriminates. Vox, a new force in Spain, harks back to the Reconquista, when Christians kicked out the Muslims. An angry, reactionary nationalism kindles suspicion, hatred and division. It is the _____ of the conservative insight that belonging to the nation, a church and the local community can unite people and motivate them to act in the common good.

① orthodoxy   ② reinforcement
③ integration   ④ antithesis
⑤ harbinger

19   What our deliberative, pluralistic democracy does demand is that the religiously motivated translate their concerns into universal, rather than religion-specific, values. It requires that their proposals must be subject to argument and amenable to reason. If I am opposed to abortion for religious reasons and seek to pass a law banning the practice, I cannot simply point to the teachings of my church or invoke God's will and expect that argument to carry the day. If I want others to listen to me, then I have to explain why abortion _____.

① is a matter of women's human rights, not of religious precepts
② makes people oblivious to the supremacy of God over human beings
③ constitutes a religious sin as well as a criminal offense
④ violates some principle accessible to all people regardless of faith
⑤ should be decriminalized and treated like any other medical procedure

20 The term "badass" — a noun and an adjective and a compound so obvious as to be almost _____ — has traditionally described dudes. The badass is "the epitome of the American male." Someone who "radiates confidence in everything he does, whether it's ordering a drink, buying a set of wheels, or dealing with women." Someone who is "slow to anger" and "brutally efficient when fighting back" and who is essentially Dirty Harry or Chuck Norris. To be badass, one must, both literally and otherwise, _____.

① inelegant — swagger ② complacent — exemplify
③ infeasible — scheme ④ impregnable — highbrow
⑤ ludicrous — democratize

21 Ask American experts how a great-power competition with China might end well, and their best-case scenarios are strikingly similar. They describe a near future in which China overreaches and stumbles. They imagine a China _____ by slowing growth at home and a backlash to its assertive ways overseas. That China, they hope, might look again at the global order and seek a leading role in it, rather than its remaking. Chinese experts also sound alike when explaining their own best-case scenario. Put crudely, it is for America to get over itself. More politely, Chinese voices express hopes that in a decade or so America will learn the humility to _____ China as an equal, and the wisdom to avoid provoking China in its Asian backyard.

① deluded — exhort ② chastened — accept
③ extricated — ignore ④ glorified — deny

22 When it comes to body weight, it may be that if you snooze, you lose. Lack of sleep seems to be related to an increase in hunger and appetite, and possibly to obesity. People who sleep less than six hours a day were almost 30 percent more likely to become obese than those who slept seven to nine hours. Recent research has focused on the link between sleep and the peptides that regulate appetite. "Ghrelin stimulates hunger and leptin signals satiety to the brain and suppresses appetite," says Siebern. "Shortened sleep time _____."

① is associated with decreases in leptin and elevations in ghrelin
② has nothing to do with difficulty awakening in the morning
③ results in increases in the hormone that stimulates leptin
④ is linked to a significant decline in BMI for both men and women

23   Natalie Angier wrote a rather sad piece in the New Yorker, saying how lonely she felt as an atheist. She clearly feels in a beleaguered minority. But actually, how do American atheists stack up numerically? The latest survey makes surprisingly encouraging reading. Christianity, of course, takes a massive lion's share of the population, with nearly 160 million. But what would you think was the second largest group, convincingly outnumbering Jews with 2.8 million, Muslims at 1.1 million, Hindus, Buddhists and all other religions put together? The second largest group, with nearly 30 million, is the one described as _____.

① nihilistic   ② esoteric
③ pantheistic   ④ secular

24   Embezzlement crime generally defined as theft or withholding of assets of another by a servant, an agent, or another person to whom possession of the assets has been entrusted. The offense has no single or precise definition. Typically, embezzlement occurs when a person gains possession of assets lawfully and subsequently _____ them. In this respect, embezzlement is to be contrasted with the crime of larceny, which requires the taking of assets from the possession of another without the latter's consent.

① augments   ② misappropriates
③ instigates   ④ aggravates

25   In almost all aspects of society, Sunni Arabs have greater economic opportunities and political rights, especially those who are members of the Al Khalifa ruling tribe. The discrimination has translated into much of the economic wealth being held by Sunnis while Shias remain economically deprived and chronically unemployed. Economic _____ led to growing frustration and resentment within the Shia community, helping to spur the 2011 protests. Furthermore, with Bahrain's economy struggling to diversify and grow, one should expect the economic inequality to continue to undermine the regime. There is not enough wealth in the country to satisfy the monarchy's allies and the poor Shia. To _____ its power base, the government has offered citizenship to various Sunni migrants. Despite not having the deep ties to Bahrain, these newly anointed citizens enjoy more economic and political rights than the Shia.

① upheaval — entrench   ② impasse — promulgate
③ recession — dismantle   ④ disenfranchisement — bolster

▌ Choose the one that best completes the sentence(s).

▶ ▶ ▶ **ANSWERS** P.351

01 Various things have been _____ away for a long time in the hopes of having a use someday.

① wolfed   ② squirreled

③ dogged   ④ butterflied

02 The border between the two countries is _____ and left-wing rebels regularly move across it undetected.

① impregnable   ② militarized

③ porous   ④ fortified

03 With every passing word, an expanding blast of spittle spews from your mouth — the more _____ the speech, the greater the spray.

① emphatic   ② tedious

③ impromptu   ④ contrite

⑤ deducible

04 Some readers consider it a(n) _____, or coming-of-age novel, because at its close Sethe, with the help of Paul D, finally begins to discover a sense of self-worth.

① bildungsroman   ② epic

③ saga   ④ novella

⑤ romantic adventures

05 Every occupation has its own _____; doctors, attorneys and economic analysts, for example, all use among themselves language which outsiders have difficulty following.

① calibers   ② detriments

③ accolades   ④ jargons

06 While there is a vast amount of information available, all that data can have the _____ effect of making us feel less aware, less informed, unsure of what to believe or whom to trust.

① perverse   ② chimerical
③ salubrious   ④ connotative

07 In a constant see-saw from one state of mind to another, she _____ between wanting to believe the story he had told her about himself and wondering whether he had deceived her about a fundamental part of his life.

① discerned   ② bridged
③ coordinated   ④ oscillated

08 The American ruling elite in a state of "_____" votes for the supply of advanced weaponry to Ukraine, turning a blind eye to lawlessness, ideological extremism, and political assassinations in the country.

① humane anxiety   ② silent abhorrence
③ unlimited emergency   ④ consistent discomfort
⑤ blissful ignorance

09 He receives a damaging letter from Mme. de Renal, denouncing Julien as a social climber and a schemer who _____ himself into wealthy families and plays on the affections of the women for his own advantage.

① insinuates   ② approbates
③ engulfs   ④ enervates

10 In some minds, social work is associated with radical, left-wing politics and others think of the social worker as a _____ with delusions of grandeur about preventing child abuse, saving people from themselves, and generally being the professional expert in helping and caring.

① woolly-minded idealist   ② cold-blooded capitalist
③ duty-conscious moralist   ④ self-deprecating altruist

11 At its 1972 peak, membership in the Boy Scouts numbered more than 6 million. Families across the country were eager to enroll their sons in the organization that _____ mentorship from older men and bonding activities with other boys, including camping trips.

① calibrated   ② touted
③ delimited   ④ nurtured
⑤ surpassed

12 The first question almost everyone repeatedly asks in regards to the financial system is whether or no longer we're headed for a recession. The second request: will the subsequent recession be a(n) _____ one, or will it be pretty benevolent by comparison?

① execrable   ② antiseptic
③ sanguine   ④ choleric

13 Hall of Fame quarterback John Elway had a pro playing career spanning 16 years and five Super Bowls and now serves as general manager of the Denver Broncos. But for many years, he has been fighting off the field with a(n) _____ medical condition that affects his hands.

① steering   ② contextual
③ invigorating   ④ snapping
⑤ debilitating

14 One of the main complaints about globalization is that the proliferation of Western styles, products, and tastes may extinguish difference. From this point of view, globalization simply represents the homogenizing of formerly _____ cultures and identities.

① clapped-out   ② disparate
③ waning   ④ amicable

15   Child abuse and spouse abuse pose a challenge to mental health authorities. Prejudice, discrimination, and racism continue to divide our pluralistic society. However, the scientific advances of our age are mocked by the _____ in our ability to understand and solve these interpersonal and societal problems.

① stasis   ② quirk
③ plethora   ④ boost

16   _____. Researchers followed people participating in email-based negotiations. One group went straight to business; members of the second began by telling their partners about themselves. Chatty negotiators reached an agreement 59% of the time, while business-centered participants succeeded only 39% of the time.

① Don't beat about the bush   ② Negotiators have a big mouth
③ Follow in your superior's step   ④ Small talk goes a long way

17   Why is a split so hard? There are many reasons. Friendships aren't monogamous, so it's easy to enjoy your other buddies even when one particular person is dragging you down. That means less pressure to act. When the ball is rolling in a long-term friendship, it's hard to stop. It's part of the rhythm of our daily lives, and the inertia is powerful. Because of this, we also tend to _____.

① prefer an enemy at hand to a friend far away
② have difficulty making friends with strangers
③ let our friends get away with bad behavior
④ befriend others until they no longer serve a use

18   What Carlyle in 1827 called the grand controversy, so hotly urged, between the Classicists and Romanticists was often revisited, generations later, when distinctions needed to be drawn in polemical reviews and manifestos. When T. E. Hulme and his Imagist circle in the first years of the 20th century, for example, dismissed the damp and _____ Romanticism of Victor Hugo and the late Victorians, they did so on behalf of a dry and hard classical style.

① gaseous   ② sleek
③ feasible   ④ grandiose
⑤ corporeal

19 The United States is often described as a _____ of culture, a colorful assemblage of tradition and history built by the nation's diverse population. Few things illustrate this as clearly as American cuisine; in the United States, food knowledge and techniques from all over the world coalesce, forming a(n) _____ landscape unlike any other.

① melting pot — bucolic
② kaleidoscope — culinary
③ homogeneity — didactic
④ lineage — eclectic

20 Should we have the choice of when to end our lives? It depends on what an individual's definition of life is. To me, life is watching the sunset with a glass of wine, dining with friends, enjoying the arts and so on. To me, life is not sitting slumped in a chair in an institution, or perhaps living with chronic pain and having my basic needs neglected by overworked staff. In short, I would like that choice to be _____.

① dispensable   ② available
③ changeable   ④ inevitable

21 The space-age technology of mobile phones has allowed us to return to the more natural and humane communication patterns of pre-industrial society, when we lived in small, stable communities, and enjoyed frequent 'grooming talk' with a tightly integrated social network. In the fast-paced modern world, we had become severely restricted in both the quantity and quality of communication with our social network. Mobile gossip restores our sense of connection and community, and provides a(n) _____ to the pressures and alienation of modern life. Mobiles are a 'social lifeline' in a fragmented and isolating world.

① immunosuppressant   ② placebo
③ stimulant   ④ antidote
⑤ narcotic

22　In Leviathan, a treatise on political obedience published in 1651, Thomas Hobbes claimed that "There is now no place for industry, because the fruit hereof is uncertain, and consequently no culture of the earth; no navigation, nor use of the commodities that may be imported by sea; no commodious building; ... no arts; no letters; no society. And, which is worst of all, continual fear and danger of violent death; and the life of man, solitary, poor, nasty, brutish, and short." Many people in France, where Hobbes wrote these words, shared his _____ vision.

① Dadaistic　　　　　　　　　　② misanthropic
③ grotesque　　　　　　　　　　④ anarchistic
⑤ apocalyptic

23　At the beginning of 20th century, it was thought that everything could be explained in terms of the properties of continuous matter, such as elasticity and heat conduction. The discovery of atomic structure and the uncertainty principle put an emphatic end to that. Then again, in 1928, physicist and Nobel Prize winner Max Born told a group of visitors to Göttingen University, "Physics, as we know it, will be over in six months." His confidence was based on the recent discovery by Dirac of the equation that governed the electron. It was thought that a similar equation would govern the proton, which was the only other particle known at the time, and that would be the end of theoretical physics. However, the discovery of the neutron and of nuclear forces knocked that one on the head too. Having said this, I still believe _____ that we may now be near the end of the search for the ultimate laws of nature.

① we need to know that we are at a dead end
② there is a mystery of the universe
③ we should have an absolute, fundamental scientific faith
④ there are grounds for cautious optimism
⑤ there must be a few flaws

24 Israel allies with friends, neutrals and former enemies whenever they share particular strategic goals. In the topsy-turvy Middle East, Israel is now sometimes a strategic partner with formerly hostile regimes in Egypt, Jordan, Saudi Arabia and other Gulf monarchies. They all share greater fears of theocratic Iran and its terrorist appendages in Lebanon, Syria and Yemen. Apparently, much of the Arab world is no longer as interested in the Palestinian desire to destroy Israel. Many Palestinian groups are allied with a despised Iran, while many Arabs believe that Israel's strength can sometimes _____.

① provoke fear and antipathy
② masquerade as weakness
③ be strategically expedient
④ get in the way of geopolitical peace

25 Singapore shows that any response to this indiscriminate virus must be inclusive. Americans on low incomes who cannot work from home and lack comprehensive health insurance have proven particularly vulnerable, as have elderly people trapped in care homes. But the virus cannot be banished from society by prioritizing the young and affluent. In Singapore, like the U.S., rich and poor take the same public transportation, use the same ride-sharing apps, prowl the same malls. "_____," says Christine Pelly, an executive committee member of Singapore's Transient Workers Count Too, a nongovernmental organization. "We benefit a lot from low-wage workers. We should look after their well-being more closely."

① We must send low-wage workers back to their homeland
② The United States should follow the example of Singapore
③ Social distancing should be further strengthened
④ The virus doesn't respect community barriers
⑤ Efforts should be made to narrow the gap between the rich and the poor

29

Choose the one that best completes the sentence(s).   ▶ ▶ ▶ ANSWERS P.356

01   The rules appeared simple, but were precise and _____ upon inspection, most of them 'gentlemanly' by nature, and all respected by the players.

① contumelious   ② sassy
③ primitive   ④ daedalian

02   When you first step out into that big world it can be a little _____, but as time goes by and you settle into the travel scene, you quickly begin to love it.

① superb   ② facile
③ daunting   ④ propitious

03   The metaphysical views of Spinoza were essentially _____, holding that God and Nature were just two names for the same single underlying reality.

① pluralistic   ② monistic
③ idealistic   ④ materialistic

04   Caffeine combats drowsiness by tricking your brain into feeling alert. It temporarily blocks adenosine, a naturally _____ brain chemical, to prevent fatigue.

① sedating   ② fascinating
③ arousing   ④ resuscitating

05   Robert Louis Stevenson once called his native Edinburgh a(n) _____ city and he was absolutely right. Any visitor senses that Edinburgh contains an intensity of heights and depths.

① precipitous   ② kaleidoscopic
③ enterprising   ④ accessible

06 Pope Francis made one of the strongest pro-life statements of his papacy when he stopped to pray silently at a symbolic "cemetery for _____ victims" about 190km southeast of Seoul.

① abortion   ② calamity
③ warfare   ④ persecution

07 It's hard to believe we've come to the tail end of this year. To _____ the year, we have chosen to feature someone who we believe is an embodiment of the catch phrase: "an ordinary person doing extraordinary things."

① cut away   ② square up to
③ round out   ④ usher in

08 Novel _____ the history of the art to which it belongs because it is at once the most complete and the most democratic of genres, coming as close as it is possible for an art-form to come to capturing the multiplicity, richness, and zest of life itself.

① bewilders   ② gainsays
③ recapitulates   ④ vaticinates

09 The photographer is not about a single moment. He is, rather, a collector of moments, staking out a location until he has _____ up enough of them to tell the story of a single place.

① squelched   ② jettisoned
③ immolated   ④ hoovered

10 Wild animals and plants are _____ as "resources" or "stocks", as if they belong to us and their role is to serve us: a notion disastrously extended by the term "ecosystem services".

① reinstated   ② epitomized
③ denunciated   ④ mitigated

11   Facebook currently derives 82 percent of its revenue from advertising. Most of that is the _____ ticky-tacky kind that litters the right side of people's Facebook profiles.

① amiable   ② desultory
③ knotty   ④ amorous
⑤ cruising

12   While the presidential candidate faces criticism for his oftentimes _____ speeches and comments, many of his supporters see his heated tone as a mark of authenticity and dependability over a decades-long career in public office.

① awry   ② nonchalant
③ phlegmatic   ④ incendiary
⑤ oblique

13   In the end, Vladimir Putin agreed to see the envoy from the Trump Administration. After a week of mutual recrimination over the war in Syria, the Russian President did not _____ Rex Tillerson, U.S. Secretary of States, during his first official visit to Moscow.

① drudge   ② hail
③ charter   ④ snub

14   Lady Luck has been good to me. I fancy she has been good to many. Only some people are _____, and when she gives them the come-hither with her eyes, they look down or turn away. But me — I give her the wink, and away we go.

① grabby   ② jovial
③ dour   ④ sapient

15   We are finding new ways of working, some of which will no doubt _____ this coronavirus crisis, and searching for new ways to meet the needs of work, family, and physical and mental health.

① outdate   ② outfit
③ outlast   ④ outrage

16 For an illustration, drive north from Warsaw into Mazowsze. The region is as gorgeous as a Chopin concerto, an undulating quilt of cereal fields and birch groves, but in the 1990s its towns were unromantically _____.

① down-at-heel   ② heel-and-toe
③ hairy-heeled   ④ well-heeled
⑤ with a low heel

17 The religious fanaticism behind the assassinations is a _____ poised to explode across the country. The embers are _____ by the opportunism of those who seek advantages in domestic politics by violently polarizing the society.

① windfall — asphyxiated   ② fireplug — flared
③ quicksand — quenched   ④ tinderbox — fanned

18 It is believed that the Inca's conquests, for the most part, were not as brutal as those of most conquering nations. The Incas insisted that those they conquered accept "Inti", the Sun, as their main god and pay homage to the Inca leaders. However, they were not forced to _____ their own gods.

① renounce   ② venerate
③ placate   ④ embrace

19 Virtual reality may be the future, but there is a great deal more to be learned about life and reality in a book than in a headset. The longer we ogle at screens of pixels and bytes, _____.

① the farther-sighted we will be
② the closer we come to Arcadia
③ the further adrift we will go
④ the more reins we will be given
⑤ the less isolated we will become

20   The history of interactions among disparate peoples is what shaped the modern world through conquest, epidemics, and genocide. Those _____ that have still not died down after many centuries, and that are actively continuing in some of the world's most troubled areas today.

① disasters toned down aftermaths   ② crashes blocked off breakthroughs

③ collisions created reverberations   ④ encounters triggered innovations

21   Online daters complained about the fickleness of their peers. Many failed to initiate conversations with those they were matched with; if they did, the other party soon disappeared. The ease with which users could make connections encouraged them to treat matches as if they were "replaceable." This stoked frustration; last October 45% of American users told us that online dating was a(n) _____ experience.

① ecstatic   ② uproarious

③ vexing   ④ lachrymose

22   Theodor Adorno offers an influential, philosophically sophisticated account of the nature of twentieth-century popular music. He is the single best source for the view that popular music is simplistic, repetitive, and boring, and that it remains this way because commercial forces manipulate it in order to _____ and manipulate the masses who passively respond to it.

① placate   ② flabbergast

③ enlighten   ④ overbear

⑤ encumber

23   There is an amusing Western misunderstanding of Arab etiquette. It is not true that sheep's eye is a typical Arab _____. The origin of this belief is said to be a British diplomat invited to dinner by a tribal sheik. The sheik showed him the eye of the sheep he was about to serve so that his guest would know the meat was fresh. Thinking he was being offered a prized treat, the diplomat ate it out of politeness. The courteous sheik didn't want to _____ and embarrass the Brit, so he ate the other eye himself.

① amulet — rectify   ② dainty — postulate

③ emblem — revise   ④ delicacy — correct

⑤ anathema — shun

24 You know, there are two kinds of atheism. Atheism is the theory that there is no God. Now, one kind is a theoretical kind, where somebody just sits down and starts thinking about it, and they come to a conclusion that there is no God. The other kind is a practical atheism, and that kind goes out of living as if there is no God. And you know there are a lot of people who affirm the existence of God with their lips, and they deny his existence with their lives. You've seen these people who have a high blood pressure of creeds and _____.

① dogmatism in their faith
② materialistic diabetes
③ an anemia of deeds
④ ideological metabolic syndrome
⑤ empirical atheism

25 Slave morality is characterized by the attitude of ressentiment — the resentment and hatred of the powerless for the powerful. Nietzsche sees ressentiment as an entirely negative sentiment — the attitude of denying what is life-affirming, saying 'no' to what is different, what is 'outside' or 'other'. Ressentiment is characterized by an orientation to the outside, rather than the focus of noble morality, which is on the self. While the master says 'I am good' and adds as an afterthought, 'therefore he is bad'; the slave says the opposite — 'He (the master) is bad, therefore I am good'. Thus the invention of values comes from a(n) _____ or opposition to that which is outside, other, different. Nietzsche says, "in order to come about, slave morality first has to have an opposing, external world, it needs, psychologically speaking, external stimuli in order to act all, — its action is basically a(n) _____."

① comparison — reaction
② aversion — impetus
③ contraposition — instigation
④ incompatibility — deterrent
⑤ detachment — disillusionment

■ Choose the one that best completes the sentence(s).　　　▶ ▶ ▶ ANSWERS P.361

01　If a commodity were in no way useful, — in other words, if it could in no way contribute to our gratification, — it would be _____ of exchangeable value, however scarce it might be.

　① feasible　　　　　　　　　② ecumenical
　③ pertinent　　　　　　　　④ destitute

02　The best way to protect migrating wildlife is to create protective corridors. Although such a corridor would not serve the entire migratory path, it would serve as a temporary _____ for some extremely mobile animals.

　① vault　　　　　　　　　　② sanctuary
　③ abyss　　　　　　　　　　④ maze

03　When the talks to tighten bank regulations started last year, central bankers and bank supervisors had to construct rules tough enough to prevent another financial crisis yet _____ enough not to strangle the banks.

　① flexible　　　　　　　　　② ancillary
　③ quenchable　　　　　　　④ morose

04　Hebrew had not been spoken in any colloquial sense or used in purely artistic rather than didactic or _____ endeavor for at least a thousand years, and its development was consequently _____.

　① studious — prompted　　　　② homiletic — arrested
　③ sleazy — accelerated　　　　④ priggish — delimited

05   The popular image of the successful man seems to favor the freely roaming jack-of-all-trades. The realities of our civilization _____ this popular image. Our industrial society _____ for more and more trained and experienced human beings.

① fortify — vies   ② cloud — trembles
③ belie — clamors   ④ spawn — caters

06   That literature mirrors society is a widely known and generally accepted proposition. But it is seldom a simple mirroring or a one to one _____, for good literature is never a case of photographic realism. Literature is rather a complex, creative re-construction of lived reality.

① correspondence   ② allusion
③ antithesis   ④ dialectic

07   A group which plays a leading role in the advance of civilization in one period is unlikely to play a similar role in the next period, for it has been too much _____ with the traditions, interests and ideologies of the earlier period to adapt itself to the demands and conditions of the next period.

① plagued   ② unfettered
③ confounded   ④ imbued

08   When a new movement in art attains a certain vogue, it is advisable to find out what its advocates are aiming at, for, however _____ and unreasonable their tenets may seem today, it is possible that in years to come they may be regarded as normal.

① prodigious   ② far-fetched
③ stale   ④ rational
⑤ innate

09 Today the boy and girl on leaving school, have a much wider choice of occupations than could be had in earlier days. Parents and children alike are often bewildered by the number of avenues which may be entered. The choice then is no light affair, no matter to be settled _____.

① pensively

② gratis

③ resplendently

④ off-hand

10 I find many men nowadays oppressed with a sense of _____, with the feeling that in the vastness of modern societies there is nothing of importance that the individual can do. This is a mistake. The individual, if he is filled with love of mankind, with a breadth of vision, with courage and with endurance, can do a great deal."

① solstice

② impotence

③ reverie

④ cosmopolitanism

11 As a result of the increasing popularity and dominance of the Google search engine, usage of the transitive verb "to google" grew _____. The _____ commonly refers to searching for information on the World Wide Web, regardless of which search engine is used.

① pervasively — syllogism

② tenuously — abracadabra

③ ubiquitously — neologism

④ meteorically — misnomer

⑤ spasmodically — coinage

12 _____ can show a range of social _____. In one study, clumsy responses to "I like your sweater" included praise upgrades ("Yes, it really brings out the blue in my eyes"), intrusive questions ("Do you really think so? Do you want to borrow it?"), and disagreement ("It's itchy, I hate it").

① Repartees — gimmicks

② Interlocutions — strata

③ Compliments — ineptitude

④ Salutations — disruption

13 A time came in the progress of human affairs when men ceased to think it a necessity of nature that their governors should be an _____ power, opposed in interest to themselves. It appeared to them much better that the various magistrates of the State should be their tenants or delegates, _____ at their pleasure.

① absolute — executable
② independent — revocable
③ alienable — empowered
④ inherited — detained

14 In Africa, with its history of detached elite, corruption and using violence to achieve goals, the path to prosperity will likely be _____. Add the looming prospect of 300 million jobless young, and the _____ for any African government looking to mitigate the turbulence is clear: The next part of Africa's development is jobs.

① slipperier — proscription
② vaster — corollary
③ bumpier — imperative
④ flatter — desideratum

15 Rich, ambitious Americans are already spending more time on what makes them fulfilled, but that thing turned out to be work. Work, in this construction, is _____, composed of the job itself, the psychic benefits of accumulating money, the pursuit of status, and the ability to afford the many expensive enrichments of an upper-class lifestyle.

① a great misfortune
② a single bliss
③ a compound noun
④ a symbol of wealth
⑤ a cure for inequality

16 Most accounts have portrayed Bolton's exit as a policy-driven clash between Trump's transactional world view and Bolton's hawkish catechism, suggesting that Trump will _____ he so palpably craves with global bad actors, such as North Korea, Iran, and the Afghan Taliban leaders, whose invitation to Camp David and its last-minute revocation last week seems to have been the proximate cause of Bolton's exit.

① improve support base
② give up his political creed
③ be now free to make the deals
④ stir up a national crisis
⑤ lose his foundation of support

17 One explanation regarding ladders and bad luck has its roots in religion. Many Christians believe in the Holy Trinity — the Father, the Son, and the Holy Ghost. This belief made the number three sacred in early times, and along with it, the triangle. A ladder leaning up against a wall forms the shape of a triangle, and walking through it would be seen as "breaking" the Trinity, a crime seen as _____ as well as potentially attracting the devil.

① halcyon   ② blasphemous
③ iconoclastic   ④ calamitous

18 The impression that the town meetings of Colonial New England were free, democratic, and civilized is _____. For one thing, those who could vote did not include women, Black people, American Indians, and White men who did not own property. In the seventeenth century it was not "the people" who ran the town meetings; it was the town selectmen. However, in early colonial Dedham, Massachusetts, there was a time when the townsfolk themselves actually made all the big decisions at town meetings. A great and noble experiment, it lasted all of three years and was abandoned by 1639, soon after the town was established.

① totally true   ② beyond doubt
③ quite rational   ④ far too simplistic
⑤ far from groundless

19 Last year in Nautilus magazine, the composer Jonathan Berger explained how sound can do that very thing Prince says it can do — stop time: Music creates discrete temporal units but ones that do not typically _____ the discrete temporal units in which we measure time. Rather, music embodies a separate, quasi-independent concept of time, able to distort or negate "clock-time." This _____ creates a parallel temporal world in which we are prone to lose ourselves, or at least to lose all semblance of objective time.

① align with — other time
② interfere with — linear time
③ account for — circulative time
④ object to — daily time

20 Two-thirds of Europeans view the past more positively than the present, and are skeptical about immigration and membership of the European Union, a survey shows. The survey found that 67 per cent of those asked were nostalgic. A total of 78 per cent of those who _____ back to the past feel that immigrants do not want to integrate into society, while 63 per cent of the non-nostalgic respondents were of that opinion.

① deviate   ② hark
③ allay   ④ berate
⑤ relish

21 The most recent study in "Addictive Behaviors" entitled "Explicit and Implicit Effects of Anti-marijuana and Anti-tobacco TV Advertisements" concluded that the exaggerated fear-based and inaccurate advertisement creates a "boomerang" effect. Instead of getting teen viewers to take the position offered in the ads, this "boomerang effect" causes teens to rebel against the stated message since it is _____ to the knowledge teens already possess regarding marijuana. Exposure to anti-marijuana advertising might not only change young viewers' attitudes positively toward the substance, but also might directly increase risk of using marijuana.

① infallible   ② susceptible
③ empirical   ④ counter
⑤ germane

22 Adler (1981), Martin (1984) and Sussman (1986) have suggested that a proximal cause of repatriation distress or at least a critical mediating variable in intensifying the repatriation distress is its unexpectedness. It is _____ to expect difficulties when returning to one's home country. Unlike the now common knowledge held by expatriates that cognitive and behavioral adjustments to life overseas are a psychological process that may at times be frustrating, disconcerting, and stressful, repatriates appear to be unprepared for the psychological distress and discomfort that accompanies a return home.

① spontaneous   ② wearisome
③ disagreeable   ④ profound
⑤ counterintuitive

23 Suppose a robber comes into a bank with a pistol, threatens to shoot one of the tellers, and walks out with money or a hostage or both. This is a case of armed robbery, and we rightly lump it together with cases of mugging and assault, morally and legally speaking, even if everybody emerges from the situation without any bruises or wounds. The reason is that there is a clear threat by means of which a person very often accomplishes what he might otherwise accomplish by _____ violence. In this case the robber not only gets as much loot but he also accomplishes pretty much the same thing with respect to degrading the persons he is dealing with.

① ulterior   ② reticent
③ overt   ④ domestic

24 In 1952 America granted self-rule to the Caribbean island of Puerto Rico, which it had obtained from Spain in 1898. Last year Congress in effect revoked that autonomy, by creating a control board capable of vetoing any item in Puerto Rico's budget. The reversal was hardly an act of _____. The island had issued $70bn in debt, far more than its stagnant economy could hope to sustain. But because Puerto Rico is not a state, its public companies could not use the bankruptcy code used by insolvent borrowers like Detroit. That raised the spectre of a chaotic default.

① financial bailout   ② imperial gluttony
③ economic stratagem   ④ public involvement

25 The proposals by Dewey, Simon, and Brim et al are all sequential in the sense that they divide decision processes into parts that always come in the same order or sequence. Several authors, notably Witte, have criticized the idea that the decision process can, in a general fashion, be divided into consecutive stages. His empirical material indicates that the "stages" are performed in _____ rather than in sequence. "We believe that human beings cannot gather information without in some way simultaneously developing alternatives. They cannot avoid evaluating these alternatives immediately, and in doing this they are forced to a decision. This is a package of operations and the succession of these packages over time constitutes the total decision-making process."

① linear   ② parallel
③ asymmetrical   ④ hierarchial
⑤ circular

01   The evening was not boring, since Peter was a real _____. I had not met such a facetious and witty person in Germany before. He told jokes non-stop: good ones as well as bad.

① valetudinarian

② wag

③ vocalist

④ bard

02   An investigation by Reuters discovered that chicken companies in the US use a wide array of antibiotics as routine feed supplements to _____ disease and promote growth.

① embolden

② excoriate

③ forestall

④ eulogize

03   The exploitation of the weak as a legitimate activity of capitalism has always been a perilous venture. It creates a fertile climate for the flourishing of fascism, itself a political philosophy that _____ the enslavement of the weak.

① eschews

② spurns

③ lauds

④ proscribes

04   Bacon's _____ style suggests the kinship between the word "essay" and the mineralogist's word "assay"; for the handful of carefully-washed words which come out in one of Bacon's essays puts one in mind of the prospector sluicing away the grit until a few clear specks of gold are left in the bottom of his pan.

① pedantic

② cryptic

③ sardonic

④ laconic

05   The United States has flown two B-52 long-range bombers through the contested airspace, a move seen as a warning by Washington that it would _____ what it considered a _____ attempt by China to expand its control over airspace in the region.

① impede — capitalist   ② accomodate — dovish
③ hail — troublesome   ④ besiege — placating
⑤ defy — provocative

06   Adam Smith recognized that the "principal architects" of policy — in his day the "merchants and manufacturers" — made sure that their own interests had "been most peculiarly attended to" however "_____" the effect on others, including the people of England.

① grievous   ② beneficial
③ compassionate   ④ empathetic

07   At times, introversion is more appropriate; at other times extraversion is more suitable. The two are mutually exclusive; you cannot hold both an introverted and an extroverted attitude concurrently. Neither one is better than the other. The ideal is to be flexible and to adopt whichever attitude is more appropriate in a given situation — to operate in terms of a dynamic _____ between the two and not develop a fixed, rigid way of responding to the world.

① asymmetry   ② analogy
③ balance   ④ anachronism

08   The earliest-known version of the expression "curiosity killed the cat", written by Ben Jonson and popularized by his frenemy William Shakespeare, goes: "Care killed the cat". With 'care' being used here to mean 'worry', the historical gist is that an anxious person (or feline) can literally worry themselves sick. It's unclear how 'care' became 'curiosity' in the late 1800s but it is clear that modern speakers almost always forget the rejoinder first published in 1905: "Curiosity killed the cat .... but satisfaction brought it back." In other words, being _____ might get you into trouble, but learning the truth is often worth the risk.

① avid   ② discontented
③ obtuse   ④ nosy

09 A second problem is governance. The ocean is subject to a patchwork of laws and agreements. Enforcement is hard and incentives are often misaligned. Waters outside national jurisdictions — the high seas — are a global commons. Without defined property rights or a community invested in their upkeep, the interests of individual actors in exploiting such areas win out over the collective interest in _____ them. Fish are particularly tricky because they move. Why observe quotas if you think your neighbour can haul in catches with impunity?

① capitalizing
② deploying
③ prodigalizing
④ husbanding
⑤ gobbling

10 Art therapy provides individuals with the opportunity to focus on their strengths in a creative manner. They create their own environment and personal world in their artwork. The artist is the master of his universe, often choosing his own themes, colors, shapes, materials, and images. The art therapist encourages individuals not to judge themselves and to let their work flow. Participants learn that _____ becomes the most important aspect of creative work.

① geometry
② aestheticism
③ verisimilitude
④ self-expression

11 It is Oliver Cromwell who is said to have requested that his portrait be done depicting him "warts and all." However, his real words, according to Horace Walpole who wrote a century after Cromwell died, were a bit less _____: "Mr. Lely, I desire you would use all your skill to paint your picture truly like me, and not flatter me at all; but remark all these roughness, pimples, wrinkles, and everything as you see me. Otherwise, I will never pay a farthing for it."

① gabby
② wary
③ naggy
④ pithy

12   In Asia, people use _____ as weapons. A Hong Kong car park has a sign on the wall saying: "The owners of this car park take no liability whatsoever for any theft or damage or any other occurrence concerning your car, whether caused directly or indirectly by us." This gives car park staff full _____ to break into your car, steal your stereo, and leave notes sneering at your taste in music.

① billboards — prohibition   ② ultimatums — admonition
③ disclaimers — permission   ④ declarations — persuasion

13   When bats fly, air flows past tiny hairs growing out of touch-receptor bumps along their wings. If a bat's wing isn't curved a certain way during flight, the air becomes bumpy. _____ The bat can then correct its course and avoid collisions, even in total darkness. Ohio University neuroscience professor John Zook recently tested this by using hair-removal cream on bats' wings. The depilated bats could fly straight, but when they attempted to make sharp turns, they would suddenly drop or jump in altitude. When the hairs grew back, the bats were again able to turn normally.

① The bat's sense of touch helps it find the way to its destination.
② The hairs detect that turbulence and convey the information to the bat's brain.
③ The bat's built-in magnetic sensor enables it to detect its location.
④ The muscles must be contracted to overcome the impact of air turbulence.

14   In some cultures it is common to use titles when talking to people who are not family or friends. Sometimes these titles show a person's profession. Or they tell us that he or she is older and should be honored. In general, North Americans are not very formal. That is true with titles, too. In everyday life, titles are not used, except for Doctor (Dr.) for a medical doctor, and sometimes Professor (Prof.) for a university professor. Naturally, Mr. and Mrs., Miss, and the newer form Ms. (pronounced Miz, and used for any woman, married or not) are used sometimes. But people in the United States and Canada are so _____ nowadays that they often use first names right away after meeting. In fact, many times even a boss or older person will ask you to use his or her first name or even a nickname.

① casual   ② tactical
③ practical   ④ conventional

15 After an unprecedented run of amateur archaeological finds in Denmark, the National Museum of Denmark has declared that it cannot keep up any more. "We are behind and at the moment we are falling further and further behind," said the museum spokesman. Recent discoveries to be _____ by the museum include a still-sharp 3000-year-old sword from the Bronze Age, an 1100-year-old gold crucifix, seven bracelets from the Viking Age — constituting the largest-ever find of Viking gold in Denmark — and a 1000-year-old rune stone found in a farmer's backyard.

① retrieved   ② processed

③ seized   ④ procured

16 When German ecologist Peter Wohlleben set out to test the long-maintained scientific belief that humans are the only species capable of feeling and expressing emotions, he already had a lifetime of _____ to challenge his doubters. In his intriguing report on animal emotions, Wohlleben draws on his own animal encounters to prove his point. We learn that roosters can deceive their hens. That mother deer grieve the death of their young. Even that horses can experience shame. From the emotional roller-coaster that a mother bird feels when her chicks empty the nest, to the gratitude a once-homeless dog expresses to its new owner, these insightful scientific proofs are both convincing and entertaining.

① anecdotes   ② parables

③ theorems   ④ calamities

17 The problem of doing justice to the implicit, the imponderable, and the unknown is of course not unique to politics. It is always with us in science, it is with us in the most trivial of personal affairs, and it is one of the great problems of writing and of all forms of art. The means by which it is solved is sometimes called style. It is style which complements affirmation with limitation and with humility; it is style which makes it possible to act effectively, but not _____; it is style which, in the domain of foreign policy, enables us to find a harmony between the pursuit of ends essential to us and the regard for the views, the sensibilities, the aspirations of those to whom the problem may appear in another light.

① reconcilingly   ② absolutely

③ conservatively   ④ flexibly

18 Workplace psychologist Jennifer Newman says she's seen a lot of cases where employees feel very guilty about making mistakes at work. Unexamined guilt can lead us to make bad decisions, but reflecting on why we're struggling with these feelings can help solve problems, says Newman. "When you have the feeling that you're disappointing people or letting them down, you have to find out whether it's true," says Newman. So if you feel guilty about something, you have to raise the question "_____", she says. Once you have the conversation with a loved one, your boss or even yourself, you can learn to get rid of the guilt.

① How far do I have to go?   ② Who on earth is on my side?

③ Where can I find an ideal job?   ④ What's really going on here?

19 In philosophy, the term 'means to an end' refers to any action (the means) carried out for the sole purpose of achieving something else (an end). It can be thought of as a _____ distinction, as no empirical information differentiates actions that are means to ends from those that are not — that are "ends in themselves." Immanuel Kant's theory of morality states that it is immoral to use another person merely as a means to an end, and that people must, under all circumstances, be treated as ends in themselves. This is in contrast to some interpretations of the _____ view, which allow for use of individuals as means to benefit the many.

① materialistic — positivistic   ② feasible — sectarian

③ tentative — pluralistic   ④ metaphysical — utilitarian

20 A new breed of computer processors that mimic the neural networks in the human brain might mean that, in a few more years or decades, there may be machines that appear to learn and think like humans. These latest advances could possibly even lead to a singularity, a term that computer pioneer John von Neumann coined and the futurist Ray Kurzweil and the science-fiction writer Vernor Vinge popularized to describe the moment when computers are not only smarter than humans but also can design themselves to be even supersmarter and will thus _____.

① facilitate our brain functions   ② create a new species of men

③ no longer need us mortals   ④ never open the humanoid era

21　The successful struggle of the American colonies for independence was in the minds of European Romanticists. _____, English Romantic poets like Coleridge and Southey planned to emigrate to the banks of the Susquehanna river in America to start a _____ farm. But what gripped the imaginations of those who were young in 1789 was, of course, the revolution in France, inspired, in part, by events in America, but vastly more _____. The French Revolution permanently transformed the opinions, political formations, party alignments, and dreams and nightmares of Europe.

① Therefore — quixotic — ravishing 　② Instead — methodical — internecine

③ Indeed — utopian — cataclysmic 　④ Moreover — canonical — apocalyptic

22　We should, and indeed do, know many things. Yet confidence in the value and truth of knowledge _____. This is especially true of historical knowledge. For example, once there was a single narrative of national history that most Americans accepted as part of their heritage. Now there is an increasing emphasis on the diversity of ethnic, racial, and gender experience and a deep skepticism about whether the narrative of America's achievements comprises anything more than a self-congratulatory story masking the power of elites.

① eludes just about everyone 　② underlies almost all knowledge

③ accrues from social diversity 　④ debunks nothing but power elites

23　No matter their 'depth' and the sophistication of data-driven methods, such as artificial neural nets, in the end they merely fit curves to existing data. Not only do these methods invariably require far larger quantities of data than anticipated by big data _____ in order to produce statistically reliable results, but they can also fail in circumstances beyond the range of the data used to train them because they are not designed to model the structural characteristics of the underlying system. We argue that it is vital to use _____ as a guide to experimental design for maximal efficiency of data collection and to produce reliable predictive models and conceptual knowledge.

① analyses — imagination 　② aficionados — theory

③ methods — antithesis 　④ abominators — hypothesis

⑤ connoisseurs — big data

24 In the decades since World War II the old intellectual absolutisms have been dethroned: science, scientific history, and history in the service of nationalism. In their place, the postwar generation has constructed sociologies of knowledge, records of diverse peoples, and histories based upon group or gender identities. And the postwar generation has questioned fixed categories previously endorsed as rational by all thoughtful men, and has _____ social behavior once presumed to be encoded in the very structure of humanness. As members of that generation, we routinely, even angrily, ask: Whose history? Whose science? Whose interests are served by those ideas and those stories? The challenge is out to all claims to _____ expressed in such phrases as "Men are ...," "Naturally science says ...," and "As we all know ...."

① discomposed — rationalities
② detribalized — generalization
③ disintegrated — humanism
④ denaturalized — universality

25 Most of the other sins of politics are derivative of this larger sin — the need to win, but also the need not to lose. Certainly that's what the money chase is all about. There was a time when money shaped politics through outright bribery; when a politician could treat his campaign fund as his personal bank account and accept fancy junkets; when big honoraria from those who sought influence were commonplace, and the shape of legislation went to the highest bidder. If recent news reports are accurate, these ranker forms of corruption have not gone away entirely; apparently there are still those in Washington who view politics as a means of getting rich, and who, while generally not dumb enough to accept bags of small bills, are perfectly prepared to take care of contributors and properly feather their beds until the time is finally ripe to _____.

① convince public officials to support or, at least, not oppose their policy positions
② extort pocket money from citizens in exchange for not enforcing law against them
③ bring an end to poverty, discrimination, oppression and other forms of injustice
④ apply the law objectively without using their personal notions of fairness or justice
⑤ jump into the lucrative practice of lobbying on behalf of those they once regulated

❚ Choose the one that best completes the sentence(s).   ▶▶▶ **ANSWERS** P.373

01   Photorealism is a form of art that involves working directly from photographs rather than from the original subjects. It acknowledges the role that the camera plays in shaping our understanding of reality, and suggests obliquely that contemporary life is often centered more around _____ objects.

① artificial than imaginary

② genuine than counterfeit

③ primitive than sophisticated

④ manufactured than natural

02   Supporters of Israel need to stop ignoring or even condoning the injustices done to the Palestinians by Israeli settlers and the military. Likewise, Palestinian supporters should not turn a blind eye to the hateful _____ propaganda produced by the likes of Hamas. Peace will continue to be _____ as long as religion continues to influence the mind-set of the belligerents involved.

① ethnocentric — feasible   ② xenophobic — elusive

③ anarchistic — promising   ④ philanthropic — visionary

03   Electronic dance music may be fueled by drugs like ecstasy, but Robinson says he is not into anything more _____ than caffeine. At heart he is an effusive nerd, obsessed with Japanese culture and his Tumblr page. He has built a massive audience, but he finds himself _____ it out. "You can't write sincere music if you're only thinking about your fans," he says.

① popular — eking   ② potent — tuning

③ innocent — sorting   ④ invalid — churning

04 For years, city officials have congratulated themselves for _____ their beach town of the crazy college kids who used to make their city the destination of choice for wild and destructive spring break parties, where they fought, destroyed property, defied police and created _____.

① lifting — washout
② clearing — felicity
③ reforming — arcana
④ ridding — mayhem

05 Granted that the learning curve in child's language acquisition can be separated into _____ phases according to the curriculum stages, what we can find in real classroom environment is actually the _____ itself in learning process.

① dependent — accomplishment
② contemplative — persistence
③ distinct — gradation
④ coterminous — liberal arts

06 Bacon brooded over some topic of social custom or behavior until he could reduce his conclusions upon it to an almost _____. That is why he so often reads like a string of mottoes and proverbs. For example, he likens the ill-natured man to "the thorn or briar which prick or scratch because they can do no other."

① arcane literature
② legal clarity
③ graphic design
④ aphoristic brevity

07 One of the oddest things about Homo sapiens is that he is alone. Though storytellers have filled the world with imaginary hominids, no sign of the real thing has ever been seen. But that was not true in the past. 40,000 years ago, there were three other species of human on Earth: Neanderthals in Europe, the "hobbits" in Indonesia, and the Denisovans, who lived in Central Asia. And now there is evidence that similar _____ existed earlier in human history, 2 million years ago, in Africa.

① subterfuge
② sleight
③ multifariousness
④ physiognomy

08 The object of the teachings of the sophists was success in one's endeavors, whether it was getting elected to some post or winning one's case in court. But teaching one how to be successful, as most Athenians clearly realized, did not necessarily mean teaching one to be just, or to know or tell the truth. How to win one's point, even if one had to be deceptive to do it, was what the sophists taught. Not surprisingly, many Athenians saw them as little more than _____.

① skeptics to the bone   ② purveyors of dishonesty
③ apostles preaching truth   ④ peddlers of sundry thoughts

09 Frank Schaefer, a Methodist preacher in Pennsylvania, officiated at his son's same-sex wedding in 2007. This act of _____ earned him a suspension. When he couldn't promise he wouldn't do it again for another same-sex couple, the United Methodist Church decided to defrock him last year. But in June the church went ahead and _____ him. A panel of judges decided it was unwise to punish the minister for something he had not yet done.

① purification — exonerated
② sacrilege — reinstated
③ allegiance — dismissed
④ baptism — consoled
⑤ consecration — reprimanded

10 Pop music fans are capricious. Soon after a new type of music appeared the same teenagers forgot all about their old favorites. Now Jonas Brothers group has fallen into _____. In a recent interview, the group's spokesman stated that the group is optimistic to regain its popularity and that people's inattention to them was not due to the performance of the group but instead because of the _____ nature of human beings, who keep changing moods.

① oblivion — mercurial   ② contempt — emphatic
③ snare — gregarious   ④ egoism — rational
⑤ glitch — exoteric

11   Shakespeare's play has been adapted in a movie. Critics of the film have emphasized the _____, bravado, and nationalistic undertones of this version. The battle scenes in the film are understated and tame, with little of the carnage that would be expected of a medieval _____. They are shot in beautiful weather, and the actors are clad in radiant colors. The scene with Henry's harsh justice is omitted.

① artistry — triptych   ② bravery — chasm
③ senescence — undulation   ④ pageantry — melee

12   W. B. Yeats is alive mainly because so many of his lines seem extraordinarily prescient and as _____ to our times as to his. Trying to frame a response to the imminent destruction by Islamic State of the ancient city of Palmyra in Syria, I recalled the _____ verses of one of Yeats's darkest meditations, 1919, written as Ireland was tearing itself apart: "Many ingenious lovely things are gone/That seemed sheer miracle to the multitude."

① pertinent — prophetic   ② immune — spurious
③ subordinate — mellow   ④ cognate — patriotic

13   *Henry V* is a play that's often produced, and most people who went through high school in the 20th century would have at least a passing acquaintance with it. Finding a new and different way to present it is quite a challenge. In this production, Damien Ryan has taken that challenge. But hackneyed adjectives like 'new and different' hardly touch on the reality of this amazing production. How Ryan managed to pull so many disparate ideas together and then present them as a(n) _____ whole _____ the imagination.

① cohesive — beggars   ② viscous — dwarfs
③ impeccable — orphans   ④ sexist — cooks
⑤ humped — crowns

14 After leaker Edward Snowden revealed the existence of massive domestic-surveillance programs operated by the NSA, the airwaves were clotted with pundits and politicians summoning a man with whom they appeared to possess only a passing familiarity. George Orwell, author of the dystopian classic 1984, warned of an all-knowing, all-seeing totalitarian state. We now know that it was a(n) _____ observation. American readers, too, saw the _____. With the Snowden disclosures dominating the news cycle, Amazon.com sales of 1984 increased 6,021 percent in a single day.

① clairvoyant — bluffs
② elusive — discrepancy
③ apathetic — controversy
④ prescient — parallels
⑤ absurd — modifications

15 You'll probably never go to Mars, swim with dolphins or sing onstage with the Wonder Girls. But if virtual reality ever _____ its promise, you might be able to do all these things — and many more — without even leaving your home. We react like that, experts say, because our brains are easily _____ when what we see on a display tracks our head movements. "We have a reptilian instinct that responds as if it's real: Don't step off that cliff; this battle is scary," Jeremy Bailenson, the founding director of Stanford's Virtual Human Interaction Lab, told me. "The brain hasn't evolved to tell you it's not real."

① does not conform with — glamorized
② rats on — magnified
③ juggles with — resurfaced
④ lives up to — fooled

16 With a new kind of heroine defiantly _____, morally courageous and fiercely independent, Charlotte Bronte brought about change in the style of fiction of the day, presenting an unconventional woman to be admired for her ability to _____ adversity. From her humble beginnings as an orphan under the care of a cruel aunt, governess Jane Eyre falls in love with her mercurial employer, the Byronic Edward Rochester. But then dark secrets of Thornfield Hall threaten to destroy everything she's worked so hard to achieve.

① disconsolate — surrender to
② virtuous — overcome
③ punctilious — eschew
④ fragile — survive

17 Children just want to be happy. So do puppies. Happy seems like a healthy, normal desire. Like wanting to breathe fresh air or shop only at Whole Foods. But "I just want to be happy" is a hole cut out of the floor and covered with a rug. Because once you say it, the implication is that you're not. The "I just want to be happy" _____ is that until you define precisely just exactly what "happy" is, you will never feel it. Whatever being happy means to you, it needs to be specific and also possible. When you have a blueprint for what happiness is, lay it over your life and see what you need to change so the images are more aligned. _____, this recipe of defining happiness and fiddling with your life to get it will work for some people, but not for others. I'm one of the others.

① red tape — Instead   ② silver bullet — Thus
③ tall talk — Moreover   ④ bear trap — Still

18 Since "group performance in problem solving is superior to even the individual work of the most expert group members," it should not be surprising that students learn better when they cooperate. But the last technique — having students help one another — raises the question of whether students with lower ability are being helped at the expense of those with higher ability. Is this true? Knowledge, happily, is not _____. Anyone who has taught or tutored knows that doing so not only reinforces one's own knowledge but often pulls one to a more sophisticated understanding of the material. The cliché about teachers' learning as much as their pupils is quite true, and the tutoring that takes place in a cooperative classroom actually benefits both the helper and the helped more than a competitive or independent study arrangement.

① a rat race   ② a zero-sum product
③ a win-win situation   ④ a norm-referenced test

19   Sylvia Plath took her life and gained immortality 50 years ago. Suicide attracts speculation and prurience like flies to rotting food. Most writers who have killed themselves — Ernest Hemingway, David Foster Wallace, Spalding Gray and Virginia Woolf, for example — established themselves before they died. Plath's fame _____ under the cloud of her death and no other writer's life has cast as much of a shadow over their work as Plath's, and it's a shadow that only darkens. Just as Marilyn Monroe is now seen as the archetypal tragic Hollywood blonde, so Plath has been flattened into the _____ of the mentally tormented poet, the betrayed woman, the tragic literary blonde.

① bloomed — prototype   ② withered — maniac
③ alleviated — protocol   ④ ratified — iconoclast

20   Modern European and American history is centered around the effort to gain freedom from the political, economic, and spiritual shackles that have bound men. The battles for freedom were fought by the oppressed, those who wanted new liberties, _____ who had privileges to defend. While a class was fighting for its own liberation from domination, it believed itself to be fighting for human freedom as such and thus was able to appeal to an ideal, to the longing for freedom rooted in all who are oppressed. In the long and virtually continuous battle for freedom, however, classes that were fighting against oppression at one stage sided with the enemies of freedom when victory was won and _____.

① against those — new privileges were to be defended
② for those — they identified themselves with the party
③ with those — their enemies suffered straight defeats
④ to those — withdrew approval for the revolutionary sentiments

21 No doubt you will ask whether there is not a contradiction between the two qualities of the intellectual: playfulness and piety. If you think of the intellectuals you know, some will occur to you in whom the note of playfulness seems stronger, others who are predominantly pious. But in all intellectuals who have any stability as intellectuals, each of these characteristics is at some point qualified by the other. Perhaps the tensile strength of the intellectual can be gauged by his ability to maintain a fair _____ between these aspects of himself. At one end of the scale, an excess of playfulness leads to triviality, to _____, to cynicism, to the failure of all sustained creative effort. At the other, an excess of piety leads to fanaticism, to messianism, to ways of life that may be morally magnificent or morally mean, but in either case are not quite the ways of intellectualism. It is of the essence of the intellectual that he strikes a balance.

① rapport — egalitarianism ② linkage — integrity
③ equipoise — dilettantism ④ antagonism — majesty

22 My job fits snugly into this category. Writing is a leaky affair, where the boundaries between _____. When I open Twitter, or watch the news on a Sunday morning, am I panning for golden nuggets of insight, taking a mental-health break, or something in between? It's difficult to say; sometimes, I don't even know. A novel that I read can become an article's lede. A history book on my desk can inspire a column. Because the scope of non-fiction journalism is boundless, every moment of my downtime could theoretically surface an idea or stray comment that becomes a story. As a result, my weekdays feel more like weekends (and my weekends feel more like weekdays) than a 20h-century reporter's.

① work and leisure are always porous
② work and leisure are necessary in the good life
③ work and leisure require a lot of effort
④ work is completely separate from leisure
⑤ work is hugely influenced by leisure

23 Today the pope urged every parish and religious community in Europe to accommodate a refugee family. But not all Italian Catholics, or their would-be political representatives, approve. Over the past few weeks, _____ between a senior prelate and a rising politician of the right. Matteo Salvini, leader of the Northern League party and advocate of a new brand of Italian nationalism, has been sparring with Nunzio Galantino, the secretary of the Italian bishops' conference. In a barbed rebuttal of anti-immigrant stereotypes, Bishop Galantino said politicians who played on xenophobic feelings were themselves "street-pedlars" or travelling salesmen hawking worthless trinkets; Mr Salvini said that as an ordinary, fallible Catholic he was at least as entitled to speak out as any "communist bishop", and that he knew many people inside the church who shared his feeling that Italians must put their own interests first.

① there has been a satisfactory agreement on the present issue
② there have been some cantankerous public exchanges
③ the pope has tried to bring about a reconciliation
④ the pope has refused to listen to conflicting opinions

24 To most of us, brought up as we have been in the world of abstractions which science has prepared for us, and in the kind of school which that world produces — schools in which almost all teaching is teaching of abstractions — the notion of poetry as knowledge, the notion of art as knowledge, is a _____ notion. Knowledge by abstraction we understand. Science can abstract ideas about apple from apple. It can organize those ideas into knowledge about apple. It can then introduce that knowledge into our heads, possibly because our heads are also abstractions. But poetry, we know, does not abstract. Poetry presents the thing as the thing. And that it should be possible to know the thing as the thing it is — to know apple as apple — this we do not understand. All we can know is a world dissolved by analyzing intellect into abstraction, not a world composed by _____ intellect into itself.

① humdrum — abstracting
② creative — logical
③ fanciful — imaginative
④ plausible — unbiased

25 Few artistic experiences are as personal as connecting with a powerful novel, so it's easy to understand why a mass-market adaptation of our favorite book can feel like a betrayal. The criticisms that result are usually justified in the case of canonical literature, but there's more to consider than just our (admittedly selfish) need to reinforce the authenticity of our experience with the source material. People are being given a new, potentially exciting way to discover an invaluable work of art, a possibility that's far more important than our footing on our intellectual high horses. If it takes Leo Tolstoy winking on a glossy cover to catch someone's eye, then let's start up the presses, because a film adaptation — even an unspeakably bad one — is uniquely capable of shoehorning a classic piece of literature back into the public's consciousness. It's far more anti-intellectual to take that kind of opportunity for granted. Here, _____.

① the movie version shouldn't be forgiven
② a film adaptation is twisted and depraved
③ critical reception is irrelevant
④ canonical literature is better than the movie

해설편

01 ④	02 ①	03 ②	04 ②	05 ①	06 ③	07 ③	08 ①	09 ①	10 ②
11 ①	12 ③	13 ①	14 ②	15 ④	16 ④	17 ③	18 ①	19 ③	20 ②
21 ②	22 ③	23 ③	24 ②	25 ②					

01 ④

콜론 다음에서 그가 증명서와 학력에 대해 거짓말을 했다고 했으므로, 그는 '속인 것'이 발견될 때까지 회사에서 근무했다고 볼 수 있다. 따라서 ④가 빈칸에 적절하다.

application n. 지원[신청](서) credential n. 자격 증명서, 성적[인물] 증명서 agonize v. 고민하다, 고뇌하다 concede v. 인정하다 dither v. 우유부단하게 행동하다, 망설이다 dissemble v. 숨기다, 감추다, 속이다

그들이 그가 속이고 있었다는 것을 알아내기까지 그는 그 회사에서 6개월 동안 근무했다. 그는 지원을 신청하면서 자신의 증명서와 학력에 대해 거짓말을 했다.

02 ①

유전적 증거가 합리적인 의심을 넘어 진실을 입증했다고 했으므로, 다윈의 진화론을 '확증'하는 데 사용되었다고 볼 수 있다.

veracity n. 정직, 성실; 진실성 corroborate v. 확증[입증]하다 capitulate v. 굴복하다 enunciate v. 명확히 발음하다 abrogate v. 취소하다; (법률·습관 따위를) 폐지[철폐]하다

유전적 증거는 다윈의 진화론을 확증하는 데 사용되었으며, 합리적인 의심을 넘어 그것의 진실성을 입증했다.

03 ②

폭력범과 성범죄자들이 아이들에게 노리는 것은 그들을 '꼬드겨(구슬려)' 뭔가 자신이 원하는 것을 하게 만드는 것이라고 추론할 수 있다.

offender n. 범법자 parry v. 슬쩍 피하다 wheedle v. 구슬리다 dither v. 망설이다 tether v. 묶다

그것은 특히 아이들을 구슬려서 뭔가를 해보려는 폭력범들과 성범죄자들에게 효과적이다.

04 ②

개선되는 변화가 점진적으로 일어나서 측정하기 어렵다는 것은 분명하게 드러나지 않는다는 말인데, but으로 이어지고 있으므로 빈칸에는 '분명하게 드러난다'라는 뜻을 가진 ②가 적절하다.

transparency n. 투명성 fickle a. 변덕스러운 stark a. 뚜렷한 vague a. 모호한 rash a. 경솔한

대개 투명성은 점진적으로만 개선되는 경향이 있으므로 측정하기 어렵지만, 이번의 변화는 특별히 뚜렷하다.

05 ①

역접의 등위접속사 but으로 두개의 문장이 연결되었으므로, 빈칸에는 malignant의 반의어에 해당하는 단어가 들어가야 한다.

malignant a. 악성의; 유해한 tumor n. 종양, 종기 benign a. (병이) 양성(良性)의; 자비로운, 친절한 infectious a. 전염성의, 전염병의; 옮기 쉬운 lethal a. 치사의, 치명적인 fetid a. 악취를 내뿜는, 고약한 냄새가 나는

처음에 의사들은 그 종양이 악성일 수도 있다고 생각했으나, 결국 양성(良性)인 것으로 판명되었다.

06 ③

고임금 일자리와 저임금 일자리는 있는데 그 중간이 부족하다고 했으므로, 일자리가 한쪽으로 기운 것이 아니라 양쪽으로 갈라진(양극화된) 것이다. 따라서 ③이 정답으로 적절하다.

lopsided a. 한쪽으로 기운 divested a. 박탈당한 bifurcated a. 둘로 갈라진 decentralized a. 분산된

그 나라의 경제는 높은 보수를 받는 엔지니어들과 낮은 보수를 받는 바리스타들을 위한 일자리는 있지만 그 사이에 속한 사람들을 위한 일자리는 충분치 않아서 여전히 양극화된 상태이다.

07 ③

자신이 손을 대는 모든 것이 비할 데 없이 중요하다는 생각에 사로잡힌 사람이라면 평소에도 '과장'하는 면이 많을 것이다.

be addicted to ~에 중독되다, 탐닉하다 be obsessed with ~에 사로잡히다 unparalleled a. 비할[견줄] 데 없는 personification n. 의인화 foresight n. 예지력, 선견지명 hyperbole n. 과장(법) euphemism n. 완곡 어구

그는 20년 전에 그랬던 것만큼이나 여전히 과장하는 것을 탐닉하고 있어서, 그가 손을 대는 모든 것이 비할 데 없이 중요하다는 생각에 사로잡혀 있다.

08 ①

while로 두 절이 연결되었고 부정어 not이 있으므로 빈칸에는 rude(무례한)와 유사한 의미의 ①이 적절하다.

obnoxious a. 불쾌한 clandestine a. 은밀한 deferential a. 공경하는 salutary a. 유익한

몇몇 경우에 그것은 에티켓의 논쟁이다. 일부 사람들은 음성메일이 불쾌하다고 말하지만 또 다른 사람들은 음성메일을 남기지 않는 것이 무례하다고 믿는다. 사실은 어느 쪽도 아니다.

09 ①

instead of는 '~대신에'라는 의미이므로, 빈칸에는 앞에 위치한 형용사 straightforward의 반의어가 들어가야 한다.

straightforward a. 똑바른; 정직한, 솔직한 buzzword n. 현학적인 전문 용어, 전문적 유행어 ambiguous a. 애매모호한 authentic a. 확실한; 진짜의 reliable a. 믿음직한; 확실한 downbeat a. 우울한, 비관적인

모호한 전문 용어 대신에 직접적인 용어를 사용하면 자신의 주장을 분명히 밝히고 다른 이들보다 훨씬 돋보이게 하는 데도 도움이 될 것이다.

10 ②

등장인물의 사유와 기억과 감각을 따라가는 것을 통해서 등장인물을 표현하는 것은, 등장인물의 모든 것을 다 알고 이야기하는 3인칭 전지적 작가시점과는 정반대 지점에 있는 재현방식이다. 고로 이런 인물의 내면을 파고드는 방식은 전지적 작가시점을 거부할 때만 가능하다.

omniscient a. 전지(全知)의, 무엇이든 알고 있는 narration n. 이야기, 서술 rejuvenate v. 다시 젊어지게 하다, 원기를 회복하다[시키다] repudiate v. 거부하다, 물리치다, 부인하다 endorse v. 시인하다, 확인하다; 배서하다, 이서하다 uphold v. 유지하다, 옹호하다

전통적인 3인칭 전지적 작가 시점에서의 이야기 서술을 거부하고서, 그들은

소설 속의 등장인물들의 변화하는 사유들, 기억들 그리고 감각들을 통해서 등장인물들을 표현하는 것을 선호했다.

11 ①

설탕이 한때는 귀했지만 지금은 기술, 식품가공 등의 발전에 힘입어 값이 싸졌다는 것은 이제는 누구나 설탕을 도처에서 쉽게 구할 수 있다는 것을 의미한다.

commodity n. 상품, 일용품, 필수품; (농업·광업의) 제1차 상품, 미 가공품; 유용한 것 millennia n. 1000년간의 기간; 천년왕국(millennium의 복수형) food processing 식품가공 ubiquitous a. 어디에나 있는, 편재하는 abstemious a. 절제하는, 검소한 dormant a. 잠자는, 휴지상태에 있는, 움직이지 않는, 활동적이지 않은 weighted a. 편중된, 치우친

설탕은 수천 년 동안 세계에서 가장 귀중한 상품들 가운데 하나였지만, 현대 지질학, 기술, 그리고 식품가공 등은 설탕을 값싸고 어디에나 있는 흔한 물건으로 만들었다.

12 ③

모두가 원치 않고 돌봐주지 않는다는 것은 '무관심'을 의미하므로 빈칸에는 ③이 적절하다.

imposture n. 사기, 협잡 acrimony n. 신랄함 nonchalance n. 무관심 dysfunction n. 기능 장애

오늘날 가장 큰 병은 암이 아니라 모두가 원치 않고 돌봐주지 않는다는 감정이다. 이러한 이웃에 대한 무관심이 가장 큰 악이다.

13 ①

조세나 금융에 대한 사항은 시민 혹은 국민들에게 공통적으로 적용되는 것이므로, 만약 이것으로 인해 좌절을 겪고 있다면 다른 나라로 가거나 국적을 포기하는 것이 하나의 해결책이 될 수 있다. 따라서 빈칸에는 ①이 들어가야 한다.

amid prep. ~의 한복판에; ~이 한창일 때에 mount v. 증가하다, 늘다, 오르다 frustration n. 좌절, 차질, 실패 taxation n. 조세; 과세제도 weighty a. 무거운, 중요한 citizenship n. 시민권, 시민의 신분 renounce v. 포기하다, 단념하다; 부인하다 affirm v. 확인하다, 단언하다; 확인하다 consider v. 숙고하다; 고려하다 imbibe v. 마시다, 흡입하다; 받아들이다, 동화하다

과세 제도와 은행과의 거래 문제에 대해 좌절감이 솟구치는 가운데, 적지만 점점 많은 수의 미국인들이 시민권을 포기하는 중대한 조치를 취하고 있다.

14 ②

질병이 걸릴 수 있는 환경을 설명하기에 적절한 표현이 필요하므로 부정적인 의미의 단어를 선택해야 한다. ①과 ③은 긍정적인 의미이므로 답이 될 수 없으며, 글의 첫 부분에서 '파산'을 언급했으므로 이것의 결과가 되는 '가난한'이라는 의미의 ②가 정답으로 가장 적절하다.

bankruptcy n. 파산, 도산 fever n. 열, 발열; 열병; 열광 typhoid n. 장티푸스 doubtlessly ad. 의심 없이 contract v. 계약하다; (병에) 걸리다; 수축시키다 well-to-do a. 유복한, 편한 살림의 impoverished a. 가난한; 허약해진; 빈약한 sanitary a. 위생적인, 깨끗한 pastoral a. 목가의, 전원생활의

존(John)이 파산한 지 2년이 지난 후, 그의 어린 딸이 열병, 곧 장티푸스에 걸렸는데, 그것은 의심할 여지없이 그 가족이 살고 있었던 가난한 환경으로 인한 것이었다.

15 ④

신진대사가 평소보다 느려진다는 내용을 통해 휴면 혹은 동면 상태에 들어가는 상황임을 추론할 수 있다.

basal a. 바닥[기초, 근본]의 metabolic a. 물질[신진]대사의, [동물]변태의 torpid a. 움직이지 않는, 활발치 못한; (동물이) 휴면하는, 동면하는 vigorous a. 정력적인, 원기 왕성한, 격렬한 robust a. 강건한, 원기 왕성한; (신념 등이) 강한, 확고한 turbulent a. 휘몰아치는, 사나운, 거친

동면상태로 들어가는 것은 동물로 하여금 자신들의 신체 에너지 비축분을 그들이 일반적인 기초대사율을 유지하고 있을 때보다 더 느린 속도로 사용하게 해준다.

16 ④

다른 사람들을 방해하는 놀이라면 '소란스럽고 귀에 거슬릴 만큼 거친' 놀이일 것임을 추론할 수 있다.

litter v. 마구 버리다 disturb v. 방해하다, 불안하게 만들다 raucous a. 소란한; 귀에 거슬리는 querulous a. 불평하는 subdued a. 가라앉은 lugubrious a. 침울한, 슬퍼하는

부모들은 여름휴가가 주는 기회를 이용해서 자녀들이 함부로 오물을 버리지 말고, 소란스러운 놀이로 다른 사람들을 방해하지 말고, 사회 규범을 잘 준수하도록 가르쳐주어야 주어야 한다.

17 ③

도약은 갑작스러운 큰 발전을 의미하는데, 빈칸 이하에서 갑자기 창의적 활동이 일어나게 된다고 했으므로 그때까지는 그 영역이 사용하지 않고 '묵히고 있던' 영역이라 할 수 있다. 따라서 빈칸에는 ③이 적절하다.

constitute v. 구성하다, 성립시키다, 만들어 내다 leap n. 도약, 큰 발전 immense a. 막대한, 광대한 rancid a. 고약한 냄새가 나는, 불쾌한 vestal a. 여신의; 처녀의 fallow a. 사용하지 않는, 묵히고 있는 suave a. 유쾌한, 온화한

혁명은 성공할 때 진정한 역사적 도약을 성립시킨다. 그때까지 사용하지 않고 있던 인류의 광대한 영역이 갑자기 인간의 창의적 활동에 개방되는 것이다.

18 ③

두 번째 문장이 쿠바에 대한 여행제한과 방문금지를 설명하므로 빈칸에는 ③이 적절하다.

tighten v. 강화하다 ban v. 금지하다 alleged a. 추정되는, 전해지는 verdict n. 평결 appropriation n. 전유(專有), 착복 sanction n. 제재 embarkment n. 출항; 싣기, 적재

미국 정부는 쿠바에 대한 제재를 강화했다. 교육 및 문화 목적의 여행을 제한했고 쿠바 군대와 금전적인 연관이 있다고 전해지는 180개 호텔과 사업체에 대한 미국 시민들의 방문을 금지했다.

19 ③

폭탄 공격을 부인하고 외국 군대의 소행으로 돌리려 하는 것은 자신들의 소행을 감추려 하는 의도로 보아야 한다. 따라서 '~을 가리다, 애매하게 하다, 이해하기 어렵게 하다'라는 의미를 가진 ③이 정답이 된다.

point out 가리키다; 지적하다 militant n. 활동가; 전투원 denial n. 부인, 부정; 거절 tactic n. 용병; 작전 extend v. 연장하다; 확장하다, 확대하다 myth n. 신화; 꾸며낸 이야기 element n. 요소, 성분; 분대 inquire v. 묻다, 문의하다 excruciate v. 고문하다; 괴롭히다 obscure v. 어둡게 하다; 가리다; 감추다 interpret v. 해석하다, 해명하다, 설명하다; 번역하다

그 신문은 현지 무장단체가 폭탄 공격에 대해 부인하는 것은 그들의 공격의 근원지를 숨기려는 일반적인 수법이며, 폭탄 공격이 외국 군대의 소행이라는 근거 없는 믿음을 퍼뜨리려는 데 있다고 지적했다.

20 ②

첫 번째 빈칸에는 and로 연결되어 있는 weighed와 유사한 의미를 가진 단어가 들어가야 한다. 두 번째 빈칸의 경우, Unlike가 이끄는 전치사구와 주절의 내용이 대조를 이루어야 하므로 carefully weighed에 대해 문맥상 반대 의미를 가진 단어가 필요하다. 숙고하는 행위는 일반적으로 시간을 들여서 하는 행위임을 감안하면 된다.

weigh v. 숙고하다, 고찰하다; 평가하다, 비교 검토하다 composition n. 구성, 조립; 작문; 저술 enthusiasm n. 열심, 열중, 열광 inspired a. 영감을 받은 vigor n. 활기, 정력 planned a. 계획된, 정연한, 조직적인 immediacy n. 직접성, 즉시성 laborious a. 힘 드는, 고된, 어려운; 근면한 endeavor n. 노력; 시도, 애씀 developed a. 고도로 발전된, 선진의 construction n. 건설, 건축; 구조, 구성

심사숙고하고 계획을 통해 만들어진 단테(Dante)의 저술과는 달리, 괴테(Goethe)의 글은 언제나 직접적이며 열정적인 감각을 지니고 있다.

---

21 ②

능률성은 일정 비용에 대한 수익의 비율이므로, 비능률이 야기되려면 비용이 제대로 지출되지 않아 수익을 감소시켜야 한다. 따라서 ②가 정답으로 적절하다.

insight n. 통찰 expenditure n. 지출 privilege n. 특권, 특전 beneficiary n. 수익자 channel v. 일정 방향으로 돌리다, 보내다 dissipate v. 흩어 없애다; 낭비하다 subdue v. 진압하다 distend v. 팽창시키다

툴록이 꿰뚫어본 점은 특권을 얻어내려 로비를 하는 데는 많은 비용이 들고 따라서 이런 지출은 수익자들에게 가야할 이득의 일부를 소실시켜 비능률을 야기한다는 점이었다.

---

22 ③

주변의 일을 알아차리지 못하는 사람은 둔한 사람이므로 빈칸에는 ③이 적절하다.

incognizant a. 알아채지 못하는 enlighten v. 계몽하다 be exposed to ~에 노출되다 dainty a. 고상한 scintillating a. 재치가 넘치는 stolid a. 둔감한, 신경이 무딘 congenial a. 붙임성 있는

그는 그가 접하게 된 신세계에 의해 너무나도 계몽되어, 주변에서 일어나는 활동들을 알아채지 못하는 둔한 인물에서 모든 일을 의식하는 사람으로 바뀌었다.

---

23 ③

역접의 접속사 But 뒤에서 '정부가 침착함을 유지해야 한다'고 하였다. 따라서 But의 앞 문장은 '국민들은 노여움으로 들끓고 있다'라는 의미가 되는 것이 적절할 것이다.

simmer v. (노여움 등으로) 들끓다 sentiment n. 정서 composure n. 침착 territorial integrity 영토 보전 bicker v. 다투다 impose v. 도입하다; 부과하다 simmer v. (노여움 등으로) 부글부글 끓다, 들끓다 sustain v. 유지하다

국민들이 반일감정으로 들끓고 있다. 그러나 정부는 침착함을 유지해야 한다. 국가안전보장회의는 오늘 일본의 역사 왜곡과 한국의 영토 보전을 해치려는 시도에 대해 한국 정부의 독트린(원칙)을 발표할 예정이다.

---

24 ②

접속사 But을 전후한 문장의 내용이 대조를 이루어야 하겠는데, simple과 harder라는 표현이 이미 대조의 조건을 완성하고 있으므로 빈칸에는 문맥상 say와 동일한 의미를 가질 수 있는 표현이 들어가야 한다. 말하는 것은 이해하는 것을 바탕으로 한 것임을 고려하면, 가장 적절한 것은 ②이다.

transform v. 변형시키다, 바꾸다 enterprise n. 기획, 계획; 기업; 진취적인 정신 reinforce v. 강화하다, 보강하다 decipher v. 판독하다, 풀다; 해독하다 encode v. 암호화하다 eschew v. 피하다, 멀리하다

정보기술이 기업의 형태의 변화를 가져온다고 말하기는 쉽다. 하지만 이런 변화가 회사와 최고 경영진에게 무엇을 요구하는지를 파악하기는 매우 어려운 일이다.

---

25 ②

be a whiner(불평꾼이 되다)와 wallow in misery(비탄에 젖어있다)가 부정적인 행동을 의미하므로 '부정성을 거부하라'는 뜻의 ②가 정답으로 적절하다.

say no to 반대하다, 거부하다 whiner n. 불평꾼 workmate n. 직장동료 hang out with ~와 사귀다 procrastinate v. 지연시키다, 꾸물거리다

부정성을 거부하라. 직장에서 불평꾼이 되지 마라. 직장동료들이 비탄에 젖어있기를 원하면 그들은 그렇게 하게 내버려두고 대신 행복한 사람들과 사귀어라. 그러면 기분이 더 좋아질 것이고 시간이 빨리 지나갈 것이다.

01 ③	02 ①	03 ②	04 ①	05 ④	06 ③	07 ④	08 ③	09 ③	10 ②
11 ③	12 ②	13 ④	14 ③	15 ②	16 ③	17 ①	18 ①	19 ③	20 ②
21 ①	22 ③	23 ③	24 ④	25 ④					

01 ③

부사 too가 단서가 된다. '나 역시도 슬퍼졌다'라고 했으므로 아이는 '슬픔'과 유사한 반응을 보였을 것이다. 그러므로 sad의 의미를 내포하고 있는 ③이 정답이 된다.

deception n. 사기, 기만, 속임 bliss n. 행복; 희열 dejection n. 낙담, 실망; 우울 animation n. 생기, 활기; 만화 영화

그 꼬마가 장난감을 잃어버렸을 때 너무도 크게 낙담해서, 나 또한 마음이 슬퍼졌다.

02 ①

이론의 타당성을 증명하는 것이 목표인 사람들에게 있어 실패란 '그 이론이 적용되지 않은 사례'가 발견되는 경우일 것이다. 그러므로 빈칸에는 '변칙적인 것, 예외적인 것'이라는 의미의 ①이 들어가는 것이 적절하다.

validity n. 정당성, 타당성; 유효함 anomaly n. 변칙적인 것, 예외적인 것; 이례 concordance n. 조화, 일치 viability n. 생존 능력, 생활력; 실행 가능성 cohesion n. 점착(粘着); 결합, 단결

이론의 타당성을 증명하는 것이 목표인 연구원들은 변칙적인 것의 발견을 실패로 판단할 가능성이 높다.

03 ②

'뜻깊은 사업'이라고 했으므로 이것을 설명하는 역할을 하는 관계대명사절은 긍정적인 결과에 대한 내용이어야 한다. 그런데, 빈칸 뒤에 목적어로 '고통'이 주어져 있으므로, 이것을 '없애주거나 덜어준다'라는 의미를 가진 단어가 들어가야 앞서 언급한 전제에 부합할 수 있다. 따라서 '경감하다, 완화하다'라는 의미를 가진 ②가 정답이 된다.

meaningful a. 의미심장한, 뜻있는; 의의 있는 fortunate a. 운이 좋은, 행운의, 행복한 assay v. 분석하다, 평가하다; 시험하다 alleviate v. 덜다, 완화하다 allude v. 암시하다, 넌지시 말하다 allure v. 유혹하다, 부추기다

나는 우리의 불우한 형제자매들의 고통을 덜어주는 데 분명 도움을 줄 수 있는 이 뜻깊은 사업을 더 많은 사람들이 지원하기를 기원한다.

04 ①

접속사 so 전후의 문장은 인과관계를 이루어야 한다. so 앞에서 '주의 깊게 통독할 시간이 없다'라고 했으므로, 결과가 되는 so 이하에서는 read through와 대조를 이루는 행위를 하게 될 것이다. 따라서 '훑어서 읽다'라는 의미의 ①이 빈칸에 적절하다.

read through 통독하다, 독파하다 skim v. 대충 훑어 보다; 스쳐 지나가다 gaze v. 지켜보다, 응시하다 span v. 걸치다; 가로지르다 flap v. 펄럭이게 하다; 손바닥으로 때리다

이 책을 주의 깊게 통독할 만한 시간은 없습니다. 따라서 저는 대충 훑어 읽기만 하겠습니다.

05 ④

빈칸 다음의 that과 콜론(:) 다음의 our belief가 동격 관계인데, 이것이 긍정적인 것이고 주어인 '고문의 사용'은 부정적인 것이므로 빈칸에는 ④가 적절하다.

torture n. 고문 entail v. (필연적 결과로서) 일으키다, 남기다, 수반 validate v. 정당화하다 incite v. 부추기다 compromise v. (명예·평판·신용 따위를) 더럽히다, 손상하다; 위태롭게 하다, 떨어뜨리다

고문의 사용은 우리를 우리의 적과 가장 많이 구별지어주는 것, 즉 모든 사람, 심지어 우리의 적조차도 기본적인 인권을 갖고 있다는 우리의 믿음을 위태롭게 한다.

06 ③

조금밖에 음식을 먹지 않았다는 주절의 내용과 Even though가 이끄는 종속절의 내용이 대조를 이루어야 하므로, 빈칸에는 '배가 고팠다'라는 의미를 가진 단어가 들어가는 것이 자연스럽다.

poorly ad. 좋지 못하게; 저조하게; 형편없이 portion n. 한 조각, 일부, 부분; 몫 surly a. 무뚝뚝한, 퉁명스러운 ravenous a. 게걸스럽게 먹는, 탐욕스러운; 몹시 굶주린 forewarn v. 미리 주의하다, 미리 경고하다; 예고하다

만찬 파티에 참석한 모든 손님들이 굶주렸음에도 불구하고, 음식이 너무나 형편없이 마련됐기 때문에 다들 조금밖에 들지 않았다.

07 ④

빈칸이 '즉석에서, 갑자기'라는 의미의 on the spur of the moment라는 표현과 순접의 접속사 and로 이어지고 있으므로, 빈칸에도 이와 유사한 의미의 단어가 쓰여야 한다.

deliver v. 배달하다; 연설하다; 해방하다 on the spur of the moment 갑자기, 즉석에서; 앞뒤 생각 없이 passionate a. (사람·말 등이) 열렬한, 열정적인; (감정이) 격렬한 wordy a. 말의; 말 많은, 장황한 cynical a. 냉소적인, 비꼬는 violent a. 격렬한, 맹렬한; 폭력적인 impromptu a. 즉석의, 즉흥적인

그가 한 연설은 즉흥적이고 갑자기 행해진 것이었지만, 그 연설은 내가 지금까지 들어본 것 중 가장 진지하고 열정적인 것 가운데 하나였다.

08 ③

콜론(:)은 부연설명, 예시, 열거 등에 쓰인다. 첫 문장의 주절의 내용, 즉 '두 사람이 더할 나위 없이 다르다'는 내용을 콜론 이하에서 부연하여 설명되어야 하는데, relaxed와 tense가 대조를 이루고 있으므로, 빈칸에는 silent의 반의어가 들어가야 한다. 따라서 정답은 '수다스러운'이라는 의미의 ③이 된다.

tense a. 긴장한; 긴박한, 절박한 anxious a. 걱정스러운, 불안한; 열망하는 calm a. 고요한; 평온한, 차분한 loquacious a. 말이 많은, 수다스러운; 떠들썩한 bleary a. (눈이) 흐린; (윤곽 등이) 흐릿한, 어렴풋한

그 두 남자는 함께 일을 매우 잘 하지만 서로 너무나 다르다. 밥(Bob)은 느긋하고 수다스러운 반면, 윌(Will)은 신경이 날카롭고 대부분의 시간을 조용하게 보낸다.

09 ③

빈칸을 포함한 부분이 '사치품'이라는 단어를 수식하고 있으므로 빈칸에는 '부자'와 관련된 단어가 들어가야 자연스럽게 호응함을 알 수 있다. 따라서 적절한 것은 ③이다.

innovation n. 혁신, 쇄신; 새로이 도입한 것 recipe n. 처방전; 조리법; 비법 affordable a. 줄 수 있는, 입수 가능한; (값이) 알맞은 gourmet n. 미식가, 식도락가 majority n. 대부분, 대다수 affluent a. 부유한 frugal a. 검약한, 소박한

밀튼 허쉬(Milton Hershey)는 분명 초콜릿을 발명하지는 않았지만, 조리법과 대량 생산을 새로이 도입함으로써 부유한 사람들을 위한 사치품을 모든 이들에게 알맞은 가격의 먹을거리로 바꾸어 놓았다.

10 ②

mince one's words가 '조심스레 말하다'는 뜻의 표현이므로 빈칸에는 ②가 들어가는 것이 적절하다.

beat around the bush 둘러말하다 mince v. 조심스레 (완곡히) 말하다, 점잔빼며 말하다 contestant n. 경기 참가자 cleave v. 쪼개다 pierce v. 꿰뚫다 sickle v. 낫으로 베다

우리는 모두 사이먼 코웰(Simon Cowell)이 특히 그의 쇼에 참가한 사람들에 관해서 둘러말하거나 조심스레 말할 사람이 아니란 것을 알고 있다.

11 ③

빈칸 다음의 they는 보험회사를 가리키는 대명사이며 보험회사의 판단에 따라 처리할 수 있는 일을 열거하고 있으므로 빈칸에는 ③이 적절하다.

insurer n. 보험 회사, 보험업자 leeway n. (무엇을 자신이 원하는 대로 하거나 변경할 수 있는) 자유, 재량 verve n. 열정, 기백 nuisance n. 폐, 성가심 indictment n. 기소, 고발

다른 많은 주(州)들은 보험회사가 누구에게 보상해야 하고 어떤 것을 보상해야 하는지, 그들이 보험료로 얼마나 청구 할 수 있는지, 심지어 경우에 따라서는 언제 보험금을 지급해야 하는지를 결정하는 데 있어 보험회사에게 많은 재량권을 준다.

12 ②

마약 범죄 조직이 범죄로 희생당한 사람들의 미망인에게 매달 지급금을 준다는 것은 일반적인 상식을 벗어난 것이므로 ②가 정답이다.

cultish a. 숭배의, 컬트적인 bible-thumping a. 열광적으로 전도하는 drug cartel 마약 범죄조직 stipend n. 정기적인 지급[지불]금 tractable a. 온순한; 다루기 쉬운 eccentric a. 괴상한, 괴짜인 philanthropic a. 인정 많은, 인자한 impeccable a. 결함 없는

극단적인 경향을 가지고 있으며 전도에 열을 올리는 마약 범죄조직인 라파밀리아는 조직원들이 마약과 술을 복용하는 것을 금지하는데, 마약 범죄로 희생당한 피해자들의 미망인에게 매달 지급금을 준다는 점에서 괴상하다.

13 ④

사람을 짐승이라 부르는 것은 일반적으로 경멸의 말이지만 나에게는 칭찬의 말이 된다는 뜻이므로 빈칸에는 ④가 적절하다.

reflex n. 반사 신경 compliment n. 칭찬의 말 confession n. 고백 grapevine n. 헛소문 bombast n. 호언장담 pejorative n. 경멸의 말

는 반사 신경이 고양이 같고(날래고) 독수리의 눈을 갖고 있으며 바람처럼 달리고 대부분의 사람들보다 더 높이 더 멀리 뛸 수 있다. 나를 짐승이라 부르는 것은 칭찬의 말이지 경멸의 말이 아니다.

14 ③

대기의 질이 나빠진 도시와 가스실의 관계는 비유의 관계이므로 첫 번째 빈칸에는 likened가 적절하고 두 번째 빈칸에는 '질이 나빠지다(급강하하다)'는 뜻으로 plunge나 plummet이 적절하다.

gas chamber 가스실 stubble n. (농작물을 베어내고 남은) 그루터기 adjacent a. 인접한 adapt v. 적응시키다 plunge v. 급강하하다(= plummet) ameliorate v. 개선되다 reduce v. 환원하다, 줄이다 liken v. 비유하다 confront v. ~에 직면하다 ascend v. 올라가다

인도의 수도 델리의 지방 정부 수장은 델리 시를 가스실에 비유했다. 인근 여러 주의 농부들이 그루터기를 태워서 생긴 연기로 인해 대기의 질이 급격히 나빠지자 학교와 많은 사무실들이 문을 닫았다.

15 ②

that의 선행사는 introductions이며 빈칸 뒤에 but이 왔으므로 '꼼꼼한 준비(meticulously rehearsed)'와 반대되는 뜻의 ②가 빈칸에 적절하다.

pitchman n. (텔레비전 등에서) 상품을 선전하는 사람 in a bind 곤경에 처한 off the cuff 준비 없이 (하는), 즉석의 on pins and needles 초조하여 on an even keel 균형을 유지한, 안정된

그 최고 경영자는 애플의 신상품을 발표하는 데 있어서 대가였으며 준비 없이 하는 것처럼 보였지만 항상 꼼꼼하게 준비된 상품 소개로 청중들을 매료시켰다.

16 ③

supposed facts and figures가 겉만 번지르르한 결과물이라는 단서에서, 특히 supposed(가정된)에서 첫 번째 빈칸에는 주관적 믿음에 해당하는 선택지를 추론 가능하고, 두 번째 빈칸은 stealthy(눈을 속이는, 은밀한)의 단서로부터 거짓의 신뢰도를 부여하는 것임을 추론할 수 있다.

facts and figures 사실과 숫자들(통계정보) glossy a. 광택 있는; 그럴 듯한 credence n. 신빙성, 믿음 merited a. 가치 있는, 당연한, 정당한 doctrine n. 교의, 교리 clandestine a. 은밀한, 숨겨진, 비밀의 tenet n. 주의, 교리 specious a. 허울만 그럴듯한 artistry n. 예술적 재능 ostensible a. 표면상의; 허울만의, 겉치레의

소위 가정된 사실과 숫자들은 학계에서의 실질적인 주의(이론)의 겉만 번지르르한 산물인데, 이들은 학계가 내린 결론에 대해 그럴듯한 믿음을 주는 것을 은밀한 목표로 삼고 있다.

17 ①

두 번째 문장의 rigid와 flexible은 정반대가 되므로 첫 번째 빈칸에는 flip(뒤집다)이 적절하고, 두 번째 빈칸에는 playful과 반대 의미인 disciplined(규율 바른)나 organized(조직화된)가 적절하다.

disposition n. 성질, 기질, 성향 flexible a. 유연한 playful a. 쾌활한, 장난스런 flip v. 뒤집다 disciplined a. 규율 바른; 훈련된 juggle v. 솜씨 있게 다루다 plastic a. 유연한 undo v. 원상태로 돌리다 organized a. 조직화된 brace v. 보강하다 slack a. 느슨한

정말로 성공적인 사람들은 종종 그들의 정신적 성향을 완전히 뒤집어버릴 수 있는 능력을 갖고 있다. 많은 분야에서, 처음에는 엄격하고 규율 바르지만 다음 일이 더 잘 되어 감에 따라 유연하고 쾌활한 것이 득이 된다.

18 ①

역접의 접속사 Although가 이끄는 양보의 부사절은 호르몬 보충제를 옹호하는 사람들과 관련된 내용이므로 이 보충제가 노화 과정을 좋은 방향으로 바꿔준다는 말이 와야 한다. 한편, 주절에는 이와 반대되는 내용이 필요하므로 이 전제에 대한 과학적인 증거는 불충분하다고 해야 한다. 그러므로 ①이 정답으로 적절하다.

proponent n. 옹호자, 지지자 supplement n. 보충, 추가 aging process 노화 작용, 노화 과정 advocate v. 옹호하다, 변호하다; 주장하다 favorably ad. 유리하게, 순조롭게; 호의적으로 scanty a. 불완전한; 불충분한 artificially ad. 인위적으로, 인공적으로 warranted a. 보증된 expeditely ad. 기민하게, 급속하게 conclusive a. 결정적인; 확실한, 단호한 discreetly ad. 분별 있게; 신중하게 reminiscent a. 추억의, 회고의; 추억에 잠기는

소수의 지지자들은 호르몬 보충제가 노화 과정을 좋은 방향으로 바꿔준다고 믿으면서 광범위한 사용을 옹호해왔지만, 대개는 이 전제를 입증하는 과학적인 증거가 불충분하다.

19 ③

열병으로 달아오르지는 않는다고 했으므로 첫 번째 빈칸에는 긍정적 감정이지만 열병에는 못 미치는 affection(애정)이나 enthusiasm(열정)이 적절하고, disesteem이 부정적인 감정이므로 두 번째 빈칸에는 무관심한 정도보다 더 부정적인 innuendo(빈정거림)나 detraction(비난)이 적절하다.

craftsman n. 장인(匠人) be no great shakes 대단한 것[사람]이 아니다 fever-heat n. 병적으로 높은 체온, 열병 disesteem n. 냉대, 경시 manifest v. 나타내다 indifference n. 무관심 affection n. 애정 panegyric n. 칭찬 antipathy n. 반감 innuendo n. 비꼼, 빈정거림 enthusiasm n. 열정 detraction n. 비난 idolatry n. 우상숭배 disinterest n. 공평무사

영국 작가들은 동료 작가들을 판단한다. 그들은 어떤 작가는 꽤 좋은 작가라고 하고 또 다른 작가는 별 볼일 없는 작가라고 말하지만, 전자에 대한 그들

의 열정이 열병 수준에 이를 때가 거의 없고, 후자에 대한 그들의 경시는 비난으로가 아니라 무관심으로 나타난다.

20
②

저녁에 기온이 불편할 정도로 떨어진다는 것은 온도의 일교차가 심하다는 것이므로 첫 번째 빈칸에는 '온화한'이라는 의미의 moderate이나 '변덕스럽다'는 의미의 mercurial이 적절하다. 그리고 모피 코트는 패션과 기능을 겸비했다고 했는데, 기능에 해당하는 stay warm이 두 번째 빈칸 앞에 왔으므로 패션에 해당하는 chic이 두 번째 빈칸에 적절하다.

mercurial a. 변덕스러운 co-opt v. 마음대로 사용하다 faux- a. 모조의, 가짜의 moderate a. 알맞은, 적당한; (기후 따위가) 온화한 innocuous a. 무해한 mercurial a. 변덕스러운 chic a. (옷 등이) 매력 있고 유행에 어울리는, 멋진 sizzling a. 타는 듯이 더운 rustic a. 투박한 brisk a. 상쾌한 pale a. 창백한

모피 코트는 변덕스러운 연안의 날씨가 밤에 불편하리만큼 쌀쌀하게 기온이 떨어지는 상황에서 패션과 기능을 겸비한 주요 트렌드였다. 남녀 모두가 멋지게 보이면서도 따뜻함을 유지하게 해 주는 모피와 인조모피 재킷을 입었다.

21
①

첫 번째 문장은 미국이 원료공급국에 비해 우월한 위치에 있다는 내용이고 두 번째 문장은 이에 대한 예시에 해당하는데, 결국 원료공급국들은 미국의 요청을 '울며 겨자 먹기' 식으로 받아들일 수밖에 없다는 맥락이다. 그렇다면 those duties는 원료공급국에는 좋지 않은, 다시 말해 부담스럽고 과중한(prohibitive) 것이며, 주어진 글은 이러한 이유로 거부하고 싶어도 그럴 수 없다는 내용이다.

leverage n. 지레 장치; (목적 달성의) 수단; 권력, 세력 negotiate v. 협상하다, 교섭하다 vulnerable a. 상처를 입기 쉬운; 비난 받기 쉬운, 약점이 있는; (유혹 따위에) 약한 countervail v. 무효로 만들다; 상쇄하다, 메우다 countervailing duty 상계관세(수출국에서 생산 (또는 수출) 보조금 등을 직접, 간접으로 받은 화물이 수입되는 것에 의해 수입국의 산업에 피해를 주거나 줄 우려가 있는 경우 이에 대항하기 위하여 통상의 관세 이외에 보조금액만큼 할증관세를 부과, 덤핑방지관세와 더불어 차별관세의 일종으로, 이에 따라 수입품의 경쟁력은 경감되고 수입국의 산업은 보호를 받음) antidumping duty (반)덤핑 관세 prohibitive a. 금지의, 금지하는 것이나 다름없는; (가격 따위가) 지나치게 높은, 과도한 emulative a. 경쟁의, 지지 않으려는 indiscreet a. 무분별한, 지각없는 dulcet a. (듣기·보기에) 상쾌한; (음색이) 아름다운, 감미로운

미국 협상가들은 불공정 무역행위에 타격을 입기 쉬운 브라질이나 스페인과 같은 원료공급국들과 협상을 하는 데 있어 힘을 가지고 있다. 이들 원료공급국들은 상계관세와 반덤핑 관세에 찬성하는 협정을 그것이 과중하다는 이유를 들어 거부하는 것이 사실상 불가능하다.

22
③

전체 글의 내용을 마지막 문장에서 밝히는 구성의 글이다. '창조의 행위는 여러 사람이 아닌 개인에 의해 이뤄지는 것'이라는 내용이므로, 빈칸에 들어갈 내용은 '개인의 창의성'에 대한 것이어야 한다. 따라서 ③이 정답이다.

collaboration n. 협동, 공동작업; 협조, 제휴 extend v. 확장하다, 넓히다 preciousness n. 귀중함, 소중함 interaction n. 상호 작용, 상호의 영향 quality n. 품질; 특성 collective activity 집단적 활동

그 어떤 것도 두 사람에 의해 창조된 적이 없다. 음악에서든, 미술에서든, 시에서든, 수학에서든, 철학에서든, 흡족한 공동 작업은 전무(全無)하다. 일단 창조의 기적이 일어나고 나면, 집단은 그것을 강화하고 넓혀갈 수는 있지만, 그 어떤 것도 발명해내지는 않는다. 귀중한 것은 한 사람의 독특한 지적 능력에 달려 있는 것이다.

23
③

옹호(변호)할 수 없는 주장은 허약한 주장일 것이므로 빈칸에는 ③이 적절하다.

distort v. 왜곡하다 condemn v. 비난하다 opponent n. 적, 상대 indefensibility n. 옹호불가능성 tenable a. 주장할 수 있는 robust a. 튼튼한 brittle a. 깨지기 쉬운 coherent a. 일관성 있는

오바마가 자기 나름의 견해를 갖고 있는 것에 나는 개의치 않는다. 그러나 그가 반대할 때면 언제나 상대편의 견해를 왜곡하고 상대편의 동기를 비난한다는 점은 그의 허약한 주장의 옹호불가능성은 말할 것도 없고 그에 대해 알아야 할 모든 것을 말해준다.

24
④

'조심스럽게 행동하다'라는 walk on eggshells의 의미를 설명한 ④가 빈칸에 적절하다.

signify v. 의미하다, 뜻하다 upset v. 화나게 하다 originate v. 시작하다, 비롯하다 diplomat n. 외교관 rank and file 부사관 및 병(兵); <비유적> 일반 시민 diplomatic a. 외교적인 dispute n. 논쟁, 말다툼 tread lightly 살금살금 걷다, 신중히 하다

계란 껍질 위를 걷는다(조심스럽게 행동하다)는 것은 다른 사람들을 화나게 하지 않기 위해 대단히 신경을 쓰는 것을 의미한다. 이 표현은 외교관들이 마치 달걀껍질 위를 걷는 것처럼, 어려운 상황에서 아주 살금살금 걷는 뛰어난 능력을 가지고 있는 것으로 설명되면서 정치 분야에서 생겨난 것으로 생각된다.

25   ④

자기들의 순수한 민주주의가 아닌 다른 형태의 정부라고 했으므로 첫 번째 빈칸은 부정적인 의미의 disdain(경멸하다)이나 demean(격하시키다)이 적절하고, 역접의 접속사 when절에서 the very opposite라 했으므로 두 번째 빈칸에는 긍정적인 의미의 touting(극구 칭찬하는)이나 proclaiming(선언하는)이 적절하다.

commentator n. 주석자, 방송해설자   corrupt a. 부패한; 타락한, 사악한 administration n. 행정부 embrace v. 포용하다 eschew v. 피하다 disdain v. 경멸하다 undermine v. 저해하다 enshrine v. 소중히 하다 tout v. 극구 칭찬하다 demean v. 품위를 떨어뜨리다 proclaim v. 공포하다, 선언하다

서구의 방송해설자들은 그들의 순수한 서구식 민주주의가 아닌 다른 모든 정부 형태를 격하시키지만, 아시아와 아프리카 전역에서 가장 실패하고 종종 가장 부패한 행정부는 현실은 정반대임(민주주의가 아님)을 보여주는데도 민주주의를 선언하는 행정부들이다.

01 ①	02 ③	03 ②	04 ②	05 ④	06 ②	07 ④	08 ②	09 ④	10 ⑤
11 ③	12 ④	13 ②	14 ③	15 ③	16 ①	17 ①	18 ③	19 ②	20 ④
21 ③	22 ④	23 ④	24 ④	25 ①					

01 ①

어떤 상황을 극복한 후에 다시 친구가 된 것이므로, 빈칸에는 그 상황에 해당하는 '좋지 못한 관계' 혹은 '좋지 못한 감정'이라는 의미를 가진 단어가 들어가는 것이 자연스럽다.

overcome v. 이기다; 압도하다, 정복하다; 극복하다, 넘어서다 rancor n. 깊은 원한; 적의; 심한 증오 comity n. 우의, 예의 amity n. 친목, 친선 rapport n. (친밀한) 관계, 조화; 동의, 일치

수지(Susie)와 톰(Tom)은 깊은 원한의 골을 극복하고 다시 친구가 되었다.

02 ③

agree의 목적어를 이루고 있는 부정사구가 등위접속사 and로 연결되어 있으므로, and 이하 역시 keep all such information confidential의 의미와 같은 맥락이 되어야 한다. 그런데, 빈칸 앞에 부정어 not이 있고 빈칸 뒤의 it이 가리키는 것은 all such information이므로, 결국 빈칸에는 keep ~ confidential과 반대되는 의미를 가진 표현이 필요함을 알 수 있다. 그러므로 '누설하다'라는 의미의 ③이 정답이다.

representative n. 대표자, 대행자, 대리인 confidential a. 은밀한, 내밀한; 기밀의 referee v. 중재하다; 심판하다 arrogate v. 침해하다; 가로채다; 사칭하다 divulge v. (비밀을) 누설하다, 밝히다 rectify v. 개정하다, 수정하다, 교정하다, 바로잡다

직원들과 대표자들은 그러한 모든 정보를 비밀로 유지하고 어느 누구에게도 누설하지 않을 것에 동의한다.

03 ②

빈칸 뒤에 이어지는 '가장 낮은 수준으로'라는 표현과 자연스럽게 호응하는 단어를 선택해야 한다. 따라서 '급락하다'라는 의미의 ②가 정답이다.

take ~ by surprise ~을 깜짝 놀라게 하다 expert n. 전문가, 숙련자 soar v. 높이 날다, 날아오르다; 급등하다 plunge v. 급락하다; (아래로) 거꾸러지다 balance v. 균형이 잡히다; 평균을 이루다 buckle v. 굽어지다; 부서지다, 무너지다

물가가 40년 만에 최저 수준으로 떨어져서 전문가들조차 놀라게 만들었다.

04 ②

선발될 사람을 미리 정해놓은 상태에서 배역을 뽑는 공개 시험을 본다면, 그것은 하나의 '웃기는 짓거리' 또는 '희화화'에 불과할 것이다.

in advance 미리 try-out n. (연기자 등의) 테스트, 오디션 no more than ~에 불과한 travesty n. 희화화, 웃기는 짓거리 mishap n. 불운한 일 prop n. 소품

각각의 역에 누구를 뽑을지 그녀가 미리 알고 있었기 때문에 그 연극을 위한 소위 "오디션"은 웃기는 짓거리에 불과했다.

05 ④

'가난과 기아'와 빈칸에 들어갈 말이 공존하는 것이 분배 면에서 잘못된 것이 되려면, 가난과 기아라는 물질 부족 상황에서는 있어서는 안 되는 것이 빈칸에 들어가야 한다. 따라서 ④가 정답이다.

distribution n. 분배, 배분 prevail v. 만연하다 frugality n. 절약 tribulation n. 고난 pacifism n. 평화주의 squandering n. 낭비

가난과 기아가 계속 만연하는데도 너무 많은 낭비가 있는 세계에는 분배에 무언가 잘못된 점이 있다.

06 ②

빈칸을 포함하고 있는 문장은 접속사 and를 통해 be more frugal이라는 표현과 연결되어 있으므로 이와 유사한 의미를 가져야 하는데, 빈칸 앞에 부정의 의미를 가진 less가 있으므로 결국 frugal의 반의어가 필요함을 알 수 있다. 따라서 정답은 ②가 된다.

accumulate v. (조금씩) 모으다, (재산 따위를) 축적하다 frugal a. 검약한, 소박한 peer n. 동료, 한패; 지위가 같은 사람 afford v. ~할 수 있다, ~할 여유가 있다 affluent a. 부유한; 풍족한 vigorous a. 원기 왕성한; 활발한; 강경한, 단호한 opulent a. 부유한; 풍부한, 풍족한 incognito a. 암행의, 잠행의; 익명의 destitute a. 빈곤한

부(富)를 축적한 사람들은 부유한 생활 방식으로 살아갈 여유가 있음에도 불구하고 그들과 사회적 지위가 같은 사람들보다 더 검소하고 덜 풍요로운 생활 방식을 가지고 살아가는 경향이 있다.

07 ④

두 번째 문장에서 physical unfitness가 문제가 안 된다는 뜻으로 말했으므로, 이것과 같은 serious illness도 여행 계획에 문제가 되지 않는다는 말이 되도록 빈칸에는 ④가 들어가는 것이 적절하다.

advance a. 사전의, 미리 하는 unfitness n. 건강하지 못함 antedate v. 앞당기다 endorse v. 보증하다; 배서하다 propel v. 추진하다 sideline v. 퇴장하게 하다, 배제하다

중한 병이 있어도 여행 계획을 배제할 필요는 없다. 사전 계획을 조금만 세우면 신체적으로 건강하지 못해도 안전하고 만족스러운 휴가를 즐길 수 있다.

08 ②

도시의 옥상정원이 왜 지옥과 같은지에 대한 이유가 대시(—) 뒤에 제시되고 있다. of 이하에 부정적인 내용들이 언급되어 있고, 특히 '아스팔트로 뒤덮여 있는 표면'이라고 했으므로, 물은 잘 '스며들지 못할' 것이다. 따라서 '반감, 혐오, 싫은 것'이라는 의미의 ②가 빈칸에 적절하다.

urban a. 도시의, 도회지에 있는 roofscape n. 옥상정원 bituminous a. 역청의, 아스팔트의 contrast n. 대조, 대비; 현저한 차이 bitter a. 모진; 호된, 가차 없는 solution n. 용해; 용액; 해결; 해법 antipathy n. 반감, 혐오, 비위에 맞지 않음 approach n. 접근; 접근법 convergence n. 집중; 수렴

도시의 옥상정원은 다소 지옥과도 같다. 그 곳은 표면이 아스팔트로 되어 있고, 극심한 기온 차이를 보이며, 바람이 매섭게 불고, 물과도 상극인, 생명이 없는 곳이다.

09 ④

'황제의 변덕을 충족시켜줌', '예스맨' 등을 고려할 때 그 행동은 '아첨하는' 것임을 추론할 수 있다.

senate n. 원로원 intent on ~에 열중하는 gratify v. 기쁘게 하다 whim n. 변덕 flippant a. 경박한 reprehensible a. 비난받을 만한 pedantic a. 현학적인 obsequious a. 아부하는, 비굴한

제국시대 로마의 원로원은 황제의 갖가지 변덕을 충족시켜줌으로써 자신의 목숨 보전에 열중하는 아첨하는 예스맨 집단에 불과했다.

10 ⑤

find 다음의 that절에서 with small men이라 했으므로 빈칸에는 이와 관련된 ⑤가 적절하다.

docile a. 유순한, 다루기 쉬운 shadow v. 어둡게 하다; 미행하다 mobilize v. 동원하다 court v. 환심을 사다, 꾀다 balloon v. 부풀게 하다 dwarf v. 작아지게 하다

국민을 자기 손안에서 더욱 유순한 도구가 되게 하기 위해 국민을 작아지게 하는 국가는 작은 국민으로는 그 어떤 큰일도 실제로 성취될 수 없다는 것을 알게 될 것이다.

11 ③

정책적 목표를 실천하기 위해 필요한 것은 그에 맞는 수단(leverage)을 강구하는 것이 될 것이다.

assurance n. 다짐, 보증 ignite v. 불을 지피다 liability n. 책임 compaction n. 꽉 채움; 간결화 leverage n. (목적을 이루기 위한) 수단 certification n. 증명

농무부 장관 피피 퀴티(Fifi Kwetey)는 정부가 벼와 카사바 생산의 가치 체인(부가가치 창출과 관련된 일련의 과정들)을 촉발시키고 연결하기 위한 수단을 제공할 것이라고 다짐했다.

12 ④

빈칸 앞의 it은 gratitude를 가리키고 빈칸 다음은 감사함의 원인이 되는 다른 사람이 항상 있다는 의미이다. 빈칸 앞에 부정어가 있으므로 빈칸에는 그런 다른 사람이 전혀 없는 상태를 나타내는 ④가 적절하다.

thankful a. 고마워하는 gratitude n. 감사 responsible a. 책임 있는, 원인이 되는 en masse 한꺼번에, 집단으로 en route 도중에 in moderation 적당히 in a vacuum 진공 상태로

받은 물건이나 일어난 일에 고마움을 느끼면 그것이 감사이다. 감사함은 진공 상태로 느낄 수 없다. 사랑하는 사람이든, 낯선 사람이든, 고위 권력가이든, 다른 사람이 항상 (감사함의) 원인이 된다.

13 ②

미국의 다국적 기업이 자국에 투자하고 그것이 국외로의 자본 도피를 막게 된다는 것은 외국에 있던 자금을 다시 본국으로 송금할 때 가능한 것이므로 ②가 빈칸에 적절하다.

stash v. (안전한 곳에) 넣어 두다[숨기다] a flight of capital 자본 도피 repatriate v. (돈·수익을) 본국으로 송금하다 divert v. (돈·재료 등을) 전용[유용]하다 freeze v. (임금가격 등을) 동결하다 waive v. 포기하다, 철회하다 allot v. 할당하다, 분배하다

미국의 다국적 기업은 해외의 안전 자산을 본국으로 송금해서 국내에 투자를 할 것인데, 이것은 국외로의 자본 도피를 막을 것이며, 결국 미국의 근로자들에게 혜택을 줄 것이다.

14 ③

필요한 시스템이 아직 준비되지 않았다고 했고 and 뒤에 also가 있으므로, 뒤에 이어지는 문장의 내용도 그 시스템이 조기에 마련될 가능성에 대해 부정적인 태도를 보이는 것이어야 한다. 그러므로 빈칸에 가장 적절한 것은 ③이다.

objective a. 객관적인; 편견이 없는; 목적의 layoff n. 일시해고, 강제 휴업 astonished a. 깜짝 놀란 committed a. 헌신적인, 열성적인 skeptical a. 의심 많은, 회의적인 adamant a. 요지부동의, 단호한, 확고한

시(市)가 성과에 기초한 공정하고 객관적인 해고를 할 수 있게 하는 시스템이 아직 분명하게 준비되지 못한 상태이며, 우리 또한 시가 다음 몇 주 안에 시스템을 만들어 낼지에 대해 회의적이다.

15 ③

보호자 자격이 아직 결정되지 않은 동안 돌보는 역할을 하는 것이므로, 양부모 혹은 친인척 보호자로 인정을 받더라도 이는 '일시적인' 것이다.

approve v. 승인하다, 찬성하다; 허가하다 foster v. 양육하다; 육성하다, 촉진하다 kinship n. 친족 관계, 혈족 관계; 유사 application n. 적용, 응용; 신청 presumptuously ad. 건방지게, 주제넘게 permanently ad. 영구히, 영속적으로 provisionally ad. 잠정적으로, 일시적으로 phlegmatically ad. 무기력하게, 냉담하게

아동보호법 하에서는 특정 개인이 양부모 또는 친인척 보호자로 잠정적으로 인정될 수 있으며, 이는 양부모 또는 친인척 보호자가 되기 위한 신청이 결정되는 동안 그들이 아이를 돌볼 수 있도록 해 준다.

16 ①

권력이 있어야만 하는 곳에 권력이 없다는 단서를 통해 정치 제도가 '제대로 작동되지 않고 있음'을 추론할 수 있다.

vote for 투표하다 claim v. 요구하다; 고소하다; 청구하다; 주장하다 on the blink 제대로 작동되지 않는 on the house (술집이나 식당에서 술·음식이) 무료[서비스]로 제공되는 on the level 정직한; 합법적인 on the ball 일이 어떻게 돌아가는지 훤히 아는[사정을 꿰고 있는]

정치 제도는 제대로 작동되지 않고 있다. 당신이 누구에게 투표를 한다고 해도 똑같은 사람이 승리하는데, 그 이유는 마땅히 권력이 있어야만 하는 곳에 권력이 없기 때문이다.

17 ①

잘못에 대해 시인했다고 했으므로, 시인하는 태도나 자세를 설명하기에 가장 적절한 단어를 찾으면 된다. '뉘우치면서'라는 의미의 ①이 빈칸에 들어가기에 가장 자연스럽다.

suspect v. 의심하다; 짐작하다 enhance v. 향상시키다; 늘리다, 더하다 contritely ad. 죄를 뉘우치면서 tediously ad. 지루하게 infuriately ad. 격분하여, 격앙되어 illicitly ad. 불법으로, 부정하게

맥과이어(McGwire)는 오랫동안 야구팬들에게 의심 받아온 것, 즉 로저 매리스(Roger Maris)의 유명한 한 시즌 기록을 깨면서 70개의 홈런을 친 1998년 시즌과 그 전후에 경기력 강화 약물을 복용했다는 사실을 뉘우치며 시인했다.

18 ③

보존과 개발의 균형을 잡아야 하는 부서에서 도움이 될 성향은 어느 쪽으로도 치우치지 않는 '중도주의'일 것이다.

serve ~ well ~에 도움이 되다 the Department of the Interior 내무부 balance v. ~의 균형을 잡다[맞추다] legitimate a. 합법적인 liberalism n. (정치·경제·종교상의) 자유[진보]주의 centrism n. (종종 C-) 중도[온건]주의, 중도 정치 fidelity n. 충실, 충성, 성실

그러나 다른 환경론자들은 그 상원의원의 중도성향이 미국 내무부에서 도움이 될 것으로 주장한다. 그곳에서 그는 토양과 생물의 보호 문제를 국가 천연자원의 합법적인 개발과 균형을 잡아야 할 필요가 있다.

19 ②

세 번째 문장의 In this way는 두 번째 문장의 전체 내용을 가리킨다. '글이 길게는 수천 년까지 전해진다'라는 내용을 나타낼 수 있는 표현이 필요하므로, 빈칸에 들어가기에 가장 적절한 것은 ②가 된다.

aspect n. 양상, 모습; 국면, 견지 millennium n. 천년간, 새로운 천년이 시작되는 시기 term v. 이름 짓다, 칭하다, 부르다 remain n. 잔존물; 유물, 유적 transpersonal a. 개인의 한계를 초월한, 개인의 이해를 초월한

오랜 시간에 걸쳐 그 영향력이 지속된다는 것이 글의 중요한 측면 가운데 하나이다. 문자화된 글은 몇 날, 몇 달에 걸쳐 변하지 않은 채로 존재할 수 있을 뿐 아니라, 한 세대에서 다음 세대까지, 심지어 수 세기, 수천 년에 걸쳐 똑같이 남아 있는 것이 가능하다. 이런 식으로 그것은 소위 일종의 "개인을 초월한 기억"으로서의 역할을 할 수 있는 것이다.

20 ④

두 번째 문장 문두에 위치한 부사 Consequently를 통해 두 번째 문장은 첫 번째 문장의 내용에 대한 결론임을 알 수 있다. 모든 소리에 대응하는 기호를 갖추고 있지 않다면, 개별 알파벳이 하나의 음을 나타내는 것이 아니라 여러 음을 나타내야 할 것이다. 따라서 정답은 ④가 된다. 실제로, 알파벳 'a'만 하더라도 hat, hate, surface, account 등에서 여러 가지로 발음됨을 쉽게 확인할 수 있다.

incomplete a. 불완전한, 불충분한 practical a. 실용적인, 실제적인 assign v. 할당하다, 배당하다; 지명하다 consequently ad. 따라서, 그 결과로서 omit v. 빠뜨리다, 빼다, 생략하다 translate v. 번역하다, 해석하다, 쉬운 말로 다시 표현하다

인간의 언어가 낼 수 있는 모든 소리에 별개의 기호를 할당하는 것은 실용적이지 않기 때문에 알파벳은 불가피하게 불완전하다. 따라서 동일한 기호가 빈번하게 2개 이상의 음의 역할을 하지 않을 수 없다.

21
③

첫 번째 빈칸에는 corrupt activities와 일맥상통하는 nepotism이나 cronyism이 적절하다. 한편, 앞에서는 푸틴측이 적에게 파시스트라는 명칭을 붙인다고 했는데 비해 마지막 부분에서는 그 대상이 푸틴의 적이 아니라 푸틴측이 되었으므로 두 번째 빈칸에는 redirect가 적절하다.

make common cause with ~와 협력하다 label v. 명칭을 붙이다, 분류하다, 낙인찍다 fascist n. 파시스트, 국수주의자 rampant a. 만연하는 appellation n. 명칭 nepotism n. 친척 편중, 동족 등용 recant v. 취소하다 pluralism n. 다원주의 backbite v. 뒤에서 험담하다 cronyism n. 편파, 연줄, 연고주의 redirect v. 방향을 고치다 legalism n. 법치주의 convert v. 전환하다

푸틴과 그와 협력하는 사람들은 소위 적들에게 파시스트라는 명칭을 거듭해서 붙인다. 그러나 러시아에서는 여러 기본 인권이 자주 무시되고 언론매체가 효과적으로 통제되며 연고주의와 부패행위가 판을 친다. 어쩌면 "파시스트"라는 명칭은 방향을 돌려 푸틴의 러시아에 붙이는 것이 적절할 것이다.

22
④

첫 번째 빈칸의 경우, 대조의 종속절을 이끄는 접속사 while이 있으므로 주절에 쓰인 '지속되다'라는 의미의 lasts와 상반된 의미를 가진 단어가 필요하다. passing 또는 fleeting이 가능하다. 한편, But 이하에서는 심리적인 측면에서는 앞 문장의 상황과 반대임을 이야기하고 있는데, 앞 문장에서는 '경험이 오래 지속되지 않는다'라고 했으므로, 두 번째 빈칸을 포함하고 있는 문장은 '경험이 오래 지속된다'라는 의미가 되어야 한다. lasts의 동의어가 필요한 것으로 볼 수 있으므로 persists 또는 endures가 가능하다.

trade-off n. 교환, 거래; (바람직하게 하기 위한 양자의) 균형 opt for ~을 선택하다 last v. 지속하다, 존속하다; 오래 가다 reverse n. 역(逆), 반대 cherish v. (마음속에) 간직하다, 소중히 여기다 passing a. 통행하는, 지나가는; 한때의, 잠깐 사이의 vanish v. 사라지다, 자취를 감추다 incessant a. 끊임없는, 그칠 새 없는 languish v. 약화되다, 시들해지다 imperative a. 명령적인; 긴급한, 절박한; 절대 필요한 persist v. 고집하다, 주장하다; 지속하다 fleeting a. 잠깐 동안의; 덧없는, 무상한 endure v. 참다; 견디다, 지탱하다

경험하는 것과 사는 것이 대립되는 상황에 직면할 때, 많은 사람들은 물질적인 이익을 선택한다. 경험이 잠깐 동안인 반면 물질적인 이익은 지속되므로, 어떤 점에서 보면 옳은 행동이다. 하지만 심리적으로는 정반대이다. 우리는 물질적인 이익에 빠르게 적응하지만, 경험은 우리가 마음속에 간직한 기억에서 오래 지속된다.

23
④

첫 번째 빈칸 앞에 however가 쓰였으므로 평소에는 생각을 잘 전달했던 그 의사가 종양학 회의에서는 생각을 잘 전달하지 못했다고 해야 적절하다. 따라서 첫 번째 빈칸에는 flubbed가 들어간다. 한편, 그 연설을 들은 청중들의 반응이 두 번째 빈칸에 적절한데, 연설에서 생각을 제대로 전달하지 못했으므로 청중들이 당황했을 것이라 추론할 수 있다. 따라서 두 번째 빈칸에는 bewilderment가 적절하다.

articulate a. (생각·느낌을) 잘[분명히] 표현하는 flub v. 실패[실수]하다, 망치다 oncology n. 종양학 bewilderment n. 당황, 당혹, 곤혹 overcome v. 압도당하다 expatiate v. 상세히 설명하다 rapture n. 환희, 열중 outline v. 개요를 서술하다 repulsion n. 반박; 거절 laud v. 칭찬하다 vertigo n. 현기증, 어지러움

수년간 많은 공개 강연을 한 바가 있어서 평소에 생각을 잘 전달했지만, 그 의사는 종양학 회의에서의 기조연설은 망치고 말았다. 그 회의에 있던 청중들이 회의 끝 무렵에 당황했음이 그들의 표정을 통해 분명해졌다.

24
④

두 번째 문장의 that이하에서 펑크록을 주류로 만들었던 밴드라고 했으므로, 큰 영향력을 줬다고 볼 수 있다. 따라서 빈칸에는 ④가 적절하다.

angst n. (삶에 대한) 불안[고뇌] take a toll ~에 큰 피해[타격]를 주다 frontman n. (음악 그룹의) 리더 seminal a. 중대한[영향력이 큰] erstwhile a. 이전의, 옛날의 derivative a. 모방한, 파생적인 recalcitrant a. 반항[저항]하는

커트 코베인(Kurt Cobain)은 지루하고 나이 든 기분이 들었다. 너바나의 노래 "Serve the Servants"에 나온 가사처럼 십대의 불안은 충분히 제 값을 했었지만, 펑크 록을 주류로 이끈 영향력이 큰 그런지 밴드의 리더로 감당했던 명성은 큰 타격을 주었다.

25
①

the mind는 지적능력을 말하므로 첫 번째 빈칸에는 cognitive(인지적인)나 mental(정신적인)이 적절하고, feeling overextended가 앞 문장에서 일주일에 5시간 이상 육아를 도운 할머니들에 해당하므로 두 번째 빈칸에는 dampens(풀 죽이다, 기를 꺾다)나 overshadows(어둡게 하다)가 적절하다.

lower v. 낮추다 child-care n. 육아 score v. 점수를 내다 extended a. 온 힘을 다한 overextended a. 과도하게 힘을 쏟은 cognitive a. 인식의 dampen v. 풀 죽이다, 기를 꺾다 ameliorate v. 개선하다, 개량하다 genetic a. 유전의 overshadow v. 어둡게 하다 insidious a. 잠행성의 enliven v. 활기차게 하다

손자손녀를 돌보는 일에 딱 적절한 양의 시간만을 보내는 것이 지적능력을 날카롭게 유지시켜주고 인지 질환이 생길 위험을 낮추어줄 수 있다. 일주일에 하루 육아를 도와주는 할머니들이 일주일에 5일 이상 손자손녀들과 보내는 할머니들보다 더 높은 지능지수 검사 점수를 받는다. 이것은 너무 힘을 쏟았다는 느낌이 드는 것이 그 할머니들의 기분을 꺾어놓기 때문이다.

01 ①	02 ②	03 ③	04 ①	05 ①	06 ④	07 ①	08 ①	09 ①	10 ③
11 ①	12 ①	13 ③	14 ①	15 ①	16 ①	17 ①	18 ②	19 ③	20 ④
21 ④	22 ②	23 ②	24 ①	25 ③					

01   ①

빈칸을 포함하고 있는 부분에는 A rather than B 구문이 적용되어 있는데, A와 B에는 각각 서로 대조를 이룰 수 있는 표현이 와야 한다. 따라서 빈칸에는 theoretical과 문맥상 대비되는 단어가 들어가야 하므로 정답은 '경험적인'이라는 의미의 ①이 된다.

theoretical a. 이론상의; 이론상으로만 가능한   evidence n. 증거, 물증 effective a. 유효한; 효과적인, 효력 있는 empirical a. 경험적인, 경험에 의한, 실험상의 hypothetical a. 가설의, 가정의 cursory a. 몹시 서투른, 조잡한, 엉성한 deficient a. 부족한, 불충분한; 불완전한

우리가 이 프로젝트에 많은 돈을 쏟아 붓기 전에, 나는 이론적이기보다는 그것이 효과가 있음을 보여주는 경험적인 증거를 보고 싶다.

02   ②

전치사 Unlike는 '~와는 달리'라는 의미이므로 calmer, more easy-going과 대조를 이룰 수 있는 단어가 빈칸에 들어가야 한다. 이런 범주에 들 수 있는 것은 ①, ②, ③이다. 이 가운데서 정답을 선택해야 하므로, 빈칸 뒤의 내용에 주목하면, 결국 '대단히 사소한 자극에도 싸우려 한다'라는 의미를 가진 단어가 정답이 되어야 한다. 따라서 빈칸에는 '화를 잘 내는'이라는 의미의 ②가 가장 적절하다.

easy-going a. 태평한, 느긋한; 게으른 colleague n. 동료, 동업자 quarrel v. 싸우다, 말다툼하다 slight a. 가벼운; 사소한, 하찮은 provocation n. 성나게 함; 도전, 도발, 자극 whimsical a. 변덕스러운, 이상한, 묘한; 마음이 잘 변하는 irascible a. 성마른, 화를 잘 내는, 성급한 gregarious a. 사교적인; 군생하는 ineffectual a. 효과 없는, 쓸데없는; 무익한; 무력

보다 침착하고 태평한 그의 동료와는 달리, 그 상원의원은 화를 잘 냈으며 매우 하찮은 자극에도 다투려 들었다.

03   ③

여러 곳에서 이주해 온 사람들로 이뤄져 있는 미국 사람들과 그렇지 않은 일본 사람들을 비교하고 있는 글이다. 여러 지역의 사람들이 혼재해 있는 상황을 나타내기에 가장 적절한 단어는 '서로 다른 구성원으로 이루어진'이라는 의미의 ③이다.

be made up of ~으로 구성되다, 조직되다 immigrant n. (외국으로부터) 이주자, 이민 artificial a. 인조의, 인위적인; 인공의 ingenious a. 재치 있는; 영리한; 교묘한; 독창적인 heterogeneous a. 이종(異種)의, 이질적인; 잡다한; 혼성의 immense a. 거대한, 막대한, 광대한

이민 온 사람들로 구성된 미국의 주민들은 일본의 그것보다 훨씬 더 이질적이다.

04   ①

제조업체는 시장에 물품을 공급하는 입장에 있으므로, 일반적으로 제조업체에게 수요는 많으면 많을수록 좋고 동종업종의 다른 공급업체는 적으면 적을수록 좋다. 주어진 문장에서는 '수요는 적고 공급은 많다'라고 했으므로, 제조업체가 매우 어려운 입장에 있었을 것이라고 추론할 수 있다. 따라서 빈칸에는 ①이 들어가야 한다.

lackluster a. 광택이 없는; 부진한, 활기가 없는 oversupply n. 공급과잉 stagger v. 비틀거리다, 휘청거리다, 무너지다 mushroom v. 갑자기 생겨나다, (불길 따위가) 확 번지다 flourish v. 번창하다, 번영하다 germinal a. 새싹의; 초기의, 미발달의

수요부진과 심각한 공급과잉이 맞물리면서 메모리칩 제조업체들은 올해 큰 타격을 받고 있다.

05   ①

avoiding과 curtailing이 주어진 문장에서 가지는 의미는 대동소이하므로, 빈칸에 들어갈 단어와 purchase가 만드는 의미는 unnecessary spending과 유사한 의미를 가져야 한다. 따라서 정답은 ①이 되는데, 왜냐하면 '충동구매' 또한 불필요한 것을 사는 데 돈을 쓰는 것이라 할 수 있기 때문이다.

minimize v. 최소로 하다; 경시하다, 얕보다 curtail v. 짧게 줄이다; 삭감하다 impulse n. (마음의) 충동, 충동적인 행위; 일시적 충격 deliberate a. 고의적인, 계획적인; 생각이 깊은, 신중한 stringent a. 엄중한; 긴박한; 강제적인 contemplative a. 관조적인; 명상에 잠기는

사치품을 최소화하고 충동구매를 피하며 불필요한 소비를 줄이는 것을 통해 저축을 할 수 있다.

06 ④

빈칸에 들어갈 표현에 대해 who 이하의 관계대명사절에서 설명하고 있으므로, 결국 who 이하의 진술 내용을 나타낼 수 있는 단어가 정답이 된다. '여러 질병에 대한 치료제를 갖고 있다고 속여서 말하는 사람들'이라는 의미를 가진 표현으로는 ④가 적절하다.

authority n. 권위, 권력; 대가; (pl.) 당국 combat v. 싸우다, 분투하다 claim n. 요구, 청구; 주장 maintain v. 지속하다, 유지하다; 주장하다 fraudulently ad. 부정한 방법으로, 속여서 cure n. 치료; 치료제 ailment n. 병; 불쾌, 불안 pharmacist n. 약사, 약제사 anthropologist n. 인류학자 charlatan n. 크게 허풍을 떠는 사람; 협잡꾼; 돌팔이 의사

공중 보건 당국은 여러 주요 질환에 대한 치료제를 가지고 있다고 부정하게 주장하고 있는 돌팔이 의사들의 주장에 맞서 싸우고 있다.

07 ①

자원이 이미 고갈된 나라는 손님을 아낌없이 후하게 대접하는 전통을 계속 유지하기가 어려울 것이다.

admittedly ad. 명백히 hospitality n. 환대 strain n. 삠, 접질림, 변형, 손상 war refugee 전쟁난민 stretch v. 늘이다, 긴장시키다, 남용하다, 왜곡하다 profuse a. 아낌없는, 후한 indiscriminate a. 무차별적인, 아무나 가리지 않는 parsimonious a. 인색한 square a. 공정한

자원이 이미 지나치게 사용된 나라에서는 후하게 대접하는 전통이 이제는 전쟁난민들로 인해 심히 손상되고 있는 것이 분명하다.

08 ①

부사 unfortunately가 부정적인 의미의 표현이므로 현(現) 지도자의 입장은 전(前) 지도자와 반대가 되어야 한다. 따라서 빈칸에는 첫 문장의 동사 encouraged와 반대 의미를 가진 단어가 들어가야 하므로, '억누르다'라는 의미의 ①이 들어가는 것이 가장 자연스럽다.

encourage v. 격려하다, 고무하다; 장려하다 suppress v. 억누르다, 억압하다; 나타내지 않다 elucidate v. (문제 등을) 밝히다, 명료하게 하다, 설명하다 animate v. 생기를 주다, 활기를 띠게 하다; 격려하다, 고무하다 epitomize v. 요약하다, 발췌하다; ~의 전형이다

그 단체의 전(前) 지도자는 독립적으로 사고할 것을 장려했다. 그러나 유감스럽게도, 현(現) 지도자는 독립적인 사고의 모든 조짐을 억누르려 애쓰고 있다.

09 ①

전자기기를 미친 듯이 좋아해서 거기에 중독되는 것에 대해 경종을 울리는 기사는 제정신이 아닌 상태에서 벗어나도록 해주는 목적을 가진 것이므로, 빈칸에는 ①이 적절하다.

addiction n. 중독 issue n. (잡지의) 호 timely a. 시의적절한 gadget-craving a. 전자기기를 몹시 갈망하는 reminder n. 생각하게 하는 것, 독촉장 sober a. 맑은 정신의 somber a. 음침한 stolid a. 둔감한 sordid a. 더러운

그 잡지의 이번 호에 실린 '기술 중독을 막는 네 가지 방법'이라는 기사는 시의적절하다. 전자기기를 미친 듯이 갈망하는 우리 사회에는 분명 이렇게 각성시켜 생각하게 하는 것이 필요하다.

10 ③

총리가 강요한 정책이 정부 지출 정책에 호의를 갖고 있는 사람들에게 짜증을 불러일으켰다면, 총리의 정책은 정부의 '지출'을 반대하는 입장의 정책이었을 것이다. 따라서 빈칸에는 spending과 상반되는 의미를 가지는 단어가 들어가야 한다. '긴축'이라는 의미의 austerity가 들어가는 것이 가장 자연스럽다. 한편, in order to keep the value of the pound에 주목해서 푸는 경우, 화폐의 가치를 유지하려면 통화의 양이 늘지 않아야 하므로, 역시 '긴축'이라는 정답을 도출할 수 있다.

impose v. (의무·세금 따위를) 부과하다; 강요하다 annoy v. 괴롭히다, 짜증나게 하다 laissez faire 자유방임주의 liberalism n. 자유주의, 진보주의 austerity n. 엄격, 간소; 내핍, 긴축 benevolence n. 자비심, 박애; 자선

파운드의 가치를 유지시키고자 총리가 강요한 긴축 정책은 정부 지출 정책에 호의를 갖고 있던 사람들을 화나게 만들었다.

11 ①

희망을 변색시키고 실망을 늘어나게 한다는 것은 마음에 상처를 남기는 것이므로 ①이 정답으로 적절하다.

inherently ad. 생득적으로, 본질적으로 promise n. 기대, 희망, 가망, 가능성 tarnished a. 변색된, 손상된 mount v. 증가하다 yawn v. 하품하다, 크게 벌어지다 traumatic a. 외상(外傷)의, 상처를 남기는 nostalgic a. 과거를 그리는 hypocritical a. 위선적인 lackadaisical a. 열의 없는

시간의 경과는 본질적으로 상처를 남기는 것이다. 청춘의 빛나는 희망은 점점 변색되고 실망은 커진다. 미래는 더 이상 무한한 가능성으로 열려 있지 않다.

12 ①

두 번째 문장은 첫 문장에 언급된 이유에 해당하는데, 영웅적인 왕에 대한 동화를 들려주는 것은 군주제를 미화하는 세뇌교육이므로 ①이 정답으로 적절하다.

fairy tale 동화 adulthood n. 성인기 monarchy n. 군주제 indoctrination n. 세뇌, 주입 endorsement n. 배서, 보증 secularization n. 세속화 enlightenment n. 계몽

많은 사람들이 자녀들에게 영웅적인 왕에 대한 동화이야기를 들려주는 데는 이유가 있다. 누구든 조기 세뇌교육을 통해서만이 어른이 되어서 현대 민주사회에서 군주제가 설 자리(존립 근거)가 있다고 믿을 수 있기 때문이다.

13 ③

판자촌(shantytown)에 본거지를 두고 근근이 살아간다(eke out an existence)는 것은 '비천하게' 살아가는 것이므로 eke out을 수식하기에는 ③이 적절하다.

depict v. 묘사하다 bleak a. 황폐한, 암담한, 냉혹한 plight n. 곤경, 궁지 army n. 군대, 무리, 집단 eke out 부족분을 채우다, 근근이 살아가다 bustling a. 분잡한 headquarter v. 본거지를 두다 muddy a. 진흙투성이의 shantytown n. 판자촌 naively ad. 순진하게 furtively ad. 남몰래 menially ad. 비천하게 glossily ad. 번드르르하게

이 드라마는 분잡한 대도시 파리에서 대부분이 교외의 진흙투성이 판자촌에 본거지를 두고 근근이 살아가는 한 작은 무리의 포르투갈 이민자들의 암담한 곤경을 묘사한다.

14 ①

but으로 연결된 마지막 절의 to remove 이하가 더 어려운 일이므로 빈칸에는 remove와 같은 의미의 ①이 적절하다. dissolve는 특히 '단체를 해산하다'는 의미로 사용된다.

disperse v. 흩어지게 하다 prosecution n. 검찰 dissolve v. 녹이다; 해산하다 coalesce v. 연합하다 unfetter v. 자유롭게 하다 suspend v. 유예하다

시위 중인 학생들은 해산되었고 검찰은 과격 운동권 학생단체를 와해시키기 위한 사법 조치를 취하고 있으나 학생운동의 뿌리를 완전히 제거한다는 것은 쉬운 일이 아닐 것이다.

15 ①

빈칸에 들어갈 called의 목적어는 네타냐후가 독직사건으로 고발당한 것을 가리키므로 being charged에 해당하는 ①이 정답으로 적절하다.

charge v. 혐의를 두다, 고발하다 bribery n. 뇌물수령, 수뢰 fraud n. 사기, 협잡 breach of trust 신뢰위반, 배임 corruption n. 부패, 독직 attempted a. 시도한, 미수의 coup n. 쿠데타(= coup d'etat) indictment n. 기소, 고발 treachery n. 반역 misdeed n. 비행(非行) demurrer n. 이의신청 clampdown n. (경찰의) 단속

이스라엘 수상 베냐민 네타냐후는 세 건의 독직사건에서 수뢰, 사기, 배임의 혐의로 고발당한 후 자신의 리더십이 도전 받게 되었다. 네타냐후 수상은 그 기소를 쿠데타 시도라고 말했다.

16 ①

모든 문제에 대해 자유롭고 공개적인 탐구를 추구한다고 하였으므로 가능한 가장 폭넓은 '자유'를 보장해야 할 것이다.

be committed to ~에 헌신하다 guarantee v. 보장하다 latitude n. (견해·사상·행동 등의) 폭, (허용) 범위, 자유 discipline n. 규율 rhombus n. 마름모 inception n. 시작 retraction n. 철회, 취소

대학은 모든 문제들에 대한 자유롭고 공개적인 탐구에 전념하기 때문에, 대학은 대학 사회의 모든 구성원들에게 말하고, 쓰고, 듣고, 도전하고, 배울 수 있는 가능한 가장 폭넓은 자유를 보장한다.

17 ①

아랍 여러 나라들이 성범죄를 저지르고 처벌을 '회피하도록' 하거나 '가벼운 형량을 받도록 해주는' 법 제도의 '허점, 빠져나갈 구멍'을 막는 조치들을 취하고 있다는 내용이다. 따라서 ①이 정답이다. '가벼운 형량을 받도록' 하는 것은 '처벌을 받지 않도록' 해주는 것과는 다르므로 ④는 정답이 될 수 없다.

dodge v. 재빨리 피하다; (부정한 방법으로) 회피하다 loophole n. (법률·계약서 등의 허술한) 구멍, 빠져나갈 구멍 close a loophole 빠져나갈 구멍을 막다 scrap v. 폐기하다, 버리다, 없애다, 철회하다 atrocity n. (특히 전시의) 잔혹 행위 shamble n. 도살장; 유혈 장면, 수라장 impunity n. 처벌을 받지 않음

8월 16일 레바논은 강간범들이 피해자와 결혼하면 처벌을 피하도록 허용하는 법을 폐지하였다. 요르단도 같은 달 같은 조치를 취하면서 "명예 살인"에 대해서는 더 가벼운 형량을 허용하는 별개의 허점을 막아버렸다. 튀니지는 "당신의 강간범과 결혼하라"는 법을 7월에 폐기했다.

18 ②

자유 무역 협정이 미국 노동자 계급에게 지위의 상실과 비통과 절망을 가져왔다는 단서로부터, 미국 제조업의 이전 근거지들의 쇠퇴가 가속화되었다는 사실을 추론할 수 있다.

stronghold n. 성채, 요새; 근거지; 본거지 manufacturing industry 제조업 bitterness n. 신랄; 쓰라림, 비통, 비꼼; 쓴 맛 cultivate v. 구축하다, 재배하다, 경작하다 precipitate v. 재촉하다, 촉진하다; 던지다; 떨어뜨리다 deter v. 그만두게 하다, 하지 못하게 하다, 방해하다 mobilize v. 동원하다; 징병하다 subdue v. 정복하다, 패배시키다; 지배권을 차지하다; 완화하다 adulterate v. 섞음질을 하다, 품질을 떨어뜨리다

미국 공화당 대선 후보는 미국 제조업의 이전 근거지들의 쇠퇴를 촉진시켰고 미국 노동자 계급에게 지위의 상실과 비통과 절망을 가져왔던 자유무역 협정을 비판하는 것을 통해서 자신의 지지를 구축하고 있다.

19 ③

but 이하의 문장에 대한 이유를 두 번째 문장에서 설명하는 구조의 글이며, 빈칸에는 두 번째 문장의 내용을 잘 나타낼 수 있는 표현이 들어가야 한다. 두 번째 문장에서 '한국 소비자의 온라인상의 활동이 대단히 많음'을 구체적인 수치를 들어 설명하고 있으므로, '활기찬'이라는 의미의 ③이 빈칸에 들어가기에 가장 자연스럽다. 이로 인해 '판매량은 적으나 소비자의 관심은 크다'라는 의미가 되어 but 전후의 문장도 자연스럽게 대조를 이룰 수 있게 된다.

account for ~을 설명하다; (~의 비율을) 차지하다 consumer n. 소비자, 수요자 slovenly a. 단정하지 못한, 초라한, 꾀죄죄한 arbitrary a. 임의의, 멋대로의; 독단적인 vivacious a. 생기가 가득한, 활기찬, 명랑한 insidious a. 음험한, 교활한; 잠행성의

한국은 전 세계 카메라 판매량 가운데 겨우 2퍼센트를 차지하지만, 캐논과 니콘은 한국의 소비자들이 단연코 가장 활발한 소비자라고 말한다. 인터넷상의 리뷰, 조회자 수, 댓글의 수는 비슷한 미국 블로그보다 최소 10배나 많다.

20 ④

sparingly, at the lowest effective dose라고 했으므로 정신병을 치료하는 데 가능하면 약을 적게 사용함을 알 수 있다. 따라서 첫 번째 빈칸에는 parsimonious가 적절하다. 그리고 사람들이 광고에 노출됨으로써 과장된 기대뿐만 아니라 잘못된 정보를 갖게 된다고 했으므로 이는 광고에 집중적인 공세(많이 노출됨)를 받기 때문이라고 볼 수 있다. 따라서 두 번째 빈칸에는 bombarded가 적절하다.

psychiatry n. 정신 의학 prodigal a. 낭비하는 hypnotize v. 최면술을 걸다 recuperative a. 회복시키는 interrogate v. 심문하다 esoteric a. 비밀의 parsimonious a. 인색한; 검소한 bombard v. 퍼붓다, 쏟아 붓다

정신병에 대한 나의 약물 치료 방법은 가능하면 아주 적은 약물의 사용 즉, 효과를 볼 수 있는 가장 적은 약물을 사용하는 것이다. 사람들은 계속해서 넘쳐나는 제약 광고에 노출되며 이것은 과장된 기대뿐만 아니라 잘못된 정보의 문화를 초래했다.

21 ④

백화점 안의 분위기를 마지막 문장이 나타내고 있다. 빈칸에는 이와 관련된 ④가 적절하다.

doorman n. (호텔·백화점의) 문 열어주는 사람 thump v. (심장이) 두근두근 뛰다 at a bargain 아주 싸게, 염가로 in the air 감돌아 cynicism n. 냉소 ataraxia n. 냉정함 mesmerism n. 최면상태 euphoria n. 행복감

백화점의 문지기는 급히 뛰어들지 말라고 주의를 주면서 사람들을 반갑게 맞아들이곤 했다. 가슴 두근거리고 두 눈을 반짝이면서 사람들은 활기차게 걸어 들어가 온갖 아름다운 물건들을 구경하면서 무엇을 사야할지 몰라 했다. 어쨌든 그들 각자는 결국 무언가를 믿지 않을 정도로 싸게 샀다. 거기에는 행복감이 감돌고 있었다.

22 ②

빈칸 이하에서, 후손에게는 우리가 과학의 측면에서 뒤떨어져 보일 것이고, 조상이 보기에는 발전해 있는 것으로 보일 것이라 했다. 이는 곧, 누구의 시각에서 보느냐에 따라 '우리가 과학의 시대에 살고 있다'라는 말은 틀린 말일 수도 있고 옳은 말일 수도 있다는 의미가 된다. 그러므로 빈칸에는 '부분적으로 옳을 뿐이다'라는 의미의 ②가 들어가야 한다. ③과 ④는 각각 '완전히 그르다', '완전히 옳다'라는 의미이므로 정답으로 부적절하다. 한편, ①을 정답으로 고르기가 특히 쉬운데, 역설이란 '소리 없는 아우성'처럼 말 자체에 모순이 있는 것을 말하므로 주어진 문장의 경우에 해당되지 않는다.

commonplace n. 평범함; 진부함; 진부한 말 predecessor n. 전임자; 선배 successor n. 상속자, 후계자, 후임자 exact a. 정확한; 엄격한; 정밀한, 엄밀한 opposite a. 정반대의 paradox n. 역설, 패러독스 partially ad. 부분적으로 groundless a. 근거 없는, 사실무근의 equivalent a. 동등한, 같은; 상당하는

우리가 과학의 시대에 살고 있다는 말은 흔히 하는 말이지만, 그것은 단지 부분적으로만 사실이다. 조상이 우리 사회를 볼 수 있다고 할 때 조상의 시각에서 보면 우리는 분명 대단히 과학적인 것으로 여겨지겠지만, 후손의 시각에서 보면 아마도 정반대로 여겨질 것이다.

23 ②

문두에 '보어 as 주어 be동사'의 양보절이 나왔고 factory work은 employment이므로 첫 번째 빈칸에는 미미한 정도를 나타내는 marginal(약간의)이나 negligible(무시해도 좋은)이 적절하고, 탈취제에 몸을 감고 피부를 문질러 씻는 것은 냄새를 없애려는 것이므로 두 번째 빈칸에는 expunge(지우다, 없애다)가 적절하다.

debilitating a. 쇠약하게 하는 dignity n. 품위 douse v. 물에 담그다, 몸을 감다 deodorant n. 탈취제 scrub v. 문지르다 raw a. 껍질이 벗겨진, 생살이 나온; 얼얼한 tangible a. 확실한 circumvent v. 회피하다 marginal a. 약간의 expunge v. 지우다, 없애다 cardinal a. 주요한 embalm v. 방부처리하다 negligible a. 무시해도 좋은, 하찮은 camouflage v. 위장하다

직장을 잃는 것이 사람을 무력하게 만들긴 하지만, 공장에서 일하는 것이 그녀에게는 형편을 약간만 나아지게 하는 것이다. 공장에서 일하는 것은 소득과 품위의식을 제공하지만 이런 것들을 얻으려고 치르는 희생이 엄청나게 크다. 매일 그녀는 작업장의 냄새를 없애기 위해 탈취제에 몸을 감으며 피부가 얼얼할 정도로 문질러 씻는다.

24 ①

첫 번째 빈칸에는 pragmatic(실용적인)과 반대되는 doctrinaire(공론적인)나 formulated(공식화된)가 적절하고, 두 번째 빈칸의 경우, than 이하가 chaos와 반대로 안정을 의미하도록 극단적인 이슬람의 성장을 무력화(neutralize)하다 혹은 사전에 방지(forestall)한다는 흐름이 되는 것이 적절하다.

combat v. ~와 싸우다 pragmatic a. 실용적인 doctrinaire a. 공론적인, 교조주의의 neutralize v. 중립화하다; 무효하게 하다 utilitarian a. 공리적인 forestall v. 미연에 방지하다 formulate v. 공식화하다, 명확하게 말하다 makeshift a. 임시변통의 expedite v. 촉진하다 endorse v. 보증하다

미국의 외교 정책 및 전략 건축가(입안자)들은 이슬람국가(IS)에 맞서 싸울 방법과 관련하여 딜레마에 봉착해 있다. 분명한 것은 그런 위협에 대한 탁상공론적인 접근은 극단적인 이슬람의 성장을 무력화시키기보다 혼란을 낳기 쉽다는 것이다. 외교정책에 보다 더 실용적으로 접근해야 할 때이다.

---

25 ③

종양학자들(종양학전문의들)은 임상실험결과(임상자료)를 과학적으로 엄격하게 전하려고 하는 반면 이것을 환자들에게 설명해야 하는 일반의사들은 '실제 세상의 일반적 양식의 글로 전하려고 한다. 따라서 빈 칸에는 '임상자료를 실제 환자에게 의미 있는 정보로 바꾼다'는 뜻의 ③이 일반 의사들에 대한 설명으로 적절하다.

oncology n. 종양학 clinical trial 임상 실험 with rigor 엄격하게 terminology n. 전문용어 fall short 모자라다, 미치지 못하다 quest n. 탐색, 추구 precise a. 정밀한, 정확한

종양학자들은 임상실험 결과의 중요성을 과학적으로 엄격하게 설명하려고 하지만, 그런 과학적 발견들을 동료학자들이 보는 학술지에 실어 전하는 데 사용되는 용어는 때때로 어떤 치료법이 환자들에게 미치는 영향을 실제 세상의 일상적인 양식의 글로 전하기에 부족하다. 보다 더 정확한 용어를 찾는 일은 종양학 전문의들과 임상자료를 실제적 의미를 가진 정보로 바꾸려고 하는 일반의사들 모두에게 필요한 지속적인 노력이다.

01 ②	02 ①	03 ②	04 ①	05 ②	06 ④	07 ②	08 ①	09 ④	10 ①
11 ②	12 ④	13 ①	14 ③	15 ③	16 ②	17 ①	18 ①	19 ④	20 ④
21 ③	22 ③	23 ④	24 ④	25 ①					

01 ②

결심을 하기에 앞서 일반적으로 하는 행위로 적절한 것을 고르면 된다. 결정을 내리기 전에는 관련된 내용을 검토하고 숙고하는 것이 일반적이므로 ②가 정답이다.

make up one's mind 결심하다 preside v. 사회를 보다, 관장하다; 주관하다 deliberate v. 숙고하다; 협의하다 counteract v. 반대로 행동하다, 방해하다; (효과 등을) 없애다; 중화(中和)하다 nullify v. 무효화하다; 폐기하다, 취소하다

줄리아(Julia)는 몇 년을 두고 숙고한 후에야 마침내 결정을 내렸다.

02 ①

much less는 '~는 말할 것도 없고'의 뜻이므로 빈칸에는 satisfy(만족시키다)보다 더욱 긍정적인 ①(기쁘게 하다)가 적절하다. ③과 ④는 고객을 위한 올바른 행위가 아니므로 부적절하다.

benchmarking n. 벤치마킹(자기 회사의 생산성 향상을 위해 다른 회사의 경영방식을 연구하는 일) client n. 고객 gladden v. 기쁘게 하다 disturb v. 방해하다 flatter v. 아첨하다 coax v. 꾀다, 설득하다

벤치마킹은 잊어버려라. 그것은 단지 다른 사람들(회사들)이 하는 것을 보여줄 뿐이고, 그것은 오늘날의 고객들을 기쁘게 하기에는 말할 것도 없고 만족시키기에도 거의 충분하지 않다.

03 ②

시저가 살던 고대 로마시대에는 시계가 없었다는 내용과 상식의 관점에서 볼 때, 당시의 공연 작품에서 시계가 울린다는 것은 시대적 배경혹은 상황과 전혀 어울리지 않는 일이다. 따라서 빈칸에는 '시대착오'라는 의미의 ②가 오는 것이 적절하다.

amphibian n. 양서 동물, 양서류 anachronism n. 시대착오; 시대에 뒤떨어진 사람 apocalypse n. 묵시, 계시; 계시록 apprehension n. 우려, 염려, 불안

『줄리어스 시저(Julius Caesar)』에서 시계가 울린다는 것은 시대착오의 좋은 본보기이다. 왜냐하면 시저(Caesar)가 살던 로마시대에는 시계가 없었기 때문이다.

04 ①

콤마 이하의 분사구문이 주절의 내용에 대해 예를 들며 부연설명하고 있다. 핵심이 되는 단어는 unfairly이며, 빈칸에는 이것과 유사한 의미를 내포하고 있는 단어가 들어가야 한다. 따라서 '편파적인, 치우친'이라는 의미의 ①이 정답으로 가장 적절하다.

tremendously ad. 굉장히, 엄청나게 unfairly ad. 부당하게, 불공평하게, 편파적으로 blame v. 나무라다, 비난하다 biased a. 치우친, 편향된, 선입견을 가진 objective a. 객관적인, 편견이 없는 unfaltering a. 확고한, 주저하지 않는, 단호한 unfeigned a. 거짓 없는, 진실한; 성실한

최근에 발견된 1880년 작(作)의 그 역사책은 대단히 편향되어 있어서 남북전쟁에 대해 남부를 부당하게 비난하고 있었다.

05 ②

빈칸에 들어갈 행위에 대해 but 이하에서 understand yourself로 표현하고 있다. 따라서 '자기성찰'이라는 뜻의 ②가 빈칸에 적절하다.

volition n. 의욕, 의지, 결의; 결단력 introspection n. 자기반성, 자기성찰 inspection n. 검사, 조사; 점검 inspiration n. 영감(靈感), 신통한 생각; 고취, 고무

어느 정도의 자기성찰은 좋다. 하지만 너무 많은 시간을 스스로를 이해하는 데 사용해서 실제로 일할 시간이 없을 정도가 되게 해서는 안 된다.

06 ④

Just as는 '~하듯이, ~인 것과 마찬가지로'라는 의미이므로, 주절의 빈칸에는 종속절에 언급된 '예측하는 것이 불가능하다'라는 의미를 내포하고 있는 단어가 들어가야 한다. '변화가 심한'이라는 의미의 ④가 들어가는 것이 가장 자연스럽다.

smash n. 대성공, 대히트 burgeoning a. 싹트기 시작한; 신흥의, 자라는 methodical a. 질서정연한, 조직적인 foreseeable a. 예견할 수 있는, 예측할 수 있는 fickle a. 변하기 쉬운, 변덕스러운; 변화가 심한

미국의 제작자들이 브로드웨이에서 대성공을 예측하는 것이 불가능하다고 말하는 것과 마찬가지로, 글로벌 시장은 변화가 매우 심할 수 있다.

07 ②

할머니 집에서는 민주당을 비난하는 것이 예수님이나 마틴 루터 킹 목사를 비난하는 것과 같다'라는 의미가 되어야 하므로, 빈칸에는 '비난'의 의미를 내포하고 있는 표현이 들어가야 한다. 따라서 ②가 정답으로 적절하다.

disrespect v. ~을 존경하지 않다, ~에 대해 결례되는 짓을 하다 chant v. ~를 부르다, 연호하다 blaspheme v. 신성 모독적인 발언을 하다 propagate v. 전파[선전]하다 endorse v. 지지하다, 보증하다 manifest v. 나타나다, 드러내 보이다

내가 아는 전부는 할머니 집에서 민주당에 대해 부정적인 말(비난)을 하는 것은 예수님의 이름을 모독하거나 마틴 루터 킹 목사에 대한 명성을 무시하는 것과 같다는 것이었다.

08 ①

접속사 While이 양보의 종속절을 이끌며 중국의 남부와 북부를 대비시키고 있는 구조이다. 종속절과 주절의 내용은 대조를 이루어야 하므로 빈칸에는 wet의 반의어에 해당하는 ①이 들어가야 한다. 한편, region을 수식하는 관계대명사절의 내용, 즉 '세계 최대의 사막이 되는 것이 임박했다'라는 내용에 근거하여 정답을 도출하는 것도 가능하다.

immense a. 거대한, 막대한, 무한한 threaten v. 위협하다; (위험 등이) 임박하다; ~할 것 같다, 징후를 보이다 desiccated a. (저장을 위해) 건조시킨; (풍토 등이) 건조한 soggy a. 물에 잠긴, 물에 젖은 tropical a. 열대성의; 몹시 더운 temperate a. 온화한; 온대성의; 삼가는, 알맞은

중국 남부는 상대적으로 습한 반면, 중국 인구의 거의 절반이 살고 있는 중국 북부는 이제 세계 최대 사막이 되는 것이 임박한 거대한 건조 지대이다.

09 ④

the massacre와 the cycle of violence는 주어진 문장에서 사실상 같은 의미인 것으로 봐도 무방하다. 첫 문장에서 대량 학살이 일어나고 있음을 밝혔으므로, suggest 이하의 deterrent message는 결국 이러한 대량 학살을 억제시키려는 메시지일 것이다. 또한 이 메시지의 대상은 학살을 자행하고 있는 사람들일 것이므로, 빈칸에는 '학살을 벌이고 있다'라는 의미를 표현할 수 있는 단어가 들어가야 한다. 이런 점에서 ①, ②, ③은 모두 학살 행위를 '피하거나 끝낸다'라는 맥락이 되어 정답으로 부적절하고, ④가 정답이 된다. 이 때, '폭력의 순환을 영속화시킨다'라는 것은 '대량 학살을 계속한다'라는 의미로 볼 수 있다.

massacre n. 대량 학살 alarming a. 놀라운, 걱정스러운 deterrent a. 단념시키는, 제지하는 shatter v. 산산이 부수다; 박살내다 cease v. 그만두다, 멈추다 bypass v. 우회하다; 회피하다 countervail v. 상쇄하다; 무효로 하다 perpetuate v. 영속시키다; 불멸케 하다

다르푸르(Darfur)에서 발생한 대량 학살의 규모는 매우 우려할만한 수준이며, 이는 그 지역을 오랫동안 파괴해온 폭력의 순환을 영속시키려는 사람들에게 가장 강력한 억지력을 가진 메시지가 전달되어야 함을 시사하고 있다.

10 ①

능력이 되는데도 벌금 납부를 하지 않는 사람이 만약 예전에도 벌금을 체납한 적이 있다면, 이 사람은 상습적으로 벌금을 체납하는 사람으로 볼 수 있다. '벌금을 체납한' 이력이 있는 사람을 나타내야 하므로 ①이 정답이 된다.

amendment n. (법안 등의) 수정, 수정안; 개정 discretion n. 판단의 자유; 자유재량; 신중, 분별 incarcerate v. 투옥하다, 감금하다 fine n. 벌금, 과료 default v. (약속·채무 따위를) 이행하지 않다, 태만히 하다 redeem v. 상각하다, 상환하다; 회복하다 connive v. 눈감아주다, 묵인하다; 공모하다 oscillate v. (마음·의견 따위가) 동요하다, 흔들리다, 갈피를 못 잡다

고속도로 교통법 개정안은 벌금 체납 이력이 있는 사람이 벌금을 지불할 능력이 있음에도 불구하고 지불을 하지 않는 경우에 그 사람을 수감할 수 있는 재량권을 법원에 줄 것이다.

11 ②

양념이 음식을 보존하는 데 도움이 되지 않는다는 단서로부터 정답을 추론할 수 있다.

seasoning n. 조미료, 양념 spice n. 양념, 향신료 mould n. 곰팡이 bereft of ~빼앗긴, 잃은 teem v. 풍부하다, 비옥하다, 가득하다 bolster up 지지하다; 보강하다; 기운 내게 하다 maim v. 불구로 만들다; 손상시키다

양념을 넣는 것이 음식을 보존하는 데 도움이 된다고 믿었던 많은 평범한 사람과 달리 대부분의 전문가들은 시장에서 파는 많은 양념들에 박테리아와 곰팡이와 효모균이 득실대고 있다는 것을 발견했다.

12 ④

but 전후 문장의 의미가 대조를 이루어야 하므로 빈칸에는 in her lifetime의 반대되는 뜻을 가진 단어가 들어가야 한다. '사후(死後)에'라는 의미의 ④가 정답이 된다.

reformer n. 개혁가 Equal Rights Amendment 남녀평등 헌법 수정안 considerable a. 중요한, 유력한; 상당한, 꽤 많은 anonymously ad. 익명으로; 작자미상으로 previously ad. 이전에, 미리, 먼저 odiously ad. 밉살스럽게, 불쾌하게, 혐오스럽게 posthumously ad. 죽은 뒤에, 사후(死後)에

많은 다른 개혁가들처럼, 1923년에 의회에 제출된 남녀평등 헌법 수정안의 입안자인 엘리스 폴(Alice Paul)은 생전에는 거의 존경을 받지 못했지만 사후(死後)에는 상당한 명성을 얻었다.

13 ①

역접의 접속부사 however가 있으므로, 세미콜론 이하하는 첫 문장의 내용과 상반되는 내용을 이루어야 한다. 따라서 '관습들이 장소에 따라서는 서로 잘 통하지 않을 수도 있다'라는 흐름이 되어야 하겠는데, at home과 abroad가 대조를 이루고 있는 것처럼, 빈칸에는 rude 혹은 bizarre와 반대되는 의미를 내포하고 있는 단어가 들어가야 한다. 그러한 의미를 가진 것은 '예의바른 태도'라는 뜻의 ①이다.

epitome n. 요약, 개략; 발췌; 전형 perceive v. 지각하다, 감지하다, 인식하다 bizarre a. 기괴한, 별스러운 urbanity n. 도회풍, 품위 있음, 세련; (pl.) 예의바른 태도 eccentricity n. (복장 따위의) 이상야릇함, 기발; 기행 coarseness n. 조잡함, 조악함; 열등함 novelty n. 진기함, 신기로움

어떤 관습들은 어디서나 통한다. 그러나 국내에서는 예의바른 행동의 전형으로 여겨지는 행동이 종종 다른 나라에서는 더할 나위 없이 무례하거나, 혹은 적어도 악의는 없을 지라도 기괴한 것으로 여겨지기도 한다.

14 ③

헬륨 가스가 양력을 공급해줄 때 비행선이 위로 올라간다고 했으므로 비행선이 땅으로 내려오기 위해서는 '양력'을 잃어야 할 것이다. 따라서 빈칸에는 lift와 같은 의미를 가진 ③이 들어가야 한다.

lift n. 들어올리기; 상승력, 양력(揚力) compress v. 압축하다, 압착하다; 축소하다 craft n. 기능, 솜씨; 항공기; 선박 propulsion n. 추진, 추진력 aviation n. 비행; 항공, 항공술 contractility n. 수축력, 수축성 resilience n. 탄성, 탄력 buoyancy n. 부력; 뜨는 성질 combustibility n. 가연성

헬륨 가스는 양력을 공급하여 비행선이 위로 올라갈 수 있게 하며, 헬륨 가스가 압축되면 비행선은 부력을 잃게 되어 착륙할 수 있다. 통제력과 추진력은 항공 연료로 가동되는 프로펠러 엔진이 공급한다.

15 ③

구석기인들이 가혹한 자연환경에서 생존했고 50세 이상 살지 못했다는 점에서 40세만 되어도 신체가 아주 노쇠하고 병약했음을 알 수 있다.

stern a. 엄격한; 가혹한 hostile a. 적대적인; (사람·사물에) 불리한; (기후·환경 등이) 부적당한, 맞지 않은 discrepant a. 모순된, 어긋나는 disparate a. 서로 다른, 이질적인 decrepit a. (사물이나 사람이) 노후한; 노쇠한 robust a. 원기 왕성한, 튼튼한

구석기인들은 가혹한 자연 환경과 치열하게 싸웠다. 생존한 사람들조차도 40대 초반에 몸이 노쇠해졌고 50을 넘긴 사람은 거의 없었다.

16 ②

빈칸 앞의 those는 다음 문장의 Big Brother에 해당하고 tools는 the leash에 해당하는데, 개에게 물리는 것을 방지하기 위해 개 끈이 필요하므로 빈칸에는 '위협'이라는 의미의 ②가 적절하다. 개 끈은 또한 개의 자유를 속박하는 것이다.

modernization n. 현대화 Big Brother 독재자 leash n. (개의) 가죽 끈, 밧줄 menace n. 위협 tribute n. 찬사 prey n. 희생물

현대화가 기술과 진보를 가져왔지만, 그것은 또한 자유를 자신의 권력에 위협이 되는 것으로 간주하는 사람들이 이용할 수 있는 도구들을 탄생시켰다. 자유는 개이고 독재자는 개 끈을 갖고 있다.

17 ①

시민권을 취소하기 위해서는 그에 대한 합당한 이유가 있어야 하며, 그 이유로는 시민권의 획득 과정이 적법하지 않았다는 것이 가장 타당하다. 따라서 정답은 '부정하게'라는 의미의 ①이 된다.

shore up 강화하다, 지탱하다 confidence n. 신용, 신뢰; 확신 immigration n. 이주, 입국, 이민 revoke v. 취소하다, 철회하다 citizenship n. 시민; 공민, 국민 most-wanted list 지명 수배자 명단 suspected a. 의심스러운, 수상한 criminal n. 범인, 범죄자 fraudulently ad. 속여서, 부정하게 provocatively ad. 약이 올라서; 도발적으로, 자극적으로 blamelessly ad. 결백하게, 비난할 점이 없게 unquestioningly ad. 의심스럽지 않게; 망설임 없이; 무조건적으로

정부는 이민 제도에 대한 우리의 신뢰를 강화하기 위한 두 가지 조치를 마련했다. 정부는 시민권을 부정하게 획득한 1,800명의 시민권을 취소하기 위해 나섰으며 30명의 전범 용의자들에 대한 1급 수배 명단을 발표했다.

18 ①

연구방법에 대해 많이 안다고 해서 반드시 연구기획을 잘 하는 것은 아니라는 말은 둘이 전혀 별개의 능력이라는 말이다. 빈칸 앞에 부정의 뜻이 내포돼 있는 far from이 있으므로 빈칸에는 ①이 적절하다.

undertake v. 착수하다 far from 전혀 ~아니다 congruous a. 일치하는 dormant a. 잠자는 incompatible a. 양립할 수 없는 disparate a. 다른, 공통점이 없는

연구방법에 대한 상당한 정보를 습득한 사람들이 자신의 연구를 기획하는 일을 어떻게 해야 하는지를 반드시 알고 있는 것은 아니다. 두 능력은 전혀 일치하지 않는다.

19 ④

작은 옹이(또는 끈실)같은 물질에서 하나의 구(sphere)로 되었다는 그것은 '합쳐져서 커진' 결과라고 볼 수 있을 것이다.

reign v. 군림하다, 지배하다 slub n. 나무의 옹이; 끈실 circumsolar a. 태양주변의, 태양주변을 도는 shaky a. 떨리는, 휘청거리는, 불안정한 slam v. 내동댕이치다; 강타하다 obliquely ad. 비스듬히 fluster v. 당황하게 하다, 안절부절 못하게 하다 abridge v. 생략하다, 단축하다 bungle v. 망치다, 망쳐놓다 accrete v. 부착하여 커지다; 하나로 합치다

지배적인 가설에 따르면, 약 45억 년 전 지구가 태양 주변 물질들이 작은 옹이 같은 상태에서 하나의 구체로 합쳐져서 커진 직후, 아직은 독자적으로 생존하기에는 불안했던 또 다른 신생 행성 하나가 비스듬한 각도로 지구와 무시무시한 힘으로 부딪혔다고 한다.

20 ④

웹사이트를 이용하는 사람들의 민감한 데이터를 보호하기 위해 사용되는 방식이라고 했으므로, 그 방식에는 safeguard(보호), encryption(암호화)이 잘 호응이 된다. 그런데 이 방식에 중대한 결함이 있다고 했으므로, 이 민감한 정보는 '공격당하기 쉬울(vulnerable)' 것이다. 따라서 두 빈칸에 모두 적절한 ④가 정답이다.

bank account 은행계좌 bug n. 결함 differentiation n. 차별화 barricade v. ~을 장애물로 막다 counterfeit n. 가짜, 위조 impregnable a. 난공불락의, 확고한 safeguard n. 보호수단; 보호 anonymous a. 익명의 quarantine n. 격리 conceal v. 숨기다, 감추다 encryption n. 암호화 vulnerable a. 공격당하기 쉬운

암호, 은행계좌, 사회보장번호 등 이용자들의 민감한 데이터를 보호하기 위해 많은 웹사이트에 의해 사용된 암호화 방식이 이러한 정보가 공격당하기 쉽도록 하는 중대한 결함을 갖고 있음이 발견되었다.

21 ③

빈칸 뒤의 내용에서 소비자의 소득증대에 관한 이야기가 나오므로 빈칸에는 경제 활성화를 위한 자극제(stimulus)와 같은 의미의 어구가 들어가야 한다. 소비자들의 소득증대를 통한 소비 증가는 경기 활성화에 기여한다.

equivalent to ~와 같음, 상응함 cornerstone n. 초석; 토대 threshold n. 문간, 입구; 시초, 출발점 a shot of adrenalin 아드레날린 주사 barometer n. 기압계; 표준

싼 기름은 세계 경제 성장에 아드레날린 주사처럼 작용한다. 배럴당 40불의 가격하락은 대략 1조 3천억 불을 생산자에게서 소비자에게로 이동시킨다. 2013년에 주유소에서 매년 3000불을 썼던 전형적인 미국의 운전자들은 1년에 800불 더 부유해 질 수 있고, 이는 2%의 임금 상승과 같은 액수다.

22 ③

'영적인 DNA를 고인과 공유한다'는 의미에 주목한다. 돌아가신 아버지의 사랑이 매순간마다 느껴진다고 고백하는 글이다.

redolent a. 향기로운; 암시하는; 상기시키는 wearied a. 피곤한; 싫증난 languorous a. 나른한, 노곤한, 피곤한 scatterbrained a. 주의가 산만한 sullen a. 무뚝뚝한 truculent a. 공격[호전]적인; (어린이 등이) 반항적인

우리는 가족들과 단순히 신체적 DNA만 공유하는 것이 아니다. 우리 아버지의 영혼이 수천, 수만 번의 순간순간 우리 앞에 스스로를 드러내시면서, 당신의 사랑을 상기시킬 때마다 우리는 고인과 영적인 DNA도 공유하는 것이다.

23 ④

폐기된 선박을 바다에 침몰시키는 것을 금지했다는 언급으로부터 정답을 추론할 수 있다.

assorted a. 여러 가지의 refuse n. 폐물, 쓰레기, 찌꺼기, 나머지 frown upon(on) 눈살을 찌푸리다, 얼굴을 찡그리다; 난색을 표시하다, 찬성하지 않다 shore up 강화하다

변기통, 쇼핑 카트, 세탁기 그리고 다른 잡다한 폐기물들이 해양 미생물들과 그들을 먹고 사는 물고기를 위한 서식지를 만들어주기 위해 바다에 던져졌다. 그러나 폐품으로 암초를 만드는 것은 이제 눈살을 찌푸리게 되는 일이 되었다. 예를 들면, 앨라배마 주는 1996년에 어부들이, 심지어는 내부의 잠재적으로 해로운 액체들을 다 비웠을 때조차도, 선박을 걸프만에 침몰시키는 것을 금지했다.

24 ④

글쓴이가 환경참사에 대한 언론의 보도 태도에 대해 의아해한다는 진술과 이어지는 글쓴이의 냉소적인 태도로부터 정답을 추론할 수 있다.

apocalypse n. 묵시, 계시; 대참사 strike v. 덮치다, 발생하다; 치다 implicit faith 맹목적인 믿음 affection n. 애정, 호의 potential n. 잠재력; 가능성 implicit a. 은연중의, 함축적인

나는 종종 환경 대참사가 발생했을 때 미디어들이 어떻게 반응할까 궁금히 여겨왔다. 나는 뉴스 프로그램들이 간단하면서도 선정적 보도를 하는 동안 왜 그러한 환경 대참사가 일어났는지 혹은 그러한 환경 대참사를 어떻게 하면 막을 수 있었는지를 설명하지 못하고 있는 모습을 상상해 보았다. 그런 다음 뉴스 프로그램들은 그들의 금융 분야 특파원들에게 이번 재난이 주가에 어떤 영향을 미칠지에 대해서 질문하고는 스포츠 뉴스로 넘어 갈 것이다. 당신도 아마 알 수 있겠지만, 나 역시 내가 일하고 이 업종(언론)에 대해서 바다와 같은 믿음 따위는 가지고 있지 않다.

25 ①

주어진 글에서 emotional lives는 feelings와 의미하는 바가 같고 thinking은 ways of reasoning과 의미가 같다고 할 수 있다. 어른들의 생각과 심리학자들의 연구 결과가 완벽하게 반대이므로 빈칸에는 ①이 들어가는 것이 적절하다.

assume v. 추정하다, 추측하다; 가정하다 radically ad. 철저하게; 근본적으로; 과격하게 accurate a. 정확한; 빈틈없는 skillful a. 능숙한, 숙련된 the other way around 반대로, 거꾸로 confirm v. 확증하다; 확인하다 deny v. 부인하다, 부정하다 context n. 전후 관계, 문맥; 맥락

어른들은 어린이들의 사고력이 덜 정확하고 능숙하지는 않을지라도 기본적으로 어른들과 동일한 반면, 어린이들의 정서적인 생활은 어른들과 근본적으로 다르다고 종종 생각한다. 사실, 어린이들을 면밀히 연구해온 심리학자들은 이것이 정반대라는 것을 알고 있다. 즉, 어린이들의 감정은 어른들의 감정과 매우 흡사하지만, 이성적인 판단을 내리는 방법은 대개 매우 다르다는 것이다.

01 ②	02 ①	03 ④	04 ③	05 ④	06 ③	07 ③	08 ②	09 ④	10 ①
11 ④	12 ④	13 ①	14 ④	15 ①	16 ③	17 ④	18 ③	19 ①	20 ④
21 ③	22 ③	23 ④	24 ②	25 ②					

01 ②

strikebound는 '파업으로 기능이 정지된'이라는 의미인데, 주어인 학교의 주된 기능을 고려하면 결국 수업을 하지 못했다는 뜻이 된다. 한편, 접속사 While이 이끄는 종속절과 주절의 내용은 대조를 이루어야 하므로, 빈칸에는 문맥상 strikebound의 반의어가 될 수 있는 표현이 들어가야 할 것이다. 따라서 '수업이 진행됐다'라는 의미가 되도록 빈칸에는 '끊임없는, 연속된'이라는 뜻을 가진 ②가 들어가야 한다.

strikebound a. 파업으로 기능이 정지된 embarrass v. 당황하게 하다, 난처하게 하다 uninterrupted a. 끊임없는, 연속된, 부단한 frozen a. 결빙한; 냉혹한; 동결된, 고정된 unduly ad. 과도하게, 심하게, 불법으로

뉴욕 소재 대부분의 학교가 파업으로 수업을 하지 못했지만, 오션 힐(Ocean Hill)에서는 수업이 중단되지 않고 계속됐다.

02 ①

주절의 주어인 the coach는 7연패를 당한 팀의 감독이므로, 지역 스포츠 신문기자들은 그 팀의 좋지 못한 성적에 대해 그를 비난했을 것이라고 보는 것이 타당하다.

losing streak (스포츠에서) 연패(連敗) denounce v. 공공연히 비난하다; 탄핵하다 enroll v. 등록하다, 명부에 기재하다 vindicate v. 진실임을 입증하다; 변호하다 affiliate v. 가입시키다; 양자로 삼다

최근 그 팀이 7연패를 당하는 동안 그 감독은 많은 지역 스포츠 담당 기자들에게 비난을 받았다.

03 ④

빈칸 뒤의 her feelings는 분사구문 속의 loving과 hating을 가리킨다. 그러므로 빈칸에는 이 두 개의 감정에 대해 분사구문 속에서 설명하고 있는 바를 요약하는 표현이 들어가야 할 것이다. '한 순간 누군가를 사랑했다가 또 다른 순간에는 그 대상을 증오하는 것'은 심리적인 동요 혹은 상반되는 감정이 함께 존재하는 것이며, 이러한 의미를 가진 단어는 ④이다.

tear v. 눈물을 흘리다; 찢다; (마음을) 괴롭히다; 분열시키다 conjecture n. 추측, 억측 delusion n. 미혹, 기만 tranquility n. 평온, 고요 ambivalence n. 반대 감정의 병존, 상반되는 감정의 교차; (심리적) 모순, 동요

한 순간은 부모님을 사랑하고 바로 다음에는 그들을 증오하게 되어 마음이 괴로웠던 마리아(Maria)는 자신의 감정적 모순에 혼란스러웠다.

04 ③

빈칸은 바로 뒤의 an exclusive news와 동격관계에 있으므로, 빈칸에는 이것과 같은 의미를 가진 단어가 들어가야 한다. 따라서 '특종'이라는 의미의 ③이 정답이 된다.

exclusive a. 배타적인; 독점적인; 유일한, 전문적인 connection n. 연결; 관계 ostracize v. 추방하다, 배척하다, 외면하다 largesse n. 증여; 선물, 과분한 부조 cynosure n. 주목의 대상; 지침, 목표 scoop n. 국자; 주걱; (신문의) 특종 sleuth n. 탐정, 형사

그가 범죄자들과 관련되어 있다는 소식이 신문에 특종, 즉 대서특필로 보도되자마자, 친구들은 그를 곧 배척하기 시작했다.

05 ④

especially when it involves~ 이하의 광고의 영향을 평가하기 어렵다는 것에 대한 예에 해당하는데, 기업 또는 국가의 명성은 확실한 형태가 없으므로 빈칸에는 ④가 적절하다.

devilishly ad. 지독히 amorphous a. 무정형(無定形)의; 무조직의 palpable a. 매우 뚜렷한, 명백한 subversive a. 전복하는, 파괴적인 repercussive a. 반향하는

광고의 영향을 평가하는 것은 특히 기업 또는 국가의 명성과 같이 확실한 형태가 없는 것과 같은 어떤 것을 홍보할 때 굉장히 까다로운 일이다.

06 ③

접속사 while이 와서 부사절과 주절의 내용이 대조되어야 하는데, while절에서 많은 회사들이 전자상거래 시장에서 10년이 넘는 동안 사업을 해왔다고 했으므로, 이와 달리 주절에 언급된 회사들은 최근 시

장에 진출했을 것이라고 볼 수 있다. 따라서 '신참자'를 뜻하는 ③이 빈칸에 적절하다.

acquisition n. (기업) 인수, 매입 faddist n. 변덕쟁이, 일시적인 유행을 따르는 사람 connoisseur n. (미술품 등의) 감식가; 전문가 neophyte n. 신참자, 초심자 hypocrite n. 위선자

이런 많은 회사들은 10년이 넘는 동안 전자상거래 시장에서 사업을 해왔지만, 다른 특히 더 규모가 큰 회사들 중 몇몇 회사들은 이제 막 시장에 진출한 신참자들이며 그들의 사업 참가는 최근 기업의 인수를 통해서 비롯됐다.

---

07   ③

빈칸은 순접의 등위접속사 and를 통해 impotence와 연결되어 있으므로, 문맥상 이 단어와 유사한 의미를 가진 단어를 정답으로 선택해야 한다. impotence가 '무능, 무기력'이라는 의미이므로, '하찮음, 사소함'이라는 의미를 가진 ③이 정답으로 적절하다.

speck n. 작은 반점, 얼룩; 작은 조각 insignificant a. 중요하지 않은, 사소한, 하찮은 impotence n. 무능, 무기력, 허약 astonishing a. 놀라게 하는, 놀라운 cupidity n. 물욕, 탐욕 grandeur n. 웅대, 장관, 화려; 위엄 minuteness n. 미세함; 사소함, 하찮음 significance n. 의의, 의미; 중요성

우주는 광활하며 인간은 어느 하찮은 혹성의 작은 먼지조각에 지나지 않는 존재이다. 그러나 우주의 힘 앞에서 우리의 미약함과 우리의 무능함을 더 깨달으면 깨달을수록, 우리 인간들이 이제껏 성취해온 업적은 그만큼 더 놀라운 것이 된다.

---

08   ②

종속절과 주절은 원인과 결과의 관계에 있다. 대부분의 웹사이트에서 실명을 요구하고 있고 IP 주소를 추적할 수 있다고 했으므로, 신원을 숨기기가 쉽지 않을 것이라는 결론을 내릴 수 있다. 그런데 빈칸 앞에 부정어 not이 있으므로 '익명의'라는 의미의 ②가 들어가야 한다.

atmosphere n. 대기; 분위기; 기분 require v. 요구하다, 규정하다; 필요로 하다 register n. 기록부; 기록, 등록 specious a. 허울 좋은, 그럴 듯한, 진실 같은 anonymous a. 익명의, 가명의 serene a. 고요한, 잔잔한; 화창한 cutthroat a. 살인의; 잔인한, 흉악한; (경쟁 등이) 치열한

대부분의 웹사이트는 최초 등록 시에 개인의 신원과 실명을 요구하며 로그인을 하지 않을 때조차도 IP 주소의 추적이 가능하기 때문에, 사이버 공간은 정부가 걱정하는 만큼 익명의 환경이 아니다.

---

09   ④

'놀랄 만큼의 민첩함'과 대조되는 표현을 골라야 하므로 '무기력'이라는 의미의 ④가 정답으로 적절하다.

---

ledge n. 가장자리; (벽에서 돌출한) 선반; 쑥 내민 곳 scale v. (아주 높고 가파른 곳을) 오르다 agility n. 민첩함 startling a. 깜짝 놀라게 하는 temperance n. 자제 petulance n. 심술 사나움 verbosity n. 수다스러움 lassitude n. 무기력

마치 자신의 말에 자극받은 것처럼, 그는 자기 위에 있는 바위의 가장자리에서 일종의 도약을 하더니, 그의 일반적인 무기력과는 놀랄 만큼 대조적으로 민첩하게 올랐다.

---

10   ①

세미콜론 다음이 그 앞을 부연 설명하고 있다. 따라서 where and how their food was produced(제품이 생산된 장소와 방식)와 관련된 의미를 가진 ①이 정답으로 적절하다.

access v. ~에 접근하다, ~를 손에 넣다, 이용하다 provenance n. 기원, 출처, 유래 dispensation n. 분배 hallmark n. 품질증명 inventory n. 재고목록

첨단기술이 소비자들로 하여금 그들이 사는 식품이 어디서 어떻게 만들어졌는지 정확하게 알 수 있게 해준다. 구매자들은 스마트폰을 이용하여 각 제품의 정확한 유래에 대한 정보를 얻게 된다.

---

11   ④

세미콜론 이후의 문장에서 '두세 번째 복역하는 사람의 수가 높다는 사실'에 대해 언급하고 있는데, 이는 곧 '범죄를 상습적으로 저지르는 비율' 혹은 '재범률'이 높다는 의미이다. 그러므로 '상습적 범행'이라는 의미의 ④가 빈칸에 들어가야 한다.

reformer n. 개혁가, 개혁론자 disturb v. 방해하다, 마음을 어지럽게 하다 indicate v. 가리키다, 지적하다, 보이다 rehabilitate v. 원상태로 되돌리다, 복원하다; 복권하다, 회복시키다 inmate n. 입원인; 수감자 penitence n. 후회; 참회, 속죄 self-surrender n. 자기포기; 몰두 accomplice n. 공범자, 연루자; 동료, 협력자 recidivism n. 상습(성); 상습적 범행

미국의 교도소를 개혁하고자 하는 이들은 상습적 범행의 비율이 높은 것 때문에 마음이 어지럽다. 두세 번째 형기를 복역하는 사람들의 수는 교도소가 수감자들을 교화시키는 데 실패했음을 보여준다.

---

12   ④

빈칸 앞에 위치한 주어 he는 첫 번째 문장에서 설명하고 있는 The individual을 가리킨다. 이러한 사람은 자신이 다른 사람들에게 진 빚을 모르고 있다고 했으므로 빈칸에는 ignorant of one's debt의 의미를 갖는 표현이 들어가야 할 것이다. 주어진 글에서 빚(debt)이란 다른 사람들에게서 받은 혜택, 은혜, 도움 등을 의미하므로, 빈칸에는 '배은 망덕'이라는 의미의 ④가 적절하다.

fancy v. 공상하다, 상상하다; 생각하다 sole a. 유일한, 단 하나의 portray v. 그리다, 묘사하다, 표현하다 timidity n. 겁, 소심함; 수줍음 probity n. 고결, 청렴 결백, 성실 autism n. 자폐증 ingratitude n. 배은망덕, 은혜를 모름

스스로 좋은 직업을 얻어 출세했다고 생각하는 사람이나 자신이 발명했기 때문에 소유권이 자신에게만 있다고 믿는 발명가 자신이 진 빚을 모르고 있다. 디킨즈(Dickens)가 『어려운 시절(*Hard Times*)』에서 묘사한 바운더비(Bounderby)라는 인물처럼, 이러한 사람은 지극히 배은망덕한 사람이다.

13 ①

상원에서 통과된 법안을 무력하게 만들도록 하원을 설득했다는 단서와 처벌이 실질적으로 무의미하다는 단서로부터 빈칸에는 처벌을 약화시켰다는 내용이 되게 하는 표현이 들어가야 함을 추론할 수 있다.

prevail on a person to do 남을 ~하도록 설득하다 manure n. 퇴비 water down 물을 타서 희석시키다, 약화시키다 chew out 호되게 꾸짖다, 야단치다 keep the tab on 감시하다 pump up 퍼 올리다; 바람을 넣다; 증대하다[시키다]; 강화하다

농업관련 이익단체들이 상원에서 통과된 법안의 최초 버전을 무력하게 만들도록 주 하원을 설득했다. 하원에 상정된 법안은 퇴비와 비료를 금지하는 법들의 위반자들에게 가하는 처벌을 많이 약화시켜서 처벌들을 사실상 무의미하게 만들었다.

14 ①

예술작품의 신비화에 반대하면서도 여전히 신비화를 유지한다는 진술로부터 정답을 추론할 수 있다.

intriguing a. 흥미로운 demystify v. 신비성을 제거하다 cryptic a. 애매한, 숨은, 비밀의, 신비한; 암호의 dogma n. 교의; 독단적 주장 pragmatism n. 실용주의

전반적으로 다다이즘의 예술작품들은 그것들이 대중적인 관점에서 예술작품의 신비성을 제거하려고 노력하지만, 그럼에도 불구하고 그들이 여전히 관찰자가 다양한 방식으로 예술작품을 해석하는 것을 허락할 정도로 충분히 신비로움을 유지한다는 점에서 흥미로운 패러독스(모순)를 제시한다.

15 ①

상을 받으려는 열망이 지나치면 상을 받아내기 위해 음모나 조작을 꾸밀 것이므로 첫 번째 빈칸에는 scheming(음모)이나 concocting(조작)이 적절하고, 상을 받으면 그것이 저자의 저술경력을 권위 있게 보증해줄 것이므로 두 번째 빈칸에는 seal(도장, 보증의 표시)이나 cachet(봉인)나 stamp(도장)가 적절하다.

authorship n. 저작자임, 저술업 scheme v. 계획을 꾸미다, 음모를 꾸미다 seal n. 봉인, 도장, 보증의 표시 hesitate v. 주저하다, 망설이다 target n. 목표 concoct v. 조작하다 scratch n. 긁힌 자국 threaten v. 위협하다 cachet n. 봉인 neglect v. 소홀히 하다; 무시하다, 경시하다 stamp n. 도장

책의 저자라는 것이 가져다주는 금전적인 보상이 너무나 적다 보니 특정한 책에 매년 수여되는 상을 받으려는 열망과 음모가 아주 많아지는데, 상을 받

은 책들은 저술 경력에 영광스러운 보증을 해줄 뿐 아니라 저자의 시장 가치를 증대시켜준다.

16 ③

know의 목적절 속에서 주어가 될 표현을 바로 앞의 주절 속에서 찾으면, 결국 philosophize의 의미를 갖고 있는 명사가 필요함을 알 수 있다. philosophize는 '사색, 연구'라는 뉘앙스를 가지고 있는 동사이므로 첫 번째 빈칸에는 consideration, speculation, supposition이 가능하다. 한편, many inventions had their birth as toys에서 toy에 주목하면, '이들 발명품들이 애초에는 가벼운 생각을 가지고 만들어졌다'는 것이 되는데, 두 번째 빈칸 앞에 부정어 no가 있으므로 '심각한, 중대한'이라는 의미의 grave 또는 weighty가 들어갈 수 있다. 따라서 두 조건을 모두 만족시키는 ③이 정답이 된다.

remarkable a. 주목할 만한, 현저한; 비범한, 뛰어난 invention n. 발명; 발명품 philosophize v. 철학적으로 사색하다 persistence n. 고집, 완고; 영속 grave a. 중대한; 근엄한 consideration n. 고려, 숙려; 고찰 satisfactory a. 만족스러운, 더할 나위 없는 speculation n. 사색; 결론; 추측 weighty a. 무거운; 중대한 supposition n. 상상, 추측; 가정, 가설 trivial a. 하찮은; 평범한

많은 발명품들이 원래는 장난감이었다는 놀라운 사실은, 생각하는 것이 심각한 결과를 초래하지 않는다는 것을 알고 있을 때 사람들이 더 자유롭게 사색한다는 것을 암시하고 있다.

17 ④

주절의 and 앞에서 '통일성을 떨쳐버렸다'라고 했으므로, and 이하는 '다양성을 인정하거나 받아들였다'라는 내용이 되어야 한다. 그러므로 uniformity와 반대되는 내용을 이야기하고 있는 ④가 빈칸에 적절하다.

dominant a. 지배적인, 유력한 shrug off (모욕·의견 따위를) 무시하다; 떨쳐버리다 myth n. 신화; 전설, 사회적 통념 uniformity n. 한결같음; 획일, 균일 provincialism n. 지방 기질, 시골 근성, 편협; 지방적 관습, 지방색 yield v. 산출하다; 양보하다, 굴복하다 centralism n. 중앙집권주의; 집중화 trait n. 특색, 특성 integration n. 통합; 완성 come to naught 무위로 돌아가다 flavor n. 맛; 멋, 정취 vibrant a. 생기 넘치는; 힘찬

'한 나라, 한 언어, 한 민족'이라는 지배 이념에도 불구하고, 오랫동안 프랑스 국민들은 통일성이라는 국가적 통념을 떨쳐버리고 지역적 정취와 관습이 여전히 살아있는 지방을 향해 나아갔다.

18 ③

just as ~, so …는 '~한 것처럼, …하다'는 뜻으로, 비슷한 성질의 것을 비교할 때 사용되는 구문이다. 미국인들이 홍역에 대해 너무 자신만하게 생각한 것처럼, 영국인들 또한 광우병을 대수롭게 여기지 않았다는 의미가 되기 위해서는 빈칸에 ③이 적절하다.

incarnation n. 구체화, 실현 let down one's guard 경계를 늦추다

미국에서 홍역의 발병이 안전하게 과거지사로 여겨진 질병에 대해 대중들이 너무 자신했을 때 어떤 일이 발생할 수 있는지를 보여준 것처럼, 훨씬 더 위험한 질병인 광우병이 인간에게 발병되는 것에 대해 영국인들은 너무 이르게 그 질병에 대한 경계를 늦추었을지도 모른다.

---

19 ①

두 번째 문장은 첫 번째 문장에 대한 반론이고, 이에 대한 부연 설명이 세 번째 문장부터 이어진다. 정책은 우수한 통찰력을 가진 정치가나 지성인이 아니라, 자신이 살고 있는 세계를 제대로 알고 있는 사람들에게 맡겨져야 한다고 했으므로 첫 문장의 주장은 잘못된 것임을 알 수 있다. 따라서 빈칸에는 ①이 적절하다.

insight n. 통찰력 spurious a. 가짜의, 위조의 agnostic a. 불가지론(자)의 congenial a. 같은 성질의, 마음이 맞는 brusque a. 무뚝뚝한, 퉁명스러운

많은 정책들은 보다 우수한 통찰력을 가졌다고 주장하는 정치나 지성인에 의해 만들어진다. 이러한 주장들은 대개 거짓이다. 모든 인간은 자신의 세계를 어떤 외부인이나 전문가보다 더 잘 알고 있다. 정책은 정책에 의해 영향을 받게 될 세상에 살고 있는 사람들에게 맡겨져야 한다.

---

20 ④

첫 번째 문장에서 하고자 하는 바는, '단조로움과 악(惡) 가운데서는 단조로움을 택하겠지만, 둘 중 하나만 있는 곳은 원하지 않는다'라는 의미이다. 이어서 다양성이 존재하고 있는 오늘날의 세상에 대해 이야기함으로써, 글쓴이는 오로지 극단적인 하나만을 취하기보다는 세상의 여러 면을 포용하길 바라는 입장을 드러내고 있다. 따라서 빈칸에는 '관용, 너그러움'이라는 의미의 ④가 들어가는 것이 가장 자연스럽다.

monotonous a. 단조로운; 한결같은, 지루한 community n. 사회, 공동체 universal a. 전세계의; 보편적인, 일반적인 variety n. 변화, 다양성; 불일치 contrast n. 대조, 대비; 현저한 차이 inebriety n. 취함, 음주벽 resignation n. 사직; 포기, 단념 justification n. 정당화; 변명, 변호 magnanimity n. 도량, 아량, 관대함; 담대함

나는 만국적인 전쟁의 세계에서 살기보다는 차라리 지루한 사회에서 살겠지만, 그 둘 중의 어느 한 사회에서 살기보다는 차라리 죽음을 택할 것이다. 내 마음은 다양성과 대조, 청색 얼굴과 녹색 얼굴을 함께 지니고 있는 오늘날의 세계에 있다. 그래서 나는 용기 있는 관용을 통해 오늘날의 세계가 보존될 수 있길 바라고 있다.

---

21 ③

더 많은 소비를 하는 것이 부자들의 본성이라고 했는데, 이것이 곧 부자들에게 자본주의가 가져다 준 보상이라 할 수 있다. '자본주의가 가져다 준 보상'을 첫 문장과 연결 지어 생각하면, 버스 대신 리무진을 타고,

---

텐트 대신 고급 아파트에서 사는 것을 의미하게 될 것이다. 따라서 만약 이들에게 이러한 생활을 하지 못하게, 다시 말해, 검소한 생활을 하도록 강제하면, 이것은 자본주의가 준 보상을 누리지 못하게 하는 것이라 할 수 있다. 따라서 빈칸에 들어갈 적절한 단어는 ③이다.

demand v. 요구하다, 청구하다 monk n. 수도승 reward n. 보수, 포상; 현상금 capitalism n. 자본주의 poise v. 균형 잡히게 하다; (어떤 자세를) 취하다, 유지하다 cement v. 강화하다; 결합하다 repeal v. 폐지하다, 철회하다, 무효로 하다 catalyze v. 촉진하다, 촉매작용을 하다

만일 부자들이 정말로 환경에 관심을 가진다면, 그들은 버스를 타고 텐트에서 살고 있을 것이다. 그러나 그것은 터무니없는 생각이다. 부자들에게 환경에 책임을 다하도록 수도승 같은 삶을 살 것을 요구할 수는 없다. 왜냐하면 그것은 자본주의의 보상을 폐지하는 것을 의미할 것이기 때문이다. 부자들은 소비를 더 많이 한다. 그것이 부자들의 본성이다.

---

22 ③

신질서가 구질서를 밀어내고 그것을 대신하는 것이므로 첫 번째 빈칸에는 supplanted(밀어내다)나 superseded(대신하다)가 적절하고, 계속성을 강조한다는 것은 과거와 현재의 동일성을 중시하는 것으로 차이를 경시하는 것이므로 두 번째 빈칸에는 overlook(간과하다)이나 downplay(경시하다)가 적절하다.

medieval a. 중세의 block v. 막다, 방해하다 continuity n. 계속성 supplicate v. 탄원하다, 간곡히 부탁하다 overlook v. 간과하다 supplant v. 밀어내다; 대신하다 accentuate v. 강조하다 supersede v. 대신하다 downplay v. 경시하다 supervise v. 감독하다 endorse v. 승인하다

역사에서 언제나 그렇듯이, 새로운 사회 제도의 모든 요소들은 신질서가 대신한 구질서에서 이미 발달해 있었다. 그러나 얼마나 많은 현대적 요소들이 중세 후기에 존재했는지와 얼마나 많은 중세적 요소들이 현대 사회에 계속 존재하는지를 아는 것도 중요하지만, 만일 계속성을 강조함으로써 중세 사회와 현대사회 사이의 근본적인 차이를 경시하려고 한다면, 그것은 역사과정에 대한 모든 이론적 이해를 방해하는 것이다.

---

23 ④

두 번째 문장 이하는 첫 번째 문장에 대한 구체적인 예에 해당하는데, 자기민족을 우월하게 여기고 다른 민족들을 배척한 사례를 언급하고 있으므로, '자기민족 중심주의'를 의미하는 ethnocentrism을 포함하고 있는 ④가 빈칸에 적절하다.

barbarian n. 야만인, 미개인 genocide n. 대량 학살 ethnic cleansing 인종청소 mythology n. 신화; 통념 insight n. 통찰, 통찰력 ethnocentrism n. 자기민족 중심주의

자기민족 중심주의가 낳은 파괴적인 결과들의 예는 역사를 통해 많이 발견된다. 유럽의 로마인들과 아시아의 중국인들은 외국인을 야만인으로 여겼다. 현대에는 독일의 독재자인 아돌프 히틀러(Adolf Hitler)가 독일인들은 "열등한" 민족들을 말살시킬 의무를 지는 우월한 민족에 속한다고 주장했다.

24 ②

두 번째 문장은 첫 번째 문장에 대한 예에 해당한다. 빈칸이 포함된 부분의 without 이하는 첫 문장의 without 이하를 부연설명하고 있으므로, 빈칸에 들어갈 표현도 disturbing the setting to which the tourists are attracted의 의미를 나타내는 것이어야 한다. 그런데 두 번째 문장에서 옐로스톤 국립공원과 만리장성을 예로 들고 있으므로 옐로스톤 국립공원을 habitat으로, 만리장성을 ancient architecture로 바꿔서 표현한 ②가 빈칸에 들어가는 것이 가장 적절하다.

destination n. 목적지, 행선지, 도착지 unique a. 유일무이한; 독특한, 특이한 accommodate v. ~에 편의를 도모하다; 융통하다, 제공하다; 숙박시키다 disturb v. 방해하다; 불안하게 하다; 저해하다 varied a. 가지가지의; 다채로운 contend v. 다투다, 경쟁하다; 싸우다 incur v. (위해를) 당하다, (손해를) 입다; (위험 등을) 초래하다 desecrate v. (신성한 것을) 훼손하다, 모독하다 lose out on ~을 놓치다

관광지는 관광객들을 매료시키는 주위 환경을 손상하지 않고 많은 관광객들을 수용하도록 노력해야 한다는 점에서 독특하다. 옐로스톤(Yellowstone) 국립공원과 중국의 만리장성과 같이 다양한 관광 장소는, 가능한 많은 사람들이 자연 서식처를 손상하거나 고대 건축물을 훼손하지 않으면서 관광명소를 경험할 수 있도록 해야 하는 이런 딜레마와 씨름해야 한다.

25 ②

indeed는 앞의 진술에 강조할 내용을 더할 때 사용되는 이른바 '첨가형 강조'의 연결어로서 '사실(실은)'로 해석된다. '성소수자 해방이 이슬람권 국가까지 도달할 것이라고 볼 수 없다'에 덧붙이는 동시에 더욱 강조하여 '가장 진보적인 국가에서도 동성애 혐오가 번질 수 있다'고 하였으므로 ②가 들어가는 것이 적절하다.

rife with ~로 가득 찬 LGBT n. 성소수자(lesbian, gay, bisexual and transgendered) homophobic a. 동성애 혐오의 backlash n. 반발, 역풍 transphobic a. 성전환자를 혐오하는

심지어 가장 동성애 친화적인 사회에서도 차별, 학대, 증오 범죄가 만연해 있다. 더구나 지난 50년 동안의 괄목할 만한 성취가 미래를 보장하지는 않는다. 역사가 일직선으로 움직이는 경우는 거의 드물다. 성소수자 해방이 필연적으로 전 세계로 확산되어, 결국 사우디아라비아와 브루나이까지 도달할 것이라고 생각해야 할 어떠한 근거도 없다. 사실, 가장 진보적인 국가들에서도 폭력적인 동성애 혐오의 역풍이 일어날 수 있다. 바로 지난주 가디언(Guardian)지는 동성애 혐오 및 성전환 혐오에 의한 증오 범죄가 지난 5년 동안 영국에서 두 배로 증가했음을 보여주는 충격적인 통계를 발표했다.

01 ④	**02** ②	**03** ②	**04** ④	**05** ②	**06** ①	**07** ②	**08** ②	**09** ②	**10** ②
11 ②	**12** ④	**13** ③	**14** ②	**15** ③	**16** ①	**17** ①	**18** ②	**19** ③	**20** ①
21 ④	**22** ①	**23** ④	**24** ④	**25** ①					

01 ④

순접의 접속사 and로 연결되어 있는 incomparable과 유사한 의미의 단어가 빈칸에 들어가야 한다. incomparable이 '견줄 데 없는'이라는 의미이므로 '전례가 없는'이라는 뜻의 ④가 가장 유사한 의미의 단어라 할 수 있다.

come across ~와 마주치다, 우연히 발견하다 vision n. 시력; 통찰력; 환상 incomparable a. 비교가 되지 않는, 비길 데 없는 knavish a. 악한 같은, 무뢰한의 stereotyped a. 진부한, 판에 박은 variable a. 변하기 쉬운; 일정하지 않은; 변화무쌍한 unprecedented a. 선례가 없는, 전례가 없는

길을 잃은 것 같은 많은 다른 젊은이들과는 비교도 되지 않고 전례도 없을 정도의 비전을 지닌 젊은이를 만나는 것은 쉽지 않다.

02 ②

사람들이 미래를 걱정하며 돈을 쓰지 않는 상황에서는 소비가 위축될 수밖에 없다. 침체를 나타내는 형용사로 적절한 것은 '빈혈의', '무기력한'이라는 뜻을 가진 ②이다.

domestic a. 가정의, 가사의; 국내의 consumption n. 소비; 소모, 소진 amnesiac a. 기억상실의, 건망증의 anemic a. 빈혈의; 침체된, 무기력한 annihilable a. 완전히 파괴될 수 있는 amendable a. 수정할 수 있는, 개정할 수 있는

사람들이 걱정하면서 돈을 쓰지 않기 때문에 한국의 국내 소비는 여전히 위축돼 있다.

03 ②

양보절을 이끄는 종속접속사 Although가 쓰였고 두 빈칸 모두가 동일 인물 주어에 대한 보어 역할을 하고 있으므로, 서로 대조를 이루는 단어가 필요하다. 따라서 서로 상반되는 의미의 단어가 짝지어져 있는 ②가 정답이 된다.

theoretically ad. 이론적으로, 이론상 testimony n. 증언; 증거 trial n. 공판, 재판 reveal v. 드러내다, 알리다; 폭로하다 intrepid a. 두려움 없는, 용맹스런, 대담한 prow a. 용맹스러운, 용감한 loyal a. 충성스러운; 성실한 hypocritical a. 위선의, 위선적인 shrewd a. 빈틈없는; 재빠른, 기민한 erudite a. 박식한, 학식 있는 loathsome a. 싫은, 지긋지긋한 hateful a. 미운, 싫은, 지긋지긋한

비록 이론적으로 그는 아주 충직한 사람이었지만, 법정 증언을 통해 그가 매우 위선적이었다는 사실이 드러났다.

04 ④

빈칸 앞의 동사 offered가 첫 번째 문장에 있는 관계대명사절의 동사 presented와 의미가 유사하다는 데 착안해야 한다. 관계대명사절의 내용은 '양 극단에 위치하는 것들을 통해 분명한 대립을 보여주었다'라는 것이므로, 빈칸에는 이러한 의미를 나타내는 단어가 쓰여야 하는데, ①과 ②의 경우, adversity와 circumstantiality가 '대립'과는 거리가 먼 단어들이므로 composed 또는 full과 호응하지 않는다. 한편, relieved와 devoid는 공히 '결여, 부족'이라는 의미를 가지고 있는데, '분명한 대립을 보여주었다'라는 말은 '중립이 없었다'라는 말로 바꿔 표현할 수 있으므로 나머지 선택지 가운데서는 ④가 정답이 된다.

stark a. 완전한, 분명한; 굳어진, 뻣뻣해진 opposition n. 대립, 반항, 반대 innocence n. 순진, 순결; 결백 criminality n. 범죄성; 범죄행위 virtue n. 덕, 선, 선행; 미덕 corruption n. 타락, 퇴폐; 부패, 부정행위 adversity n. 역경, 불운 circumstantiality n. 상황, 사정 relieved a. 안도하는, 다행으로 여기는 polarity n. 양극성; 정반대, 대립 devoid a. ~이 전혀 없는, 결여된 neutrality n. 중립; 불편부당

무죄와 유죄, 미덕과 타락, 선과 악 사이의 분명한 대립을 보여주는 멜로드라마가 인기가 있는 정확한 이유는 중립이 없는 세계를 관객에게 제시했기 때문이다.

05 ②

'so ~ that …' 구문이 원인과 결과를 나타내는 문장을 이끌고 있다. that 이하에서 '바라고 원하는 것을 정확하고 명료하게 말할 수 없다'라고 했으므로, 빈칸에는 이것의 원인을 나타낼 수 있는 단어가 필요하다. 결국 accurately, distinctly와 반대되는 의미를 가진 형용사가 와야 하므로 정답은 ②가 된다.

convey v. 나르다, 전달하다 distinctly ad. 명료하게, 뚜렷하게 will v. 바라다, 원하다, 의도하다 garish a. 야한, 화려한 nebulous a. 흐린, 불투명한; 애매모호한 palpable a. 손으로 만질 수 있는; 매우 뚜렷한, 명백한 perfunctory a. 형식적인; 겉치레의; 피상적인

칸트(Kant)는 현명하게 다음과 같이 썼다. "행복의 개념은 너무도 애매모호해서, 모든 사람이 행복을 얻으려 하지만 그가 정말로 바라는 것과 원하는 것을 결코 정확하고 명료하게 전할 수 없다."

내가 동의를 하지 않을 때마다 그렇게 거만하게 굴려고 한다면, 저는 당신과 함께 일하고 싶지 않습니다. 당신이 수년간에 걸쳐 이룬 연구와 경험은 존중합니다만, 당신의 거만한 태도는 받아들 수 없습니다.

06 ①

정부의 기능 중 하나가 밀항(밀입국)을 단속하는 것이므로 정부가 없으면 밀항이 방해받지 않고 마구 벌어질 것이다. 따라서 ①이 정답으로 적절하다.

function v. 제 역할을 다하다, (제대로) 기능하다 smuggle v. 밀수[밀항]하다 smuggling gang 밀항 알선 집단 load v. 싣다, 태우다 unmolested a. 방해받지 않는 encumbered a. 방해받는 unrequited a. 보답이 없는 incapacitated a. 자격(능력)을 잃은

리비아에 제구실을 하는 정부가 없다는 것은 밀항 알선 집단들이 점점 더 많은 수의 이주자들(밀입국자들)을 바다를 건너기에 적합하지 않은 배에 태우면서 대체로 방해받지 않고 활약한다는 것을 의미했다.

07 ②

마지막 문장에서 대명사 It은 Time을 가리키고, words는 앞 문장의 spoken language를 가리킨다. 결국, 마지막 문장은 세 번째 문장에 대한 재진술 문장으로 볼 수 있는데, 마지막 문장에서 '진실을 말한다'라고 했으므로, 세 번째 문장에서도 동일한 이야기를 해야 할 것임을 짐작할 수 있다. 그런데 빈칸 앞에 부정어 less가 있으므로 truth와 반대되는 의미를 가진 표현을 찾아야 하며, ②가 이러한 의미에 가장 근접한다.

plainly ad. 명백하게, 솔직하게; 수수하게 convey v. 나르다, 운반하다; 전하다 loud and clear 분명하게, 명료하게 manipulate v. 조종하다; 조작하다; 능숙하게 다루다 be subject to ~을 받기 쉽다; 걸리기 쉽다 acquisition n. 취득, 획득, 습득 perversion n. (의미의) 곡해; 남용, 악용 synchronism n. 동시 발생, 병발(併發); 동시성 hush n. 침묵, 조용함

시간은 말한다. 시간은 오히려 말보다도 더 분명하게 말한다. 시간이 전하는 메시지는 명료하게 전달된다. 시간은 의식적으로 덜 조작되기 때문에 말로 표현된 언어보다 덜 왜곡된다. 시간은 말이 거짓을 늘어놓는 곳에서 진실을 외칠 수 있다.

08 ②

태도와 관련해서 첫 문장에서 언급하고 있는 내용을 참고해야 한다. get on one's high horse는 '거만하게 굴다'라는 의미이므로, 이러한 의미를 내포하고 있는 형용사 ②가 빈칸에 들어가야 한다.

get on one's high horse 뽐내다, 거만하게 굴다 disagree v. 일치하지 않다; 의견이 다르다 complaisant a. 고분고분한; 공손한 supercilious a. 거만한, 젠체하는, 사람을 깔보는 puerile a. 어린애 같은, 철없는 provident a. 선견지명이 있는; 신중한; 절약하는

09 ②

눈에 보이지 않는(invisible) 산업으로 돈을 번다고 했고 재능을 자랑하지 않는다고 했으므로 이 도시는 '은밀한' 곳이라 할 수 있다.

flaunt v. 자랑하다, 과시하다 pinched a. 초췌한 furtive a. 은밀한, 내밀한 wanton a. 타당한 이유 없이 고의적인 bucolic a. 목가적인

예로부터 언제나 그 도시는 금융업과 보험업 같은 눈에 보이지 않는 산업으로 돈을 벌었고, 사람들이 재능을 자랑하는 곳이 아니다.

10 ②

책을 탄압하려 한 것이 오히려 그 책이 더 많이 팔리는 결과를 가져왔으므로, 정부의 대응은 어리석고 잘못된 것이었다고 할 수 있다.

suppress v. 억압하다, 진압하다; (감정을) 누그러뜨리다 on the ground(s) of ~의 이유로, ~의 구실로 blasphemy n. 신에 대한 불경; 독설 boost v. 밀어 올리다; 후원하다 enormously ad. 대단히, 매우, 막대하게 profit v. 이익을 보다, 소득을 얻다 piracy n. 해적행위, 저작권 침해; 무허가 행위 imbecility n. 저능; 어리석음, 어리석은 행동 acumen n. 예민, 총명, 날카로운 통찰력 ignominy n. 치욕, 불명예

문화부 장관은 불경스런 내용이라는 이유로 그 소설을 탄압하려 들었지만, 그 책의 판매고를 엄청나게 올려주는 결과만 가져 왔다. 저자는 정부 측의 바보 같은 대응으로 상당한 이익을 보았다.

11 ②

further가 결정적인 단서가 된다. 빈칸 뒤에서 언급하고 있는 '최고의 뮤추얼 펀드 회사의 기함급 펀드의 매매 금지 조치' 또한 부패 스캔들처럼 주식시장에 악영향을 끼치는 것이므로, 빈칸에는 앞서 비슷한 의도로 쓰인 동사 rocked보다 좀 더 강한 의미를 가진 단어가 들어가야 한다. 그러므로 빈칸에는 '소용돌이치게 하다'라는 의미의 ②가 적절하다.

rock v. 요동치다, 흔들리다 corruption n. 타락; 퇴폐; 부패 scandal n. 추문, 스캔들 move n. 조치, 행동 ban v. 금하다, 금지하다 flagship n. 기함; 가장 중요한 것; 본사, 본점 writhe v. 몸을 비틀다, 굽히다 roil v. (마음을) 어지럽히다; (사회를) 소란케 하다; 노하게 하다 hoodwink v. (남의 눈을) 속이다, 현혹시키다 revolve v. 회전시키다; 순환하다

금년 초 부패 스캔들로 요동쳤던 인도의 주식시장은, 이 나라 최고의 뮤추얼 펀드 회사의 기함급 펀드의 매매 금지 조치로 인해 더더욱 소용돌이쳤다.

12　　　　　　　　　　　④

첫 번째 빈칸은 주절의 행위에 대해 동시동작 혹은 연속동작의 분사구문으로 이어지고 있으므로 주절의 동사인 underestimated와 유사한 의미의 단어가 필요하다. disregarding 또는 disdaining이 가능하다. as a good actor 부분으로 인해 eulogizing이나 complimenting을 선택하기 쉬우나, 비난하는 내용이 주절에 이미 나와 있는 상태인 점과 현재 정치를 하고 있는 사람에게 이전 직업인 배우를 들먹이는 것은 칭찬이 아니라 비난이라는 점에 유의해야 한다. 한편, 두 번째 빈칸의 경우, 다른 사람이 써준 원고를 그대로 읽는 사람을 말하고 있으므로, puppet 또는 simpleton이 가능하다. 상기 두 조건을 모두 만족시키는 정답은 ④가 된다.

opponent n. 적, 적수, 상대 consistently ad. 시종일관, 지속적으로; 모순 없이 underestimate v. 과소평가하다; 얕보다 eulogize v. 칭찬하다, 칭송하다; 기리다 deity n. 신(神), 신성(神性) disregard v. 무시하다; 경시하다 hermit n. 수행자; 은둔자 compliment v. 칭찬하다, 경의를 표하다; 축하하다; 아첨의 말을 하다 puppet n. 작은 인형, 꼭두각시 disdain v. 경멸하다, 멸시하다 simpleton n. 바보, 얼간이

레이건(Reagan)이 정치인으로 활동했던 동안 그의 정적들은 끊임없이 그를 과소평가했으며, 그를 훌륭한 배우, 즉 다른 사람들이 대신 써 준 대본을 읽기만 할 수 있는 바보라고 경멸했다.

13　　　　　　　　　　　③

to accept와 to give는 모두 첫 번째 빈칸을 수식하고 있다. 따라서 첫 번째 빈칸에는 '잘못된 것에 대한 책임은 자신이 지고, 잘된 것에 대한 공로는 부하에게 돌릴 줄 아는 태도'를 설명할 수 있는 단어가 와야 한다. self-sacrifice, bounty, humility가 가능하다. fairness는 공명정대한 것이므로 앞서 언급한 태도와 거리가 있다. 한편, 책임은 자신이 지고 공은 다른 사람에게 돌리는 것이 모두 지도자의 훌륭한 자질로서 언급되고 있는 글이므로, 두 번째 빈칸의 경우, 동일한 맥락을 나타내는 표현인 likewise 또는 accordingly가 쓰일 수 있다. 상기 두 조건을 모두 만족시키는 것은 ③이다.

conviction n. 신념, 확신; <법> 유죄의 판결 publicly ad. 공공연하게, 공개적으로 responsibility n. 책임, 책무, 의무 subordinate n. 부하, 하위에 있는 사람 credit n. 신용; (협력 따위의) 공적; (공적에 대한) 감사 triumph n. 승리; 업적, 위업 self-sacrifice n. 자기희생 bounty n. 관대함, 활수함; 박애 paradoxically ad. 역설적으로 humility n. 겸손, 겸양; 비하 likewise ad. 똑같이, 마찬가지로 fairness n. 공평함, 공명정대 accordingly ad. 따라서, 그러므로

나의 소신은 지도자라면 누구나 자신이 선택한 부하들의 실수를 자신이 책임질 일로 공개적으로 인정하고, 그리고 그와 마찬가지로 업적에 대해서는 그들의 공으로 공개적으로 돌릴 정도의 겸손함을 가져야 한다는 것이다.

14　　　　　　　　　　　②

두 번째 문장의 sarcasm과 같은 의미의 형용사인 ②가 빈칸에 들어가기에 적절하다.

sarcasm n. 빈정거림, 신랄함 conflict n. 충돌 feverish a. 열광적인 caustic a. 신랄한, 빈정대는 brazen a. 뻔뻔스러운 quirky a. 기발한

신뢰받지만 신랄한 동료가 당신의 창의성을 향상시켜줄 수 있을 것이다. 신랄함을 이해할 수 있는 사람들이 더 창의적이고 문제를 더 잘 해결할 수 있다. 그러나 충돌을 피하기 위해 신랄함은 서로 믿는 사람들 사이에 사용하는 것이 가장 좋다.

15　　　　　　　　　　　③

But 앞에서 '하고 싶은 것을 마음대로 할 수 있는' 왕국에 대해 기술하고 있으므로, 그 뒤에는 이러한 상황과 상반되는 내용의 진술이 와야 한다. '마음껏 누리는 자유를 제한 당하게 된다'라는 의미를 만드는 ③이 정답으로 가장 적절하다.

ridiculous a. 우스운, 어리석은 harsh a. 거친; 사나운; 모진 conventional a. 전통적인, 인습적인; 상투적인 loosen v. (규제 따위를) 완화하다, 관대하게 하다 satiate v. 물리게 하다, 물릴 정도로 주다 qualify v. 자격을 주다, 적합하게 하다; 한정하다, 제한하다 lubricate v. 기름을 바르다, 기름을 치다; 미끄럽게 하다

우리들만이 지배하고, 현명하건 어리석건, 어렵건 쉽건, 인습적이건 이상하건, 원하는 것을 무엇이나 할 수 있는 온전한 왕국을 우리들은 가지고 있다. 그러나 그 왕국을 벗어나자마자, 우리들의 행동의 자유는 다른 사람들의 자유에 의해 제한을 받게 된다.

16　　　　　　　　　　　①

불면증을 없애기 위해 복용하는 약이 실제로는 적절한 수준의 수면에 빠지게 하는 효과가 없다는 내용이 앞에 있으므로, 잠이 드는 것은 아니지만 그와 유사한 상태를 만드는 효과가 있을 뿐이라는 맥락이 되어야 한다. 따라서 '진정되다'라는 의미를 만드는 ①이 정답으로 가장 적절하다.

insomnia n. 불면증 turn to ~에 의지하다 over-the-counter a. 처방전 없이 구입할 수 있는 prescription n. 명령, 규정; 법규; 처방, 처방전 pill n. 알약 proper a. 적당한, 타당한 sedate v. 진정시키다, 안정시키다 sober a. 술 취하지 않은, 맑은 정신의 adulterate v. 질을 나쁘게 하다 somber a. 어둠침침한; 흐린; 음침한, 우울한

불면증을 이겨내기 위해 수백만 명의 미국인들이 약 — 처방전이 필요한 약과 그렇지 않은 약 모두 — 에 의존하고 있다. 제임스 민라드(James Minrad) 박사는 "어떤 약을 쓰더라도 정상적으로 잠이 들게 하진 않습니다. 알약을 복용한다고 해서 적절한 수면의 수준에 이를 수 있는 것은 아닙니다. 단지 마음이 진정되었을 뿐입니다"라고 말하고 있다.

17 ①

'가난한 사람들이 행복한 게 아니라, 불편, 곤란, 슬픔이 생활의 일부가 되어 버려서, 부자들보다 더 잘 참아내고 있는 것'이라고 했으므로, '가난한 사람들은 이러한 것들을 많이 경험한 까닭에 한두 번 정도 더 경험해도 대수롭지 않을 정도로 무뎌졌다'라고 해야 자연스러운 흐름의 문장이 된다.

bear v. 지탱하다; 견디다, 참다 discomfort n. 불쾌, 불안; 싫은 일 blow n. 강타, 구타; (정신적) 타격, 불행, 재난 dull v. 둔하게 하다, 무디게 하다; (고통 따위를) 완화시키다 demur v. 이의를 제기하다, 반대하다 stir v. 분발하게 하다; 자극하다 delude v. 미혹시키다, 속이다

사람들은 가난한 사람들이 부자들보다 행복하다고 흔히 믿고 있다. 그들은 그렇지 않다. 불편, 곤란, 슬픔이 평상시 생활의 일부가 돼 버려서, 그들이 부자들보다 훌륭하게 참아내고 있는 것뿐이다. 많은 불행으로 인해 무뎌진 사람에게 불행이 한 번 더 찾아오는 것은 대수롭지 않은 법이다.

18 ②

영화의 자살 장면에서 '몸 안으로 들어가는 칼이나 상처, 혹은 내장이 나가떨어지는 장면' 등이 보이지 않고, 피를 흘리면서 쓰러지는 모습만 볼 수 있다면, 이것은 감독의 '표현상의 절제'가 드러나는 것으로 볼 수 있다.

evident a. 분명한, 명백한, 뚜렷한 stage v. 무대에 올리다, 상연하다 suicide n. 자살, 자살행위 sequence n. 장면, 시퀀스; 연속, 연쇄 director n. 지도자; 영화감독, 연출가 stomach n. 위(胃); 복부, 배 wound n. 상처, 부상 organ n. 기관(器官) tumble v. 넘어지다; 굴러 떨어지다 noble n. 귀족 sink v. 가라앉다, 침몰하다 smear n. 얼룩, 오점; 명예훼손, 비방 suspense n. 걱정, 불안; (영화 등에 의한) 긴장감, 서스펜스 restraint n. (표현상의) 절제, 억제; 제지, 금지 ribaldry n. 품위가 낮음, 상스러움; 음담패설 solecism n. 문법 위반, 파격 어법; 결례

미이케(Miike)의 표현상의 절제는 고상하게 연출된 자살 장면인 첫 장면부터 분명하게 드러난다. 감독은 칼이 그 사람의 배 안으로 들어가는 것이나 그 결과 생긴 상처, 또는 내장이 나가떨어지는 것을 전혀 보여주지 않는다. 자살하는 그 고귀한 사람이 얼룩진 피 속으로 조용히 쓰러지는 모습이 위로부터 차분하게 보여질 뿐이다.

19 ③

no more A than B 구문은 양자 부정의 의미가 있으므로, A와 B에 해당되는 표현은 동일한 맥락 하에 진술되어야 한다. 따라서 첫 번째 빈칸의 경우, than 이하에서 동사로 주어져 있는 avoid와 같은 의미를 가진 단어가 들어가야 한다. forestall 또는 prevent가 가능하다. 한편, judgements는 impressions와 같은 의미로 쓰인 것이므로, 두 번째 빈칸에는 first와 같은 의미를 가진 단어가 들어가야 한다. inchoate 또는 initial이 가능하다. 결과적으로, 상기 두 조건을 모두 만족시키는 정답은 ③이다.

first impression 첫인상 alter v. 변경하다, 바꾸다 accumulate v. 모으다, 축적하다 perceive v. 지각하다, 감지하다; 인식하다 accept v. 받아들이다; 수락하다 inchoate a. 이제 막 시작한, 초기의; 불완전한 forestall v. 앞질러 방해하다; 기선을 제압하다 ultimate a. 최후의, 궁극의; 최종적인 prevent v. 막다, 방해하다 initial a. 처음의, 최초의 ensconce v. 안치하다; 숨기다, 감추다 succulent a. 즙이 많은; 흥미진진한

어떤 사람에 대한 정보를 일정한 기간에 걸쳐 추가적으로 축적함에 따라 때때로 첫인상이 바뀌기는 하지만, 눈에 보이는 물체나 가락이 주어져 있을 때 그것을 보고 듣는 것을 피할 수 없는 것과 마찬가지로, 초기에 이뤄진 이러한 판단의 형성과 빠른 성장을 막는 것은 불가능하다.

20 ①

빈칸 앞의 this는 앞 문장의 내용을 받는 지시어이다. 앞 문장에서 '생각하는 것은 인간에게 부자연스럽고 힘든 활동이다'라고 했으므로, 빈칸에는 unnatural and laborious의 의미가 내포된 단어가 들어가야 한다. '반감, 혐오; 매우 싫어하는 대상'이라는 의미를 가진 aversion이 이에 가장 부합하는 단어이다.

unnatural a. 부자연스런; 이상한, 기괴한 laborious a. 힘이 드는, 곤란한; 고심한 manifest a. 명백한, 일목요연한, 분명한 prosperous a. 번영하는, 성공한 aversion n. 반감, 혐오; 아주 싫은 대상이나 물건 propriety n. 타당, 적당; 예의바름, 교양 empathy n. 감정 이입, 공감 fondness n. 맹목적인 사랑; 맹신

두 다리로 걷는 것이 원숭이에게 부자연스럽고 힘든 것만큼, 생각하는 것은 인간에게 부자연스럽고 힘든 활동이다. 이렇게 생각하는 데 노력을 들이는 것에 대한 인간의 기피가 사생활에서와 마찬가지로 공공 생활에서도 명백하기 때문에, 인간은 편안하고 풍요로운 시대에는 역사적인 사고를 많이 하지 않는다.

21 ④

학문적으로 중요한 환경은 학식을 갖추는 데 도움이 될 것이므로, 첫 번째 빈칸에는 contributive 또는 conducive가 가능하다. 한편, because절의 주어 부분은 '학생 스스로 재능을 계발하는 것'과 비교되고 있으므로, 두 번째 빈칸에는 이것과 대비를 이룰 수 있는 단어가 필요하다. '학생 스스로 재능을 계발하는 것'과 반대되는 개념은 '학생이 해야 하는 것을 교수가 시키는 것'이며, 이것은 또한 첫 문장의 tell their students what to write과 일맥상통한다. 따라서 두 번째 빈칸에는 indoctrination이 들어가야 한다.

strive v. 노력하다; 얻으려고 애쓰다 establish v. 확립하다, 제정하다 critical a. 비평의, 평론의; 위기의; 중대한 thorough a. 철저한; 완전한 creative a. 창조적인; 건설적인 scholarship n. 학문; 학식; 장학금 encouraging a. 장려하는; 유망한 faculty n. 능력, 기능; 재능 independently ad. 독립적으로; 무관하게 crucial a. 결정적인, 중대한 autonomy n. 자치; 자치권; 자치 국가 contributive a. 기여하는, 공헌하는, 이바지하는 fulmination n. 맹렬한 비난, 질책; 폭발 baneful a. 파괴적인, 치명적인; 사악한 enlightenment n. 계발, 계몽; 교화 conducive a. 도움이 되는; 이바지하는 indoctrination n. 주입; 가르침; 교화

훌륭한 교수들은 절대로 학생들에게 무엇을 써야 하는지 말하지 않는다. 대신에 그들은 빈틈없고 창의적인 학식에 도움이 되는, 학문적으로 중요한 환경을 조성하려 애쓴다. 왜냐하면 주입을 통해 학생을 교육하는 것은 학생 스스로 재능을 개발하게 하는 것만큼 효율적이지 않기 때문이다.

22　　　　　　　　　　　　　　①

꽃이 매우 풍부하게 존재한다는 점, 부유한 자들과 가난한 자들 모두 꽃을 가질 수 있다는 점 등이 단서가 된다. 빈칸이 들어 있는 문장은 '꽃이 모든 사람들에게 똑같이 공평하게 주어져 있다'라는 의미가 되어야 하는데, 빈칸 앞에 부정어 not이 있음에 유의하면 '독점'의 의미를 가진 ①이 빈칸에 들어가는 것이 가장 자연스럽다.

gratitude n. 감사, 사의 providence n. 섭리; 신(神); 선견지명 profusely ad. 아낌없이, 풍부하게 require v. 요구하다, 명하다; 규정하다; 필요로 하다 appreciate v. 평가하다, 판단하다; 진가를 인정하다 monopolize v. 독점하다 tout v. 강매하다; 성가시게 권유하다 jettison v. (긴급 상황에서 배·항공기에서) 짐을 버리다; (방해물·부담 등을) 버리다 festoon v. 꽃줄로 잇다, 꽃줄로 꾸미다

꽃을 사랑하는 사람은 행복하다. 신(神)이 주신 이 선물이 그 무엇보다도 풍부하게 주어졌다는 것을 감사해야 한다. 꽃은 아무도 독점할 수 없다. 가난한 사람들도 부유한 사람들과 마찬가지로 꽃을 가질 수 있다. 꽃을 사랑하고 감상하는 데는 터너(Turner)의 그림이나 미켈란젤로(Michelangelo)의 조각상을 감상하고 찬미하는 데 필요할 그러한 교육이 필요하지 않다.

23　　　　　　　　　　　　　　④

예술의 사회와의 관계를 중요하게 생각하지 않는다는 것은 예술이 사회에 별로 필요하지 않고 사회를 벗어난 순수하게 개인적인 것으로 본다는 말이므로, 첫 번째 빈칸에는 gratuitous(불필요한)가 적절하고, 두 번째 빈칸의 경우에는 uncontrolled(통제되지 않는)나 autonomous (독자적인)가 적절하다.

playful a. 장난스런 manifestation n. 표현 radical a. 근본적인, 철저한, 급진적인, 과격한 individuality n. 개성 absolutely ad. 절대적으로, 정말로 conditioning n. 조건 붙이기 quintessential a. 전형적인 pragmatic a. 실용적인 purposeful a. 고의적인 uncontrolled a. 통제되지 않는 ideological a. 관념학의; 이데올로기의 restricted a. 한정된, 제한된 gratuitous a. 무료의; 불필요한 autonomous a. 독립한, 독자적인

예술과 사회의 관계의 중요성을 부인하거나 적어도 최소화할 사람은 예술을 완전히 불필요하거나 장난스런 활동으로 간주하는 사람들과 예술을 가장 철저한 개성의 표현으로 간주하는 사람들과 예술을 모든 조건부여(제약)를 탈피하는 정말로 독자적인 영역으로 간주하는 사람들이다.

24　　　　　　　　　　　　　　④

빈칸 앞에 위치한 관계대명사 which의 선행사는 앞 문장 전체이다. 개종자에게 가하는 보복과 보복 위협은 흔했다고 했고, 경찰도 때때로 보복 행위를 막지 않으려 하거나, 그러한 일을 저지른 사람들을 처벌하지 않았다고 했으므로, 개종자에게 가해지는 보복 행위를 묵인하거나 당연하게 여기는 분위기가 생겨났을 것으로 미루어 짐작할 수 있다. 이러한 의미를 가진 것은 ④이다.

reprisal n. 보복, 앙갚음 threat n. 위협, 협박 convert n. 개종자 harassment n. 괴롭힘, 학대 charge v. 고소하다, 고발하다 commit v. 저지르다, 범하다 clue n. 실마리, 단서 restrict v. 제한하다, 한정하다; 금지하다 climate n. 풍토, 분위기; 기후 impunity n. 처벌을 받지 않음

개종자들에게 가하는 보복과 보복 위협은 흔했다. 종교적 소수집단의 구성원들은 폭력과 괴롭힘을 당했으며, 경찰은 때때로 그런 행위를 막는 것을 거부하거나 그런 행위를 저지른 사람들을 고소하지 않았다. 이로 인해 종교적 소수집단에 대한 폭력 행위를 처벌하지 않는 풍토가 생겨났다.

25　　　　　　　　　　　　　　①

빈칸 앞의 this public performance of theirs는 네 번째 문장의 mask와 같은 의미로 쓰인 것이다. 글에서는 유명 인사가 세상에 보이는 모습을 '가면'으로 묘사하고 있으므로, 밖으로 드러나는 모습을 그들의 속에 있는 참모습과 일치한다고 생각해서는 안 될 것이다. 따라서 빈칸에 적절한 표현은 ①이 된다.

passion n. 열정, 열심; 매우 좋아하는 것 celebrated a. 유명한; 세상에 알려진 prestige n. 위신, 명성, 신망 acquire v. 획득하다, 얻다 account n. 계산; 판단; 중요성 come across 우연히 만나다 conceal v. 숨기다, 비밀로 하다 correspond v. 일치하다, 부합하다 acquired a. 후천적인 inborn a. 타고난, 천부적인

사람들이 유명 인사를 몹시 만나고 싶어 하는 것에 대해 나는 항상 이상하게 생각해 왔다. 당신이 친구에게 유명한 사람들을 알고 있다고 말할 수 있음으로 인해 얻게 되는 명성은 당신 자신은 하찮은 사람이란 것을 증명해 줄 뿐이다. 유명 인사들은 우연히 만나는 사람들을 다루는 솜씨를 발휘한다. 그들은 세상을 향해 가면, 그것도 종종 인상적인 가면을 내보인다. 그렇지만 자신들의 참된 자아를 조심해서 잘 감춘다. 그들은 사람들이 자신들에게 기대하는 역할을 하며, 노력을 통해 그 역할을 아주 잘하는 법을 익힌다. 하지만, 그들이 노력해서 공공연하게 내보이는 바가 숨은 인간성과 일치한다고 생각한다면 당신은 바보다.

01 ①	02 ①	03 ④	04 ②	05 ④	06 ②	07 ③	08 ①	09 ①	10 ①
11 ①	12 ④	13 ①	14 ④	15 ③	16 ④	17 ④	18 ②	19 ③	20 ③
21 ④	22 ④	23 ③	24 ②	25 ④					

01 ①

고인을 추모하는(venerate one's memory) 장례식에서 고인의 부인이 참석자들에게 하는 말은 일종의 고별사(valediction)라고 할 수 있다.

valediction n. 고별사, 작별인사 impromptu a. 즉흥적인, 즉석에서 행하는 venerate v. 공경하다, 추앙하다 memory n. (죽은 사람에 대한) 기억 attendee n. 참석자 convocation n. (특히 교회나 대학 관계자들의) 집회[대회]; 소집 homage n. 존경, 경의 epiphany n. 직관, 통찰

예식을 마칠 때쯤, 장군의 부인이 즉석에서 고별사를 하였는데, 고인이 된 장군에 대한 기억을 진심으로 추모하였고 많은 참석자들에게 감동을 주었다.

02 ①

illegal이 핵심 단어이다. 불법적인 기부금을 받는 것은 윤리적으로 옳지 못한 일이므로, 빈칸에는 '(도덕의) 위반'이라는 의미의 ①이 들어가는 것이 적절하다.

accept v. 받아들이다; 수락하다 illegal a. 불법의, 위법의 campaign n. 군사행동; 선거운동, 유세 contribution n. 기부, 기부금; 기여, 공헌 ethics n. 윤리학; 도덕 candidate n. 후보 breach n. 갈라진 틈; (도덕·약속의) 위반, 불이행 plot n. 음모, 책략; 줄거리 obedience n. 복종, 순종 accolade n. 칭찬, 영예; 표창

불법 선거 기부금을 받는 것은 공직 선거에 뛰어든 후보자들 사이에서 심각하면서도 너무나도 흔히 발생하는 윤리 위반이다.

03 ④

앞 문장에서 콧구멍 속에서 발생하는 감염에 대해 이야기하고 있으므로, 두 번째 문장의 congestion은 코 속에 생긴 울혈증을 의미함을 알 수 있다. 그러므로 빈칸에도 코와 관련 있는 단어인 ④가 와야 한다.

infection n. 전염, 감염 nostril n. 콧구멍 congestion n. 밀집, 혼잡; <병리> 충혈, 울혈 respiratory a. 호흡의, 호흡 기관의 dermal a. 피부의, 피부에 관한 tactile a. 촉각의; 만져서 알 수 있는 feral a. 야생의, 야생으로 돌아간; 야성적인 nasal a. 코의; 콧소리의

사실 감염의 90퍼센트 이상은 콧구멍 속에서 발생한다. 울혈증과 같이 코에 문제가 생기면 귀와 호흡기도 감염될 수 있다.

04 ②

아무도 볼 수 없는 외딴 섬에서의 만남이라면, 그 만남 역시 아무도 볼 수 없고 또한 알 수도 없을 것이다. 그러므로 빈칸에는 anyone could not see의 의미를 내포하고 있는 단어가 들어가야 하며, 정답은 ②가 된다.

deserted a. 사막의; 불모의, 황량한; 인적이 끊긴 adulterous a. 불륜의, 간통의 clandestine a. 비밀의, 은밀한, 남모르게 하는 diurnal a. 주간의, 낮의; 낮에 활동하는; 매일의 lascivious a. 음탕한, 호색의, 외설적인

그 젊은 연인들은 아무도 자신들을 알아보지 못하는 외딴 섬에서 은밀한 만남을 가지기로 계획을 세웠다.

05 ④

컵 아래에 밑받침이나 받침 접시를 사용하는 것을 목재가구와 연관 지어 생각하면, 이는 결국 가구가 '훼손되지' 않도록 하기 위한 행동임을 알 수 있다.

coaster n. 받침 접시; 비탈용 썰매 saucer n. 받침 접시, 받침 fell v. (나무를) 베어 넘어뜨리다; 쳐서 넘어뜨리다 prop v. 버티다, 기대 놓다; 지지하다 polish v. 닦다, 윤을 내다; 다듬다 mar v. 흠가게 하다; 손상시키다, 망쳐놓다

목재가구에 흠이 가지 않도록 여러분들의 컵 아래에 밑받침이나 받침 접시를 사용해 주십시오.

06 ②

주체가 여성이고 이제 대학에 입학하려고 하므로 독신남자 혹은 학사의 의미를 가진 ③은 적절하지 않으며, ④의 '장학생'도 빈칸 뒤에 이어지는 표현, 즉 '어느 대학을 다녀야 할 지에 관해'라는 내용과 부자연스럽게 이어진다. 정답은 ②가 되며, 어느 대학을 다녀야 할 지에 대해 고민스러운 입장에 있음을 말하고 있는 내용이 된다.

apply v. 적용하다, 응용하다; 지원하다, 신청하다 accept v. 받아들이다; 수락하다 attend v. 출석하다, 참석하다; (학교에) 다니다 alacrity n. 기민함, 민첩함 quandary n. 곤혹, 당혹, 궁지 bachelor n. 독신남자; 학사 honor student 우등생

자신이 지원했던 3개 대학에서 자신을 받아들였을 때, 그녀는 어느 대학을 다녀야 할지에 관해 어찌 할 바를 몰랐다.

07 ③

아버지의 사상이 허무맹랑한 것이라고 생각하게 되었다면, 그것에 대해 아버지는 유감스러워했을 것이다.

chimerical a. 공상적인, 터무니없는; 기상천외의 immerse v. ~에 몰두하다 creed n. 교리, 신조 utilitarianism n. 공리주의 chagrin n. 유감, 원통함 euphoria n. 극도의 행복감, 희열 frowziness n. 지저분함, 곰팡내가 남 temerity n. 무모함, 만용

그의 아버지의 공리주의 신조에 물들어 있었던 청소년기를 지난 뒤, 밀(Mill)은 그의 아버지에게는 매우 유감스럽게도 불구하고 공리주의가 약속하는 행복이 허무맹랑하다는 것을 깨달았다.

08 ①

because절의 and 이하에서 '실명이 알려지길 원하지 않았다'라고 했으므로, 실명이 아닌 다른 이름을 쓰려 했을 것이라 유추할 수 있다. real name과 반대되는 개념의 ①이 정답이 된다.

label v. 명칭을 붙이다, 분류하다; 낙인찍다 unladylike a. 숙녀답지 않은, 귀부인에게 있을 수 없는 pseudonym n. 익명, 필명 terminology n. 전문용어; 용어법 metaphor n. 은유(隱喻) quill n. 깃촉, 깃촉펜

19세기에 많은 여성 작가들은 필명을 사용했다. 왜냐하면 그들은 '숙녀답지 않다'라는 꼬리표가 붙는 것을 두려워했고 자신들의 실명이 알려지길 원하지 않았기 때문이다.

09 ①

빈칸 앞의 형용사 false는 빈칸에 들어갈 단어의 방법이 바람직하지 않다는 것을 의미하며, and 이하에서는 결과적으로 '두 가지 측면들을 동시에' 치료한다고 했다. 따라서 빈칸에는 '둘로 나눈다'라는 의미를 내포하고 있는 표현이 들어가야 한다. '이분법'이라는 의미의 ①이 빈칸에 적절하다.

addiction n. 중독, 탐닉 psychiatrist n. 정신과 의사 recognize v. 알아보다, 인지하다; 인정하다 physiological a. 생리학의; 생리적인 psychological a. 심리학의; 정신적인 aspect n. 양상, 모습, 외관 simultaneously ad. 동시에, 일제히 dichotomy n. 분열; 이분법 diagnosis n. 진단 prognosis n. 예상, 예측; 예후 logomachy n. 언쟁, 말다툼; 설전

중독 전문 정신과 의사들은 중독을 생리학적, 정신적 측면들로 양분하는 것이 잘못된 것임을 오랫동안 인식해 왔으며, 그래서 이 둘을 동시에 치료한다.

10 ①

국제관계 분야의 전문가임에도 불구하고 흥미로운 주제마저도 학생들로 하여금 졸면서 산만하게 강의한다는 단서로부터 지루한 강의의 교수임을 추론할 수 있다.

lackluster a. 광택이 없는; 흐리멍텅한; 활기 없는 conspicuous a. 눈에 잘 띄는; 분명한 meticulous a. 소심한, 작은 일에 신경을 쓰는, 매우 신중한

국제관계 분야의 뛰어난 전문가임에도 불구하고 Andrew Ashworth는 옥스퍼드 대학의 재미없는 교수이다. 심지어 흥미진진한 국제 현안들에 대해 강의를 할 때조차도 그의 강의는 너무나 밋밋해서 학생들을 졸게 하거나 산만하게 만든다.

11 ①

after so many years 이하는 서구 문학계가 그에게 관심을 가지기 이전의 상황에 대해 언급해야 한다. 이에 대해 첫 번째 문장에서 진술하고 있는데, '자국에서는 위대한 작가로 인정받은 것과 다른 나라에서는 거의 알려져 있지 않은 것'이 그것이다. 오직 자국에서만 인정을 받은 것은 그의 명성이 변방에만 머물러 있었다는 것이므로, 빈칸에는 ①이 들어가는 것이 가장 적절하다. 한편, ③의 경우, '자국에서는 그가 인정을 받았다는 사실'과 배치되므로 정답으로 부적절하다.

recognize v. 알아보다; (공로 따위를) 인정하다 discover v. 발견하다; 알다, 깨닫다 establishment n. 설립, 창립; 권력기구, 체제; 주류파 wilderness n. 황야, 황무지, 미개척지 translator n. 번역자; 통역 negligence n. 태만; 부주의; 무관심 limelight n. 석회광(光); (the-) 주목의 대상

그는 자기 나라에서는 위대한 작가로 널리 알려져 있었지만, 그 나라 밖에서는 거의 알려져 있지 않은 사람이었다. 그렇게 오랜 세월 동안 변방에 머물러 있던 그를 지금 서구 문학계가 갑자기 발견해 관심을 보이고 있다.

12 ④

where 이하의 내용을 통해 유추할 수 있다. '소도시에서는 재밌는 일이 전혀 일어나지 않는다고 생각한다'라는 말에는 소도시를 무시하거나 비하하는 뜻이 내포되어 있다. 그러므로 ④가 정답이다. 한편, 사전적으로 provincial 안에는 '편협한, 촌티가 나는' 등의 비하하는 의미가 실제로 있으며, 이것을 통해서도 정답을 도출하는 것이 가능하다.

provincial a. 지방의, 시골의; 시골티 나는; 편협한 term n. 용어; 조건; 기간 centralize v. 중심에 모으다; 집중시키다; 집중되다 esteem n. 존중 존경; 경의 affection n. 애정, 호의; 감동; 영향 nostalgia n. 향수(鄕愁); 옛날을 그리워함 contempt n. 경멸, 모욕; 치욕

특히 영국이나 프랑스 같이 고도로 중앙 집중화된 국가에서는 '지방'은 언제나 경멸을 나타내는 말이었는데, 이런 나라에서는 런던 시민이나 파리 시민이 셰필드나 리옹 같은 소도시에서는 재미있는 일이 결코 일어날 수가 없다고 생각하는 경향이 있다.

13　　　①

let alone 뒤에는 앞 문장의 내용, 즉 '내가 어디에 있고 어떤 위험에 처해 있는지를 가족이 모르고 있는 것'에 더하여, 가족들이 모르고 있던 또 다른 사실에 대한 내용이 이어져야 한다. 따라서 빈칸에는 앞 문장의 unaware와 문맥상의 의미가 같은 표현이 들어가야 하며, ①이 이러한 의미를 갖고 있는 단어이다.

mournful a. 슬픔에 잠긴; 애처로운 echo v. 메아리치게 하다; 울리다 peak n. (뾰족한) 끝; 산꼭대기 unaware a. 눈치 채지 못하는, 알지 못하는, 모르는 let alone ~은 말할 것도 없고; ~은 물론이고 oblivious a. 염두에 없는; 알아차리지 못하는 belligerent a. 호전적인; 교전중인 captious a. 헐뜯는, 흠잡기 좋아하는 heedful a. 주의 깊은, 조심성 있는; 마음 쓰는

도와달라는 나의 애처로운 울음소리가 그 협곡의 꼭대기에 있는 절벽을 가로질러 울려 퍼졌다. 당시 나의 가족은 내가 어디에 있는지와 내 목숨을 앗아갈 위험을 알아차리지 못한 것은 물론, 내가 실종되었다는 것도 알지 못한 채 편안하고 따뜻한 침대에서 여전히 잠들어 있었다.

14　　　④

otherwise가 있으므로 첫 번째 빈칸과 forceful은 두 번째 빈칸과 undramatically와 서로 대조를 이루어야 한다. 따라서 ④의 '생생한'과 '산문적으로, 무미건조하게'가 적절하다.

naked a. 적나라한, 있는 그대로의 parable n. 우화, 비유 grim a. 엄한, 모진, 소름끼치는 justify v. (행위, 주장을) 정당화하다 forceful a. 힘 있는, 효과적인 undramatically ad. 극적이지 못하게, 인상 깊지 않게 rosy a. 낙관적인 graphically ad. 사실적으로 pensive a. 생각에 잠긴 epically ad. 서사시적으로 laconic a. 간결한 verbosely ad. 장황하게 vivid a. 생생한 prosaically ad. 산문적으로, 무미건조하게

이것은 적나라한 우화가 아니며 우리가 실재하는 마을과 사람들의 인상을 받는다는 사실은 소름끼치는 공포감을 준다. 그래서 픽션(소설) 형식은 그렇지 않으면(픽션이 아니면) 무미건조하고 평범하게 나타내져야 할 것을 생생하고 힘 있게 만듦으로써 정당화된다.

15　　　③

사람들이 잘못 생각하고 있다는 말은 첫 번째 문장의 that절의 진술이 틀렸다는 것이다. 따라서 첫 번째 문장의 의미를 다른 말로 표현하면 'in fact, beauty is a lot to do with the efficient functioning of a city.'가 된다. 결국 도시가 효율적으로 운영되기 위해선 미적인 요소도 무시해선 안 된다는 의미가 되므로, 빈칸에는 beauty의 동의어 혹은

그와 유사한 의미를 포함하고 있는 단어가 들어가야 한다.

erroneously ad. 잘못되어, 틀리게 efficient a. 능률적인, 효과가 있는, 유효한 function v. 작용하다, 역할을 다하다 coincide v. 일치하다; 동시에 일어나다 significance n. 의의, 의미; 중요성 economy n. 절약, 검약; 효율적 사용; 경제 security n. 안전, 안심; 보안 aesthetics n. <철학> 미학(美學) logistics n. <군사> 병참술, 병참학; (업무의) 세부 계획

사람들은 도시가 역할을 효율적으로 수행하는 것과 아름다움은 거의 관련이 없다고 매우 잘못 생각하는 경향이 있다. 그러나 경찰이 안고 있는 가장 큰 골칫거리는 도시에서 가장 구질구질한 구역과 대단히 자주 일치한다. 도시를 설계할 때, 다른 여러 가지 중에서 사회적으로 매우 중요한 것은 설계되는 그 거리들의 미적(美的) 측면이다.

16　　　④

'too ~ to …' 구문에 부정의 의미가 내포되어 있음에 유의한다. to give 이하의 내용은 '변화의 요소를 제공해 주지 못한다'라는 말인데, 변화가 없다는 것은 종전과 동일하다는 것이므로, 결국 '독서와 정신노동자들의 일상적인 일과가 다르지 않다'라는 맥락이 된다. 그러므로 '~와 유사하다'라는 의미의 ④가 정답이다.

diversion n. 딴 데로 돌림, 전환; (자금의) 유용; 기분 전환, 오락 vast a. 광대한, 거대한, 막대한 varied a. 가지각색의; 다채로운 defect n. 결점, 결함; 부족 brainworker n. 정신노동자, 두뇌노동자 element n. 요소, 성분, 구성 요소; 원소 indifferent a. 무관심한, 냉담한 in the power of ~에 좌우되는 akin a. 혈족의; 같은 종류의

가장 일반적인 기분전환의 형태는 책을 읽는 것이다. 그 광활하고 다채로운 벌판에서, 수많은 사람들이 정신적인 위안을 얻는다. 그러나, 독서는 한 가지 중요한 결점을 갖고 있다. 즉, 책은 정신노동자들의 일상적인 일과 너무나도 유사하기 때문에, 꼭 필요한 변화의 요소를 실생활에 제공해 줄 수 없다는 것이다.

17　　　④

첫 번째 빈칸 다음의 when절이 지각인식 주장의 근거가 희박함을 의미하므로 첫 번째 빈칸에는 skepticism(회의, 의심)이 적절하다. 한편, or 다음의 when절도 그 앞의 when절처럼 부정적이어야 하므로 두 번째 빈칸에는 untried(시험해보지 않은, 확인되지 않은)가 적절하다. 따라서 ④가 정답이다.

perceptual recognition 지각인식(신체감각으로 하는 인식) challenge n. 이의, 도전 transcend v. 초월하다 sense modality 감각 양상(양식) optimism n. 낙관 immature a. 미숙한 cynicism n. 냉소 certified a. 증명된 pragmatism n. 실용 routine a. 틀에 박힌 skepticism n. 회의, 의심 untried a. 시험해보지 않은, 확인되지 않은

따분한 일상생활에서 지각인식의 주장들은 언제든 이의가 제기될 수 있으며 그 주장들이 그 주장들을 기초로 하여 알게 될 것으로 합리적으로 예상할 수 있는 것이 아니거나 그 주장들 자체가 확인되지 않은 감각양상에 기초해 있을 때는 회의적으로 다루어져야 한다.

18 　　　　　　　　　　　　　　　②

because절에서 변화의 시기를 살아간다고 했으므로 뉴스에 대해 즉, 새로운 혹은 달라진 점에 대해 계속 잘 알고 있어야 할 것이다. 따라서 '계속 정통하다'라는 의미의 ②가 정답으로 적절하다.

historic a. 역사적으로 중요한 impact n. 영향 look askance at 곁눈질(의심의 눈길)을 보내다 stay on top of ~에 계속 정통하다 turn a deaf ear to 들으려고 하지 않다 put a new face on 면목을 일신하다

시간은 귀중하고 그래서 사람들은 분주하다. 우리는 피할 수 없고 무시할 수 없는 엄청난 영향을 미치는 사건들이 일어나는 가운데 역사적 변화의 시기를 살아가고 있기 때문에 뉴스에 정통하고 있어야 한다는 것을 모두 알고 있다.

19 　　　　　　　　　　　　　　　③

but 이하의 문장은 앞 문장의 The inaccuracy of the testimony에 관해 부연 설명하는 역할을 한다. 따라서 첫 번째 빈칸에는 문맥상 inaccuracy와 동일한 의미를 가질 수 있는 단어가 들어가야 한다. falsehood 또는 distortion이 가능하다. 한편, 두 번째 빈칸에 들어갈 단어는 뒤에 주어진 전체 문장의 내용을 통해 찾아야 한다. '증언의 왜곡이나 부정확성이 사건에 대한 목격자의 독특한 재해석 방법에 의한 것이고, 그러한 재해석 방법은 그가 살아온 과정이 영향을 미친다'라는 내용인데, 이 말을 뒤집어 생각하면, '개인의 살아온 과정을 알면 사건의 재해석 방법을 알 수 있고, 사건의 재해석 방법을 알면 왜 증언이 부정확했는지를 알 수 있다'라는 것이 된다. 그러므로 부정확한 증언도 일정한 규칙과 연유가 있다는 결론이 도출되며, 빈칸 앞에 부정어 not이 있으므로, '무작위의, 임의의'라는 의미의 random이 두 번째 빈칸에 적절하다.

inaccuracy n. 부정확, 정밀하지 않음; 잘못, 틀림 testimony n. 증언; 증거, 증명 eyewitness n. 목격자, 증인 falsehood n. 허위; 틀린 생각, 거짓말 exhaustive a. 고갈시키는, 소모적인; 총망라한, 철저한 credibility n. 신용, 신뢰성 mandatory a. 의무적인, 강제적인 distortion n. 왜곡; 곡해 random a. 되는 대로의, 임의의 confidentiality n. 기밀성, 비밀유지 persuasive a. 설득력 있는, 구변이 좋은

목격자가 하는 증언이 부정확하다는 것은 법률 심리학에서 잘 알려져 있다. 그러나 그러한 왜곡은 임의적인 것이 아니다. 그것은 당연히 목격자가 사용했던 독특한 사건의 재해석 방법으로부터 나오는 것이며, 그가 사용한 독특한 사건의 재해석 방법은 그가 어떤 삶을 살아왔느냐에 좌우된다.

20 　　　　　　　　　　　　　　　③

strove to preserve와 was careful not to break라 했으므로 첫 번째 빈칸에는 delicate(깨지기 쉬운)가 적절하고, doing so가 아름다운 영역을 깨뜨리는 것을 가리키는데 이것은 순수함과 호기심을 없앨 것이므로 두 번째 빈칸에는 snuff out(소멸시키다)나 scrape out(문질러 지우다)가 적절하다.

innocence n. 순진, 무구 realm n. 영역 purity n. 순수함 curiosity n. 호기심 antique a. 골동품의 sort out 가려내다 glazed a. 유약이 칠해진 spell out 명확히 설명하다 delicate a. 깨지기 쉬운 snuff out 소멸시키다 chipped a. 이가 빠진 scrape out 문질러서 지우다

그는 어린 소녀의 순진무구함을 깨지기 쉬운 도자기처럼 다루었다. 그는 믿음, 사랑, 미, 친절 등 모든 좋은 것을 가능한 한 오래도록 보존하려 애썼다. 그는 어린아이다운 경이의 이 아름다운 영역을 깨뜨리지 않으려 조심했다. 왜냐하면, 그렇게 하는 것은 어린 시절의 본질인 순수함과 호기심을 소멸시킬 것이기 때문이었다.

21 　　　　　　　　　　　　　　　④

첫 번째 문장은 양지와 어두움은 아무 선입견이 없는 아이에게는 똑같이 무섭지 않은 것이라는 말이므로 두 번째 문장은 어두움과 관련한 무서운 이야기로 어두움을 양지와 구별 지어서는 안 된다는 말이 되어야 한다. 따라서 빈칸에는 ④가 적절하다. 빈칸 다음의 them은 양지와 어두움을 가리킨다.

limitation n. 제한, 한정 illumination n. 조명 distinction n. 구별, 차별

아이들은 혼자 두면 넓은 양지에서와 마찬가지로 어두움에서도 무서워할 수 없을 것이다. 그들은 놀기 위해 후자(양지)를 환영하는 만큼 잠자기 위해 전자(어두움)를 환영할 것이다. 후자(양지)보다 전자(어두움)에서 더 많은 위험과 끔찍한 일이 일어난다는 이야기로 이 둘을 구별해서는 안 된다.

22 　　　　　　　　　　　　　　　④

빈칸을 포함하고 있는 마지막 문장은 글 전체의 결론에 해당하며, not A but B 구문이 쓰였음에 유념해야 한다. not A but B 구문에서 A와 B에는 대조를 이루는 표현이 오는데, A에 해당하는 how much we know how to do는 첫 번째 문장의 the ability 이하의 내용을 의미하므로, 빈칸에는 두 번째 문장의 a style of life, a way of behaving in various situations와 동일한 의미를 나타내는 표현이 들어가야 함을 짐작할 수 있다. 따라서 정답은 ④가 된다.

intelligence n. 지성; 이해력; 정보 indicator n. 표시기; 지표 behave v. 행동하다, 예절 바르게 행동하다 various a. 가지가지의, 여러 가지의; 여러 방면의 test n. 시험; (판단·평가의) 기준, 시금석 improve v. 개량하다, 개선하다, 향상시키다

지능에 대해 이야기할 때, 우리는 어떤 종류의 시험에서 좋은 점수를 받을 수 있는 능력이나 심지어 학업을 잘 해나갈 수 있는 능력의 뜻으로 말하는 것이 아니다. 이런 것들은 기껏해야 더 크고 더 깊으며 훨씬 더 중요한 어떤 것을 나타내 주는 표지에 불과하다. 지능이라고 하면 그것은 하나의 생활양식, 다양한 상황에서의 행동 방식을 의미한다. 지능을 판별하는 진정한 시금석은 어떤 일의 수행 방식을 얼마나 많이 알고 있느냐가 아니라 어찌 해야 할 지 모르는 상황에서 어떻게 행동하느냐 하는 것이다.

23 ③

rather than으로 연결되므로 첫 빈칸에는 calm(진정시키다)과 반대 의미의 jangle(소란케 하다)이 적절하고, 진정효과가 무엇 때문인가를 설명하고 있으므로 두 번째 빈칸에는 '진정제'라는 의미의 sedative나 tranquilizer가 적절하다.

jitter n. 신경과민, 초조감 nerve n. 신경, 용기 ritual n. 의식, 반드시 지키는 일 conditioned a. 조건반사적인(자동적으로 일어나는) toughen v. 강하게 하다 cushion v. 완화하다 jangle v. 소란케 하다 enervate v. 약화시키다 panacea n. 만병통치약

차(茶)에는 신경과민을 일으키는 카페인이 들어있지만 차가 신경을 소란케 하기보다 진정시키는 것 같은 때가 분명히 있다. 차를 만들어 마시는 일에 의지하는 것이 스트레스가 많은 때에 일어나는 거의 조건반사적인 반응이 되었다. 그러나 그 진정효과는 차의 화학적인 면과 무관할지 모른다. 한 잔의 차를 천연 진정제가 되게 하는 것은 차를 만들어 마시는 일 자체와 그와 연관된 사회적인 측면들이다.

24 ②

첫 번째 문장의 내용을 두 번째 문장과 세 번째 문장에서 부연설명하고 있는 구조이다. 두 번째 문장과 세 번째 문장은 각각 디플레이션 시기에 '이득을 얻는' 채권자와 고정 수입자에 대한 내용이므로, 빈칸에는 '이득을 얻는 것'과 관련된 내용이 들어가야 한다. 이러한 의미를 가진 것은 ②뿐이다. 한편, 두 번째 문장과 세 번째 문장이 동일한 맥락이므로, 두 번째 문장의 gets back more purchasing power와 동일한 의미를 가지는 표현을 찾는 방식으로 접근하는 것도 가능하다.

deflation n. 통화 수축, 디플레이션 creditor n. 채권자 fixed a. 고정된, 일정한 at the expense of ~의 비용으로; ~을 희생하여 debtor n. 채무자 purchasing power 구매력 income n. 수입, 소득

디플레이션 시기에는 채권자와 고정 수입을 받는 사람들이 채무자와 수익을 받는 사람들 덕택으로 이득을 얻게 되는 경향이 있다. 만약 채권자가 돈을 빌려준 시기와 그 돈을 상환 받는 시기 사이에 물가가 하락한다면, 그는 빌려준 돈보다 더 많은 구매력을 얻게 된다. 계속 일을 하면서 월급이 깎이지 않은 교사는 자신의 실질적인 수입이 증가했다는 것을 알 것이다.

25 ④

빈칸이 들어 있는 문장의 주어가 '조작하는 사람'이므로 그가 하는 행위는 '조작' 혹은 '인위적으로 만들어내는 행위'일 것이다. 이러한 의미를 가지고 있는 것은 ④뿐이며, engineer가 manipulate와 같은 의미로 쓰였다.

acquainted a. 아는, 아는 사이인; 정통한 various a. 가지각색의; 여러 가지의 philosophy n. 철학 marvel v. 놀라다, 감탄하다 suit v. ~에 적합하다, 어울리다 dominant a. 지배적인; 유력한; 현저한 manipulator n. 교묘히 다루는 사람, 조종자 dissenter n. 불찬성자, 반대자 introduce v. 받아들이다, 수입하다, 도입하다 consent n. 동의, 허가, 승낙

다양한 철학을 알게 되면 알게 될수록, 인간 정신이 이들 철학을 이용하여 그 정신의 특별한 동기에 적합한 것을 만들어내는 능력에 감탄하게 된다. 중국의 지배적인 철학이 어떤 것이었던 간에 여론의 조작자들은 그들의 사상에 동의하도록 조종할 수 있었을 것이라는 게 나의 생각이다. 공자의 사상을 모택동의 가르침에 대한 길잡이로 제시하는 것이 그리 어려운 것은 아니라고 생각한다.

01 ①	02 ①	03 ④	04 ②	05 ②	06 ④	07 ①	08 ④	09 ③	10 ④
11 ③	12 ②	13 ③	14 ①	15 ②	16 ①	17 ②	18 ③	19 ④	20 ②
21 ③	22 ③	23 ②	24 ③	25 ②					

01 ①

cabins in forests를 수식하는 형용사로는 '전원의, 목가적인'을 뜻하는 ①이 의미상 가장 적절하다.

chalet n. 샬레, 오두막 bucolic a. 전원의 gaudy a. 야한, 천박한 sumptuous a. 사치스러운, 화려한 dilapidated a. 황폐해진, 황폐

뻐꾸기 시계에 대해 생각할 때, 사람들은 숲속에 있는 전원의 오두막 또는 산중턱에 있는 조용한 목조 주택 안에 있는 정교하게 나무로 만들어진 시계의 이미지를 상상할지도 모른다.

02 ①

우리를 구속할 수 없는 것에 우리가 예속되었다고 느끼듯이 우리가 마음대로 할(지배할) 수 있는 것 앞에서 그것을 아무렇게도 할 수 없다는 무력감을 느낀다는 뜻이므로 빈칸에는 ①이 적절하다.

enslave v. 예속시키다 bind v. 구속하다, 속박하다 powerless a. 무력한 dominion n. 지배 qualm n. 불안, 주저함 obeisance n. 복종, 경의 patronage n. 후원, 보호

우리는 우리를 구속할 수 없어야 할 여러 조건에 예속된 느낌이 들고 우리가 지배할 능력을 가진(지배할 수 있게 된) 여러 세력 앞에 무력감을 느낀다.

03 ④

주절에서 긍정적으로 charming이라 했으므로 역접의 though절에서는 brusque와 over-serious처럼 부정적인 의미의 ④가 빈칸에 적절하다.

royal watcher 왕실연구가 brusque a. 퉁명스러운 aide n. 보좌관 winsome a. 매력 있는 jocund a. 명랑한 plucky a. 용기 있는 cantankerous a. 심술궂은

찰스 왕세자는, 비록 그가 또한 심술궂고, 때로로 보좌관들에 대해 퉁명하고, 지나치게 진지하다고 왕실연구가들은 말하지만, 매력적일 수도 있다.

04 ②

콤마 이하의 'so ~ that …' 구문 앞에는 being이 생략되어 있으며, 콤마 이하는 앞 문장에 대한 부연설명이다. 그러므로 빈칸에는 all-knowing과 같은 의미를 가진 단어가 들어가야 하며, ②가 정답이 된다.

all-knowing a. 모든 것을 아는 dissident a. 의견을 달리하는 omniscient a. 전지의, 무엇이든지 알고 있는 interim a. 중간의; 임시의 unctuous a. 상냥한, (사람을) 살살 녹이는; (겉으로만) 열심인 체 하는

조지 오웰(George Orwell)의 저명한 소설 『1984』에서 '빅 브라더'는 그가 통제하는 세상에서 사생활이 전혀 존재하지 않을 정도로 모든 것을 알고 있는 전지전능한 정치 지도자이다.

05 ②

that is 혹은 that is to say 뒤에는 앞 문장에 대해 부연설명하는 내용이 오므로, 빈칸에서부터 used까지는 바로 앞의 morally neutral을 부연설명 혹은 재진술하는 내용이어야 한다. 그런데 to the value of the ends for which the means are used가 morally의 의미와 호응하므로, 빈칸에는 neutral과 문맥상 유사한 의미를 가지는 단어가 들어가야 한다. 중립적이라는 것은 어느 편도 들지 않는 것이므로, 어느 쪽에도 관심이 없다는 것과 일맥상통한다. 따라서 ②가 정답이 된다.

morally ad. 도덕적으로; 사실상 neutral a. 중립적인, 어느 편도 들지 않는; 불편부당한 means n. 방법, 수단 differential a. 구별이 되는, 차별적인; 특이한 indifferent a. 무관심한, 마음에 두지 않는, 냉담한 intertwined a. 뒤얽힌, 밀접하게 관련된 officious a. 참견하는, 간섭하는

과학 자체는 도덕적으로 중립적일 뿐 아니라, 다시 말해 수단을 사용하는 목적의 가치에 대해 관심이 없을 뿐만 아니라, 도덕적으로 그 어떤 방향도 제시할 수 없다.

06 ④

that 관계절의 내용이 기존의 것을 다시 생각해보게 만든 것이라 했는데, 다시 생각해보아야 한다는 것은 그만큼 기존의 것이 낙후된 것임을 말하며 이 기술이 기존의 것을 파괴하는 셈이므로 빈칸에는 ④가 적절하다.

podcasting n. 팟캐스팅(아이팟(iPod)과 방송(broadcasting)이 결합된 신조어로, 컴퓨터와 휴대용 미디어 플레이어를 이용하여 정기적으로 배달되는 오디오, 비디오 형태의 방송을 청취할 수 있는 기술) reconsider v. 다시 생각해보다, 재고하다 preconception n. 선입견 conventional a. 전통적인 declining a. 쇠퇴하는 있는 precarious a. 불확실한; 위험한 disruptive a. 파괴적인, 와해성의

팟캐스팅은 일부 라디오 방송 사업 관계자들로 하여금 시청자들, 소비, 생산, 분배 등에 관한 일부 기존의 관행들과 선입견들을 다시 생각해보게 만든 와해성(혁신) 기술이다.

---

07 ①

전치사 to 이하에 쓰인 both A and B 구문에는 와인 서적이 도움이 될 사람을 크게 두 개의 부류로 나눈 단어가 들어가야 한다. and 이하에서 '경험이 많은 전문가'를 언급하고 있으므로 and 앞 부분은 '경험이 일천한 초심자'가 되는 것이 적절하다. 그러므로 expert의 반의어인 ①이 정답이 된다.

amiable a. 호감을 주는; 붙임성 있는; 상냥한 comprehensive a. 포괄적인; 이해가 빠른 overview n. 개관, 개략 experienced a. 경험 많은, 노련한 connoisseur n. 감식가, 전문가 novice n. 풋내기; 초보, 무경험자 miser n. 구두쇠 zealot n. 광신자 glutton n. 대식가, 폭식가; 열성가

친근한 문체로 쓰인 그 책은 유럽산 와인에 관해 포괄적인 개요(槪要)를 제시하고 있는데, 이것은 사실상의 초보자나 경험 많은 감식가 모두의 마음을 끌게 될 것이다.

---

08 ④

두 번째 문장에서 and 전후는 원인과 결과의 관계에 있으며, see the whole world as a source of a work of art가 문맥상 의미하는 것은 첫 번째 문장의 make art out of everyday junk이다. 결국, and 이하의 문장은 '많은 다른 예술가들이 그 유명 예술가처럼 일상의 쓰레기로부터 예술을 창조해 내고 있다'라는 것이 되고, 이는 그의 예술품 제작 기법이 다른 이들에게 전해졌다는 것을 뜻한다. 따라서 빈칸에는 '다른 이들에게 퍼져나간다'라는 의미를 가지고 있는 단어가 필요하며, ④가 이러한 의미를 가진 단어이다.

junk n. 쓰레기; 잡동사니; 폐물 blunt a. 무딘; 둔감한; 퉁명스러운 obdurate a. 완고한, 고집센 protean a. 변화무쌍한; 다방면의 contagious a. 전염성의; 전파하는; 만연하는

그 예술가는 거리에서 발견한 일상생활의 쓰레기로부터 작품을 만드는 것으로 유명했다. 사물을 바라보는 그의 시각은 전파력이 있었으며, 이제는 많은 다른 예술가들도 온 세상을 예술 작품의 원천으로 여기고 있다.

---

09 ③

접속사 while이 이끄는 절의 의미는 주절과 대조를 이룬다는 점에 착안한다. while절에서는 이리저리 흔들리는 성격에 대해 말하고 있으므로, 빈칸에는 굳은 의지를 나타내는 표현이 들어가야 할 것이다. 따라서 정답은 '불요불굴의'라는 뜻의 ③이며, 결국 be tossed about와 반대되는 의미의 단어를 찾는 문제라고 할 수 있다.

complexity n. 복잡성; 복잡한 일 personality n. 개성, 인격; 성격 be tossed about 흔들리다 bird n. 배드민턴의 공, 셔틀콕 corpulent a. 뚱뚱한, 살찐, 비만한 fastidious a. 까다로운, 괴팍스러운 indomitable a. 불요불굴의, 요지부동의 munificent a. 인색하지 않은, 아낌없이 주는

우리는 사람의 성격의 복잡함을 거의 이해하지 못하고 있다. 예를 들어, 우리는 왜 어떤 사람들은 어려서부터 의지가 굳은 반면 또 다른 사람들은 배드민턴 경기의 공처럼 일이 생길 때마다 흔들리는지를 정말로 알지 못한다.

---

10 ④

비행기 추락시의 충격으로 인해 사망자의 시신은 온전하지 못해 사진을 잘못 찍으면 사망자의 인간으로서의 존엄을 해치기가 쉽다. 따라서 첫 번째 빈칸에는 '해치다'는 의미의 offending이나 insulting이나 harming이 적절하고, 추락사고 현장 사진이므로 두 번째 빈칸에는 bleak(황폐한)나 somber(음울한)가 적절하다

impress v. 감명을 주다 breathtaking a. 깜짝 놀랄만한 posthumous a. 사후의 dignity n. 존엄 aircraft crash 비행기 추락 uphold v. 지지하다 bleak a. 황폐한 offend v. 해치다 flippant a. 경박한 ensure v. 보증하다 luminous a. 빛나는 insult v. 모욕하다; 해치다 somber a. 음울한 harm v. 해치다 methodical a. 질서정연한

그가 찍은 사진은 나에게 깊은 감명을 준다. 그 사진들은 사망자의 사후 존엄을 해치지 않으면서도 깜짝 놀랄만하다. 비행기 추락사고 현장을 찍은 이 음울한 사진들이 그 현장에 대한 그 어떤 다른 분석보다 더 훌륭하며 더 깊이가 있다.

---

11 ③

but 앞에서 개선해야할 단점에 관심이 집중되는 것은 당연하다고 했으므로 빈칸에는 장점도 즐기라는 내용이 들어가야 한다. 따라서 '가장 특기할 점을 즐기다'라는 의미의 ③이 정답으로 적절하다.

attract v. 마음을 끌다 draw in 끌어들이다, 꾀어 들이다 shrug off the magnets 자석(마음을 끄는 것)을 떨쳐버리다 dwell on the drawbacks 단점에 대해 곰곰이 생각하다 revel in the highlights 가장 특기할 점을 즐기다 grope for the hidden blots 숨겨진 흠을 찾다

당신의 집을 본 순간 마음에 드는 점이 무엇이었나? 양지바른 마당이었나, 매혹적인 베란다였나, 원목 마룻바닥이었나? 일단 거기 들어와 살면 개선할 점에 관심이 집중되는 것은 당연하지만, 당신을 거기로 끌어들였던 가장 특기할 점들을 즐길 것도 꼭 기억하라.

12   ②

마지막 문장의 내용이 단서가 된다. 경찰이 무장을 함으로써 범죄자들도 무장을 하게 된다는 것이므로, 이것은 나쁜 현상이 되풀이되는 것이다. 따라서 빈칸에는 '악순환'이라는 의미의 ②가 들어가는 것이 적절하다.

organization n. 조직; 구성, 편제 armed a. 무기를 소지한; 무장한 criminal n. 범인, 범죄자 encounter v. 우연히 만나다, 마주치다, 조우하다 silver lining 구름의 흰 가장자리; 밝은 희망[전망] vicious circle 악순환 rule of thumb 어림짐작, 경험에 바탕을 둔 방법 pat on the back 격려의 말, 칭찬의 말

근무 중에 무장을 하고 있는 경관의 수가 점점 늘어나는 것에 대해 우려하고 있다고 뉴욕 경찰청장이 말했다. "물론 경찰도 자신을 보호하길 원하겠지만, 사실은 이것은 악순환입니다. 무장한 경찰을 만나게 될 것이라 생각하는 범죄자들이 무기를 가지고 다니게 될 가능성이 더 높아지기 때문입니다."

13   ③

by 이하의 such a thought가 가리키는 것은 앞 문장의 내용, 즉 '해리가 부자가 됐을 때면 자신과 남편은 이미 죽고 없을 것이라는 생각'이다. 자신이 커서 엄마를 호강시켜 주겠다는 아들의 말에 위와 같은 대답을 한다면 그것은 아들의 기를 꺾게 될 것이다. 따라서 빈칸에 가장 적절한 단어는 ③이다.

faintly ad. 희미하게, 힘없이 churchyard n. (교회에 부속되어 있는) 묘지 youthful a. 젊은, 발랄한; 젊은이 특유의 enthusiasm n. 열심, 열중; 열광, 의욕 utterance n. 발언; 말씨, 어조 uplift v. 양양하다 ignite v. 점화하다; 흥분시키다 dampen v. 적시다; 풀이 죽게 하다, 기를 꺾다 enliven v. 활기차게 하다, 기운을 돋우다

"제가 부자가 되면, 엄마는 더 이상 일을 안 해도 될 거예요"라고 해리(Harry)는 말했다. 엄마는 힘없이 미소 지을 뿐, 기대하지는 않았다. 해리가 부자가 되기도 전에 남편과 자신은 마을 교회 묘지에 묻혀 영면을 취하고 있을 것 같은 생각이 들었다. 그러나 그런 생각을 입 밖에 내어 해리의 젊은 열정을 꺾어놓고 싶지는 않았다.

14   ①

기소를 구해야 할 검사가 이상하게 보이는 상황이 빈칸에 와야 한다. 검사가 피고인 측 변호사처럼 보이는 것이 이상한 것이다.

protest n. 항의[반대, 이의], 시위 indictment n. 기소 testimony n. 증언 grand jury 대배심 eerily ad. 섬뜩하게, 기분 나쁘게 a defense attorney 피고인 측 변호사(법정 대리인) biased a. 치우친 victim n. 희생자, 피해자 suspect n. 용의자

심각한 그 시위는 검사가 기소를 구하는 그의 역할을 잘 수행했느냐 몹시 부적절하게 했느냐에 관한 것이었다. 왜 그는 그러한 조치를 취하였는가? 왜 그는 윌슨이 대배심 앞에서 증언을 하였을 때 적극적으로 그를 심문하지 않았는가? 왜 이상하게도 그는 결과를 발표할 때 마치 피고인 측 변호사처럼 보였는가?

15   ②

Or의 전후로 서로 다른 모습을 보이는 자아의 측면을 이야기하고 있다. 빈칸이 when절에 속해 있으므로, 앞 문장의 when절의 내용과 대조를 이루는 표현을 찾으면 된다. Or 앞 문장의 when절에서는 '술에 취했을 때나 격분했을 때, 혹은 완전히 지쳤을 때'를 이야기하고 있는데, 이것과 대조를 이루는 것으로는 '절주; 절제; 냉정, 침착' 등의 의미를 가진 ②가 적절하다.

argument n. 논의, 논증, 논거 ponder v. 숙고하다, 깊이 생각하다, 곰곰이 생각하다 authentic a. 진짜의; 믿을 만한 rude a. 버릇없는, 무례한 bigoted a. 편협한, 고집불통의 enrage v. 격분시키다, 노하게 하다 exhausted a. 다 써 버린, 소모된; 지친 tamp v. 다져서 굳히다, 눌러 담다 unsavory a. 고약한; 불쾌한; (도덕적으로) 불미스러운 impulse n. 충동; 추진력, 자극 insistency n. 주장, 고집, 강조; 강요 sobriety n. 절주; 절제; 냉정, 침착 convulsion n. 경련; 격동, 변동 snit n. 흥분, 흥분상태, 초조

그 논쟁은 흥미로운 것이며, 심리학자들이 오랫동안 숙고해온 것이다. 참된 자아는 누구인가? 우리가 술에 취했을 때나 격분했을 때, 혹은 완전히 지쳤을 때 나타나는 그 무례하거나 편협한 자아인가? 아니면 다른 99퍼센트의 시간 동안의 자아, 즉 스스로의 고약한 충동을 내리누르도록 해주는 침착함이 드러날 때의 자아인가?

16   ①

The local poll은 지금 막 치러진 선거이고 national elections는 미래의 선거이므로 빈칸에는 '서곡', '전조'라는 의미의 ①이 적절하다.

contest v. 경쟁하다, 겨루다 boycott v. 배척하다, 참가를 거부하다 poll n. 투표 worrying a. 걱정 되는 lock up 가두다, 구금하다 prelude n. 서곡, 전조 replica n. 복사, 복제 profile n. 윤곽 attestation n. 증거 epitome n. 축도, 전형

탄자니아의 집권당은 야당이 정부를 선거조작혐의로 고소하며 거부한 지방 선거에서 경쟁을 벌인 전체 의석 중 99%를 차지했다. 그 지방 선거 투표는 내년에 있을 전국 선거에 대한 걱정스런 서곡이다. 정부는 야당 당원들과 기자들을 구금했다.

17   ②

두 번째 문장의 independent judgment는 다른 사람들의 생각이나 사회적 통념에서 벗어난 독립적인 판단이므로 사회적 편견에서 벗어난 것이라 할 수 있다. 따라서 첫 번째 빈칸에는 prejudice(편견)가 적절하고, 편견에서 벗어나지 못해 민주주의가 잘 작동하지 않는다는 것은 혼란을 의미하므로 두 번째 빈칸에는 shambles(혼란)나 shreds(산산조각)가 적절하다. 따라서 ②가 정답이다.

enlightened a. 계몽된 electorate n. 유권자 free of ~가 없는 ingrained a. 뿌리 깊은 as it is 사실, 실제로는 consumerism n. 소비자중심주의, 소비자운동 drown v. 익사시키다, 압도하다 ignorance n. 무지(無知) cradle n. 요람 prejudice n. 편견 shambles n. 도살장, 난장판, 혼란 insolence n. 오만 fetter n. 속박 temperance n. 절제 shred n. 조각, 파편

민주주의는 유권자들이 계몽되어 뿌리 깊은 편견이 없는 경우에만 제대로 작동한다. 실제로는, 소비자운동이 사람들의 독자적인 판단 능력을 말살시켰다. 그 결과, 민주주의는 미국과 호주에서뿐 아니라 일본과 유럽에서도 혼란에 빠져있다.

---

18 ③

restricting the business to owner-drivers에 반대되게 첫 번째 빈칸에는 liberalize(자유화하다)가 적절하고, which 관계절의 동사가 가정법 형태인 것에서 알 수 있듯이 실현되지 못한 제안이므로 두 번째 빈칸에는 dumped(버렸다)가 적절하다.

illustrate v. 설명하다, 예시하다 cabby n. 택시운전사 bring to a halt 정지시키다, 멈추게 하다 blockade v. 봉쇄하다 parliamentarian n. 국회의원 fleet n. 함대, 선단, 회사 전체 차량 privatize v. 민영화하다 skip v. 거르다, 빠뜨리다 boost v. 후원하다 buttress v. 보강하다 liberalize v. 자유롭게 하다 dump v. 버리다 demarcate v. 한계를 정하다 reinstate v. 원상회복시키다

택시영업을 자유화하자는 최근의 한 제안은 이태리에서 개혁에 대한 저항이 얼마나 강할 수 있는가를 잘 보여준다. 화가 난 택시운전사들은 도로를 봉쇄하여 로마를 마비시켰다. 의회 의원들은 결국 제안의 가장 중요한 부분을 폐기했는데, 택시영업을 자가 운전자에 국한시키지 않고 거대한 택시 회사들의 탄생을 가능하게 했을 제안이었다.

---

19 ④

세포벽이 얇을 때 소리가 자유롭게 이동할 것이므로 첫 번째 빈칸에는 thinning(얇아지게 하는 것)이 적절하고 성가신 소리를 제거하는 것은 그런 소리를 죽이는 것이므로 두 번째 빈칸에는 stifling(질식시키는)이나 dampening(풀죽게 하는)이 적절하다.

fungus n. 곰팡이 spruce n. 가문비나무, 전나무 top plate 상판 resonant a. 울리는, 공명하는 soften v. 물렁하게 하다 amplify v. 증폭시키다 thicken v. 두껍게 하다 stifle v. 질식시키다 harden v. 단단하게 하다 buoy v. 띄우다 thin v. 얇아지게 하다 dampen v. 풀죽게 하다

곰팡이는 바이올린 상판을 만드는 데 사용되는 유일한 목재인 노르웨이 전나무의 세포벽을 얇아지게 하여 소리가 더 자유롭게 움직일 수 있도록 해줄 수 있다. 무게가 더 가볍다는 것은 음색이 더 크고 더 울린다는 것을 의미한다. 곰팡이는 또한 너무 높은 성가신 소리를 제거하여, 소리를 죽이는 목재의 기능을 배로 증대시킨다.

---

20 ②

포스터를 거는 과정에서 전체 사용량이 줄었다고 한 것은 서로 비교하는 것이 효과적임을 말하므로 첫 번째 빈칸에는 overleap(무시하다)나 underrate(과소평가하다)가 적절하고, 서로 비교해서 더 나은 다른 사람의 행동을 따라하는 것이 더 큰 발전을 가져다주므로 두 번째 빈칸에는 canny(영리한, 좋은)나 impeccable(나무랄 데 없는)이 적절하다.

hanger n. (상점 안의) 포스터 undermine v. 저해하다, 몰래 손상시키다 fatuous a. 어리석은 overleap v. 저해하다 canny a. 어리석은 underrate v. 과소평가하다 chancy a. 불확실한, 위험한 overblow v. 과대평가하다 impeccable a. 나무랄 데 없는

우리는 사람들을 그들의 동료와 비교하는 것의 영향력 있는 효과를 무시해서는 안 된다. 한 에너지 회사는 사원들이 각자 얼마나 많은 에너지를 사용하는지를 비교해볼 수 있도록 사무실 문에 월별 사용량 포스터를 걸었는데, 그 과정이 전체 사용량을 3.5% 감소시켰다. 진화론적으로는 우리 주위의 사람들이 비슷한 상황에서 한 행동을 하는 것이 좋다.

---

21 ③

버트런드 러셀과 그의 말을 인용한 필자의 요지는, 사람들이 벌이고 있는 경쟁은 흔히 '생존 경쟁'과 동의어인 것처럼 여겨지고 있지만 사실은 그렇지 않으며, 단지 '다른 사람과의 경쟁에서 질지도 모른다'는 두려움 때문에 타인과의 경쟁에 뛰어들고 있다는 것이다. 그러므로 빈칸에는 '~와의 경쟁에서 이기다'는 의미의 표현이 들어가는 것이 적절하다.

misrepresent v. 잘못 표현하다, 와전하다 disguise v. 가장하다; 꾸미다, 속이다 outshine v. ~보다 더 뛰어나다 taunt v. 놀리다, 조롱하다 spare v. (불쾌한 일을) 모면하게 해주다 dismiss v. (사람들을) 물러가게 하다, 해산시키다

우리는 때때로 경쟁하려는 충동을 생존의 기본 욕구인 것처럼 가장함으로써 경쟁을 잘못 표현한다. 오래 전에 버트런드 러셀(Bertrand Russell)은 "종종 생존 경쟁인 것으로 불리는 그것은 실제로는 성공을 위한 경쟁적 분투일 뿐이다. 사람들이 그 분투에 가담할 때 두려워하는 것은 그들이 다음 날 아침 먹을 것을 구하지 못할 수도 있다는 것이 아니라, 그들의 이웃보다 더 뛰어나지 못할지도 모른다는 것이다."라고 지적했다.

---

22 ③

역접(But then) 이전의 주제어는 '독서에 대한 열정'이지만, 역접의 접속사 이후에는 '다시는 책을 읽고 싶지 않았다'라고 했으므로 독서에 대한 일종의 '반감, 혐오, 거부감'이 생긴 것이라고 추론할 수 있다.

take hold 대단히 강력해지다 devour v. 게걸스럽게 먹어 치우다 mandatory a. 의무적인 capitulation n. 항복 penchant n. 취미, 성향 deferment n. 연기 repulsion n. 반감, 혐오 relish n. 즐거움; 흥미

크리스티나 치푸리치(Cristina Chipurici)는 4살 때 읽는 것을 독학했다. 새로 발견한 열정이 강렬해졌을 때, 그녀는 부모님의 집에 있는 모든 책을 다 읽어버렸다. 그런데 그때 무슨 일이 일어났다. "내가 초등학교에 입학하고 독서가 의무화되자, 나는 우리 담당 언어 선생님 때문에 그 활동에 대한 거부감을 갖게 되었고, 그 때문에 다시는 책을 읽고 싶지 않았다."라고 그녀는 말한다.

capital punishment 사형 racial a. 인종의, 민족의 prejudice n. 편견, 선입관
execute v. 실행하다, 실시하다; 처형하다 unjustly ad. 부당하게; 부정하게
deserve v. ~할 만하다, 받을 만한 가치가 있다 sentence n. 판결, 선고 valid
a. 정당한 근거가 있는, 확실한, 타당한 ethical a. 윤리적인, 도덕상의 trivial a.
하찮은, 사소한; 대수롭지 않은

흑인에 대해 상당한 인종적인 편견이 있었고 사형을 당한 대부분의 사람들
은 흑인이었다는 이유로 사형을 반대하는 주장을 하는 사람들이 더러 있다.
많은 사례에 있어 사형제도가 부당하게 이용되었다는 것은 의심할 바 없다.
그러나 오늘날 인종적 편견은 그다지 크지 않다. 사형은 그러한 판결을 받을
만한 모든 사람에게 적용될 수 있다. 1947년 이후 사형 집행된 47명 가운
데 흑인은 17명뿐이었다. 흑인으로서, 나는 인종편견 주장은 더 이상 타당
하지 않다고 생각한다.

---

23   ②

빈칸 다음의 But을 기준으로 전후의 세 개의 문장이 각각 대조를 이루
는 내용을 진술하고 있음을 알 수 있다. 즉, At home you can never,
with the best will in the world, forget it은 in foreign countries
your fellows are unreadable과 대조를 이루고, Habit has rendered
your own people as immediately plain and clear as your own
language는 The less obvious products of upbringing escape your
notice와 대조를 이루고 있다. 그러므로 빈칸에는 The accent, the
vocabulary, the inflection of voice, and the gestures, tell you
nothing과 반대되는 의미의 표현이 들어가야 하며, 따라서 정답은 ②
가 된다.

render v. ~로 만들다, ~이 되게 하다; 표현하다, 묘사하다 plain a. 분명한, 명백한
unreadable a. 판독하기 어려운, 뜻이 불명료한 obvious a. 명백한, 명료한
upbringing n. 양육, 교육 inflection n. 굴곡; 음조의 변화, 억양 sufficient
a. 충분한, 족한 recall v. 생각해내다, 상기하다; 소환하다

해외여행의 즐거움 또는 위험 가운데 하나는 계급의식을 잃어버린다는 사실
이다. 본국에서는 아무리 그렇게 하려 해도 그 의식을 결코 잊을 수 없다. 습
관은 언어만큼이나 명백하고도 분명하게 즉시 자신이 속한 계급을 나타내주
기 때문이다. 말 한 마디 몸짓 하나로도 충분하다. 그러나 다른 나라에서는
상대방이 어떤 사람인지 짐작이 가지 않는다. 교육으로 얻은 성과들 중에서
보다 눈에 덜 띄는 점은 알아차리는 것이 불가능하다. 악센트, 어휘, 소리의
억양, 몸짓 같은 것으로는 아무 것도 파악할 수 없다.

---

24   ③

첫 문장에서 색깔이 빛의 파장에 의해 생겨난다고 했고, 빛이 물체에
닿으면 파장 중 일부가 그 물체에 흡수되고 나머지는 반사된다고 했으
므로 물체에 반사된 빛으로 인해 그 물체가 색을 띠게 되는 것이다. 따
라서 물체 자체는 색깔을 포함하지 않는다고 볼 수 있으므로 빈칸에는
③이 적절하다.

wavelength n. 파장 absorb v. 흡수하다, 빨아들이다 multitude n. 다수 think
of A as B A를 B라고 여기다 intrinsic a. 고유한 in oneself 본래, 본질적으로

색깔은 여러 가지 빛의 파장에 의해 만들어진다. 빛이 물체에 닿으면 일부 파장
은 그 물체에 흡수된다. 나머지는 반사되어 우리 눈에 하나의 특정한 색깔로 보
이게 된다. 공기 중에서 모든 파장은 결합하여 흰빛이 된다. 빛이 유리로 된 스펙
트럼을 통과할 때 그것은 여러 파장으로 분리되며, 흰 빛을 구성하고 있는 많은
색깔들이 드러나게 된다. 만약 당신이 색깔을 어떤 특정한 물체에 들어 있는 하
나의 고유한 특성이라고 생각하고 있다면, 파장에 관한 이 모든 이야기가 혼란스
러울 수 있다. 물체는 본질적으로 색깔을 포함하고 있는 것이 아니다.

---

25   ②

사형제도가 한때는 부당하게 이용되었지만, 현재에는 인종적 편견도
크지 않으며, 최근 사형 집행된 사람들 가운데 흑인의 비율이 그리 높
지 않았음을 수치를 통해 구체적으로 밝히고 있다. 따라서 빈칸에는 인

01 ③	**02** ①	**03** ④	**04** ②	**05** ①	**06** ③	**07** ①	**08** ③	**09** ①	**10** ③
11 ①	**12** ①	**13** ②	**14** ③	**15** ②	**16** ③	**17** ④	**18** ①	**19** ③	**20** ②
21 ④	**22** ③	**23** ③	**24** ③	**25** ④					

01 ③

빈칸에 들어갈 단어는 햄릿이 immobilized한 상태가 되게 만든 직접적인 원인이 되는데, 수단의 전치사 by 이하의 indecision도 동일한 역할을 하고 있다. 그러므로 빈칸에는 문맥상 indecision과 같은 의미를 가질 수 있는 단어가 들어가야 한다. 결정을 내리지 못하는 우유부단함은 확실한 말을 피하고 얼버무리는 행위와 유사하다고 할 수 있다. 따라서 ③이 정답이 된다.

constant a. 변치 않는, 일정한, 항구적인 immobilize v. 움직이지 않게 하다, 고정하다 indecision n. 우유부단, 주저함 revenge n. 복수, 보복 fortitude n. 꿋꿋함, 용기, 강건함, 불굴의 정신 equivocation n. 얼버무림, 확언을 피함 catharsis n. 카타르시스, 감정의 정화작용

계속해서 애매한 태도를 보임으로써, 햄릿(Hamlet)은 종종 우유부단함으로 인해 행동을 실천에 옮기지 못하는 인물이 돼 버렸다.

02 ①

속물근성이 드러났다면, 그가 어떤 태도를 보였기 때문일까를 묻는 문제이다. 부정적인 의미의 단어가 필요하므로 ①이 정답으로 적절하다.

snobbishness n. 속물근성 obvious a. 명백한, 명확한, 명료한 inferior n. 손아랫사람, 하급자; 열등한 것 hauteur n. 오만, 자만 benignity n. 인자, 친절한 행위 perspicacity n. 명민, 총명, 통찰력 epistle n. 편지, 서한

사회적으로 자신보다 열등하다고 간주하는 사람들에게 말할 때의 오만함을 목격하는 모든 사람들에게 그의 속물근성은 분명하게 드러난다.

03 ④

특정 잡지가 검열관에 의해 독자들이 보지 못하게 거부되었다는 것은 검열관이 보기에 독자들이 보아서는 안 되는 부적절한 잡지라는 말이므로 ④가 정답으로 적절하다.

censor n. 검열관 adjudge v. 결정하다, 판결하다 reproduction n. 재생, 복제물, 전재(轉載) hermetic a. 밀봉한, 밀폐한; 신비한 garish a. 화려한 fusty a. 진부한 salacious a. 외설스런

그 잡지는 이집트 화가 위암 엘-마스리가 그린 그림들을 그 잡지에 전재한 (옮겨 실은) 것을 너무 외설스럽다고 결정한 검열관들에 의해 그 나라 독자들에게는 거부되었다.

04 ②

신용카드로 구매하는 것을 음주에 빗대어 설명하고 있는 글이다. 신용카드로 물건을 살 때엔 당장 현금이 필요하지 않으므로 기분 좋게 쇼핑을 할 수 있지만, 이후에 대금이 청구되면 그것을 갚느라 힘이 들게 마련이다. 따라서 빈칸에는 술을 마신 후 다음날 겪게 되는 좋지 않은 점에 관한 단어가 들어가야 하며, '숙취'라는 의미의 ②가 가장 자연스럽다.

drunk a. 술에 취한 initial a. 처음의, 시작의; 초기의 buzz n. 얼큰히 취함; 열중하는 것, 열광 lift n. (정신의) 앙양, 기분의 고조 delight n. 기쁨, 즐거움 hangover n. 숙취(宿醉); 잔존물, 유물 reinforcement n. 강화, 보강, 증원 exhortation n. 간곡한 권유, 충고, 경계

신용카드로 구매하는 것은 술을 마시는 것과 같다. 처음 얼큰하게 취할 때엔 기분이 좋아지지만 다음 날이면 숙취로 고생한다.

05 ①

두 번째 문장에서 카페 같은 공공장소에서 소리치며 인사하고 멈추지 않고 떠든다고 했으므로, 빈칸에는 din, yelling의 의미를 내포하고 있는 단어가 들어가야 한다. 따라서 ①이 정답이다.

temperamental a. 타고난; 신경질적인; 변덕스러운 din n. 떠듦; 소음 yell v. 고함치다, 소리 지르다, 외치다 vociferous a. 큰소리로 외치는, 소란한, 시끄러운 gullible a. 속기 쉬운, 잘 속는 lethargic a. 노곤한; 활발치 못한; 혼수상태의 puritanical a. 청교도적인, 금욕주의적인

그리스인들은 매우 신경질적이고 소란스럽다. 소리치며 인사하는 것뿐만 아니라 떠드는 소리도 쉴 새 없이 카페에서 들을 수 있다.

06 ③

After절에서 페퍼 스프레이로 아이를 진압했다고 했고 but 이하에서 그것이 필요한 최소한의 강제력이었다고 했으므로 아이의 어머니는 그것이 과잉진압이었다는 취지로 말한 것이 되어야 한다. 'should have

과거분사'가 '~했어야 했는데'라는 뜻이므로 빈칸에는 과잉진압과 반대되도록 '말로 설득하다'라는 의미의 ③이 들어가는 것이 적절하다.

pepper n. 후추 pepper spray 최루액 분사기 subdue v. 진압하다 confer v. 의논하다 argue v. 다투다 reason v. 말로 설득하다 side v. 편들다

경찰이 8살 난 통제 불능의 아이를 페퍼 스프레이를 사용하여 진압하고 나자 아이의 어머니는 경찰이 아이를 붙들고 그냥 말로 설득했어야 했다고 말했지만, 나는 페퍼 스프레이는 필요한 최소한의 강제력이었다고 생각한다.

07 ①

연료비가 얼마나 들 것인지 전혀 알 수 없는 이유로는 '가격의 등락이 심하기 때문'이 가장 적절하다. 따라서 ①이 정답이다. ③의 경우, 항공사의 수입으로부터 상당한 액수를 뺏어간다는 내용과 배치되며, 부사 notoriously와도 자연스럽게 어울리지 않는다.

take A out of B B에서 A를 공제하다[빼다] huge a. 거대한; 막대한 chunk n. 큰 나무 도막; 큰 덩어리; 상당한 양 revenue n. 소득, 수입 notoriously ad. 널리 알려져서 volatile a. (가격·가치 등이) 심하게 변동하는; 휘발성의; 폭발하기 쉬운 spurious a. 가짜의, 위조의; 겉치레의 inexpensive a. 비용이 들지 않는, 값이 싼 stagnant a. 흐르지 않는, 괴어 있는; 썩은; 불경기의

연료비는 항공사의 수입에서 상당한 액수를 뺏어갈 뿐 아니라, 변동이 심한 것으로 악명이 높다. 매달 항공사들은 연료비가 정확히 얼마나 들 것인지 알 길이 없다.

08 ③

세미콜론 이하는 우연한 발견을 인정하는 사람들에 대한 부연설명이므로, 주어의 자리인 빈칸에는 an accidental discovery의 동의어가 필요하다.

reluctant a. 마음 내키지 않는, 꺼리는 accidental a. 우연한, 우발적인, 뜻밖의 component n. 성분, 구성요소 invention n. 발명; 발명품 rapture n. 큰 기쁨, 환희 coinage n. 주화; 화폐주조; 신조어 serendipity n. 뜻밖의 발견; 우연한 발견을 하는 능력 sagacity n. 총명, 명민

몇몇 과학자들과 발명가들은 우연히 발견한 것을 보고하는 것에 대해 마음 내키지 않아 하지만, 사실, 우연한 발견은 과학적 발견과 발명의 주된 요소라고 그것의 역할을 솔직하게 인정하는 다른 과학자들과 발명가들도 있다.

09 ①

부연설명의 역할을 하고 있는 콜론 뒤의 문장들은 초창기 여객기의 모습을 이야기하고 있다. '출장요리, 바, 피아노' 등에서 떠오르는 이미지는 '호사스러움, 사치, 호사' 등일 것이므로, 당시에는 '항공여행 = 사치'의 관계가 성립했다고 할 수 있다. 따라서 빈칸에는 '같은 뜻을 나타내는'이라는 의미의 ①이 적절하다.

clipper n. 장거리 쾌속 비행정; 대형 여객기 cater v. 음식을 준비하다; 조달하다, 장만하다 wet bar 자택에 설치한 바 synonymous a. 동의어의, 같은 뜻의, 같은 것을 나타내는 reserved a. 보류한; 사양하는, 삼가는; 내성적인 itinerant a. 순회하는, 이리저리 이동하는 premature a. 조숙한; 시기상조의, 너무 이른

항공여행이 사치스러움과 같은 의미이던 시절이 있었다. 팬 아메리칸 항공사의 첫 번째 대형 여객기들은 파리의 맥심 레스토랑에서 나온 출장 요리를 제공하였고, 보잉 747이 도입된 초창기에 과감하게 위층으로 올라가봤다면, 피아노와 작은 바를 발견할 수 있었을 것이다.

10 ③

빈칸 뒤에서 '누구의 말을 인용하는지 청중들이 이해할 것으로 알고서'라고 했으므로 빈칸에는 '인용하는 말이 누구의 말인지를, 즉 그 말의 출처를, 밝히는 것(the act of saying that something was written, said, painted etc by a particular person)'이라는 뜻의 ③이 적절하다.

nomination n. (후보자로의) 지명 candidate n. 입후보자 Senate n. 상원 quote v. 인용하다 authorization n. 권한 부여 rendition n. 번역, 해석 attribution n. 귀착시킴, 귀속, 귀인(歸因); 출처를 밝힘) premedition n. 미리 생각하기

에이브러햄 링컨이 1858년 연방 상원의원 선거에서 일리노이 주 공화당 후보 지명을 수락했을 때 그는 청중들이 그가 누구의 말을 인용하는지 이해할 것으로 알고서 자신의 연설에 예수의 말을 출처를 밝히지 않고 사용했다.

11 ①

새로운 법의 처벌 대상은 '아이를 오랜 기간 동안 돌보지 않고 내버려둬서 아이의 안전을 의도적으로 무시한 사람'이다. 이 표현에서 핵심이 되는 단어는 neglects이며, 따라서 빈칸에는 이러한 의미를 내포하고 있는 형용사가 들어가야 한다. 정답은 '의무에 태만한'이라는 의미를 가진 ①이다.

adopt v. 채택하다, 채용하다 punish v. 벌하다; 응징하다 so-called a. 소위, 이른 바 mandatory a. 명령의; 의무적인, 강제적인 sentence n. 판결, 선고 willfully ad. 고의적으로, 계획적으로 neglect v. 무시하다, 간과하다; 게을리 하다 unattended a. 보살핌을 받지 않는, 내버려 둔 derelict a. 직무 태만의, 무책임한; 유기된 solicitous a. 갈망하는, 걱정하는 mercenary a. 돈을 목적으로 일하는; 고용된 pedantic a. 아는 체하는, 현학적인

미시건 주(州)는 의무를 태만히 한 부모를 벌하는 강력한 새 법을 채택했다. 소위 "나 홀로 집에 법률"이라고 불리는 이 법에 의하면, 아이를 오랜 기간 동안 돌보지 않고 내버려둬서 아이의 안전을 의도적으로 무시한 사람은 누구나 90일간의 강제 징역형에 처해진다.

12 ①

빈칸이 포함된 두 번째 문장은 첫 번째 문장을 재진술한 것이다. 따라서 빈칸에는 'can find no organic cause for the pain'과 문맥상 같은

의미를 나타낼 수 있는 단어가 필요하다. 통증에 대해 몸에서 원인을 발견할 수 없다면 그 원인이 심리적이라는 것이므로, 정답은 '심인성의'라는 뜻의 ①이다.

indignant a. 분개한, 성난 insult v. 모욕하다, 무례한 짓을 하다 physician n. 의사, 내과의사 organic a. 유기적인, 조직적인; 근본적인 interpret v. 해석하다, 판단하다 term n. 기간, 임기; 용어; 조건 nonexistent a. 존재하지 않는, 실재하지 않는 symptom n. 징후, 조짐, 전조(前兆) underlying a. 기초가 되는, 근원적인 psychogenic a. 심인성(心因性)의, 정신에서 일어나는, 정신 작용[상태]에 의한 morbid a. 병적인; 음울한 invalid a. 병약한, 허약한 amnesic a. 건망증의

환자들은 의사가 통증에 대해 기질적 원인을 발견할 수 없다고 말하면 화를 내거나 모욕감을 느낀다. 그들은 '심인성'이란 말을 자신들이 있지도 않은 증상에 대해 불평하고 있다는 말로 해석하는 경향이 있다. 그들은 여러 형태의 통증들이 근원적인 신체적 원인이 없이 발생한다는 사실에 대해 교육받을 필요가 있다.

13 ②

MTV가 이전에는 흑인 아티스트들의 음악을 방영하는 것을 거부했지만, 마이클 잭슨의 노래와 뮤직 비디오의 인기를 인정한 이후엔 팝과 R&B쪽으로 선회했다고 했으므로, 그 이후 흑인 아티스트들이 방송에 출연하는 데 있어 '길을 열어주었다'라는 흐름이 되어야 적절하다.

dominate v. 지배하다, 통치하다, 위압하다 airtime n. (특정 주제의) 방송 시간 popularity n. 인기; 대중성 orient v. 일정한 방향으로 향하게 하다; 적응시키다 exposure n. 공개석상에 나타남, 출연 wreak havoc on ~을 엉망으로 만들다, 파괴하다 pave the way for ~의 길을 열다; ~을 용이하게 하다 keep close tabs on ~을 엄중하게 감시하다 take the place of ~을 대신하다, 대리하다

이전에 락 뮤직 비디오가 주류를 이뤄왔던 MTV가 릭 제임스(Rick James)와 같은 유명한 흑인 아티스트에게는 방송시간을 할애하지 않았다. 그러나 마이클 잭슨(Michael Jackson)의 노래와 뮤직 비디오의 인기를 인지하자마자, MTV는 팝과 R&B쪽으로 선회하였고, 이것은 이후에 휘트니 휴스턴(Whitney Houston)과 프린스(Prince) 같은 차세대 흑인 가수들의 길을 열어 주었다.

14 ③

미국의 정치담론에서 극우 폭력자들은 다른 이름으로 부른다는 것에서 테러리즘이 이슬람 과격파만을 지칭하는 용어라는 것을 추론할 수 있다.

discourse n. 담론; 대화; 담화, 토론, 강연 reserved a. 보류된, 제한된, 삼가 하는; 특별한 목적을 위해 따로 확보된; 미리 예약된 abandoned a. 버림받은; 자포자기한; 자유분방한 provoked a. 화난, 약이 오른 mollified a. 화가 누그러진, 감정이 진정된

미국 정치담론에서, 테러리즘은 종종 이슬람에 대한 폭력적인 해석을 추종하는 사람들을 위해 따로 확보된 꼬리표로 여겨진다. 반면, 인종에 기초한 극단적인 극우 이데올로기의 이름으로 폭력을 저지른 사람들은 때때로 문제가 있는 젊은이 혹은 범죄자로 묘사된다.

15 ②

글 속에 나오는 미국 언어학자의 입장은 "Leave your language alone"에 나타나 있는데, 이 말의 뜻은 '세련되거나 정교한 스타일로 말하려는 노력'에 반대하는 것이라 할 수 있다. 그러므로 빈칸에는 '반대' 혹은 '거부'의 의미를 가진 단어가 포함된 표현이 들어가야 한다. hostility가 들어 있는 ②가 정답으로 가장 적절하다.

conflict n. 투쟁, 충돌, 대립; 불일치 linguistics n. 언어학 humanistic a. 인문학의 refinement n. 세련됨, 우아함, 고상함 linguist n. 언어학자 urge v. 재촉하다; 주장하다, 강조하다 elaborate a. 정교한, 정성껏 만든 oral a. 구술(口述)의 unusual a. 이상한; 유별난, 색다른, 진기한 hostility n. 적의(敵意), 적개심 predilection n. 편애, 매우 좋아함 inequity n. 불공평, 불공정

언어학과 인문학적 목표 또는 스타일의 세련됨 사이에 필연적으로 상충하는 점은 없지만, 실제로 많은 미국 언어학자들은 일반 대중들에게 "언어를 그냥 내버려두라"고 촉구해 왔으며, 평범한 사람들이 말로 하는 꾸밈없는 의사소통보다 더 정교한 스타일에 대해서는 적대감을 표명해 왔다.

16 ③

유권자는 선거를 할 수 있는 자격이 있고 등록된 사람을 말하고, 선거는 지식의 많고 적음과 무관하므로 첫 번째 빈칸에는 eligible(자격 있는)이나 registered(등록된)가 적절하고 learned(박식한)나 illiterate(문맹의)는 부적절하며, 인도는 다양하다고 한 것은 인도의 경향(성향)이 한 가지가 아니라는 말이므로 두 번째 빈칸에는 '경향'이라는 의미의 bent나 pulse가 적절하다.

voter n. 유권자, 투표자 diversity n. 다양성 Maoist a. 모택동주의의 insurgency n. 모반, 폭동 foremost a. 으뜸의, 가장 중요한 subsidy n. 보조금 learned a. 박식한 perk n. 특전 illegible a. 읽기 어려운 bent n. 경향 eligible a. 자격 있는 pulse n. 맥박; 기분, 경향 illiterate a. 문맹의 foible n. 약점 registered a. 등록된 margin n. 변두리

인도의 자격 있는 유권자 수가 8억을 넘고 인도의 다양성이 크다는 점을 감안할 때, 인도가 가진 경향은 한 가지가 아니다. 한 주에서는 유권자들의 생각에 모택동주의식 폭동이 가장 중요할지 모르지만, 또 다른 주에서는 가장 중요한 것이 농민들을 위한 보조금일지도 모른다.

17 ④

첫 번째 빈칸은 A rather than B 구문에 포함되어 있다. 이 구문에서 A와 B에는 대조를 이루는 표현이 오므로, 결국 빈칸에는 judgement와 문맥상 상반되는 의미의 단어가 필요하다. urge 또는 compulsion이 가능하다. 한편, 충동적으로 말을 하는 것은 경솔한 행동이라 할 수 있으므로 두 번째 빈칸에는 rash 또는 imprudent가 들어갈 수 있다. 상기 두 조건을 모두 만족시키는 ④가 정답으로 적절하다.

afterwards ad. 나중에, 그 후에 acknowledge v. 인정하다; 승인하다, 용인하다; 고백하다 fusillade n. 일제사격, 연속사격; (질문 등의) 연발 enamored a.

매혹된, 사랑에 빠진 urge n. 몰아침, 충동 vicious a. 사악한; 타락한; 악의 있는 prudence n. 신중, 세심, 분별 rash a. 분별없는, 경솔한 compulsion n. 강요, 강제; 강박적 충동, 누르기 어려운 욕망 imprudent a. 경솔한, 무분별한

혼자 남게 되었을 때, 그 의사는 자신이 인터뷰에서 한 말이 매우 마음에 들지 않았다. 그는 판단에 의해서보다는 충동적으로 이야기했다. 그리고 그렇게 말하는 사람들이 대개 그러하듯이, 그는 자신이 경솔했다는 것을 나중에 스스로 인정할 수밖에 없었다.

18 ①

두 개의 'if절, 주절'이 but으로 연결된 구조이므로 이 둘을 비교하여 두 번째 빈칸에는 앞의 applaud와 유사한 의미의 commend(칭찬하다), eulogize(찬사를 드리다)가 적절하고, 칭찬을 오래도록 기억한다는 것은 그 칭찬을 자발적이고 진정한 것으로 받아들인다는 말이므로 첫 번째 빈칸에는 이와 반대되게 exacted(강요된)나 induced(유발된)나 promoted(촉구된)가 적절하다.

applaud v. 박수갈채하다 compliment n. 칭찬 civility n. 예의바름 space n. 사이, 시간, 잠시 intervene v. 사이에 끼다, 끼어들다 exact v. 강요하다 commend v. 칭찬하다 slash v. 삭감하다 venerate v. 존경하다 upgrade v. 승격시키다, 개량하다 eulogize v. 칭찬하다, 칭송하다 induce v. 야기하다, 유발하다 denounce v. 비난하다 promote v. 진전시키다, 조장하다 remind v. ~에게 생각나게 하다

만일 어떤 사람의 연설을 듣고 그가 자리에 앉는 순간에 박수를 보내면 그는 당신의 칭찬을 일반적인 예의가 요구하는 바에 의해 강요된 것으로 받아들일 것이지만, 만일 얼마간의 시간 간격을 두고 나서 그의 연설의 장점에 대해 그를 칭찬하면 그는 당신의 칭찬을 오래도록 기억할 것이다.

19 ③

첫 번째 빈칸은 글 속의 상황과 인용문 속의 말을 근거로 적절한 표현을 선택해야 한다. 죽지 않았는데 자신이 사망했다는 오보가 실린 상황이고, '내가 죽었다는 글을 내가 읽었다'라는 말에는 상대를 조롱하거나 비꼬는 의미가 있으므로 sarcastically가 적절하다. 한편, 죽은 사람은 더 이상 잡지를 받아서 읽을 수 없을 것이므로, 두 번째 빈칸에는 '구독자'라는 의미의 subscribers가 들어가야 한다.

incorrectly ad. 부정확하게, 올바르지 않게 delete v. 삭제하다, 지우다 haphazardly ad. 우연히, 무턱대고, 아무렇게나 publisher n. 출판업자; 출판사 vigorously ad. 격렬하게 defector n. 도망자; 배반자 sarcastically ad. 빈정거리며, 비꼬면서 subscriber n. 기부자; 신청자; 구독자 imminently ad. 임박하여, 일촉즉발로 correspondent n. 기자, 통신원; 특파원

영국의 작가이자 시인인 러디어드 키플링(Rudyard Kipling)은 지나치게 일을 많이 하는 것이 지나친 음주만큼 나쁘다고 믿는다. 1907년에 키플링은 최연소이자 영국인으로서는 최초로 노벨 문학상을 수상했다. 어떤 잡지에 그의 사망에 관한 오보가 실리자, 그는 "내가 죽었다는 얘기를 방금 읽었다. 구독자 명단에서 내 이름을 삭제하는 것을 잊지 말라"고 비꼬아 말했다.

20 ②

매년 이혼 건수가 같은 해 결혼 건수의 약 절반일 뿐, 전체 결혼의 절반이 이혼으로 끝나는 것은 아니라는 내용을 잘못된 사망률 계산을 예로 들면서 이야기하고 있다. 한 해 동안 죽거나 태어난 사람에 해당되지 않는 사람, 즉 '계속해서 살고 있는 사람'을 무시한 채 사망률을 계산하는 것이 잘못된 것처럼, 이혼율도 해당 기간 동안 새로 결혼하거나 이혼하지 않고 '계속해서 결혼생활을 하고 있는 사람'을 무시한 채 산출해서는 안 된다는 의미이다. 그러므로 빈칸에는 ②가 들어가야 한다.

compute v. 계산하다, 측정하다 ignore v. 무시하다, 묵살하다 figure n. 숫자, 수치 single n. 단일; 독신자 intact a. 그대로인, 손상되지 않은 engagement n. 약속, 계약; 약혼 temporary a. 일시적인; 순간의, 덧없는 separation n. 별거, 이별; 분리

미국에서 맺어진 결혼 가운데 50퍼센트가 결국 이혼으로 끝난다는 말이나 글을 몇 번이나 접해 보았는가? 그것은 사실이 아니다. 매년 이혼 건수가 같은 해 결혼 건수의 약 절반이라는 것이 사실이긴 하다. 그러나 그것은 죽는 사람의 수를 태어나는 사람의 수와 비교하여 사망률을 계산하는 것과 같다. 그것은 그 12개월 동안 태어나지도 죽지도 않은 사람들을 무시하고 있는 것이다. 50퍼센트라는 이혼율 수치도 그대로 유지되고 있는 결혼의 수를 무시하는 것이다.

21 ④

첫 번째 빈칸은 원인과 결과의 의미를 가지는 'so ~ that …' 구문에 속해 있다. 빈칸이 들어 있는 문장은 바로 뒤에 위치한 all efforts to obtain it hopeless와 동일한 의미를 가져야 하므로, hopeless의 동의어에 해당하는 단어가 와야 한다. futile 또는 vain이 가능하다. 한편, 행복이 작은 즐거움을 누리는 데 있지만 만약 우리가 크고 자극적인 쾌락을 찾으려 한다면 이런 것을 발견하기가 어렵게 되거나 무시하게 될 것이다. 따라서 두 번째 빈칸에는 neglect 또는 overlook이 들어갈 수 있다.

scatter v. 흩뿌리다, 흩어버리다 futile a. 쓸 데 없는, 무익한, 헛된, 효과 없는 overemphasize v. 지나치게 강조하다 quixotic a. 돈키호테식의; 열광적인; 공상가의, 비실제적인 stymie v. 방해하다, 훼방 놓다, 좌절시키다 uncanny a. 엄청난; 초인적인, 초자연적인 neglect v. 무시하다; 간과하다; 소홀히 하다 vain a. 헛된, 무익한 overlook v. 바라보다; 눈감아주다, 너그럽게 봐주다

행복은 크고 아름다운 보석같이 그렇게 비범하고 너무나도 희귀해서 그것을 찾고자 하는 행동이 헛되고 그것을 얻으려는 모든 노력이 희망 없는 그런 것이 아니다. 행복은 그것들을 모아서 서로 조립하고 나면 즐겁고 우아한 전체를 형성하는 보다 작고 평범한 보석들로 이루어져 있다. 행복은 인생의 평범한 길을 따라 흩어져 있는 작은 즐거움을 누리는 데 있는 것이다. 그런데, 우리는 어떤 크고 자극적인 쾌락을 찾으려는 나머지 이런 것들을 못보고 지나치기가 쉽다.

22　　　　　　　　　　③

두 번째 문장 이하는 첫 번째 문장에 대한 부연설명에 해당한다. 첫 문장에서 '연극에는 social cohesion이 필요하다'라고 했는데, 이것은 '청중과의 유대 관계'를 의미하는 것이므로, 결국 빈칸에는 cohesion과 유사한 의미를 가진 단어가 들어가야 한다. '결속'이라는 의미의 ③이 가장 적절하다.

maximum a. 최대의, 최고의; 극대의 fulfillment n. 이행, 수행; 성취, 달성 cohesion n. 결합, 단결, 유대 predicate v. 단언하다, 단정하다; 진술하다; 입각시키다, 기초를 두다 response n. 응답, 대답; 반응 prerequisite n. 선행조건, 필요조건 hegira n. 도피, 도주 seclusion n. 격리, 은퇴, 은둔 solidarity n. 결속, 단결 decorum n. 예의 바름, 예법; 단정함

연극이 최대한의 성과를 이뤄내기 위해서는 가치, 상징, 통념과 관련해서 고도의 사회적 유대가 필요하다. 연극은 인생에 대한 모종의 이해에 입각해야 하며, 그 과정을 청중이 공유해야 한다. 다른 어떤 예술보다도 연극은 반응을 공유하는 예술이다. 극장에서는 청중과의 결속력이 그가 무대 위에서 일어나는 일에 연루되기 위한 선결조건이다. 전자(前者) 없이는 후자(後者)가 그다지 훌륭해질 수 없다.

23　　　　　　　　　　③

저성장, 생산과잉 등의 영향으로 우월한 입장에 놓인 소비자가 할인된 가격으로 물건을 구입할 수 있게 된 것은 맞으나, 그러한 경향이 계속되면 낮은 임금과 낮은 구매력, 경기 침체로 이어질 수 있다는 내용이다. 경기가 침체되면 앞서 언급한 상황들이 계속 반복될 것이다. 따라서 빈칸에는 '악순환을 일으킨다'라는 의미를 나타낸 ③이 들어가는 것이 가장 적절하다.

lowball a. 실제보다 싸게 어림한 sluggish a. 게으른, 부진한, 불경기의 growth n. 성장; 증대, 발생 excess n. 과다, 과잉; 잉여, 초과 capacity n. 용량, 능력, 재능 depressed a. 억압된, 풀이 죽은; 불경기의 desperate a. 자포자기의; 무모한; 필사적인 short-change v. 거스름돈을 덜 주다; 속이다 overall a. 종합적인, 전반적인 lift v. 부양하다, 올리다 norm n. 기준; 규범; 수준, 평균 spiral n. 나선; (물가·임금 등이) 연쇄적 변동, 악순환 induce v. 꾀다; 야기하다, 유발하다

가격 할인의 시대를 환영한다. 성장률이 정체되고, 생산능력은 넘쳐나고, 경기회복에 대한 기대가 꺾인 상황에서, 상품 및 서비스 — 특히, 노동력, 주택, 그리고 레스토랑 음식 — 구매자들은 자신이 어떤 가격을 제시해도 절박한 입장에 놓인 판매자가 받아들일 수밖에 없다고 생각하게 되었다. 그러나 그렇게 할인된 가격에 물건을 사려고 하는 것은 위험한 악순환을 일으킬 수 있다. 고용주가 근로자에게 임금을 덜 주면 근로자는 소비를 줄여야 하고 전반적으로 경제는 침체된다.

24　　　　　　　　　　③

빈칸 앞에 위치한 주어 부분의 내용, 그리고 이어지는 문장의 내용은 모두 '사형 집행의 내용과 횟수를 공개하지 않는다는 사실'에 관한 것이다. 이것은 집행 과정이 투명하지 않다는 의미이므로 빈칸에 들어갈 적절한 표현은 ③이다.

underreport v. 너무 적게 보고하다 execution n. 실행; 사형 집행, 처형 hanging n. 교살, 교수형 fortify v. 요새화 하다; 강화하다; 확고히 하다 official n. 공무원; 임원 notify v. 통지하다, 통고하다 beforehand ad. 미리, 사전에 defendant n. 피고 trial n. 공판, 재판; 시도 access n. 접근, 면접, 출입 thorough a. 철저한; 면밀한; 완전한 appeal n. 상소, 항고, 상고 crack down on ~에 단호한 조치를 취하다; 탄압하다; 호되게 혼내다, 비난하다 brutality n. 잔인성, 무자비함 reflect v. 반영하다, 나타내다 transparency n. 투명성; 명료함 convey v. 나르다, 운반하다, 운송하다 incompetence n. 무능력; 부적격

이라크 정부가 사형 집행의 횟수를 적게 신고하는 것은 집행 과정의 투명성이 대체적으로 결여된 점을 반영한다. 교수형은 바그다드에 위치한 요새화된 장소에서 비밀리에 집행된다. 오직 소수의 관리들만이 사전에 집행 통지를 받고 처형된 사람들의 이름은 공개되지 않는다. 인권단체는 사형선고를 받은 피고인들이 공정한 재판을 받고 철저한 항소 절차를 밟을 수 있을지에 대해 염려하고 있다.

25　　　　　　　　　　④

두 번째 문장에 나온 젊은이가 나환자에게 보인 행동은 사랑의 행동이며 그 후 그는 아무것도 두려워하지 않게 되었다고 했으므로 빈칸에는 ④가 적절하다.

leprosy n. 나병 impel v. 재촉하다, 몰아대다 gaily ad. 화려하게 caparison v. 장식마의를 입히다, 성장(盛裝)시키다 embrace v. 얼싸안다, 포옹하다 leper n. 나병 환자, 문둥이 keep ~ within bounds ~가 도를 넘지 않게 하다 sensitive a. 민감한, 예민한

두려워하는 사람에게 더 많이 사랑하고자 한다면 덜 두려워하게 될 것이라고 말해주는 것으로는 분명 충분치 않을 것이다. 나병이 지금보다 훨씬 더 큰 공포의 대상이었던 시대에 어떤 부유한 망나니 젊은이는 길에서 갑작스런 어떤 거역할 수 없는 감정에 휩싸여 화려하게 차려 입힌 자신의 말에서 내려와 나환자를 얼싸안았다. 그날부터 그는 아무것도 두려워하지 않았다. 그러나 우리 중에 그런 거역할 수 없는 감정의 엄습을 당하는 사람은 거의 없다. 어떻게 하면 보통 사람들이 공포를 없애지는 않더라도 적어도 도가 지나치지는 않게 하여 개인과 국가의 일에 있어 공포가 아니라 이성이 더 강한 역할을 하게 만들도록 도와줄 수 있을까? 이것이 인류가 직면한 가장 중요한 문제이다.

01 ④	02 ④	03 ④	04 ②	05 ③	06 ①	07 ④	08 ③	09 ③	10 ④
11 ②	12 ③	13 ④	14 ②	15 ③	16 ④	17 ④	18 ③	19 ①	20 ②
21 ④	22 ①	23 ①	24 ④	25 ③					

01 ④

영국 관광객이 노르웨이에서 본국으로 돌아갈 뱃삯만 갖고 있는 상황을 가장 잘 나타낼 수 있는 단어를 고르면 된다.

validate v. 정당함을 입증하다; 비준하다, 확인하다 engross v. 몰두시키다, 열중시키다 shun v. 피하다, 비키다 strand v. 좌초시키다; 궁지에 몰다; 오도 가도 못하게 하다

한 관광객이 주머니에 영국으로 돌아갈 뱃삯을 지불할 만큼의 돈만을 가지고서 노르웨이에서 오도가도 못 하게 되었다.

02 ④

세미콜론이 이유를 나타내는 접속사 for의 역할을 하고 있다. 따라서 세미콜론 이하는 왜 비판이 칭찬인지를 설명하는 내용이 되어야겠는데, 칭찬 자체가 긍정적인 개념이고 또 a belief와 동격인 that절이 긍정적인 내용이므로, 빈칸에 부정적인 의미의 동사가 들어가선 안 된다. 따라서 ①, ②, ③은 모두 부적절하다. 결국, '나타내다'라는 의미로 쓰인 ④가 정답이 된다.

criticize v. 비판하다, 비평하다 compliment n. 경의, 칭찬; 아첨; 영광스러운 일 disprove v. 반증을 들다, 그릇됨을 증명하다 expunge v. 지우다, 삭제하다, 말살하다 defy v. 도전하다; 반항하다, 무시하다 evidence v. 증언하다; 명시하다, 겉으로 나타내다

자기나라를 비판하는 것은 자기나라를 칭찬하는 것이다. 그 비판은 자기나라가 지금보다 더 잘 할 수 있다는 믿음을 보여주는 증거이기 때문에 칭찬인 것이다.

03 ④

해부학적으로 어깨와 이어져 있는 부위를 뜻하는 표현은 dorsal이다.

anatomy n. 해부학 shoulder joint 어깨관절(견관절) faunal a. 동물지(誌)의 endocrine a. 내분비의 osmotic a. (물리·화학) 삼투(성)의 dorsal a. (해부학에서) 등(부분)의; 등 모양의 n. 등지느러미; 척추

개구리 해부에서, 어깨의 주요 근육들은 등 부분에서 뻗어 나와 어깨 관절을 지나 팔까지 이어져 있다.

04 ②

but 전후 문장이 내용상 대조를 이루어야 한다. 앞 문장을 부정한 결과가 abandons the flattery인데, 동사 abandon은 부정적인 의미를 가지고 있으므로, 빈칸에는 abandons the flattery에서 abandons를 삭제한 의미, 즉 flattery의 의미를 내포하고 있는 단어가 들어가야 한다. '아첨꾼'이라는 의미의 ②가 정답이 된다.

abandon v. 버리다; 포기하다, 단념하다 flattery n. 아첨, 아부 pediatrician n. 소아과의사 adulator n. 아첨꾼; 사대주의자 prig n. 깐깐한 사람; 학자인 체하는 사람 apprentice n. 도제(徒弟); 수습공

그 시장은 지역의 사업가들에게 말할 때는 보통 아첨꾼이지만, 드물게는 아첨을 버리고, 자기 의견을 솔직히 말한다.

05 ③

'체포를 피해 브뤼셀로 도주한 후에'라고 했으므로 그들을 처벌하려는 본국에서는 그들을 돌려보내달라고 브뤼셀(벨기에) 정부에 요청할 것이다. 따라서 빈칸에는 ③이 적절하다.

adviser n. 조언자, 고문 flee v. 달아나다, 도망하다 naturalization n. 귀화 enfranchisement n. 해방 extradition n. 도주범인 인도 amnesty n. 사면

게다가, 카탈로니아 대통령 카를레스 푸지데몬과 4명의 고문은 체포를 피해 브뤼셀로 도주한 후에 도주범인 인도 요청에 직면해있다.

06 ①

연설을 해서 사람의 감정을 격동케 하는 것은 선동가이므로 빈칸에는 ①이 적절하다.

oration n. 연설 direct v. 향하게 하다 arouse v. 불러일으키다, 자극하다 demagogue n. 선동가, 선동정치가 autocrat n. 독재자 conspirator n. 공모자 kingpin n. 두목; 주요인물

선동가들은 국민을 향해 연설을 하여 그들의 열정과 편견과 감정을 불러일으킴으로써 연설을 통해 권력을 획득하는 사람들이다.

07   ④

conflicts 이하에 병치되고 있는 세 개의 of구(句)에는 and를 사이에 두고 각각 반의어 표현이 위치해 있다. 그러므로 빈칸에는 abstraction의 반의어가 들어가야 한다.

integral a. 완전한, 빠진 것이 없는; 필수의 resolution n. 결심, 결의; 해결, 해답 conflict n. 투쟁; 충돌, 대립, 불일치 abstraction n. 추상, 추상개념 general a. 일반의, 보통의; 총괄적인 particular a. 특별한; 특정한; 개별적인 denotation n. 명시적 의미, 원뜻 connotation n. 함축, 언외(言外)의 뜻 practicality n. 실용성, 실용주의; 실용적인 일 consequence n. 결과, 결말; 중요성 amalgam n. 혼합물; 합성물 concreteness n. 구체적임, 실체적임

한 편의 시(詩)가 갖는 완전한 통일성이란, 추상성과 구체성, 보편성과 특수성, 명시적 의미와 함축적 의미의 대립이 그 예술작품 안에서 성공적으로 해결되는 것에서 기인하는 통일성을 의미한다.

08   ③

심리검사에서 지능이 높을수록 도덕수준도 높은 것으로 나타나는 것은, 그 검사에서 어떤 식으로든 지능에 대한 평가가 이뤄지고 있다는 것을 의미한다. 따라서 빈칸에는 지능과 유사한 범주에 드는 단어 혹은 문맥상 지능을 대신할 수 있는 표현이 필요하다. '추론'이라는 의미로 쓰인 ③이 빈칸에 들어가기에 가장 적절하다.

psychological a. 심리학상의; 정신적인 indicate v. 가리키다, 지적하다, 보이다 correlation n. 상호관계 intelligence n. 지성; 이해력, 사고력 ethical a. 윤리의, 도덕의 standard n. 표준, 기준; 규격 method n. 방법, 방식; 순서 rely on ~에 의지하다, 의존하다 subject n. 신하; 과목, 환자, 피실험자 evaluate v. 평가하다 portray v. 그리다, 묘사하다 glossary n. 용어풀이, 용어사전 defalcation n. 횡령, 유용; 결점, 단점 ratiocination n. 추리, 추론 subjectivity n. 주관성, 자기 본위, 주관

심리검사를 해 보면 지능과 윤리적 기준 간에 상호 연관성이 상당히 높다는 사실이 나타나는데, 그것은 제시된 상황을 평가하는 데 있어 피실험자의 추론에 의존하는 시험 방법 때문이다.

09   ③

마지막 부분의 another family member가 단서가 된다. 따라서 빈칸에는 ③이 적절하다.

school district 교육구 assign v. 할당하다, 임명하다 work location 근무지 supervision n. 감독 meritocratism n. 능력주의 provincialism n. 지방우선주의 nepotism n. 친척등용, 족벌주의, 정실인사 bureaucratism n. 관료주의

그 교육구의 친척 등용 관련 정책은 "그 어떤 직원도 그 직원의 또 다른 가족 식구에게 보고하거나 그의 직접적인 감독 하에 있게 될 근무지나 직위에 임명되어서는 안 된다."는 것이다.

10   ④

두 번째 문장에서 '주위의 많은 위험을 과대평가하는 것 같다'고 했는데, 이것은 그들이 자신들은 해악에 쉽게 피해를 입는다고 생각한다는 말이다. 앞에 little이 있으므로 빈칸에는 ④가 적절하다.

to the contrary 그와 반대로의, 그렇지 않다는 adolescent n. 청소년 if anything 어느 쪽이냐 하면 오히려 overestimate v. 과대평가하다 impious a. 불경한 immutable a. 불변의 infirm a. 약한 invulnerable a. 상처입지 않는

그렇지 않을 거라는 강한 믿음에도 불구하고, 청소년들이 자신들은 해악에 상처입지 않는다고 생각한다는 것을 보여주는 과학적 자료는 거의 없다. 사실, 어느 쪽이냐 하면 오히려 그들은 그들 주위의 많은 위험을 과대평가하는 것 같다.

11   ②

마지막의 their나 them은 비정상적으로 태어난 아이들을 가리키는데, 이들을 버린다는 것은 비정상적인 출생의 치욕을 '없애는' 것이므로 빈칸에는 ②가 적절하다.

abnormal a. 비정상적인 habitually ad. 상습적으로, 끊임없이 in one's interests ~를 위하여 disgrace n. 불명예, 치욕 bolster v. 강화하다 expunge v. 지우다 requite v. 되갚다 outface v. 대항하다, 도전하다

빅토리아 시대에는 미혼모들과 비정상아의 엄마들은 아이를 주어버림으로써 출생의 치욕을 지우는 것이 아이를 가장 위하는 일이라고 늘 설득 당했다.

12   ③

while절과 주절은 내용이 반대가 되어야 한다. 주절에서 가족이 TV 때문에 하나로 결속되는 것은 아니라고 했으므로, while절에서는 반대로 흩어지지도 못하게 한다는 의미가 되는 것이 적절하다. 따라서 빈칸에는 dispersing이 들어가야 하며, 'bring ~ together'의 문맥상 반의어를 찾는 문제라 할 수 있다.

contribution n. 기여, 공헌; 기부, 기부금 equivocal a. 애매모호한, 다의적인; 확실하지 않은 scathe v. 상처 입히다, 해치다 converge v. 한 점에 모이다, 수렴하다 disperse v. 흩어지다, 해산하다 reunite v. 다시 모이다, 모으다

가족생활에 대한 텔레비전의 기여는 애매모호한 것이다. 왜냐하면, 텔레비전은 실제로 가족구성원들이 뿔뿔이 흩어지지 못하게 해 주었지만, 그들을 결속하는 데 이바지하지도 못했기 때문이다.

13 ④

대통령이 야당을 비난한 것이 선거법 조항을 위반하는 것이라면, 그 선거법 조항에서는 이러한 행위를 하지 못하도록 규정하고 있을 것이다. 그러므로 빈칸에는 첫 번째 문장의 condemnation의 동의어에 해당하는 단어가 들어가야 하며, 정답은 ④가 된다.

condemnation n. 비난, 유죄판결 obligation n. 의무, 책임 neutral a. 중립의; 불편부당한, 공평한 infringe upon ~을 침해하다 article n. 물품; 기사; 조항 ban v. 금하다, 금지하다 adjuration n. 선서; 간원 extollment n. 극찬 archenemy n. 대적(大敵), 최대의 적 aspersion n. 비방, 중상

대통령이 야당을 반(反) 개혁 세력으로 비난한 것은 선거 운동에서 중립을 지켜야 하는 공무원의 의무에 역행하는 것이며 상대 정당에 대한 비난을 금지하고 있는 선거법 조항을 위반하는 것이다.

14 ②

빈칸은 think of A as B 구문에 속해 있으며, as 이하가 states에 대해 설명하는 부분임을 염두에 두고서 이어지는 문장을 보아야 한다. 빈칸 이하에서, whose의 선행사는 civilizations이고 대명사 they가 가리키는 것은 states이다. states에 대해 'appear and disappear'로 기술하고 있는데, 이것은 '국가가 존속하는 기간이 문명에 비해 짧으며, 그 흥망이 반복됨'을 말하는 것이다. 따라서 빈칸에는 이러한 속성을 설명할 수 있는 단어인 ②가 들어가야 한다.

in terms of ~의 관점에서, ~의 견지에서 civilization n. 문명, 문화 subordinate a. 예하의, 하위의; 종속하는 phenomenon n. 현상, 사건 (pl. phenomena) bosom n. 가슴; 흉부; 애정 perpetual a. 영속적인; 부단한 ephemeral a. 하루밖에 못 가는, 단명한 terrestrial a. 지구의; 흙의; 세속적인 tantalizing a. 애타게 하는, 감질나게 하는

이것이 내가 여러분들에게 역사를 국가의 관점에서가 아니라 문명의 관점에서 보고, 국가를 문명의 품 안에서 나타났다가 사라지는, 문명의 삶 안에서 종속적이고 일시적인 정치 현상으로 생각하라고 부탁해온 이유 중 하나이다.

15 ③

주어진 글에서 '모든 것을 지배하는 운명 = 신의 몸짓'의 관계가 성립한다. 이것에 대해 나이가 들면서 더 이해하게 된다고 했으므로, 젊었을 때에는 그 본질에 대해 제대로 몰랐을 것이라 할 수 있다. 한편, 운명은 예정되어 있는 것이므로, 빈칸에는 예정되어 있는 것과 상반되는 의미를 가진 표현이 들어가야 한다. 따라서 정답으로 가장 적절한 것은 '하찮은 우연'이라는 의미의 ③이다.

destiny n. 운명, 숙명 enormous a. 거대한, 막대한 calling n. 소명, 천직 niggardly a. 인색한; 빈약한, 불충분한 pittance n. 기부; 약간의 음식, 약간의 수당 trifling a. 하찮은, 시시한 horrendous a. 무서운, 끔찍한

모든 것을 지배하는 운명이 어떤 때는 팔꿈치로 가볍게 밀고, 어떤 때는 손가락으로 가리키며, 어떤 때는 가슴을 치는 것을 우리는 나이가 들면서 더 이해하게 된다. 25살에는 하찮은 우연이라고 생각했던 것을, 75세에는 그것이 신(神)의 엄청난 몸짓이었다는 것을 알게 된다.

16 ③

첫 문장에서 is built into(만들 때 적용하여 만들다)라 했고 세 번째 문장에서 '구형이어서 고칠 수 없다'고 했으므로, ③의 '계획적인 진부화'가 적절하다.

be built into ~에 붙박이로 만들어지다 run out (재고가) 바닥나다, (기한이) 다하다 outmoded a. 유행에 뒤진, 구식의 contradict v. 모순되다, 위배되다 detection n. 발견, 간파 attrition n. 마찰, 마모 planned obsolescence 계획적 진부화(신상품의 판매를 촉진하기 위해 구상품을 계획적으로 진부한 것이 되게 하는 기업행동)

계획적 진부화 방식은 우리가 구입하는 거의 모든 상품을 만드는 데 적용된다. 그것은 보증기간이 지난 후 곧 고장 난 우리 집 세탁기를 생각나게 한다. 세탁기가 구형이어서 고칠 수 없다는 말을 들었다. 3년도 채 안 된 세탁기였다. 이런 낭비적인 관행은 분명 자원 보존 노력에 위배된다.

17 ②

고통이나 의미 없는 삶에서 벗어날 수 있는 것이 인간의 기본적인 권리라면, 부모나 보호자는 그런 상황을 경험하고 있는 사람으로부터 그 고통을 덜어주려 해야 할 것이다.

relief n. 경감, 제거; 안심, 위안; 구제 meaningless a. 무의미한, 의미 없는 guardian n. 감시인; 보호자; 후견인 encourage v. 격려하다, 고무하다 request v. 구하다; 청하다; 부탁하다 entrust v. 맡기다, 위탁하다 tragic a. 비극적인; 비참한 denigrate v. 더럽히다; 모욕하다 spare v. 절약하다, 아끼다; (불행·수고 따위를) 끼치지 않다, 덜다 exacerbate v. 악화시키다; 격분시키다

그러므로, 고통이나 의미 없는 삶에서 영원히 벗어나는 쪽을 택할 수 있는 권리는 사람의 기본권인 듯 보이며, 또한 부모나 그 밖의 보호자들은 그들이 보호하고 있는 사람에게서 쓸데없는 고통 혹은 비극적인 삶을 덜어 주도록 요구할 권리를 가져야 할 뿐만 아니라 그렇게 되도록 요구해야 하는 책임을 받아들여야 할 것으로 보인다.

18 ③

주절의 주어인 트빌리시(Tbilisi)는 그루지야의 수도이며, 이 글에서는 그루지야 정부를 의미한다. 분사구문의 내용을 통해 그루지야 정부는 러시아 정부(Moscow: 러시아의 수도)를 비난하는 입장에 있음을 확인할 수 있는데, 유럽 연합도 자신과 같은 입장을 표명하길 원할 것이므로 두 번째 빈칸에는 Accusing의 의미를 내포하고 있는 condemnation 또는 blame이 들어갈 수 있다. 한편, the EU should 뒤에는 not A but B 구문이 쓰였는데, 이 구문에서 A와 B에는 서로 의미상 대조를 이루는

표현이 와야 하므로 첫 번째 빈칸에는 but 이하의 내용, 즉 '비난을 표명하는 것'과 반대되는 의미를 나타내는 표현이 들어가야 할 것이다. 용서하거나 유화적인 자세를 보이는 것이 이에 해당할 수 있으므로, 첫 번째 빈칸에는 pardon 또는 appease가 가능하다. 상기 두 조건을 모두 만족시키는 정답은 ③이 된다.

accuse v. 고발하다, 고소하다; 비난하다 aggression n. 공격, 침략 territory n. 영토 clear-cut a. 선명한, 명쾌한 aggravate v. 악화시키다; 화나게 하다 regret n. 유감; 후회 pardon v. 용서하다; 관대히 봐주다 pretext n. 구실, 핑계 appease v. 달래다, 진정시키다 condemnation n. 비난; 유죄판결 excoriate v. 피부를 벗기다; 통렬히 비난하다 blame n. 비난, 책망

러시아가 영토 안으로 유도 미사일을 발사하여 자국에 대한 '침략 행위'를 저질렀다고 비난한 그루지야 정부 당국은, 유럽연합이 러시아 정부를 달래려 해서는 안 되며, '강하고 분명한' 비난의 메시지를 보내야 한다고 말했다.

---

19 ①

soaring unemployment, a political crisis는 모두 부정적인 의미의 표현이므로, 이 표현과 함께 동사 faces의 목적어 역할을 하고 있는 첫 번째 빈칸에도 부정적인 의미를 가진 단어가 와야 한다. quagmire 또는 dilemma가 가능하다. 한편, crisis를 수식하는 관계대명사절은 A rather than B 구문을 이루고 있는데, 이 때 A와 B는 서로 대조를 이루어야 하므로 두 번째 빈칸에는 cooperation과 대조를 이룰 수 있는 단어가 필요하다. divisions 또는 disunion이 가능하다. 두 조건을 모두 만족시키는 정답은 ①이 된다.

insurmountable a. 극복할 수 없는, 넘을 수 없는 soar v. 치솟다, 날아오르다 crisis n. 위기, 중대국면, 난국 exacerbate v. 악화시키다; 노하게 하다 spur v. 박차를 가하다; 자극하다 quagmire n. 꼼짝할 수 없는 곤경, 궁지; 수렁 division n. 분할; 분배; 분열; 불화 dilemma n. 딜레마, 궁지 elation n. 의기양양; 크게 기뻐함 union n. 결합, 일치; 단결 impasse n. 곤경, 막다른 골목 heyday n. 전성기 disunion n. 분리, 분열; 불화, 내분

그의 지역은 극복할 수 없어 보이는 경제적 곤경, 치솟는 실업률, 그리고 그 대륙에서 더 큰 협력을 이끌기 보다는 분열을 악화시킨 정치적 위기에 직면해 있다.

---

20 ②

'갈아내면 우중충한 갈색의 가루가 된다'라고 한 것에서 '날개 자체가 색을 가지고 있는 것이 아님'을 알 수 있고, 빈칸 이하에서 '빛이 날개에 부딪치는 방식에 의해 아름다운 색으로 보인다'라고 한 것을 통해 '실제로는 없는 색이 있는 것처럼 보인다'는 것을 알 수 있다. 이것은 일종의 착시임을 말하고 있는 것이므로 ②가 정답이다.

iridescent a. 무지개 빛깔의; 보는 각도에 따라 색깔이 변하는 drab a. 우중충한 갈색의; 단조로운, 재미없는 hue n. 빛깔, 색조 structural color 구조색(색깔이 없는 물질이 그 결정구조에 의해 만들어내는 색) gorgeous a. 호화로운; 찬란한, 화려한 reflect v. 반사하다, 비치다; 반영하다; 반성하다 absorb v. 흡수하다; 열중하게 하다 partial a. 부분적인; 불공평한, 편파적인 metamorphosis n. 변태; 변성 optical a. 시각적인, 눈의, 시력의 illusion n. 환영(幻影), 환각; 착각

---

gene n. 유전자 mutation n. 돌연변이, 변종 breeding n. 번식; 양육; 교양

중남미 열대 우림에서 발견되는 모르포 나비는 보는 각도에 따라 색깔이 변하는 푸른 날개로 유명하다. 그러나, 이 날개를 갈아내면 우중충한 갈색의 가루가 된다. 이 나비의 색은 구조색이라 불리는 착시 현상이다. 즉, 빛의 파동 가운데 일부는 반사되고 다른 어떤 것들은 흡수되는 등, 빛이 날개에 부딪치는 방식에 의해 아름다운 색이 생겨나는 것이다.

---

21 ④

접속사 but 전후 문장의 내용이 대조를 이루어야 하므로, 첫 번째 빈칸에는 앞 문장의 throw away or part with와 상반되는 행위 혹은 심적 상태를 나타내는 단어가 들어가야 한다. content 또는 satisfied가 가능하다. and perhaps 이하의 내용, 즉, '스스로의 참모습을 말해주지 않는 것'은 허영심이나 자기도취와 관련된 것이므로, 두 번째 빈칸에는 vainglory 또는 vanity가 들어갈 수 있다. 따라서 정답은 ④가 된다.

distinguish v. 구별하다, 식별하다 dissatisfied a. 불만스러운; 불만을 나타내는 vainglory n. 자만, 자부; 허영, 허세 livid a. 납빛의, 검푸른, 창백한; 격노한 denouement n. (소설·희곡 등의) 대단원; 고비; (분쟁 따위의) 해결, 결말 casuistry n. 궤변 content a. 만족하는, 감수하는 vanity n. 덧없음, 상함; 허무; 헛됨

사람은 시간이 맞지 않는 쓸모없는 시계를 내던지거나 남에게 줘버릴지도 모른다. 그러나 그는 자신의 정신이 너무나도 병들어서 옳고 그름을 구별할 수 없을지라도, 또 정신이 그 허영심으로 인해 거의 쓸모없게 되어 자기 정신의 참모습을 결코 일러준 일이 없을지라도 그것에 가끔 만족하곤 한다.

---

22 ①

빈칸의 앞에서 언급한 '일거리가 없다'라는 내용과 뒤에서 언급하고 있는 '돈 걱정'과 '식습관의 변화' 등의 내용을 통해, 현재 돈에 쪼들려 하고 있음을 알 수 있다.

cheap a. 값싼 available a. 이용할 수 있는, 쓸모 있는; 입수할 수 있는 architectural a. 건축의, 건축학의 eggplant n. <식물> 가지; 진한 보라색 feel the pinch 돈에 쪼들려 고통을 당하다 call the shots 명령하다, 지휘하다 go against the grain 성미에 맞지 않다, 못마땅하다 take fortune at the tide 좋은 기회를 이용하다

먹고 살 만큼은 되지만 저축을 많이 하기에는 빠듯합니다. 최근 4주 동안이나 일거리가 없었기 때문에, 주부들은 돈에 쪼들리고 있습니다. 아직까지는 실제로 배를 곯는 일은 없지만 돈 걱정을 많이 한다고 제니퍼(Jennifer)는 말하고 있습니다. 그래서 그녀의 가족들은 식습관을 바꿔 더 이상 고기나 닭고기를 먹지 않고, 무엇이든 값싸고 구하기 쉬운 것, 즉 쌀, 가지, 바나나를 더 먹습니다.

23   ①

Since로 시작되는 마지막 문장에서 현직 대통령의 재선 성공률이 상당히 높았음을 이야기하고 있다. 따라서 오바마의 재선 가능성이 높거나 상대 후보인 롬니의 승리 가능성이 힘든 이유도 결국 오바마가 현직 대통령이라는 점에서 찾을 수 있다. 빈칸에는 '현직의'라는 의미의 ①이 들어가야 하며, 결국 sitting의 동의어를 찾는 문제라 할 수 있다.

fundamental a. 근본적인, 중요한 oath n. 맹세; 서약 sitting a. 현직의, 재직하고 있는 incumbent n. 현직자, 재직자, 재임자 minority n. 소수파, 소수당; 소수민족 infidel n. 무신론자; 이교도 influential n. 영향력 있는 인물

오바마(Obama) 대통령이 재선에 성공할 가능성이 높은 근본적인 이유가 있는데, 그것은 밋 롬니(Mitt Romney)가 근본적으로 어려운 도전에 직면해 있는 것과 같은 이유이다. 그것은 오바마가 현직 대통령이라는 점이다. 1789년에 조지 워싱턴(George Washington)이 취임 선서를 한 이래로, 31명의 현직 대통령이 선거에 뛰어들어 그 가운데 21명이 승리했다.

24   ④

주어진 글은 사람의 본모습이 그가 쓴 글이나 그림에서 드러난다는 내용으로, 이는 '글이나 그림에서는 사람들이 현실에서 쓰는 위선의 가면을 쓸 수 없다'는 말과 일맥상통한다. 따라서 빈칸에는 문맥상 '가면'이라는 의미를 가질 수 있는 단어, 즉 글에 쓰인 surface 혹은 mask와 같은 의미를 가지는 단어가 들어가야 한다. 가장 적절한 것은 '허세'라는 의미를 가진 ④가 된다.

reveal v. 드러내다; 폭로하다; 밝히다; 누설하다 intercourse n. 교제, 교섭; 거래 inference n. 추리, 추측, 추론 unconscious a. 무의식의; 모르는 assume v. (태도, 임무 등을) 떠맡다; 취하다; 사칭하다, 가장하다 in due course 당연한 순서를 따라; 머지않아, 때가 되면, 그러는 동안에 defenceless a. 무방비의; 방어할 수 없는 expose v. 노출시키다; 폭로하다, 드러내다; 내놓다 vacuity n. 공허; 진공; 방심 dotage n. 망령, 노망 recrimination n. (상대방의 비난에 맞서서 하는) 비난, 맞대응 faultiness n. 과실 있음, 잘못됨; 불완전 pretentiousness n. 자부, 자만; 허세

사람의 작품은 그 사람의 본모습을 드러낸다. 교제를 함에 있어서, 사람은 세상이 받아들이길 바라는 외양을 보여주기 때문에, 그 사람의 참모습을 알 수 있으려면 그가 무의식중에 행하는 사소한 행동을 통해 유추해 볼 수밖에 없다. 때때로 사람들은 그들이 짐짓 그런 체하는 가면을 너무나도 완벽하게 쓰고 있기 때문에 얼마 지나지 않아 실제로 그 가면의 인간이 되어 버리기도 한다. 그러나 그가 쓴 책이나 그림 속에는 그의 참모습이 적나라하게 드러난다. 그의 허세는 마음의 공허함을 드러내게 될 뿐이다.

25   ③

이신론자들은 신이 세계를 창조했지만 이 세계가 운영되는 것에 대해서는 간섭하지 않았다고 생각했다. 이들은 신을 시계 제작자로 봤는데, 시계가 만들어진 후에는 시계가 작동되는 데 있어 더 이상 시계 제작자를 필요로 하지 않을 것이므로 빈칸에는 그 자체적으로 운영된다고 한 ③이 적절하다.

deism n. 이신론(理神論)(신을 세계의 창조주로 인정하나 세계를 지배하는 인격적 존재로 인정하지 않고 계시나 이적을 부정하는 이성적 종교관) preside over 관리하다, (사업 등을) 통할[지배]하다 orderly a. 순서 바른, 정돈된 realm n. 영역, 범위 intervene v. 개입하다, 간섭하다 mortal n. 인간, 죽음을 면할 수 없는 것

과학혁명은 1700년대 인기를 얻었던 이신론이라고 알려진 신념체계에 기여했다. 이신론자들은 강력한 신을 믿었는데 신은 질서 있는 세계를 만들고 관장했지만 세계가 돌아가는 것에 대해 간섭하지 않았다. 이신론자들은 신을 시계 제작자로 보았는데, 신은 세계를 세우고 세계를 운영할 수 있는 자연법을 제공하며, 그 자체적으로 (수학적으로 증명될 수 있었던 자연 법칙 하에) 운영되도록 했다. 그러한 이론은 체계적인 종교 안에서 있을 장소가 없었다.

01 ④	**02** ①	**03** ②	**04** ④	**05** ③	**06** ④	**07** ③	**08** ②	**09** ①	**10** ③
11 ④	**12** ③	**13** ①	**14** ②	**15** ③	**16** ③	**17** ②	**18** ②	**19** ③	**20** ①
21 ①	**22** ②	**23** ④	**24** ③	**25** ②					

01 ④

관용 표현인 break a leg은 '행운을 빈다'라는 의미이므로 격려의 말이라 할 수 있다. 따라서 ④가 정답이 된다. 만약 이 표현의 의미를 정확하게 몰랐다면, 빈칸 뒤의 '자신감이 솟아나게 했다'라는 내용을 통해 유추할 수 있다.

audition n. 오디션; 청각, 청력 lift v. 올리다, 들다; 들어 올리다; 향상시키다 confidence n. 신용, 신임, 신뢰; 확신; 자신감 invective n. 욕설, 악담, 독설 admonishment n. 훈계, 권고, 충고 malediction n. 저주, 악담, 중상, 비방 encouragement n. 격려, 장려

집을 떠나기 전에, 오빠는 내게 오디션에서 '성공하길 빈다'라고 말했다. 좀처럼 하지 않는 격려의 말을 오빠에게서 들었기에 나는 정말로 자신감이 솟아올랐다.

02 ①

당국이 위조지폐를 찾았다고 했으므로, 그가 지명 수배를 받고 있는 것은 '위조'와 관련된 혐의로 인한 것임을 알 수 있다.

counterfeit money 위조지폐 want v. (경찰이) 지명 수배하다 forgery n. (문서·지폐의) 위조 charge n. 기소, 고발 bribery n. 뇌물 assault n. 폭행, 습격 misdemeanor n. 경범죄

당국은 그들이 그의 차에서 위조지폐를 찾았으며 그가 위조 혐의로 지명 수배를 받고 있다는 사실을 이내 알게 됐다고 말한다.

03 ②

no matter how는 양보절을 이끄는 표현이므로, 빈칸에는 offended와 문맥상 반대되는 의미를 가진 단어가 필요함을 알 수 있다. 그러므로 정답은 innocuous이며, '화나게 할 만한 악의가 없음에도 불구하고 상대방을 화나게 할 수도 있다'라는 맥락이 된다.

exercise v. 행사하다, 발휘하다; 운동하다 intentionally ad. 의도적으로, 고의로 guarantee v. 보증하다, 확실히 하다, 보장하다 offend v. 화나게 하다, 불쾌하게 하다 pester v. 괴롭히다, 고통을 주다 innocuous a. 해가 없는; 악의 없는 hackneyed a. 낡은; 진부한 factual a. 사실의, 실제의, 실제에 입각한

당신의 유머가 아무리 악의가 없다고 생각하더라도 누군가의 감정을 상하게 하는 것은 거의 확실하므로, 의도적으로 유머를 이용할 때에는 신중을 기해야 한다.

04 ④

두 번째 문장에서 가방에서 진통제를 꺼내 던졌다고 했는데, 이는 더 이상 약을 먹을 필요가 없을 만큼 통증이 호전됐기 때문일 것이다. 그러므로 빈칸에는 '진정되다'라는 의미의 ④가 들어가야 한다.

notice v. 알아채다, 인지하다 sap v. 활력을 없애다, 약화시키다 gradually ad. 차차, 점차 toss v. 던지다, 흔들다 painkiller n. 진통제 loom v. 어렴풋이 보이다, 어렴풋이 나타나다 sprout v. 싹이 트다, 발아하다; 갑자기 자라다; 성장하다 ascend v. 올라가다, 높아지다 subside v. 가라앉다, 침전하다; 잠잠해지다, 진정되다

몇 주 안에, 나는 골프 경기의 기쁨을 앗아가고 있었던 아래쪽 등의 통증이 서서히 가라앉고 있음을 느꼈다. 얼마 있지 않아 나는 진통제를 골프가방에서 꺼내 던져 버렸다.

05 ③

노숙자 보호시설의 이전과 확장 계획이 뜻밖의 난관에 부딪혔다는 내용 뒤에 접속사 but이 주어져 있으므로, but 이하에는 '계획이 정상적으로 추진될 수도 있다'와 같은 긍정적인 내용이 이어져야 한다. 그런데 'A가 B하는 것을 막다'라는 뜻의 표현 keep A from B는 그 자체에 부정의 의미가 내포되어 있으므로, 결국 빈칸에는 '계획 추진이 잘되지 않을 수도 있다'라는 의미의 표현, 즉 첫 문장의 hit a snag와 문맥상 같은 의미를 가질 수 있는 단어가 들어가야 한다. 정답으로 적절한 것은 '계획이 틀어지다'라는 뜻의 ③이다.

relocation n. 재배치 expansion n. 팽창, 신장; 확장, 확대 shelter n. 피난장소, 은신처; 엄폐 hit a snag 뜻밖의 장애에 부딪치다; 생각지도 않은 문제에 다다르다 gumption n. 상황 대처 능력; 진취적인 기상, 의기 unravel v. 풀어지다; 명백해지다 disentangle v. 풀리다, 해결되다; 해방되다 derail v. 계획이 틀어지다, 탈선하다, 일탈하다 hasten v. 서둘러 가다, 서두르다

바카빌(Vacaville)에 위치한 노숙자 보호시설의 이전과 확장 계획은 뜻밖의 난관에 부딪혔지만, 상황을 대처할 여지가 조금은 있어 보이며, 시에서 지원해 준다면 그 계획은 실패하지 않을 수도 있을 것이다.

06   ④

빈칸에 들어갈 단어의 의미를 as절의 내용을 통해 되짚어 볼 수 있다. as절에서는 '확산되어 다른 사람에게 전해지는 것'을 이야기하고 있는데, 이러한 의미를 가진 표현은 ④이다.

strike v. ~에게 인상을 주다 spread v. 퍼뜨리다, 유포시키다 ad infinitum 무한히, 영구히 prolific a. 다산의; 비옥한; 다작하는 migratory a. 이동하는, 이주하는 picayune a. 보잘것없는, 무가치한 viral a. 바이러스성의; 전염성의

어떤 영상이 사용자들에게 멋지다거나 흥미롭다는 인상을 주면, 그것은 스스로 생명력을 띄게 되고, 확산되어 친구에게서 친구에게로 끝없이 공유되어 가면서 '전염성을 가지게' 된다.

07   ③

평화회담을 '다시 시작'하겠다고 했으므로, 2001년 이래로 그 회담은 '교착' 또는 '답보' 상태에 있었을 것이라 할 수 있다.

come into office 취임하다 determined a. 단단히 결심한; 결연한, 단호한 relaunch v. 다시 선보이다, 새롭게 선보이다 effectively ad. 효과적으; 실질적으로, 사실상 assume v. (태도·임무 등을) 떠맡다; 가장하다; 사칭하다 conflate v. 융합하다, 혼합하다 align v. 정렬시키다, 일직선으로 하다 stall v. 시동을 꺼뜨리다; 지연시키다; 교착 상태에 빠뜨리다 interlock v. 서로 맞물리다, 연동하다

오바마(Obama)는 2001년 초 이스라엘의 아리엘 샤론(Ariel Sharon) 총리가 취임한 이래로 사실상 교착상태에 빠져있었던 평화 협상을 다시 시작하기로 굳게 마음먹은 채 취임했다.

08   ②

빈칸에는 '감기보다 더 불길하고 나쁜 병이 된다'는 의미가 되도록 ②가 들어가는 것이 적절하다. 부비강염과 천식은 전염병이 아님에 유의한다.

morph v. 변하다 sinusitis n. 부비강염(축농증) asthma n. 천식 fugitive a. 도망가는; 일시적인 sinister a. 사악한 insipid a. 김빠진, 활기 없는 contagious a. 전염성의

보통의 치료에 반응하지 않는 감기 환자들이 많다. 이런 경우, 감기가 부비강염이나 천식 같은 더 나쁜 것으로 변할 위험이 있다.

09   ①

주어진 글에서 '문제를 해결하기 위한 조치'는 문맥상 경제위기를 해결하기 위한 방책으로 보아야 한다. 이러한 조치들은 경제 위기를 피하게 해 줄 것이므로 빈칸에는 ①이 들어가야 한다.

approve v. 승인하다, 찬성하다 measure n. 수단, 방책; 조치 loan n. 대부; 대부금, 융자 potential n. 잠재력; 가능성 disaster n. 재해, 재난, 참사 stave off 저지하다; 피하다; 연기하다 lay off 일시 해고하다; 쉬다, 휴식하다 palm off ~을 거짓으로 속이다 call off (주의를) 딴 곳으로 돌리다; 취소하다

민간 경제 단체장은 대출이 원활히 이뤄지기 시작하고 잠재적인 국가 경제 위기를 피하기 위해서는 문제를 해결하기 위해 내놓은 조치를 어떤 식으로든 의회가 빨리 승인해야 한다고 말했다.

10   ③

두 번째 문장은 첫 번째 문장에 대한 예에 해당한다. 상대의 몸에 있는 기생충을 잡아주는 것은 이타적인 행동인데, 이것을 교대로 한다고 했으므로 빈칸에는 '상호주의'라는 의미의 ③이 가장 적절하다.

apparent a. 명백한; 겉치레의 altruism n. 이타주의 kin n. 친척, 친족 pick out 고르다; 선발하다 parasite n. 기생충; 식객 reverse v. 거꾸로 하다, 반대로 하다; 교환하다, 전환하다 animosity n. 원한, 악의, 증오 jingoism n. 맹목적 애국주의 reciprocity n. 호혜, 상호주의 fealty n. 충성, 성실, 신의

명백한 이타주의가 친족 간에 행해지는 것이 아닐 때, 그것은 상호주의에 바탕을 두는 것일 수 있다. 원숭이는 자신의 등을 다른 원숭이에게 돌려 그로 하여금 기생충을 잡게 하는 경향이 있다. 얼마 후에 그 역할은 바뀔 것이다.

11   ④

Money, debt 등의 표현으로부터 빈칸에 '금전의'라는 의미의 ④가 적절함을 추론할 수 있다.

household n. 세대, 가구, 가계 cite v. 인용하다, 열거하다, 언급하다 marital a. 결혼의 somatic a. 육체의 vocational a. 직업의 pecuniary a. 금전의

돈이 우리의 가장 큰 걱정거리이다. 전 세계의 총 가계 부채가 미화 약 44조 달러에 달한다. 개인적인 금전 문제는 또한 전 세계 시민들 중 거의 절반의 가장 큰 스트레스 원인으로 거론되기도 한다.

12   ③

대부분의 영미 문학 강좌가 문화적 다양성을 반영하지 못한다는 단서로부터 정답을 추론할 수 있다.

insinuate v. 암시하다, 넌지시 말하다 exhilarate v. ~의 기분을 들뜨게 하다 stifle v. 질식시키다 foment v. 촉진하다, 조성하다, 선동하다

문화적 다양성을 반영해 오고 있지 않는 대부분의 영미 문학 강좌들은 우리의 다문화적인 특징들에서 핵심인 지적인 개방성을 질식시켰다.

13   ①

순접의 접속사 and를 통해 빈칸과 have the opposite effect라는 표현이 연결되어 있으므로, 빈칸에도 이와 유사한 의미를 가진 단어가 들어가야 한다. 따라서 '역효과를 내다'라는 의미의 ①이 정답이 된다.

boost n. 밀어올림; 밀어줌, 후원, 지지; 인상, 증가 piggyback v. 기대다, 편승하다 opposite a. 맞은편의, 정반대의; 역(逆)의 effect n. 결과; 효과; 영향 intend v. 의도하다; 기도하다; 예정하다 backfire v. 예상을 뒤엎다, 역효과를 내다; 실패하다 reckon v. 헤아리다; 기대하다 infringe v. 침해하다, 위반하다 spur v. 박차를 가하다, 몰아대다

부모님의 신용카드 계좌를 이용해 자신의 신용점수를 올리려고 하는 젊은이들은 그런 조치가 자신들에게 역효과를 가져올 수 있으며 실제로는 의도한 것과 정반대의 효과를 낼 수 있다는 것을 알게 될 것이다.

14   ②

분사구문으로 된 voting 이하에서 '대신에 반대하는 분자들에게 표를 던졌다'고 했으므로 빈칸에는 '버렸다'는 뜻의 ②가 적절하다.

stunning a. 기절할 만큼의, 엄청난 shift n. 변화, 변동, 추이, 교체 insurgent n. 폭도, 반란자; <정치> (정당내의) 반대 분자 resurrect v. 소생시키다 ditch v. 버리다 underpin v. 지지하다 mar v. 손상시키다

엄청난 세대교체 속에서 수백만 명의 젊은 프랑스인들은 수 세대 동안 프랑스를 지배해온 사회주의 정당과 보수 정당을 버리고 대신에 마크롱 같은 (이 정당들에) 반대하는 분자들에게 표를 던졌다.

15   ③

대형 언론사를 멸종한 동물인 공룡에 비유하고 있다. 이유의 종속절을 이끌고 있는 as절에 '시청률과 발행 부수가 거침없이 추락하고 있다'라고 했으므로, 언론사들이 직원들을 정리하고 있다는 말이 되어야 한다. 그래야만 첫 번째 문장에서 언급한 '제 수명을 단축하고 있다'라는 표현과 자연스럽게 호응한다. 따라서 ③이 정답이 된다.

pull out the stops 필사의 노력을 하다 lumbering a. (육중한 덩치로) 느릿느릿 움직이는; 방대한; 둔감한 rating n. 평가, 견적; 시청률 circulation n. 순환, 유통; 발행부수 inexorably ad. 거침없이; 냉혹하게 slide v. 미끄러지다, 미끄러져 가다 replenish v. 채우다, 다시 채우다, 보충하다 pamper v. 하고 싶은 대로 하게 하다, 응석을 받아주다 slash v. 대폭 줄이다, 삭감하다 hallow v. 신성하게 하다; 숭배하다

대형 언론사들이 전체적인 형세를 바꾸기 위해 필사의 노력을 하고 있지만, 그런 언론사들은 그 과정에서 제 수명을 단축하고 있는지도 모른다. 행동이 굼뜬 옛 언론 공룡들은 시청률과 발행 부수가 거침없이 추락함에 따라 직원을 정리해오고 있으며 온라인 뉴스 매체에 밥그릇을 빼앗기는 것을 지켜보고 있다.

16   ③

빈칸에 들어갈 단어의 목적어가 the need for further study or explanation of them임에 유의한다. 동물에게는 이성이 없고 그들은 오로지 본능에 의해서만 행동한다고 믿는다면, 복잡한 연구나 설명이 필요하지 않다고 여기게 될 것이다. 그러므로 그러한 필요성을 '없애다, 사라지게 하다'라는 의미를 표현할 수 있는 단어가 필요하다. 정답으로 적절한 것은 '감추다'라는 의미를 가진 ③이다.

govern v. 통치하다, 다스리다; 지배하다 faculty n. 능력, 재능 reason n. 이유; 도리; 이성, 지성 instinct n. 본능; 타고난 소질; 직감 attribution n. (원인 따위를 ~에) 돌림, 귀속(歸屬); (사람·사물의) 속성 necessitate v. 필요로 하다; (결과를) 수반하다 beleaguer v. 에워싸다, 포위공격하다; 괴롭히다 disguise v. 변장하다, 가장하다; 숨기다, 감추다 articulate v. 똑똑히 발음하다; 분명히 말하다

인간의 행동은 이성의 기능이 지배하고 동물의 행동은 본능의 기능이 지배한다고들 한다. 그러나 동물의 행동을 본능으로 돌리는 바로 이것이 이 말을 사용하는 대부분의 사람들에게서 동물을 좀 더 연구하고 설명해야 할 필요성을 감춰버린 듯하다.

17   ②

빈칸 앞에 위치한 must be의 주어는 the politics of insults, character assassination and the use of intemperate language이다. and 앞 부분에서 이러한 것들이 민주주의를 파괴하고 있다고 했으므로, 민주주의의 날을 기념하러 온 사람들은 이런 것들에 반대하고 막으려는 입장을 표명했을 것이다. 따라서 빈칸에는 '막다, 저지하다'라는 의미를 가진 ②가 적절하다.

participant n. 참가자, 관여자 forum n. 공개 토론회; 포럼 insult n. 모욕, 무례 assassination n. 암살; (명예의) 훼손 intemperate a. 무절제한; 과도한, 난폭한 fledgling a. 풋내기의, 미숙한 nonplus v. 난처하게 하다, 당황하게 만들다 stem v. (흐름을) 막다, 저지하다; 멈추게 하다 uphold v. 지지하다, 시인하다, 변호하다 cloister v. 수도원에 가두다; 은둔시키다

올해 세계 민주주의의 날을 기념하여 경제문제연구소(IEA)가 주최한 공개 토론회에 참석한 사람들은 모욕, 인신공격, 그리고 폭언의 정치가 막 태동한 그 나라의 민주주의를 급속하게 파괴하고 있으며 그것들을 시급히 막아야 한다는 것을 모두 인정했다.

18   ②

the way they practice their faith에서 대명사 they가 가리키는 것은 Muslim이므로, 이 표현은 그 다음 문장의 Islamic traditions와 사실상 같은 의미이다. Islamic traditions가 '매우 다양하다'라고 한 것에 대해 빈칸이 들어 있는 문장도 같은 의미를 나타내야 하는데, 빈칸 앞에 부정어 not이 있으므로 결국 vary의 반대 의미를 내포하고 있는 단어가 필요하다. 따라서 '완전히 통일된'이라는 의미의 ②가 정답이 된다.

confuse v. 혼동하다, 헷갈리게 하다, 잘못 알다 grave a. 중대한, 예사롭지 않은 planet n. 행성 vary v. 변화하다, 변하다; 가지각색이다, 서로 다르다 influence v. 영향을 미치다, 감화하다 whopping a. 터무니없이 큰 monolithic a. 단일거석의; 완전히 통일된, 한 덩어리를 이룬 antiquated a. 낡아빠진; 노후한; 오래된; 구식의, 시대에 뒤진 sciolistic a. 겉만 번지르르한 지식의, 수박 겉핥기식의, 천박한 학문의

많은 미국인들이 지금 이슬람과 알 카에다(al-Qaida)를 혼동하고 있는 것은 심각한 실수이다. 지구상의 4명 중 1명은 회교도이다. 그러나 회교도들이 자신들의 신앙을 실천하는 방식이 완전히 통일돼 있는 것은 아니다. 규모가 큰 여타 종교 신앙처럼, 이슬람 전통도 곳곳에 따라 크게 다르며, 현지 문화의 영향을 자주 받는다.

19 ③

until 앞에서 이야기하고자 하는 것은 '덧없음' 또는 '일시성'이다. until 이하는 앞의 내용을 인생 전체에 확장시켜 얻을 수 있는 결론에 해당하므로, 역시 '덧없음' 혹은 '일시성'에 관한 내용이어야 한다. 빈칸 앞에 부정어가 있으므로 이와 반대되는 의미, 즉 '의미심장함' 혹은 '연속성'을 뜻하는 단어가 들어가야 하며, 따라서 정답은 ③이 된다.

absorbing a. 흡수하는; 열중하게 하는 appetite n. 식욕; 욕구 passion n. 열정; 격정; 열망 tide n. 조수, 조류; 흥망성쇠 empty v. 비우다, 없어지게 하다 opprobrium n. 불명예, 치욕 quibble n. 핑계, 구차한 변명 continuity n. 연속, 연속성 quintessence n. 정수, 진수, 전형

나이가 들어가면서, 우리는 그 때는 사람을 열중시키는 흥미 있는 일로 보였던 것이 사실은 우리를 잠깐 동안 휩쓸고서 사라지는 욕망 혹은 정열이었다는 것을 알게 된다. 그리하여 드디어, 우리의 인생은 조수(潮水)에 의해 물거품으로 채워졌다가는 곧 말라버리고 마는 바위 사이의 물웅덩이처럼 연속성이 없는 덧없는 것이라는 것을 알게 된다.

20 ①

유럽인들과는 달리, 중국인들이 빅맥 햄버거를 문화적 제국주의로 인식하지 않는 것은 '미국의 것'이라는 색깔을 없애고 자신들의 것으로 받아들였기 때문일 것이다. 따라서 첫 번째 빈칸에는 internalized 또는 domesticated가 올 수 있다. 한편, 미국의 색채가 묻어나지 않게 했다면, 아이들은 그것을 미국의 것이 아닌 자국의 브랜드로 여길 것이므로, 두 번째 빈칸에는 domestic이 들어가는 것이 적절하다. 따라서 정답은 ①이 된다.

terrifying a. 무서운; 예사롭지 않은 imperialism n. 제국주의 invasion n. 침입, 침략; 침해 identify v. 확인하다; (신원을) 판정하다; 감정하다; 동일시하다 internalize v. (다른 집단의 가치관 따위를) 받아들여 자기의 것으로 하다 domestic a. 국내의, 자국의; 국산의 excommunicate v. 파문하다, 제명하다, 축출하다 domesticate v. 길들이다; (외국의 습관 따위를) 자기 나라에 받아들이다 vanquish v. 정복하다, 극복하다 proxy a. 대리의, 대리에 의한

유럽인들은 빅맥(Big Mac) 햄버거를 모조리 미국의 문화적 제국주의에 대한 무서운 징후로 보는 경향이 있을지 모르지만, 중국인들은 그러한 침략을 대체로 환

영하며 받아들였으며, 실제로는 자신들의 것으로 만들었다. 최근에 실시한 한 설문조사에서, 12세 이하의 중국 어린이들 가운데 거의 절반이 맥도날드를 자국 브랜드로 인지하고 있었다.

21 ①

두 번째 문장에서 while절은 현실(reality)을 나타내고 주절의 believes는 사람들의 인식(perception)을 나타내므로 빈칸에는 '현실과 인식'이라는 의미의 ①이 적절하다.

enduring a. 지속하는 perception n. 인식, 지각 conservatism n. 보수주의 liberalism n. 진보주의, 자유주의

광범위한 경기 회복에 있어 가장 오래 지속되는 특성은 현실과 인식 사이의 차이였다. 성장과 고용이 증가하고 있는데도 미국인 4명 중 약 1명만이 경제가 더욱 튼튼해지고 있다고 믿는다. 이유는 분명하다. 고소득층을 제외하고는 개인소득이 늘고 있지 않기 때문이다.

22 ②

중산층 젊은이들이 공부에 대해 걱정을 하지 않는 것은 졸업 후의 진로나 방향이 보장되어 있기 때문일 것이다. 주체가 중산층 젊은이들의 부모이므로, 빈칸에는 '연줄을 이용하다', '배후에서 영향력을 행사하다'라는 의미의 ②가 들어가는 것이 가장 적절하다.

scholarship n. 학문, 학식; 장학금 graduate v. 졸업하다 a great deal of 매우 많은, 다량의 motivation n. 자극, 유도; 동기부여; 열의, 욕구 degree n. 계급, 신분, 지위; 학위 be in red 적자를 내다 pull strings 배후에서 조종하다; 연줄을 동원하다 toe the line 출발선에 서다; 규칙을 지키다; 책임을 지다 go over the top 단호한 수단을 쓰다, 돌격하다

내가 경험한 대학 생활에 의하면, 중산층 젊은이들은 장학금을 받으면서 공부하는 데 관심이 없었다. 그들 가운데 상당수는 졸업 후에 자신들을 위해 연줄을 이용할 수 있는 부모를 두고 있는 까닭에 공부에 대해 관심을 둘 이유가 없었다. 반면에 노동자 계층의 학생들은 학위를 취득하기 위한 열의가 많이 있었다.

23 ④

첫 번째 빈칸 앞 문장에서 테마파크가 직원들에게 제공하는 혜택이 언급되어 있으므로 첫 번째 빈칸에는 perks(혜택)가 적절하다. 그리고 이런 혜택의 제공이 직원들의 충성심을 유지시켜 준다고 했는데, 두 번째 빈칸 뒤에서 신입사원을 채용하고 훈련시키는 데 드는 비용을 낮춘다는 것은 결국 이직률과 연관된 것이므로 두 번째 빈칸에는 turnover(이직률)가 적절하다.

little-known a. 거의 알려지지 않은 attraction n. 인기거리, 어트랙션 compensation package (급여와 복리후생을 포함한) 보수 altruistic a. 이타주의의 audit n. 회계감사 reward n. 보상 facilities n. 편의시설 boredom n.

지루함 subsidy n. 보조금 acquisition n. 취득, 획득 perk n. 임직원의 특전[혜택] turnover n. 이직률; 거래액

놀이기구를 운영하고 기념품을 판매하는 등의 일은 통상적으로 최저임금보다 조금 더 벌뿐이다. 그러나 무료입장권, 새로운 놀이기구를 먼저 이용할 수 있는 특권과 같이 거의 알려지지 않은 혜택들이 테마파크 직원을 위한 보상혜택 중 큰 부분이 되어왔다. 고용주는 단순히 이타적인 이유 이상으로 특혜를 제공하는데, 그런 추가적인 혜택은 근로자들의 충성심을 유지시켜주며, 직원들의 이직률을 낮추고 신입사원을 채용하고 훈련시키는 데 드는 비용을 낮추는 데 도움이 된다.

---

24 ③

빈칸은 recommendation에 대한 동격절을 이루고 있다. 미국의 안전에 위협이 될 수 있는 것으로 분류됐던 포로들을 석방하거나 이송하는 것은 국방부의 권고와 상반된다고 했으므로, 국방부의 권고 내용은 이들에 대한 석방 혹은 이송을 반대하는 것이라 할 수 있다. 석방이나 이송에 대한 반대 개념은 '계속해서 구금 상태에 있게 하는 것'이므로, 빈칸에는 ③이 들어가야 한다.

prisoner n. 죄수; 포로 release v. 해방하다, 석방하다; 면제하다; 풀어놓다 transfer v. 옮기다, 이동하다; 양도하다 pose v. 자세를 취하게 하다; 적절히 배치하다; (문제 등을) 제기하다 threat n. 위협, 협박; 징조 detainee n. 억류자 classification n. 분류; 등급 매기기 contradict v. 부정하다, 부인하다; ~에 모순되다 recommendation n. 추천; 권고, 건의 intervene v. 방해하다; 조정하다, 중재하다 category n. 범주, 종류; 부류 ultimately ad. 최후로, 마침내

부시(Bush) 대통령과 오바마(Obama) 대통령 시대에 관타나모(Guantanamo) 수용소에서 석방되거나 이송된 포로들 가운데 160명 이상은 이전에 '미국에 위협이 될 가능성이 크다'라고 여겨졌던 사람들이었다. 이전에 '위험성이 큰 것으로' 분류되었음에도 불구하고 이런 억류자들을 석방하거나 이송하기로 한 결정은 이런 부류의 포로들은 구금상태에 있어야 한다는 국방부의 권고와 배치되는 것이었다.

---

25 ②

이상적인 세계의 반대편에 있는 것은 종말론적인 세계라 할 수 있으므로 ②가 정답으로 적절하다.

solarpunk n. 미래를 긍정적인 측면에서 바라보는 새로운 운동 apocalypse n. 대참사, 대사건; 세계의 종말 felicity n. 대단한 행복, 지복 fairyland n. 동화의 나라, 도원경; 더없이 아름다운 곳

"깨끗하고 재생 가능한 에너지로 추동되는 지속가능한 세계를 상상해보십시오. 그리고 태양의 방사능을 동력삼아 이동하는 커다란 우주선들, 나노기술에 의한 바이오 연료 생산, 광합성을 하는 인간의 도래 등을 상상해보십시오. 솔라펑크의 눈부신 푸른 세계에 온 것을 환영합니다." 친환경적인 기술, 경제 이데올로기, 사회학, 공상과학 소설, 건축, 그리고 심지어 패션 등의 혼합물인 솔라펑크는 문화적인 운동이라기보다는 (유토피아를 지향하는) 야심에 찬 마음의 태도이자 생활방식으로 남아 있다. 그러나 솔라펑크라는 용어의 인기는 세계의 종말이라는 대참사에 대한 대안에 대한 갈망을 확증하고 있는 것이다.

TEST 13

01 ④	02 ①	03 ③	04 ④	05 ②	06 ①	07 ③	08 ③	09 ②	10 ②
11 ③	12 ④	13 ②	14 ④	15 ③	16 ②	17 ③	18 ②	19 ②	20 ④
21 ④	22 ④	23 ④	24 ③	25 ④					

01 ④

rather than 다음의 truth-seeking으로 보아, 사설이 진실의 추구라는 목적을 따르지 않고 있다면 그것 외의 목적을 가지고 있다고 봐야 하므로, '저의가 있는'이라는 의미의 ④가 정답이 된다.

subscriber n. 기부자; 응모자, 신청자, 예약자; 구독자 editorial n. 사설, 논설 periodical n. 정기간행물, 잡지 square a. 공명정대한, 올바른, 정직한; 단호한 veracious a. 진실을 말하는, 성실한, 정직한 brusque a. 무뚝뚝한, 통명스러운 tendentious a. 목적이 있는, 저의가 있는; 불공평한, 선전적인

이 정기간행물 속의 사설은 진실을 추구한다기보다는 어떤 목적을 염두에 두고 있다고 많은 구독자들이 생각하고 있다.

02 ①

빈칸 뒤에 비교급 than이 왔으므로 부시가 준비된 원고를 읽을 때보다 준비 없이 의사를 전할 때 더 잘한다는 말이 되어야 한다. 따라서 ①이 빈칸에 적절하다.

off-the-cuff ad. 준비 없이, 즉석에서 topsy-turvy ad. 거꾸로, 앞뒤[상하, 선후]가 뒤바뀌어 in a nutshell 아주 간결하게 for a lark 재미삼아

최근 출연에서 부시는 준비된 원고를 읽었을 때보다 준비 없이 의사를 전할 때 더 편안하고 인상적인 모습을 보여줬다.

03 ③

빈칸 뒤의 분사구문에서 언급된 내용을 가장 포괄적으로 설명할 수 있는 단어가 필요하다. 약탈과 방화 등은 무차별적인 폭력행위의 범주에 들어가므로, 정답은 ③이 된다.

racial a. 인종의, 종족의 tension n. 긴장; 흥분, 노력 explode v. 폭발하다; 파열하다 trigger v. 방아쇠를 당기다; (일련의 사건·반응 등을) 일으키다, 유발하다 loot v. 약탈하다 rob v. 훔치다, 강탈하다 dedication n. 봉헌, 헌신 nonentity n. 존재하지 않음, 허무; 하잘것없는 사람 mayhem n. 신체 상해; 무차별 폭력; 대혼란, 아수라장 armistice n. 휴전, 정전(停戰)

인종간의 긴장상태가 폭발하여 무차별적인 폭력으로 나타났는데, 그리하여 화가 난 흑인들은 코리아타운에서 한국인이 소유하고 있는 상점을 불 지르고 약탈하고 강탈하였다.

04 ④

which 이하는 '본사 건물'이라는 표현을 수식하고 있는데, '로비에 전시할 수 있다'라고 했으므로 실제 건물이 아닌 모형이 필요할 것이다.

headquarters n. 본사, 본부 estimated a. 평가상의, 견적상의 repose n. 휴식, 휴양; 침착, 평정 remnant n. 나머지, 잔여; 찌꺼기 recluse n. 은둔자, 속세를 떠난 사람 replica n. 복사, 복제; 모형

우리가 로비에 전시할 수 있는 본사 건물의 모형을 여러분들이 만들어 주길 바랍니다. 가능한 빨리 예상 비용을 알려 주십시오.

05 ②

순접의 접속사 and가 빈칸 앞에 있으므로, 빈칸에 들어갈 단어는 the accepted notions와 같거나 유사한 의미를 가진 것이어야 한다. 따라서 '선입견'이라는 의미의 ②가 정답이다.

afresh ad. 새로이, 다시 discard v. 버리다, 폐기하다 accepted a. 일반에게 인정된 notion n. 관념, 개념; 생각, 의견 flesh n. 살; 육체 preamble n. 서문, 머리말 prejudice n. 편견, 선입견 hyperbole n. 과장; 과장된 말 apothegm n. 격언, 경구

화가들은 세상을 새롭게 보길 원하며, 살결은 분홍빛이고 사과는 노랗거나 붉다는 기존의 모든 생각과 선입견을 벗어버리길 원한다.

06 ①

빈칸은 그 배우의 특징을 수식할 수 있는 형용사가 필요한데, '속내를 드러내지 않는다'고 했으므로 말수가 적은 사람임을 알 수 있다. 따라서 ①이 빈칸에 적절하다.

play one's cards close to the vest 불필요한 위험을 피하다; 속내를 드러내지 않다 curt a. 짧은, 간략한 laconic a. 간명한; (사람이) 말수가 적은 versatile a. 재주가 많은; 변덕스러운 flamboyant a. 현란한, 화려한 seclusive a. 틀어박혀 있기를 좋아하는, 은둔적인

텍사스 출신으로 존슨은 여전히 샌안토니오의 외곽에 살고 있는데, 말수가 적은 그 영화배우는 항상 속내를 드러내지 않아 왔지만, '할리우드 리포터'지에 그의 신작 영화에 대해 어느 정도 간략한 의견을 말했다.

농업의 시작과 함께 신석기 시대의 인구는 급격히 증가하여 사람들은 더 이상 자기 마을 공동체 구성원을 다 알 수는 없게 되었다. 그 결과로 나타난 소외가 사회 불안을 낳았다.

07 ③

into more open construction이라는 표현이 단서가 된다. into는 상태의 변화, 추이, 결과를 나타내는 전치사이고, more open이라는 비교급 표현 속에는 현재보다 바람직한 상태로의 변화의 의미가 내포되어 있다. 그러므로 '개선'의 의미를 가지고 있는 단어가 필요하며, 정답은 ③이 된다.

parallel v. ~에 평행하게 하다; ~에 필적시키다 construction n. 건설, 건축; 구조, 구성 focus v. 초점을 맞추다, 집중하다 borderline a. 경계선상의, 경계의; 결정하기 어려운 inland a. 내륙의 retrovert v. 뒤로 구부리다 wither v. 시들게 하다, 쇠퇴하게 하다 revamp v. 수선하다; 개조하다; 개혁하다, 쇄신하다 postulate v. 가정하다; 요구하다

더욱이, 세계화 시대에 발맞춰 나가기 위해 대한민국의 국가 구조를 좀 더 개방적인 구조로 개혁해 나갈 것이며, 동부, 서부, 남부 해안 지역과 같은 경계 지역 및 내륙 대도시 지역의 개발에 집중할 것입니다.

08 ③

컵 밑바닥에 무언가가 숨어 있을 것 같아 내용물을 다 마시지 못하는 경향이 있다면, 그러한 경향은 안에 무엇이 들어있는지 알 수 없는 경우에 특히 심할 것이라 예상할 수 있다. 이러한 상황을 만드는 것은 컵이 불투명한 경우이다.

container n. 그릇, 용기(容器) stem v. 유래하다, 일어나다, 생기다, 시작하다 paranoid a. 편집증의, 편협한, 과대망상의 lurk v. 숨다, 잠복하다 exotic a. 외래의, 외국산의; 이국적인 opaque a. 불투명한 elliptical a. 타원형의; 생략된

나는 컵에 든 내용물을 밑바닥까지 다 마시기가 어려운데, 불투명한 컵이면 특히 더 그러하다. 이런 이상한 행동의 이유는 컵 밑바닥에 숨어있을지도 모르는 것에 대해 내가 병적인 망상을 갖고 있다는 데 있다.

09 ②

The resulting은 의미상 결과의 접속사를 대신하고 있으므로, 빈칸에는 앞 문장에서 말한 현상, 즉, 마을 사람들끼리 잘 모르는 것으로부터 생길 수 있는 현상과 관련된 단어가 와야 하며, 또한 이것은 사회 불안을 초래하는 원인으로 작용할 수 있는 것이어야 한다. 이런 조건에 맞는 것은 '소외'라는 의미의 ②이다.

advent n. 도래, 출현; 시작 Neolithic a. 신석기의 resulting a. 결과적인 disorder n. 혼란, 무질서; (사회적·정치적) 소동, 소란 strangulation n. 질식, 협착 estrangement n. 소외, 소원(疏遠), 불화 martyrdom n. 순교; 순교자적 고통 expulsion n. 추방; 제명, 제적; 배제

10 ②

빈칸 다음의 goal이 destination과 같은 의미이므로 빈칸에는 fixed와 같은 의미의 ②가 들어가는 것이 적절하다.

set out on 길을 떠나다, 출발하다 eye-opening a. 놀라운 destination n. 목적지 stray v. 옆길로 빗나가다 by-way n. 옆길 goal n. 목적지 overriding a. 최우선적인 preordain v. 미리 정하다 impassable a. 통행할 수 없는 foretell v. 예언하다

모든 해답을 찾을 것이라는 기대 없이 끝없는 길을 나서는 것은 일정한 목적지로 여행하는 것보다 언제나 더 놀랄만한 일이었는데 그것은 미리 정해진 목적지보다 더 보람될지 모르는 옆길로 자유롭게 들어서게 해주기 때문이다.

11 ③

주어진 글에서 분사구문과 주절은 인과관계에 있다. 많은 수가 곧 퇴직할 상황에 놓여 있는 직업은 평균연령이 높은 직업, 다시 말해 노령화가 심한 직업이라고 할 수 있다. 그러므로 정답은 ③이 되며, a large percentage of librarians that would soon be retiring과 같은 뜻을 나타내는 단어를 고르는 문제라 할 수 있다.

article n. 물품; 기사, 논설; 조항 profession n. 직업; 고백, 선언 note v. 적어두다; 주목하다, 알아차리다 librarian n. 도서관 직원, 사서 retire v. 은퇴하다, 퇴직하다; 후퇴하다, 철수하다 exodus n. 집단적 대이동; (이민 등의) 출국, 이주 professionalize v. 직업화하다, 전문화하다 masculinize v. 더 남자답게[남자같이] 만들다 gray v. 백발이 되다, 노령화하다 feminize v. 여성스럽게 만들다, 여성화하다

지난 몇 년에 걸쳐, 여러 기사에서 상당수의 사서들이 곧 은퇴하게 될 것이라는 사실에 주목하면서, 이 직업의 노령화 추세에 우려를 표명해 왔다. 그러나 지금은 대규모 인력 이탈에 대한 걱정은 필요 없어 보인다.

12 ④

by recognizing의 주체가 관계대명사 who가 아니라 전체 문장의 주어인 He임에 유의해야 한다. 문장을 살펴보면, 빈칸 뒤의 that절에는 veteran에 대한 부정적인 내용이 언급되어 있고, by recognizing 이하의 that절에는 veteran에 대해 긍정적인 내용이 주어져 있음을 알 수 있다. 앞서 언급했듯이 by recognizing의 주체는 전체 문장의 주어인 He이므로, '긍정적인 면을 인정함으로써 부정적인 생각을 불식시킨다'라는 맥락이 되는 것이 자연스럽다. ①과 ③에 쓰인 동사 confirm과 spread는 '불식시키는 것'과 반대 개념이며, ②에 쓰인 명사 acclaim은 부정적인 내용을 담고 있는 that절과 동격을 이루는 것이 어색하기 때

문에 정답에서 제외된다. 따라서 '고정관념을 깨뜨리다'라는 의미의 ④가 빈칸에 가장 적절하다.

veteran n. 퇴역군인, 참전용사 troubled a. 난처한, 당황한; 거친, 떠들썩한 recognize v. 알아보다, 인정하다, 인식하다 deployment n. (부대의) 배치, 전개 confirm v. 확실히 하다, 확증하다; 확인하다 hearsay n. 소문, 풍문 blemish v. 더럽히다, 흠을 내다 acclaim n. 찬사; 갈채, 환호 myth n. 신화; 전설; 꾸며낸 이야기 stereotype n. 고정관념; 상투적인 수단

퇴역군인들이 군사 훈련과 부대 배치 등에서 중요한 리더십과 사회생활 기술을 터득했음을 인정함으로써, 그는 퇴역군인이 거친 시한폭탄이거나 스스로 생각할 수 없는 로봇이라는 고정관념을 깨뜨리고 있다.

13 ②

어떤 사람이 아무런 지식 없이 특정 의견에 동의했다면, 그 사람은 그 어떤 반대 의견에도 제대로 대처할 수 없을 것이고 대답도 할 수 없을 것이다. 따라서 빈칸에는 ②가 들어가야 한다. ④의 경우, 빈칸 뒤의 대명사 it이 '자신이 동의하기로 한 의견'을 가리키므로, 동의하는 의견에 대한 해결책을 제시한다는 의미가 되어 적절하지 않다. 이것이 답이 되자면, 빈칸 뒤에 of it이 없어야 한다.

assent v. 동의하다, 찬성하다 undoubtingly ad. 의심하지 않고, 확신을 갖고 ground n. 기초, 근거, 이유, 동기 superficial a. 표면적인, 외견상의; 피상적인 objection n. 반대; 이의, 반론 practical a. 실제상의; 실용적인, 쓸모 있는 tenable a. 공격에 견딜 수 있는; 유지할 수 있는 critical a. 비평의; 비판적인; 위기의 plausible a. 그럴 듯한, 정말 같은 solution n. 용해; 용액; 해결, 해법

자기들이 사실이라고 생각하는 의견을 어떤 한 사람이 의심 없이 동의하면, 그 사람이 그 의견의 타당한 근거를 전혀 알지 못하고 가장 피상적인 반대 주장에 대해서도 그 의견을 조리 있게 방어할 수 없을 지라도 그것으로 충분하다고 생각하는 그런 부류의 사람들이 있다.

14 ④

어떤 대책의 유효기간이 끝나서 피해가 발생했다면 그 대책의 효력이 지속되도록 하는 조치가 미리 취해졌어야 했을 것이다. 따라서 빈칸에는 ④가 적절하다.

federal a. 연방의 unemployment benefit 실업수당 emergency measure 비상대책, 긴급조치 recession n. 불경기, 경기침체 expire v. (기간이) 끝나다, 만기가 되다 condemn v. 비난하다 devise v. 고안하다; 발명하다 enforce v. 실행하다 abolish v. 폐지하다 renew v. 갱신하다

심한 불경기 때 통과된 비상대책의 유효기간이 12월 28일에 끝나자 130만 명이 넘는 미국인들이 연방정부의 실업수당을 잃게 되었다. 정부는 의회가 그 대책을 갱신하지 못한 것을 비난했다.

15 ③

집에 온 사람들은 이전에 살고 있던 사람들의 아이들이 그린 그림인 줄을 알 지 못한 채, 글쓴이의 아이가 한 것으로 오해하고서 칭찬을 했던 것이다. 그러므로 빈칸에는 ③이 들어가야 적절한데, culprit이 이 문맥에서는 '범죄를 저지른 사람'이라는 의미가 아니라 '어떤 사건을 일으킨 장본인'이라는 의미로 쓰였다.

transfer v. 옮아가다, 이동하다; 갈아타다 former a. 이전의, 앞의 occupant n. 점유자, 거주자 comment v. 논평하다, 의견을 말하다 layman n. 속인, 평신도; 아마추어, 문외한 outcast n. 추방당한 사람, 부랑인 culprit n. 범인; 피의자; (문제를 일으킨) 장본인 witness n. 증언; 증인, 목격자

우리 가족이 3년 전에 집을 옮겼을 때, 이전에 살던 사람들에게는 유치원에 다니는 아이가 둘 있었는데, 그 아이들이 문과 벽에 크레용 자국을 남겨 놓았었다. 그 때 이후로, 우리 집에 온 사람들은 종종 4살짜리 내 아들이 그렇게 했다고 생각하고서 그림을 잘 그린다고들 말해 왔다.

16 ②

첫 번째 문장의 내용에 대해 두 번째 문장에서 부연해서 설명하는 구조의 글이다. 빈칸 뒤에 위치한 관계사절에서, 대명사 it이 가리키는 것은 첫 번째 문장의 trial by jury이므로 빈칸에는 첫 번째 문장에 쓰인 beginning과 동일한 의미를 가진 단어가 들어가야 한다. 그러므로 ②가 정답이 된다.

beginning n. 시작; 발단, 기원 trial n. 공판, 재판, 심리; 시도 jury n. 배심; 심사원 establish v. 확립하다, 설립하다, 개설하다 progeny n. 자손; 제자, 후계자; 결과 germ n. 미생물, 병균; 조짐, 기원, 근원 consummation n. 완성, 성취, 완료; 극치 microbe n. 세균; 미생물

배심원에 의한 재판의 기원을 찾기 위해서는 헨리(Henry) 2세 시대로 거슬러 올라가야 한다. 그가 살던 시대 이전에도 그러한 재판이 발전해 온 근원이 존재하고 있었으나, 현대의 형태로 발전할 수 있도록 확립한 것은 그가 최초였다.

17 ③

빈칸에는 앞 문장에서 언급한 난투극 혹은 충돌을 지칭할 수 있는 단어가 필요하며, 적절한 것은 '실랑이, 승강이'라는 의미의 ③이다. 난투극과 실랑이가 자연스럽게 호응하지 않는다고 생각할지 모르나, 감독 입장에서는 좋지 않은 사건을 축소해서 표현하고자 했을 것임을 감안해서 보아야 한다.

scuffle v. 난투하다; 허둥대다 skirmish n. 전초전, (우발적인) 작은 전투; 작은 충돌 put a stop to ~을 멈추다, 중지시키다, 끝내다 consternation n. 소스라침, 당황, 섬뜩 놀람 ramification n. 파문, 영향, 결과 altercation n. 논쟁, 격론; 실랑이 contusion n. 타박상; 멍듦

악수를 하기 위해 미드필드 부근으로 모인 양 팀은 스테이션 캠프 팀의 선수석 앞에서 난투극을 벌이기 시작했는데, 이 충돌은 양 팀의 코치진과 경찰들이 나서고서야 중단시킬 수 있었다. 스테이션 캠프 팀의 감독 홀린즈워스(Shaun Hollinsworth)는 "실랑이가 어떻게 시작되었는지 보지 못 했습니다"라고 말했다.

18 ②

But 전후의 문장은 대조를 이루어야 한다. But 이하에 6개월 이상의 공백에 대해서는 채용하는 사람들이 의구심을 갖고 묻기 시작할 것이라는 언급이 있으므로, 그 앞에는 몇 달간의 공백은 무방하다는 내용이 와야 한다. 그러므로 빈칸에는 But 이하의 문장에 있는 void 혹은 그 뒤의 문장에 나오는 gap과 유사한 의미를 가지는 단어가 들어가는 것이 적절하다. ②가 정답이다.

recruiter n. 신병 모집인, 모병관; 모집인 void n. 진공; 공간 employment n. 고용; 직업, 일 jeopardize v. 위태롭게 하다, 위험한 지경에 빠뜨리다 prospect n. 전망, 경치; 예상, 기대 disquisition n. 논문; 강연 hiatus n. 틈; (연속된 것의) 중단, 휴지기 espionage n. 정찰; 간첩행위 arrogation n. 사칭; 횡탈, 월권, 횡포

몇 달간 일을 하지 않은 기간이 있는 것은 전혀 신경 쓸 것이 못 된다. 그러나 채용하는 사람들이 당신의 직무 이력에서 6개월 이상 비어 있는 기간을 발견하게 되면 대체로 그에 관해 질문을 하기 시작할 것이다. 이력에서 공백 기간이 있다는 것을 일단 인식하고 나면, 그것이 장래의 성공 가능성을 위태롭게 하지 않도록 위험관리를 어느 정도는 해야 한다.

19 ②

parliamentary perks의 내용이 a travesty 다음의 that절에 구체적으로 나와 있으며, 이러한 특권에 대해 a travesty라는 부정적 의미로 표현하고 있는 상황이다. 따라서 퍼듀카 의원이 의원의 특권에 대해 부정적인 입장이라면, 첫 번째 빈칸에는 '비판'하는 단어가, 두 번째 빈칸에는 '시인'하는 단어가 들어가야 한다. 또한 만약 동조하는 입장이라면, 첫 번째 빈칸에는 '지지'하는 단어가, 두 번째 빈칸에는 '부인'하는 단어가 들어가야 한다. 이러한 조건을 충족시키는 것은 ②뿐이다.

parliamentary a. 의회의; 의회에서 제정된, 의회의 관례에 의거한 perk n. 특전, 혜택; 임시 수입, 팁 travesty n. 졸렬한 모조품, 서툰 흉내; 익살스런 변장 parliamentarian n. 하원의원 be entitled to ~할 자격이 있다 pension n. 연금 supportive a. 지지가 되는 argue v. 논하다; 주장하다 critical a. 비평의; 비판적인; 위기의 acknowledge v. 인정하다, 고백하다 expectant a. 기다리고 있는, 기대하고 있는 prophesy v. 예언하다; 예측하다 censorious a. 비판적인; 검열관 같은 negate v. 부인하다, 부정하다, 취소하다

의회의 특권에 대해 비판적인 입장을 보여 왔던 상원의원 마르코 퍼듀카(Marco Perduka)는, 한 차례의 임기를 채우는 의원에게 다른 사람이었으면 40년을 일했어야 할 정도의 연금을 받을 자격을 주는 것은 웃기는 일임을 시인하고 있다.

20 ④

마지막 두 문장에서 '현대인들이 조상의 유산인 위험에 대한 공포심으로 인해 사회 현실을 오해하여 현실이 아닌 환각의 세계를 만든다'고 했는데, 이것은 정확한 현실 파악을 '방해하는' 것이므로 빈칸에는 ④가 적절하다.

predator n. 포식자, 육식동물 marauder n. 약탈자 legacy n. 유산 unwittingly ad. 부지중에 phantom n. 유령, 환각, 망상 poise v. (자세를) 취하다 be poised to V ~할 태세(각오)이다 innocuous a. 무해한, 악의 없는 indemnify v. 보상(보장)하다 sublime v. 승화시키다 regenerate v. 재생하다 encumber v. 방해하다

육식동물이나 약탈자 무리들과 같은 과거 선사시대의 적들이 이제는 더 이상 우리의 일상적 생존에 위험이 되지 않지만, 우리는 이러한 위험들에 노출되어 두려워했던 우리 조상들의 유산에 방해받고 있다. 우리는 개개인들이 우리를 지배하고 기만하고 착취할 태세인 환각의 세계를 부지불식 중에 만든다. 우리는 사소하거나 악의 없는 사건이나 경미한 도전을 중대한 공격으로 오해할지도 모른다.

21 ④

첫 번째 문장은 과거의 상황을 이야기하고 있고, Now 이하에서는 현재의 상황을 이야기하고 있다. 현재와 과거의 상황이 대조를 이루어야 하겠는데, 두 번째 문장에서 'DNA를 만지작거려 뜻대로 바꿀 수 있다'라고 했으므로, 첫 번째 문장은 '과거에는 이것이 불가능했다고 생각했다'라는 내용이어야 한다. 따라서 '바꿀 수 없는, 조작할 수 없는'이라는 의미인 ④가 정답이다.

code n. 법전; 규약, 규칙 epigenetics n. 후생유전학 influence v. 영향을 미치다; 좌우하다 genetic code 유전 정보 tinker with ~을 어설프게 만지작거리다, 서투르게 수선하다 bend v. 알맞게 바꾸다 to one's will ~의 뜻대로, 맘대로 labile a. 변하기 쉬운, 변화를 일으키기 쉬운, 불안정한 heterodox a. 이단의, 정통이 아닌 longwinded a. 숨이 긴; 장광설의 ironclad a. 철갑을 입힌; 깨뜨릴 수 없는, 엄격한

우리는 DNA를 우리, 우리 자식들, 손자들이 지키고 살아야 하는 엄격한 규약 같은 것으로 생각했다. 이제는 강력한 환경 조건이 단 한 세대 만에 유전 정보에 영향을 미칠 수 있음을 보여주는 새로운 후생유전학의 증거들로 인해, 우리는 DNA를 만지작거릴 수 있고 우리 뜻대로 그것을 바꿀 수 있는 세상을 상상할 수 있게 되었다.

22 ④

마지막 문장에서 '번성하던 시기에는 위대한 대통령으로 남는 인물이 거의 없다'라고 한 점이 단서가 된다. 이 말을 달리 표현하면, '임기 동안 위기가 많은 경우에 위대한 대통령으로 남게 될 가능성이 크다'는 것이며, 그렇기 때문에 클린턴은 9.11 사건이 자신의 재임 기간에 일어나지 않은 것에 대해 아쉬워했던 것이다.

acquaintance n. 지식; 면식; 아는 사람, 아는 사이 frustrated a. 실망한, 좌절된 founder n. 창립자, 설립자; 창시자 predecessor n. 전임자; 선배 priority n. 보다 중요함; 우선권, 우선사항 disaster n. 재해, 재난, 참사

빌 클린턴(Bill Clinton)의 한 지인은 클린턴이 9.11 사건이 자신의 재임 기간에 일어나지 않은 것에 실망감을 느꼈다고 말한 적이 있다. 대통령이 위대해질 수 있는 가장 좋은 기회는 전쟁이나 재난의 시기 동안 집권하고 있는 것이기 때문에 그것은 이해가 가는 말이다. 미국을 건국한 초기의 대통령들을 제외하면, 미국이 번성하던 좋은 시기의 위대한 대통령은 시어도어 루즈벨트(Theodore Roosevelt)뿐이다.

23
④

이집트인들, 페르시아인들, 세계 모든 곳의 사람들은 곧 지역마다의 민족들을 말하는데, 페르시아인들이 자기민족을 중심에 두고 거기서 멀리 사는 사람들일수록 덜 존중했다고 했으므로, 첫 번째 빈칸에는 이와 관계 있는 ethnocentrism(자기민족 중심주의)이 적절하고 두 번째 빈칸에는 lower esteem(더 낮은 존중)이 적절하다.

characterize v. 특징짓다 presumably ad. 아마 hold ~ in esteem ~를 존중하다 anachronism n. 시대착오 rapt a. (생각 따위에) 정신이 팔린, 골몰[몰두]한 xenophobia n. 외국인 혐오 bondage n. 속박; 굴종 nationalism n. 민족주의, 국수주의 contempt n. 경멸, 모욕 ethnocentrism n. 자기민족 중심주의 esteem n. 존중, 존경

자기민족중심주의는 역사상 예로부터 인간 사회의 특징이 되어왔다. 고대 이집트인들은 "사람"인 그들 자신과 아마도 인간에 좀 못 미치는 존재인 다른 민족을 구별 지었다. 고대 페르시아인들은 페르시아로부터 멀어질수록 거기 사는 사람들을 점차적으로 덜 존중했다. 세계 모든 곳의 사람들은 그들 자신과 자신들의 방식을 다른 사람들과 그들의 방식보다 어떻게든 더 낫거나 다 우위에 있다고 생각하는 경향이 있다.

24
③

But 이하에 '다윈과 유사한 이론을 정립한 사람이 나타났다'라는 내용과 '나중에는 자신의 발견에 도움을 준 선배들을 깨닫게 되었다'라는 내용이 있으므로, 다윈이 처음에는 자신이 아무도 생각하지 않은 발견, 다시 말해 '독창적인' 발견을 하고 있다고 생각했을 것이다. 따라서 빈칸에는 ③이 들어가는 것이 적절하다.

formulate v. 공식화하다; 명확하게 말하다 hypothesis n. 가설, 가정; 억측 naturalist n. 박물학자, 자연주의자 predecessor n. 전임자; 선배 pungent a. 매운, 얼얼한; 날카로운 putative a. 상상속의, 추정되는, 억측의 unique a. 유일무이한; 독특한 autochthonous a. 토착의, 자생적인

다윈(Darwin)은 자신이 완전히 독창적인 발견을 하고 있다고 생각하면서 『종의 기원』을 발표했다. 그러나 그가 책을 마무리 짓기 전에, 다른 젊은 박물학자인 월러스(Wallace)가 내놓은 유사한 가설이 그의 관심을 끌었다. 두 사람 모두 맬서스(Malthus)의 『인구론』에서부터 실마리를 얻었다는 사실이 드러났다. 다윈이 재판(再版)을 발행하였을 때에는, 그는 마침내 (이러한 발견을 하는 데 도움을 준) 앞서 간 모든 이들을 깨닫게 되었다.

25
④

두 번째 문장 이하에서는 '예술 활동을 하는 데 필요한 창의성 혹은 창작력은 나이가 들면서 쇠하며, 젊은 시절에 나타나는 왕성한 창작력, 독창성을 보고 예술가의 길로 들어섰다가 후일에 젊은 시절만큼의 예술적 능력을 나타내지 못하게 되어 힘든 세월을 보내는 사람이 많음'을 이야기하고 있다. 이것은 '예술적 영감은 젊은 시절에 누리는 특권과 같은 것 혹은 젊은이에게 가장 왕성한 것'임을 말하고 있는 것이다. 따라서 빈칸에 들어가기에 적절한 표현은 ④가 된다.

tragedy n. 비극, 비극적인 사건 spectacle n. 광경, 장관; 구경거리 vast a. 광대한, 거대한, 막대한 mislead v. 그릇 인도하다, 현혹하다 passing a. 지나가는; 현재의; 한때의, 잠깐 사이의 fertility n. 비옥; 다산(多産), 풍부; 독창성 devote v. (노력·시간 따위를) 바치다; 내맡기다 invention n. 발명; (예술적) 창작, 창조 desert v. 버리다, 돌보지 않다 unfit v. 부적당하게 하다, 어울리지 않게 하다 humdrum a. 평범한, 단조로운, 지루한 calling n. 신의 부르심, 소명, 천직; 생업 harass v. 괴롭히다, 애먹이다 wearied a. 지친, 피곤한; 싫증난 beat out (보도·이야기 등을) 급히 쓰다 bitterness n. 쓴맛; 신랄함; 슬픔, 괴로움 ally v. 동맹하게 하다; 결합시키다 poverty n. 가난, 빈곤; 부족 inspiration n. 영감(靈感); 고취, 고무

청춘은 영감(靈感)이다. 예술 활동의 비극들 가운데 하나는 얼마 있다 사라지고 마는 이러한 독창성을 보고서 길을 잘못 들어 평생을 창작하는 일에 바치는 많은 사람들의 모습이다. 그들의 창의력은 나이가 들면서 없어지고, 이제 와서 이보다 시시한 일을 할 수는 없으므로, 뇌가 더 이상 가져다 줄 수 없는 소재를 얻기 위해 머리를 쥐어짜내는 긴 세월을 맞이하게 된다. 씁쓸하지만, 언론이나 교직처럼 예술과 관련된 일로 생계를 유지할 수 있다면 다행한 일이다.

TEST 14

01 ③	02 ①	03 ④	04 ②	05 ①	06 ③	07 ③	08 ②	09 ①	10 ④
11 ④	12 ①	13 ④	14 ①	15 ①	16 ②	17 ①	18 ②	19 ③	20 ②
21 ①	22 ②	23 ①	24 ④	25 ④					

01 ③

lament는 '애가(哀歌, elegy)'의 의미로 쓰였다. 어떤 노래를 듣고 '애가'라는 인상을 받았다면 그 노래는 '애처로운' 음조의 노래였을 것이다.

impression n. 인상, 감명, 감상 lament n. 비탄, 한탄, 애도; 비가, 애가 minatory a. 협박적인, 위협의 platonic a. 순정적인; 이상적인, 관념적인 plangent a. 울려 퍼지는; 구슬프게 울리는 somnolent a. 졸린, 최면의

우리는 그 노래의 가사들을 이해할 수 없었지만, 가수들의 애처로운 음조로부터 그것이 어떤 종류의 애가(哀歌)라는 인상을 받았다.

02 ①

신중하게 고려하지 않았음이 드러난다고 했으므로, 빈칸에 들어갈 단어는 결국 '신중하지 못한'이라는 문맥상 의미를 가질 수 있는 것이어야 한다. '어리석은'이라는 의미의 ①이 가장 적절하다.

remark n. 주의, 주목; 소견, 비평 consideration n. 고려, 고찰; 참작 asinine a. 우둔한, 고집이 센, 완고한 truculent a. 공격적인, 호전적인; 반항적인 scintillating a. 번득이는; 재기가 넘치는, 재미있는 piercing a. 꿰뚫는; 통찰력 있는

너의 어리석은 말은 네가 이 문제에 대해 진지하게 고려하지 않았음을 분명히 드러내준다고 나는 생각한다.

03 ④

이유를 나타내는 because절에서 '지금까지 만들어진 것과 아주 달랐다'라고 했으므로, 빈칸에는 이와 유사한 의미를 가진 단어가 들어가야 한다. 따라서 '혁신적인'이라는 의미의 ④가 빈칸에 가장 적절하다.

submit v. 제출하다, 제공하다, 맡기다 approval n. 승인, 찬성; 인가, 허가 cricket n. <스포츠> 크리켓; 귀뚜라미 previously ad. 이전에, 본래; 먼저, 미리 earthbound a. 땅에 고착한; 세속적인, 평범한 thoroughgoing a. 철저한, 완전한 hard-boiled a. 냉철한, 현실적인, 고집 센 ground-breaking a. 혁신적인, 획기적인

승인을 받기 위해 제출했을 때, 사람들은 그 디자인이 혁신적이라고들 말했는데, 왜냐하면 그것이 종전에 만들어진 그 어떤 크리켓 대회 트로피와도 아주 달랐기 때문이다.

04 ②

Courage가 가져올 수 있는 일반적인 결과 혹은 효과를 검토해야 하는데, 빈칸 앞에 부정어 not이 있으므로 '용기, 배짱, 담력' 등을 가진 행동과 반대 의미를 갖는 단어가 필요하다. 따라서 '겁을 내다, 움츠려들다'라는 뜻의 ②가 정답이 된다.

radical a. 근본적인; 급진적인, 과격한 policy n. 정책, 방침 initially ad. 처음에, 최초로 recession n. 퇴거, 후퇴; 경기 후퇴 the Great Depression 대공황 stint v. 절약하다, 검약하다 flinch v. 주춤하다, 겁을 내다 rant v. 폭언하다, 고함치다; 야단치다 aspire v. 열망하다, 포부를 갖다

처음에 그의 급진적인 경제 정책이 대공황 이래 최악의 경기침체를 가져다주었을 때, 용기가 그로 하여금 움츠려들지 않게 해주었다.

05 ①

콤마 이하는 앞 문장에서 진술한 '딱정벌레의 당기는 힘'이 사람의 경우라면 어느 정도에 해당하는지를 알려주고 있는 내용으로 보아야 한다. 그러므로 빈칸에는 '~에 상응하는 것, 동등한 것'이라는 뜻인 ①이 적절하다.

reveal v. 밝히다, 드러내다, 누설하다 beetle n. 투구벌레, 딱정벌레 lift v. 올리다, 들어 올리다 equivalent n. 동등한 것, 상당하는 것; 등가물 balance n. 저울; 평균, 균형 contour n. 윤곽, 외형 disparity n. 부동(不同), 부등(不等), 불균형

새로운 연구 결과, 힘센 딱정벌레는 체중의 1141배 되는 것을 끌어당길 수 있다는 사실이 밝혀졌는데, 이것은 체중 70kg의 사람이 80톤의 물건을 들어 올리는 것에 해당한다.

06 ③

부사 accidently가 쓰인 점과 승객으로 인해 공범이 된 정황을 고려하면, 이러한 상황은 그가 의도한 것이 아니라 뜻하지 않게 이뤄진 것이다. 그러므로 빈칸에는 ③이 쓰여야 한다.

accidentally ad. 우연히, 뜻밖에, 문득 accomplice n. 공범, 연루자, 한패 murder n. 살인; 살인사건 passenger n. 승객, 여객 berserk a. 광포한, 맹렬한 jaded a. 몹시 지친, 넌더리 난 unwitting a. 모르는; 무의식의; 고의가 아닌 dishonest a. 부정직한, 불성실한

그 차의 운전사는 자신의 승객이 경쟁 관계에 있는 갱단의 단원을 총으로 쏘는 바람에 살인 사건에 우연히 뜻하지 않은 공범이 되었다.

07 ③

was 이하의 문장에서 not A but B 구문이 쓰였다. 이 구문에서 A와 B에는 각각 서로 대조를 이루는 의미의 표현이 와야 하므로, 빈칸에는 tightly organized 혹은 well-planned와 반대되는 의미를 가진 단어가 들어가야 함을 알 수 있다. 주어진 선택지 중 '계획에 의한' 것의 반대 개념으로 가장 적절한 것은 '자발적으로' 일어난 것이다. 정답은 ③이 된다.

rising n. 반란, 봉기 premeditated a. 미리 생각한, 계획적인 emeritus a. 명예직의, 명예퇴직의 spontaneous a. 자발적인, 마음에서 우러난; 임의의 vehement a. 격렬한, 맹렬한; 열정적인

렉싱턴(Lexington) 전투는 우리 대부분이 배웠던 것처럼 농부들의 자발적인 반란이 아니라 빈틈없이 조직화되고 잘 계획된 사건이었다.

08 ②

is 이하에 열거되고 있는 보어는 동일한 맥락 하에 있으므로 빈칸에도 individual과 contemplative와 유사한 의미 혹은 성격을 가진 단어가 필요하다. ②가 여기에 가장 부합한다. 한편, 책이나 이야기의 창조에만 전적으로 관심이 있다면, 다른 일 혹은 다른 사람에게는 관심이 없을 것이므로, 교제를 싫어할 것이라 볼 수 있으며, 이런 접근으로도 정답을 유추해낼 수 있다.

individual a. 개개의; 개인적인; 독특한 contemplative a. 명상적인, 관조적인 amiable a. 붙임성 있는, 상냥한 retiring a. 교제를 싫어하는, 수줍은; 은퇴하는 amorphous a. 무정형의, 특색이 없는 bestial a. 짐승의; 흉포한, 야만스런

자신의 능력이 허용하는 한 완벽하게 이야기나 책을 만들어내는 일에만 전적으로 관심을 가지고 있는 문학가는 일반적으로 상당히 개인적이고 사색적이며 교제를 싫어한다.

09 ①

마지막 문장은 이전 문장들의 내용을 요약하는 역할을 하고 있다. 고등학교 졸업생 가운데 대학에 진학하는 비율이 이전에 비해 크게 늘었다면, 대학 진학이 이제는 필수적인 과정, 즉 누구나 의례히 경험해야 하는 과정이 된 것으로 볼 수 있다. 이것은 '통과의례'라는 말로 나타낼 수 있으며, 통과의례는 영어로 rite of passage로 표현한다.

roughly ad. 거칠게, 함부로; 대략 graduate n. 졸업생; 대학원 학생 passage n. 통행, 통과; 통로 rite of passage 통과의례 trend n. 경향, 동향; 추세 reconciliation n. 화해; 단념; 조화, 일치 commitment n. 범행; 위임; 공약, 약속; 헌신

요즘에는 대학이 정말로 달라졌다. 50년 전에는 전체 고등학교 졸업생의 대략 15퍼센트가 대학에 진학했다. 지금은 전체 고등학교 졸업생 가운데 70퍼센트까지가 대학에 간다. 그래서 이 일은 하나의 통과의례가 되어버렸다.

10 ④

두 번째 문장이 사이버공간(인터넷)에 비해 옛날의 뉴스공급원이 불리하다는 부정적인 말이고 첫 번째 문장과 역접의 However로 연결되므로, 첫 번째 문장은 신문 등 옛 뉴스공급원은 인터넷에도 불구하고 영향력이 여전하다는 긍정적인 내용이 되는 것이 적절하다. 빈칸 앞에 not이 있으므로 빈칸에는 ④가 들어가야 한다.

cyberspace n. 사이버공간 interactive a. 상호작용하는 dodge v. 피하다 inflate v. 부풀리다 portend v. 미리 알리다 eclipse v. 무색하게 하다

2000년에 인터넷이 신문이나 라디오나 텔레비전의 영향을 무색케 하지 못했다. 그러나 사이버공간은 옛날의 뉴스 공급원에 비해 이점이 있었다. 인터넷은 상호작용하는 매체인 것이다.

11 ④

세미콜론 이하의 문장에서 바로 앞 문장에 대한 부연설명을 하고 있다. 이전의 입장에서 물러서려 하지 않는다면, 협상은 '오도 가도 못하는 상태', 즉 '교착상태'에 빠져 있을 것이다. 그러므로 ④가 정답이 된다.

negotiation n. 협상, 교섭, 절충 budge v. 의견을 바꾸다; 몸을 움직이다 consensus n. 일치; 합의, 여론 context n. 문맥; 전후 관계; 배경, 정황, 환경 cession n. 할양; 양도 stalemate n. 막다름, 교착상태

관련 당사자들은 좋은 결과를 이끌어내기 위해 열심히 노력했다. 그러나 노조와 사용자간의 협상은 교착상태에 빠지고 말았다. 어느 쪽도 이전에 발표한 입장에서 조금도 물러서려 하지 않고 있기 때문이다.

12 ①

'투우의 측면들 중 하나'와 '소의 피가 튀기는 것'은 동격 관계이므로 빈칸에는 ①이 적절하다.

color-blind a. 색맹인 enrage v. 화나게 하다 cape n. 어깨 망토 bold a. 뚜렷한, 선명한 hue n. 색상 mask v. 숨기다, 감추다 bullfight n. 투우 splatter n. 튀기기 gruesome a. 무시무시한 auspicious a. 상서로운 mellow a. 감미로운 impregnable a. 난공불락의

소는 색맹이다. 그래서 투우를 하는 소는 아마도 망토의 색깔이 아니라 망토의 빠른 움직임에 의해 분노가 유발될 것이다. 그런데 왜 선명한 색상(빨강)인가? 일부 사람들은 그것(빨강)이 투우의 더욱 무시무시한 측면들 중 하나인 소의 피가 튀기는 것을 감추는 데 도움을 준다고 말한다.

13　　④

but 전후의 내용이 대조를 이루어야 한다. 매년 출판되는 수천 권의 책 가운데 소수만이 오래 주목을 끈다는 맥락이 되어야 하므로, many of them이 주어로 주어져 있는 첫 번째 빈칸에는 instant, transitory, momentary가 들어갈 수 있다. 한편, 사람들의 마음에서 사라지기 전에 일반적으로 책을 볼 수 있는 장소에서 먼저 사라질 것이므로, 두 번째 빈칸에는 '서가(書架)'라는 의미의 the shelves가 가장 적절하다. 따라서 정답은 ④가 된다.

attract v. 끌다; 매혹하다 gradually ad. 차차, 점차 instant a. 즉시의, 즉각적인; 긴박한 pandemonium n. 지옥; 아수라장 transitory a. 일시적인, 덧없는, 무상한 itinerary a. 순회하는; 여정의, 여행의 momentary a. 순간의, 찰나의, 덧없는 shelf n. 선반, 시렁; 책꽂이, (책장의) 칸

매년 수많은 책들이 출판되지만, 그 가운데 상당수가 오직 일시적으로 주의를 끌다가 점점 서가(書架)와 독자들의 마음으로부터 사라지고 만다.

14　　①

앞 문장의 내용을 포괄적으로 표현하고 있는 단어가 빈칸에 들어가야 한다. 앞 문장에서는 많은 영리한 젊은이들이 해외로 나간 후에 본국으로 돌아오지 않고 있는 상황에 대해 이야기하고 있으므로, 빈칸에 들어갈 적절한 표현은 '두뇌유출'이라는 의미의 ①이다.

youngster n. 젊은이, 청소년 emigrate v. (타국으로) 이주하다, 이민하다 immigrant n. 이주자, 이민 phenomenon n. 현상; 사건 significantly ad. 중대하게, 중요하게; 의미심장하게 brain drain 두뇌 유출 mammonism n. 배금주의 cultural lag 문화지체현상 human alienation 인간소외

더 나은 교육을 받기 위해 이민을 가는 수천 명의 영리한 이 젊은이들 가운데 상당수는 졸업 후에도 해외에 머무르며, 직업을 구하고, 이민자로서 남은 삶을 살아간다. 두뇌 유출은 특히 EU에 가입한 이후에 루마니아에서 생겨나고 있는 현상이다.

15　　①

Although가 이끄는 종속절의 내용과 주절의 내용은 대조를 이뤄야 한다. 종속절에서 '확정된 가격을 말하기는 어렵다'라고 했으므로, 주절의 내용은 '대략적인' 가격을 알려주겠다는 흐름이 되어야 한다. 그러므로 이 문제는 fixed의 문맥상 반의어를 찾는 문제가 되며, '대략적인', '어림의'라는 의미를 가진 ①이 정답이 된다. 한편, 마지막 문장의 내용에 주목하면, 결국 이 대략적인 수치가 참고 가격을 말하는 것이며, 참고 가격이란 말 그대로 참고만 할 수 있는 가격이므로 '확정되지 않은 대략적인' 수치를 의미하게 된다.

fixed a. 고정된, 일정불변의 price quote 시세, 시가 figure n. 숫자; 합계; 모양; 인물 detail n. 세부, 세부적인 목록; 상세 indicative price 참고가격 ball-park a. 대략적인, 어림의; 거의 정확한 strict a. 엄격한; 엄밀한, 정확한 pecuniary a. 금전의, 재정상의

아래는 당신을 위해 우리가 가격에 맞출 수 있는 여러 가지 방안들입니다. 고정된 시세를 말씀드리기는 매우 어렵지만, 대략적인 수치를 알려드릴 수는 있습니다. 당신이 찾고 있는 것의 세부사항을 보내주시면, 참고 가격을 알려 드리겠습니다.

16　　②

샐러드를 먹는 목적이 많은 채소와 과일을 먹는 것일지도 모른다고 했으므로 지방이 적은 샐러드도 적당히 '절제한' 것이라고 볼 수 있다. 하지만 마지막 문장에서 샐러드의 맛이 좋을수록 그것들을 게걸스럽게 먹는다고 했으므로 샐러드와 함께 소금, 고기, 치즈 등을 곁들인다고 볼 수 있다. 따라서 이런 음식을 '배제하지' 않는다고 볼 수 있다.

lean a. (고기가) 지방이 적은, 살코기의 abstemious a. (식사·술을) 삼가는, 절제하는 garnish n. (요리의) 고명, 곁들이는 것 gobble v. 게걸스럽게 먹다 meticulous a. (주의 따위가) 지나치게 세심한, 매우 신중한 ornament v. 꾸미다, 장식하다 abstemious a. 절제하는, 자제하는 preclude v. 제외하다; 방해하다 cosmopolitan a. 세계주의의; 전 세계적인 season v. 간을 맞추다, 양념하다 extravagant a. 낭비벽이 있는 avert v. (눈·얼굴 따위를) 돌리다, 비키다; (타격·위험을) 피하다, 막다

심지어 나의 지방이 적은 샐러드도 적당히 절제한 것일 뿐이다. 그 목적은 채소와 과일을 많이 섭취하는 것일 수도 있지만, 소금, 고기, 치즈 등의 다양한 것들을 (샐러드에) 곁들이는 것을 배제한 것은 아니다. 결국 내 샐러드의 맛이 좋을수록 내가 그것들을 게걸스럽게 먹어치울 확률이 높아진다.

17　　①

투자하려는 국가가 정책의 일관성이 부족하다면 투자자 입장에서는 확신을 가질 수 없고 머뭇거리게 될 것이므로, 첫 번째 빈칸에는 uncertainty 또는 dither가 가능하다. 한편, 해당 국가의 정부 입장에서는 자국에 대한 우려를 불식시키려 할 것이므로, allay 또는 soothe가 두 번째 빈칸에 들어갈 수 있다. 두 조건을 모두 만족시키는 정답은 ①이다.

analyst n. 분석가 consistency n. 일관성, 언행일치; 조화 uncertainty n. 불확정, 불확실 allay v. (불안 따위를) 가라앉히다; (슬픔 등을) 누그러뜨리다, 경감시키다 confidence n. 신용, 신뢰 soothe v. 달래다, 위로하다, 진정시키다 dither n. 망설임; 초조, 안절부절 intensify v. 격렬하게 하다; 증강시키다 stipend n. 수당, 급료; 연금 surmise v. 추측하다, 짐작하다

작년에 잠비아 정부가 교체된 이래로, 그곳에 대한 투자 결정을 내리는 데 있어서 점점 더 많은 논쟁이 있어 왔다. 일부 분석가들은 비록 현 정부가 그러한 염려를 누그러뜨리려 노력해 왔지만, 정책 일관성이 부족하기 때문에 투자자에게 불확실성을 초래할 수 있다고 주장하고 있다.

18   ②

부연설명의 역할을 하는 표현 in other words 다음의 they는 빈칸이 들어 있는 문장의 주어인 These gods를 지칭하며, agriculture는 the earth and the grain과 같은 의미로 쓰였다고 볼 수 있다. 이들이 농사를 '보호하는' 역할을 한다고 했으므로, 빈칸에는 protectors의 속성, 즉 '보호'의 의미를 가진 단어가 들어가야 한다. ②가 정답이다.

rite n. 의례, 의식 pray v. 빌다, 기원하다; 간청하다; 기도하다 altar n. 제단, 제대 guardian god 수호신 grain n. 곡물, 곡류 sycophantic a. 알랑대는, 아첨하는 tutelary a. 수호하는, 보호하는, 후견하는 cantankerous a. 심술궂은, 툭하면 싸우는 waggish a. 익살맞은, 우스꽝스러운

왕은 나라의 수호신을 모신 제단에서 비를 내려달라는 기도를 올리는 의식을 거행했다. 이 수호신들은 또한 땅과 그 땅이 만들어내는 곡식을 보호하는 신령들로 여겨졌다. 다시 말해, 그들은 농사를 보호하는 이들이었으며, 따라서 비를 내리게 하려는 노력을 하는 데 있어서 가장 중심이 되는 이들이었다.

19   ③

두 번째 문장에서 '냉전(cold war)이 지속적인 적대 상태를 의미한다'라고 했는데, war가 '적대 상태'를 가리키므로, cold에는 '지속적인(sustained)'이라는 의미가 있는 것으로 이해할 수 있다. 한편, 빈칸에 들어갈 단어에 대해 두 번째 문장의 it means 이하에서 sustained truce로 나타내고 있는데, 앞서 살펴본 바대로 sustained는 cold라는 말로 대체할 수 있고 truce는 그 의미상 적대 상태의 반대인 '평화 상태'를 뜻하는 것으로 볼 수 있으므로, 이를 통해 Cold Peace라는 낱말을 만들어낼 수 있다. 따라서 정답은 ③이 된다.

phrase n. 말, 표현; 어법 reflect v. 반영하다, 나타내다; 반성하다, 숙고하다 sustained a. 지속적인, 일련의 hostility n. 적의, 적개심; 적대행위 short of ~까지는 가지 않는, ~에 부족한 truce n. 정전(停戰), 휴전 settlement n. 정착, 안정; 화해, 해결 latent a. 잠재적인, 숨어 있는, 보이지 않는 pop v. 불쑥 나타나다 conversation n. 대화, 회화

새로운 분위기를 반영하는 새로운 표현이 지난주에 유럽 전역으로 퍼지고 있었다. 그것은 냉전(冷戰)중의 소강상태라는 말이다. 냉전이 제 3차 세계대전에 버금가는 지속적인 적대 상태를 의미하는 것처럼, 이 말은 화해가 없는 지속적인 정전(停戰) 상태를 의미한다. 드러나지 않고 표현되지 않았던 이 분위기가 갑자기 공개적으로 불거졌으며, 『런던 옵저버』지에 따르자면 이제 "유럽 전역에 걸쳐서 정보에 해박한 정치 대화의 주된 소재가 되고 있다."

20   ②

'적대 행위 가능성', '유전공학(유전적 조작)', '음모론' 등의 진술을 통해 전염병을 '인간의 사악한 의도에 의한 조작'의 결과물로 보는 시각이 존재함을 추론할 수 있다.

loom v. 어렴풋이 나타나다 advent n. 출현, 등장 conspiracy n. 음모 trial and error 시행착오 tinker v. 어설프게 손보다 malevolence n. 악의, 증오 contact n. 접촉 contamination n. 오염 confession n. 고백 exposure n. 노출; 폭로 deployment n. 배치

그러나 어떤 사람들의 마음속에는, 바이러스보다 더 큰 어떤 것 편에서의 적대 행위 가능성이 어렴풋이 나타나고 있다. 1970년대 유전공학이 출현한 이후 음모론자들은 에이즈에서 에볼라, 메르스에서 라임병, 사스에서 지카에 이르기까지 거의 모든 새로운 전염병들을 인간의 어설픈 조작과 악의의 결과로 지적했다.

21   ①

흥미를 느끼지 못한다면 무관심하거나 태연자약한 관점으로 사물을 바라볼 것이므로 첫 번째 빈칸에는 equanimity 또는 apathy가 들어갈 수 있다. 한편, '애착을 가지게 될 만큼 이 세상과 인생이 마음에 들거나 흥미롭지는 않다고 생각했다'라는 것은 세상에 대한 부정적 인식을 나타내는 표현이므로, 두 번째 빈칸에는 meanly 또는 badly가 가능하다. 두 조건을 모두 만족시키는 것은 ①이다.

agreeable a. 기분 좋은, 유쾌한; 마음에 드는 properly ad. 올바르게, 정확하게; 적당하게 blade n. (풀의) 잎; (칼의) 날 equanimity n. (마음의) 평정, 침착, 냉정 meanly ad. 천하게, 초라하게; 비열하게 apathy n. 냉담, 무관심 provocation n. 성나게 함; 도발, 자극 enmity n. 증오, 적의; 불화, 반목

애착을 가지게 될 만큼 이 세상과 인생이 마음에 들거나 흥미롭지는 않다고 생각한다거나, 인생의 끝을 태연자약하게 지켜본다고 사람들이 말하는 것을 들었을 때, 나는 그들이 결코 올바르게 살지 못했으며 또한 그들이 그토록 천하게 생각하는 세상을 맑은 눈으로 바라보지 못했거나, 혹은 그 안에 있는 어떤 것도, 풀잎 하나라도 제대로 보지 못했다는 생각이 든다.

22   ②

세 번째 문장의 'I love to be alone.'이라는 표현을 통해 첫 번째 빈칸에는 love처럼 긍정적인 의미를 가진 단어 혹은 이것과 문맥상 같은 의미를 가질 수 있는 단어가 들어가야 함을 알 수 있다. wholesome 또는 salutary가 가능하다. 한편, 사람들과 함께 있는 것보다 혼자 있는 것이 더 좋다는 맥락의 글이므로, 두 번째 빈칸에는 alone의 의미를 가진 단어가 필요하다. privacy 또는 solitude가 가능하다. 두 조건을 모두 만족시키는 정답은 ②가 된다.

company n. 동석한 사람들; 교제; 회사 wearisome a. 피곤하게 하는; 넌더리나는, 싫증난 dissipate v. 흩어져 없어지다, 사라지다 companionable a. 벗으로 삼기에 좋은, 사교적인; 다정한 abroad ad. 외국으로, 해외로; 외출하여 chamber n. 방, 침실, 응접실; 회관 inscrutable a. 불가사의한, 수수께끼 같은 privacy n. 사적 자유, 프라이버시; 비밀 wholesome a. 건강에 좋은; 건전한 solitude n. 고독 foolhardy a. 저돌적인, 무모한 gregariousness n. 군거적임, 사교적임 salutary a. 유익한, 건전한 homage n. 존경; (봉건시대의) 충성; 주종 관계

나는 더 많은 시간을 혼자 보내는 것이 유익하다고 생각한다. 다른 사람들과 함께 있으면, 가령 그가 가장 친한 친구라 하더라도, 곧 따분해지고 마음이 산만해진다. 나는 혼자 있는 것을 좋아한다. 고독만큼 사귀기 편한 상대를 나는 아직 만나지 못했다. 우리는 대개 자신의 거실에 있을 때보다 밖으로 나가서 사람들 사이를 돌아다닐 때 더욱 외로워진다.

---

23   ①

문맥상 '미국과 비슷한, 동등한 수준'에 도달했다는 내용을 만들도록 하는 표현이 들어가는 것이 적절하다.

denial n. 부인, 부정 irrelevance n. 무관함 copycat n. 흉내쟁이 parity n. 동등함 arrogance n. 오만 divergence n. 분기 convergence n. 수렴 singularity n. 특이점 promptness n. 신속

중국의 기술에 대한 미국의 태도는 지난 20년 동안 몇 가지 부인 단계를 거쳤다. 처음에는 미국과 무관하다는 태도였고, 다음으로 중국 기업들은 종종 흉내쟁이나 산업 스파이쯤으로 여겨졌고, 최근에는 중국이 자국의 해안을 결코 벗어나지 못한 채 독특한 종들만 자라고 있는 기술계의 갈라파고스섬 정도로 간주되었다. 이제는 중국이 비슷한 수준에 도달하고 있다는 두려움으로 표시되는 네 번째 단계가 시작되었다. 미국 기술의 "제국적 오만" 시대는 끝나가고 있다고 실리콘 밸리의 한 인물은 말한다.

---

24   ④

두 번째 문장 이하는 첫 번째 문장의 내용에 대한 부연설명에 해당한다. 칼뱅주의가 기독교적인 정신이 아니었다고 했으므로 빈칸에는 부정적인 표현이 들어가야 한다. 그러므로 ②와 ③을 먼저 정답에서 제외할 수 있다. 한편, '천국에 갈 사람들과 그렇지 못한 사람들은 태초에 이미 정해졌다'라는 것은 칼뱅 나름의 주장에 해당하므로, '저항'이라기보다는 '왜곡'에 가깝다고 봐야 한다. 따라서 정답은 ④가 된다.

Calvinism n. 칼뱅주의(프랑스의 종교개혁자 칼뱅에게서 발단한 기독교 사상) aggrandize v. 확대하다, 확장하다; ~의 힘을 증대하다 visible a. 눈에 보이는; 명백한; 뚜렷한 signifier n. 의미하는 것, 나타내는 것 tenet n. 주의, 교의(敎義) reprobate a. 신에게 버림받은; 사악한, 타락한, 불량한 damned a. 저주받은 embrace v. 포옹하다; 맞이하다, 환영하다 resistance n. 저항, 반항; 반대 obedience n. 복종; 순종 reluctant a. 마음 내키지 않는, 마지못해 하는 distortion n. 왜곡, 곡해

칼뱅주의는 결코 기독교적인 정신이 아니었다. 그것은 기독교적인 정신을 적극적으로 왜곡한 것이었으며, 눈에 보이는 속세의 부(富)를 신(神)의 사랑이 표현되어 나타난 것으로 만듦으로써, 부자의 힘을 더 크게 만들어주었다. 칼뱅(Calvin)의 핵심적인 교의는 천국에 갈 사람들과 그렇지 못한 사람들은 태초에 이미 정해졌다는 것이다. 신에게서 버림을 받은 사람들은 항상 저주를 받도록 되어 있었기 때문에 버림을 받았다는 것이다. 두말 할 필요 없이, 제네바의 부유한 시민들은 이것을 환영하며 받아들였다.

---

25   ④

두 번째 문장의 But 이하에서 '두 사건은 관련이 있다'라고 했으므로, 이와 대조를 이루는 앞 문장은 '관련이 있는 것으로 보기 힘들다, 즉, 단지 우연의 일치였다'라는 내용이 되는 것이 적절하다. 따라서 '우연의 일치, 동시발생'이라는 의미를 가진 ④가 정답이 된다. 더불어, the fact 이하의 내용이 두 사건이 동일한 날짜에 일어난 것에 관한 것이므로, coincidence가 들어가면 문맥이 매끄럽게 연결되는 것 또한 확인할 수 있다.

attribute v. ~의 탓으로 하다, ~의 행위로 돌리다 reform n. 개혁, 개정 anniversary n. 기념일 harrowing a. 비참한; 끔찍한, 참혹한 nonetheless ad. 그럼에도 불구하고, 그래도 eliminate v. 제거하다, 배제하다 onerous a. 번거로운, 귀찮은, 성가신 requirement n. 요구, 필요; 필요물 prompt v. 자극하다, 격려하다; 촉구하다 bedlam n. 대혼란, 아수라장 rule of thumb 경험의 법칙, 어림짐작 furor n. 벅찬 감격; 격정 coincidence n. (우연의) 일치; 동시발생

쿠바 대통령 라울 카스트로(Raúl Castro)가 냉전시대의 가장 끔찍한 순간, 즉 쿠바 위기가 시작된 지 50번째 기념일이었던 10월 16일 화요일에 대규모 이민 개혁을 단행한 사실이 우연의 일치가 아니라고 하긴 힘들다(우연의 일치이다). 그러나 그럼에도 불구하고 그 두 사건은 관련이 있다. 쿠바의 밖을 여행하고자 하는 국민들에게 번거로운 출국비자를 요구하는 관행을 철폐하는 카스트로의 개혁은, 미사일 위기가 어떻게 지난 50년간 양국 정부가 쿠바의 입출국을 봉쇄하도록 했는지를 떠올리게 한다.

01 ①	**02** ①	**03** ③	**04** ④	**05** ④	**06** ④	**07** ④	**08** ④	**09** ③	**10** ②
11 ②	**12** ②	**13** ③	**14** ②	**15** ③	**16** ④	**17** ①	**18** ③	**19** ④	**20** ①
21 ③	**22** ③	**23** ③	**24** ④	**25** ④					

01 ①

이슬람에 대해 반감을 품고 있는 단체가 주어로 주어져 있다. 이런 단체들은 비록 허위라 하더라도 회교와 관련돼 있는 조직에 대해 부정적인 내용을 '유포하려' 할 것이다. 따라서 빈칸에 들어갈 적절한 단어는 ①이다.

islamophobic a. 이슬람을 싫어하는; 이슬람 공포증의 spurious a. 가짜의, 위조의; 겉치레의 accusation n. 비난, 규탄; 죄명; 고발 threaten v. 위협하다, 협박하다 disseminate v. 널리 퍼뜨리다, 선전하다; 유포하다 dissimulate v. 숨기다, 모르는 체하다 encumber v. 방해하다, 지장을 주다; (의무 등을) 지우다 intercept v. 가로채다; 저지하다, 차단하다

이슬람에 대해 반감을 품고 있는 단체들은 이슬람 지하드(jihad)가 미국의 안전을 위협하고 있다는 허위적인 규탄내용을 널리 퍼뜨린다.

02 ①

and 앞에서 '워릭 대학 주식회사'로 '부르고 있다'라고 했다. 빈칸에는 이렇게 불리는 사실 혹은 그 명칭을 가리키는 단어가 필요하다. 따라서 ①이 정답이 되며, 주어진 글은 대학을 기업처럼 부르는 것에 대해 부총장들은 거부감을 갖고 있지 않다는 내용이다.

chancellor n. 대법관; 수상; 대학총장, 학장 compliment n. 경의, 칭찬; 아첨 criticism n. 비평, 비판, 평론 appellation n. 명칭, 호칭 varsity n. 대학, 대학 대표팀 disparity n. 불일치, 불균형 infamy n. 악평, 오명

실제로, 워릭(Warick)은 현재 워릭 대학 주식회사로 불리고 있는데, 대부분의 부총장들은 그러한 호칭을 비판이 아니라 칭찬으로 여길 것이다.

03 ③

'아무리 못난 엄마라도 죽어 없는 것보다는 낫다'라는 말은 '살아있는 것만으로도 엄마로서의 최소한의 역할은 하고 있다'라는 의미라 할 수 있다. 이것은 올바른 양육, 아이에게 모범적인 생활을 보여주는 것 등, 엄마가 맡아서 해야 할 다른 중요한 역할에는 크게 관심이 없다는 것이며, 따라서 엄마의 역할에 대한 기준이 매우 낮음을 나타내는 것이라 할 수 있다.

motherhood n. 모성, 모성애 zest n. 풍미, 맛; 열의, 열정 finesse n. 교묘한 처리; 기교; 술책, 책략 benchmark n. 기준, 척도; 표준가격 grid n. 격자, 쇠창살

마돈나(Madonna)는 "내가 아무리 못난 엄마라 해도 죽어 없는 것보단 낫잖아요."라는 말을 하여 엄마의 역할에 대한 낮은 기준을 보여주었다.

04 ④

기사의 내용 중 많은 부분이 왜곡된 것을 알게 됐을 때 해당 신문사가 취하는 가장 자연스러운 조치는 기사 내용을 정정하거나 철회하는 것이다.

publish v. 발표하다; 출판하다 article n. 품목; 기사, 논설; 조항 falsify v. 위조하다, 변조하다; 속이다, 왜곡하다 improvise v. 즉석에서 하다; 즉흥연주를 하다 fumble v. 분명하지 않게 이야기하다, 말을 더듬다; 더듬다 consolidate v. 결합하다; 강화하다 recant v. 철회하다, 취소하다

그 신문은 많은 정보가 왜곡된 것을 알게 됐을 때 게재된 기사를 철회할 수밖에 없었다.

05 ④

far from 뒤에 위치한 동명사 being의 주체는 주절의 주어인 nature이며, far from은 '전혀 ~이 아닌, ~이 아니라 오히려 (그 반대인)'이라는 뜻으로 대조의 의미를 가지고 있다. 주어가 동일한 상황이므로, 빈칸에는 bountiful과 반대되는 의미를 가진 단어가 들어가야 한다. 따라서 ④가 정답이 된다.

bountiful a. 활수한; 관대한, 인정 많은; 윤택한, 풍부한 extinction n. 사멸, 절멸; 멸종 inexplicable a. 설명할 수 없는, 불가해한 fugacious a. 덧없는, 변하기 쉬운; 손에 잡히지 않는 therapeutic a. 건강유지에 도움이 되는; 치료법의 parsimonious a. 빈약한, 모자란; 인색한

다윈(Darwin)은 자연이 너그러움과는 거리가 멀고, 매우 인색하여 모든 종(種)이 대규모의 죽음과 멸종의 위험에 처해있음을 보여주었다.

06 ④

'중립적인(neutral)'과 대립·대조적인 의미를 가졌으며, '자극(stimuli)'과 어울리는 표현을 고른다. 중립적이라는 것은 덜 두드러졌다는 말이다.

probe n. 탐색침(과학적인 조사기록에 쓰이는 길고 가느다란 기구) stimuli n. stimulus(자극)의 복수형 auditory a. 청각적인 viable a. 실행 가능한, 실용적인 tactile a. 촉각적인 salient a. 두드러진; 돌출된

보통 불안한 참가자는 중립적 자극들을 대신하는 탐색침들보다는 두드러진 자극들을 대신하는 탐색침들에 대한 반응이 더 빠를 것이다.

07 ④

첫 번째 문장에서는 부모의 헌신과 사랑, 두 번째 문장에서는 나의 부족함을 나타내고 있다. 더 많은 노력을 하는 것은 부모님의 기대에 부응하는 것이고, 이는 곧 부모의 사랑과 헌신에 보답하는 것이 되므로, 빈칸에는 ④가 들어가야 한다. ①의 경우, '만회하다, 벌충하다' 등의 의미를 가지므로, 목적어로 '나의 부족함, 실수, 불효' 등에 해당하는 표현이 왔을 경우에 정답이 될 수 있다.

retrieve v. 만회하다, 회수하다; 보상하다, 벌충하다 retrocede v. 반환하다, 돌려주다 remit v. 송금하다; 하급법원으로 환송하다; 면제하다 reciprocate v. 주고받다, 교환하다; 보답하다

나의 부모님은 일주일 내내 매일 12시간을 일하셔야 겨우 나를 학교에 보낼 돈을 벌 수 있다. 그러나 나는 부모님이 바라는 만큼 좋은 아이가 못될 때가 더러 있다. 이제부터는 부모님의 사랑에 보답하기 위해 더 많은 노력을 하고 싶다.

08 ④

생산성을 높이는 것과 비용을 줄이는 것은 수익 증대 효과 면에서는 같지만 서로 중점적으로 생각하는 것이 다른 행동이라 할 수 있다. 대조를 나타내는 표현 rather than이 쓰인 것으로 보아, 캐세이 퍼시픽은 전자를, 다른 회사들은 후자를 택한 것으로 보는 것이 적절하다. 따라서 빈칸에는 '삭감하다'라는 의미의 ④가 들어가야 한다.

pressure n. 압력, 압박; 곤란 amenity n. 쾌적함; (pl.) 쾌적한 설비; 예의 focus v. 초점을 맞추다; 집중하다 productivity n. 생산성, 생산력 personnel n. 전직원, 인원 mutter v. 속삭이다; 불평을 말하다 recoup v. 벌충하다, 메우다 juxtapose v. 나란히 놓다, 병렬하다 trim v. 잘라내다, 없애다; (예산·인원을) 삭감하다

모든 항공사들이 비용 절감의 압박을 받아왔다. 그러나 캐세이 퍼시픽 (Cathay Pacific)은 많은 항공사들이 그래 왔던 것처럼 각종 설비를 줄이는 데 의존하기 보다는 직원들의 생산성을 높이는 데 초점을 맞추었다.

09 ③

빈칸을 포함하고 있는 부분은 순접의 접속사 and를 통해 his love of being alone과 연결되어 있으므로, 글의 흐름상 and 앞 부분이 이 표현과 유사한 의미를 나타낼 수 있도록 해야 한다. 그런데, 빈칸 뒤의 interference from outsiders는 being alone과 반대되는 개념이므로, 결국 빈칸에는 love의 반의어에 해당하는 표현이 들어가야만 and 이하와 순접의 흐름으로 연결될 수 있을 것이다. 따라서 빈칸에는 '혐오, 반감'이라는 의미의 ③이 들어가야 한다.

attach v. 붙이다, 부여하다; 애착심을 갖게 하다 affection n. 애정, 호의; 감동; 영향 interference n. 방해, 훼방; 간섭 licentiousness n. 방종, 방탕 sophism n. 궤변 detestation n. 증오, 혐오; 몹시 싫은 것 hype n. (과장된) 선전, 과대광고

영국인은 항상 자신의 집에 애착을 느끼는데, 이는 가족에 대한 애정 때문이라기보다는 외부 사람들로부터 간섭받길 싫어하고, 혼자 있길 좋아하고, 남의 일에 간섭하지 않으려는 것 때문이다.

10 ②

첫 번째 빈칸은 순접의 접속사 and를 통해 명사 greed와 연결되어 있으므로, '탐욕'과 유사한 의미 혹은 이것처럼 부정적인 의미를 가진 단어가 필요하다. bigotry 또는 obscenity가 가능하다. 한편, 전치사 by 이하는 탐욕과 같이 부정적인 것을 숨기기 위한 수단에 해당되는데, 자신의 잘못을 감추거나 두드러지지 않게 하기 위해서는 남의 잘못이나 부정을 부각시킬 것이므로, 두 번째 빈칸에도 부정적인 의미의 단어가 들어가야 한다. 따라서 atrocious 또는 malicious가 가능하다. 상기 두 조건을 모두 만족시키는 ②가 정답으로 적절하다.

greed n. 탐욕, 욕심 incite v. 자극하다, 격려하다 고무하다; 선동하다, 부추기다 leniency n. 관대함, 자비로움 atrocious a. 흉악한, 잔학한 bigotry n. 편협; 심한 편견 heinous a. 가증스러운; 흉악한, 극악한 obscenity n. 외설, 음란 philanthropic a. 박애주의자의 euphoria n. 행복감, 희열 malicious a. 악의 있는, 심술궂은

오늘날, 사람들은 평화적인 종교의 이름으로 대중들로 하여금 흉악한 짓을 저지르도록 선동함으로써 자신의 완고함과 탐욕을 감추는 데 종교를 이용하고 있다.

11 ②

저수지가 버틸 수 없는 상황이 도래하기 전에 기술자들과 구조대원들이 하고 있는 작업은 제방을 쌓는 일이라고 보는 것이 가장 적절하다.

prevent v. 막다, 방해하다; 예방하다 repeat n. 되풀이함, 반복 disaster n. 재해, 재난, 참사 expert n. 전문가 irresistible a. 저항할 수 없는, 견딜 수 없는 pressure n. 압력; 압박 reservoir n. 저장소, 저수지 hydrology n. 수문학(水文學) dike n. 둑, 제방 paddock n. (마구간에 딸린) 작은 방목장; 경마장 부속의 울친 잔디밭 corral n. 가축의 우리, 축사

그런 재난이 반복되는 것을 막기 위해 구조대원들과 기술자들은 비가 오기 전에 방어용 제방을 완공시키려고 있는데, 전문가들은 비가 온다면 그 저수지에 더 버티기 어려운 압력을 가하게 될 것으로 우려하고 있다.

---

12   ②

주어진 글에서 쉬운 일로서 열거한 것을 풀이해서 요약하면, 결국 '다른 사람들에 맞춰가면서 사는 것과 다른 사람들에 개의치 않고 자신이 원하는 대로 사는 것'이다. 역접의 접속사 but 이하에는 쉽지 않은 일을 해내는 것에 대한 내용이 와야 하는데, 주어진 글 속에서 그 방법을 찾으면, 앞서 언급한 두 가지를 종합적으로 모두 잘 해내는 것이 이에 해당될 것이다. 그런데, 빈칸 앞 부분의 in the midst of crowd가 '다른 사람들에 맞춰가면서 사는 것(after the world's opinion)'을 언급한 것이므로, 빈칸에는 '다른 사람들에 개의치 않고 자신이 원하는 대로 사는 것(to live after our own)'을 뜻하는 표현이 들어가야 할 것이다. ②가 이러한 의미를 나타내는 정답이 된다.

isolation n. 고립; 격리, 분리 crowd n. 군중; 민중, 대중 dependence n. 의지함, 의존; 종속 상태; 신뢰 singularity n. 특이성, 기이함; 단독, 단일 independence n. 독립, 자립, 자주 solitude n. 고독; 외로움 multitude n. 다수; 군중, 군집 communality n. 공동체적 일치; 공동체의 상태

세상 속에서 세상의 의견을 따라 사는 것은 쉬운 일이고 홀로 살면서 자신의 의견을 따라 사는 것도 쉬운 일이다. 그러나 위대한 사람은 군중 속에서 홀로 지내는 생활의 독립성을 최대한 즐겁게 유지하는 사람이다.

---

13   ③

두 번째 문장은 첫 번째 문장의 내용을 예를 통해 재진술하는 역할을 하고 있다. but 이하의 내용이 첫 번째 문장의 내용과 일치해야 하겠는데, 빈칸 앞에 부정어 not이 있으므로, 결국 빈칸에는 첫 번째 문장의 chained always by the laws of cause and effect와 반대 의미를 갖는 표현이 들어가야 한다. 따라서 ③이 정답으로 적절하다.

chain v. 속박하다, 구속하다 skyscraper n. 마천루, 고층건물 refrain v. 그만두다, 삼가다, 참다 murder n. 살인; 살인사건 escape v. 달아나다, 모면하다, 벗어나다 consequence n. 결과; 결말; 중요성 compel v. 강제하다, 강요하다, 억지로 ~시키다 likewise ad. 똑같이, 마찬가지로

당신은 자유롭다고 생각하겠지만, 실제로는 항상 인과법칙에 구속되어 있다. 당신 마음대로 고층건물에서 뛰어내리거나 1주일 동안 아무 것도 먹지 않을 수도 있지만, 그 결과로부터는 마음대로 벗어날 수 없다.

---

14   ②

remove의 목적어 them은 reject의 목적어 '빈칸+place-names'를 가리키고, 이것은 첫 문장의 Offensive toponyms를 가리킨다. 따라서 빈칸에는 offensive와 가까운 의미인 ②가 적절하다.

---

offensive a. 모욕적인 toponym n. 지명(地名) cartographer n. 지도제작자 revise v. 수정하다 update v. 최신의 것으로 하다, 갱신하다 outmoded a. 구식의 derogatory a. 경멸적인 hackneyed a. 진부한 enigmatic a. 수수께끼 같은

모욕적인 지명이 최근 수십 년 사이에 훨씬 더 드물어졌다. 지도제작자들은 새로운 지도를 만들면서 경멸적인 지명을 거부할 뿐 아니라 옛 지도를 수정하고 갱신하면서 그런 지명을 체계적으로 제거하기도 한다.

---

15   ③

두 번째 문장의 the move는 첫 번째 문장의 a decision 이하의 내용을 가리킨다. 이러한 법안에 대해 야당뿐만 아니라 여당 일각에서도 반대 의견을 내고 있다면, 의회의 승인을 받지 못하고 시행되지 못한 채로 있을 것이다. 따라서 빈칸에는 '(법률 등이) 미결상태로 남아 있음'을 뜻하는 ③이 들어가야 한다.

cabinet n. 내각; 고문단 investment n. 투자, 출자 retail n. 소매(小賣) opposition n. 반대, 반항; 대립; 야당 protest n. 항의, 이의 제기; 주장 ally n. 동맹국, 연합국; 협력자 move n. 운동; 행동, 조처 ruling a. 지배하는; 우세한, 주요한 continuance n. 영속, 존속; 계속 momentum n. 운동량, 타성, 여세 abeyance n. 중지, 정지; 미정 tedium n. 싫증, 지루함

작년 11월에, 내각에서는 다국적 소매업에 최대 51퍼센트까지 외국인의 직접 투자를 허용하는 결의안을 채택했다. 그러나 그 법안은 야당뿐만 아니라 집권 통일진보연합의 협력자들 일부에서도 이의를 제기하여 미결 상태에 있어 왔다.

---

16   ④

알 카에다의 공격이 10년 넘게 재개되지 않아 테러리즘에 대한 생각이 다소 느슨해졌음을 이야기하고 있다. 테러에 대한 염려보다는 일상의 걱정들이 우선하게 된 것이므로, 이는 곧 이러한 일상적인 걱정들이 테러리즘에 대한 걱정을 대신하게 된 것을 의미한다고 할 수 있다. 따라서 빈칸에는 ④가 들어가야 한다.

excuse v. 용서하다; 면제하다; 변명하다 relaxed a. 긴장을 푼, 누그러진 mortgage n. 저당; 융자, 대부금 anthrax n. 탄저균 coax v. 감언으로 설득하다, 어르다, 달래다 intimidate v. 겁을 주다, 위협하다, 협박하다 proliferate v. 증식시키다, 급격히 늘리다 supplant v. 대신하다; 탈취하다, 밀어내다

미국인들이 테러리즘이 대체로 급박한 위험이 아닌 것으로 생각하더라도 너그러이 봐줄 수 있다. 공격 이후에 10년이 흘렀지만, 알 카에다(Al Qaeda)는 아직 미국을 다시 공격하지 않고 있다. 공항에서의 보안검색은 보다 느슨해진 것 같으며, 취업과 담보 대출에 대한 염려가 탄저병과 자살 폭탄 테러범에 대한 걱정을 밀어냈다.

17 ①

과거와 현재를 대조하고 있는 글이다. 그러므로 첫 번째 빈칸에는 두 번째 문장의 still on top과 반대되는 의미를 표현할 수 있는 단어가 필요하고, 두 번째 빈칸에는 개과천선을 통해 만들고자 하는 이미지에 해당하는 단어가 들어가야 한다. 따라서 ①이 정답이 된다.

ultimately ad. 궁극적으로; 결국, 마침내 conscious a. 의식하고 있는, 알고 있는 flagging a. (기력이) 쇠약해지는, 쇠퇴 기미의 palatable a. 맛있는, 풍미가 좋은; 바람직한 docile a. 가르치기 쉬운; 유순한 ebb v. (열정·정신·불빛 따위가) 점점 쇠하다; 약해지다 aggressive a. 호전적인; 진취적인, 적극적인 culminate v. 정점에 이르다; 최고점에 달하다 pugnacious a. 싸움하기 좋아하는, 호전적인

과거에는 스눕 독(Snoop Dogg)이나 아이스 큐브(Ice Cube)와 같은 래퍼들이 그들의 명성이 쇠퇴하는 시점에서 개과천선을 했었지만, 오늘날의 래퍼들은 바람직한 이미지가 결국 사업에 더욱 유리하다는 것을 알고 있기 때문에 그들이 정상에 있을 때 개과천선을 하려는 의식적인 노력을 하고 있다.

18 ③

새로운 연구가 진행되면서 기존의 연구 결과를 뒤집는 경우가 잦음을 이야기하고 있으므로, 생물의학적 연구는 '변덕스러운 지침'이라고 할 수 있다. 따라서 ③이 정답이 된다. 한편, 연구내용이 바뀔 수 있다고 해서 연구 그 자체를 희생이 따르는 노력으로 보는 것은 지나친 비약이 되므로 ④는 정답으로 부적절하다.

risk v. 감행하다, 위험을 무릅쓰고 ~하다 whiplash n. 채찍 끝; 편달(鞭撻), 자극, 충격 lower v. 낮추다, 내리다, 낮게 하다 release v. 방면하다; 개봉하다, 공개하다, 발표하다 resource n. 자원, 물자; 수단, 방책 rigorous a. 가혹한; 엄격한 methodology n. 방법론, 방법학 fickle a. 변하기 쉬운; 변덕스러운 costly a. 값이 비싼; 희생이 큰, 타격이 큰 endeavor n. 노력, 진력; 시도

의학 연구와 관련한 뉴스를 쫓아다보면 충격을 각오해야 한다. 마늘이 해로운 콜레스테롤의 수치를 낮춘다고 하나, 더 많은 연구 끝에 그렇지 않다는 사실이 알려졌다. 아침을 잘 먹으면 하루에 섭취하는 총 열량을 줄이는 효과가 있다더니 지난주에 발표된 연구에서는 그렇지 않다고 한다. 생물의학적 연구결과는 현 시점에서 보면 변덕스러운 지침서이다.

19 ④

주어진 글에서 odd, abnormal, strange가 의미하는 바는 동일하다. 이 단어들은 사용하는 사람에 따라 의미가 달라질 수 있는 주관적인 단어라고 했으므로, 빈칸에는 아이들의 행동이 객관적으로 이상한 것이 아니라 '주관적인 어떤 기준'에 미치지 못한 것일 뿐이라는 것을 의미하는 표현이 필요하다. 즉, '적응을 잘 하는 아이들을 기준으로 자신의 아이가 그에 미치지 못한 것을 이상하게 받아들인다'라는 맥락이 되는 것이 자연스러우므로, 빈칸에는 ④가 들어가는 것이 적절하다.

to some extent 어느 정도까지는, 다소 odd a. 홀수의; 이상한, 기묘한, 뜻밖의 term n. 기간, 임기; 조건, 조항; 용어 normal a. 정상의, 보통의; 표준적인

abnormal a. 보통과 다른, 정상이 아닌; 불규칙한 subjective a. 주관의, 주관적인 interpretation n. 해석, 설명; 판단 varied a. 가지가지의, 가지각색의; 다채로운 well-adjusted a. 잘 적응한 academic a. 학원의; 학구적인 achievement n. 성취, 달성; 위업; 학력 conform v. 적합하다, 순응하다; 따르게 하다 deviate v. (규칙, 원칙 따위에서) 벗어나다, 빗나가다, 편향(偏向)하다 expectation n. 기대; 예상

우리 자신과 주변 사람들을 살펴본 후라면 모든 사람이 어느 정도는 이상하다는 것을 인정할 수밖에 없다. '정상적인'과 '비정상적인'이라는 용어는 쓰는 사람에 따라 그 의미가 다르게 해석될 수 있는 주관적인 단어이다. 그래서 아이들의 이상한 행동이 걱정될 때, 그것은 어쩌면 '잘 적응된' 아이들의 바람직한 생활 모습에 대한 우리 자신의 기대에서 아이들이 벗어나 있기 때문일지도 모른다.

20 ①

두 번째 문장부터 여러 부류의 사람들이 치른 희생(price)을 설명하므로 첫 번째 빈칸에는 tumult(폭동)나 distress(재난)가 적절하고 콜론 다음이 심리적이고 정신적인 희생을 의미하므로 두 번째 빈칸에는 psychic(심리적인)이나 intangible(무형의)이나 ethereal(정신적인)이 적절하다.

melee n. 난투, 혼잡 scramble v. 서둘러 움직이다 arrange v. 정리하다, 주선하다 angst n. 불안한 마음, 고뇌 tumult n. 폭동 psychic a. 심리적인 feast n. 축제 intangible a. 무형의 distress n. 고민, 걱정; 재난 monetary a. 화폐의, 통화의 venture n. 모험 ethereal a. 정신적인

폭동과 관련된 거의 모든 사람들이 밤의 난투극으로 인해 모종의 희생을 치르고 있었다. 그 지역의 부모들은 공립학교 수업이 취소되자 서둘러 집으로 가 아이들을 돌보고 식사를 마련해주었다. 동네 근로자들은 공장이 매일 밤 일찍 문을 닫음으로 인해 급료를 받지 못하는 희생을 치렀다. 멀리서 지켜보는 미국인들의 경우, 그 희생은 지도자들이 해결책은 내놓지 않고 걱정만 하는 또 한 번의 위기가 찾아왔구나 하는 심리적인 것이었다.

21 ③

두 번째 문장의 But 이하에서 접속사 whereas가 이끄는 종속절과 주절의 내용은 대조를 이루어야 하는데, at the mercy of와 master가 의미상 이미 대조를 이루고 있는 상황이므로, 첫 번째 빈칸에는 문장 끝에 있는 natural forces와 동일한 의미를 가진 단어가 들어가야 한다. 두 번째 빈칸의 경우, at the mercy of가 포함된 문장과 순접의 접속사 and로 연결되므로, 이 표현과 유사한 의미를 나타내는 단어가 들어가야 할 것이다. 따라서 첫 번째 빈칸에는 정관사와 함께 '자연력'이라는 의미를 갖는 elements가 들어가야 하며, 두 번째 빈칸에는 '의존'이라는 뜻의 dependence가 들어가는 것이 적절하다. ③이 정답이다.

plough v. (쟁기로) 갈다, 일구다 sow v. (씨를) 뿌리다, 심다 reap v. 거둬들이다, 수확하다 acquire v. 얻다, 획득하다 climate n. 기후; 풍토, 환경 aplomb n. 침착, 태연자약; (마음의) 평정 stigma n. 치욕, 오명(汚名); 불명예 nemesis n. 천벌, 인과응보 the elements 자연력 dependence n. 의존, 종속; 신뢰, 믿음

paranormal a. 초자연적인, 과학적으로 설명할 수 없는 omnipotence n. 전능; 무한한 힘

자신이 소유한 토지를 경작하는 농부의 일은 실로 다양하다. 그는 밭을 갈기도 하고, 씨를 뿌리기도 하며, 수확을 하기도 한다. 그러나 그는 자연력의 지배를 받으며, 그는 자신이 자연의 힘에 의지하고 있다는 점을 매우 잘 인식하고 있다. 반면에, 현대적인 기계를 작동시키는 사람은 자신에게 힘이 있다고 인식하여, 인간이 자연력의 노예가 아닌 지배자라는 느낌을 가지게 된다.

22 ③

빈칸 다음에 이어지는 미국의 초기 역사에 대한 부정적인 진술들로부터 정답을 추론할 수 있다.

presidium n. (구소련의) 최고 회의 간부회; (비정부 기관의) 이사회(理事會) morass n. 소택지, 저습지(低濕地); 곤경, 난국 stock n. 차꼬(죄수를 매던 형구); 재고; 비축물자; 주식; 가축 stockade n. 방책 peonage n. 날품팔이, 잡역부 gray zone 이도저도 아닌 상태

이제 나는 우리가 성자들의 최고 간부회의에 의해서 인도되는 천사들의 나라가 절대 아니라는 점을 인식하고 있다. 초창기 미국은 도덕적인 늪지였다. 신생국가에 살고 있는 다섯 명 중 한 명은 노예였다. 가난한 사람들을 위한 정의는 차꼬(사람을 신체로 구속하는 일종의 고문도구)와 방책을 의미했다. 여성들은 실질적인 잡역부로서 고통받았다. 이교도들은 추방을 강요받거나 그보다 더 나쁜 대우를 받았다. 원주민들은 — 인디언들은 — 그들의 땅에서 쫓겨났고 그들의 운명은 '눈물로 얼룩진 강제이주'와 파기된 조약 속에 내던져졌다.

23 ③

두 번째 문장과 세 번째 문장에서 '작가들이 전자책처럼 컴퓨터 화면으로 출판되는 것보다는 종이로 만든 책으로 자신의 글이 먼저 출판되길 원하고 있음'을 말하고 있다. 다시 말해, 아직은 종이책이 죽지 않고 존재감을 가지고 있다는 의미이므로, 글 전체 내용을 요약하는 마지막 문장의 빈칸에는 '위신'이라는 뜻의 ③이 들어가는 것이 가장 자연스럽다.

tweak v. 살짝 바꾸다, 변경하다 imaginative a. 상상의; 가공의; 상상력이 풍부한 overly ad. 과도하게, 지나치게 hospitable a. 환대하는, 환영하는, 우호적인 literary a. 문학의, 문학적인 transmit v. 전달하다, 전송하다 carry v. 지니다; 수반하다; (속성 등을) 가지고 있다 circulation n. 유통, 유포; 순환 servility n. 노예근성, 비굴 prestige n. 위신, 명성, 신망; 중요성 epithet n. 별명, 통칭

만약 우리가 존 레논(John Lennon)의 노랫말을 "종이가 없다고 상상해 봐요"로 바꾼다면, 상상력이 풍부한 문학을 어떻게 마음 속에 그릴까? 바로 지금, 처음으로 출간되는 문학 작품들에게 인터넷은 그다지 환영받지 못하고 있는 듯하다. 대부분의 작가들은 비록 그들의 글을 컴퓨터를 통해 작업하고 출판사 측에 컴퓨터를 통해 전달했다 하더라도, 여전히 그들의 글이 화면보다는 종이 위에 먼저 나타나는 것을 더 보고 싶어 한다. 종이는 여전히 위신을 지키고 있는 셈이다.

24 ④

마지막 문장에서 '다음에 누군가가 좋아하는 레스토랑을 물으면 40곳 가운데 한 곳을 가르쳐 줄 것이다'라고 했는데, 빈칸 뒤에는 100곳 이상의 레스토랑이 제시되고 있으므로, 결국 이 곳들 가운데 40곳을 추려냈다고 보아야 한다. 그러므로 빈칸에는 '골라내다'라는 의미의 ④가 가장 적절하다.

one-size-fits-all a. 널리[두루] 적용되도록 만든 process n. 진행, 경과, 절차; 과정 potential a. 잠재적인; 가능한 modify v. 수정하다, 변경하다; 조정하다, 제한하다 impart v. 주다, 나누어주다; 전하다 tarry v. 머무르다; 기다리다 winnow v. 고르다, 골라내다, 분석하다, 검토하다; (쓸모없는 것을) 제거하다

"그래서, 당신이 가장 좋아하는 레스토랑이 대체 어디입니까?"라고 수도 없이 사람들이 내게 물어 보았다. 모든 경우에 다 좋은 레스토랑은 없다. 내가 좋아하는 레스토랑도 수십 곳이다. 선호하는 100곳이 넘는 레스토랑을 개인적으로 제일 좋아하는 40곳으로 추려내는 데는 여러 달이 걸린다. 다음에 누군가가 내게 물어보면, 그에게 그 40곳 가운데 한 곳을 가르쳐 줄 것이다.

25 ④

빈칸 앞의 your long 부분이 단서이다. 빈칸이 포함된 문장에서 this가 가리키는 것은 '어떤 사람이 당신에게 한 비난'이므로, 빈칸에는 '그 사람이 들어 마땅한 비난을 아흔 아홉 번이나 삼갔던 것'을 나타내는 단어가 들어가야 한다. 따라서 refrain의 의미를 내포하고 있는 단어가 와야 하며, '인내', '자제'라는 의미의 ④가 가장 적절하다.

so-and-so n. 아무개, 모(某) horrid a. 무서운; 매우 불쾌한 refrain v. 그만두다, 삼가다, 참다 utter v. 발언하다, 말하다 well-deserved a. 충분한 자격이 있는; (벌·보상 등이) 응당한 criticism n. 비평, 비판, 평론 unguarded a. 부주의한, 방심하고 있는, 마음 놓고 있는 declare v. 선언하다, 단언하다; 발표하다 reward n. 보수, 포상; 현상금; 보답 escapade n. 모험; 탈선, 탈선적 행위; 장난 quirk n. 변덕; 핑계 tirade n. 긴 연설, 장광설 forbearance n. 삼감, 자제; 인내

어떤 사람이 당신에 관해 끔찍한 말을 했다는 소리를 들으면, 당신은 그 사람이 응당 받아 마땅한 비판을 아흔 아홉 번이나 삼갔던 점은 기억하고, 백 번째에 무심코 그 사람에 관한 사실을 말해버린 것은 잊어버린다. 당신은 자신이 그처럼 많이 참아준 것에 대한 보답이 이것인가라고 생각할 것이다. 그러나, 그 사람의 입장에서 보면, 당신의 행동은 그 사람의 행동에 대해 당신이 느끼는 것과 완전히 마찬가지이다. 그는 당신이 말하지 않았던 아흔 아홉 번에 대해서는 알지 못하고, 당신이 말을 한 백 번째만을 알고 있을 뿐이다.

01 ④	02 ②	03 ①	04 ①	05 ③	06 ③	07 ③	08 ①	09 ④	10 ③
11 ④	12 ④	13 ④	14 ②	15 ③	16 ①	17 ③	18 ②	19 ③	20 ①
21 ④	22 ①	23 ④	24 ③	25 ④					

01 ④

since가 이유의 절을 이끌고 있다. 어떤 대상으로부터 선택을 할 때 어려움이 없다면, 무엇을 선택할 지 확실히 결정이 난 상태이거나 대상이 선택의 여지가 거의 없는 경우에 그러할 것이다. 따라서 빈칸에는 ④가 들어가는 것이 자연스럽다.

selection n. 선발, 선택; 발췌 content n. 내용, 내용물; 목차, 목록 heterogeneous a. 이종(異種)의; 서로 다른 성분으로 된 standoffish a. 쌀쌀한, 냉담한; 불친절한 sylvan a. 숲의; 나무가 무성한 homogeneous a. 동종의, 동질의, 균질의

그 상자에서 선택을 하는 것은 그리 어렵지 않다고 생각한다. 내용물이 모두 같은 종류이기 때문이다.

02 ②

첫 번째 문장의 내용에 관한 예를 두 번째 문장에서 들고 있는 구조의 글이다. 안전에 문제가 있고, 편의시설이 거의 없는 상황을 요약할 수 있는 단어가 필요한데, 이런 점은 모두 서비스의 질이 좋지 않음을 말하고 있으므로 빈칸에는 ②가 들어가야 한다.

costly a. 값이 비싼, 비용이 많이 드는 iffy a. 의심스러운, 불확실한 security n. 안전; 보안, 방위 comfort n. 위로, 위안; 안락 fiduciary a. 신용상의; 피신탁인의 shoddy a. 조잡한, 질이 나쁜, 싸구려의 sophisticated a. 고도로 세련된 prodigal a. 낭비하는; 방탕한; 풍부한

국제항공운송협회(IATA)는 아프리카의 공항들이 세계에서 가장 비용이 많이 드는 공항에 속하며, 질이 떨어지는 서비스를 제공한다고 전하고 있다. 나이로비 공항은 안전이 의심스러우며 편의시설이 거의 없다.

03 ①

해를 끼치려고 의도한 행동이 좋은 결과를 가져왔다면, 본래 '의도하지 않은' 다른 결과를 가져온 것이다. 그러므로 빈칸에는 intended의 반의어, 즉 unintended의 의미를 내포하고 있는 단어가 들어가야 하며, 정답은 '우연히'라는 뜻의 ①이다.

intend v. 의도하다, 기도하다; ~할 작정이다 harm n. 해악; 손해, 손상; 불편 intention n. 의향, 목적; 의도, 의지 inadvertently ad. 무심코, 우연히; 태만하게 recklessly ad. 무모하게, 개의치 않고 discursively ad. 산만하게, 두서없이 emphatically ad. 강조하면서; 눈에 띄게

어떤 행동이 해를 끼치려고 의도된 것이지만 우연히 좋은 결과를 야기한다면, 그것은 선의로 행해진 행동의 결과와 같게 판단될 수 있을 것이다.

04 ①

지구 온난화와 한파는 서로 대조를 이룬다. 거침없이 말하는 사람이 한파를 증거로 들었다고 했으므로 지구 온난화를 '헛소문'으로 생각할 것이다.

outspoken a. 노골적으로[거침없이] 말하는 dismiss v. (고려할 가치가 없다고) 묵살[일축]하다 canard n. 헛소문, 유언비어 snap n. (날씨의) 일시적인 급변, (특히) 갑작스러운 추위 incubus n. 큰 걱정거리 jeopardy n. 위험 juggernaut n. 엄청난 파괴력, 불가항력

거침없이 말하는 그 남자는 지구 온난화를 헛소문이라고 일축했으며, 갑작스러운 한파를 증거로 들었다.

05 ③

전제가 옳다는 것을 알 때 결론을 의심 없이 믿게끔 만드는 논거라면, 그 논거는 허점이 없고 논리적인 논거일 것이다. 빈칸에는 이러한 의미를 가진 단어가 들어가야 하며, '설득력 있는'이라는 의미의 ③이 가장 적절하다.

intuitively ad. 직관에 의해, 직관적으로 argument n. 논의, 논증; 논거; 주장 premise n. <논리> 전제(前提) reasonable a. 이치에 맞는, 온당한; 분별 있는 discordant a. 조화하지 않는, 일치하지 않는; 불협화음의 farfetched a. 억지스런, 부자연스러운; 에둘러 말하는 cogent a. 적절한; 설득력 있는, 강력력이 있는 queasy a. 구역질나게 하는, 역겨운

직관적인 관점에서 볼 때, 설득력 있는 논거에서는, 전제가 사실이라는 점을 안다면 그 결론을 믿는 것이 이치에 맞을 것이다.

06　③

소크라테스가 examined life를 높이 평가했다고 돼 있으므로, 빈칸에는 examined와 관련이 깊은 ③이 적절하다.

proclaim v. 선언하다, 공포하다 examined life 성찰하는 삶 account n. 설명 clarify v. 명료하게 하다 illuminate v. 조명하다 gruesome a. 무시무시한 quaint a. 기이한 reflective a. 반성적인, 사려 깊은 secondhand a. 간접적인

소크라테스가 성찰하는 삶의 미덕을 선언한 후 지금까지 철학의 과제는 인간실존에 대한 반성적인 설명을 제시하는 것, 인간의 삶을 명료하게 하고 밝게 조명하는 것이었다.

07　③

주어진 글의 분사구문은 앞 문장에서 이야기한 것을 부연설명 하는 역할을 하고 있다. 대중문화의 이미지를 이용하고자 했다고 했으므로, 강조하는 내용은 popular와 관련된 것이다. '대중적인' 것은 사람들에게 널리 퍼져 있는 평범한 것이라 할 수 있으므로 ③이 정답이다. 한편, as opposed to elitist를 기준으로 본다면, elitist와 상반되는 의미의 형용사를 찾아야 하며, 이런 방법으로도 정답을 도출해 낼 수 있다.

aim v. 겨냥하다; 겨누다; 목표로 삼다 as opposed to ~에 대립하는 것으로서; ~와는 대조적으로 emphasize v. 강조하다; 역설하다 element n. 요소, 성분 irony n. 풍자, 반어법; 빈정댐 sophisticated a. 세련된, 정교한; 복잡한 piquant a. 얼얼한; 야무진, 통쾌한 banal a. 평범한, 진부한 squeamish a. 몹시 딱딱한, 결벽한, 신경질적인

팝 아트는 예술에서 엘리트 문화와 상반되는 입장에 있는 대중문화의 이미지를 이용하고자 했으며, 흔히 반어 기법을 이용하여 모든 주어진 문화에서 평범한 요소를 강조했다.

08　①

믿기 어렵다는 말은 의외의 성질을 보였다는 것이므로 빈칸에는 brazen과 상반되는 의미의 ①이 적절하다.

brazen a. 철면피한, 뻔뻔스런 cop v. (+to) 인정하다(= admit), 고백하다(= confess) bashful a. 수줍어하는 indolent a. 나태한 garrulous a. 수다스런 jovial a. 쾌활한

믿기 어렵지만, 세계에서 가장 낯 두꺼운 코미디언과 강력한 지도자조차도 자신들도 연기나 연설을 하고 있지 않을 때는 수줍음을 많이 탄다고 인정한다.

09　④

빈칸은 순접의 등위접속사 and로 연결된 병렬구조의 안에 속해 있으므로, 전후의 tensions, dispute와 유사한 성격 혹은 의미의 단어가 들어가야 한다. '알력, 불화'라는 뜻의 ④가 정답으로 적절하다.

relation n. 관계, 관련 plague v. 괴롭히다, 애태우다; 고통을 주다 tension n. 긴장, 긴장상태 border n. 테두리, 가장자리; 경계, 국경 dispute n. 분쟁, 분규; 말다툼, 싸움 preference n. 좋아함, 편애; 우선권 intimacy n. 친밀함, 친교 privation n. 결여, 결핍; 궁핍; 박탈, 상실 friction n. 마찰; 알력, 불화

중국과 인도사이의 관계는 통상과 관련된 긴장, 국경 분쟁, 그리고 인도의 라이벌인 파키스탄에 대한 중국의 정치적, 군사적 지원으로 인한 갈등으로 오랫동안 골치를 썩어 왔다.

10　③

연구 대상으로서의 '학습 방법과 문화 사이의 관계'를 수식하기에 자연스러운 표현을 찾는 문제이다. 여기서 '연구 대상'이라는 말에 중점을 둬야 하는데, 그런 점에서 ①, ②, ④는 그 의미상 부자연스럽다. 따라서 빈칸에는 ③이 적절하며, causal link는 '인과관계'라는 의미이다.

relationship n. 관계, 관련 clear-cut a. 윤곽이 뚜렷한, 명쾌한 identify v. 확인하다; 판정하다, 감정하다; 동일시하다 perspective n. 전망; 시각, 견지 examine v. 시험하다; 검사하다; 검토하다 caustic a. 부식성의; 신랄한, 통렬한 causal a. 인과 관계의; 원인의 casual a. 우연한; 뜻밖의; 격식을 차리지 않은 carping a. 흠 잡는, 잔소리하는

대단히 많은 연구에서 학습 방법과 문화 사이의 관계를 검토해 왔다. 비록 명확한 인과관계는 확인되지 않았지만, 검토할 만한 가치가 있는 몇 가지 관점들이 있다.

11　④

다리지 않은 옷이 유행되길 바라는 것은 옷을 다리는 것을 싫어하기 때문일 것이며, 옷을 다리는 것도 routine household chores에 포함된다고 할 수 있다. 그 의미를 좀 더 확장해서 보면, 이 은행가는 routine household chores를 귀찮게 여기는 게으른 사람이라고 할 수 있다.

when it comes to ~에 관해서라면 routine a. 일상의, 판에 박힌 chore n. 자질구레한 일, 허드렛일 (pl.) 가사(家事) fashionista n. 패션에 관심이 많고 최신 스타일을 선호하는 사람 declare v. 선언하다, 발표하다, 공언하다 unironed a. 다리미질을 하지 않은 crafty a. 교활한, 간교한, 나쁜 꾀가 많은 meticulous a. 지나치게 세심한, 매우 신중한 penniless a. 무일푼의, 몹시 가난한 sluggish a. 게으른, 나태한

일상적인 집안일에는 대단히 게으른 투자 은행가 롭 가뤼(Rob Garrus)는 이번 봄/여름 기성복 컬렉션을 주시하고 있다. 그는 패셔니스타들이 다리지 않은 옷들이 유행이라고 말하기를 바라고 있다.

12　④

두 번째 문장에서 우리들이 누리는 쾌락을 때때로 '중단해 볼 것'을 권하고 있다. 첫 번째 문장에서 '식욕'을 언급하고 있으므로, 빈칸에는 먹는 즐거움을 중단하는 것에 해당하는 단어가 들어가는 것이 적절하다. 따라서 '단식'이라는 의미의 ④가 정답이 된다.

homage n. 존경; 충성 majesty n. 위엄; 권위 appetite n. 식욕; 성욕; 욕구 arrange v. 결정하다; 마련하다, 준비하다 regularly ad. 정기적으로, 일정하게; 규칙적으로 preserve v. 보전하다, 유지하다; 보존하다; 잊지 않다 intensity n. 강렬, 격렬; 긴장, 집중 euphuism n. 미사여구, 아름다운 말과 화려한 문체 attrition n. 마찰, 마모; 약화, 감소 anorexia n. 신경성 식욕 부진증, 거식증 fasting n. 단식, 금식

단식은 식욕이라는 권위에 대해 경의를 표하는 행위이다. 그래서 나는 우리가 — 친구, 음식, 연인 등 — 우리의 쾌락이 주는 강렬함과 그것들을 되찾는 순간을 잊지 않기 위해 정기적으로 우리가 누리는 쾌락을 중단해 보아야 한다고 생각한다.

13 ④

글 끝 부분에 있는 suggests 이하의 내용은 '문제가 뿌리 깊이 박혀 있다'라는 의미로, 이는 곧 '이 문제가 고질적인 것이어서 해결이 쉽지 않다'라는 의미를 내포하고 있다. 따라서 사람들의 의심 혹은 불신을 가시게 하는 것도 어려웠을 것이므로, 빈칸에는 '누그러뜨리다, 진정시키다'라는 의미의 ④가 들어가는 것이 가장 적절하다.

observer n. 관찰자, 관측자; 입회인, 옵저버 take notice of ~을 알아차리다, 주목하다 commitment n. 범행, 수행; 위임; 공약; 약속; 헌신 inflate v. 부풀리다; 팽창시키다 betoken v. 전조가 되다, 보이다; 나타내다 cogitate v. 숙고하다, 궁리하다, 고안하다 assuage v. (슬픔 따위를) 누그러뜨리다, 진정시키다, 완화시키다; (식욕 등을) 만족시키다

국제 관측통들은 유로(euro)화를 지켜내기 위해 "필요한 일은 뭐든지" 하겠다는 드라기(Draghi)의 약속에 주목했다. 그러나 위기가 발생한지 2년 반이 지났는데도 유로를 지켜내겠다는 약속에 대한 사람들의 의심을 유로화 지역의 지도자들이 누그러뜨리지 못한 점은, 그 문제가 뿌리 깊이 박혀 있는 것임을 시사하고 있다.

14 ②

첫 문장은 'so ~ that …' 구문을 이루고 있으며, 이 구문은 인과관계를 나타낸다. 슬픔에 잠긴 부모라는 주제가 영화의 주요한 테마로 굳어져 왔다면, 그것의 결과로는 '오늘날 그러한 주제가 진부한 것이 된 것'이 가장 적절하다. 이는 두 번째 문장의 "Such grief isn't new"라는 문장을 통해서도 확인할 수 있다.

grieve v. 몹시 슬퍼하다, 비통해 하다 staple n. 주요한 테마; 주요소, 주요 산물 demonstrable a. 증명할 수 있는, 명백한 grief n. 슬픔, 비탄; 통탄할 일 preponderance n. 우위; 우세; 우월; 다수 compelling a. 주목하지 않을 수 없는; 강한 흥미를 돋우는; 강제적인 chagrin n. 유감, 원통함, 분함 cliché n. 진부한 표현, 상투적인 문구 fiasco n. 낭패, 큰 실수 plagiarism n. 표절, 도용

슬픔에 잠긴 부모들은 너무나도 자주 영화의 테마가 돼 버려서 현재 그런 주제들은 확실히 진부하다. 그런 슬픔은 영화에서 새로운 것이 아니지만, 이런 이야기들이 다수를 차지하는 것은, 타인의 고통에 대해서 주목하지 않을 수 없는 무언가가 있다고 영화제작자들이 믿고 있음을 시사하고 있다.

15 ③

'선물 교환이 비효율적임'을 말하고 있는 첫 문장이 주제문이며, 나머지 문장들은 왜 그런지에 관해 이야기하는 부연설명에 해당한다. 빈칸을 포함하고 있는 문장도 선물 교환의 비효율적인 면을 언급해야 하는데, 미리 자신이 받을 선물을 스스로 골라서 내가 무엇을 받을지를 이미 알고 있다면, 선물이라는 이름으로 무언가를 교환하는 행위 자체가 속임수라 할 만하다. 따라서 빈칸에 들어갈 정답은 ③이 된다.

inefficient a. 효과 없는; 비능률적인 via prep. ~을 경유하여, ~을 거쳐 registry n. 기입; 등록, 등록부 decent a. 버젓한, 알맞은, 남부럽지 않은; 일정 수준의 unwanted a. 불필요한, 쓸모가 없는 hallucination n. 환각; 환상; 망상 annuity n. 연금 charade n. 빤히 들여다보이는 속임수; 허위, 위장 vicissitude n. 변화, 변천

선물 교환은 대단히 비효율적이다. 모든 사람들이 선물 목록을 통해 선물을 고르지 않는 한, 누군가가 원치 않는 선물을 받을 가능성이 크다. 그리고 만약 모든 사람들이 미리 자신이 받을 선물을 골랐다면, 그리하여 놀라는 일이나 그것과 관련해 생각할 일이 많지 않다면, 선물을 교환한다는 생각은 빤히 드러나 보이는 속임수와 같은 것이다.

16 ①

where절에서 한쪽의 나쁜 소식이 다른 쪽에 고통을 유발한다고 했는데, 이는 양자(兩者)가 부정적인 측면에서 같은 입장에 있다는 것이다. 그러므로 첫 번째 빈칸에는 symbiosis 또는 synergy가 적절하다. 한편, 기업이나 가계가 채무를 불이행하면 금융가는 향후 신용대출 이용 가능성을 제한하거나 금지시킬 것이므로 두 번째 빈칸에는 restrict 또는 dwindle이 가능하다. 따라서 상기 두 조건을 모두 만족시키는 ①이 정답이 된다.

negative a. 부정적인; 금지의, 반대의 induce v. 권유하다; 야기하다, 유발하다 default n. 채무불이행; 태만, 불이행 availability n. 이용도, 유효성, 효용 symbiosis n. 공생; 공생 관계, 협력 관계 restrict v. 제한하다, 한정하다; 금지하다 antagonism n. 적대, 대립, 반감 dwindle v. 축소하다; 감소시키다 synergy n. 상승작용, 시너지 ordain v. 정하다; 규정하다 metabolism n. 물질대사, 신진대사 stabilize v. 안정시키다, 고정시키다

금융업과 경제는 지금 일종의 부정적인 공생관계에 갇혀 있어서, 한쪽의 나쁜 소식이 다른 쪽에 고통을 유발한다. 채무불이행이 금융가로 하여금 신용대출 이용가능성을 제한하게 하고, 이것이 더 많은 채무불이행을 야기하고 있다.

17 ③

자동화와 과로 문화로 인해 일터에서 인간다움이 사라지고 있다고 했으므로, 인간다움을 회복하기 위해서는 '일에서 벗어난다'는 말이 필요하다.

be in short supply 부족하다 unveil v. 정체를 밝히다 amend v. 수정하다 unplug v. 플러그를 뽑다, ~에서 막힌 것을 제거하다 reward v. 보답하다

많은 일터에서 인간다움이 부족하다. 자동화와 과로 문화로 인해 인간다움이 몰아내어졌기 때문이다. 아담 웨이츠는 인간다움을 회복하는 놀라운 방법에 대해 쓰고 있다. 그것은 사람들에게 자신의 일에서 완전히 벗어날 수 있는 시간과 격려를 해 주는 것이다.

---

18 ②

빈칸을 기준으로, 앞 부분에서는 지나온 것에 연연하고 있음을 이야기하고 있고, 뒷 부분에서는 앞에 놓여 있는 것이 중요하다는 것을 이야기하고 있다. 두 문장이 내용상 대조를 이루므로 빈칸에는 '반대로'라는 의미의 ②가 들어가는 것이 가장 적절하다.

twilight n. 땅거미, 황혼; 새벽녘 faint a. 어렴풋한, 희미한 beam n. 대들보; 광선 illuminate v. 조명하다; 밝게 하다, 비추다 obscurity n. 어두컴컴함; 어둑한 곳; 세상에 알려지지 않음; 무명 aspiration n. 열망, 포부 anxiety n. 걱정, 근심, 불안 insight n. 통찰력, 간파 hopefully ad. 희망을 걸고; 바라건대, 아마 conversely ad. 거꾸로, 반대로 inevitably ad. 불가피하게, 필연적으로 rapidly ad. 빠르게, 재빨리, 신속하게

현대인은 자신이 빠져나온 땅거미 속을 열심히 돌아보면서, 그것의 희미한 빛이 자신이 향해 들어가고 있는 어둠을 비춰주길 바란다. 그러나 그와는 반대로, 자신의 앞에 놓여 있는 길에 대한 포부와 염려가 뒤에 놓여 있는 것에 대한 통찰력을 날카롭게 하는 것이다.

---

19 ③

두 번째 문장의 '청년이 폭발 계획을 성공시키지 못했다'라는 내용이 단서가 된다. 성공하지 못했으므로, '폭발 계획'이라는 표현을 수식하고 있는 빈칸에는 '미연에 방지되어 미수에 그쳤다'라는 의미가 되도록 ③이 들어가는 것이 적절하다.

arrest n. 체포, 억류 accuse v. 고발하다, 고소하다 determine v. 결심시키다; 결심하다; 정하다 incident n. 사건, 일어난 일 chilling a. 냉담한, 쌀쌀한 reminder n. 생각나게 하는 것; 메모 roseate a. 쾌활한; 낙관적인 lopsided a. 한쪽으로 기운, 균형이 안 잡힌, 남 다른 데가 있는 foil v. 좌절시키다, 미연에 방지하다 ravage v. 약탈하다, 황폐하게 하다

불발에 그친 폭발 계획에 연루된 것으로 고발된 21세의 방글라데시 청년을 이번 주에 체포한 것은 테러리스트들이 미국을 공격하려는 마음을 먹고 있음을 보여주는 가장 최근의 증거이다. 그는 자신의 야심찬 계획을 성공시키지는 못했다. 그러나 뉴욕에게 있어 그 사건은 아직도 뉴욕이 최우선 공격 목표에 속해 있음을 오싹하게 상기시키고 있다.

---

20 ①

아시아 국가들이 중국을 견제하고 있다는 점이 두 번째 문장에 나타나 있으므로, 첫 번째 문장은 "중국을 이용해 미국을 견제하기보다 미국을 추종한다"라는 내용이 되어야 한다. 따라서 첫 번째 빈칸에는 '대항세력'이라는 단어가 적절하며, 두 번째 빈칸에는 미국에 '편승한다'라는 의미를 만드는 단어가 들어가야 한다.

strategic a. 전략의, 전략상 중요한 primacy n. 제일, 수위; 탁월 balance n. 평균, 균형, 평형 counterweight n. 대항세력, 균형을 이루는 힘, 평형추 bandwagoning n. (우세한 쪽·시류에) 편승 countercoup n. 반격, 역(逆) 쿠데타 cope with ~을 대처하다, 극복하다 counterblast n. 강력한 반발, 반대기류, 역풍 grapple with ~을 붙들고 씨름하다, 해결하려고 고심하다 counterfeit n. 가짜, 위조 물건; 모조품 side with ~의 편을 들다

아시아 대부분의 나라들은 중국의 부상을 미국 제일주의에 대한 전략적 대항세력으로 이용하기보다는 조용히 미국에 편승하고 있는 것처럼 보인다. 동시에, 많은 아시아 국가들은 중국에 견줄 균형을 창출해 내기 위해 서로 거래를 하고 있다.

---

21 ④

모든 사람이 각자에 대한 가장 훌륭한 비평가라고 했으므로, 어떤 책에 대해서 모든 학자들이 아무리 침이 마르도록 칭찬하더라도, 정작 본인의 흥미를 끌지 못한다면 의미가 없을 수도 있다. 따라서 첫 번째 빈칸에는 zealous 또는 unanimous가 올 수 있다. 두 번째 빈칸이 포함되어 있는 마지막 문장은 첫 번째 문장을 재진술한 것이므로, 빈칸에는 critic의 의미를 가질 수 있는 단어가 필요하다. bench, judiciary, judge가 가능하다. 상기 두 조건을 모두 만족시키는 정답은 ④가 된다.

critic n. 비평가, 평론가 criticism n. 비평, 비판, 평론 blunder n. 큰 실수, 대실책 eminent a. 저명한, 유명한 split a. 갈라진, 분열된 bench n. 의석; 판사석; 재판관 precarious a. 불확실한, 믿을 수 없는 judiciary n. 사법부; 재판관 zealous a. 열심인, 열광적인, 열성적인 felon n. 중죄인, 흉악범, 악한 unanimous a. 만장일치의, 이의 없는

모든 사람이 각자에 대한 가장 훌륭한 비평가이다. 학자들이 어떤 책에 관해 무어라 말하든, 아무리 만장일치로 그 책을 칭찬하더라도, 만약 그 책이 당신의 흥미를 끌지 못하면 당신과 아무 상관이 없다. 비평가들도 흔히 실수를 하며, 비평의 역사는 가장 저명한 비평가들조차도 저지르고 만 과오들로 가득 차 있으며, 또한 책을 읽는 당신이 지금 읽고 있는 책이 당신에 대해 갖는 가치의 최종적인 판단자라는 사실을 잊어서는 안 된다.

---

22 ①

술부의 내용이 그녀를 부정적으로 생각했다는 내용이므로 첫 번째 빈칸에는 Sceptics(회의론자)나 Detractors(비방자들)나 Antagonists(적대자들)가 적절하고, 앞 문장에서 의심과 두려움으로 괴로워하는 사람들에게 도로시의 글을 읽어보라고 조언했다고 했는데, 이는 도로시가 마음의 고통을 받는 사람들에게 힘이 되어주는 자질이 있다는 말이므로 두 번째 빈칸에는 tonic(힘을 돋우는)이나 exhilarating(활력을 주는)이 적절하다.

deadline n. 마감시간 winded a. 숨 가쁜, 숨을 헐떡이는 arch a. 교활한, 간교한 sentimentalist n. 감상(感傷)주의자 ladle out 가리지 않고 마구 주다 sceptic n. 회의론자 tonic n. 튼튼하게 하는, 원기를 돋우는 detractor n. 비방하는 사람 downbeat a. 우울한, 비관적인 electric a. 전기의, 자극적인 antagonist n. 적수, 경쟁자 enervate v. 기력을 빼앗다 proponent n. 지지자 exhilarating a. 유쾌하게 하는, 상쾌한

마감시간을 놓친 적이 없는 도로시 딕스는 숨 가쁜 기색을 보이지 않았다. 그녀의 칼럼을 한 번도 읽어보지 않은 회의론자들은 그녀를 그다지 똑똑하지 못한 사람들에게 마구 조언을 해주는 교활한 감상주의자로 여겼다. 그러나 한 심리치료 교수는 의심과 두려움에 시달리는 여자들에게 매일 도로시의 글을 읽어보라고 조언했다. 사람들에게 힘이 되어주는 그녀의 자질을 인정하여, 전국 의료 여성 협회는 그녀를 명예회원으로 삼았다.

---

23   ④

첫 번째 빈칸과 관련하여 '경제 식물학의 시대'라고 하였으므로 식물의 '유용성'이 식물 연구의 최대 관심이었을 것으로 추론할 수 있다. 두 번째 빈칸과 관련하여 제국주의 지배국 영국 정부가 자국의 경제 식물학자들을 얼마나 후원하고 있는지 모르고, 그런 사람을 체포하여 수난을 자초하였으므로 피식민지인 인도의 시킴 왕의 행동은 제국주의에 맞서는 '무모한 행위' 또는 '만용'이었다고 추론할 수 있을 것이다.

botany n. 식물학 prominent a. 두드러진 taxonomist n. 분류학자 but then 그도 그럴 것이, 그렇긴 해도, 하긴 patronage n. 후원 trespass v. 침입하다 punitive a. 징벌의 espionage n. 스파이[간첩] 행위 peculiarity n. 특성 fastidiousness n. 까다로움, 결벽 vagary n. 변덕, 일시적 기분 temerity n. 무모함, 만용

사실 식민지 팽창기인 18세기와 19세기는 국가 경제에 대한 새로운 식물의 유용성이 순수한 분류학자들을 제외한 모든 사람들의 마음속에서 두드러졌던 경제 식물학의 시대였다. 그도 그럴 것이, 탐험가들이 누렸던 후원은 인도를 통치하고 있던 영국 정부가 식물을 찾아 자신의 영지에 침입한 후커(J.D. Hooker)를 체포한 시킴(Sikkim) 왕을 무릎 꿇게 하고(굴복시키고) 다르질링(Darjeeling) 지역을 그의 만용에 대한 징벌적 벌금의 차원에서 빼앗았을 정도였다.

---

24   ③

For example 이후의 내용은 사람들의 실수로 인한 잘못된 철자의 쓰임이 일반적으로 쓰이게 된 어휘의 예에 해당한다. 따라서 빈칸이 포함된 문장은 '철자에 관해 실수가 너무 많이 일어나서, 그것이 언어의 한 부분으로 받아들여지게 되었다'는 내용이 되어야 문맥상 적절하다.

linguist n. 언어학자 etymology n. 어원; 어원학, 어원 연구 folk etymology 민간 어원 inevitably ad. 불가피하게, 필연적으로 apron n. 앞치마 mishear v. 잘못 듣다, 잘못 알아듣다 additionally ad. 게다가 onomatopoeic a. 의성의; 의성어의 hiccup n. 딸꾹질 mistakenly ad. 잘못하여, 실수로 associate with ~와 관련되다, 어울리다 cough v. 기침하다 accepted a. 일반적으로 인정된, 용인된 alternative a. 양자택일의, 대신의; 선택적인 habituate v. 익다, 익숙하게 하다; 습관을 들이다 slip one's tongue 실언을 하다 ruin v. 파괴하다, 파멸시키다

언어학자들이 어휘와 어구에 관한 어원학을 논할 때마다 민간 어원이 필연적으로 발생한다. 이따금씩 영어를 쓰는 사람들이 실수를 너무 자주 하여 실수가 언어의 한 부분이 된다. 예를 들어, "apron"이라는 단어는 중세영어의 "napron"이 종종 잘못 들린 데서 비롯되었다. 뿐만 아니라 의성어인 "hiccup"은 너무 자주 기침과 잘못 관련지어져서, 현재는 "hiccough" 또한 용인된 대체 가능한 철자가 되었다.

---

25   ④

자신의 모든 것을 쏟아 부은 소설작품이 얼마 지나지 않아 사람들에게서 잊혀지는 현실을 소설가가 받아들이긴 쉽지 않다고 했다. 만약 그렇다면, 소설가가 바라는 것은 '자신의 작품이 오래도록 기억되는 것', 혹은 나아가 '생전이 아니라면 사후에라도 이름을 떨치는 것'이라 할 수 있으며, 이것이 바로 마지막 문장에서 언급한 The belief in posthumous fame이다. 문맥상 바로 앞 문장의 a secret hope가 가리키는 바도 이와 동일하므로, 빈칸에 들어갈 표현은 posthumous fame을 나타낼 수 있게 하는 것이어야 한다. 결국, '작품이 자신의 세대를 지나 여러 세대에 걸쳐 남아 있게 된다'는 의미를 만드는 ④가 이것에 가장 근접한 의미의 표현이다.

reconcile v. 화해시키다; 조화시키다; 단념하게 하다 reconcile oneself to ~을 감수하다 anxious a. 걱정하는, 불안한; 열망하는 toil n. 수고, 노고, 고생 posthumous a. 사후(死後)의; 저자의 사후에 출판된; 유복자로 태어난 harmless a. 무해한; 악의 없는 vanity n. 덧없음, 무상함; 허무; 허영 harsh a. 거친, 난폭한; 가혹한

소설의 평균 수명은 90일이라고 출판업자들은 말한다. 자신의 모든 것 뿐만 아니라 여러 달 동안의 고역을 쏟아 넣었던 책이 서너 시간 만에 읽혀진 다음 그렇게 짧은 기간 만에 잊혀진다는 사실을 받아들이기는 쉽지 않다. 비록 큰 이익이 되지는 않겠지만, 적어도 자기 작품의 일정 부분이라도 사후 한두 세대 정도 남아있기를 은근히 바라지 않을 정도로 시시한 작가는 없다. 사후에 이름이 남을 거라는 신념은 예술가로 하여금 살아생전에서의 실망과 실패를 받아들일 수 있게 해주는 해롭지 않은 허영이다.

01 ③	02 ③	03 ④	04 ④	05 ④	06 ①	07 ①	08 ②	09 ④	10 ①
11 ②	12 ③	13 ④	14 ④	15 ④	16 ③	17 ③	18 ②	19 ②	20 ②
21 ③	22 ③	23 ①	24 ②	25 ④					

01 ③

마지막 라운드까지 접전을 이루고 있는 상황에서 어린 상대의 체력을 오랫동안 챔피언이었던 사람이 이겨내지 못했을 것이므로 빈칸에는 ③이 적절하다.

toe-to-toe ad. 정면으로 맞선 자세로 stamina n. 정력, 체력 stymie v. 훼방놓다, 좌절시키다 decimate v. 대량 살육하다 galvanize v. ~의 기운을 북돋우다 ostracize v. 국외로 추방[배척]하다

두 명의 복서는 마지막 라운드까지 정면으로 맞서서 싸웠으며 마지막 라운드에서 복싱계의 오랜 챔피언은 그의 어린 상대의 체력에 결국 굴복했다.

02 ③

만성적인 외상과 같은 것이라면 병사들이 겪을 수 있는 부상의 위험에 관한 언급이라고 추측할 수 있다. 단기적 영향과 만성적 병증을 언급하는 것으로 볼 수 있으므로 '파급 효과, 영향, 결과' 등을 의미하는 ③이 정답으로 적절하다.

ramification n. 파문, 영향, 결과 chronic a. 만성적인, 고질적인 traumatic a. 외상성의; 외상 치료의 encephalopathy n. 뇌병증 requirement n. 필요조건 liabilities n. 부채, 채무 surge n. 급상승, 급등

나는 내가 진찰하는 모든 병사들에게 단기적인 영향들과 만성적인 외상성 뇌병증과 같은 것들에 대해 이야기해 준다.

03 ④

처음으로 이뤄진 어떤 행위를 설명한 후에 그 행동이 가져 온 결과에 대해 이야기하는 구조의 글이다. 빈칸에는 '그 행위를 그대로 따라서 하다'라는 의미를 만드는 단어가 들어가는 것이 자연스럽다. follow suit은 '남이 하는 대로 하다, 선례를 따르다'라는 의미이므로 정답은 ④가 된다.

Kabbalah n. 유대교 신비주의 종파 signature n. 서명, 사인 wrist n. 손목 prompt v. 자극하다, 격려하다, 고무하다; 촉구하다 flurry n. 질풍, 돌풍; 눈보라; 혼란, 동요 follow suit 선례를 따르다

마돈나(Madonna)가 1998년에 처음으로 카발라(Kabbalah)교의 상징인 붉은 끈으로 된 팔찌를 착용하기 시작했으며, 그 결과 많은 유명연예인들이 앞 다투어 그녀의 선례를 따랐다.

04 ④

두 번째 문장에서 개선책을 찾고 있다고 했으므로, status quo(현재의 상태)는 바람직하지 않은 것이어야 한다. 따라서 빈칸에는 ④가 적절하다.

reminiscence n. 회상, 추억 epiphany n. 직관적 깨달음, 통찰 (평범한 사건이나 경험을 통해 직관적으로 파악하는 진실의 전모) improvisation n. 즉흥 연주 nemesis n. 인과응보, 천벌, 강적

현재의 상태는 우리의 적(敵)이다. 우리는 전통적인 모델을 갖고 더 좋게 만들 수 있는 방법을 끊임없이 찾고 있다.

05 ④

장기 미해결 사건을 해결하게 된다면 실추된 명성을 회복시킬 수 있을 것이다.

be fed up with ~에 넌더리나다 misrepresent v. 잘못 전하다, 거짓 설명을 하다 cold case 나쁜 상황, 궁지, 장기 미해결 사건 tarnish v. 더럽히다 cement v. 강화하다 relish v. 즐기다 redeem v. 되찾다, 회복하다

셜록 홈즈는 부주의한 비평가들이 자신을 잘못 설명해온 것에 넌더리나서, 그의 마지막 장기 미해결 사건을 해결함으로써 자신의 명성을 되찾으려고 시도했다.

06 ①

rare와 usually가 의미상 대조를 이루고 있음에 유의한다. 첫 번째 문장에서 용서가 드물다고 했으므로, forgiveness의 반의어에 해당하는 표현이 빈칸에 들어가야 한다.

forgiveness n. 용서, 관대함 rare a. 드문, 진기한; 희귀한 vengeance n. 복수, 원수, 앙갚음 dismay n. 당황, 경악; 낙담 bootleg n. 불법 제조하는 것, 해적판 cringe n. 위축; 굽실거림; 아첨, 비굴한 태도

오늘날, 용서는 드문 일이 됐다. 무언가 나쁜 일이 일어나면, 대개 우리는 화가 나고 종종 보복할 생각이 떠오르게 된다.

---

07   ①

so that은 결과의 부사절을 이끌고 있으며, 와인, 커피, 케첩 등은 앞 문장에서 언급한 물과 기름의 예에 해당한다. 앞에서 이러한 물과 기름이 들러붙지 않게 해 준다고 했으므로, 거기에 대한 결과로는 '털어낼 수 있다'가 적절하며, 또한 그래야만 as if절의 표현과도 자연스럽게 호응한다.

molecule n. 분자 latch onto ~에 달라붙다, 꼭 쥐다 fiber n. 섬유, 실; 소질, 기질 spill n. 엎지름, 엎질러짐; 엎지른 흔적, 더러움 lint n. 실 보푸라기 brush off ~을 털어버리다, 치우다 write off 막힘없이 쓰다 lock up 감금하다, 가두다; 폐쇄하다 soak up 빨아들이다, 흡수하다; 이해하다

폴리머 털은 물이나 기름 분자들이 섬유에 달라붙지 않게 하여, 포도주나 커피 혹은 케첩을 흘러도 마치 액체로 된 보푸라기인 것처럼 털어낼 수 있다.

---

08   ②

첫 번째 문장의 의미를 달리 표현하면, 일반인들도 파파라치에게 사진이 찍히는 대상이 되고 있다는 것이다. 두 번째 문장은 첫 번째 문장의 진술에 대해 보다 구체적으로 설명하는 역할을 하고 있으므로, 빈칸은 바로 뒤의 shots와 함께 '파파라치에게 사진이 찍힌다'라는 의미를 나타낼 수 있어야 한다. 그런데, 파파라치가 찍는 사진은 사진을 찍는 줄 모르고 찍히는 경우이므로, 이것은 '포즈를 취하지 않고' 사진을 찍는 셈이다. 따라서 ②가 들어가야만 앞서 설명한 내용에 부합되는 의미를 만들 수 있다.

pap v. (파파라치가) 몰래 사진을 찍다 cotton on to ~을 이해하다, 깨닫다; 좋아지다 crave v. 열망하다, 갈망하다; 요구하다, 간청하다 request n. 요구, 의뢰 ordinary a. 보통의; 평범한 folk n. 사람들; 가족; 평민 diagonal a. 대각선의, 비스듬한, 사선의 unposed a. 포즈를 취하지 않은 penny-wise a. 푼돈을 아끼는

파파라치에게 '몰래 사진을 찍히는' 것은 더 이상 유명 인사들만의 영광이 아니다. 뉴욕에 본사를 둔 메소드라즈(Methodlzaz)라는 업체는 일반대중이 포즈를 취하지 않은 채 찍힌 사진을 열렬히 원한다는 것을 파악하고 지금 일반인들의 신청을 받고 있다.

---

09   ④

cover story는 주어진 글에서 '진실의 은폐나 호도를 위해 조작된 이야기'라는 의미로 쓰였다. 이러한 사전적 의미를 안다면, 조작된 이야기의 목적 혹은 속성과 같은 맥락의 의미를 가진 gloss over를 만드는 정답 ④를 쉽게 찾아낼 수 있다. 만약 그러한 의미를 모른다면, 자유민주주의를 대표하는 국가인 미국이 '중요 협력자가 군부 독재자라는 사실'을 어떻게 하고 싶겠는가를 추론해서 정답을 도출해야 한다.

cover story 표지 기사; 진실의 은폐나 호도를 위해 조작된 이야기 awkward a. 서투른, 미숙한; 불편한; 난처한, 거북한 mull over ~에 대해 심사숙고하다, 곰곰이 생각하다 take over (일 따위를) 이어받다, 인수하다 turn over 방향을 바꾸다; 뒤집다 gloss over (흠·과오 등을) 은폐하다, 속이다

페르베즈 무샤라프(Pervez Musharraf) 대통령에 대한 미국의 지지는 미국의 가장 중요한 협력자 중의 하나가 공교롭게도 군부 독재자라는 거북한 사실을 은폐하고자 조작된 이야기와 항상 동반되어 나타났다.

---

10   ①

두 번째 문장의 this time은 첫 번째 문장의 adolescence를 가리킨다. 두 문장의 내용을 연결 지어 생각해보면, 첫 번째 문장에서 언급하는 여러 변화들은 사춘기 아이들이 어른이 되는 과정에서 겪는 독특한 양상이라 할 수 있다. 그러므로 빈칸에는 '특징'이라는 의미의 ①이 적절하다. 한편, 첫 번째 문장에서 언급한 변화들에 대해 좋고 나쁨을 논하지 않았으므로 maelstrom은 정답으로 부적절하다.

physical a. 육체의, 신체의; 물질적인; 자연의 emotional a. 감정의, 감정적인 cognitive a. 인식의, 인식력 있는 adolescence n. 사춘기, 청춘기 evolve v. 서서히 발전하다; 진화하다 mature a. 익은, 성숙한; 심사숙고한 hallmark n. 특징, 특질; 품질증명 obverse n. (화폐 등의) 표면; 앞면; (사실 등의) 이면; 상대되는 것 maelstrom n. 큰 동요, 대혼란; 큰 소용돌이 coterie n. (사교·연구 등을 위해 자주 모이는) 한패, 동아리

급격한 신체적, 정서적, 인지적, 사회적 변화는 사춘기의 특징이다. 이 시기 동안 아이들은 성숙하고 독립적인 젊은 성인으로 성장한다.

---

11   ②

두 번째 문장의 내용에서 단서를 찾을 수 있다. inconsolable과 enraged는 각각 depressed와 angry보다 강한 의미의 표현인데, 우울해하거나 화를 내고 말아야 할 상황에서 슬픔에 잠기거나 격분한다면, 그것은 감정이나 잘 제어하지 못한다는 것을 의미한다고 보아야 한다. 앞에 부정의 의미를 내포하고 있는 inability가 있으므로, 빈칸에는 '조절하다'라는 의미의 ②가 들어가는 것이 적절하다.

define v. 규정짓다, 한정하다; 정의를 내리다 explosive a. 폭발하기 쉬운, 격정적인 depressed a. 우울한, 슬픈; 억압된 inconsolable a. 위로할 길 없는, 슬픔에 잠긴 enraged a. 화가 난, 격분한 preclude v. 방해하다; 미리 배제하다, 제외하다 calibrate v. 구경을 재다; 조정하다, 대조하다 conjecture v. 추측하다, 억측하다, 어림으로 말하다 procrastinate v. 미루다, 연기하다

경계성 인격 장애를 특징짓는 것 — 그리고 그것을 대단히 폭발하기 쉬운 것으로 만드는 것 — 은 환자가 자신의 감정과 행동을 조절하지 못한다는 점이다. 우울하거나 화가 나게 하는 상황에 부딪혔을 때 경계성 인격 장애 환자들은 종종 슬픔을 가누지 못하거나 격분하게 된다.

12 ③

불쾌한 사건은 무시해버리거나 정서적 협박이 아닌 충분한 대화를 나누는 등, 두 번째 문장 이하의 내용이 대인관계상 지켜야할 예절에 관한 것이므로 빈칸에는 ③이 적절하다.

tense a. 긴장시키는 incident n. 사건 talk out 끝까지 기탄없이 이야기하다 blackmail n. 공갈, 협박 emotional blackmail 정서적 협박(상대방의 죄책감, 의무감, 동정심 등을 이용하여 상대방을 자기 뜻에 굴복시키는 행위: 예를 들어 '나를 버리면 죽어버리겠다'는 말) surmise n. 추측 inference n. 추론 decorum n. 예절 audacity n. 뻔뻔스러움

우리 사회에는 비록 시간이 지나면서 변할 수는 있어도 예절 규칙들이 있다. 가까운 사람들과의 스트레스 많고 긴장된 상황들을 피하려면 불쾌한 사건들을 무시해버리는 것이 때로는 가장 좋다. 이렇게 할 수 없으면, 그 사람과 끝까지 이야기해야 하며 정서적 협박에 호소해서는 안 된다.

13 ④

공화정이란 왕이 없는 정치 체제인데, 빈칸 전후에서 국민들이 왕을 없애기를 원치 않았다고 했으므로, 당시에 공화정 사상이 지배적이었던 것은 아니라고 할 수 있다. 빈칸 앞에 부정어 not이 있으므로 '우세한, 주요한'이라는 의미인 ④가 정답이 된다.

vague a. 어렴풋한, 막연한, 애매한 liberty n. 자유; 해방, 석방 possess v. 소유하다, 가지다, 점유하다; (감정·관념 등이) 지배하다, ~의 마음을 사로잡다 curiously ad. 신기한 듯이; 기묘하게 get rid of ~을 면하다, 벗어나다; 쫓아버리다 republic n. 공화국; 공화제 sham a. 모조의, 가짜의, 허위의 neoteric a. 현대의, 최신의 savvy a. 사리를 이해한, 정통한, 경험 있고 박식한 regnant a. 통치하는, 지배적인; 우세한, 주요한

자유에 대한 막연한 갈망이 18세기를 살고 있던 프랑스 국민들을 사로잡았다. 그러나 기이하게도, 철학자들도 국민들도 왕을 없애기를 원치 않았다. 공화정 사상은 당시에 지배적인 사상이 아니었으며, 사람들은 여전히 이상적인 군주를 갖기를 희망했다.

14 ④

마지막 문장은 not A but B 구문의 형태를 이루고 있으며, 이 표현에서 A와 B에 해당하는 표현은 서로 반대되는 의미를 담고 있는 것이어야 한다. 그러므로 move와 대조적인 의미를 가진 단어가 빈칸에 들어가야 하며, '움직임'과 상반되는 의미를 내포하고 있는 형용사인 ④가 정답이 된다.

audience n. 청중, 관객 necessarily ad. 필연적으로, 필연적 결과로서 grip v. 꽉 쥐다; 마음을 사로잡다; 이해하다 meditation n. 묵상, 명상; 숙고, 고찰 argument n. 논의, 논증; 논거 mobile a. 움직이기 쉬운, 이동성이 있는 bibulous a. 술을 좋아하는, 술꾼의; 흡수성의 mendacious a. 허위의, 거짓의 static a. 정적인, 정지상태의

연극은 계속해서 관객의 흥미를 북돋워주어야 하며, 만약 그렇지 않으면 상연되는 도중에 실패하기 때문에, 드라마는 모든 예술 가운데 가장 사회적이며, 그런 까닭에 필연적으로 많은 사람들을 향해 이야기하며, 또한 그들의 마음과 감정을 사로잡을 수 있는 무언가를 말하고 있다. 연극은 정적(靜的)인 명상이어서는 안 되며, 움직여야 한다. 단순한 논쟁이어서는 안 되고 행동해야만 한다.

15 ④

threshold의 문맥상의 의미를 묻는 문제라고 할 수 있다. 주어진 문장에서는 '임계'라는 의미로 쓰였으며, 이것은 '어떤 현상이 다르게 나타나기 시작하는 경계'를 뜻한다. 이 말을 주어진 글에 적용시켜 보면, '긴장이나 피로가 정해진 한계에 이르러 밖으로 드러나게 되는 것'이므로, 빈칸에는 ④가 들어가는 것이 가장 적절하다.

threshold n. 문지방, 입구; 시초; 한계점 ache n. 아픔, 쑤심 trigger v. 일으키다, 유발하다; 발사하다 tension n. 긴장; 긴장상태 migraine n. 편두통 supposititious a. 가짜의, 몰래 바꿔친, 가정의 delusive a. 미혹시키는; 기만하는; 망상적인 omnibus a. 여러 가지 항목을 포함하는, 일괄적인 tell-tale a. 고자질하는; 내막을 폭로하는, 숨기려 해도 숨길 수 없는

모든 종류의 통증 가운데 '임계' 통증보다 더 중요하게 이해해야 하는 것은 없다. 거의 모든 사람에게 긴장 혹은 피로가 특정 한계점에 이를 때마다 숨길 수 없이 드러나는 통증이다. 그것은 편두통의 형태를 띨 수도 있다.

16 ③

not A but B 구문을 'B, not A'의 형태로 표현할 수 있는 것처럼 not because A but because B 구문 또한 'Because B, not because A'의 형태로 쓸 수 있으며, 이 때 A와 B에는 문맥상 대조를 이루는 표현이 들어가는 것이 일반적이다. 주어진 글에서 only because 이하는 앞서 언급한 형태를 취하고 있으므로, 빈칸에는 he is told to do them과 반대되는 의미를 가진 표현이 들어가야 한다. '지시를 받는 것'의 반대 개념은 '스스로의 의사에 의해 행동하는 것'이므로 빈칸에는 '자신 안의 욕구'라는 뜻의 ③이 적절하다.

genie n. (아라비안나이트의) 요정, 마귀 astounding a. 깜짝 놀라게 할만한, 아주 대단한 prodigy n. 경이, 비범함; 비범한 사람, 천재 coercion n. 강요, 강제; 위압 impulse n. 충동, 욕구; 자극, 추진력 scheme n. 계획, 책략

정치가와 과학자의 관계는 『아라비안나이트(the Arabian Nights)』의 마법사와 그의 지시를 따르는 요정 지니(genie)의 관계와 같다. 지니는 만약 자신이 도와주지 않는다면 마법사는 결코 할 수 없을 놀라운 일들을 한다. 그러나 지니는 자신 안의 그 어떤 욕구 때문이 아니라 단지 그런 일들을 하라는 지시를 받기 때문에 그런 놀라운 일들을 한다.

17 ③

리히텐슈타인에서 사용하고 있는 독일어 단어는 다른 곳에서 사용할

수 없는 것이라고 했으므로, 이 곳은 그러한 단어가 유일하게 보존되어 있는 곳이라 할 수 있다. 그러므로 빈칸에는 '보호구역'이란 의미의 ③이 들어가야 한다.

treat n. 큰 기쁨, 예기치 않은 멋진 경험 unusable a. 사용할 수 없는 feudal a. 봉건시대의; 중세의 aristocratic a. 귀족의; 당당한 form of address 직함, 칭호 scourge n. 하늘의 응징, 천벌; 불행을 가져오는 것 labyrinth n. 미궁, 미로 refuge n. 피난, 보호; 피난소, 은신처 abattoir n. 도살장; 육체를 학대하는 곳

리히텐슈타인(Liechtenstein)은 여러 가지 이유로 멋진 경험을 하게 해 준다. 한 가지는 훌륭한 개인 소장 예술작품을 보는 것이다. 또 하나는 다른 곳에서는 사용할 수 없을 독일어 단어를 쓸 기회를 갖는 것이다. 전 세계에서 유일하게 독일어를 말하는 봉건국가인 리히텐슈타인은 귀족 호칭에 대한 전통적 독일어의 마지막 보호구역이다.

---

18 ②

첫 번째 문장에서 조니 워커가 유럽연합의 통합을 회의적으로 보는 이들의 시각에 동조할 것이라고 했으며, 마지막 문장에서 스카치위스키의 새로운 시장은 유럽을 벗어난 곳에 있다고 했다. 그러므로 유럽연합 통합 회의론자들이 주장하는 바는 '영국은 유럽을 벗어나야 성공할 수 있다'가 될 것이다. 빈칸 뒤의 재귀대명사 itself는 Britain을 가리키므로, 빈칸에는 '속박을 풀다'라는 의미의 ②가 들어가는 것이 적절하다. ①의 경우, 'dissuade + 목적어 + from ~ing'의 형태로 쓰임에 유의한다.

make one's name 유명해지다, 이름을 떨치다 Eurosceptic n. 유럽연합 통합 회의론자 contention n. 논쟁, 말다툼; 주장 be better off ~ing ~하는 편이 낫다 ailing a. 병든, 병약한, 건전치 못한 affluent a. 부유한, 유복한 dissuade v. 단념시키다, 만류하다 unshackle v. 차꼬를 벗기다, 속박을 풀다; 자유롭게 하다 galvanize v. 갑자기 활기를 띠게 하다 resurrect v. 소생시키다, 부활시키다; 부흥시키다

대영제국의 무역로를 따라 이름을 떨쳤던 조니 워커(Johnnie Walker)는 유럽연합 통합 회의론자들의 주장을 지지할 것으로 보인다. 그들은 영국이 국제무대에서 성공하기 위해서는 병든 유럽연합으로부터 벗어나는 편이 낫다고 주장하고 있다. 결국, 새로운 스카치위스키 소비자들을 발견할 수 있는 가장 큰 희망은 새로운 부유층인 인도와 중국 사람들에게 있다는 것이다.

---

19 ②

while이 이끄는 절의 내용이 주절의 내용과 대조를 이루어야 한다. 주절에서 부유한 소수의 사람들이 경기 회복을 경험했다고 했으므로, 주절 주어와 반대되는 개념인 majority를 주어로 하는 종속절의 빈칸에는 recovery와 반대되는 의미를 가진 단어가 와야 한다. 따라서 '경기후퇴, 불황'이라는 의미의 ②가 정답이 된다.

describe v. 묘사하다, 기술하다; 말로 설명하다 fundamental a. 기초의, 기본의; 근본적인 affluent a. 풍부한; 유복한 moderate a. 절제하는, 삼가는; 알맞은, 적당한 mire v. 진구렁에 빠뜨리다; 곤경에 처하게 하다 flush n. 홍조; 상기, 흥분; 활기, 한창때; 부자 recession n. 퇴거, 후퇴; 경기후퇴 tenure n. (지위·직분 등의) 보유; 보유권; 재직기간, 임기 gibberish n. 뭐가 뭔지 알 수 없는 말, 횡설수설

현재의 경제상황을 충분히 빠르게 진행되고 있지 않을 뿐인 회복기로 설명하는 것은 완전히 잘못된 것이다. 사실은, 미국 인구 가운데 소수의 사람들이 - 주로 가장 나이가 많고 부유한 사람들이 해당된다 - 거의 3년 동안 적당한 정도의 회복을 경험한 반면, 대다수는 여전히 완전한 불황에 빠져 있다.

---

20 ②

이세돌과 알파고의 역사적 대국에 대한 묘사이다. 이세돌이 멋진 수를 두자 알파고가 당황했다는 내용이 첫 번째 빈칸이고, 두 번째 빈칸에는 놀란 알파고가 이상한 수를 두었다는 내용을 만드는 표현이 들어가야 한다. 마지막 빈칸은 a billion과 합하여 알파고를 가리켜야 한다. 모두를 만족시키는 것은 ②이다.

gouge v. 파내다 extemporaneous a. 즉흥적인 bungle n. 실수 blink v. 깜짝 놀라서 보다 horrendous a. 끔찍한 circuit n. 회로 debilitate v. 쇠퇴하다 terrific a. 빼어난 glimpse v. 얼핏 보다 jaded a. 몹시 지친

리는 바둑판의 한가운데 근처에 백돌을 놓는다. 이 수는 알파고의 방어선을 효과적으로 갈라놓는다. 알파고는 놀라서 처다본다. 물론 문자 그대로의 의미는 아니다. 하지만 그 다음 수는 끔찍한 수다. 리는 십억 개의 회로가 적이 아니라 알파고의 프로그래머이자 알파고를 대신하여 바둑판에 돌을 놓는 황(Huang)이 적인 것처럼 황을 노려본다.

---

21 ③

두 번째 빈칸부터 채울 수 있다. 축출된 독재자들로부터 교훈을 얻지 못했다고 했는데, 독재자가 축출되면 그들이 누리는 상황이 달라지거나 혹은 더 이상 그것을 누리지 못하게 될 것이므로, 두 번째 빈칸에는 decay 또는 disappear가 가능하다. 두 번째 문장의 comprehend의 목적절이 첫 문장에 언급된 교훈의 내용이며, 이들이 교훈을 얻지 못하는 것은 현재 누리고 있는 것에 너무 익숙해져 있기 때문으로 보는 것이 타당하다. 따라서 첫 번째 빈칸에는 accustomed 또는 inured가 가능하다. 두 조건을 모두 만족시키는 정답은 ③이 된다.

dictator n. 독재자, 절대 권력자 remove v. 제거하다; 해임하다; 죽이다 inner circle 핵심층, 중추 세력 corner v. 구석에 두다; 궁지에 빠뜨리다 tyrant n. 폭군, 압제자; 전제군주 status quo 현상(現狀) accustomed a. 습관의; 익숙한 vaunt v. 자랑하다, 뽐내다, 허풍떨다 wreak v. (원수를) 갚다, (벌을) 주다, (분노를) 터뜨리다 decay v. 쇠하다, 쇠퇴하다; 썩다, 부패하다 inure v. 익숙하게 하다, 단련시키다 disappear v. 사라지다; 없어지다 stultify v. 어리석어 보이게 하다, 무의미하게 하다; 망쳐 버리다 rejoice v. 기뻐하다, 좋아하다, 즐기다

아사드(Assad)는 '아랍의 봄(Arab Spring)'으로 축출된 다른 독재자로부터 교훈을 얻지 못했는데, 그들 가운데 대다수는 핵심권력이라는 거품 너머에서 벌어지고 있는 사실을 접하지 못하고 있었을 가능성이 높다. 궁지에 빠진 많은 독재자들은 오랜 세월 동안 모든 것을 완전히 통제하는 데 젖어 있었던 까닭으로, 심지어는 1년 반에 걸친 무자비한 전투 후에도 수십 년에 걸쳐 만들어 온 현재 상황이 연기 속에 사라질 수 있다는 사실을 이해하기가 여전히 어려울 지도 모른다.

22 ③

앞서 언급한 living on the street의 행위를 하는 사람들을 의미하는 단어가 첫 번째 빈칸에 들어가야 한다. vagabonds 또는 vagrants가 가능하다. 한편, 거리에서 사는 사람들이 거리를 항상 주시하고 있는 경우, 지켜보는 사람이 있기 때문에 거리가 더 안전하게 될 것이라 추론할 수 있으므로, 두 번째 빈칸에는 secure 또는 livable이 쓰일 수 있다. 두 조건을 모두 만족시키는 정답은 ③이다.

prohibit v. 금지하다 obviously ad. 명백하게, 명확하게 turn a blind eye to ~을 눈감아주다 reckon v. 계산하다; 생각하다, 추정하다 presence n. 존재, 실재; 참석 neighborhood n. 근처, 이웃; 지역 footpad n. 노상강도 secluded a. 외딴, 세상에서 격리된; 한적한 vagabond n. 방랑자, 유랑자; 부랑자 vibrant a. 활기찬; 진동하는 vagrant n. 부랑자; 방랑자 secure a. 안전한, 위험 없는 scavenger n. 청소부; 폐품 수집자 livable a. 살기 좋은, 살기에 알맞은

길거리에서 사는 것은 금지되어 있지만 그런 부랑자들이 말썽을 피우지 않는 한 지역 경찰은 명백하게 그 관행을 눈감아준다. 나는 그들의 눈이 가장 확실하게 거리를 주시하고 있으므로, 그들의 존재가 실제로 동네를 더 안전하게 만든다고 생각한다.

23 ①

마지막 문장의 의미를 살펴보면, 개인이 자신이 속해 있는 문화로부터 대단히 큰 영향을 받는다는 것이며, 달리 표현하면, '개인은 자신이 속해 있는 문화에 동화 혹은 조화되어 간다'라는 것이다. 따라서 빈칸에는 ①이 들어가는 것이 가장 적절하다.

first and foremost 제일 먼저 standard n. 표준, 기준; 규격; 모범 custom n. 풍습, 관습, 관행 accommodation n. 숙박시설; 편의; 적응, 조화, 순응 cacophony n. 불협화음; 불쾌한 음조, 소음 flivver n. 값싼 물건; 낙제; 실패; 날조 upheaval n. (사회 등의) 대변동, 동란, 격변

개인의 인생사는 가장 먼저 자신이 속해 있는 사회에서 전통적으로 전해 내려 온 양식과 기준에 대한 조화라고 할 수 있다. 태어나는 순간부터 그가 태어난 곳의 관습은 그의 경험과 행동을 형성한다. 그가 성장하여 문화 활동에 참여할 수 있게 되는 무렵이면, 그 문화의 습관이 그의 습관이고, 그 문화의 믿음은 그의 믿음이며, 그 문화에서 불가능한 것은 그에게도 불가능하다.

24 ②

글의 전체적인 흐름과 'thus cannot be declared insane'라는 단서로부터 정답을 추론할 수 있다.

psychiatrist n. 정신과의사 invoke v. 기원하다; 호소하다; 불러내다, 연상시키다; 가져오다, 야기하다 insanity n. 정신이상; 매우 어리석음 absurdity n. 불합리, 어리석음

조셉 헬러는 세계 제 2대전을 배경으로 군인들을 향한 부조리한 관료주의의 억압들을 묘사하고 있는 1961년작 『Catch-22』를 통해 "Catch 22"라는

용어를 만들어 냈다. 이 용어는 소설 속 등장인물로 군의관인 Doc Daneeka에 의해서 소개된다. 그는 비행을 할 수 없을 만큼 미쳤다는 판정을 받아 위험한 임무로부터 벗어나기를 희망하며, 정신 이상여부를 판정해달라고 정신감정을 요청하는 조종사에게, 그러한 요청을 하는 것은 그 자체로 정신이상이 아님을 보여주고 있으며 따라서 (그로서는 조종사에게 조종사가) 미쳤다는 판정을 내려줄 수 없다는 사실을 설명하기 위해서 "Catch 22"이라는 용어를 사용한다. 이 용어는 또한 상호 연관된 갈등이나 상호의존적인 조건 때문에 출구가 보이지 않는 딜레마나 어려운 상황을 의미한다.

25 ④

사회적 존재인 인간은 좋은 평판을 얻고 비난을 피하고자 필연적으로 다른 사람들을 의식한다는 내용이다. 빈칸이 들어 있는 문장의 the point는 앞 문장의 the generality of mankind stand in awe of public opinion, while conscience is feared only by the few를 가리키는데, 다른 사람을 의식한다는 점을 반어적으로 표현하고 있는 ④가 빈칸에 가장 적절하다. ①은 다른 사람들을 배려하라는 의미이므로, 다른 사람들을 의식하는 것과는 차이가 있는 표현이다.

possess v. 소유하다, 가지고 있다; 지니다; (관념 등이) 지배하다 reputation n. 평판; 명성 condemnation n. 비난, 유죄판결 undoubtedly ad. 틀림없이, 확실히 substantial a. 실질적인; 많은, 대폭적인; 견실한 preserve v. 보전하다, 유지하다; 보존하다 delicacy n. 섬세함, 정교함; 미묘함 expose v. 노출시키다, 드러내다 generality n. 일반적 원칙; 일반성; 대다수 awe n. 경외, 두려움 conscience n. 양심, 도덕관념 cynical a. 냉소적인, 비꼬는 brevity n. 간결; 짧음

사람은 사회적 존재이므로 동료들의 판단에 신경을 쓴다. 가족, 이웃, 친구들로부터 좋은 평판을 얻고, 사회의 비난을 피하는 것이 선행을 하는 동기임에 틀림없다. 플리니우스(Pliny)는 상당한 진실을 갖고서 그러한 상황에 대해 다음과 같이 말했다. "세상 사람들 앞에 있을 때처럼 혼자 있을 때 점잖은 행동을 하는 사람은 거의 없다." 여론 앞에서는 떨지만 양심을 무서워하는 사람은 적은 것이 사실이다. 아랍의 한 격언이 이 점을 신랄하게 요약해주고 있다. "아는 사람이 없는 동네에 가서 멋대로 행동해라."

01 ④	**02** ④	**03** ④	**04** ④	**05** ④	**06** ③	**07** ②	**08** ④	**09** ②	**10** ②
11 ②	**12** ③	**13** ①	**14** ④	**15** ④	**16** ④	**17** ②	**18** ③	**19** ④	**20** ⑤
21 ③	**22** ③	**23** ②	**24** ⑤	**25** ②					

01 ④

사실상 troubleshooter의 사전적 의미를 묻는 문제라 할 수 있다. 이 단어는 '분쟁을 조정하는 역할을 하는 사람'을 뜻하므로, 그에게 요청한 것은 '중재하는 일'이라고 생각할 수 있다.

troubleshooter n. 분쟁 조정자; 수리기사 call upon ~을 부탁하다, 요구하다 dispute n. 토론; 논쟁, 말다툼, 싸움 turn in 제출하다 give in 굴복하다 chide v. 꾸짖다, 비난하다 intercede v. 중재하다, 조정하다

회사의 분쟁 조정 담당자는 회사와 그 도시간의 관계에 금이 가게 한 싸움을 중재해달라는 요청을 받았다.

02 ④

주어진 글의 경우, 빈칸이 없다 하더라도 글의 이해에 전혀 문제가 되지 않는 상태에 있다고 할 수 있다. 그러므로 이 문제는 빈칸 뒤의 동사인 condemned와 가장 자연스럽게 호응하는 부사를 찾는 문제로 볼 수 있다. 따라서 '가차 없이'라는 의미의 ④가 가장 적절하다.

standard n. 표준, 기준; 규범, 모범 condemn v. 비난하다, 나무라다, 책망하다 leniently ad. 관대하게, 가볍게 contingently ad. 우연히; 불시에; 부수적으로 tepidly ad. 미지근하게; 열의 없이 relentlessly ad. 가차 없이, 혹독하게

일반적인 기준으로는 가차 없이 비난받게 될 사람에게 아이러니하게도 얼마나 많은 선함이 있는지를 보여주는 것이 나에게는 자주 즐거운 일이었다.

03 ④

Although가 이끄는 종속절과 주절의 내용이 대조를 이루어야 한다. '병으로 인해 원래의 식욕과 성격이 무뎌졌다'라고 했으므로, 종속절에는 무뎌지기 이전의 식욕과 성격에 대한 내용이 언급되어야 할 것이다. 강한 식욕에 상응하는 것이 gluttonous인 것처럼, 빈칸에는 강한 성격에 상응하는 표현이 들어가야 한다. 따라서 '다투기 좋아하는'이라는 의미의 ④가 들어가는 것이 가장 자연스럽다.

gluttonous a. 게걸스런, 많이 먹는 blunt v. 둔감하게 하다, 무디게 하다 appetite n. 식욕; 욕망 temper n. 기질, 천성; 기분 reticent a. 과묵한; 삼가는

reflective a. 반사하는; 반영하는; 숙고하는 lukewarm a. 미지근한; 미온적인, 냉담한 contentious a. 다투기 좋아하는, 논쟁하기를 좋아하는

그는 평상시에 음식 욕심이 많고 다투길 좋아했지만, 그의 병은 그의 식욕과 기질 모두를 무디게 만들었다.

04 ④

Though가 이끄는 종속절과 주절의 내용은 대조를 이루어야 하는데, 정답을 찾는 데 있어 단서가 되는 표현은 동사 shared이다. 이것은 '함께 하다, 공유하다'라는 의미이므로, 빈칸에는 이와 대조를 이루는 '분리' 혹은 '차이'를 나타내는 단어가 들어가야 한다. 따라서 정답은 ④가 된다.

numerous a. 다수의, 수많은 desultory a. 산만한, 단편적인; 일관성이 없는 jocund a. 명랑한, 쾌활한, 즐거운 lugubrious a. 애처로운, 가엾은; 우울한 disparate a. 다른, 공통점이 없는, 별개의

사회적 배경이 서로 다른 출신이었음에도 불구하고, 그 신혼부부는 많은 공감대를 형성하고 있었다.

05 ④

유복한 집안 출신이라면, 빈곤이나 가난을 경험한 적이 없었을 것이다. 그러므로 정답은 ④가 되며, affluent와 반대되는 의미를 내포하고 있는 단어를 찾는 문제라 할 수 있다.

affluent a. 풍부한; 유복한 suffer v. 경험하다; 견디다, 참다 symmetry n. 대칭, 균형, 조화 malady n. 질병; (사회적) 병폐, 폐해 imputation n. (책임 따위의) 씌우기, 전가; 비난, 오명(汚名) deprivation n. 탈취, 박탈; 상실; 궁핍, 빈곤

진아(Jin-ah)는 매우 유복한 집안 출신임에 틀림없다. 나는 그녀가 살아오는 동안 그 어떤 빈곤도 겪어 본 적이 없을 것이라고 생각한다.

06 ③

빈칸 다음이 but으로 연결되므로 네안데르탈인들이 묘사되어 온 모습과 실제 고고학 증거가 말하는 모습이 대조를 이루어야 한다. 상징적

사고를 할 수 있었다는 것은 지적 수준이 높았다는 것을 의미하므로, 빈칸에는 '우둔한'이라는 의미의 ③이 적절하다.

portray v. 그리다, 묘사하다 archaeological a. 고고학의 evidence n. 증거; 증언; 흔적 unearth v. 발굴하다, 파내다; 발견하다 symbolic a. 상징적인; 기호의 miscreant a. 악한, 사악한 gargantuan a. 거대한; 엄청난 imbecile a. 우둔한, 저능한 sanguine a. 낙천적인; 혈색이 좋은, 다혈질의

네안데르탈인들은 오랫동안 저능한 것으로 묘사되어왔지만, 영국 과학자들이 발굴한 고고학 증거는 그들이 상징적 사고를 할 수 있었음을 시사하고 있다.

07 ②

노벨상 수상자를 추천한 사람이 어떤 사람들인지를 누설할 수 있는 내부 관계자라면, 당연히 그에 관한 정보를 알고 있거나 전해 받은 사람일 것이다. 따라서 빈칸에는 '은밀하게 통지를 받는'이라는 의미의 ②가 적절하다.

committee n. 위원회; 위원 nominator n. 지명자, 임명자, 추천자 national assembly 국회, 의회 dean n. 수석 사제; 학장 leak v. (비밀 등을) 누설하다, 흘리다 insider n. 내부의 사람, 회원; 내막을 아는 사람, 소식통 prim a. 꼼꼼한; 새침 떠는 privy a. 비밀스럽게 관여하는, 비밀히 통지를 받는 primordial a. 원시의; 최초의 punitive a. 형벌의, 징벌의, 응보의

노르웨이 노벨상 위원회는 의회, 대학교 학장과 교수 등에서 추천자를 초빙한다. 추천자들은 그에 관한 정보를 비밀리에 전달받은 내부 관계자가 누설하지 않는 한 50년 동안 기밀로 유지된다.

08 ④

인상주의는 존재의 부단한 움직임 속에서 어느 한 (인상적인) 순간을 정지 포착하는 것이다. 부단히 움직인다는 것은 불안정하고 위태로울 수밖에 없다.

impressionistic picture 인상주의 그림 deposit n. 침전물; 층; 예금; 보증금 perpetuum mobile n. (음악) 상동곡; <비유적> 영원히 움직이는 것 representation n. 재현, 대표; 나타냄, 상징 precarious a. 위험한; 불안정한; 불분명한; 기초가 단단하지 않은 contend v. 주장하다; 다투다, 경쟁하다; 싸우다 adamant a. 요지부동의, 단호한 callous a. 굳어진, 딱딱한; 무감각한 detrimental a. 해로운, 유해한

모든 인상주의 그림은 계속해서 움직이는 존재의 어느 한 순간을 정지 포착하여, 서로 갈등하는 힘들이 작용하는 가운데 위태롭고 불안정한 균형 상태를 묘사한다.

09 ②

treated 이하는 순접의 접속사 and를 통해 shunned와 연결되어 있으므로, 사람들이 일반적으로 기피하는 대상에 해당하는 단어가 들어가야 한다. 이런 조건에 가장 부합하는 의미를 가진 ②가 정답이 된다.

shun v. 피하다, 비키다 harbinger n. 선구자; 전조(前兆) pariah n. 추방당한 사람, 천민, 하층민; (사회에서 버림받은) 부랑자 trencherman n. 대식가 equestrian n. 기수(騎手), 곡마사

많은 사람들은 아직도 에이즈(AIDS)에 대해 무지하다. 나는 에이즈 환자들의 가족이 기피당하고 사회의 부랑인 취급을 받지 않도록 사람들을 교육시키기 위해 더 많은 것들이 행해질 수 있다고 생각한다.

10 ②

두 번째 문장에 나온 direct knowledge와 direct acquaintance가 단서이다. 다른 사실이나 증거, 또는 추론을 매개로 하지 않고 사물과 직접 접촉하여 느낌으로 지식을 얻을 수 있는 능력은 '직관'이다. 따라서 정답은 ②가 되며, 결국 direct knowledge와 direct acquaintance에 대한 동의어를 찾는 문제라 할 수 있다.

acquaintance n. 지식, 익히 앎; 면식; 아는 사람 primary a. 주요한, 첫째의; 최초의 genius n. 천재; 비범한 재능; 특수한 재주 intuition n. 직관; 직관적 통찰 syllogism n. 삼단논법, 연역법 dilettantism n. 취미로 하는 일, 도락; 아마추어 예술; 얕은 지식

그것은 예술가의 직관과 같은 것이다. 다시 말해, 그것은 있는 그대로의 세상에 대한 직접적인 지식이며, 세상의 사물에 대해 직접적으로 아는 것이다. 그리고 이것이 예술가의 주된 지식이다.

11 ②

and then 앞 부분의 내용을 요약하면, '지금은 보답할 수 없고 나중에 여건이 되면 보답할 수 있다'라는 내용이다. 보답을 한다는 것은 배은망덕하지 않음을 의미하는데 빈칸 앞에 부정어 not이 있으므로, 빈칸에는 ②가 들어가야 한다.

reward v. 보답하다, 보상하다; 보수를 주다 inheritance n. 상속, 계승; 상속재산 income n. 수입, 소득 lanky a. 홀쭉한, 호리호리한 unappreciative a. 감사하지 않는; 감상할 줄 모르는 lavish a. 아낌없는, 활수한; 사치스러운 mournful a. 슬픔에 잠긴; 쓸쓸한; 애처로운

당신의 노고에 대해 지금은 보답해드릴 수 없지만, 한두 달 후면 제가 상속을 받고 수입을 마음대로 할 수 있게 될 것이니, 그때는 적어도 제가 배은망덕하지는 않다는 것을 보여드리겠습니다.

12 ③

마지막 문장의 과학자, 도덕가, 종교 집단은 모두 바로 앞 문장에서 언급한 '현대 의학 및 종교'와 관련된 사람 혹은 단체이다. 이들에 의해서 칭송을 받았다고 했으므로, 첫 문장의 주체인 It은 논쟁을 해결하거나 불식시키는 역할을 했을 것이다. 따라서 빈칸에는 '(긴장·위험 등을) 완화하다'라는 의미의 ③이 들어가야 한다.

landmark n. 경계표지; 획기적인 사건; 역사적 건물 divisive a. 구분하는, 분석적인; 불화를 일으키는 laud v. 기리다, 찬양하다, 찬미하다 ethicist n. 도덕가, 윤리학자 ferment v. 발효시키다; 들끓게 하다, 자극하다 inveigle v. 유혹하다, 유인하다; 꾀다 defuse v. (폭탄의) 신관을 제거하다; (긴장, 위험 등을) 완화하다 downplay v. 경시하다, 얕보다

그것은 모든 면에서 획기적인 업적이었으며, 현대 의학과 종교의 가장 분열적인 논쟁을 완화시켜주었다. 과학자, 도덕가, 그리고 종교 집단들은 그것을 칭송해 마지않았다.

13 ①

빈칸 앞의 but은 except의 의미로 쓰인 전치사이다. 다른 사람은 갈 수 없는 곳에 출입할 수 있는 과학자라면, 그러한 자격을 부여받거나 승인을 얻은 사람들일 것이다. 따라서 빈칸에는 ①이 들어가는 것이 가장 자연스럽다.

naturalist n. 박물학자; 자연주의자 reserve n. 비축; 예비; 보류; 보호구역 inventory n. 물품 명세서; 목록, 천연자원 조사 일람 accredited a. 공인된, 인정된; 용인된 unaffiliated a. 연계가 없는, 무파벌의 mesmerized a. 매혹된 retired a. 은퇴한, 퇴직한

크라카토아(Krakatoa) 섬은 박물학자의 낙원이 되었으며, 네덜란드인들은 그곳을 자연보호구역으로 만들어, 승인 받은 과학자들 이외에는 아무도 발을 들여놓지 못하게 했다. 그들은 크라카토아 섬에 서식하는 생물의 완전한 목록을 만들어냈다.

14 ④

맨 끝에 위치한 두 개의 when절을 잘 비교하여 정답을 도출해야 한다. 마지막에 위치한 when절은 그 앞의 when절을 재진술한 것인데, can no longer remain과 have ceased의 의미는 사실상 동일하므로, 빈칸에는 experience them과 문맥상 같은 의미를 갖는 표현이 들어가야 함을 알 수 있다. 이 때, them은 friends를 가리키므로, 결국 빈칸에는 '친구를 경험한다'라는 의미를 가질 수 있는 표현이 들어가야 할 것이다. 친구를 경험하는 동안에는 친구와의 친밀도가 높을 것이므로 ④가 빈칸에 들어가기에 가장 적절한 표현이다.

criticism n. 비평, 비판 cease v. 그만 두다, 멈추다; 그치다 inspiration n. 영감; 고취, 고무, 격려 critical a. 비평의, 평론의; 위기의 appreciative a. 감식력 있는; 고마워하는 solitude n. 고독, 외로움 intimacy n. 친밀함, 친교; 절친함

예술 작품을 체험하는 것을 그쳤을 때에 비로소 예술 작품에 대한 비판이 시작되듯이, 친구에 대한 비판도 친구를 경험하는 행위를 그쳤을 때, 다시 말해 우리의 마음이 친밀함의 절정에 더 이상 있을 수 없을 때에야 비로소 시작된다.

15 ④

러시아의 외환 예금이 작년 이래로 25억 달러 감소했음을 감안하면, 러시아가 금의 판매를 촉진하는 것은 금을 팔아 얻게 되는 달러를 가지고서 부족해진 외환예금을 메우려 하기 때문으로 보아야 한다.

step up 촉진하다, 빠르게 하다 bullion n. 금괴, 은괴; 순금, 순은 influx n. 유입(流入); 밀어닥침, 쇄도 analyst n. 분석가, 분해자 speculate v. 추측하다; 사색하다, 숙고하다 foreign deposit 외환 예금 embezzle v. 유용하다, 착복하다; 횡령하다 peculate v. 횡령하다, 유용하다 liquidate v. (빚을) 청산하다, 갚다, 변제하다 procure v. 획득하다, 마련하다

러시아는 서방에서의 금 판매를 촉진하고 있다. 취리히의 금괴 거래업자들은 10월에 거의 2억 달러 어치의 금이 스위스로 유입됐다고 전하고 있다. 분석가들은 러시아의 금 판매가 작년 말 이래로 25억 달러 감소한 외환 예금을 조달하기 위한 것이라 추측하고 있다.

16 ④

어떻게 그런 것에서부터 놀라운 결과물을 만들어냈는지'를 감탄해 마지않았다면, 최초의 아이디어는 그다지 뛰어나지 않은 '변변찮은 것'이었다고 봐야 한다.

fragment n. 파편, 조각, 단편 theme n. 주제, 화제; 테마 marvel v. ~을 기이하게 느끼다; 감탄하다; 놀라다 miraculous a. 불가사의한, 신기한, 놀랄만한 virtuoso n. 예술의 거장, 대가 adroitness n. 교묘함; 솜씨 좋음 contraband n. 밀수품; 불법 거래 clumsiness n. 서투름, 꼴사나움, 세련되지 않음

베토벤(Beethoven)은 항상 옆에다 두고 있는 공책에다 조각조각의 선율을 써 두고, 오래 세월에 걸쳐 그것들을 검토하고 발전시켜 나갔다. 종종 그의 처음 아이디어들은 매우 서투른 것이어서, 학자들이 그가 어떻게 그런 것들로부터 마침내 놀랄만한 결과를 발전시켜 냈는지에 대해 감탄할 정도였다.

17 ②

어떤 종류의 비평이 유용하다면, 또 다른 어떤 것은 그렇지 않을 것이다. 따라서 빈칸에는 useful과 반대되는 의미의 단어가 들어가야 하며, 정답은 ②가 된다.

criticism n. 비평, 비판, 평론 profess v. 공언하다, 단언하다; 고백하다; 주장하다 elucidation n. 설명, 해설 critic n. 비평가, 평론가 comparatively ad. 비교적; 꽤, 상당히 perform v. 실행하다, 이행하다; 수행하다; 공연하다 satisfactorily ad. 만족스럽게, 더할 나위 없이 profane a. 불경스런, 모독적인; 세속의 otiose a. 불필요한, 무효의; 쓸모없는; 한가한, 게으른 chivalrous a. 기사도의; 여성에게 정중한 variegated a. 변화가 많은, 다채로운

비평은 항상 의도하고 있는 목적을 명확히 밝혀야 한다. 따라서 비평가의 역할은 그에게 매우 들어맞는 것처럼 보인다. 또한 그가 자신의 임무를 만족스럽게 수행하고 있는지와 대체로 어떤 종류의 비평이 유용하고 어떤 것이 쓸모없는 지를 판단하는 것은 비교적 쉬운 일이다.

18 ③

두 번째 문장은 '생필품 가격에 불을 지피고 있다'라고 한 첫 문장의 내용에 대해 구체적인 예를 제시하는 역할을 하고 있다. 그러므로 peak, high, advance처럼 물가 상승과 관련 있는 단어가 빈칸에 들어가야 하며, '(가치가) 급등하다'라는 의미의 ③이 정답이 된다.

extreme a. 극도의, 심한; 최대의 drought n. 가뭄; 부족, 결핍 light a fire under ~을 부추기다, 압력을 넣다 commodity n. 일용품, 필수품, 물자 rally v. 달려가다; 시세를 회복하다 high n. 최고치; 최고 기록 settle v. 내려앉다, 가라앉다; 진정되다 bungle v. 서투른 방식으로 하다; 실패하다; 실수하다 spike v. 못을 박다; (가치가) 급등하다 jaywalk v. 무단횡단하다

러시아와 우크라이나에는 가뭄이 들고 파키스탄과 캐나다에는 홍수가 나는 등, 올해 전 세계적인 기상이변이 물가를 부추기고 있다. 밀의 가격이 6월 이후에 급등했고, 게다가 옥수수 가격은 23개월 만의 최고치에, 커피 가격은 13년 만의 최고치에 이르렀으며, 면화는 1995년 이래 최고 가격으로 올랐다.

19 ④

세 번째 문장의 On the other end of the spectrum(정반대의 경우에)은 부부가 서로 의존하는 경우를 말하므로 첫 번째 빈칸에는 falter(비틀거리다)나 tumble(넘어지다)이 적절하고, 이상적인 관계는 의존적이면서도 독립적인 관계를 말하는데 but 앞에서 의존 관계를 언급했으므로 두 번째 빈칸에는 autonomous(독립적인)가 적절하다.

falter v. 비틀거리다 subordinate a. 종속하는 scramble v. 기어오르다 adjunctive a. 부속된, 부수적인 withstand v. 저항하다 detached a. 떨어진, 분리된; 초연한 tumble v. 넘어지다 autonomous a. 독립적인, 자치권이 있는

너무 많은 독립성을 가진 부부는 서로 충분한 관계를 가지지도 서로에게 충분히 의존하지도 않는다. 관계가 깨어져도 양쪽 모두 스스로의 힘으로 무사하다. 정반대의 경우에는 그 관계가 깨어지면 양쪽 모두 넘어진다. 각자가 상대방을 필요로 하지만 또한 스스로의 힘으로 설 수 있을 만큼 충분히 독립적인 그런 관계가 이상적이다.

20 ⑤

일종의 정의 문제이다. 가난과 부의 차이를 크게 느끼면 '탐욕'이 생겨날 것이다. lust는 다른 형태의 욕망이다. 유명해지고 싶은 욕망은 '허영'이라 부른다.

misery n. 불행 obscurity n. 불명료; 무명의 상태 wrath n. 분노 sloth n. 나태 gluttony n. 폭식 lust n. 욕정 envy n. 질투, 시기 prudence n. 신중, 검약 avarice n. 탐욕 vainglory n. 자만심, 허영심

인간 삶의 불행과 무질서의 가장 커다란 원천은 영구적인 한 상황과 다른 상황의 차이를 과대평가하는 것에서 생겨나는 것 같다. 탐욕은 가난과 부 차이를 과대평가하는 것이고, 야심은 사적인 영역과 공적 영역의 차이를 과대평가하는 것이고, 허영은 무명과 광범위한 명성의 차이를 과대평가하는 것에서 비롯된다.

21 ③

첫 번째 빈칸 앞의 that right는 프라이버시에 대한 권리를 의미한다. 전화번호부에 있는 번호들을 아무나 쉽게 얻을 수 있다면, 그것은 프라이버시에 대한 권리를 침해하는 것이므로, 첫 빈칸에는 usurped 또는 seized가 들어갈 수 있다. 한편, 프라이버시가 쉽게 침해당하는 것은 민주주의가 지향하는 것에 반(反)하는 것이므로, 두 번째 빈칸에는 counter만이 들어갈 수 있다.

apparatus n. 장치, 기계, 기구 obtain v. 얻다, 획득하다 avert v. (얼굴 따위를) 돌리다, 비키다; (위험을) 피하다, 막다 fallow a. 묵히고 있는, 휴한(休閑) 중인; 미개간의; (이용 가치가 있는데도) 사용하지 않는 guarantee v. 보증하다, 확실히 하다 hypercritical a. 혹평하는 usurp v. 빼앗다, 찬탈하다, 강탈하다 counter a. 반대의, 거꾸로의 seize v. 붙잡다; 빼앗다, 탈취하다 apposite a. 적당한, 적절한

프라이버시는 이 나라 모든 사람들이 자신이 가질 권리가 있다고 생각하는 것이다. 예를 들어, 전화번호부에 올라있는 전화번호를 누구나 손쉽게 입수할 수 있게 해주는 전자 데이터 수집 장치에 의해 그 권리가 너무나 쉽게 침해당하는 것은 이 민주국가가 지지하는 모든 것에 역행하는 것일 따름이다.

22 ③

두 번째 문장 이하에서는 어떤 행위에 대한 인간의 실제 목적과 그에 수반되는 부작용들이 나열되고 있다. 목표로 삼은 것과는 '다른' 결과에 의해 인간이 피해를 입는 경우들이므로, 빈칸에는 이러한 상황을 포괄적으로 설명할 수 있는 ③이 들어가는 것이 적절하다.

aim v. 목표로 삼다, 마음먹다 pesticide n. 농약, 살충제 get rid of ~을 제거하다, 없애다 unspoiled a. 손상되지 않은, 해를 입지 않은 poison v. 독살하다; 해독을 끼치다, 악화시키다 boredom n. 지루함, 권태 merciful a. 자비로운, 인정 많은 providence n. 섭리; 신(神) doleful a. 슬픈, 씁쓸한 misnomer n. 틀린 이름; 부적절한 명칭; 잘못 부름 discrepancy n. 불일치; 모순 opportune a. 형편이 좋은, 시의적절한 ambiguity n. 모호함, 불명료함

인간이 목표로 삼은 바와 그가 실제로 얻게 되는 것에는 너무나도 자주 가슴 아픈 불일치가 존재한다. 인간은 벌레와 잡초를 없애고자 농약을 뿌리지만, 그럼으로써 새들과 물고기, 꽃이 피어 있는 나무를 죽이고 만다. 때가 묻지 않은 자연을 발견하고자 차를 타고 먼 거리를 가지만, 공기를 오염시키고 그러는 중에 죽기도 한다. 육체노동에서 벗어나고자 기계를 만들지만, 기계의 노예가 되고 권태로움을 겪는다.

23 ②

임금동결을 부정적인 것으로 보게 만든 발표에 대해 빈칸 바로 뒤에서 The reverse is true라고 했으므로, In fact 이하에는 '임금을 동결하는 것이 실제로는 긍정적인 면을 가지고 있다'라는 내용이 이어져야 한다. 주어가 benefits이므로, '늘어나다'라는 의미의 ②가 들어가는 것이 적절하다.

defective a. 결함이 있는, 불완전한 presentation n. 증여, 수여; 공개; 발표 interpret v. 해명하다, 설명하다; 통역하다 involve v. 연좌시키다, 관련시키다 substantial a. 실질적인; 많은, 대폭적인 sacrifice n. 희생; 제물 reverse n. 역(逆), 반대 maintain v. 유지하다, 지속하다; 주장하다 existing a. 현존하는, 현재의 reasonable a. 분별 있는; 온당한, 적당한 purchasing power 구매력 canvass v. 선거운동을 하다; 권유하다 accrue v. 자연증가로 생기다, (이익·결과가) 생기다; (이자가) 늘어나다 macerate v. 야위다, 쇠약해지다 slacken v. (활동 따위가) 줄다, 약해지다

결함이 있는 발표를 통해, 정부는 임금동결이 관련된 모든 사람들, 특히 그 것을 감당할 여유가 없는 사람들의 상당한 희생을 수반하는 것으로 해석되게끔 했다. 그 반대가 진리이다. 사실, 현재의 임금 수준을 유지함으로써 모든 사람들에게 상당한 이득이 생겨날 것이다. 왜냐하면, 만약 이것이 합리적인 시기에 이뤄진다면, 실질 임금 혹은 구매력이 늘어날 것이기 때문이다.

차라리 어느 정도 반대의견을 갖고 싶다. 나는 차라리 누군가가 내게 따지는 것이 좋다. 한 조직에서 두 사람이 똑같이 생각한다면 한 사람은 없어도 된다는 사실을 명심하자.

---

24 ⑤

"주변 환경에 비해 자격 미달인 것보다 자격 과잉인 것이 더 좋다."라는 단서로부터 정답을 추론할 수 있다.

phoenix n. 피닉스, 봉황, 자신을 불태움으로써 재로 돌아간다는 전설의 새 premise n. 전제, 기본적인 가정 aphorism n. 경구(警句), 잠언(箴言), 격언, 금언(金言) foresee v. 예견하다 oar n. 노, 노젓는 사람 vinegar n. 식초

중국에는 '봉황의 꼬리가 되느니 닭의 머리가 되는 것이 더 좋다'는 속담이 있다. 이 경구(警句)의 가정은 ─ 주변 환경에 비해 자격 미달인 것보다 자격 과잉인 것이 더 좋다는 ─ 널리 받아들여지는 것으로서 거의 모든 문화에 이와 유사한 경구가 존재한다. 미국인들과 영국인들은 큰 연못에서 작은 개구리가 되는 것보다 작은 연못에서 큰 개구리(혹은 물고기)가 되는 것이 더 좋다고 종종 공공연하게 말한다.

---

25 ②

첫 네 문장의 내용은 조직과 상사에 충성하여 무조건적으로 의견을 따르기보다는 반대 의견을 개진하는 것이 낫다는 것이다. 마지막 문장은 이러한 의견을 종합하는 역할을 하는데, 앞서 언급한 관점에서 보면, '두 사람이 모두 항상 의견이 같다면 한 사람이면 충분하므로 굳이 두 사람이 있을 필요는 없다'라는 결론을 내릴 수 있다. 따라서 빈칸에 들어갈 표현으로는 ②가 적절하다.

threat n. 위협, 협박; 우려 adopt v. 채용하다, 채택하다 belittle v. 얕잡다, 하찮게 보다 loyalty n. 충의, 충성, 성실 disagreement n. 불일치; 논쟁, 불화 argument n. 논의, 논증, 논거 organization n. 조직, 구성; 기구, 조직체 exactly ad. 정확하게, 엄밀하게 achieve v. 이루다, 달성하다, 성취하다 get along without ~없이 지내다 dispense with ~없이 지내다, ~을 필요하지 않게 하다

사람이 발전하는 데 있어서 가장 심각한 위협은 아무 탈 없이 일하고, 실수를 하지 않으려 조심하는 것에서 비롯된다. 때때로 우리가 '안일한' 태도를 취할 때, 우리는 직장 상사와 조직에 충성하기 때문에 그의 뜻에 따른다고 스스로에게 변명한다. 충성심을 과소평가하려는 생각은 결코 없지만, 나는

01 ②	02 ④	03 ①	04 ①	05 ②	06 ①	07 ③	08 ④	09 ①	10 ②
11 ④	12 ①	13 ①	14 ⑤	15 ①	16 ③	17 ①	18 ①	19 ③	20 ③
21 ④	22 ①	23 ①	24 ③	25 ①					

01 ②

슬픈 어린 시절을 보냈음을 지금 시점에서 알려면, 그 근거가 되는 표정 혹은 모습도 '슬픈' 것이어야 한다. 그러므로 빈칸에는 ②가 들어가야 하며, sadness의 의미를 내포하고 있는 단어를 찾는 문제라 할 수 있다.

sadness n. 슬픔, 비애 portrait n. 초상화; 상세한 묘사 countenance n. 용모, 표정; 지지, 후원 notice v. 알아채다; 주의하다; 통고하다 sadistic a. 가학적인, 사디스트적인 rueful a. 후회하는; 슬픔에 잠긴; 가엾은, 애처로운 salient a. 현저한, 두드러진 gorgeous a. 호화로운; 찬란한, 화려한

다른 사람들은 그 모든 것을 눈치 채지 못했지만, 그 화가는 슬픈 표정을 하고 있는 그 소년이 그린 초상화에서 어린 시절에 겪은 슬픔을 포착해냈다.

02 ④

sophistication과 shallowness가 문장 안에서 대조를 이루고 있다. 천박함이 그가 근본적으로 가진, 다시 말해 '안에 숨어 있는' 면모라면, 그와 대비되는 고도의 세련됨은 '밖으로 드러나는' 면모일 것이다. 그러므로 빈칸에는 fundamental에 대해 반의어적 의미를 가진 ④가 들어가야 한다.

casual a. 우연한, 뜻밖의; 일시적인, 임시의 acquaintance n. 지식, 면식; 아는 사이, 아는 사람 deceive v. 속이다, 기만하다 sophistication n. 궤변을 논함; 세상 물정에 익숙함, (고도의) 지적 교양, 세련됨 recognize v. 알아보다; 인지하다; 인정하다 fundamental a. 기초의, 기본의; 근본적인 shallowness n. 얕음; 천박함, 피상적임 pinnacle n. 작은 뾰족탑; 절정, 정점 revulsion n. (감정 따위의) 격변, 급변 asperity n. 신랄함; 퉁명스러움 veneer n. 겉치장, 허식

그를 깊이 알지 못하는 사람들은 밖으로 드러나는 그의 세련됨에 속아서 기저에 깔려 있는 그의 천박한 면모를 인식하지 못했다.

03 ①

그가 거부한 행동의 내용이 곧 정복자가 원했던 행동일 것이다. 그러므로 빈칸에는 앞 문장의 abase himself in the eyes of his followers의 의미를 나타낼 수 있는 단어가 들어가야 하는데, 빈칸 뒤의 대명사 him

은 abase 뒤의 himself와 동일인이므로, 결국 빈칸에는 abase의 의미를 가진 단어가 와야 함을 알 수 있다. 따라서 '굴욕감을 주다'라는 의미의 ①이 정답이 된다.

stubborn a. 완고한, 고집 센; 완강한 refusal n. 거절, 거부; 사퇴 abase v. 깎아내리다, (지위 등을) 낮추다; 창피를 주다 irritate v. 초조하게 하다, 노하게 하다; 흥분시키다 conqueror n. 정복자, 승리자 humiliate v. 욕보이다, 창피를 주다, 굴욕을 주다 incarcerate v. 투옥하다, 감금하다 manacle v. 수갑을 채우다, 속박하다 commandeer v. 징집하다, 징용하다; 징발하다

불행하게도, 자신을 따르는 자들이 보는 앞에서 스스로를 낮추길 거부한 그의 태도는 정복자를 더 화나게 만들었다, 왜냐하면 그 정복자는 그에게 굴욕감을 안겨주고 싶었기 때문이다.

04 ①

주절에 '축하하고자 했다'라는 내용이 있으므로, 그 이유가 되는 표현이 와야 하는 빈칸에는 긍정적인 의미의 단어가 필요하다. 따라서 '대성공'이라는 의미의 ①이 정답이다.

broker n. 중개인, 브로커; 주식 중개인 drop by 잠깐 들르다, 불시에 찾아가다 congratulate v. 축하하다 coup n. 타격; 불의의 일격; (사업 등의) 대성공; 쿠데타 down-fall n. 낙하, 추락; 몰락, 멸망 trepidation n. 공포, 전율; 당황; 불안 tribulation n. 재난, 고난, 시련; 고민거리

그가 큰 성공을 거뒀다는 소식이 다음날 월스트리트 곳곳에 전해지자마자, 그의 동료 중개인들 모두는 축하하기 위해 그를 방문했다.

05 ②

But으로 시작되는 두 번째 문장에서 '유색인종들이 미국을 환경 친화적으로 만드는 데 좀 더 직접적으로 연관되어 있다'라고 했으므로, 첫 번째 문장의 빈칸에는 유색인종과 대비되는 표현, 즉 백인을 의미하는 단어가 들어가야 한다.

driving force 추진력 color n. (피부의) 빛, 유색, (특히) 흑색; 안색 stake n. 내기, 이해관계, 관여 at stake 위험에 처하여, 문제가 되어; 관련이 되어 bankrupt a. 파산한, 지급능력이 없는 white a. 백인의; 보수적인 hectic a. 얼굴에 홍조를 띤; 열광적인, 매우 바쁜 ethnic a. 인종의, 민족의; 인종 특유의

미국의 새로운 녹색 경제를 이끌어 나가는 힘은 거의 전적으로 백인에게 있다. 그러나 유색인종들이 미국을 환경 친화적으로 만드는 데 훨씬 더 많이 직접적인 관련을 맺고 있다.

---

06 ①

결과절의 명사 주어는 앞 절의 내용을 요약 반복하는 역할을 하고 있다. 앞의 내용이 별것 아닌 것을 자랑한다는 것이므로, 빈칸에는 boasting과 같거나 유사한 의미를 가진 단어가 들어가야 한다. '허세'라는 의미의 ①이 정답이 된다.

terrible a. 무서운, 가공할; 지독한; 가혹한, 엄한 boast v. 자랑하다, 떠벌리다 accomplishments n. 업적, 성취 renowned a. 유명한 bluff n. 허세, 으름장; 허세부리는 사람 rectitude n. 정직, 청렴; 올바름 diffidence n. 수줍음, 자신 없음 tempestuousness n. 소란, 야단법석

그는 자신이 조금이라도 잘한 것이 있으면 엄청나게 떠들어 대는 지독한 버릇이 있어서, 그의 허세는 그 작은 대학 전체에서도 유명하게 되었다.

---

07 ③

that is 이하에는 not A but B 구문이 쓰였으며, 이 구문에서 A와 B에 해당되는 자리에는 서로 대조를 이루는 표현이 와야 한다. 따라서 빈칸에는 emptiness의 반의어에 해당하는 단어가 들어가야 하며, '충만'이라는 의미의 ③이 가장 적절하다. 한편, that is는 부연설명의 역할을 하는 표현이므로, that is 전후의 표현을 비교하여, absence가 emptiness와 호응하는 것처럼 presence와 의미상 호응하는 단어를 찾는 식으로 접근하여 정답을 도출하는 것도 가능하다.

earn v. 벌다; 획득하다, 얻다 silence n. 침묵; 고요함 absence n. 부재, 결석, 결근 presence n. 존재, 실재; 출석 emptiness n. 공허, 비어있음 repast n. 식사; 식사량 reconnaissance n. 정찰, 수색, 답사 repletion n. 충만; 만원; 포식 repulsion n. 격퇴; 반박, 거절

우리는 침묵을 손에 넣어야 하고, 침묵을 위해 노력해야 하며, 침묵을 부재(不在)가 아니라 존재(存在)로, 다시 말해 공허가 아니라 충만으로 만들어야 한다.

---

08 ④

and를 전후하여 부정사구가 나열되어 있는데, and는 순접의 접속사이므로 두 부정사구가 의미하는 바는 동일하거나 같은 흐름 하에 있어야 한다. 한편, 주어진 동사 control과 present의 의미가 대조를 이루고 있으므로, 빈칸에는 simple unvarnished facts와 반대되는 의미를 가진 단어가 들어가야 할 것이다. 그러므로 과장하거나 윤색하여 말하는 것을 의미하는 ④가 정답이 된다.

unvarnished a. 꾸밈없는, 솔직한, 소박한 vagary n. 기발한 행동, 엉뚱한 짓, 기행(奇行); 변덕 understatement n. 줄잡아 말함, 줄잡아 하는 표현 axiom n. 자명한 이치, 공리; 격언, 금언 embellishment n. 장식; 수식, (이야기 등의) 윤색; (과장을 섞어) 재미있게 함

재판관은 그들에게 평소처럼 윤색해서 말하는 것을 자제하고 순전히 꾸밈없는 사실만을 진술하도록 요청했다.

---

09 ①

주차장에 뿌린 밀가루를 탄저균과 같은 생물학 테러행위와 관련된 것으로 생각했다면, 사람들은 피신하거나 그 장소에서 벗어나려는 행동을 했을 것이다. 그러므로 ①이 정답이다.

ophthalmologist n. 안과의사 sprinkle v. 뿌리다; 끼얹다, 흩다 flour n. 밀가루; 가루, 분말 ensuing a. 계속되는, 잇따라 일어나는, 결과로서 계속되는 felony n. 중범죄 charge n. 책임, 의무; 고발, 고소; 죄과 evacuate v. 피난하다, 철수하다; 소개(疏開)하다 converge v. 한 점에 모이다; 몰려들다 consort v. 교제하다, 사귀다; 일치하다, 조화하다 disport v. 놀다, 장난치다

한 안과의사와 여동생이 코네티컷(Connecticut)주(州) 이케아(Ikea)의 한 주차장에 밀가루를 뿌렸다. 뒤이어 생물학 테러에 대한 공포가 퍼져 수백 명의 사람들이 피신해야 했다. 두 사람은 지금 중범죄 혐의로 기소될 입장에 처해 있다.

---

10 ②

징역형을 선고 받았다고 했으므로, 그녀가 입게 될 옷은 죄수복일 것이다.

custody n. 보관, 관리; 구금, 구류 sentence v. 판결하다, 형을 선고하다 county n. 군(郡), 주(州) jail n. 교도소, 감옥, 구치소 variety n. 변화, 다양성; 종류 stripe n. 줄무늬; 줄무늬 옷, 죄수복 gray n. 회색, 잿빛

판사는 파리스 힐튼(Paris Hilton)이 이번 시즌에 수감되어야 한다고 판결하며, 군(郡) 교도소에서 45일간 복역하도록 선고했다. 그는 "패리스 힐튼은 그녀의 다양한 패션으로 유명한데, 이번 시즌에는 죄수복이 될 것이다"라고 말했다.

---

11 ④

'믿지(그렇게 생각하지) 않는다(we don't believe)'고 말하는 것은 의심하는 '회의적인' 태도이므로 빈칸에는 ④가 적절하다.

by default 그렇지 않아야 할 특별한 경우가 아니면, 기본적으로 sophisticated a. 세련된, 지성적인 disingenuous a. 불성실한 creative a. 창의적인 equivocal a. 모호한 lukewarm a. 미온적인 skeptical a. 회의적인

오늘날, 지성적으로 보일 가장 안전한 방법은 기본적으로 회의적인 태도를 취하는 것이다. 우리는 그렇게 생각하지 않는다고 말할 때 지성적으로 여겨지고 그렇게 생각한다고 말할 때 불성실하게 여겨진다.

12 ①

일반적으로, 수요가 많으면 가격이 오르고 공급이 많으면 가격이 내리게 된다. helped 이하에서 가격의 상승에 대해 이야기하고 있으므로, demand를 수식하고 있는 빈칸에는 '많음' 혹은 '지속'의 의미를 가진 형용사가 들어가야 한다. 따라서 '그칠 줄 모르는 수요'라는 의미가 되게 하는 ①이 빈칸에 가장 적절하다.

promote v. 진척시키다; 증진하다, 조장하다, 장려하다 benchmark n. (일반적인) 기준, 척도; 표준 가격 voracious a. 게걸스레 먹는, 식욕이 왕성한; 탐욕적인; 물릴 줄 모르는 malodorous a. 악취를 풍기는; (법적·사회적으로) 인정할 수 없는 judicious a. 신중한, 현명한, 판단력이 있는 unpretentious a. 잘난 체 하지 않는, 자만하지 않는, 가식 없는

지난해 중국 자동차 제조회사와 조선 회사의 그칠 줄 모르는 수요로 철강가격이 치솟았고, 포스코(POSCO)는 열연강판의 표준 가격을 1톤당 약 510달러로 52퍼센트 올리게 되었다.

13 ①

마지막 문장에서 마약 과다복용으로 사망한 사람이 작년까지 계속 증가했음을 말하고 있다. 빈칸 앞에 부정어가 있으므로, ①이 정답으로 적절하다.

addicted a. 중독된 opioid n. 아편, 마약 heartbreaking a. 가슴 아픈 statistic n. 통계자료 epidemic n. 유행병, 유행 overdose n. 과다복용 set a record (최고) 기록을 세우다 abate v. 수그러들다, 가라앉다 persist v. 지속하다 surge v. 급증하다 bud v. 시작하다 gnaw v. 부식하다

미국에서는 매 25분마다 마약에 중독된 아기가 태어난다. 그 가슴 아픈 통계자료는 수그러들 기미를 보이지 않는 어떤 유행의 한 증세일 뿐이다. 작년의 마약 과다복용 사망자 수 33,000명은 그 또한 최고기록이었던 그 전 해에 비해 16퍼센트 증가한 수치였다.

14 ⑤

뒤에서 '헬리콥터처럼'이라 했으므로 빈칸에는 '공중에 멈춰 떠 있다'라는 의미의 ⑤가 적절하다.

hummingbird n. 벌새 kingdom n. <생물> …계(界); (학문·예술 등의) 세계, 분야 diminutive a. 아주 작은 aerial a. 공기의, 공중의 acrobat n. 곡예사 beat v. 치다 anatomy n. 해부학, 해부학적 구조 mid-air n. 공중, 상공 soar v. 높이 날아오르다 haunt v. (귀신이) 출몰하다 overhang v. ~위로 쑥 내밀다 grovel v. 넙죽 엎드리다, 굴복하다 hover v. 공중에 멈춰 떠 있다

벌새는 동물계에서 가장 빠른 새는 아니지만 이 아주 작은 공중 곡예사들은 다른 그 어느 새보다 더 빠르게 초당 200회까지 날개를 칠 수 있다. 벌새의 다른 해부학적 구조와 아울러 이 기술로 인해 벌새는 헬리콥터처럼 공중에 멈춰 떠 있을 수 있고 심지어 뒤로 날 수도 있다.

15 ①

두 번째 문장의 At the same time은 이 글에서 '그러나, 그렇기는 하나'라는 의미로, however와 같은 맥락으로 쓰였다. 따라서 첫 번째 문장과 두 번째 문장은 서로 대조를 이루는 구조를 가지고 있다는 점을 염두에 두고 문제를 풀어야 한다. 첫 번째 빈칸에는 두 번째 문장의 acknowledged와 대조를 이룰 수 있는 어구인 lampooned 또는 discrowned가 들어갈 수 있으며, 두 번째 빈칸에는 첫 번째 문장의 his allies와 대조를 이룰 수 있는 어구인 adversaries 또는 opponents가 쓰일 수 있다. 따라서 정답은 ①이 된다.

ally n. 협력자, 자기 편 sly a. 교활한, 음흉한 acknowledge v. 인정하다; 승인하다 acumen n. 총명, 날카로운 통찰력 lampoon v. 비아냥거리다, 풍자하다 adversary n. 적, 상대편, 대항자 rhapsodize v. 광상시를 짓다; 열광적으로 이야기하다 opponent n. 적수, 반대자, 상대 discrown v. 퇴위시키다, 권위를 빼앗다 buddy n. 친구, 동료, 동지 lionize v. 치켜세우다, 떠받들다 confidant n. 절친한 친구, 믿을만한 친구

미국의 42대 대통령으로서 그는 심지어 자기 편 사람들한테서도 (맥도날드 점원처럼) 빅맥 스카프를 하고 색소폰을 부는 교활한 남부 변호사라는 비아냥거림을 받았다. 그러나, 그의 적들조차도 그의 매력과 지성과 정치적 통찰력을 인정했다.

16 ③

두 번째 문장의 This가 가리키는 것은 첫 번째 문장 전체의 내용이다. 영어 말하기 시험에 통과하는 것을 통해 요구하는 바는 영어로 말을 잘 하는 것이라 볼 수 있다. 그러므로 빈칸에는 '정통한'이라는 의미의 ③이 가장 적절하다. ②는 '수다스럽고 군말이 많다'라는 뉘앙스로, 영어로 말을 잘 한다는 것과는 다소 거리가 있는 개념이다.

association n. 협회, 조합; 연합; 관련 require v. 요구하다, 명하다, 규정하다; 필요로 하다 athlete n. 운동선수, 경기자 mandate v. 명령하다, 요구하다 inarticulate a. 똑똑히 말을 못하는, 발음이 분명치 않은; 의견을 말하지 않는 garrulous a. 수다스러운, 말이 많은 conversant a. 정통한; 친교가 있는 ethereal a. 공기 같은; 천상의, 하늘의

모든 주요 스포츠 협회에서 운동선수들에게 영어로 대화를 나누는 것에 능통하다는 것을 입증하도록 한다면 미국의 스포츠는 어떻게 보이게 될까? 이것이 LPGA가 2년 이상 투어에 참여해 왔던 골프 선수들에게 영어 말하기 시험에 반드시 통과하도록 하는 새로운 규칙을 통해 근본적으로 요구하고 있는 것이다.

17 ①

마지막 문장이 군인에게 요구되는 것과 투표자에게 요구되는 것이 다르다는 뜻이므로 이 둘을 비교한 것은 잘못임을 알 수 있다. 따라서 첫 번째 빈칸에는 fallacious(잘못된)나 asinine(우둔한)이 적절하고 두 번째 빈칸의 경우에는 군인에게 요구되는 복종으로서 uncritical(무비판적인)이나 unflinching(움츠리지 않는, 단호한)이 적절하다.

draw a parallel 비교[대비]를 하다 evaluate v. 평가하다 prerequisite n. 선결조건 obedience n. 복종 fallacious a. 잘못된 uncritical a. 무비판적인 convincing a. 설득력 있는 unflinching a. 움츠리지 않는 asinine a. 우둔한 vacillating a. 우유부단한 intriguing a. 흥미로운 evanescent a. 순간의

조국의 전투에 나가 싸울 수 있는 나이의 사람은 투표할 수 있는 나이라고 말하는 것은 완전히 잘못된 비교를 하는 것이다. 사실에 기초해 평가할 수 있는 능력이 적절한 투표 연령의 선결조건이다. 군인에게 요청되는 것은 무비판적인 복종인데 그것은 당신이 투표자에서 원하는 것이 아니다.

18 ①

전치사 from 이하에는 심리 치료에 관여하고 있는 동료들을 화나게 하는 행동이 나열되어야 하므로, 첫 번째 빈칸에는 debunking 또는 inveighing against가 가능하다. 두 번째 빈칸의 경우, 심리치료를 없애려는 입장에 있는 사람들이 주어로 쓰였기 때문에, 빈칸 전후의 faddish와 harmful과 같이 부정적인 뉘앙스의 단어가 필요하다. 그러므로 unproved 또는 malignant가 가능하다. 상기 두 조건을 모두 만족시키는 정답은 ①이다.

ire n. 분노 colleague n. 동료, 동업자 prevent v. 막다, 방해하다 loosely ad. 느슨하게, 엉성하게; 부정확하게 root out 뿌리 뽑다, 근절하다 faddish a. 일시적으로 유행하는, 변덕스러운 potentially ad. 잠재적으로, 가능성 있게 debunk v. 정체를 폭로하다, 가면을 벗기다; 헐뜯다 unproved a. 증명되지 않은 inveigh v. 통렬히 비난하다, 호되게 매도하다 ingenuous a. 솔직한, 성실한; 천진난만한 garner v. 모으다, 축적하다 state-of-the-art a. 최첨단의, 최신식의, 최신기술의 ponder v. 숙고하다, 깊이 생각하다 malignant a. 악의 있는; 악성의, 유해한

동료들이 분노하고 있음에도 불구하고, 느슨한 조직을 갖춘 소수의 학계 심리학자들은 심리 치료를 근절시키는 한편 공개적으로 그것을 헐뜯고 있다. 이들은 이러한 심리 치료를 일시적인 유행이며, 입증되지도 않았고, 어떤 경우에는 해로울 수도 있다고 보고 있다.

19 ③

투자자들의 돈을 돌려준 것은 월스트리트에서 돈을 벌 수 있는 기회가 없다고 생각했기 때문일 것이므로, 첫 번째 빈칸에는 '결여, 부족'의 의미를 나타낼 수 있는 lacking in 또는 barren of가 들어갈 수 있다. 한편, 마지막 문장에서 '시장이 파산한 것'을 언급하고 있는데, 이것은 월스트리트에 기회가 없을 거라는 그의 생각이 적중한 것이므로, 두 번째 빈칸에는 prescient 또는 clairvoyant가 가능하다. 상기 두 조건을 모두 만족시키는 ③이 정답이 된다.

detachment n. 초연함, 초월; 공평 fabulous a. 전설적인; 엄청난; 멋진, 굉장한 unselfish a. 이기적인 아닌, 사심이 없는 exempt a. 면제된; 면역의 bureaucratic a. 관료적인; 관료정치의; 요식적인 lacking a. 부족한, 부족하여 fatuous a. 어리석은, 얼빠진 barren a. 불모의, 메마른; 무익한; ~이 없는, ~을 결여한 prescient a. 선견지명이 있는, 미리 아는 fervent a. 열렬한, 강렬한 clairvoyant a. 투시의, 투시력의; 통찰력이 있는

초연함은 버핏(Buffet)이 성공을 거둔 비밀 가운데 하나였다. 헤지 펀드 매니저로서 엄청난 대박을 터뜨린 후인 1969년에, 그는 월스트리트에 더 이상의 기회가 없다고 생각해서 투자자들의 돈을 돌려주었다. 이것은 선견지명이 있는 것뿐만 아니라 이타적인 행동이었다. 시장은 파산하고 말았다.

20 ③

시위의 성격은 독일의 안(案)에 반대하는 것인데, 독일의 계획안은 채무국의 지출을 줄이도록 하는 것이다. 그러므로 빈칸이 들어 있는 문장에서 말하고 있는 조치란 결국 '지출을 줄이는' 조치를 가리킨다고 할 수 있다. 빈칸에는 앞 문장의 cut spending enough의 의미를 내포하고 있는 단어가 들어가야 하며, '긴축, 경비 절감'이라는 의미의 ③이 정답이 된다.

clash v. 충돌하다; 격렬한 소리를 내다 fiscal a. 국고의, 재정의, 회계의 unity n. 통일; 일관성; 단일성 veto v. 부인한다, 거부하다; 금지하다 budget n. 예산; 예산안 debtor n. 채무자; 신세를 진 사람 inhumane a. 잔인한, 몰인정한, 비인도적인 panache n. 당당한 태도, 겉치레, 허세 impeachment n. 비난; 탄핵; 고발 retrenchment n. 단축, 축소; 삭제, (인원) 삭감; 경비 절감 comity n. 예의; 예양 (禮讓)

유럽의 지도자들이 브뤼셀에서 만나 보다 엄격한 재정 통합을 지지하는 독일의 계획안을 검토함에 따라, 수만 명의 그리스 시위대들이 거리에서 충돌했다. 독일의 안(案)은 채무국들이 지출을 충분히 줄이지 않는 경우 그 국가들의 예산안을 거부할 권리를 유럽연합에게 주게 된다. "우리는 가혹하고 비인간적인 긴축 조치에 반대하는 시위를 벌이고 있습니다"라고 아테네에서 교사로 일하고 있는 이라 디아만티디(Ira Diamantidi)가 말했다.

21 ④

첫 번째 빈칸에 들어갈 단어를 두 번째 문장에서 he has forbidden himself로 달리 표현하고 있다. 이것은 금지하고 통제하는 행위이므로 continence 또는 censorship이 들어갈 수 있다. 두 번째 빈칸의 경우, '스스로 금지시킨 행동을 다시 했을 때 난처하게 생각하는 것'을 종교적 관점에서는 '무엇이 생겨난 것'으로 보겠는가를 묻고 있다. nirvana는 종교적 용어이긴 하나, '열반'이라는 의미이므로 스스로를 구속하는 것과는 거리가 있으며, '양심'이라는 의미의 conscience가 보다 적절하다. 따라서 정답은 ④가 된다.

recrudescence n. 재발, 도짐; 재연 forbid v. 금지하다, 허락하지 않다, 용납하지 않다 relationship n. 관계, 관련 establish v. 확립하다, 설립하다, 개설하다; 제정하다 continence n. 자제; (특히 성욕의) 절제, 극기, 금욕 nirvana n. 열반, 해탈 objurgation n. 질책, 비난, 꾸짖음 brawl n. 말다툼; 대소동 buffoonery n. 익살, 해학, 저속한 농담 turpitude n. 간악함, 비열함; 비열한 행위 censorship n. 검열 (제도) conscience n. 양심, 도덕관념

문제가 있는 행동들에 있어서, 아이는 곧 자신의 어떤 행동들에 대해 나름의 검열을 의식하게 된다. 그는 스스로가 금지시킨 행동을 다시 하게 되면 난처하게 생각한다. 심리학자들에게 있어, 이것은 아이와 사회적 환경 사이에 확립된 관계의 결과인 초자아(超自我)이다. 그러나 종교 교육자들에게 이것은 양심이 발전하는 징후이다.

22 ①

두 번째 문장은 첫 번째 문장의 내용에 대한 예에 해당한다. '전달할 글자 단위로 돈을 지불하고 항상 내용이 잘못 전달될 위험이 있었을 때에 메시지가 간결했다'는 것은, '정보를 전달하는 데 있어 비용이 많이 들거나 그 방법이 어려운 것일수록, 전달되는 메시지의 내용이 부실할 수밖에 없었다'라는 것을 의미한다. 이는 전자와 후자가 서로 역(逆)의 관계에 있음을 나타내므로, 첫 번째 빈칸에는 inverse 또는 converse가 들어갈 수 있다. 두 번째 빈칸은 '간단명료한'이라는 의미의 to the point와 순접의 접속사 and로 연결되어 있으므로, 이것과 같거나 유사한 의미를 가진 단어가 들어가야 한다. concise 또는 condensed가 가능하다. 상기 언급한 두 조건을 모두 만족시키는 정답은 ①이다.

relationship n. 관계, 관련 expense n. 지출, 비용; 손실 telegraph n. 전신, 전보 garble v. (사실을 왜곡시키기 위하여) 부정한 취사선택을 하다; (기사를) 멋대로 고치다; 오전(誤傳)하다 transmission n. 회송, 전달; 매개 to the point 요령 있는, 적절한; 간단명료한, 간결한 complexity n. 복잡성, 복잡함 affect v. 영향을 주다, 악영향을 끼치다 irrelevant a. 부적절한, 무관계한 inverse a. (위치·관계 등이) 반대의, 역(逆)의, 도치의 concise a. 간결한, 간명한 direct a. 직접적인; 노골적인; 솔직한 dilapidated a. 황폐한, 헐어빠진; 남루한, 초라한 designated a. 지정된 condensed a. 응축한; 간결한, 요약한 converse a. 역(逆)의, 거꾸로의 rambling a. 산만한, 되는 대로 퍼져 나가는; 횡설수설하는

통신의 비용 및 어려움과 전달되는 내용의 질(質)은 반비례 관계에 있다. 전보 교환원에게 글자 단위로 돈을 지불하고, 항상 내용이 잘못 전달될 위험이 있었을 시절에는, 메시지가 간결하고, 간단명료했다. 하지만, 길이나 내용의 복잡함이 메시지를 전달하는 비용에 영향을 주지 않는 때에는, 부적절하고 불필요한 통신을 막을 수 없게 된다.

23 ①

두 번째 문장은 첫 번째 문장에 대한 예시 혹은 부연설명에 해당하므로, 두 번째 문장에서 강조하고 있는 바가 첫 번째 빈칸에 들어가야 한다. 또한 두 번째 빈칸 앞에 thus가 있으므로, 여기에도 두 번째 문장의 내용에서 강조하고 있는 내용을 함축할 수 있는 단어가 들어가야 한다. 조지 그레이 바너드에 대한 일화는 '그가 자신이 하고 있던 일에 모두하고 있었다'라는 것이므로, 결국 두 빈칸 모두 '몰입' 혹은 '집중'과 관련된 단어가 들어가야 한다. 이러한 짝으로 이뤄진 것은 ①이다.

distract v. (주의 등을) 흩뜨리다, (딴 데로) 돌리다; 괴롭히다 sculptor n. 조각가 bewilder v. 당황하게 하다 literally ad. 글자 뜻 그대로; 아주, 사실상 exceptionally ad. 이례적으로, 특별히, 대단히 intentness n. 집중됨; 열심임, 여념 없음 immersed a. 몰두한; 잠긴, 묻힌 intransigeance n. 타협하지 않음, 비타협적인 태도 maladroit a. 솜씨 없는, 서투른 concentration n. 집중; 전념 gauche a. 솜씨가 서투른, 세련되지 않은 foible n. 약점, 결점, 흠 absorbed a. 마음을 빼앗긴, 열중한

당신이 알고 있는 성공한 사람으로서 누구보다도 어떤 일을 잘 할 수 있는 사람을 선택해서 그가 그 일을 하는 동안 그 사람의 주의를 뺏으려고 한번 해 보아라. 위대한 조각가로 널리 여겨지고 있는 고(故) 조지 그레이 바너드 (George Gray Barnard)는 작업 중에 친구들이 들렀을 때 그들을 아예 보지

못함으로써 친구들을 당황하게 만들곤 했다. 자신이 하고 싶은 일에 이처럼 열중하게 되지 않으면, 그 일을 빼어나게 잘 할 수 있는 가망성은 거의 없다.

24 ③

그는 내게 "만일 네가 여기에 있는 나의 동료의원들이 나쁘다고 생각한다면, 너는 그들을 이곳으로 보낸 사람들도 보아야만 한다."라고 말했다는 단서로부터 글쓴이가 유권자, 즉 국민에 대해 무작정 긍정적으로 생각하지는 않는다는 사실을 추론할 수 있다. 따라서 ③이 정답으로 적절하며, ④ deify는 지나친 표현이다.

the state legislature 주 입법부(주 의회) senator n. 상원의원 acquaint v. 알리다; 사람을 소개시키다; 알게 하다 wily a. 약삭빠른, 교활한 gallery n. (테니스·골프 등의) 관객, 구경꾼; 청중; 방청인 demonize v. 악마처럼 만들다, 악마가 되게 하다 underestimate v. 과소평가하다, 얕보다 romanticize v. 공상적[낭만적]으로 하다[보다, 말하다, 묘사하다], 낭만화하다 deify v. 신으로 섬기다; 신성시하다; (부·권력을) 중요시하다 supercede v. 대신하다, 대체하다; 승계하다

나는 '국민'을 낭만화 시키지도 않는다. 텍사스 대학 학생의 신분으로 내가 주 의회에 관한 기사를 쓰기 시작했을 때, 한 약삭빠르고 나이 든 주 상원의원은 내게 주 의회가 어떻게 돌아가는지를 알려주겠다고 제안했다. 우리는 주 상원 의사당 의원석 뒤에 서 있었고 그는 의사당 여기저기에 흩어져 있는 그의 동료 의원을 가리켰다. 그가 가리킨 상원의원들은 카드를 치고, 낮잠을 자고, 방청석에 앉아 있는 예쁘고 젊은 방청객 여성에게 윙크를 했다. 그리고 그는 내게, "만일 네가 여기에 있는 나의 동료의원들이 나쁘다고 생각한다면, 너는 그들을 이곳으로 보낸 사람들(즉 유권자인 일반 국민들)도 보아야만 한다."라고 말했다.

25 ①

미국에서 소프트 타깃을 대상으로 한 테러 공격이 없다고 했으므로 미국인들은 테러 공격에 무사안일하게 행동할 것이라고 볼 수 있다. 따라서 엄중한 대책이 취해진다면 미국인들은 받아들이지 못할 것이므로 빈칸에는 ①이 적절하다.

soft target 소프트 타깃(테러리스트의 공격에 취약한 사람이나 장소 등) unarmed a. 무기가 없는, 무장하지 않은 surveillance n. 감시, 감독 draconian a. 엄중한, 가혹한 countermeasure n. 대책 upshot n. (최종적인) 결과, 결말 hard target 강인 표적(테러단체들의 목표물을 구분할 때 방어 능력이 강해 침투나 공격이 어려운 정부기관이나 공공기관을 의미) tolerate v. 참다, 견디다 disdain v. 경멸하다 jeopardize v. 위태롭게 하다 censor v. 검열하다 depreciate v. 비난하다

미국에서 소프트 타깃을 보호하는 일을 하는 소수의 보안요원들은 무기가 없고, 훈련되어 있지 않으며, 의욕이 없다. 카메라 감시 시스템(그 시스템이 어쨌든 설치되어 있지만)은 불규칙적으로만 확인해보는 경향이 있으며, 카메라를 확인해 볼 때, 보안 요원들은 일반적으로 잠재적인 테러리스트들보다는 물건을 훔칠 가능성이 있는 사람들과 문제를 일으킬 것 같은 사람들에 주력한다. 미국에서 소프트 타깃에 대한 공격이 없어짐에 따라 미국인들은 이스라엘 사람들이 불평 없이 받아들이는 엄중한 대책을 전혀 참아내려 하지 않는다. 그 결과, 지독한 이중적 역설을 낳는다. 미국에서 소프트 타깃을

대상으로 한 공격이 없었다는 분명한 사실은 소프트 타깃에 대한 위험을 증가시킨다. 하드 타깃의 공격에 대비하여 더욱 보강할수록 소프트 타깃이 공격을 받을 가능성이 더욱 커진다.

TEST 20

01 ②	02 ③	03 ②	04 ①	05 ④	06 ①	07 ①	08 ①	09 ②	10 ①
11 ④	12 ④	13 ②	14 ③	15 ②	16 ②	17 ③	18 ③	19 ①	20 ④
21 ②	22 ④	23 ①	24 ④	25 ③					

01 ②

as 이하에서 암수가 평생 동안 짝으로 지낸다고 했으므로, 이는 곧 '일부일처제'를 의미한다. 따라서 ②가 정답이다.

maintain v. 지속하다, 유지하다; 주장하다 relationship n. 관계, 관련 mate v. 부부가 되다, 결혼하다; 교미하다 bilateral a. 쌍방의, 양측의; 양쪽면이 있는 monogamous a. 일부일처의 flimsy a. 무른, 취약한; (근거가) 빈약한; 천박한; 하찮은 promiscuous a. 난잡한, 문란한

놀랄 만큼 많은 수의 동물들이 암컷과 수컷이 평생을 짝으로 지내는 일부일처(一夫一妻) 관계를 유지하고 있다.

02 ③

뒤에 이어지는 문장에서 그와 결혼한 것을 후회했다는 내용이 있으므로, 일반적인 관점에서 가장 부정적인 의미를 가지고 있는 단어를 선택하면 된다. '하찮은 사람'이라는 의미의 ③이 들어가는 것이 적절하다.

claim v. 요구하다, 청구하다; 주장하다 convert n. 개종자, 전향자; 귀의자 mogul n. 중요인물, 거물 cipher n. 암호; 부호; 하찮은 사람 veterinarian n. 수의사

나중에, 그녀는 자신의 전 남편이 완전히 하찮은 사람이었다고 주장했으며, 왜 자신이 그와 결혼했는지를 어이없어 했다. 그러나 모든 것이 너무 늦었다.

03 ②

순접의 접속사 and를 통해 '노쇠한'이라는 의미의 senile과 빈칸이 연결되어 있으므로, 이와 유사한 의미를 갖는 단어가 빈칸에 들어가야 한다. '나이가 들어서 비실비실하거나 휘청거린다'라는 의미를 가진 ②가 들어가는 것이 가장 자연스럽다.

senile a. 노쇠한; 노망이 든 merit v. (상·벌·감사·비난 등을) 마땅히 받을 만하다 touchy a. 성미 까다로운; 다루기 힘든 doddering a. 비실비실한, 휘청휘청하는 naive a. 천진난만한, 순진한, 소박한 nubile a. 결혼적령기의, 나이가 찬

그가 아직은 비실비실하고 노쇠한 늙은이가 아니지만, 그의 생각과 견해는 더 이상 우리가 오래 전에 그에게 보냈던 존경을 받을 만한 자격이 되지 못한다.

04 ①

아동보호기금의 설립자 입장에서는 아동에 대한 지원이 부족한 상황을 매우 비판적으로 바라볼 것이므로, 빈칸에는 '비난하다, 헐뜯다'라는 의미의 ①이 적절하다.

founder n. 창립자, 설립자 financial a. 재정의, 재무의; 금융상의 moral a. 도덕의, 윤리의, 도덕적인 decry v. 공공연히 비난하다, 비방하다, 헐뜯다 dissimulate v. 숨기다, 모르는 체 하다, 시치미 떼다 simulate v. 가장하다; 흉내를 내다 ruminate v. 되새기다, 반추하다, 곰곰이 생각하다

아동보호기금의 설립자 매리언 라이트 에델만(Marian Wright Edelman)은 오늘날 미국에서 아이들에 대한 재정적, 윤리적 지원이 부족한 것을 강도 높게 비난하고 있다.

05 ④

Although가 이끄는 종속절의 내용과 주절의 내용이 대조를 이루어야 한다. 주절의 내용은 그녀를 만나고자 '오랜 시간 동안 노력하고 계획했다'라는 것이므로, 이와 대조를 이루는 개념은 '우연에 의한' 만남이다.

encounter n. 만남, 조우 hang around 귀찮게 달라붙다; 어슬렁거리다, 배회하다 haunt n. 자주 드나드는 곳, 늘 왕래하는 곳; 출몰하는 곳; 서식지 turn up 모습을 나타내다 predestined a. 예정된, 운명으로 정해진 insipid a. 싱거운; 김빠진, 맛없는; 무미건조한 vapid a. 맛이 없는, 김빠진; 활기 없는 fortuitous a. 우연의, 예기치 않은

그는 그들의 만남이 우연인 척했지만, 사실 그는 그녀가 나타나길 바라면서 그녀가 자주 나타나는 곳 주위를 2주 동안 배회하고 있었다.

06 ①

came 이하에 not A but B 구조의 표현이 쓰였는데, 이때 일반적으로 A와 B는 의미상 대조를 이루어야 하므로, 주어진 글의 빈칸에는 but 앞 부분에 있는 direct의 문맥상 반의어에 해당하는 단어가 들어가야 함을 알 수 있다. 누군가가 직접적으로 한 말의 반대 개념은 소문처럼 떠도는 말이라고 할 수 있으므로, '출처가 의심스러운'이라는 의미의 ①이 정답으로 적절하다.

comment n. 논평, 비평; 견해 subject n. 주제, 문제; 학과, 과목 go the rounds 순회하다; (소문 따위가) 퍼지다, 전해지다 apocryphal a. 출처가 의심스러운; 거짓의, 진짜가 아닌 gingerbread a. (가구·건물 따위가) 야한, 값싼 explicit a. 뚜렷한, 명백한; 노골적인 voyeuristic a. 훔쳐보는 취미의, 관음증의

그 주제에 관한 라이언(Ryan)의 견해는 직접적인 진술에서 나온 것이 아니라 계속해서 떠돌고 있던, 출처가 의심스러운 이야기에서 나온 것이었다.

---

07 ①

빈칸 뒤에 이어지고 있는 though절에서 처음 찾아가는 곳이라 했으므로, the beaten path, 즉 자주 다니던 길에서 '벗어나는' 것이다.

beaten path 밟아 다져진 길; 익숙한 길 grimy a. 때 묻은, 더러워진 shantytown n. 판자촌; 빈민가 neighborhood n. 근처, 인근, 이웃; 지역 stray off 옆길로 빗나가다, 벗어나다 step on to ~로 나아가다 sweep over 압도하다, 휩쓸다; 만연하다 secure against ~에 대비해서 지키다

필리핀에서 휴가를 보내던 32세의 그 스튜어디스는, 비록 처음 찾아가는 그 더러운 판자촌이 안전한 지역은 아니었지만, 자주 다니던 길에서 벗어나 다른 곳을 가볼 수 있는 기회를 가지게 되어 기뻤다.

---

08 ①

경찰이 고소당한 상황에서 그 사건에 대한 심리를 진행하겠다는 법원의 결정을 반대했다면, 그 논거는 '경찰 공무원의 신체수색은 정당하였다' 또는 '공무원으로서의 활동에 대해서는 책임 추궁을 면한다'는 것이라고 추론할 수 있다.

sue v. 고소하다 engage in ~에 관여하다 violation n. 침해 constitutional a. 헌법적인 dissent v. 반대하다 qualified a. 자격이 있는; 조건부의 qualified immunity 공무원 면책권 immunity n. 면제, 면책특권 consent n. 동의 repatriation n. 송환 prosecution n. 기소 acceptance n. 수용

한 여성과 그녀의 10살 아이는 헌법상의 권리를 침해하면서까지 신체수색에 관여했다는 이유로 경찰관들을 고소했다. 법원은 그 사건이 진행되도록 허락했다. 앨리토(Alito)는 경찰이 조건부 면책권(공무원 면책권)을 가지고 있다고 주장하며 반대했다.

---

09 ②

무고한 사람을 죽이는 행위는 그들이 속한 단체에 해가 될 것이다. 따라서 빈칸에는 '명예 등을 손상시키다'라는 의미인 ②가 들어가야 한다.

beloved a. 가장 사랑하는, 귀여운, 소중한 justify v. 옳다고 하다, 정당화하다 destructive a. 파괴적인; 파멸적인 buttress v. 지지하다, 보강하다 tarnish v. 흐리게 하다; (명예 등을) 더럽히다, 손상시키다 denote v. 나타내다; 표시하다; 의미하다 brandish v. (칼·채찍을) 휘두르다; 야단스럽게 나타내 보이다

무고한 사람들을 폭탄으로 죽이는 이슬람 강경파들이 나의 사랑하는 조국

인도네시아의 이미지를 더럽히고 있다. 그들은 종교를 이용해 자신들의 파괴행위를 정당화하려고 한다.

---

10 ①

첫 문장에서 다른 사람들과 온갖 정보를 기꺼이 공유하려고 한다고 했는데, 이것은 사적인 것(정보든 순간이든)이 없어짐을 말하므로 빈칸에는 (공개적으로) '드러내다'는 의미의 ①이 적절하다.

acquaintance n. 아는 사람, 지인 astonishing a. 놀랄 만한, 놀라운 intimate a. 친밀한, 개인적인, 사적인 divulge v. (비밀을) 누설하다, 폭로하다 savor v. 맛보다; ~의 기미가 있다 lavish v. (돈·애정 따위를) 아낌없이 주다, 아끼지 않다; 낭비하다 reminisce v. 추억에 잠기다

오늘날 우리가 친구들과 지인들만이 아니라 소셜 미디어를 통해 전혀 모르는 사람들과도 기꺼이 공유하려는 종류의 정보는 놀랄만하다. 모든 사적인 순간은 아무리 사적이어도 사람들 앞에 드러낼 수 있다.

---

11 ④

두 번째 문장은 첫 번째 문장에 대한 부연설명에 해당한다. 첫 번째 문장의 flattery와 두 번째 문장의 praise가 동일한 의미로 쓰였으므로, 빈칸에는 앞 문장의 nauseating과 유사한 의미의 단어가 들어가야 한다.

nauseating a. 메스꺼운, 역겨운 flattery n. 아첨, 추켜세우기; 감언 match v. ~에 필적하다, 호적수가 되다; 어울리다 heap v. 쌓아올리다, 쌓다; 축적하다 pernicious a. 해로운, 유해한; 치명적인, 파괴적인 titular a. 이름뿐인, 유명무실한 grisly a. 섬뜩한, 소름끼치는 fulsome a. 지나친, 역겨운; 집요한; 완전한

스탈린에게 메스꺼울 정도로 아첨했다는 점에서 루즈벨트는 처칠에 충분히 필적하는 인물이었다. 루즈벨트처럼 처칠도 그 공산주의자 살인마에 대해 역겨운 찬사를 쌓아올렸고 스탈린과의 개인적인 우정을 갈망했다.

---

12 ④

자신의 국가를 스스로 경영해야 한다는 격한 감정은 다른 국가의 도움 없이는 생존이 불가능한 현실 앞에 잦아들기 마련이다. 가슴 부푼 이상이 차가운 현실에 의해 한풀 꺾이게 되는 것을 떠올리면 된다. 그러므로 빈칸에는 ④가 들어가는 것이 가장 적절하다.

intense a. 격렬한, 심한, 맹렬한 widespread a. 널리 퍼져 있는; 광범위한 patron county 후견국가 blessing n. 축복; 행복; 승인, 허락 deviate v. 벗어나게 하다, 일탈시키다 vilify v. 비방하다, 헐뜯다 adumbrate v. ~의 윤곽을 나타내다; (생각 등을) 막연히 나타내다; 예시하다 temper v. 부드럽게 하다; 경감시키다, 진정시키다

자신들의 나라가 보다 자유롭게 내정을 챙길 수 있어야 한다는 격한 감정이 그 위성 국가 국민들 사이에 널리 퍼져 있지만, 후견 국가의 은전(恩典) 없이는 생존할 수 없다는 현실이 이것을 누그러뜨리고 있다.

13 ②

빈칸에 들어갈 표현은 콤마 앞의 the weakest form of anger와 동격 관계에 있으므로, 이와 유사한 의미의 표현이 필요하다. 따라서 정답은 ②가 되며, the weakest form of가 diluted와 호응하고 anger가 range와 호응함을 확인할 수 있다.

formulate v. 공식화하다; 명확하게 말하다 definition n. 한정, 명확; 정의, 설명 annoyance n. 성가심, 불쾌함; 곤혹, 괴로움 persistent a. 고집하는, 완고한; 영속하는 overtone n. 담겨진 뜻, 부대적 의미, (말 따위의) 함축 instinctive a. 본능적인, 직관적인 dilute v. 묽게 하다, 희박하게 하다 rage n. 격노, 격정 intrusive a. 거슬리는; 강제하는, 훼방하는 sheer a. 완전한, 순전한, 단순한

불쾌함에 대해 실용적인 정의를 명확하게 내리는 것은 연구자들에게 있어 항상 어려운 문제이다. 어떤 사람은 그것을 가장 약한 형태의 화, 간단히 말하자면 강도가 약해진 분노라고 한다. 다른 사람들은 혐오감, 반감, 그리고 심지어는 공포가 함축된 것이라고 말한다.

14 ③

lead to는 '~를 초래하다'라는 의미이므로, 이 표현이 쓰인 문장에서는 주어가 원인, 목적어가 결과에 해당하게 된다. 주어진 글의 lead to 이하에서는 '더 값싼 에너지를 찾아 이전하게 될 수도 있다'라는 결과를 제시해 놓고 있으며, 이에 대한 원인은 가격의 상승과 연관이 있는 것이어야 할 것이다. 한편, 가격이 오르려면 수요가 증가하거나 공급이 감소해야 하는데, 빈칸 뒤의 nuclear power는 전기를 '공급'하는 것이므로, 빈칸에 '감소시킨다'라는 의미를 가진 표현이 들어가야만 '공급의 감소'라는 개념이 완성될 수 있다. 따라서 '단계적으로 철폐하다'라는 의미의 ③이 정답이 된다.

catastrophe n. 대단원, 파국; 큰 재해; 대이변 relocate v. 다시 배치하다; 새 장소로 옮기다, 이전시키다 stick to ~에 달라붙다, 집착하다; 충실하다 capitalize on ~을 활용하다, 기회로 삼다 phase out ~을 단계적으로 철거하다, 단계적으로 폐지하다 trigger off (사건 등을) 일으키다, 유발하다; 계기가 되다

일본의 후쿠시마 원전 참사 이후 원자력 발전소를 단계적으로 폐쇄하기로 한 독일 정부의 결정은 일부 독일 주요기업들이 보다 값이 저렴한 에너지를 찾아 다른 곳으로 이전하는 결과를 초래할 수 있을 것이다.

15 ②

빈칸에는 provides a definition의 행위를 하는 사람에 해당하는 단어가 들어가야 한다. 마지막 문장의 a dictionary definition이라는 표현을 참고하면, '사전 편찬자'라는 의미의 ②가 들어가는 것이 가장 적절하다.

definition n. 한정, 명확; 정의, 설명 unsatisfactory a. 마음에 차지 않는, 만족스럽지 못한 characterize v. 특색을 이루다, 특징을 지우다; 성격을 나타내다 bibliographer n. 서지학자, 목록편찬자 lexicographer n. 사전 편찬자 maestro n. 대음악가; (예술 따위의) 대가, 거장 bigwig n. 중요 인물, 높은 사람, 거물

16 ②

일부 사람들에게 유대교의 전통은 배타적 정신을 갖고 있었다고 했으므로 다른 종교에 대해 무관심했을 것이다. 따라서 기독교인과 이슬람 사람들을 전도시키는 것을 피하려고 했을 것이다.

shun v. 피하다, 비키다 ethos n. 기풍, 풍조, 특질 exclusion n. 배제, 제외, 배타 terrestrial a. 지상의; 세속적[현실적]인 proselytize v. (남을 자신의 종교로) 개종시키다, 전도하다 belligerent a. 교전 중인; 호전적인 sanctify v. ~을 신성하게 하다, 축성하다 sacrifice v. 희생하다, 제물로 바치다

유대교의 전통은 아브라함의 사촌들인 기독교와 이슬람의 전도(남을 자신의 종교로 개종시키려는)성향을 피해왔다. 그러나 그렇게 하면서, 그것은 일부 사람들에게 배타적 정신을 갖고 있는 것으로 보였다.

17 ③

빈칸이 들어 있는 문장에 대한 내용을 마지막 문장에서 부연설명하고 있다. 마지막 문장에서는 간의 지방을 없앨 수 있는 방법을 이야기하고 있으므로, 빈칸에는 마지막 문장에 쓰인 동사 cut의 동의어에 해당하는 단어가 들어가야 한다. 따라서 '없애다, 제거하다'라는 의미를 가진 ③이 정답이 된다.

diabetes n. 당뇨병 fatty a. 지방질의, 지방이 많은, 기름진 liver n. 간(肝) moderate a. 삼가는, 절제하는; 알맞은, 적당한 dilate v. 팽창시키다; 넓히다 douse v. 물에 처넣다, 물을 끼얹다 prune v. (가지 등을) 잘라내다; (불필요한 부분을) 제거하다; (비용 따위를) 바싹 줄이다 forge v. (쇠를) 불리다, 단조(鍛造)하다; 위조하다

만일 과체중에다 당뇨병이 있다면, 당신은 아마도 지방간일 것이다. 그러나 간의 지방을 없애는 방법이 있다. 존스 홉킨스 대학의 연구원들은 자전거 타기, 걷기, 혹은 달리기를 일주일에 세 번 적당한 정도로 하면, 간의 지방을 40퍼센트까지 없앨 수 있다는 사실을 발견했다.

18 ③

두 번째 빈칸부터 채울 수 있다. '체내에 칼슘이 부족할 때에는 칼슘을 보충하기 위해 음식을 많이 먹게 된다'라고 했다. 칼슘 섭취량이 충분할 때에는 그럴 필요를 느끼지 않아 음식을 더 먹고 싶은 욕망을 억제할 것이므로, 두 번째 빈칸에는 curb 또는 stifle이 적절하다. 한편, 음식을 더 먹고 싶지 않게 되면 결국 체중 감량에 도움이 될 것이므로, 첫 번째 빈칸에는 shed가 들어가야 한다. 따라서 정답은 ③이 된다.

intake n. 섭취; 섭취량; 빨아들임, 흡입 detect v. 발견하다; 간파하다; 탐지하다 compensate v. 보상하다; 보충하다; 상쇄하다 spur v. 자극하다, 격려하다; 박차를 가하다 sufficient a. 충분한, 족한 replicate v. 반대편으로 접다; 사본을 뜨다, 모사하다 excrete v. 배설하다, 분비하다 bloat v. 부풀게 하다; 우쭐하게 하다 curb v. 억제하다, 구속하다 shed v. 흘리다; 벗어버리다; 퍼뜨리다; 버리다 stifle v. 질식시키다, 숨이 막히게 하다 dilate v. 팽창시키다; 넓히다 suture v. (상처 따위를) 봉합하다

체내 칼슘 수치가 낮으면, 칼슘 섭취를 늘리는 것이 체중을 줄이는 데 도움이 될 수도 있다. 뇌는 칼슘이 부족할 때를 감지하여 음식물 섭취를 자극하여 부족분을 보충하는 것으로 여겨지고 있다. 충분히 칼슘을 섭취하면 더 먹고 싶은 욕망이 억제되는 것처럼 보인다.

19   ①

우울증은 마음의 병이므로 배우자로부터 마음에 상처를 받는 비판의 말을 듣지 말아야 재발되지 않는다고 할 수 있다. 마음에 상처를 주는 것과 관련된 의미를 가진 두 동사로 짝지어진 것은 ①이다.

criticism n. 비판 predictor n. 예언자, 예보자 relapse v. 병이 재발하다, 도지다 depression n. 우울증 disparage v. 깔보다, 얕보다; 헐뜯다 humiliate v. 욕보이다, 굴욕감을 주다 bemoan v. 슬퍼하다, 한탄하다 deplore v. 한탄하다, 개탄하다 entertain v. 대접하다, 환대하다 flatter v. 아첨하다 venerate v. 존경하다; 공경하다 commend v. 칭찬하다

비판은 관계를 만들기도 하고 깨뜨리기도 한다. 결혼한 성인의 경우 우울증의 재발 가능성을 가장 잘 예측해내는 것은 "배우자가 당신에 대해 얼마나 비판적입니까?"라는 질문에 그들이 보이는 반응이다. 건강을 유지하는 환자들보다 재발한 환자들이 배우자를 상당히 더 비판적인 것으로 평가했다. 헐뜯거나 모욕을 주지 않고 비판하는 것이 중요하다.

20   ④

such that 전후의 내용은 인과관계에 있어야 한다. 교육의 영향이 엄청나게 크다면 사람들은 배운 것을 '무조건적으로' 믿게 될 것이므로, 첫 번째 빈칸에는 unconditionally 또는 uncritically가 올 수 있다. 한편, 두 번째 문장의 문두에 역접의 접속사 But이 있으므로, 앞 문장의 first 이하에서 언급한 내용을 부정하여, '사실은 그렇지 않다'라는 내용으로 이어지는 것이 적절하다. 빈칸 앞에 부정어 neither가 있는 점을 고려하면, manifest 또는 self-evident가 들어갈 수 있을 것이다. 두 조건을 모두 만족시키는 정답은 ④가 된다.

possession n. 소유; 점유; 점거; 점유권 consideration n. 고려, 숙려, 고찰; 동정 proposition n. 제안, 제의, 건의; 진술, 주장 giddily ad. 어지럽게, 아찔하게 manifest a. 명백한, 분명한, 일목요연한 considerately ad. 동정심 있게; 신중하게 tentative a. 시험적인, 임시의; 주저하는; 불확실한 unconditionally ad. 무조건적으로, 절대적으로 falsify v. 위조하다; 속이다; 거짓임을 입증하다 uncritically ad. 무비판적으로 self-evident a. 자명한, 따로 설명할 필요가 없는

우리들 대부분이 보통 교육의 영향을 너무나도 크게 받은 까닭에, 첫째, 자유는 좋은 것이며, 둘째, 자유의 소유는 우리의 행복을 더 크게 만들어 줄 것 같다는 것을 우리가 다소 무비판적으로 믿는 경향이 있어 왔다. 그러나 잠깐만 생각해보면 이런 주장은 둘 다 자명한 사실이 아니란 것이 드러날 것이다.

21   ②

첫 번째 빈칸이 들어 있는 문장 앞의 세미콜론은 이유의 접속사 for를 대신하고 있다. 우리가 스스로를 사회의 다른 구성원들과 연관 지어 인식하지 않는 것은 스스로를 그들과 별개인 '독립적인' 개인으로 보기 때문일 것이므로, 첫 번째 빈칸에는 autonomous 또는 self-governing이 들어갈 수 있다. 한편, 두 번째 빈칸이 들어 있는 문장은 예전과 오늘날을 비교하고 있는데, 세미콜론 앞에서 '가족전체에게 부끄러운 일이었다'라고 했으므로, 세미콜론 뒤에서는 '개인이 비난받거나 부끄러워해야 할 일이 되었다'라는 맥락으로 이어져야 한다. shame의 의미를 내포하고 있는 단어가 필요하므로 blameworthy 또는 reproachable이 쓰일 수 있다. 상기 두 조건을 모두 만족시키는 정답은 ②가 된다.

perceive v. 지각하다, 감지하다, 인식하다 context n. 전후 관계, 문맥; (사건 등에 대한) 경위, 배경 so-and-so n. 아무개, 모(某) evident a. 분명한, 명백한, 뚜렷한 criminal a. 범죄의; 죄가 있는 immoral a. 부도덕한, 행실이 나쁜 crotchety a. 별난 생각을 갖고 있는, 변덕스러운 draconian a. 엄중한, 가혹한 autonomous a. 자치권이 있는, 자치의; 자율의 blameworthy a. 비난받을 만한, 질책당할 만한 self-governing a. 자치의, 자제하는 gung-ho a. 멸사봉공의; 무턱대고 열심인, 열혈적인; 감정적인 pigheaded a. 고집이 센, 성질이 비뚤어진 reproachable a. 비난할 만한

우리는 스스로를 사회를 구성하는 배경의 한 부분으로, 아무개 씨의 딸로서, 어느 가정의 일원으로 인지하지 않는다. 왜냐하면 우리는 독립된 개인이기 때문이다. 이것은 범죄나 비도덕적인 행동을 한 경우에 분명해진다. 옛날에는 그런 행동은 일가족 전체에 부끄러운 일이었다. 그러나 오늘날에는 오로지 당사자만이 비난받아야 하는 것으로 간주된다.

22   ④

많은 희생자를 발생시킨 국가의 혁명을 통해 사람들은 민주주의를 꿈꾸기 시작했다고 했다. 하지만 마지막 문장에서 볼 수 있듯이, 정부는 국민들의 민주주의에 대한 희망은 유지시키면서 억압적인 정책을 폈으므로, 국가의 행동은 국민들을 대상으로 한 '속임수'라고 할 수 있다. 그러므로 첫 번째 빈칸에는 hoax 또는 swindle이 들어갈 수 있다. 한편, 그 속임수는 독재적 방식을 유지하면서 혁명의 이름을 '가장한' 것으로 요약될 수 있으므로, 두 번째 빈칸에는 affected 또는 feigned가 가능하다. 따라서 두 조건을 모두 만족시키는 ④가 정답이 된다.

revolution n. 혁명, 변혁 staggering a. 비틀거리는; 어마어마한, 경이적인 toll n. 통행료; 희생자, 희생 estimated a. 평가상의, 견적상의 dictatorial a. 독재자의; 오만한 repressive a. 억누르는, 억압적인 tactic n. 작전, 방책, 수단 stamp out ~을 밟아서 끄다; 진압하다 extinguish v. 끄다, 진화하다; 소멸시키다 swindle n. 사기, 사취 mitigate v. 누그러뜨리다; 완화하다 convalescence n. 차도가 있음; 회복, 회복기 affect v. 영향을 주다; 감동시키다; 가장하다, ~인

체하다 extremity n. 끝; 파멸의 직전; 난국 ameliorate v. 개선하다, 개량하다 hoax n. 사람을 속이기, 짓궂은 장난; 날조 feign v. ~인 체하다; 속이다

그 나라의 마지막 혁명은 100만 명으로 추정된 사망자를 포함하는 어마어마한 사상자를 낳았다. 그러나 또한 국민들로 하여금 민주주의를 꿈꾸기 시작하게끔 하였다. 국민들이 그 대신 얻은 것은 혁명의 이름을 가장하여 예전의 독재 방식을 유지하는 정치체제가 행한 잔혹한 속임수였다. 정부는 투쟁하고자 하는 국민들의 수많은 의지를 근절하기 위해 억압적인 수단을 이용했다. 그러나 그들의 희망을 꺼버리지는 못했다.

overuse v. 지나치게 쓰다, 남용하다 stale a. 상한, 신선하지 않은; 케케묵은, 흔해빠진 ineffective a. 효과 없는, 쓸모가 없는 inappropriate a. 부적당한, 온당하지 않은 literate a. 읽고 쓸 수 있는; 교양 있는 recondite a. 심원한, 난해한

속어가 사람들에게 주는 가장 큰 매력은 새로운 느낌을 주는 것이다. 어떤 생각을 새롭고 색다른 표현으로 들으면 재미가 있다. 그러나 수백 번 반복해서 들으면 그 새로운 느낌은 바래진다. 속어가 신선함과 생기를 잃기 때문이다. 속어 표현의 일생은 처음 생겨나서, 과도하게 사용되었다가, 진부해지고, 얼마 있지 않아 생명력을 잃는 것이다. 오래도록 남게 될 말과 글에 종종 속어가 비효과적이고 적절하지 못한 이유가 여기에 있다.

23 ①

강한 언어를 사용함으로써 '생활이 언제나 흥미롭고 엄청난 일들로 가득 차 있어야 한다'라고 생각하게 된다면, 평범한 일들로 가득 차 있다는 현실은 초라하게 보이거나 부족하다고 생각될 것이다. 정상적인 것도 터무니없이 높이 설정된 잘못된 기준으로 보면 비정상적인 것이 되거나 가치가 없는 것이 될 것이므로, 빈칸에 들어갈 가장 적절한 표현은 ①이 된다.

symptomatic a. 징후인; 전조가 되는; 나타내는 malaise n. 막연한 불안, (특정 상황, 집단 내에 존재하는 설명하기 힘든) 문제들 affect v. 악영향을 미치다; 영향을 주다; 감동시키다 dazzling a. 눈부신, 현혹적인 fabulous a. 전설적인; 터무니없는, 엄청난 routine a. 판에 박힌, 일상의 absurd a. 불합리한, 부조리한, 터무니없는 conception n. 개념, 생각; 이해 wanting a. 부족한; 빠져 있는 devaluate v. 가치를 내리다, 평가절하하다 descry v. (관측·조사하여) 발견하다, 찾아내다; 어렴풋이 식별하다 habituate v. 익숙하게 하다, 습관을 들이다 inculcate v. (사상·지식 따위를) 가르치다, 되풀이하여 가르치다, 설득하다

강한 언어를 사용하는 것은 사람들에게 악영향을 미치고 있는 특정 문제들을 나타내 주고 있는데, 이러한 것들은 사람들로 하여금 생활이 언제나 흥미롭고, 활력이 넘치고, 눈부시며, '엄청난' 경험들로 가득 차 있어야 한다고 생각하게 만든다. 이것은 분명히 터무니없는 생각이다. 모든 사람들은 자신의 시간 가운데 상당히 많은 부분을 일상의 평범한 일을 하면서 보낸다. 그러므로 우리가 정상적인 것에 대해 불합리한 개념을 갖게 되고, 우리의 생활을 이러한 잘못된 기준을 통해 평가하며, 우리 자신이 뭔가 부족하다고 느끼기 때문에, 강한 언어를 사용하는 것은 우리로 하여금 스스로의 생활의 가치를 떨어뜨리도록 한다.

25 ③

현재 과학적 발견이 비전문가들에 의해서도 나온다고 했으며 마지막 문장의 주절에서 과학자들은 비전문가들이 참여할 수 있도록 하며 자료를 활용한다고 했으므로 비전문가들의 견해를 적절히 받아들이고 있음을 알 수 있다. 빈칸 앞에 instead of가 있으므로 과학자들이 비전문가들의 견해에 대한 '부정적인' 뜻인 ③이 빈칸에 적절하다.

toil away 피땀 흘려 일하다 pristine a. 원래의, 옛날의 chamber n. (특정 목적용) -실(室) grunt work 지루하고 고된 일 brainwork n. 머리 쓰는 일, 정신노동 noncredentialed a. 자격이 없는 unschooled a. 교육 받지 않은, 훈련 받지 않은, 경험 없는 wannabe n. 명사[스타]가 되고 싶어 하는 사람 bona fide a. 진심의, 성실한, 선의의 sift through 꼼꼼하게 살펴 추려내다 ponder over ~에 관해 숙고하다 merit n. 가치; 장점 without reserve 거리낌 없이; 무조건으로 bristle at ~에 발끈하다 hypothesis n. 가설, 가정

다음 세상을 바꿀 과학적 발견은 일반적인 전문 실험실에서 열심히 일을 하는 연구자뿐 아니라 안락의자에서 편안하게 연구를 하는 아마추어로부터 나올지도 모른다. 오늘날 수천 명의 시민 과학자들은 이미 크라우드소싱 사이트의 요청으로 지루하고 고된 일과 정신노동, 심지어 응용과학연구의 자금 조달에까지 나서고 있다. 그리고 신용이 떨어지고 전문 교육을 받지 않은 비전문가들의 견해에 대해 발끈하는 대신 성실한 과학자들은 비전문가들이 참여할 수 있도록 하며, 그들의 자료를 철저히 검토하여, 심지어 그들의 분야에 참여하기도 한다. 그리고 이들 중 일부는 중요한 문제를 해결한다.

24 ④

마지막 문장의 대명사 That은 바로 앞 문장의 내용을 가리키며, 앞 문장의 핵심 내용은 '속어 표현이 과도하게 사용되다가 금방 신선함을 잃고 사라진다'라는 것이다. 새로운 느낌이 금방 사라지고 만다면, 나중에 그 표현을 접하게 되는 이들은 해당 표현 속의 새로운 느낌을 전혀 느끼지 못할 것이므로 그 만큼 가치가 덜 하게 될 것이다. 속어가 가진 새로운 느낌이 오래 가지 못한다면, 오래도록 남게 될 글 혹은 말에는 속어를 사용하지 않는 편이 낫다는 결론을 내릴 수 있다.

attraction n. 매력, 유혹, 사람을 끄는 힘 slang n. 속어; 전문어, 술어 phrase v. 말로 표현하다, 진술하다 unusual a. 이상한, 유별난, 색다른 repetition n. 되풀이, 반복 novelty n. 신기함, 진기함; 새로움 wear off (차츰) 사라지다, 없어지다 sparkle n. 불꽃; 광채, 광택; 재치, 생기

01 ③	02 ④	03 ④	04 ①	05 ②	06 ③	07 ③	08 ①	09 ②	10 ②
11 ①	12 ④	13 ①	14 ②	15 ②	16 ④	17 ④	18 ①	19 ④	20 ②
21 ③	22 ①	23 ②	24 ①	25 ②					

01 ③

기독교 신앙과 이슬람교 신앙은 별개의 것이며 상식적으로도 양립할 수 없는 것이므로, 만약 이슬람교를 받아들인다면 기독교 신앙은 포기해야 할 것이다. 따라서 빈칸에는 '부인하다'라는 의미의 forswear가 들어가야 하며, and 뒤에 위치한 동사 embrace에 대한 문맥상의 반의어를 찾는 문제라 할 수 있다.

knight n. 기사, 무사 Christianity n. 기독교 신앙 embrace v. 포옹하다; 맞이하다, 환영하다; 받아들이다 hail v. 환호로써 맞이하다; 인사하다, 축하하다 baptize v. 세례를 베풀다, 세례명을 붙이다 forswear v. 맹세코 그만 두다; 맹세코 부인하다 refurbish v. 다시 닦다; 일신하다, 쇄신하다

그 나라에서, 사로잡힌 기사들은 기독교신앙을 부인하고 이슬람교를 진실한 신앙으로 받아들여야만 죽음을 면할 수 있었다.

02 ④

빈칸에는 '효율성(efficiency)'과 상반되는 의미를 가진 표현이 와야 할 것이므로 ④가 정답으로 적절하다.

cherish v. 애호하다; 사랑하며 키우다; 소중히 하다 efficiency n. 능력, 능률, 효율성 profligacy n. 방탕, 품행 불량; 낭비; 대량 frugality n. 절약, 검소 chagrin n. 억울함, 원통함, 분함 presumption n. 가정, 추측; 대담함, 뻔뻔스러움

우리는 우리 자신에게 효율성을 소중히 여기라고 말한다. 그러나 우리는 그 설계의 원리가 지나치게 소모적인 그런 수송체계를 만들어왔다.

03 ④

어떤 일을 하던 사람이 다른 일을 함께 하게 되는 경우, 이전에 하던 일은 하지 않게 되거나 혹은 그 비중이 줄어들기 마련이다. 주어진 글에서는 배우가 극단의 미술감독 일을 하게 된 상황이므로, 이전에 하던 직업 가운데 배우로서의 비중은 줄어들 것이다. 따라서 '부차적인 것이 되다'라는 의미의 ④가 정답이 된다.

hint v. 넌지시 비추다, 암시하다 leading a. 일류의, 탁월한 come to heel 뒤에서 따르다, (규칙·명령 등에) 충실히 따르다 play truant 무단결석하다, 농땡이 부리다

come in handy 편리하다, 곧 쓸 수 있다 take a back seat 한 걸음 물러나다, 남에게 맡기다; 부차적인 것이 되다

시드니의 일류 극단에서 미술감독 역할을 새로 맡게 됨으로써 배우로서의 자신의 커리어는 줄어들 수도 있을 것이라고 케이트 블란쳇(Cate Blanchet)이 금요일에 넌지시 비췄다.

04 ①

있는 그대로 말하는 것이 두려웠다고 했고 또한 직접적인 언급을 피하고자 했다고 되어 있으므로, call a spade a spade 혹은 direct reference의 의미와 상반되는 의미를 가진 단어가 빈칸에 들어가야 한다.

call a spade a spade 사실 그대로 말하다, 직언하다 resort v. (어떤 장소에) 다니다; 드나들다; 의지하다, 호소하다 reference n. 문의, 조회; 언급; 관련 circumlocution n. 에둘러 말함, 완곡한 표현 lullaby n. 자장가 lexicon n. 사전; (특정한 작가·작품의) 어휘; 어휘 목록 valediction n. 고별, 고별사

그는 있는 그대로 말하는 것이 두려웠으며, 자기가 가진 주제에 대해 직접적인 언급을 피하고자 완곡한 표현을 썼다.

05 ②

빈칸에는 involvement의 동의어 혹은 그와 유사한 의미를 가진 단어가 들어가야 한다. ②가 여기에 부합하는 단어이다.

affair n. 일, 용건, 사건 involvement n. 관련, 연루, 연좌 superior n. 윗사람, 상관, 선배 corollary n. 추론; 당연한 결과 complicity n. 공모, 공범; 연루 throe n. 고민; 진통, 산고 schism n. 분리, 분열; 불화

나는 이 일을 공모한 사실을 당신이 오래도록 비밀로 할 수 있을 것이라 생각하지 않는다. 따라서 당신이 연루됐음을 상사에게 즉시 인정하는 것이 현명할 것이다.

06 ③

to see 이하에는 delighted의 원인이 되는 내용이 와야 한다. see 뒤에 위치한 대명사 him은 일전에 무례한 행동을 했던 사람이므로, 빈칸에는 부정적인 의미의 단어가 오는 것이 적절하다. 문맥상 '벌을 받았다'라는 의미의 ③이 들어가는 것이 자연스럽다.

vividly ad. 생생하게; 선명하게 rudeness n. 버릇없음, 무례 reincarnation n. 재생, 환생 paean n. 기쁨의 노래, 찬가; 환호성 comeuppance n. 당연한 벌, 인과응보 eclat n. 대성공, 명성, 평판

그의 무례함을 우리 모두가 일찍이 생생하게 목도한 후에, 우리는 그가 인과응보의 벌을 받는 것을 보고 무척 기뻤다.

07 ③

두 번째 문장 이하는 용서하는 행위가 가지는 의미에 대한 내용이라 할 수 있다. 빈칸이 포함된 that절의 주어인 they는 all forgivers를 가리키므로, 그들이 잃게 되는 충동은 용서와 반대되는 행위에 관한 것으로 봐야 한다. 따라서 빈칸에는 ③이 들어가는 것이 적절하다.

restore v. 되찾다; 복구하다, 복원하다; 부활시키다 self-worth n. 자기가치, 자존감 urge n. 충동; 자극, 압박 relegate v. 추방하다; 지위를 떨어뜨리다, 좌천시키다 rejuvenate v. 도로 젊어지다, 원기를 회복하다 retaliate v. 보복하다, 앙갚음하다 revoke v. 철회하다, 취소하다; 해약하다

결국, 용서하는 모든 사람들은 동일한 일을 하게 되는데, 그들은 가해자에게 자존감을 회복시켜주고, 빚을 탕감해주며, 보복하고 싶은 충동을 잃을 정도의 평화를 경험한다.

08 ①

두 번째 문장은 첫 번째 문장에 대한 부연설명에 해당한다. 첫 번째 문장에서 tentative와 provisional의 의미를 nothing으로 부정하고 있으므로, 두 번째 문장의 빈칸에는 이 두 형용사와 의미적으로 반대인 단어가 들어가야 한다. 따라서 ①이 정답으로 가장 적절하다.

tentative a. 시험적인, 임시의 provisional a. 일시적인, 잠정적인; 임시의 critical a. 비평의, 비판적인; 위기의; 중대한 pronouncement n. 선언, 공고, 발표; 의견, 견해 radical a. 근본적인, 철저한; 과격한 confidently ad. 확신을 갖고, 자신만만하게 remissly ad. 태만하게, 부주의하게 perversely ad. 고집스럽게, 심술궂게 surreptitiously ad. 은밀하게, 비밀히

무어(Moore)가 초기에 했던 비판적 발언에는 시험적이거나 잠정적인 것이 전혀 없었다. 그녀는 당시에 시(詩) 분야에서 새롭게 급진적으로 발전하고 있던 것을 확신을 갖고서 다루었다.

09 ②

빈칸에는 라피트가 불법거래를 처리한 방법을 나타내주는 부사가 들어가야 한다. 불법거래를 하면서도 자신만은 법망을 피할 수 있었던 것은 그러한 거래를 매우 교묘한 방법으로 처리했기 때문일 것이다. 따라서 빈칸에는 ②가 들어가는 것이 자연스럽다.

clandestine a. 비밀의, 은밀한 lawless a. 무법의, 불법적인 clutch n. 붙잡음, 파악 escape v. 달아나다, 모면하다, 벗어나다 overtly ad. 공공연하게, 명백하게 adroitly ad. 솜씨 좋게; 기민하게, 교묘하게 gauntly ad. 수척하게; 황량하게, 쓸쓸하게 waywardly ad. 변덕스럽게; 제멋대로

장 라피트(Jean Lafitte)는 이런 은밀한 불법 거래를 매우 교묘하게 처리했기 때문에, 그의 형제들은 종종 법망에 걸려들기도 했지만 자신은 항상 모면했다.

10 ②

두 문장이 역접의 접속사 but으로 연결되어서 두 문장이 대조되어야 한다. 일부 사람들은 미국의 국기에 대한 모독행위를 반역적으로 생각하지만, 또 다른 사람들은 그것들이 단순한 상징물에 지나지 않다고 생각해야 한다. 빈칸 앞에 refuse to가 있으므로 빈칸에는 desecration과 반대되는 의미의 ②가 들어가는 것이 적절하다.

desecration n. 신성 모독 treasonous a. 반역의, 모반의 seminal a. 창의성이 풍부한; 생산적인 sacrosanct a. 신성불가침의 obsequious a. 아첨[아부]하는; 비굴한 dubitable a. 의심스러운; 불확실한

일부 사람들은 미국 국기에 대한 신성 모독 행위를 반역적이거나 심지어는 테러 행위로 간주하지만, 다른 사람들은 단순한 상징물로 생각되는 것을 신성한 것으로 취급하는 것에 반대한다.

11 ①

첫 문장에서 인터넷 검색에 많은 시간을 보냈다고 했는데, 두 번째 문장에서 이베이에서 물건을 아주 저렴하게 구입했다고 했으므로 인터넷 검색에 오랜 시간을 보낸 것에 운이 따랐다고 볼 수 있다.

providential a. 천우신조의; 행운의, 운이 좋은 raucous a. 쉰 목소리의, 귀에 거슬리는 scathing a. 냉혹한, 가차없는 irascible a. 성미가 급한, 성마른

인터넷 검색에 오랜 시간을 보낸 것은 운이 좋았던 것으로 증명되었다. 대부분의 장비가 미국에서 구매하면 일반적으로 덜 비쌌지만, 일부 장비를 이베이에서 매우 저렴하게 구입했다.

12

①

you cannot 이하는 앞 부분의 내용을 부연설명하고 있다. 강요나 협박에 의해 저지른 범죄는 처벌을 받지 않는다고 했으므로, 빈칸에는 forced or threatened의 의미를 내포하고 있는 단어가 필요하다. 이러한 의미를 가진 것은 ①이다.

contract n. 계약, 약정 voidable a. 비울 수 있는; 무효로 할 수 있는 convict v. 유죄를 입증하다, 유죄를 선언하다 threaten v. 협박하다, 위협하다 commit v. 저지르다, 범하다; 위임하다, 위탁하다 crime n. 범죄, 법률위반 duress n. 구속, 속박, 감금; 강박 menopause n. 폐경기, 갱년기 parturition n. 분만, 출산 stupor n. 무감각, 인사불성

속박된 상태에서 서명한 계약은 무효로 할 수 있다. 중범죄의 경우에는 이런 항변이 소용없을 수도 있지만, 강요나 협박에 의해 범죄를 저질렀음을 입증할 수 있으면 유죄판결을 받지 않을 수 있다.

13

①

자기주장을 관철한다는 것은 이 글에서는 부부간의 말다툼에서 이긴다는 말이다. 그것은 상대가 결함 때문에 진다는 말이 되며 사랑에 눈꺼풀이 있다는 것은 사랑한다면 상대의 결함을 눈감아줄 수 있어야 한다는 말이므로 빈칸에는 '흠이 없는'이라는 의미의 ①이 적절하다.

win one's point 주장을 세우다, 주장을 관철하다 do well to V ~하는 것이 좋다 bear in mind 명심하다 spotless a. 결함이 없는, 완벽한 heedless a. 경솔한 restless a. 침착하지 못한 dauntless a. 겁 없는

말다툼에서 자기주장을 관철하는 것으로는 당신의 배우자가 흠이 없지 않다는 것을 증명할 뿐이다. 함께 행복하게 살기를 진정으로 원하는 부부는 사랑에는 눈뿐 아니라 눈꺼풀도 있다는 옛말을 명심하는 것이 좋을 것이다.

14

②

빈칸 앞의 대명사 this는 앞 문장에서 언급한 미담의 내용을 가리키는데, 이것과 gloom and doom은 대조를 이루는 개념임에 주목해야 한다. 밝고 희망적인 이야기를 언론 매체에서 많이 싣는다면 우울하고 파멸적인 이야기를 상쇄시킬 수 있을 것이므로, ②가 정답으로 적절하다.

tragedy n. 비극, 비극적인 사건 gloom n. 우울, 침울; 슬픔 doom n. 운명, 숙명 solidify v. 단결시키다, 응고하다; 굳히다 offset v. 상쇄하다, 상계하다, 벌충하다 concatenate v. 사슬같이 잇다; (사건 따위를) 연결시키다 cull v. 따서 모으다; 발췌하다

개인적인 비극을 선(善)을 향한 힘으로 바꿈으로써, 그녀는 수많은 사람들의 생각을 바꾸어 놓았다. 언론 매체가 이런 이야기를 더 많이 실어서 우리 귀에 매일 흔하게 들리는 것 같은 어둡고 파멸적인 면을 상쇄하도록 하지 않는 것은 대단히 유감스러운 일이다.

15

③

첫 문장에서는 법이 제안, 발의된 상태이다. 두 번째 문장의 주절에서는 법이 집행되는 면을 보이고 있는데, 법을 어길 수 있으려면 그 법이 효력을 가지는 상태, 다시 말해 비준된 상태에 있어야 하므로, 빈칸에는 ③이 들어가는 것이 적절하다.

illegal a. 불법의, 위법의; 반칙의 propose v. 신청하다, 제안하다, 제의하다 psychologist n. 심리학자 fine n. 벌금, 과료 fabricate v. 제조하다; 날조하다, 조작하다 abrogate v. 취소하다, 폐지하다; 파기하다 ratify v. 비준하다, 재가하다, 확증하다 prognosticate v. 예지하다, 예언하다, 예측하다

자기 이름이 다른 사람의 애완동물의 이름과 똑같아서 우울함을 느끼는 아이들이 더러 있다는 심리학자들의 말이 있은 후, 브라질에서는 애완동물에게 사람의 이름을 부여하는 것을 불법으로 규정하는 법안이 최근 발의되었다. 그 법이 비준되면, 법을 어기는 애완동물 주인은 벌금을 물거나 사회봉사 활동을 해야 할 것이다.

16

④

두 번째 문장 이하는 첫 번째 문장의 진술, 특히 인종적 갈등의 내용을 보다 구체적으로 설명하는 역할을 하고 있다. 갈등은 양자(兩者) 사이에 발생하는 것이므로, 많은 흑인들이 직책을 차지하고자 경쟁에 뛰어든 상황을 달갑지 않게 여기는 사람들의 태도나 행위에 해당하는 표현이 필요하다. 그러므로 빈칸에 가장 적절한 것은 '반발'이라는 의미의 ④가 된다.

competition n. 경쟁; 시합 promotion n. 승진, 진급; 장려, 판촉 racially ad. 인종적으로 conflict n. 충돌, 대립, 불일치; 전투 vie v. 다투다; 경쟁하다 fiat n. (권위에 의한) 명령; 인가 concurrence n. 찬동, 일치; 협력; 동시발생 blandishment n. 감언, 유혹; 추종 backlash n. 반동, 반발, 반격

미국에서 직장 내 승진 경쟁은 종종 인종적으로 논쟁이 일어나기 쉬운 갈등의 근원이 되고 있다. 많은 아프리카계 미국인들이 직책을 차지하고자 경쟁하기 시작하고 있고, 한정된 수의 일자리를 놓고 더 이상의 경쟁을 원하지 않는 사람들로부터 반발이 일어나고 있다.

17

④

석유를 판매함으로써 얻는 수익이 줄어드는 것은 수요가 줄어들거나 판매를 할 수 없는 여건이 늘어나는 경우이다. 첫 번째 빈칸에 들어갈 단어의 동사로 expands가 주어져 있으므로, 빈칸에는 '통상금지'라는 의미의 embargo 또는 '억제'라는 의미의 check가 들어갈 수 있다. 한편, 두 번째 빈칸은 '석유생산에 있어서 피해를 입히는' 주체에 해당하므로, 부정적인 의미의 단어가 필요하다. anarchy, peril, sanctions가 가능하다. 따라서 정답은 ④가 된다.

revenue n. 소득, 수익 expand v. 퍼지다, 넓어지다; 팽창하다, 성장하다 investment n. 투자, 출자 sector n. 분야, 방면, 영역 dry up ~을 바싹 말리다;

고갈되다, 바닥나다 inflict v. (상처·고통 따위를) 입히다, 가하다 long-term a. 장기적인 potential n. 잠재력, 가능성 check n. 저지, 억제; 방해; 저지하는 것 nomenclature n. 명명법; 학명; 술어, 전문어 clout n. 강타, 타격; 강한 영향력 anarchy n. 무정부; 무정부상태; 무질서 demand n. 요구, 청구; 수요 peril n. 위험; 모험 embargo n. 통상금지; 보도금지 sanction n. 인가; 제재, 제재 규약

이란산 석유에 대한 금수조치가 확대되고 이란의 석유산업 분야에 대한 투자가 고갈되어 감에 따라, 이란의 석유 수익은 감소하고 있으며 훨씬 낮은 수준으로 떨어질 수도 있다. 경제 제재 또한 이란의 장기적인 석유 생산 잠재력에 점점 더 많은 피해를 입히고 있다.

---

18 ①

리듬을 탄다는 것은 '어떤 상황이 규칙적으로 순환한다'라는 의미이다. 정서적으로 리듬을 탄다는 것은 우울한 느낌과 즐거운 느낌이 규칙적으로 번갈아 나타난다는 것을 의미하게 되므로, 첫 번째 빈칸에는 rotating 또는 alternate가 가능하다. 지적으로 리듬을 타는 경우도 정서적으로 리듬을 타는 경우처럼 대조를 이루는 상태가 교대로 일어나야 할 것이므로, 두 번째 빈칸에는 빈칸 뒤에 위치한 명사 concentration 의 반의어가 필요하다. relaxation, recess, respite가 가능하다. 상기 언급한 조건을 모두 만족시키는 정답은 ①이다.

physiologically ad. 생리학적으로, 생리적으로 rhythmical a. 율동적인, 리드미컬한; 규칙적으로 순환하는 depression n. 의기소침, 우울; 침울; 불경기 exhilaration n. 들뜬 기분, 유쾌, 상쾌; 흥분 concentration n. 집중, 전념 alternate a. 번갈아 하는, 교대의 relaxation n. 이완; 경감, 완화 verdant a. 푸릇푸릇한, 신록의; 경험이 없는 recess n. 쉼, 휴식; 휴정 rotating a. 선회하는 centralization n. 집중화 immutable a. 변경할 수 없는, 불변의 respite n. 연기, 유예; 휴식

생리적으로, 우리는 리듬을 탄다. 우리는 좋은 건강상태를 유지하기 위해 규칙적으로 먹고, 자고, 숨쉬고, 놀아야 한다. 또한 우리는 정서적으로도 리듬을 탄다. 심리학자들이 우리들 대부분이 상대적인 우울과 즐거움을 교대로 느낀다고 말하고 있기 때문이다. 지적으로도 우리는 또한 리듬을 탄다. 왜냐하면 우리는 집중한 후에 반드시 휴식을 취해야 하기 때문이다.

---

19 ④

정부는 국민에 대한 감시를 계속할 것이고, 사생활은 필연적으로 사라져 버릴 것이라고 했다. 이러한 상황에서 바랄 수 있는 최선은 그 감시 주체에 대한 통제와 감시라고 할 수 있다.

naive a. 순진한, 천진난만한 communism n. 공산주의 anarchy n. 무정부 상태; 무질서 상태 patriotism n. 애국심 improve v. 개선되다; 향상되다 privacy n. 사적 자유, 사생활, 프라이버시 inevitably ad. 불가피하게, 필연적으로 privatize v. 민영화(民營化)하다 evaporate v. 증발하다; 자취를 감추다 communize v. 공산화하다; (토지·재산 따위를) 국유화하다 enlighten v. 계몽하다, 교화하다

만약 정부가 당신의 일거수일투족을 감시하고 있다고 생각한다면, 그것은 어리석은 생각이다. 그러나 만약 정부가 너무 착하거나 너무 정직해서 감시

하려 들지 않는다고 생각한다면, 그것은 순진한 생각이다. 범죄, 공산주의, 테러, 무정부 상태, 호전적인 적과의 전쟁이라는 명분으로, 혹은 단순히 애국심이라는 이름으로 정부는 우리를 감시해 왔으며, 앞으로도 우리를 감시할 것이다. 기술이 발달함에 따라, 우리의 사생활은 필연적으로 사라져 버릴 것이다. 따라서 우리가 바랄 수 있는 최상의 것은 바로 그 감시자를 감시하는 힘이다.

---

20 ②

애플이 우려하고 있다는 것에서 애플은 스포티파이에 대해 '비판적인' 입장을 취하고 있다는 점을 알 수 있고, 비판의 핵심은 스포티파이의 기계적인 접근이 음악이 가진 인간적인, 다시 말해 정신적인 측면을 '약화시킨다'는 것이므로 이를 참조하면 정답은 ②가 적절하다.

decline v. 거절하다 allude to 암시하다 drain out 고갈시키다 reproach n. 비난 evade v. 피하다, 면하다 critique n. 비평, 비판 erode v. 침식하다 condescension n. 겸손, 생색 evacuate v. 소개(疏開)시키다 hurrah n. 만세 exhort v. 훈계하다 depreciation n. 평가절하 eavesdrop v. 엿듣다

스포티파이(Spotify)를 꼭 집어 말하지는 않았지만, 쿡은 스트리밍 음악이 인간적인 느낌을 잃어가고 있는 데 대해 애플이 우려하고 있다고 말했다. 이는 스포티파이가 내용을 부각시키는 데 알고리즘을 많이 이용하고 있는 것을 넌지시 암시하는 것이다. 쿡의 말은 스포티파이에 대한 애플의 유서 깊은 비판적인 입장을 잘 보여 주고 있다. 다시 말해 스포티파이의 알고리즘이 우리 삶에 음악이 차지하고 있는 정신적인 역할을 앗아가고 있다는 것이다. 쿡은 "우리는 인간성이 음악에서 빠져나가 고갈되고 있는 것에 우려하고 있다."라고 말한다.

---

21 ③

두 번째 문장에서 '사업의 영역과 우정의 영역에서 확연히 다른 점'을 이야기하고 있으므로, 첫 번째 빈칸에는 '구별하다, 구분하다'라는 의미를 가진 단어가 들어가는 것이 적절하다. demarcate 또는 differentiate가 올 수 있다. 한편, '두 영역이 확실하게 구분이 된다'라는 내용 뒤에 Yet 이 왔고, Business has its social morality 이하 전체에서 사업과 우정의 영역이 중첩되는 면이 제시되고 있으므로, 두 번째 빈칸에는 '경계가 명확하지 않다' 혹은 '두 영역이 겹치는 부분이 있다'라는 의미를 나타낼 수 있는 단어가 와야 한다. intermediary 또는 intermediate가 가능하다. 상기 두 조건을 만족시키는 정답은 ③이다.

sphere n. 영역, 범위 obtain v. 얻다, 획득하다 bargain n. 매매, 거래; 계약 morality n. 도덕, 도의; 윤리성 aspect n. 양상, 모습; 국면, 정세 deserve v. ~할 만하다, ~을 받을 가치가 있다 epitomize v. 요약하다, 발췌하다 reciprocity n. 상호성, 상호관계 underlie v. 기초가 되다, 근저에 있다; 우선하다 classify v. 분류하다, 등급으로 나누다 superlative a. 최상의, 최고의; 과도한, 과장된 synthesize v. 종합하다; 합성하다 intermediary a. 중간의; 중급의 demarcate v. 경계를 정하다; 한정하다, 구분하다 intermediate a. 중간의, 개재하는; 중간에 일어나는 differentiate v. 구별하다, 식별하다; 차별하다 extramural a. 성벽 밖의, 교외의

유럽 문화에서, 우리는 사업의 영역을 우정의 영역과 구분한다. 전자(前者)는 가능한 한 가장 좋은 거래를 얻어내는 것이 옳다고 주장하는 반면, 후자(後者)는 거래라는 관점에서 다루길 거부한다. 그럼에도 불구하고, 중간 영역은 있다. 사업에는 사회적 윤리가 있다. '호의로' 이뤄지는 일들도 있으며, '공정한' 가격이라는 개념도 있다. 우정이 반드시 물질적인 측면을 무시하는 것도 아니다. '도움을 받았으면 갚아야 한다'라는 말은 많은 호의적인 행동의 기저에 깔려 있는 상호성의 존중을 요약하고 있는 말이다.

22 ①

첫 번째 빈칸의 경우, 바로 다음 문장의 reduced visibility에서 볼 수 있듯이 가시성이 제한된다는 말이 필요하다. 두 번째 빈칸은 흙탕물처럼 물이 뿌옇다는 말이 필요하다.

breathtaking a. 놀랄만한 marine a. 바다의 deadline n. 마감시간 penetrate v. 관통하다 wave surge 큰 파도 stir v. 휘젓다 silt n. 침니(침적토의 일종) compromise v. 훼손하다 murky a. 흐릿한, 분명치 않은 impound v. 가두다 shroud v. 가리다, 감추다 cantorial a. 합창 지휘자의 flare v. 불타오르다 effulgent a. 빛나는 shrink v. 수축하다 reinstate v. 원래대로 만들다

대부분의 사람들은 수중 촬영을 직업으로 하는 사람들에 대해 이리저리 헤엄치면서 근사한 해양생물들을 사진 찍을 수 있다니 참 운이 좋은 사람들이라고 생각한다. 하지만 그들의 예술은 일이기도 하다. 마감시간을 맞추기 위해서는 많은 지식과 창의성이 필요한데, 그 주된 이유는 수중의 가시성이 훼손되기 때문이다. 거친 바다는 여러 가지 이유로 가시성을 제한한다. 하나는 거친 바다 표면은 좀 더 많은 햇빛을 반사해서, 물속까지 들어오는 빛이 줄어든다. 또 하나의 이유는 큰 파도가 바다 밑바닥의 침니나 모래를 휘저어, 물을 뿌옇게 만든다.

23 ②

소셜 미디어의 부정적 영향을 언급한 문장에 이어서 순접(and)으로 이어지는 내용이므로 소셜 미디어를 '멀리한다'는 내용이 들어가는 것이 적절하다.

impact n. 영향, 충격 detox v. 해독하다 exhilarate v. 원기(기운)을 북돋우다 depression n. 우울증 nerd n. 광(狂), 매니아

최근 들어 소셜 미디어가 우리의 정신 건강에 부정적 영향을 미친다는 이야기들을 많이 듣게 됨에 따라, 새해의 시작을 디지털 해독의 기회로 볼 수도 있다. 소셜 미디어는 우리를 어느 때보다 더 연결되게 만들고 도파민 분비를 촉진하여 기분을 들뜨게 만들 뿐만 아니라, 어떤 이들의 경우에는 우울증, 불안 및 외로움의 증세와도 관련되어 있다고 초기 연구들은 지적하고 있다.

24 ①

바로 앞 문장에서 '대수학에 대해 거의 알지 못하는 사람을 불러들인다 해도 아무런 도움도 받지 못한다'라고 했으므로, 대수학을 모르는 사람 여럿이 협력하여 내놓은 답은 유능한 수학자가 푼 답에 비해 가치가 없을 것임을 미루어 짐작할 수 있다.

erroneous a. 잘못된, 틀린 uninformed a. 알려지지 않은, 정보를 받지 못한 hold v. 생각하다, 주장하다 algebra n. 대수학 approve v. 승인하다, 찬성하다; 허가하다 unanimous a. 만장일치의, 이의 없는 vote n. 투표, 표결 competent a. 적임의, 유능한 mathematician n. 수학자 count for nothing 보잘 것 없다, 아무 쓸모가 없다 infallible a. 전혀 틀림이 없는

대중이 불완전한 지식을 갖고 있는 문제에 있어서, 중론(衆論)은 똑같이 무지한 개인의 의견과 마찬가지로 오류에 빠지기 쉽다. 그렇지 않다고 생각하는 것은 다수의 무지를 모으면 지혜를 얻을 수 있다고 생각하는 것과 같다. 대수학을 전혀 모르는 사람은 대수학에 대해 자신만큼 알고 있는 이웃사람을 불러들인다 해도 대수학 문제를 푸는 데 있어 아무런 도움도 받지 못한다. 그리고 백만 명의 이와 같은 무지한 사람들의 만장일치의 투표로 인정을 받은 답이라 해도, 한 사람의 유능한 수학자의 답에 비하면 아무런 가치도 없는 것이다.

25 ②

빈칸 이하의 문장에서는 정치권과 금융기관이 서로 결탁해 있는 상황에 대해 예를 들어 설명하고 있다. 금융기관에 대해 정부가 고발을 하지 못하는 것은 정부가 해당 기관들로부터 공공연하게 혜택을 받았기 때문으로 보아야 하며, 이런 점을 가장 잘 나타내는 단어는 '연줄, 정실인사' 등의 의미를 가진 ②이다.

criminal a. 범죄의; 죄가 있는; 형사상의 charge n. 고발, 고소 file v. (신청·항의 등을) 제출하다, 제기하다 executive n. 행정부, 행정관; 경영진, 임원 institution n. 시설, 기관; 제도, 관습; 학회 detail v. 상술하다, 열거하다 suspicious a. 의심스러운, 수상쩍은; 의혹을 품은 flood v. 넘치게 하다, 범람시키다 donation n. 증여, 기부; 기증품 jingoism n. 맹목적 애국주의 cronyism n. 편파, 편애, 편들기; 연고주의; 정실인사 elitism n. 엘리트 의식, 엘리트주의 capitalism n. 자본주의

월스트리트(Wall Street)의 부패를 없애겠다는 오바마(Obama) 대통령의 약속에도 불구하고, 금융기관의 고위 임원에 대해 연방정부는 단 한 차례도 형사고발을 하지 않았다. 왜 그런 것일까? 한 마디로 말하자면 연줄 때문이다. 골드만 삭스(Goldman Sachs)를 예로 들어보자. 2008년에 골드만 삭스의 직원들은 버락 오바마의 선거 운동에 가장 많은 기부금을 낸 사람들에 속했다. 더욱이, 상원의 상임분과위원회에서 골드만 삭스의 의심스러운 부채담보부증권(ABACUS) 거래에 대해 자세히 열거한 보고서를 발표했을 때, 골드만 삭스 경영진 일부는 기부금을 통해 오바마의 선거자금을 대기 시작하고 있었다.

01 ②	02 ④	03 ③	04 ①	05 ②	06 ①	07 ②	08 ②	09 ③	10 ①
11 ③	12 ④	13 ④	14 ④	15 ①	16 ②	17 ③	18 ②	19 ③	20 ④
21 ②	22 ①	23 ①	24 ③	25 ①					

01 ②

세미콜론이 이유의 접속사의 역할을 하고 있다. 세미콜론 이하에서 '교훈이 시의 내용보다 인상적이다'라고 했는데, 여기서 the lines가 앞 문장의 literary qualities에 호응하므로, 빈칸에는 the lesson과 호응할 수 있는 단어가 들어가야 함을 알 수 있다. 그러므로 '교훈'이라는 의미를 내포하고 있는 didactic이 정답이 된다.

quality n. 품질; 성질, 특성 overshadow v. 그늘지게 하다, 가리다; 볼품없이 보이게 하다 literary a. 문학의; 문예의, 학문의 memorable a. 기억할 만한, 잊기 어려운; 중대한 scathing a. 냉혹한, 가차 없는, 통렬한 didactic a. 가르치기 위한, 교훈적인 acerbic a. 신, 떫은; 표독한, 신랄한 oblique a. 비스듬한; 간접적인, 에두른

그의 시(詩)가 가진 교훈적인 특성이 문학적인 특성을 가리고 있다. 왜냐하면 그의 작품에서 그가 가르치고 있는 교훈이 시구(詩句) 자체보다 더 인상적이기 때문이다.

02 ④

강연이 주제에서 벗어난 것을 사람들이 개의치 않아 했던 이유를 세미콜론 이하에서 설명하고 있다. the topic of the day가 official theme을 가리키므로, 빈칸에는 'lectures wandered away'를 설명할 수 있거나 그러한 의미를 가진 단어가 들어가야 한다. '여담'이라는 의미의 ④가 적절하다.

wander v. 헤매다; 방랑하다; 옆길로 빗나가다, 탈선하다 official a. 공식적인; 공인된 theme n. 주제, 화제; 테마 fascinating a. 황홀하게 하는, 매혹적인; 대단히 흥미로운 apologue n. 우화, 교훈담 victual n. 음식, 양식 homily n. 설교; 훈계 digression n. 본제를 벗어나 지엽으로 흐름; 여담; 탈선

르누아르(Renoir) 교수의 강의가 공식적인 주제에서 벗어났을 때, 아무도 신경 쓰지 않았다. 왜냐하면 그의 여담이 그 날의 강연주제보다 항상 더 흥미로웠기 때문이다.

03 ③

정직한 것 같아 보였던 사람에게 충격을 받았다면, 그것은 그가 정직하지 않은 행동을 했기 때문일 것이다. 따라서 빈칸에는 honest and straightforward와 상반되는 의미를 가진 단어가 들어가야 한다. '표리부동, 이중적인 태도'라는 의미를 가진 ③이 정답이 된다.

dismay v. 당황하게 하다, 놀라게 하다, 낙담시키다 patron n. 보호자, 후원자; 고객 straightforward a. 올바른; 정직한, 솔직한 verity n. 진실, 진실성; 진실의 진술; 사실 fray n. 소동, 싸움; 논쟁 duplicity n. 표리부동, 사기, 이중성 hypnosis n. 최면, 최면술

사람들은 자신들을 후원하던 사람이 이 문제에 이중적인 태도를 보인 것을 알게 됐을 때 충격을 받고 크게 낙담했는데, 그는 그들에게 항상 정직하고 솔직하게 보였기 때문이다.

04 ①

'so ~ that …' 구문은 인과관계의 문장을 이끈다. 박물관의 폐쇄와 소장품의 기부를 고려하고 있는 상황을 재무적 관점과 결부시켜 보면, '재무 상태가 좋지 않다'라는 결론이 나온다. 그러므로 빈칸에는 '절망적인, 암울한'이라는 의미의 ①이 들어가는 것이 가장 적절하다.

financial a. 재정의, 재무의 trustee n. 피신탁인; 수탁자, 보관인; 평의원, 이사 shut down 문을 닫다, 멈추다, 정지시키다 donate v. 기증하다, 기부하다 institution n. 협회, 시설, 기관; 제도, 관습 bleak a. 황폐한; 암울한, 절망적인 promising a. 가망 있는, 유망한 ostentatious a. 과시하는, 화려한 sturdy a. 건장한, 착실한; 튼튼한, 건강한

미국 민속 박물관의 재무 상황이 너무 암울해져서, 박물관의 이사들은 박물관을 닫고 다른 기관에 소장품을 기부하는 것을 고려하고 있다.

05 ②

국민을 떠받쳐주었다고 했으므로 '힘'을 느끼게 하는 것이다. 따라서 마지막 문장의 vitality(활기)와 유사한 의미의 ②가 정답으로 적절하다.

unquenchable a. 끌 수 없는, 억누를 수 없는 sustain v. 떠받치다, 유지하다 vitality n. 활기, 생기 edacity n. 왕성한 식욕 verve n. 힘, 활기 torpor n. 무감각 qualm n. 불안한 마음, 주저함; 양심의 가책

십 년 동안 쿠바의 큰 자원은 국민이었는데, 주위의 모든 것이 무너져 내리는 것 같은 때에도 국민의 끌 수 없는 활력이 어떻게든 그들을 떠받쳐주었다. 아직도 그곳에는 토요일 밤의 활기가 있다.

---

06 ①

소수뿐만 아니라 주류인 다수의 주장들도 censorship(검열)의 위험이 있다는 내용으로부터 빈칸을 추론할 수 있다.

censorship n. 검열 proponent n. 제안자, 발의자 muzzle v. 재갈을 물리다 safeguard v. 보호하다 substantiate v. 증명하다, 실증하다 convince v. 납득시키다, 확신시키다

검열의 위험에 빠진 건 소수들뿐만이 아니다. 주류들, 심지어 다수의 주장들과 전에는 상식적이고 무해한 농담까지도 점점 그런 주장을 하는 자들의 입에 재갈을 채우고 있다.

---

07 ②

outstanding moderator가 갖출 만한 긍정적 자질로, 뒤에 오는 diplomatically and tactfully와 의미가 통하는 단어를 골라야 한다. '교묘한 처리, 솜씨'라는 의미의 ②가 정답으로 적절하다. prowess의 경우, 긍정적인 의미를 가지고 있긴 하나, 주로 물리적 용맹함을 뜻하므로 부적절하다.

outstanding a. 걸출한, 뛰어난; 현저한 moderator n. 중재자, 조정자; (토론회의) 사회자 diplomatically ad. 능란하게, 세련되게; 외교적으로 tactfully ad. 재치 있게; 솜씨 좋게 on track 제대로 진행되고 있는, 바르게 haggle n. 입씨름, 언쟁 finesse n. 교묘한 처리, 솜씨; 술책, 책략 prowess n. 용감; 용감한 행위 succor n. 구조, 구원; 구원자, 원조자

애드리아나(Adriana)는 토론 사회자로서 매우 뛰어났는데, 그녀가 지나치게 과열된 그 논쟁을 매우 솜씨 좋게 다루었고, 능수능란하고 재치 있게 대화가 공정하고 제대로 진행되게끔 했기 때문이다.

---

08 ②

but 이하의 내용을 그 다음 문장에서 부연해서 설명하고 있는 구조의 글이다. 두 번째 문장에서 '이기고자 하는 열의가 없어졌다'라고 했는데, 이것을 바탕으로 하면, 그들의 경기 내용은 '활력이 없었을' 것이라 짐작할 수 있다.

powerhouse n. 발전소; (운동 경기에서) 최우수 팀 incorrigible a. 상습적인, 뿌리 깊은; 제멋대로의 effete a. 활력을 잃은, 지친; 쇠약해진 effusive a. 토로하는, 감정이 넘쳐나는 듯한; 과장된 exuberant a. 열광적인, 열의가 넘치는; 원기 왕성한

나는 그들이 한때는 이 나라에서 가장 뛰어난 풋볼 팀이었다고 생각한다. 그러나 요즘 들어 그들의 경기는 힘이 완전히 빠져 있다. 추측컨대, 너무 쉽게 많이 이긴 것이 그들의 열의, 다시 말해 이기고자 하는 욕망을 잃어버리게 만든 것 같다.

---

09 ③

두 번째 문장에서 whereas 전후의 내용은 대조를 이뤄야 한다. whereas 이하에 부정적인 의미의 내용이 있으므로 빈칸에는 긍정적인 의미의 표현이 들어가야 할 것이다. 따라서 ①과 ②를 정답에서 먼저 제외시킬 수 있다. 한편, 첫 번째 문장과 두 번째 문장의 주절은 Thus라는 부사를 통해 인과관계로 연결되어 있는데, 오프라인 소매업이 일부지역을 제외하고는 모두 낙후되어 있는 상황이라면, 온라인 사업이 그런 상황을 보완하는 역할을 할 수 있을 것임을 추론할 수 있다. 따라서 빈칸에는 ③이 들어가는 것이 보다 자연스럽다. ④의 경우, 앞의 문장에서 온라인 회사의 도약에 대해 이미 언급한 경우에 한해 정답이 될 수 있다.

retail v. 소매하다 fragment v. 파편이 되게 하다, 분해하다, 산산조각이 되다 underdeveloped a. 발달이 불충분한, 저개발의 disrupt v. 붕괴시키다, 분열시키다 deadlock n. 막다름, 교착상태 void n. 공간; 허공; 무(無) 공백, 공허감

중국에서는 오프라인 소매업이 동쪽 해안 부근의 대도시들을 제외하고는 여러 조각으로 나뉘어져 있고 또한 낙후되어 있다. 그래서 온라인 회사들이 서구 여러 나라에서는 기존의 산업을 종종 붕괴시켰지만, 중국에서는 오프라인의 부족한 부분을 메울 가능성이 더 높다.

---

10 ①

역접의 접속사 but 전후에서 이야기하는 내용은 대조를 이루어야 한다. but 이하에서, 'with ~ by the employer'는 주절의 내용을 뒷받침해주는 부가적 사항들에 해당하며, 실제로 말하고자 하는 중요한 내용은 it is not bad이다. 따라서 but 앞 부분의 빈칸에는 'not bad'와 상반되는 의미, 즉 문맥상 bad의 의미를 가지는 단어가 와야 한다. 주어가 '매달 받는 50만원의 급여'이므로, '보잘것없다'라는 의미의 ①이 적절하다.

wage n. 임금, 노임; 급료 accommodation n. 숙박 시설; 편의; 적응; 조절 transport n. 수송, 운송 employer n. 고용주, 사용자 paltry a. 보잘것없는; 시시한, 하찮은 hefty a. 무거운; 크고 건장한, 억센; 많은 prodigious a. 거대한; 막대한; 놀라운 excessive a. 과도한; 지나친, 엄청난

한국의 임금과 비교하면 그녀가 매달 벌게 될 50만원은 보잘 것 없게 보일지 모르지만, 그곳에서의 저렴한 생활비용, 하루 5시간 근무, 고용주가 일체로 제공하는 숙박과 교통을 감안하면 나쁘지 않은 조건이라고 그녀는 말했다.

---

11 ③

첫 번째 문장에서는 노예 병사들이 엄격한 행동규범을 따라야 했음을

말하고 있다. In addition은 '첨가, 부가'의 의미이므로, 그 다음 문장에 는 첫 문장에서 언급한 '제약'의 연장선에서 강도가 보다 센 것을 언급 해야 한다. never marrying이 빈칸에 들어갈 단어를 부연하여 설명하 는 역할을 하고 있으므로, 결국 '독신의'라는 의미의 ③이 정답이 된다.

adhere v. 고수하다, 집착하다; 신봉하다 strict a. 엄격한, 엄한; 정밀함 code n. 법전; 규약, 규칙 obedience n. 복종, 순종 paramount a. 최고의, 주요한; 탁월한 harsh a. 사나운; 모진, 가혹한; 난폭한 punishment n. 형벌, 처벌; 징계 promiscuous a. (성 관계가) 문란한, 난잡한, 혼잡한; 뒤죽박죽인 pragmatic a. 활동적인; 실제적인, 실용적인 celibate a. 독신의, 독신주의의 diaphanous a. 비치는, 투명한; 어렴풋한

대체로, 노예 병사들은 엄격한 행동 규범에 충실했는데, 그 규범에 따르면 복종과 예의를 최고로 쳤고 위반에는 무조건 가혹한 처벌이 뒤따랐다. 뿐만 아니라, 그들은 결코 결혼을 하지 않은 독신주의의 삶을 살아야 했다.

12
④

양보의 접속사 even if절에서 '남편을 떠나기 어려운 상황'에 대해 언급 하고 있으므로, 주절은 '그럼에도 불구하고 토를 달거나 지체하는 일이 없이 친정으로 가는 것에 동의한다'라는 내용이 되어야 자연스럽게 글 이 이어진다. 따라서 정답은 ④가 되며, ②의 경우 '화가 나서'라는 의미 이므로 동사 agree와 자연스럽게 호응하지 않는다.

to the effect that ~이라는 취지로 installment n. 할부; 할부금, 납입금 purchase money 구입 대금, 대가 up to time 제시간대로, 제때에 dowry n. 신부의 혼인 지참금 in a fit of spleen 홧김에 elope v. 가출하다, 도망가다 ado n. 야단법석, 소동

아내의 친정가족이 신부 구입대금에 대한 납입금이 제때에 지불되지 않았기 때문에 친정으로 돌아와야 한다는 취지의 전갈을 아내에게 보내면, 아내는 비록 남편을 사랑하고 남편을 떠나기 어려워도 별 소란을 일으키지 않고 순 순히 동의한다.

13
④

간접적으로 마시게 되는 담배연기가 건강에 어떠할지를 상식적으로 생 각하면 된다. 적절한 것은 '해로운'이라는 의미의 ④이다.

secondhand a. 간접적인; 중고의, 고물의 mixture n. 혼합; 혼합물 exhale v. (숨을) 내쉬다, (공기 등을) 내뿜다; 발산시키다 involuntarily ad. 모르는 사이 에, 본의 아니게 inhale v. (공기 등을) 빨아들이다, 흡입하다, 들이마시다 exacerbate v. 악화시키다; 노하게 하다 respiratory a. 호흡의, 호흡성의 infection n. 전염, 감염; 전염병 asthma n. 천식 viable a. (계획 따위가) 실행 가능한, 실용적인; (태아 등이) 살아갈 수 있는, 생명력 있는 listless a. 열의 없는, 무관심한, 냉담한 deranged a. 미친, 정상이 아닌 adverse a. 거스르는, 반대하 는; 불리한, 해로운

비흡연자가 간접적으로 마시게 되는 연기는 타고 있는 담배, 파이프, 시가의 끝에서 나오는 연기와 흡연자들의 폐에서 뿜어져 나온 연기의 혼합물이다. 비흡연자들은 그것을 의도하지 않게 들이마시게 되며, 그것은 암, 호흡기 전

염병, 천식을 비롯해서, 여러 가지 건강상의 해로운 결과들을 초래하거나 악 화시킬 수 있다.

14
④

Religious types와 Sceptics는 모두 두 번째 문장의 '종교를 설명하고 자 하는 사람들'에 속한다. 세 번째 문장 이하에서 이들의 견해가 상충 되는 측면을 이야기하고 있으므로, 종교를 설명하는 것은 '쉽지 않은 문 제'라 할 수 있다.

ubiquitous a. 도처에 존재하는, 편재(偏在)하는 universal a. 보편적인, 일반적 인; 공통의 ubiquity n. 도처에 있음, 편재 reflection n. 반영, 반성, 숙고; 반사 underlying a. 근본적인; 기초가 되는 sceptic n. 회의론자 flavor n. 맛, 풍미; 운치, 정취 cargo cult 적하(積荷) 신앙(조상의 영혼이 배, 비행기로 돌아와 백인에 게서 해방시켜 준다는 신앙) rationale n. 근본적 이유; 이론적 근거 pathos n. 애절감, 비애감, 애수, 애수의 정 mirth n. 환희, 명랑; 유쾌함 conundrum n. 수수께끼; 난문제

종교는 도처에 존재하지만, 보편적인 것은 아니다. 그 점이 종교를 설명하려 는 사람들에게 어려운 문제이다. 종교적인 사람들은 편재성(偏在性)을 언급 하면서, 종교가 사물의 본질을 실제로 반영하고 있음을 이것이 증명한다고 주장한다. 회의론자들은, 이 주장이 사실이라면, 종교가 가톨릭 교회와 사도 교회부터 파푸아뉴기니의 적하(積荷) 신앙에 이르기까지 왜 이렇게 다양한 지를 의아하게 여긴다.

15
①

첫 번째 문장과 두 번째 문장은 암의 확산에 대한 이론과 실제에 대해 이야기하고 있으며, 세 번째 문장과 네 번째 문장은 이러한 현상에 대 해 부연해서 설명하는 역할을 하고 있다. 두 번째 문장의 빈칸에도 첫 번째 문장에서 언급하고 있는 'spread' 현상을 지칭할 수 있는 표현이 들어가야 하는데, 주어진 글이 암에 대한 것임을 감안하면 암이 다른 곳으로 퍼지는 것을 지칭하는 표현, 즉 '전이'를 의미하는 단어가 들어 가는 것이 자연스럽다. 따라서 정답은 ①이며, cells spread 혹은 네 번 째 문장의 의미를 포함하고 있는 단어를 찾는 문제로 볼 수 있다.

prostate n. 전립선 lymph node 림프절 tumor n. 종양; 종기 lymphatic system 림프계 bloodstream n. 혈류, 혈류량; 활력 metastasis n. 전이(轉移) carcinogen n. 발암물질 occlusion n. 폐색, 폐쇄, 차단 incision n. 절개; 베기, 칼자국 내기

이론적으로는, 전립선암은 몸의 어느 곳으로든 퍼져나갈 수 있다. 그러나 실 제로는 전립선암 전이의 대부분은 림프절과 뼈에서 일어난다. 그와 같은 암세 포의 확산은 암세포가 전립선의 종양으로부터 떨어져 나오는 경우에 발생한 다. 암세포들은 림프계나 혈류를 통해 신체의 다른 부분으로 전해질 수 있다.

16 ②

첫 번째 문장의 주장에 대해 두 번째 문장에서 예를 들어 설명하는 구조의 글이다. 인체의 뼈의 이름을 암기해야 할 때, 두개골, 목뼈와 등뼈, 양팔의 뼈 등등으로 묶는 것은 부위별로 암기하는 것이라 할 수 있다. 이러한 방법을 가장 잘 나타낸 것은 ②가 된다. ①은 중요도를 평가하는 것이고, ③은 특징을 찾아내는 것이며, ④는 딱 들어맞는 경우를 생각해낸다는 것이므로 모두 정답으로 부적절하다.

skeleton n. 골격; 해골; 골자, 윤곽 efficient a. 능률적인; 효과적인 skull n. 두개골 memorize v. 암기하다, 기억하다 haphazardly ad. 우연히, 함부로, 되는 대로 assess v. (재산·수입 따위를) 평가하다, 사정하다 establish v. 확립하다, 설치하다, 설립하다 identify v. 확인하다, 인지하다; 동일시하다 feature n. 특징, 특색; 두드러진 점 figure out 계산하다; 이해하다; 생각해내다

일련의 사실들을 기억해야 할 때, 우선 먼저 그것들을 몇 개의 집단으로 묶어보도록 하여라. 인체의 골격을 이루는 뼈의 이름을 말해야 한다면, 그 이름들을 아무렇게나 암기하지 말고 먼저 두개골의 뼈들을 외우고, 다음엔 목과 등의 뼈, 그 다음 양팔의 뼈, 등등으로 해나가는 것이 더 효과적일 것이다.

17 ③

집주인들이 상호간의 계약을 맺는 것은 첫 번째 문장에 언급한 문제점을 미연에 방지하기 위해서일 것이다. 두 번째 문장의 existing views는 첫 번째 문장의 views from surrounding homes' front porches, back decks, bedroom windows, etc.를 가리키므로, 빈칸에도 두 번째 문장에 쓰인 동사 obstruct와 문맥상 유사한 의미를 가진 단어가 들어가야 할 것이다. 따라서 '덮어서 감추다'라는 의미의 ③이 정답이 된다.

property n. 재산; 소유물; 성질, 특성 touchy a. 화를 잘 내는, 과민한; 민감한 porch n. 현관, 입구 deck n. 갑판; 납작한 지붕 mutual a. 서로의; 공동의, 공통의 obstruct v. 막다, 차단하다; 방해하다 supplement v. 보충하다; 추가하다 antedate v. (날짜·시기 등이) ~보다 선행하다; 예상하다, 내다보다 obliterate v. 지우다, 말살하다; 흔적을 없애다 ornament v. 꾸미다, 장식하다

이웃이 새로 와서 주변 집들의 현관문, 뒤편의 지붕, 침실의 창문 등으로부터 전망을 완전히 덮어버리는 3층 집을 세워 올리려 하는 경우, 집주인들은 매우 예민해질 수 있다. 그래서 집주인들은 종종 기존의 전망을 방해하는 그 어떤 건축물도 짓지 못하도록 상호간에 계약을 맺기도 한다.

18 ②

또 다른 관리가 아주 '적절한 동의어'로 묘사했다고 했으므로, 결과적으로 빈칸에는 bellicose와 같은 맥락의 어구가 들어가야 함을 알 수 있다. bellicose가 '호전적인, 싸우기 좋아하는'이라는 뜻이므로, 싸움 또는 전쟁과 관련된 어구를 찾으면 된다.

aim v. 겨냥하다, ~을 향하다 territory n. 영토; 땅, 지역 bellicose a. 호전적인, 싸우기 좋아하는 rhetoric n. 수사법, 화려한 문체; 과장; 미사여구, 수사적 기교

synonym n. 동의어, 유의어 indication n. 지시; 암시, 표시; 징조 announcement n. 발표, 공고, 고지 tumescent a. 부어오른, 팽창한; 과장된 warmongering a. 전쟁 도발의 red-tape a. 절차에 얽매인, 관료적인, 형식주의적인 felicitous a. (말·표현이) 교묘한, 적절한

그것이 남한, 하와이, 미국령 괌을 겨냥한 미사일이었다고 북한이 발표했을 때, 미국 국방성은 그것을 '호전적인 수사(修辭)'로 묘사했다. 미국 방위성의 또 다른 관리는 '호전적인'의 아주 적절한 동의어를 사용해서 북한의 발표를 묘사했다. "우리는 현시점에서 그것이 전쟁 도발적인 수사라는 것 외에는 언급할 게 없습니다."

19 ③

첫 번째 문장에서 현재의 나쁜 상황에 대해 언급했으며, 두 번째 문장의 동사로 hope를 썼음에 유의한다. hope에는 바람직한 방향으로의 변화를 기대하는 의미가 내포되어 있으므로, 이 동사가 이끄는 that절의 내용과 주어진 글의 첫 번째 문장의 내용은 대조를 이룰 것이다. 첫 번째 문장에서 현재의 상황을 음흉하고 불성실한 금권주의로 규정하고 있는데, 미래 세대의 정치인들은 그렇지 않길 바랄 것이므로, 두 번째 빈칸에는 insidious and perfidious와 대조를 이루는 upright 또는 principled가 적절하다. 한편, without messing up its economy는 기대하고 있는 미래의 모습을 나타내고 있으므로, 현재 상황에 해당하는 첫 번째 빈칸에는 부정어 without을 삭제한 상황, 즉 messing up의 의미를 가지고 있는 단어가 들어가야 한다. 따라서 shambles 또는 straits가 적절하다. 상기 언급한 사항을 모두 만족시키는 ③이 정답이 된다.

insidious a. 교활한, 음험한; 잠행성의 perfidious a. 불성실한, 배반하는 plutocracy n. 금권정치, 금권주의 mess up 혼란시키다, 엉망으로 만들다 updraft n. 상승기류 versatile a. 재주가 많은; 융통성 있는, 다방면의 moiety n. (재산 따위의) 절반; 일부분; 몫 principled a. ~주의의; 원칙에 의거한; 도의에 의거한 shambles n. 도살장; 난장판; 무질서 상태 upright a. 강직한, 정직한 strait n. (pl.) 궁핍, 곤란 crooked a. 구부러진; 부정직한, 마음이 삐뚤어진

서구 민주국가들은 그야말로 음험하고 불성실한 금권주의 국가로 변해버렸으며, 그들의 경제는 혼란에 빠져있다. 우리는 미국과 유럽의 정직한 신세대 정치인들이 경제를 혼란에 빠뜨리지 않고 국가를 경영하는 방법을 모색하기를 바란다.

20 ④

첫 번째 빈칸에 들어갈 행위를 이어지는 문장들에서는 recalcitrantly acts against the captain or any of his officers와 disobedience로 표현하고 있다. 따라서 첫 번째 빈칸에는 이와 유사하거나 동일한 의미를 가진 Defiance 또는 Insubordination이 들어갈 수 있다. 한편, 빈칸 다음의 such as an illegal order or mentally ill officer는 선원에게 부당한 상황일 것이므로, 이는 곧 불복종 행위에 대해 정상 참작이 가능할 수 있는 상황일 것이다. 따라서 두 번째 빈칸에는 palliative 또는 extenuating이 가능하다. 상기 언급한 두 조건을 모두 만족시키는 ④가 정답이 된다.

mutiny n. (함선·군대 등에서의) 폭동, 반란 impose v. (의무·벌 따위를) 지우다, 과(課)하다 recalcitrantly ad. 반항하여, 반대하여 disobedience n. 불순종, 불복종 warrant v. 보증하다, 보장하다; 정당화하다 illegal a. 불법의, 위법의 defiance n. 도전; 저항; 반항 dilatory a. 더딘, 꾸물거리는; 지연하는, 늦은, 시간을 끄는 camouflage n. 위장, 변장; 기만. 속임 swarthy a. (피부 등이) 거무스레한, 가무잡잡한 cajolery n. 구슬림, 감언, 아첨 palliative a. 완화하는, 경감하는; 정상을 참작할 만한 insubordination n. 불순종, 반항 extenuating a. 죄를 가볍게 하는, 참작할 수 있는

항해중인 배 위에서 일어나는 불복종은 반란이라고 불린다. 선장이나 항해사 중 어느 누구에게라도 반항하는 행동을 하는 선원에게는 특별법에 의해 엄격한 처벌을 부과하고 있다. 그러나 선원은 그의 불순종이 위법적인 명령이나 정신병이 있는 항해사와 같은 경우처럼 정상을 참작할 수 있는 상황으로 인한 정당한 행위였음을 입증할 수는 있다.

21 ②

유로는 유럽의 화폐를 물리적으로 통합한 것(forced togetherness)이므로, 첫 번째 빈칸 이하에 언급된 여러 나라의 화폐는 유로의 출범과 함께 더 이상 사용하지 않게 된다. 그러므로 첫 번째 빈칸에는 각각 '~없이 지내다', '~와 단절하다'라는 의미를 만드는 dispensed와 broke up이 들어갈 수 있다. 한편, 희망에 반하는 현상이 발생하고 있다고 했으므로, 두 번째 빈칸에는 각각 '부담', '혼란'이라는 의미를 가진 millstone과 whirlpool이 가능하다. 두 조건을 모두 만족시키는 정답은 ②가 된다.

launch n. 진수; 발사; 개시, 시작 cleanse v. 깨끗이 하다, 제거하다 warring a. 서로 싸우는, 교전 중인 efficiently ad. 능률적으로, 효율적으로, 유효하게 peseta n. 페세타(스페인의 화폐) franc n. 프랑(프랑스, 벨기에, 스위스의 화폐) guilder n. 길더(네덜란드의 화폐) if anything 어느 쪽이냐 하면; 오히려 togetherness n. 통일; 연대감; 친목 revive v. 소생시키다, 되살아나게 하다 prejudice n. 편견, 선입관; 적대감 be besieged with 둘러싸이다, 공세를 받다 nostrum n. 만능약; (정치·사회 문제 해결의) 묘책, 묘안 dispense with ~를 필요 없게 하다, ~없이 지내다 millstone n. 맷돌; 무거운 짐, 부담 break up with ~와 관계를 끊다; (낡은 사고방식 등을) 버리다 gimmick n. 눈속임의 장치, 트릭 be infatuated with ~에 열중한, 홀린 whirlpool n. 소용돌이, 혼란, 소동

지난 1999년 유로화가 출범했을 때, 유럽이 페세타, 프랑, 길더, 그리고 독일 마르크와 같은 유서 깊은 통화를 없앤 만큼 효과적으로 그 적대적이었던 역사도 청산할 것이라는 기대가 높았다. 하지만 오히려 정반대의 현상이 발생하고 있다. 유로화는 많은 회원국들에게 무거운 짐이 되었으며, 강제적인 통일은 국가 간에 적대감을 되살아나게 하고 있다.

22 ①

첫 번째 빈칸에 들어갈 표현은 바로 뒤의 organism과 함께 식물을 지칭할 수 있어야 한다. 식물의 특징은 '한 곳에 머물러 있는 채 사는 것'이므로 stationary 또는 motionless가 올 수 있다. 한편, '마약을 사용하는 사람은 식물이 된다'라는 첫 문장의 내용을 참고하면, 결국 '식물이 다시 동물이 되어간다'라는 것은 마약을 하지 않게 된다는 것을 의미

한다고 볼 수 있다. 따라서 두 번째 빈칸에는 '마약을 끊는 것'과 연관된 표현이 필요함을 알 수 있다. '금단현상' 혹은 '마약사용의 중지'라는 의미의 withdrawal 또는 cold turkey가 적절하다. 상기 언급한 조건을 모두 만족시키는 정답은 ①이다.

junk n. 쓰레기, 폐물; 헤로인, 마약 turn A into B A를 B로 바꾸다, 되게 하다 organism n. 유기체, 생물 libido n. 성적인 충동, 리비도 replace v. 제자리에 놓다, 되돌리다; 대신하다 intense a. 격렬한, 심한, 맹렬한; 열정적인 discomfort n. 불쾌, 불안; 불편, 곤란 transition n. 변천, 변화; 과도기 stationary a. 움직이지 않는, 정지된; 변화하지 않는 withdrawal n. 철수, 취소; 철회; 금단현상 motionless a. 움직이지 않는, 정지한 fanaticism n. 광신, 열광, 열중 down-to-earth a. 실제적인, 현실적인; 철저한; 솔직한 cold turkey n. 갑작스런 약물 중단에 의한 신체적 불쾌감 botanical a. 식물의, 식물학의 quarantine n. 격리; 검역소; 고립화

마약은 그것을 사용하는 사람을 식물로 변하게 만든다. 식물은 고통을 느끼지 못하는데, 움직이지 않는 생물에게는 고통이 아무런 역할을 하지 못하기 때문이다. 인간이나 동물의 관점에서 볼 때, 식물은 성적 충동을 갖고 있지 않다. 마약은 성적 충동을 대신한다. 아마도 금단현상에서 생기는 강한 불쾌감은 식물이 동물이 되는 변화, 즉, 고통을 느끼지 못하고, 성욕도 없고, 시간도 없는 상태에서 성욕, 고통, 시간이 존재하는 상태로의 변화, 다시 말해 죽음에서 다시 생명이 되어 가는 변화를 말해주는 것이다.

23 ①

However 바로 뒤에 '좀 더 자세히 들여다보면'이라는 표현이 있는데, 이것은 However 앞에서 언급하고 있는 견해, 즉 첫 번째 문장의 think의 목적절의 내용이 '깊이 생각하지 않은' 것임을 의미하게 된다. 따라서 빈칸에는 looking more closely에 대해 반대 의미를 내포하고 있는 '근시안적인'이라는 의미의 ①이 들어가야 한다.

organization n. 조직, 단체; 기구, 체제 implementation n. 이행, 수행; 완성, 성취 on the surface 표면적으로, 얼핏 보기에는 over-budget a. 예산 초과의 follow suit 선례를 따르다 dimension n. 차원; 관점; 일면 myopic a. 근시의, 근시안적인 burlesque a. 익살부리는, 해학의, 웃기는 auspicious a. 길조의, 상서로운 polemic a. 논쟁의; 논쟁을 좋아하는

많은 조직의 리더들은 사업 관리자가 사업 실행에서의 성패(成敗)에 전적으로 책임이 있는 것으로 잘못 생각하고 있다. 표면적으로는, 그러한 근시안적인 견해가 맞는 것처럼 보일 지도 모른다. 많은 임무가 지연되고 예산을 초과한다면, 당연히 전체 사업이 선례를 따르게 될 것이기 때문이다. 하지만, 좀 더 자세히 들여다보면, 사업 관리는 사업 실행의 성공을 위해 반드시 필요한 여러 가지 것들 가운데 단지 한 측면에 지나지 않는다는 사실이 분명하게 드러난다.

24 ③

빈칸 뒤의 this ritual은 '아기가 태어났을 때, 주변 사람들과 재산을 함께 나누고 담배 연기를 하늘로 올려 보냈던 원시 의례'를 가리킨다. 오늘날의 경우에는 시가를 나누어준다고 했는데, 이것은 앞서 언급한 원시

의례 가운데, '무언가를 나누어주는 행위'와 '담배 연기를 하늘로 올려 보내는 행위'가 합쳐져 다른 형태로 나타난 것으로 볼 수 있다. 그러므로 빈칸에는 '변형, 변종'이라는 의미의 ③이 들어가는 것이 적절하다.

primitive a. 원시의, 초기의; 태고의 ceremony n. 의식, 식; 의례 blessed a. 신성한; 축복 받은, 행복한 community n. 공동 사회, 공동체; 지역 사회 avoid v. 피하다, 회피하다 envy n. 질투, 선망, 시기 drift v. 표류하다, 떠돌다 appeasement n. 진정, 완화; 달램 distribution n. 분배, 배급, 배포 celebrate v. 축하하다; 찬양하다, 찬미하다 ritual n. 의식, 제식 springboard n. 도약판; 새로운 출발점, (발전을) 촉진시키는 것 drawback n. 결점, 약점 variant n. 변체 (變體), 변형; 변종, 이형(異形) taboo n. 금기(禁忌), 금단, 꺼림

원시 의례에서 아기의 탄생으로 축복을 받은 사람은 동료와 신(神)들의 시기를 피하기 위해 그의 재산을 지역 주민과 함께 나누었다. 의기양양한 아버지의 담배 파이프에서 하늘로 날려 올라가는 연기는 천상의 신들을 달래는 역할을 하는 것이었다. 오늘날 아버지들이 아기의 탄생을 축하하기 위해 시가를 나누어주는 것은 이 의식이 현대에 변형되어 나타난 것으로 간주할 수 있을 것이다.

---

25 ①

어떤 단체에 대한 좋지 않은 편견에 대해 '그 단체 출신의 위인이 있다'라는 말로 대응하는 것은 잘못된 접근법이라는 내용에 관해 네 번째 문장까지 언급하고 있다. 마지막 문장은 해결책에 해당한다. 위인과 대비되는 개념인 악당과 바보를 가질 수 있는 권리를 언급하는 것을 보면, '단체에 위인이 있느냐 악당이 있느냐는 그다지 중요하지 않으며, 그가 속한 단체에 대한 좋지 않은 편견, 혹은 비난을 없애는 것이 중요하다'라는 것, 즉 전체가 매도당하지 않는 것이 중요함을 알 수 있다. 그러므로 정답은 ①이 되며, 첫 문장의 with prejudice against a group에 대해 문맥상의 반대되는 의미의 표현을 찾는 문제라 할 수 있다.

prejudice n. 선입견, 편견 Jew n. 유대인, 유대교도 come up with ~을 제안하다, 생각해내다 defender n. 방어자, 옹호자 approach n. 접근; 접근법, 해결방법 minority n. 소수파, 소수당; 소수자의 무리 genius n. 천재; 비상한 재주 scoundrel n. 악당, 깡패 condemn v. 비난하다, 나무라다 mischief n. 해악; 악영향, 손해 bias n. 선입관, 편견

누군가가 가톨릭교도, 유대인, 이탈리아인, 흑인 집단과 같은 어떤 단체들에 대해 편견을 가지고 말할 때마다, 다른 누군가는 흔히 "아인슈타인(Einstein)을 보라!" "카버(Carver)를 보라!" "토스카니니(Toscanini)를 보라!" 등의 통상적인 변호의 말을 들고 나온다. 이들 옹호자들의 의도는 좋다. 그러나 그들의 접근 방식은 잘못된 것이다. 그것은 나쁘다고 말할 수 있을 정도다. 소수 집단이 원하는 것은 그들 중에 천재들을 가질 권리가 아니라, 바보와 악당들이 있지만 집단 전체가 비난받지 않을 권리이다.

TEST 23

01 ③	02 ②	03 ④	04 ②	05 ③	06 ①	07 ①	08 ④	09 ①	10 ①
11 ④	12 ③	13 ①	14 ①	15 ①	16 ②	17 ①	18 ②	19 ③	20 ④
21 ③	22 ③	23 ③	24 ④	25 ④					

01 ③

Instead of의 목적어를 이루는 표현에서 핵심이 되는 것은 directly이다. 그런데 Instead of는 '~대신에'라는 의미이므로, 주절의 빈칸에는 directly와 반대되는 의미를 가진 단어가 들어가는 것이 적절하다. 따라서 '생각을 솔직하게 말하지 않는'이라는 뜻의 ③이 정답으로 가장 적절하다.

dislike v. 싫어하다, 미워하다 subject n. 주제, 제목, 화제; 과목 pithy a. (표현 등이) 힘찬, 함축성 있는; 간결한 terse a. (문체·표현 따위가) 간결한, 간명한 mealy-mouthed a. (자신의 생각을) 솔직하게 말하지 않는 compendious a. 간결한, 간명한

자신이 좋아하지 않았던 것에 대해 직접적으로 질(Jill)에게 말하는 대신, 잭(Jack)은 솔직하지 않은 말을 몇 마디 던지고는 화제를 바꾸려 했다.

02 ②

빈칸에 들어갈 표현의 성격을 such as 이하에서 부연하여 진술하고 있는 구조이다. 따라서 빈칸에는 '일상회화에서 사용한다'라는 의미를 가진 colloquial이 들어가는 것이 가장 적절하다. 한편, '공식적인 글에 적절하지 않다'라는 내용에 초점을 맞추면, 빈칸에는 formal에 대해 대조적인 의미를 가진 단어가 들어가야 함을 알 수 있다.

formal a. 형식에 맞는; 공식의; 의례상의, 예식의 present v. 나타내다; 제출하다, 건네다 spoil v. 망쳐놓다, 손상시키다 recondite a. 심원한, 알기 어려운, 난해한 colloquial a. 구어체의, 회화체의; 일상회화의 blasphemous a. 불경한, 모독적인 pusillanimous a. 무기력한, 소심한, 겁 많은

당신이 대개 일상회화에서 쓰는 것과 같은 구어체 표현을 공식적인 논문에서 사용하면 얻고자 하는 결과를 망치게 된다.

03 ④

because절에서는 판사가 엄한 판결을 내린 까닭을 설명해야 하는데, 범죄자가 자신의 죄에 대해 반성이나 가책을 느끼지 않은 것이 그 이유로 가장 타당하다.

sentence v. 판결을 내리다 heinous a. 가증스런; 흉악한, 악질의 sedition n. 난동, 선동; 치안방해 tithe n. 십일조; 작은 부분 iniquity n. 부정, 불법; 죄악 compunction n. 양심의 가책, 후회; 죄책감

판사는 특히 엄한 판결을 내렸는데, 그 범죄자가 자신의 저지른 흉악한 범죄에 대해 전혀 죄책감을 느끼는 기색을 보이지 않았다고 생각했기 때문이다.

04 ②

접속사 but 전후의 내용이 대조를 이루어야 한다. but 이하에 '도덕적인 면모'를 말해주는 내용이 있으므로, but 앞에서는 이것과 상반되는 모습을 나타내야 한다. 따라서 '속이다'라는 의미를 가진 ②가 빈칸에 오는 것이 가장 적절하다.

as it were 말하자면, 이를테면 eminently ad. 뛰어나게; 현저하게 ethical a. 도덕상의; 윤리적인 mollycoddle v. 과잉보호하다, 온갖 응석을 다 받아 주다 cozen v. 속이다, 속여 빼앗다 betroth v. 약혼하다, 약혼시키다 endorse v. 배서하다; 승인하다; 찬성하다

말하자면, 그는 시시한 카드 게임에서는 친구를 속이려 들겠지만, 사업적 거래에서는 대단히 도덕적인 부류의 사람이었다.

05 ③

빈칸에 들어갈 단어를 두 번째 문장에서 설명하고 있다. '6개월 만에 20년이 늙어버린 것 같았다'라는 내용에서 핵심이 되는 표현은 'aged'이므로, 이 의미를 자체에 내포하고 있는 단어가 빈칸에 들어가야 한다. 따라서 ③이 정답이 된다.

unprepared a. 준비가 없는; 준비가 되어 있지 않은 zephyr n. 서풍; 솔솔 부는 바람 canard n. 허위보도, 와전 decrepitude n. 노쇠, 노후 muddle n. 혼란, 난잡; 어리둥절함

내가 알게 된 옛 친구의 노쇠한 상태는 전혀 예상 밖이었다. 내가 보기에, 그는 6개월 만에 20년이 늙어버린 것처럼 보였다.

06 ①

첫 문장에서 '인습타파주의자인 잡스가 진부한 사고방식을 배격한다'라고 했다. 두 번째 문장의 빈칸 뒤에 conventional ideas와 반대되는 의미의 new experiences가 주어져 있으므로, 빈칸에는 attack and overthrow에 대해 반대 의미를 가지는 단어가 필요하다. 따라서 '좋아한다'라는 의미의 표현을 만드는 ①이 적절하다.

iconoclast n. 우상 파괴자, 인습 타파주의자 aggressively ad. 공격적으로; 적극적으로, 진취적으로 overthrow v. (정부·제도 등을) 뒤엎다, 전복시키다; 폐지하다 conventional a. 전통적인; 인습적인; 진부한 affinity n. 좋아함, 서로 잘 맞음; 유사, 친근성 contretemps n. 뜻하지 않는 불행, 뜻하지 않은 사고 rebuff n. 거절, 퇴짜; 좌절 drudgery n. 고된 일, 단조롭고 고된 일

잡스(Jobs)는 진부한 사고방식을 적극적으로 찾아서 공격하고 전복시키는 전형적인 인습타파주의자이다. 그리고 인습타파주의자들, 특히 성공한 사람들은 새로운 경험을 좋아한다.

07 ①

indoor waste disposal과 indoor plumbing이 글 속에서 의미하는 바는 사실상 같다. 두 번째 문장에서 '16세기가 되어서야 실내 화장실이 실제로 만들어졌음'을 이야기하고 있으므로, 이러한 것을 만들려는 시도로서 그 이전에 행해졌던 것은 모두 실패했다고 할 수 있다. 그러므로 빈칸에는 '실패한'이라는 의미의 ①이 들어가는 것이 적절하다.

disposal n. 처분, 처리; 양도, 매각 inspired a. 영감을 받은, 영감에 의한; 멋진 water closet 수세식 화장실 indoor plumbing 실내화장실 aborted a. 유산한; 미발달의; 실패한 medieval a. 중세의; 중고의 impeccable a. 결함이 없는, 완벽한; 죄를 범하지 않은 trenchant a. 통렬한, 신랄한; 명쾌한, 설득력 있는

배설물을 실내에서 처리하려는 시도가 기원전 2,500년에도 실패한 적이 있음이 발견되었다. 존 해링턴(John Harrington)경이 16세기에 획기적인 수세식 화장실 설계를 만들어내고 나서야 실내 화장실을 실행할 수 있는 현실이 되었다.

08 ④

빈칸 뒤에 confusion이라는 부정적인 의미의 표현이 있음에 유의하면, 빈칸에는 첫 문장과 세 번째 문장에서 강조하고 있는 simple, clear, direct와 반대되는 의미를 내포하고 있는 단어가 들어가야 함을 알 수 있다. 그러므로 '에둘러서 하는 표현'이라는 의미의 ④가 정답이 된다.

term n. 기간, 임기; 조건; 용어 confusion n. 혼동; 혼란; 당황 condolence n. 애도; 조사(弔辭) obituary n. 사망기사, 사망광고 euphony n. 기분 좋은 소리, 기분 좋은 음조 euphemism n. 완곡어법, 완곡어구

아이들이 이해할 수 있는 꾸밈없는 말로 죽음을 설명하는 것이 그들이 대처하도록 도와주는 데 매우 중요하다. 완곡하게 표현하는 것은 혼동을 더 할 뿐이다. 설명할 때엔 분명하고 직접적으로 해야 한다.

09 ①

inasmuch as가 이유의 절을 이끌고 있음에 유의하면, 선정적 보도로 유명한 언론의 제안에 어떤 태도를 보였겠는가를 생각하면 된다. '선정적인 보도'가 부정적인 개념이므로 그 제안에 대해 호의적인 입장을 보이지 않았을 가능성이 크다고 할 수 있는데, 빈칸 앞에 부정어 not이 있으므로, '흔쾌히 받아들인다'라는 의미를 가진 ①이 들어가야 한다.

proposal n. 신청; 제안; 제의, 건의 inasmuch as ~이므로, ~인 까닭에 sensationalization n. 선정적으로 표현함 quality n. 질, 품질, 특성; 자질 amenable a. 순종하는, 쾌히 받아들이는 garish a. 야한, 화려한 dire a. 무서운; 비참한 venial a. (죄나 과실 따위가) 용서할 수 있는, 가벼운, 경미한

흥미롭게도, 콜롬비아 대학은 퓰리처(Pulitzer)의 제안을 즉각적으로 흔쾌히 받아들이진 않았는데, 왜냐하면 퓰리처의 신문들은 언론의 질적인 측면보다는 선정적 보도로 더 잘 알려져 있었기 때문이다.

10 ①

첫 문장은 오늘날의 출판업자들이 과거에 비해 도덕적으로 타락했음을 수사 의문문의 형식을 통해 표현하고 있다. 따라서 빈칸에는 부정적인 의미의 단어가 들어가야 하겠는데, 타락한 사회를 출판물이 반영하고 있는 것이 아니라면, 출판물 자체가 타락한 것이라 할 수 있으므로, 빈칸에는 앞에 쓰인 명사 decline과 유사한 의미를 가진 단어인 ①이 들어가는 것이 가장 적절하다.

moral a. 도덕의, 윤리의 standard n. 표준, 기준; 모범 garbage n. 쓰레기, 폐기물; 잡동사니 reflect v. 반사하다; 반영하다, 나타내다 decline n. 쇠퇴; 퇴보; 타락 decadence n. 타락; 퇴폐 connivance n. 묵과, 간과; 묵인 deference n. 복종, 존경, 경의 ennui n. 권태, 지루함

출판업자들이 윤리적 기준을 가지고 있던 때에 비해 지금은 무슨 일이 일어난 것일까? 오늘날 그들이 인쇄해내는 쓰레기는 사회적 가치의 쇠퇴를 반영하는 것일까 아니면 그것은 그들 스스로 만들어 낸 타락인 것일까?

11 ④

첫 문장의 dead set on은 '~에 굳게 마음을 먹은, 굳게 결심한'이라는 의미이다. 빈칸이 '결심'이란 의미의 determination을 수식하고 있으므로, 이것이 가진 의미를 보다 강화하는 형용사가 들어가면, dead set on과 완전히 같은 의미를 가지게 된다. '변경할 수 없는, 멈출 수 없는'이라는 의미의 ④가 자연스럽게 호응한다.

dead set on ~에 전력투구하는, ~에 굳게 마음을 먹은 determination n. 결심, 결의; 결정 naval a. 해군의; 군함의 willingly ad. 기꺼이, 자진해서 navigation n. 운항, 항해; 항해술 partially ad. 부분적으로; 편파적으로 finance v. 자금을 공급하다; 융자하다 impecunious a. 돈이 없는, 무일푼의 intemperate a. 무절제한, 과도한; 난폭한 irresolute a. 결단력이 없는, 우유부단한 inexorable a. 멈출 수 없는, 변경할 수 없는; 무정한, 냉혹한

진아(Jin-ah)는 자신이 직접 손으로 만든 보트를 타고 태평양을 횡단하리라고 굳게 마음먹고 있다. 그녀의 굳은 결심은 한 해군 장교의 도움을 얻어냈는데, 그는 그녀에게 기꺼이 항해술을 가르쳐 주었고 자금을 일부 지원해 주었다.

12 ③

두 번째 문장에서 '생긴 지 얼마 되지 않은' 작은 회사라고 했으므로, 첫 번째 빈칸에는 upstart와 같은 의미를 가진 newborn 또는 nascent가 들어갈 수 있다. 한편, 시골지역은 이 철도회사가 서비스를 제공하는 장소, 곧 영업활동을 하는 곳이라 할 수 있으므로, 두 번째 빈칸에는 realm, niche, sphere가 가능하다. 상기 두 조건을 모두 만족시키는 정답은 ③이다.

rural a. 시골의, 지방의; 촌스러운 exceptionally ad. 예외적으로, 특별히, 대단히 upstart a. 벼락출세한, 건방진; 최근에 나타난 newborn a. 갓 태어난; 신생의 residue n. 나머지, 찌꺼기 conglomerate a. 밀집하여 뭉친; 복합적인 realm n. 왕국, 국토; 영역, 범위 nascent a. 발생하고 있는; 초기의 niche n. 활동 범위, (특정) 분야, 영역 old-line a. 보수적인; 유서 깊은, 전통 있는 sphere n. 영역, 범위

드림 레일(Dream Rail)은 대형 철도회사들이 몇 가지 이유로 오래 전에 운행을 포기했던 시골지역을 영업 무대로 하고 있는 신생 철도회사이다. 드림 레일의 주식은 갓 생긴 작은 회사 치고는 대단히 좋은 결과를 내고 있다.

13 ①

빈칸의 전후에 '정직하지 않은' 행위들에 해당하는 단어들이 나열되어 있으므로, 빈칸에는 hoaxes와 forgeries와 유사한 속성 혹은 의미를 가진 단어가 들어가야 한다. 따라서 '거짓맹세, 위증'이라는 의미의 ①이 가장 적절하다.

confess v. 고백하다, 자백하다; 실토하다 proclaim v. 선언하다, 포고하다, 공포하다 testament n. 유언, 유언장; 계약; (사실·정당성 등에 대한) 입증, 증거 deceit n. 속임, 사기; 허위 revenge n. 보복, 복수, 앙갚음 tempting a. 유혹하는; 구미가 당기는, 매혹적인 elaborate a. 공들인, 정교한 hoax n. 사람을 속이기, 짓궂은 장난, 날조 forgery n. 위조, 위조죄 enormous a. 거대한, 막대한 ripple effect 파급효과, 연쇄작용 perjury n. 거짓맹세, 위증; 위증죄 profession n. 고백, 선언 augury n. 점복(占卜), 점; 전조, 조짐 oblation n. 봉헌, 봉납; 공물

어린 워싱턴(Washington)은 "결코 거짓말을 할 수는 없습니다"라고 선언함으로써 체리 나무를 자신이 베어 쓰러뜨렸음을 고백했다. 그 이야기는 미국인들이 얼마나 정직을 중요시하는가를 보여주는 증거라 할 수 있다. 그러나 많은 사람들에 있어, 허위가 돈, 명예, 복수, 혹은 권력을 좌우하며, 이러한 것들은 사람의 마음을 대단히 끄는 것으로 드러난다. 역사에서, 이것은 종종 엄청난 파급효과를 가져온 정교한 날조, 위증, 위조 등을 초래했다.

14 ①

빈칸이 들어 있는 문장의 주어는 앞 문장에서 언급한 샌디 프랭크 엔터테인먼트사(社)다. 비록 대단히 인기 있는 만화라 하더라도, 자극적인 장면이나 내용이 시청자에게 적절하지 않다고 생각했다면 그런 장면이 있는 에피소드는 삭제하고 방영하려 했을 것이다. 따라서 빈칸에는 ①이 들어가야 한다.

premiere v. (영화 등을) 처음으로 공개하다 feature v. ~의 특징을 이루다, 특색 짓다 graphic a. 사실적인, 생생한 profanity n. 신성을 더럽힘, 모독 villain n. 악인, 악한; 악역 deem v. 생각하다, 간주하다 domestic a. 가정의; 국내의, 자국의 bowdlerize v. (저작물의) 불온한 문구를 삭제하다 anneal v. (강철 등을) 달구어 식히다; 단련하다 impugn v. 비난하다, 공격하다, 반박하다 annex v. 부가하다, 추가하다; 합병하다

1972년에 『독수리 5형제(Science Ninja Team Gatchaman)』가 일본 TV에 첫선을 보였다. 사실적인 폭력장면, 다방면에 걸친 신성모독 행위, 성전환을 한 악한 등을 특징으로 하는 그 작품은 당시에 가장 인기 있는 만화 시리즈 가운데 하나였다. 샌디 프랭크(Sandy Frank) 엔터테인먼트 사(社)에서 1978년에 그 시리즈를 입수했으나, 자국 시청자가 보기에는 지나치게 사실적이고 폭력적이라고 생각했다. 그래서 그들은 일부 에피소드는 완전히 삭제했다.

15 ①

첫 번째 문장이 주제문이며, 나머지 문장들은 모두 첫 문장의 진술에 대한 예시에 해당한다. 첫 문장의 내용을 두 번째 문장에 대입하면, 다사다난했던 청교도 혁명의 기간은 밀턴에게 작가로서의 영감을 자극하기 보다는 오히려 피폐시키는 역할을 했을 것임을 알 수 있다. 그러므로 빈칸에는 '상상력이 부족한'이라는 의미의 ①이 적절하다.

eventful a. 사건 많은, 파란 많은 exhaust v. 고갈시키다, 다 써 버리다; 지치게 하다 stimulate v. 자극하다, 활발하게 하다, 북돋우다 atmosphere n. 분위기, 주위의 상황 legitimate a. 합법적인, 정당한; 합리적인, 이치에 닿는 diplomatic a. 외교의, 외교관계의 sterile a. 메마른, 불모의; 흉작의, 불임의; 상상력이 부족한 skittish a. 겁이 많은; 활발한; 변덕스러운 fecund a. 다산의; 비옥한; 상상력이 풍부한; 풍성한 muggy a. 무더운, 후텁지근한

다사다난한 삶은 자극하기보다는 피폐하게 하는 역할을 한다. 1640년에 매우 전도유망한 시인이었던 밀턴(Milton)은 매우 많은 사건이 발생했던 청교도 혁명의 환경에서 상상력이 부족한 20년을 보냈다. 첼리니(Cellini)는 흥미진진한 생활로 인해 그가 될 수 있었던 위대한 화가가 되지 못했다. 마키아벨리(Machiavelli)가 외교 관련 일을 계속 할 수 있었더라면 그가 과연 위대한 책들을 저술할 수 있었을 지를 의심하는 것도 당연하다.

16 ②

마지막 문장에서 status as a convicted criminal과 civil abilities가 대비를 이루고 있다. 범죄인 전력을 가지고서는 제대로 된 시민으로서의

자격을 가질 수 없고, 시민으로서의 자격을 되찾기 위해서는 범죄인 전력이 없어야 하겠는데, restore가 무언가를 더하여 주는 개념이므로, 빈칸에는 '무언가를 덜거나 없애주는 개념의 동사'가 필요하다. 따라서 '면제하다, 용서하다'라는 의미의 ②가 정답으로 적절하다.

commute v. 교환하다, 변환하다; (벌, 의무를) 감형하다, 경감하다 sentence n. 판결, 선고; 형벌 pardon n. 용서, 허용; 특사(特赦), 사면 grant v. 주다, 부여하다; 허가하다 status n. 상태, 지위, 자격; 신분 convicted a. 유죄선고를 받은 criminal n. 범인, 범죄자 restore v. 되찾다; 복구하다, 복원하다 civil a. 시민의; 문명의 upbraid v. 신랄하게 비판하다 absolve v. 용서하다; 면제하다; (의무 등을) 해제하다 stigmatize v. 오명을 씌우다, 낙인찍다; 비난하다 capsize v. 뒤집히다, 전복시키다

감형은 형벌을 줄여주는 행위이다. 대통령은 복역을 시작하기도 전에 형벌을 줄일 수 있는 권한을 가지고 있다. 일반사면 또한 형벌을 줄여줄 수 있다. 그러나 사면은 형(刑)을 복역한 후에도 매우 흔하게 주어진다. 그리고 감형과는 달리, 사면은 유죄판결을 받은 범죄인이라는 신분을 면하게 하여 시민으로서의 자격을 회복시켜 줄 수도 있다.

17 ①

고대 그리스의 신과 영웅에 대한 전설이 오늘날에도 영향을 미치고 있다고 설명하며, 고대 그리스 신화에 영향을 받은 슈퍼히어로의 예를 마지막에 들고 있으므로, 이런 만화책에 등장하는 슈퍼히어로가 그리스 신화에 영향을 받았다고 한 ①이 빈칸에 적절하다.

pagan a. 이교(도)의; 우상 숭배의 peninsula n. 반도 reference n. 참조, 참고 oblique a. 간접의, 에두른, 완곡한 stamp n. 특징, 흔적 impose v. 부과하다; 강요하다, 강제하다 archetype n. 원형(原型) divine a. 신성한; 신성의 moral a. 도덕의, 윤리의

고대 그리스인들의 이교도 종교가 더 이상 에게해 반도의 국가 신앙은 아니지만, 그리스의 신과 영웅의 전설에 대한 내용은 우리 문화에 계속해서 영향을 미치고 있다. '판도라의 상자', '하피(얼굴과 몸은 여자 모양이며 새의 날개와 발톱을 가진 추악하고 탐욕스러운 괴물)', '헤라클레스(초인적인)'는 고대 신화와 관련되어 오늘날에도 많이 사용되는 표현 중 하나이다. 그리스의 영향은 또한 더 간접적인 방식으로 발견될 수 있다. 예를 들면, 수많은 해설자들은 현대 만화책에 등장하는 슈퍼히어로들이 그리스 신화의 특징을 지니고 있음을 발견했다.

18 ②

두 번째 문장에서 앞 문장의 내용 즉, 특수부대원의 신원을 공개한 것을 비난하고 있으므로, 첫 번째 빈칸에는 이와 같은 행동을 '인기에 영합하는 것' 혹은 '요란스럽게 떠벌리는 것'으로 규정하게 하는 grand-standing 또는 ballyhooing이 가능하다. 한편, 두 번째 빈칸에 들어갈 표현은 명사 slogan을 함께 수식하고 있는 관계사절과 의미가 자연스럽게 통해야 한다. dated 또는 trite가 '매우 많이 들어왔다'라는 표현과 자연스럽게 호응할 수 있다. 상기 언급한 조건을 모두 만족시키는 정답은 ②가 된다.

detail n. 세부; 상세; 세부 묘사 raid n. 급습, 습격 release v. 방출하다, 해방하다; 개봉하다, 발표하다 identify v. 확인하다; 판정하다; 동일시하다 retaliation n. 보복, 앙갚음 hush-hush v. 쉬쉬하다, 극비로 하다 foolproof a. 고장이 없는; 실패 없는, 절대 확실한 grand-stand v. 인기를 노리는 연기를 하다 dated a. 시대에 뒤떨어진, 구식의 ballyhoo v. 요란스럽게 선전하다, 떠벌리다 browbeaten a. 겁먹은, 주눅이 든 dillydally v. 빈둥거리며 지내다, 꾸물거리다 trite a. 진부한, 케케묵은

우리 지도자들과 언론매체는 오사마 빈 라덴(Osama bin Laden)에 대한 기습공격에 관해 점점 더 많은 세부사항을 공개함으로써, 그의 죽음에 대해 대중들의 인기에 영합하고 있다. 왜 특수부대 씰(Seal) 6팀의 신원을 공개하여, 테러리스트들이 팀원들과 그 가족들을 찾아내어 보복할 수 있도록 하고 있는가? 우리는 지금 전쟁 중에 있다. "헤픈 입이 배를 가라앉힌다"라는 말은 우리가 수도 없이 들어 온 진부한 표현이기도 하지만 우리가 다시 배워야 할 교훈이기도 하다.

19 ③

두 번째 문장의 They는 첫 문장에 언급한 세 국가를 가리키는데, 이들이 간섭이라는 개념 자체에 반대해왔다고 했으므로, 불간섭 원칙은 이들 국가에는 대외정책의 기준이나 지침과 같은 것이라 할 수 있다. 그러므로 첫 번째 빈칸에는 bedrock 또는 touchstone이 가능하다. 한편, 민간인 보호나 독재자 축출과 같은 명분이 있더라도 국제사회가 간섭하는 것을 반대한다고 했는데, 이는 이들 국가에게는 인도주의적인 고려사항이 주권 수호를 위한 불간섭에 비해 '덜 중요하기' 때문일 것이다. 따라서 두 번째 빈칸에는 '부차적인'이라는 의미의 auxiliary 또는 '하위의'라는 의미의 subordinate가 가능하다. 상기 두 조건을 모두 만족시키는 것은 ③이다.

nonintervention n. 불간섭, 불개입, 방임 multilateral a. 다변(多邊)의, 다각적인 explicitly ad. 뚜렷이, 명백히; 노골적으로 oppose v. 반대하다, 대항하다; 적대하다 notion n. 관념, 개념; 의견, 생각 civilian n. 민간인 remove v. 옮기다; 제거하다, 없애다 dictator n. 독재자, 절대 권력자 humanitarian a. 인도주의의, 박애주의의 sovereignty n. 주권; 통치권 moniker n. 별명, 별칭 auxiliary a. 보조적인; 예비의 crux n. 핵심; 난제 preferable a. 차라리 나은, 바람직한 bedrock n. 기초, 기본원리 subordinate a. 종속적인, 하위의 touchstone n. 표준, 기준 tantamount a. 동등한, 같은, 상당한

브라질, 인도, 남아프리카공화국의 경우, 불간섭 원칙이 모든 다자간 대외정책의 기초가 되고 있다. 그 국가들은 민간인 보호와 독재자 제거를 위해 국제 사회가 간섭한다는 개념 자체를 명백하게 반대해왔는데, 왜냐하면 (그들에게는) 인도주의적 고려 사항들이 외국의 간섭으로부터 국가의 주권을 지키는 것보다 하위의 것이기 때문이다.

20 ④

세 번째 문장의 what they are saying은 두 번째 문장에 나온 '객관적 진실은 없고 주관적인 생각만 있다'는 말이고 이것은 진실에 대한 상대주의이며, 이것의 false한 면, 즉 자기모순성을 네 번째 문장의 세미콜론 이하에서 보여준다. 따라서 빈칸에는 ④가 적절하다.

state of affairs 사물이나 일의 상태, 사태 assertion n. 단언, 주장 presume v. 추정하다, 가정하다 absolutism n. 절대주의 self- fulfilling a. 자기성취적인 relativism n. 상대주의 self- contradictory a. 자기모순적인

진실은 사실인 것이나 세상에서 사물이나 일의 실제 상태인 것이다. 일부 사람들은 객관적인 진실은 없고 주관적인 믿음(생각)만이 있을 뿐이라고 말한다. 그러나 역설적이게도, 이 주장은 그들이 하고 있는 말이 거짓이라고 추정한다. 그들은 그들의 주장이 실제로 객관적으로 진실이라고, 즉 객관적인 진실은 없다는 것이 객관적으로 진실이라고 주장하고 있는 것이다. 진실에 대한 상대주의는 자기 모순적이다.

---

21   ③

첫 번째 빈칸은 증오 범죄의 양상을 설명하는 부분에 속해 있는데, 범위를 넓게 보자면, 범죄의 원인이 될 수 있는 tantrums와 grudge 모두 빈칸에 들어갈 수 있다. 한편, 두 번째 빈칸 뒤에 위치한 대명사 they는 a string of losers with a common goal to grab headlines를 가리키는데, 바로 앞 문장에서 이들이 원하는 것은 '전 세계가 멈춰 서서 자신들에게 주목하는 것'이라 했으므로, 빈칸에는 take notice of의 의미를 내포하고 있는 단어가 들어가야 한다. attention이 이에 부합하며, 따라서 정답은 ③이 된다.

burst n. 돌발, 격발; 폭발 emerging a. 최근 생겨난 specific a. 특유한; 일정한; 상세한, 구체적인 frenzied a. 열광한, 격앙한, 광적인 stage v. (정치 운동 등을) 계획하다, 행하다 take notice of ~을 알아차리다, 주의하다, 주목하다 oblige v. 의무적으로 ~하게 하다; 은혜를 베풀다 crave v. 열망하다, 갈망하다 habiliment n. 옷, 복장 nuisance n. 폐, 성가심, 귀찮음; 성가신 것 qualm n. 양심의 가책; 불안, 염려 curiosity n. 호기심; 골동품 tantrum n. 역정, 울화 attention n. 주의, 주목, 관심 grudge n. 적의, 악의; 원한, 유감 remission n. (죄의) 용서, 사면; 면제

매우 눈에 띄는 증오 범죄가 최근에 크게 늘어난 가운데, 새로 생겨난 양상은 특정한 반감에 대한 것보다는 헤드라인 장식이라는 공통된 목표를 가진 패배자들이 자행하는 광적인 울화 표출과 관련이 있는 것처럼 보인다. 그들이 이런 일을 자행하는 것은 영광의 순간, 즉 세계가 멈춰 서서 자신들을 주목하고 있다는 느낌을 갖기 위해서이다. 사회는 제정신이 아닌 사람들에게 그들이 갈망하는 관심을 줄 수밖에 없는 것처럼 보인다.

---

22   ③

빈칸 이하는 빈칸에 들어갈 표현과 동격 혹은 부연설명의 관계에 있다. 그러므로 빈칸에는 communication when words fail or are wholly inadequate의 의미를 포함하고 있는 표현이 들어가야 하며, 이러한 조건에 가장 부합하는 것은 ③이다.

expanse n. 광활한 공간; 넓은 장소 marble n. 대리석 ethereal a. 천상의; 아주 우아한, 영묘한 aesthetic n. 미학; 미적인 특징 reign v. 지배하다; 영향력을 행사하다 inadequate a. 부적당한; 불충분한 substantialize v. 실체화하다; 실현하다, 실제로 나타내다 flaunt v. 자랑하다, 과시하다 ineffable a. 말로 나타낼 수 없는, 이루 말할 수 없는 assuage v. 누그러뜨리다, 진정시키다, 완화시키다 discord n. 불화, 불일치; 내분, 알력

반 고흐(Van Gogh)의 『별이 빛나는 밤(The Starry Night)』의 넓은 바다처럼 흐르는 하늘, 로댕(Rodin)의 섬세한 손길에 의해 대리석으로 조각되어 탄생된 인간상, 드가(Degas)의 발레리나가 보여주는 우아한 모습은 모두 아름다움이 모든 것을 지배하는 세계에서 감정과 본질을 전달한다. 예술은 말로 표현할 수 없는 것을 표현하기 위한 인간의 수단, 즉 말로써는 나타낼 수 없거나 완전히 부적절 할 때 의사소통하는 수단으로서의 역할을 오랫동안 해왔다.

---

23   ③

빈칸 앞의 주어 These tours에 대해 첫 번째 문장에서 eerie, scary 등의 형용사를 이용해 설명하고 있다. 또한 이 여행은 공동묘지와 유령이 출몰하는 건물을 돌아다니는 테마의 여행이므로, 어린이들에게는 '무서운' 것일 수 있을 것이다. 그러므로 정답은 ③이 되며, eerie, scary, spine-chilling 등의 동의어를 찾는 문제로 볼 수 있다.

eerie a. 섬뜩한, 무시무시한; 기괴한 downright ad. 철저히, 완전히 scary a. 무서운, 두려운 pop up 별안간 나타나다 bewitching a. 매혹시키는, 황홀하게 하는 cemetery n. 묘지, 공동묘지 haunted a. 유령이 출몰하는; 고뇌에 시달린 spine-chilling a. 등골이 오싹해지는 shadowy a. 어두운; 아련한; 어렴풋한 creepy a. 기어 다니는, 느릿느릿 움직이는; 오싹한 benighted a. 밤이 된, 길이 저문; 어리석은, (문화·시대에) 뒤진; 미개한 invidious a. 비위에 거슬리는, 불쾌한; 불공평한 spooky a. 유령 같은; 유령이 나올 것 같은, 무시무시한 restive a. 고집 센, 다루기 힘든, 난폭한

뉴올리언스에서는 신비하고, 섬뜩하고, 대단히 무서운 테마의 여행이 인기가 있으며, 넋을 빼놓는 오래된 공동묘지와 유령이 출몰하는 건물을 관광객들이 돌아볼 수 있게 하는 여행사들이 많이 생겨났다. 이러한 여행의 경우, 어린 아이들에게는 매우 무시무시한 것일 수도 있지만, 뉴올리언스의 역사에 관한 이야기를 들으면서 어두운 거리와 건물 그리고 오싹한 공동묘지를 돌아다닐 수 있는 등골이 오싹해지는 기회를 매우 좋아하는 어른들도 있다.

---

24   ④

첫 번째 문장과 두 번째 문장에서 각각 thesis와 belief의 동격절을 이끄는 that절의 내용을 통해 판단해야 한다. 두 개의 that절 '모두 사람의 정신은 태어날 때에는 백지상태임'을 말하고 있으므로, 빈칸에는 '백지상태의 무구한 마음'이라는 의미의 ④가 들어가는 것이 적절하다. without built-in mental content 혹은 blank or empty 등의 의미를 내포하고 있는 표현을 고르는 문제로 볼 수 있다.

epistemological a. 인식론의, 인식론상의 thesis n. 논제, 제목, 주제; 명제 content n. 내용; 목차, 목록 perception n. 지각, 지각작용; 인식 phrase n. 관용구; 표현 blank a. 백지의; 텅 빈 magnum opus (문학·예술 따위의) 대작, 걸작; (개인의) 주요 작품 non sequitur 불합리한 추론, 그릇된 결론 terra incognita 미지의 나라, 미개척 영역 tabula rasa (어떤 일의 진행에 대해) 정해진 의견이 없는 상태; (인간이 태어날 때와 같은) 백지 상태의 무구한 마음

백지 이론은 개개인이 미리 만들어져 있는 정신적인 내용을 지니지 않은 채 태어나며 그들의 지식은 경험과 인식으로부터 생겨난다는 인식론적 명제이다. 이것은 존 로크(John Locke)에 의해 유명해지게 되었는데, 그는 정신이

백지 상태 혹은 비어 있는 채로 태어난 다음 경험에 의해 그 위에 기록이 된다는 자신의 믿음을 설명하는 데 이 표현을 사용했다. 그것은 또한 교육 분야에 있어서와 본성 대 양육의 이슈를 논하는 데 사용되어 왔다.

---

25   ④

첫 번째 빈칸의 경우, 바로 앞의 The same이 단서가 된다. 바로 앞 문장에서 사적인 정보 보호를 위한 '경계'를 늦추지 말 것을 이야기하고 있으므로, 빈칸에는 이 문장 속의 단어 precaution에 대한 동의어 혹은 이와 유사한 의미를 가진 단어가 들어가야 할 것이다. alertness 또는 vigilance가 가능하다. 한편, 마지막 문장은 정보 보호를 위한 학교의 조치에 '상응하는' 사용자의 의무에 관한 것이므로, 두 번째 빈칸에는 incidental, accessory, concomitant가 가능하다. 상기 두 조건을 모두 만족시키는 것은 ④이다.

dorm n. 기숙사 access n. 접근, 출입; 접근 수단 precaution n. 조심, 경계; 예방책 hook up to ~에 접속하다 register v. 기록하다, 기입하다; 등록하다 responsibility n. 책임, 책무, 의무 pilferage n. 좀도둑질 incidental a. 부수하여 일어나는; 부차적인; 임시의, 우연의 alertness n. 빈틈없음, 조심성 있음 verbatim a. 말 그대로의, 축어적인 anathema n. (가톨릭에서의) 파문(破門); 저주; 증오 accessory a. 부속의, 보조적인, 부대적인 vigilance n. 조심, 경계 concomitant a. 동반하는, 부수하는; 공존하는

기숙사에서 살면 다른 사람들이 당신의 컴퓨터를 이용할 가능성이 커진다. 그러므로, 사적인 정보를 보호하기 위해서는 경계를 늦추지 않는 것이 현명하다. 컴퓨터가 캠퍼스 네트워크에 연결되어 있는 경우에도 동일한 경계가 요구된다. 학교에서는 사용자로 하여금 컴퓨터를 등록시키고 암호를 만들도록 함으로써 개인 파일이 저장되는 공간을 보호한다. 사용자들은 그에 수반되는 책임을 갖고서, 암호를 바꾸고, 작업시간이 끝나면 로그아웃을 하고, 자료를 저장할 때에는 주의를 기울여야 한다.

01 ②	**02** ②	**03** ③	**04** ③	**05** ③	**06** ②	**07** ④	**08** ②	**09** ②	**10** ②
11 ②	**12** ③	**13** ③	**14** ③	**15** ②	**16** ③	**17** ④	**18** ④	**19** ①	**20** ①
21 ①	**22** ①	**23** ③	**24** ④	**25** ③					

01 ②

빈칸 다음의 if가 '양보'의 접속사여서 '비록 느리게 나아가고 나아가다가 서다가 하는 변덕을 부리기도 했지만 그 방향으로 나아간다는 원칙은 항상 지켰다'는 의미이므로, 빈칸에는 '어김없이'라는 의미의 ②가 적절하다.

fitfully ad. 단속적으로, 변덕스럽게 fortuitously ad. 우연히 inexorably ad. 냉혹하게, 어김없이, 요지부동으로 expeditiously ad. 신속하게 waywardly ad. 변덕스럽게

미국이 완벽하지는 않지만, 최근까지 미국은 비록 서서히 그리고 변덕스럽게라 해도 어김없이 항상 전반적으로 정의와 위대함의 방향으로 나아갔다.

02 ②

Even though가 이끄는 양보의 종속절에서 '사실이 명백하게 드러났다'라고 했으므로, 이것과 대조를 이뤄야 하는 주절에서는 '그러한 명백한 사실을 부정했다'라는 맥락으로 글이 이어져야 한다. 따라서 '얼버무리다'라는 의미의 ②가 들어가는 것이 가장 자연스럽다.

harsh a. 거친; 사나운; 모진 obvious a. 명백한, 명료한 related a. 관계있는, 관련되어 있는 pundit n. 학자; 박식한 사람 irrelevant a. 부적절한, 무관계한 succumb v. 굴복하다, 압도되다 prevaricate v. 얼버무려 넘기다, 발뺌하다, 속이다 persevere v. 참다, 견디다, 버티다 recede v. 물러나다, 퇴각하다, 멀어지다

공식적인 자료를 통해 냉혹한 사실이 명백해졌음에도 불구하고, 관련돼 있는 정치인들과 학자들은 계속해서 얼버무리고 있다. 그들 가운데 일부는 그것이 전혀 무관하다고까지 말하고 있다.

03 ③

두 번째 문장의 주절과 연속동작을 나타내는 leaving 이하의 분사구문은 원인과 결과의 관계에 있다. '밤낮 계속된 공습이 적 지상군의 힘을 빼앗았다'라고 했으므로, 그 결과는 '힘이 완전히 빠진 상태가 되는 것'이다. 그러므로 정답은 enervate의 과거분사인 ③이 된다.

offensive n. 공격, 공세 altitude n. 높이, 고도; 해발 soften up (적의) 저항력을 약화시키다; 누그러지다 sap v. 수액을 짜내다; 약화시키다, 활력을 없애다

advance v. 전진하다; 진격하다 invigorate v. 원기를 돋우다, 격려하다 debauch v. 타락시키다; (여자를) 유혹하다 enervate v. 기력을 빼앗다, 힘을 약화시키다 defile v. 더럽히다, 모독하다

지상 공격 이전에, UN군은 고고도 폭격기를 이용해 적 부대의 힘을 약화시켰다. 밤낮으로 계속된 공습은 적 지상군의 힘을 빼놓았으며, UN군이 진격했을 때엔 그 힘이 완전히 빠져 있었다.

04 ③

빈칸에 들어갈 표현은 바로 앞의 Rain, snow처럼 '목적지까지 가는 여정을 더 길어지도록' 만드는 날씨를 나타낼 수 있어야 하므로, '궂은, 험악한'이라는 뜻의 ③이 들어가는 것이 가장 적절하다.

contend v. 다투다, 경쟁하다, 싸우다 the elements 자연력; 폭풍우 factor n. 요인, 요소 delay n. 지연, 지체, 연기 iridescent a. 무지개 빛깔의, 진주빛의 libelous a. 명예훼손의, 중상하는 inclement a. (날씨가) 험악한, 거칠고 궂은, 혹독한 hirsute a. 털이 많은, 덥수룩한

폴로(Polo)의 가족들 또한 자연력과 싸워야 했다. 비, 눈, 그리고 그 밖의 험악한 날씨로 인해 베니스에서 중국까지의 여행은 3년 반이 걸렸다. 이렇게 지연되도록 했던 또 다른 요인은 마르코(Marco)가 도중에 거의 1년 동안 매우 심하게 앓았다는 점이다.

05 ③

오만함 혹은 자만이 가져오는 나쁜 결과에 대해 이야기하고 있는 글이다. 첫 번째 문장에 쓰인 pride를 두 번째 문장에서는 self-conceit라는 말로 바꿔 표현한 것을 알 수 있는데, 따라서 세 번째 문장의 빈칸에도 결국 pride의 의미를 갖고 있는 단어가 들어가야 할 것이다. 그러므로 '오만함, 지나친 자신감'이라는 의미의 ③이 정답이 된다.

unwarranted a. 보증되지 않은; 부당한, 부적절한, 불필요한 lethal a. 치명적인, 치사의 self-conceit n. 자만심, 자부심, 허영심 corrode v. 부식하다, 침식하다; 약화시키다 distinguish v. 구별하다, 식별하다, 분간하다; 두드러지게 하다 genuine a. 진짜의; 진심에서 우러난 sham a. 가짜의, 허위의 tyranny n. 폭정, 정제정치 beget v. 낳다; 생기게 하다, 초래하다 dig v. 파다; 발굴하다, 파헤치다 grave n. 무덤 tyrant n. 폭군, 전제군주 caprice n. 변덕, 줏대 없음 parochialism n. 지방근성, 파벌주의; 편협 hubris n. 지나친 자신, 오만 pulchritude n. (육체의) 아름다움

정치지도자들의 부적절한 자만심은 치명적이다. 절대적인 통치자들의 자만은 옳은 것과 그른 것 혹은 진짜와 가짜를 구별하는 그들의 능력을 약화시키는 경향이 있다. 그리고 때로는 폭정이 낳은 오만함이 그런 폭군들의 무덤을 파게 된다.

06 ②

마지막 문장은 '폭발물질이 고착물질을 통해 빈칸에 들어갈 단어의 성질을 갖게 됨으로써' 얻을 수 있는 결과에 해당한다. 고착물질은 '폭발물질을 여러 모양으로 만들어 낼 수 있게' 해주는 역할을 하는 것이므로, 빈칸에는 '펴서 늘일 수 있는'이라는 의미의 ②가 들어가야 한다.

variety n. 변화, 다양; 불일치; 종류 explosive n. 폭약, 폭발성 물질 binder material 접합물질, 고착물질 mold v. 주조하다; 본뜨다; 반죽하여 만들다 fluorescent a. 형광을 발하는, 형광성의 malleable a. 펴서 늘일 수 있는; 유순한, 영향을 잘 받는 feculent a. 탁한, 흐린; 더러운 rancid a. 고약한 냄새가 나는; 불쾌한

C4는 플라스틱 폭약의 일종이다. 플라스틱 폭약의 기본 개념은 폭발물질을 플라스틱 고착물질과 섞는 것이다. 고착제는 중요한 역할을 한다. 고착제는 모양을 만들어 낼 수 있는 성질을 폭발물질이 매우 많이 갖게끔 만든다. 그 폭발물질을 반죽하여 여러 가지 다른 모양으로 만들어 폭발의 방향을 바꿀 수도 있다.

07 ④

빈칸에 들어갈 단어에 대한 구체적인 내용은 '소련이 동부유럽을 점령하지 않았다고 주장한 것'이며, 이것을 두 번째 문장에서는 the mistake로 표현하고 있다. 그러므로 빈칸에도 mistake의 동의어 혹은 이러한 의미를 포함하고 있는 단어가 들어가야 할 것이다. '실언, 과실'이라는 의미의 ④가 빈칸에 가장 적절하다.

claim v. 요구하다, 청구하다; 주장하다 occupy v. 차지하다; 점령하다; 종사시키다 majority n. 대부분, 대다수; 과반수 newscast n. 뉴스방송 focus v. 초점을 맞추다; 집중하다 support n. 지지, 원조, 후원, 찬성 dip v. 가라앉다; 내려가다; 내리막이 되다 squabble n. 시시한 언쟁, 말다툼 slander n. 중상, 비방; 비난, 명예훼손 doublespeak n. 거짓말, 속임수 gaffe n. 과실, 실수, 실언

1976년 선거에서, 제럴드 포드(Gerald Ford) 대통령은 지미 카터(Jimmy Carter)와의 토론 중에 소련이 동부유럽을 점령하지 않았다고 주장하는 실언을 했다. 대부분의 시청자들은 포드가 토론에서 승리했다고 생각했지만, 뉴스에서 그 실수에 초점을 맞춘 후에는 포드에 대한 지지가 줄어들었다.

08 ②

두 번째 문장의 '사실은 고네릴과 리건이 배은망덕하다'라는 말 속에는 '리어왕은 막내인 코델리아가 배은망덕하다고 생각했다'라는 뜻이 내포되어 있다. 빈칸은 명사가 들어갈 자리이므로 ungrateful의 의미를 내포하고 있는 명사가 필요하며, '배은망덕한 사람'이라는 의미의 ②가 정답이 된다.

palace n. 궁전, 왕궁 in rags 누더기가 되어, 누더기를 입고 ungrateful a. 은혜를 모르는, 감사할 줄 모르는 realize v. 실현하다; 실감하다 genuine a. 진짜의; 진심에서 우러난, 성실한 reunion n. 재회; 화해 neophyte n. 신개종자; 신참자, 초심자 ingrate n. 은혜를 모르는 사람, 배은망덕한 사람 raconteur n. 이야기꾼, 이야기를 잘 하는 사람 virago n. 잔소리가 많은 여자, 바가지 긁는 여자

리어(Lear)는 자신의 세 딸 가운데 막내인 코델리아(Cordelia)가 은혜를 모르는 사람이라고 생각한다. 사실은, 리어를 자신들의 궁전에서 쫓아내고 폭풍우가 몰아치는 추운 밤에 누더기를 입은 채 집도 없이 굶주리게 만든 고네릴(Goneril)과 리건(Regan)이 배은망덕한 이들이다. 리어는 코델리아의 진심어린 효심을 그들의 짧은 재회에서 너무 늦게 깨닫는다.

09 ②

첫 번째 문장에서는 로렌스가 대통령을 암살하려 한 혐의로 기소되었다고 했는데, 마지막 문장에서는 투옥되거나 형이 집행되는 대신 '정신병원으로 보내졌다'라고 했으므로, 정신이상을 이유로 그에게 죄를 묻지 않은 것으로 볼 수 있다. 따라서 빈칸에는 '무죄방면하다, 석방하다'라는 의미가 되도록 ②가 들어가는 것이 적절하다.

charge v. 고발하다, 고소하다; 비난하다 assassination n. 암살 delusional a. 망상적인 insanity n. 광기, 발광, 정신이상 commit v. 위임하다, 맡기다; 범하다; (정신병원·시설 따위에) 보내다, 수용하다 asylum n. 보호시설, 수용소; 정신병원 imprison v. 투옥하다, 감금하다; 구속하다 acquit v. 석방하다, 무죄로 하다 edify v. 교화하다, 품성을 높이다 castigate v. 징계하다; 혹평하다; 첨삭하다

리처드 로렌스(Richard Lawrence)는 미국 대통령 앤드류 잭슨(Andrew Jackson)에 대한 암살 기도로 기소된 최초의 인물이었다. 로렌스는 자신이 영국의 왕이고 잭슨이 자신의 아버지를 죽였다고 믿고 있는 등, 과대망상증이 있는 것으로 밝혀졌다. 그는 정신이상을 이유로 석방되어 정신병원으로 보내졌다.

10 ②

마지막 문장은 글 전체를 통해 내릴 수 있는 결론에 해당한다. '미국에서 인기 있는 피자 토핑에는 여러 가지가 있으며, 안초비의 경우, 미국에서는 가장 인기가 없지만, 이것이 인기 있는 나라도 있다'는 내용을 통해, '피자 토핑에 대한 기호는 세계적으로 다양하다'라는 결론을 내릴 수 있다. 그러므로 빈칸에는 ②가 적절하다.

come as a shock 쇼크를 느끼다; 정신적 충격을 받다 perennial a. 연중 끊이지 않는; 여러 해 계속 하는 favorite n. 마음에 드는 것, 인기가 있는 것 anchovy n. 안초비 consistently ad. 시종일관, 모순 없이 dainty a. 고상한, 맛좋은; 까다로운 eclectic a. 취사선택하는, 절충주의의; (하나의 입장에) 얽매이지 않는, (취미 따위가) 폭넓은 platitudinous a. 시시한 말을 하는, 평범한, 진부한 tawdry a. 야한, 값싸고 번지르르한

페퍼로니가 미국에서 가장 인기 있는 피자 토핑이라는 사실은 아마 그다지 놀라운 일이 아닐 것이다. 지속적인 인기를 끄는 다른 것들은 특제 치즈, 소시지, 버섯, 피망, 양파 등이다. 안초비의 경우 몇몇 나라에서는 매우 인기가 좋지만, 미국에서는 가장 인기 없는 토핑의 자리를 꾸준히 유지하고 있다. 사실, 피자 토핑에 대한 기호는 전 세계에서 확실히 그 폭이 넓다.

11 ②

첫 번째 문장에서는 유럽에 산책하기에 좋은 길이 많다는 내용을 이야기하고 있고, 두 번째 문장에서는 몇몇 나라에 walking traditions가 있음을 이야기하고 있다. 세 번째 문장 이하에서는 두 번째 문장에서 언급한 산책하는 전통을 가지고 있는 나라들에 대해 스위스와 스페인을 예로 들며 설명하고 있다. 그러므로 빈칸에는 walking이나 hiking의 의미를 가진 단어가 들어가는 것이 적절하다. 따라서 '산책'이라는 의미의 ②가 정답이 된다.

meandering a. 굽이쳐 흐르는, 정처 없이 지나는 boulevard n. 넓은 가로수길, 넓은 산책길; 대로 criss-crossed a. 종횡으로 선이 그어진; 엇갈린 trail n. 자국, 발자국; 오솔길 converge v. 한 점에 모이다, 몰려들다; 집중하다 square n. 정사각형; 광장 stroll v. 어슬렁어슬렁 걷다, 산책하다 greet v. 인사하다; 환영하다 masquerade n. 가면무도회; 가장용 의상; 겉치레, 허구, 구실 promenade n. 산책, 산보; 행진 vista n. 길게 내려다 본 경치; 전망; 추억 thoroughfare n. 통로; 주요도로; 왕래, 통행

유럽 도시들에는 산책을 하기에 이상적인 구불구불한 길과 넓은 산책로들이 있다. 몇몇 나라들에는 도보 여행을 하는 휴가 중에 발견하게 되면 매우 즐거운 일이 될 만한 산책 전통이 있다. 언덕과 산이 하이킹을 할 수 있는 길들로 가득 차 있는 스위스가 그 한 예가 된다. 또 다른 멋진 산책 전통은 스페인에서 이뤄지고 있는 저녁 산책인데, 이때에는 온 가족이 중앙 광장에 모여 가볍게 거닐고 서로 인사를 나눈다.

12 ③

마지막 문장에서 암 치료에 있어 큰 진전이 될 수 있기를 희망한다고 했으므로 빈칸에는 '(암의) 소실, (병의) 완화, 차도'를 의미하는 ③이 적절하다.

ongoing a. 진행하는 lymphoma n. 림프종 advanced a. (밤이) 이슥한, 깊어진 digression n. 탈선 absolution n. 면죄 remission n. (암의) 소실, (병의) 완화, 차도 prostration n. 쇠약

환자 자신의 혈액세포를 암 킬러로 바꾸어주는 면역요법 치료제가 미국 식품의약국 승인절차를 신속히 밟아가고 있다. 진행 중인 임상실험에서 그 치료제는 표준 치료제에 반응하지 않았거나 계속 재발을 한 말기 림프종 환자에게 투여되었다. 석 달이 되었을 때 83퍼센트의 환자가 완쾌 중에 있었다. 실험이 계속됨에 따라 과학자들은 그 요법이 암 치료에 있어 또 하나의 큰 진전이 될 수 있기를 희망한다.

13 ③

두 번째 문장에서 설명하고 있는 그룹은 실제로는 아무런 효과가 없는 가짜 장치를 이용하여 치료를 받은 셈인데, 이것은 첫 번째 문장에서 언급하고 있는 치료 과정이 효과가 있는지를 알아보기 위한 비교 과정이라 할 수 있다. 따라서 이 문제는 '실험 결과가 제대로 도출되었는지의 여부를 판단하기 위해 어떤 조작이나 조건도 가하지 않은 집단'을 무엇이라 하는지를 묻는 문제이며, '대조군'이라는 의미의 ③이 정답이다.

acne n. 여드름 undergo v. (영향·검사 따위를) 받다, 입다; 경험하다; 견디다 irradiation n. (열선) 방사; (자외선 따위의) 조사, 투사(投射); 방사선 요법 expose v. 노출시키다, 쐬다; 드러내다; 폭로하다 placebo n. 위약(偽藥); 위안, 아첨 device n. 고안; 계획; 책략 inflammatory a. 염증성의; 선동적인, 열광시키는 lesion n. 외상, 손상; 장애 significant a. 중대한, 중요한; 의미심장한 volunteer n. 지원자, 독지가 response n. 응답, 대답; 반응 control n. 지배; 관리; 억제, 제어; (실험 결과의) 대조 표준 subsequence n. 뒤이어 일어남, 계속하여 일어나는 사건

한 연구에서, 일단(一團)의 여드름 환자들은 세라젬 메디시스(Ceragem Medisys)에서 만든 LED 장치를 이용하여 파란색과 붉은색 전구에서 나오는 광선을 4주 동안 매일 두 차례에 걸쳐 2분 30초씩 쬐었다. 그 사이에 대조군은 치료효과가 없는 가짜 장치에 노출시켰다. 12주 후에, 치료 그룹은 염증성 여드름에 의한 손상과 비염증성 여드름에 의한 손상 모두 각각 77퍼센트, 54퍼센트 감소했다. 반면, 대조군 그룹에서는 의미 있는 변화가 없었다.

14 ③

빈칸 앞 부분에서 마이클 잭슨이 이뤄 낸 뛰어난 성과에 대해 이야기하고 있으므로, 첫 문장에서 언급한 잭슨 브라더스보다 '더 많은 명성을 얻었다'라는 맥락으로 이어지는 것이 자연스럽다. 그러므로 빈칸에는 ③이 들어가야 한다.

debut n. 데뷔, 첫 무대, 첫 출연 release v. 개봉하다, 공개하다, 발표하다 platinum a. 음반이 100만장이 팔린 dismember v. 손발을 자르다, 해체하다 disabuse v. ~의 어리석음을 깨우치다, (그릇된 관념·잘못 따위를) 깨닫게 하다 eclipse v. 가리다; 어둡게 하다; (~의 명성 따위를) 가리다, 무색하게 하다, 능가하다 acclimate v. 순응시키다; 익히다

마이클 잭슨(Michael Jackson)은 1964년에 잭슨 브라더스(The Jackson Brothers)에서 데뷔했는데, 이 그룹은 70년대부터 잭슨이 탈퇴한 80년대 중반까지 명성을 높였다. 1979년, 마이클 잭슨은 그의 다섯 번째 스튜디오 앨범인 "오프 더 월(Off the Wall)"을 발표했는데, 이 앨범은 호주 차트 정상에 올랐고, 미국과 영국을 비롯한 몇몇 나라에서는 5위 안에 들었다. 그 앨범은 아주 빠르게 100만장 판매를 기록했고, 자신의 형들의 명성을 능가하게 되었다.

15 ②

빈칸에 들어갈 단어에 대해 마지막 문장에서 설명하고 있다. '아첨을 하는 사람이 자신의 아부하는 행동이 뻔히 드러나지는 않게 하면서도 다른 사람의 환심을 얻는 것'을 나타내는 표현을 찾아야 하므로, ②가 가장 적절하다.

susceptible a. 민감한, 영향 받기 쉬운, 무른 brownnose v. 환심을 사다, 알랑거리다, 아첨하다 recognize v. 알아보다, 인지하다; 인정하다, 감사하다 suck up 알랑거리다, 아첨하다 The jig is up 이젠 다 틀렸다, 끝장이다 effective a. 유효한, 효과적인, 유력한 scheme n. 계획, 기획; 설계, 음모 obvious a. 명백한, 명료한; 눈에 잘 띄는 beginner's luck 초심자에게 따르는 행운 ingratiator n. 비위를 맞추는 사람, 환심을 사는 사람 prisoner's dilemma 죄수의 딜레마(공범 두 명이 상대를 배신하고 자백하여 감형을 받느냐, 상대를 믿고 입을 다무느냐는 협력 · 비협력의 곤경) all or nothing 양자택일, 전부냐 제로냐

환심을 사려고 알랑거리는 행동에 약하긴 해도, 우리가 항상 속아 넘어가는 것은 아니다. 아첨하는 사람은 도를 넘어 지나치게 되기 쉽다. 아첨하는 사람이 개인적인 이익을 위해 알랑거리고 있음을 사장이 알아차리게 되면, 그것으로 완전히 끝이다. 효과적으로 아첨하는 사람은 선을 넘지 않으려 조심하고 자신의 계획이 뻔히 보이지 않도록 주의를 기울인다. 심리학자들은 이 문제를 아첨꾼의 딜레마라고 부른다. 이것은 아첨꾼이 선을 넘거나 자신의 계획이 드러나게 하지 않으면서도 누군가의 마음에 들려 노력하는 것을 일컫는다.

16 ③

주어진 글에서, 첫 번째 빈칸 뒤의 명사 order는 '순서'라는 의미로 쓰였다. '분배를 늘리기 위해 성장이 반드시 일어나야 한다'라는 말은 '성장이 있은 후에 분배를 늘려야 한다'라는 의미이며, 이 표현에는 그 순서가 바뀌어선 안 된다는 뜻이 내포되어 있다. 빈칸 뒤에 has not worked라는 부정적인 표현이 있으므로, 첫 번째 빈칸에는 '순서가 바뀌는' 것을 의미하는 reverse가 들어가야 한다. 한편, 두 번째 문장은 이러한 순서를 지키지 않은 결과가 가져온 사례에 해당하므로, 부정적인 의미의 단어가 들어가야 한다. catastrophe, desuetude, debacle이 가능하다. 따라서 정답은 ③이 된다.

dictum n. 공식견해; 언명, 단정; 금언 distribution n. 분배, 배당; 배포 one-sided a. 한쪽으로 치우친, 불공평한; 일방적인 injection n. 주입, 주사; (자금 등의) 투입 strategy n. 병법, 전략, 작전 decade n. 10년간 depraved a. 타락한, 사악한; 불량한 catastrophe n. 파국; 대이변, 큰 재해; 대실패 adventitious a. 우연의, 외래의 desuetude n. 폐지, 폐지상태, 폐용(廢用), 불용 reverse a. 반대의, 거꾸로의; 역(逆)의 debacle n. (군대 따위의) 패주; (정부 등의) 붕괴; (시장의) 도산 ignoble a. 비열한, 천한 appropriation n. 충당, 할당; 착복

분배를 늘리기 위해서는 성장이 반드시 일어나야 하며, 그 순서가 거꾸로 되면 전혀 효과가 없다는 경제발전 관련 격언을 우리는 기억해야 한다. 새로운 성장에 대한 합당한 전략 없이 무상 복지 프로그램만을 일방적으로 쏟아 부은 결과, 최근에는 그리스에서, 수십 년 전에는 페론주의 하에 있던 아르헨티나에서 완전한 경제 붕괴가 초래됐다.

17 ④

첫 번째 빈칸에는 뒤에 위치한 admirable과 비슷한 의미의 표현이 필요하고 두 번째 빈칸은 complain과 비슷한 의미의 표현이 필요하다.

single-minded a. 목적이 단 하나의, 일치단결한; 단순한 stress n. 시련, 곤경 welter n. 혼란 woe n. 고통 slaughter n. 학살 bogus a. 가짜의 plod v. 터벅터벅 걷다 heinous a. 흉악한 mesmerize v. 최면을 걸다, 매혹시키다 wistful a. 동경하는 듯한 balk v. 방해하다 transcendent a. 뛰어난 cavil v. 이의를 제기하다 stout a. 단단한 garner v. 축적하다

사람들은 여성들이 하나만 생각한다고 말한다. 보통은 그것은 단점일 수 있겠지만 대단한 위기의 순간에는 모든 미덕 중에서도 가장 훌륭하고 찬탄할 만한 것일지도 모른다. 나는 지나간 이번 전쟁과 그 전쟁에서 우리나라의 여성과 다른 나라의 여성들이 했던 역할에 대해 생각해 본다. 세상이 고통과 학살의 혼란에 있을 때는 그 누구도 여성들의 단순성에 대해 이의를 제기하거나 불평하지 않았다.

18 ④

첫 번째 빈칸에는 암에서 완치됐음을 공개적으로 선언하는 사람의 태도나 기분을 나타내는 표현이 와야 하므로, '기분이 들떠 있음'을 나타내는 effervescent 또는 ebullient가 가능하다. 한편, '암 환자의 경우, 치료 후 적어도 2년이 지나야만 위험에서 벗어난 것으로 볼 수 있다'라는 의사들의 말에 비추어 보면, 종양제거 수술 4개월 후에 완치를 선언한 차베스의 말은 너무 일찍 마음을 놓거나 상황을 지나치게 낙관적으로 본 것이라 할 수 있다. 그러므로 두 번째 빈칸에는 complacent 또는 rosy가 들어갈 수 있다. 두 조건을 모두 만족시키는 정답은 ④가 된다.

declare v. 선언하다, 발표하다, 공언하다 remove v. 제거하다; 옮기다; 해임하다 malignant timor 악성종양 address n. 주소; 인사말, 연설 socialist n. 사회주의자 treatment n. 취급; 처리; 치료 assertion n. 단언, 단정; 주장 effervescent a. 비등성의, 거품이 이는; 활기찬, 열띤 gloomy a. 어두운; 음울한 despondent a. 낙담한, 의기소침한 complacent a. 자기만족의; 마음속으로 즐거워하는; 안심한 disquieting a. 불안한, 걱정이 되는 ripe a. 익은, 원숙한 ebullient a. 비등하는; 원기 왕성한 rosy a. 유망한, 낙관적인

악성종양 제거 수술을 받은 지 4개월이 지난 후, 차베스(Chavez)는 목요일에 자신이 암에서 완치됐다고 선언했다. "저는 아무 병에도 걸려 있지 않습니다."라고 차베스는 한 연설에서 말했다. 기세등등한 그 사회주의자의 발표에도 불구하고, 치료가 끝난 지 적어도 2년이 지나기 전에는 암 환자가 위험에서 벗어난 것으로 간주할 수 없다고 의사들은 말하고 있다. "암이 완치됐다는 그의 주장은 현 시점에서는 지나치게 낙관적인 것입니다"라고 한 암 관련 전문가는 말했다.

19   ①

'이러한 가장 실존적인 관심사'가 앞 문장에 나온 죽음 문제의 해결을 의미하므로 첫 번째 빈칸에는 '부응하다, 영합하다'는 뜻의 pandered나 catered가 적절하고, 마지막 문장이 죽은 자를 사후 세계로 보내는 신앙과 종교의식을 사람들은 자신의 문화 속에서 미리 알게 된 상태에서 죽음을 맞이한다는 의미이므로 두 번째 빈칸에는 uninitiated(충분한 경험/지식이 없는)이나 unprimed(준비되어 있지 않은)가 적절하다.

resignation n. 체념 existential a. 존재에 관한, 실존의 It is safe to say that ~라고 말해도 괜찮다[무방하다](= It is not too much to say that) mark n. 특징 ritual n. 의식(儀式) embalm v. 방부 처리하다 buckle v. 굽어지다, 굴복하다 undaunted a. 기죽지 않은 accrue v. 생기다 unheralded a. 전달[보고] 되지 않는, 예상 밖의

죽음이 공포를 의미하든 조용한 체념 속에 받아들여지든, 생명의 종식을 존재의 종식으로 받아들이기는 어려운 것 같다. 모든 주요 종교들은 이러한 가장 실존적인 관심사에 영합하는 신앙을 제공해주었다. 지금껏 알려진 그 어떤 사회에서도 사회 구성원들이 사전 지식 없이 죽음을 맞이하도록 방치되어 있지는 않다고 말해도 무방하다. 그렇게 방치되기는커녕 오히려, 죽음 너머의 영역으로 적절히 나아가도록 보장해주는 신앙과 의식(儀式)들을 사람들에게 제공해주는 것이 인간 문화의 한 특징인 것이다.

20   ①

네 번째 문장의 So에 유의한다. 이 문장에서 진술하고 있는 "국제회의가 열린 것과 그 회의에서 독일의 배상금 지급을 당분간 '소멸시키는' 조치를 취한 것"은 그 앞 문장에서 언급하고 있는 '후버 대통령의 제안'에 따른 것으로 봐야 하므로, 첫 번째 빈칸에는 cancel의 의미를 내포하고 있는 moratorium 또는 reprieve가 가능하다. 한편, '로잔 조약은 독일의 배상금 지불의 끝을 기록하게 되었다'라는 말은 '로잔 조약 이후에는 독일이 배상금을 지불한 적이 없다'라는 것으로, 결국 히틀러가 권좌에 오른 이후 배상금 지불을 이행하지 않았다는 의미가 된다. 따라서 두 번째 빈칸에는 '거부'나 '부정'의 의미를 갖고 있는 repudiated 또는 disapproved가 가능하다. 상기 두 조건을 모두 만족시키는 정답은 ①이다.

responsibility n. 책임, 책무, 의무 reparation n. 보상, 배상; 배상금; 수선 propose v. 제안하다, 제의하다; 신청하다 conference n. 회담, 협의, 의논 moratorium n. 모라토리엄, 지급정지, 지급유예 repudiate v. 거부하다, 거절하다; 부인하다; (채무) 이행을 거부하다 fallout n. 부산물, 부수적인 결과 disapprove v. 불가하다고 하다; 비난하다 reprieve n. 집행유예; 일시적 경감, 일시적 구제 defray v. 지불하다, 지출하다; 부담하다 decoy n. 유인하는 장치, 미끼; 유인 장소 salvage v. 구조하다; 구하다, 지키다

전후(戰後) 계획안 하에서, 독일은 배상금 지불에 있어 모든 책임을 지게 되었다. 그러나 나중에 대공황이 독일을 엄습했다. 1931년에 후버(Hoover) 대통령은 정부 사이의 모든 부채에 대해 1년간의 유예기간을 둘 것을 제안했다. 그리하여 1932년 6월, 스위스 로잔(Lausanne)에서 국제회의가 열렸고, 세계 경제가 호전될 때까지 독일의 모든 배상금을 소멸시켰다. 로잔 조약은 독일의 배상금 지불의 끝을 기록하게 되었는데, 왜냐하면 1933년에 히틀러가 권좌에 오르면서 모든 배상금에 대한 지급을 거부했기 때문이다.

21   ①

마지막 문장의 내용은 결국 '전쟁이 끊임없이 계속되고 있다'라는 것인데, 이는 패배한 쪽에서 전쟁을 통한 복수나 보복을 갈구했기 때문일 것이다. 따라서 첫 번째 빈칸에는 reprisal 또는 retribution이 가능하다. 한편, 이 때 '복수'라는 것은 또 다른 전쟁을 시작할 명분 혹은 근거가 되는 것이므로, 두 번째 빈칸에는 이러한 의미를 가진 foundation 또는 basis가 쓰일 수 있다. 두 조건을 모두 만족시키는 정답은 ①이다.

fervently ad. 열심히, 열렬하게 victorious a. 승리를 거둔, 이긴 defeat v. 쳐부수다; 좌절시키다 poverty n. 가난, 빈곤; 결핍 reprisal n. 앙갚음, 보복 foundation n. 창립, 설립; 기초, 토대; 근거 amity n. 친목, 친선, 우호관계 basis n. 기초, 토대; 이유, 근거 infelicity n. 불행, 불운; 부적절 swagger n. 으쓱거리며 걷기, 활보; 뽐냄 retribution n. 응보, 보복, 앙갚음; 징벌, 천벌 cessation n. 정지, 중지

이제 양측에서 승리하게 해달라고 신(神)에게 열렬히 기도하고 있는 전투 군대를 잘 살펴보도록 하자. 이긴 군대는 승리한 것에 대해 신에게 감사한다. 그러나 패배한 군대는 복수하게 해달라고 계속해서 신에게 기도한다. 그런 까닭에, 전쟁이 끝나자마자 또 다른 전쟁이 일어날 수 있는 근거를 마련하게 되는 것이다. 사실, 모든 전쟁을 종식시킬 전쟁 ─ 빈곤에 맞선 전쟁 ─ 특히 최악의 빈곤에 속하는 인간 정신과 마음의 빈곤에 맞선 전쟁은 아직 있었던 적이 없다.

22   ①

기존의 근무 제도를 '과거의 유산' 그리고 '사용자와 직원 모두에게 좋지 않은 것'으로 기술하고 있으므로, 현대자동차가 시행하고자 하는 새로운 교대근무제를 긍정적으로 보고 있음을 알 수 있다. 따라서 이 제도를 다른 기업에서도 시행하길 원할 것이므로, 빈칸에는 '흉내 내다'라는 의미의 ①이 들어가는 것이 적절하다.

shift n. 변천; 변화, (근무의) 교대; 교대시간 abolish v. 폐지하다, 철폐하다 graveyard shift (교대근무에 있어서의) 야간 근무 legacy n. 유산, 물려받은 것 ultimately ad. 결국, 마침내, 궁극적으로 employer n. 고용주, 사용자 employee n. 종업원, 직원 introduce v. 받아들이다, 수입하다; 소개하다 emulate v. 겨루다, 다투다; 흉내를 내다 discontinue v. 그만두다, 중지하다 remand v. 돌려보내다, 귀환을 명하다 retard v. 속력을 늦추다, 지체시키다

지난주에, 현대자동차는 야간근무를 폐지하고 근무시간을 감축하기 위한 새로운 교대근무제에 대해 2주간의 시험 운영을 시작했다. 긴 근무시간은 과거의 유산이며 궁극적으로는 사용자와 직원 모두에게 해를 끼친다. 현대자동차는 그 새로운 교대근무제를 3월에 도입할 계획이다. 현대자동차의 사례를 다른 기업들도 모방할 필요가 있다.

23   ③

assume의 목적어로 주어져 있는 두 개의 that절이 인과관계에 있음을 부사 therefore를 통해 알 수 있다. 회계 규칙이 엄격하다면, 결과를 자

의적으로 해석할 여지가 적다고 생각했을 것이므로, 정답은 '여유, 자유(재량)'라는 의미의 ③이다.

assume v. 추정하다, 추측하다, 가정하다 accounting n. 회계, 회계보고, 결산 fairly ad. 상당히, 꽤 rigid a. 엄격한, 융통성이 없는 auditor n. 회계 감사관 interpret v. 설명하다, 해석하다 ambiguity n. 애매성, 애매모호함 expense n. 지출, 비용; 경비 estimate v. 평가하다, 어림하다, 추정하다 fictitious a. 허구의, 지어낸 bias n. 편견, 선입견; 편향 distort v. 비틀다, 왜곡하다 peroration n. 연설의 마무리 부분; 장황한 연설 referendum n. 국민투표 leeway n. (공간·시간·활동 등의) 여지, 여유, 자유재량의 폭 paradigm n. 보기, 범례, 모범

대부분의 사람들은 회계원칙이 상당히 엄격하며, 따라서 회계 감사관이 결과를 해석하는 데 있어 그렇게 많은 재량을 갖고 있지는 않다고 생각한다. (그러나) 사실은 상당한 모호함이 존재한다. '비용은 무엇인가?'와 '투자는 무엇인가?'라는 아주 명백한 질문조차 해석하기 나름이다. 예를 들어, 어느 가상의 가구에서 지불해야 하는 소득세를 추정해 달라는 머니 매거진의 요청을 받았을 때, 회계사들의 대답은 범위가 약 3만 7천 달러부터 6만 8천 달러까지에 이르렀다. 그러한 범위는 회계 감사원들의 편견이 결과를 왜곡할 수 있다는 것을 의미한다.

---

24   ④

첫 문장에서 '다른 사람들의 행동이 우리가 생각하는 동기와 무관한 경우가 상당히 많다'라고 했고, 세 번째 문장에서 '우리가 판단한 사실들과 그 사실들에 관련된 다른 사람들의 동기에 대해 의심을 해보는 것이 좋은 일'이라고 했으므로, 다른 사람의 행위에 대한 첫 판단은 나중에 더 자세히 알게 되면 잘못된 것으로 드러나는 경우가 많다고 볼 수 있다.

annoyance n. 불쾌감, 괴로움, 곤혹 spring v. 생기다, 발생하다, 일어나다 have nothing to do with ~와 전혀 관계가 없다 assign v. 할당하다; 부여하다; 지정하다; ~의 탓으로 하다 smother v. 숨 막히게 하다, 질식시키다 distrust v. 믿지 않다; 의심하다 recall v. 생각해내다, 상기하다; 소환하다 conclusion n. 결말, 종결; 결론 so-and-so n. 아무개, 모(某) absurdly ad. 불합리하게; 터무니없이, 우스꽝스럽게 annoying a. 성가신, 귀찮은 wide of the mark 얼토당토않은; 과녁을 빗나간

우리를 화나게 하는 다른 사람들의 행동들 중 대부분은 우리가 생각하는 동기와 무관하다. 오셀로(Othello)는 손수건에 관한 오해 때문에 데스데모나(Desdemona)를 목 졸라 죽였는데, 만약 5분만 차분히 이야기했더라면 오해는 깨끗이 풀렸을 것이다. 우리가 판단한 사실들을 의심해보는 것은 좋은 버릇이고, 그 사실들에 관련된 다른 사람들의 동기에 대해 의심을 해보는 것은 더더욱 좋은 일이다. 어떤 사람이 이런저런 일을 한 이유에 대한 나의 첫 판단이 좀 더 자세히 알았을 때 터무니없이 빗나가지 않았던 경우는 거의 없다.

---

25   ③

빈칸을 포함하고 있는 문장에는 'just as ~ so …' 구문이 쓰였으며, 이것은 '~와 마찬가지로 …하다'라는 의미이다. 최악의 범죄자들을 처형하지 않는 사회가 범죄자들에게 꼼짝 못하게 된다면, 국가가 어떤 입장을 보일 때 호전적인 정권에 휘둘리겠는가를 생각하면 된다. 범죄자들이 상대가 결코 자신의 생명을 빼앗지는 않는다는 것을 알고서 범죄를

저지르는 것처럼, 국가도 상대가 결코 전쟁을 통해 자신들을 해하지 않는다고 생각하는 경우에 그 나라를 꼼짝 못하게 할 것이다. 그러므로 빈칸에는 ③이 들어가는 것이 가장 적절하다.

outlaw v. 불법이라고 선언하다, 금지하다 death penalty 사형 reverence n. 숭배, 존경, 경의 moral a. 도덕의, 윤리의; 양심적인 confusion n. 혼동, 혼란 custody n. 보관, 관리; 구금 treasure v. 비축해두다; 소중히 하다; 마음에 새기다 possession n. 소유; 소유물, 소지품 guarantee v. 보증하다; 보장하다; 확언하다 declare v. 선언하다, 발표하다, 공언하다 at the mercy of ~에 좌우되어 warlike a. 전쟁의; 호전적인 regime n. 정권; 정부; 제도 qualm n. 불안한 마음, 양심의 가책; 불안, 염려 necessary evil 필요악

사형 제도를 불법화하는 현대 사회는 생명에 대한 경외감이라는 의미가 아니라 도덕의 혼란이라는 의미를 전하는 것이다. 사형 제도를 불법화할 때, 우리는 살인자에게 아녀자나 노인과 같이 우리가 보호하면서 살피고 있는 무고한 사람들에게 그가 무슨 짓을 하더라도 그의 가장 소중한 재산인 그의 생명은 안전하다는 것을 말해주는 것이다. 우리는 그것을 미리 보장해주고 있는 것이다. 어떤 경우에도 전쟁을 하지 않겠다고 선언하는 국가가 호전적인 정권에게 꼼짝 못하게 되듯이, 최악의 범죄자들을 처형하지 않는 사회는 무고한 사람들을 죽이고도 가책을 느끼지 않는 범죄자들에게 꼼짝 못하게 될 것이다.

01 ①	02 ①	03 ②	04 ③	05 ②	06 ④	07 ②	08 ①	09 ④	10 ③
11 ④	12 ①	13 ③	14 ①	15 ④	16 ④	17 ②	18 ①	19 ④	20 ①
21 ②	22 ②	23 ②	24 ④	25 ②					

01

① ①

but 이하에서 '실질적인' 관심사에 대해 언급하고 있으므로, 앞 문장에서는 '실질적이지 않은' 목적에 대한 내용이 오는 것이 적절하다. 그러므로 빈칸에는 really에 대해 문맥상 반대 의미를 내포하고 있는 단어가 들어가야 하며, '표면적인'이라는 의미의 ①이 정답이 된다.

expedition n. 탐험, 원정, 파견 ostensible a. 외면상의, 표면적인 uncouth a. 거칠고 천한; 세련되지 않은; 황량한 fawning a. 아양을 부리는; 아첨하는 gruesome a. 무시무시한, 소름끼치는, 섬뜩한

이 원정의 표면적인 목적은 새로운 땅을 발견하는 것이지만, 우리는 실제로는 우리의 상품을 팔 수 있는 새로운 시장을 찾는 데 관심이 있다.

02

① ①

주어진 글의 전치사구와 주절은 각각 회의 시작 전과 회의 개시 후의 모습을 나타내고 있다. 그런데, In spite of는 역접의 전치사구이므로 빈칸에는 주절의 핵심 표현과 반대되는 의미를 가진 단어가 들어가야 할 것이다. 주절에서 '심각한 내용의 협의'를 할 수 있었다고 했으므로, 이것과 반대되는 의미를 가진 것은 '수다'라는 의미를 가진 ①이다.

delegate n. 대표자, 대리인, 대의원; 파견 위원 negotiation n. 협상, 교섭, 절충 conference n. 회담, 협의; 의논 palaver n. 교섭, 상담; 수다, 아첨 petition n. 청원, 탄원, 진정; 탄원서 paucity n. 소수; 소량, 결핍 parley n. 회담, 교섭, 협상

회의 전에 있었던 온갖 수다에도 불구하고, 대표자들은 다음 순간 회의석상에 앉았을 때에는 심각한 내용의 협의를 진행할 수 있었다.

03

② ②

다른 주체가 내린 결정을 무효로 할 수 있다면, 그 단체 혹은 조직이 결정을 내리는 위치에 있어서 더 우위에 있을 것이다. 의사의 결정을 조지아 주에서 뒤집을 수 있다면, 조지아 주 당국이 더 우월한 위치에서 결정할 권한을 갖고 있다고 볼 수 있으므로, 빈칸에는 '결정권자'라는 의미의 ②가 들어가는 것이 적절하다.

rule v. 통치하다; 규정하다; 판결하다 override v. 무시하다, 거절하다; 무효로 하다 handicapped a. 신체적 장애가 있는, 불구의 bogeyman n. 도깨비, 악귀, 무서운 것 arbiter n. 중재인, 조정자; 결정권자 entourage n. 측근, 수행원, 동료 mortician n. 장의사

주(州) 당국이 의료 결정에 대한 '최종 결정권자'이므로 장애아에 대해 얼마만큼의 치료가 필요할지에 대한 의사의 결정을 조지아(Georgia)주가 뒤집을 수 있다고 항소순회법원이 올해 봄에 판결했다.

04

③ ③

연구자 명단의 첫 자리를 제공하는 것은 권위를 침해한 것에 대한 보상 혹은 속죄의 의미로 보는 것이 타당하다. 따라서 빈칸에는 ③이 들어가는 것이 가장 자연스럽다.

encroach v. 침입하다; 잠식하다, 침해하다 authority n. 권위, 권력, 위신; 권한 honored a. 명예로운 offense n. 위반, 반칙; 기분을 상하게 하는 것; 모욕 exhilarate v. 원기를 돋우다, 유쾌하게 하다 expatiate v. 상세히 설명하다, 부연하다 expiate v. 속죄하다, 보상하다 expurgate v. (책의 불온한 대목을) 삭제하다

이 프로젝트를 추진하는 동안 제가 당신의 권위를 침해했다고 생각합니다. 그래서 저는 연구자 명단의 영예로운 첫 자리를 당신에게 드립니다. 그것이 제 무례함을 속죄하기에 충분하길 바랍니다.

05

② ②

처음 이마를 내려쳤을 때엔 제대로 잘라내지 못했지만, 시체를 굴려서 돌려놓은 후에는 단번에 두개골을 쪼갰다'라는 내용이다. 시체를 돌리기 전, 즉 이마가 위쪽을 향해 있었을 때에 자르는 일을 제대로 하지 못한 것은, 대상이 되는 것을 마주 한 상태에서는 자르는 행위를 하는 것이 힘들었거나 혹은 그 일을 망설였다는 것으로 볼 수 있다. 그러므로 빈칸에 들어갈 수 있는 가장 적절한 표현은 ②가 된다.

chop n. (도끼나 칼로) 내리치기, 절단 forehead n. 이마, 앞머리 task n. 일, 임무, 작업 roll over 구르다, 자빠뜨리다 effective a. 유효한, 효과적인 split v. 쪼개다, 찢다, 분할하다 skull n. 두개골, 머리 drollery n. 익살스러운 짓, 익살, 해학 hesitancy n. 주저, 망설임 simplicity n. 단순, 간단, 평이; 검소 audacity n. 대담무쌍, 뻔뻔스러움

이마를 향해 첫 번째로 여러 번 내려쳤을 때엔 뼈를 관통하지 못했는데, 이는 아마도 그 일을 망설였음을 보여주는 증거라 할 수 있다. 시체를 굴려서 돌려놓은 후, 다음번에 내려쳤을 때엔 보다 효과적이었다. 일격으로 두개골을 밑바닥까지 쪼갰다.

---

06 ④

시체를 파내서 먹는 행위와 사람을 죽여서 소금에 절이는 행위는 모두 '식인 행위'를 설명하고 있는 진술이다. 그러므로 ④가 정답이다.

colony n. 식민지; 집단, 부락 starve v. 굶주리다, 굶어죽다 account n. 설명; 이야기, 기술; 근거 corpse n. 시체, 송장 exhume v. 파내다; (특히 시체를) 발굴하다; 찾아내다 salt v. 소금을 치다, 절이다 flesh n. 살; 육체 execute v. 실행하다, 실시하다; 사형을 집행하다, 처형하다 chauvinism n. 쇼비니즘, 맹목적 애국주의 famine n. 기근, 흉작, 배고픔 cremation n. 소각, 화장 cannibalism n. 식인풍습; 동족끼리 서로 잡아먹음; 만행

식인풍습이 식민지의 "굶주리는 시기"에 일어났다는 사실은 의심의 여지가 거의 없었다. 시체를 파내서 먹고, 남편이 아내를 죽여서 살을 소금에 절인 것에 관한 이야기를 적어도 여섯 곳에서 기술하고 있다.

---

07 ②

LP판과 앨범 표지가 과거의 우리와 우리의 음악적 경험을 '기억나게 해주는' 것이므로 빈칸에는 reminders와 관련 있는 ②가 적절하다.

go beyond ~에 그치지 않다, ~이상이다 tangible a. 만져서 알 수 있는, 확실한 reminder n. 기억나게 하는 것 friable a. 부서지기 쉬운 evocative a. 불러내는, 떠올리는, 환기시키는 pastoral a. 전원의, 목가적인 insurgent a. 모반의, 폭동을 일으키는

우리는 플라스틱 레코드판이 만들어내는 더 풍부한 소리를 선호하지만 우리의 플라스틱 레코드판 사랑은 소리에 그치지 않는다. LP판은 젊었을 적의 우리를 확실히 기억나게 해주며 앨범 표지는 (옛적의) 음악적 경험을 환기시켜주는 시각적 추가물이다.

---

08 ①

마땅히 주목해야 할 자료에 주의를 기울이지 않고 주장하는 것은 생각이 없는 '태평한' 주장이라 할 수 있으므로, 빈칸에는 ①이 적절하다.

target v. 표적으로 삼다, 겨냥하다 disproportionate a. 불균형의, 어울리지 않는 blithely ad. 생각 없이 태평하게, 분별없이 dejectedly ad. 낙심하여 wrathfully ad. 화가 난 듯 judiciously ad. 현명하게

퍼거슨 시장은 대부분이 백인인 시 경찰이 흑인들을 표적으로 삼아 터무니없이 많은 수의 검문검색을 행해왔다는 것을 명백히 보여주는 자료에는 전혀 주목하지 않고 퍼거슨 시가 인종간의 조화를 이루고 있다고 생각 없이 태평하게 주장했다.

---

09 ④

첫 문장에서 종교는 주된 요인이 아니었다고 했으므로 빈칸에는 종교적 색채가 없는 ④가 들어가는 것이 가장 적절하다.

uprising n. 봉기 protester n. 시위자 take to ~에 가다 implementation n. 실행 pervasive a. 만연한 blasphemy n. 신성모독 secularization n. 세속화 heresy n. 이단 depravation n. 부패

시리아에서 알아사드에 대항한 봉기가 시작되었을 때 종교는 주된 요인이 아니었다. 2011년 3월에 시리아의 시위자들이 거리로 뛰쳐나왔을 때 그들은 민주적 이상의 실행과 만연한 부패의 종식을 구하고 있었다.

---

10 ③

첫 번째 빈칸에는 '둘 사이를 멀어지게 하다'는 뜻이 되게 하는 wedge가 적절하고, 두 번째 빈칸의 경우 그 뒤에서 '감정이 단단해져 있었다'고 했으므로 빈칸에는 unresolvable(해결할 수 없는)이 적절하다.

hedge n. 울타리, 장벽, 방지책 indispensable a. 필수불가결한 linkage n. 연결 장치 irreversible a. 돌이킬 수 없는 wedge n. 쐐기 drive a wedge between (문제 따위가 둘 사이를) 이간시키다 unresolvable a. 해결할 수 없는 leverage n. 지렛대, 수단 impalpable a. 감지할 수 없는

그녀는 20년 동안 오빠와 단 한 번 말을 했었다. 그들은 차로 30분이 채 안 걸리는 거리를 두고 서로 떨어져 살았지만, 아버지가 돌아가신 후 둘 사이를 멀어지게 한 다툼은 해결할 수 없는 것 같았고 감정은 콘크리트처럼 단단해져 있었다.

---

11 ④

첫 번째 빈칸 다음에서 otherwise pure(그렇지 않으면 순수할)라 했으므로 첫 번째 빈칸에는 '오점'이라는 뜻의 blemish나 stain이 적절하다. 한편, 두 번째 문장의 주어 it은 '과격집단들의 개입'을 가리키는데, 정권은 이것을 국가를 해치려는 음모로 보았을 것이므로 두 번째 빈칸에는 debilitate(약화시키다)나 perturb(교란하다)가 적절하다.

brigade n. 여단, 부대 exile v. 추방하다 uprising n. 봉기 tyranny n. 학정, 독재 scheme n. 계획, 책략, 음모 misstep n. 실수 bolster v. 강화하다 blemish n. 오점 revamp v. 개혁하다 feat n. 공적 debilitate v. 약화시키다 stain n. 오점, 얼룩 perturb v. 교란시키다

반란군과 추방된 야당지도자들에게는 과격집단들의 개입이 그렇지 않으면 순수할 반독재 봉기에 대한 불행한 오점이었다. 독재정권에게 그것은 외국의 자금 지원을 받아 나라를 뒤흔들려는 음모의 증거였다.

12 ①

빈칸 앞의 대명사 they는 scammers를 가리킨다. 기업공개가 있을 것이라는 헛소문을 퍼뜨려 투자자들로부터 많은 돈을 끌어 모은 사기꾼이 그 돈을 가지고 어떻게 하겠는가를 묻는 문제라 할 수 있다. '도망가다, 달아나다'라는 의미의 ①이 가장 자연스럽게 호응한다.

IPO 기업공개, 주식공개 get in on the ground floor 처음부터 관여하여 유리한 지위를 차지하다 substantial a. 실질적인; 많은, 대폭적인 profit n. 이익, 수익, 소득 scammer n. 사기꾼, 난봉꾼 upcoming a. 다가오는, 곧 있을 abscond v. 도망하다, 달아나다 grieve v. 몹시 슬퍼하다 wail v. 울부짖다, 소리 내어 울다, 통곡하다 preponderate v. 한쪽으로 기울다, 영향력이 있다

기업공개는 '처음부터 유리한 입장에 있게 하'여 상당한 이득을 볼 수 있는 기회를 제공하기 때문에, 그것을 좋아하는 투자자들이 더러 있다. 하지만 사기꾼들은 주식을 공개할 계획이 전혀 없거나 아예 존재하지 않는 회사의 기업공개가 있을 것이라는 말을 퍼뜨린다. 그런 다음엔 투자자의 돈을 가지고 달아난다.

13 ③

진부한 표현이 지나치게 많은 대화의 속성 혹은 성격을 묻는 문제라 할 수 있다. 빈칸에는 cliché라는 단어가 가진 의미를 내포하고 있는 단어가 들어가야 하므로, ③이 정답이 된다. 한편, 마지막 문장은 빈칸이 들어있는 문장에서 언급하고 있는 문제점의 해결책에 해당하는데, 여기서 creative를 언급하고 있으므로, 이 단어의 반의어를 찾는 식으로 정답을 도출하는 것도 가능하다.

cliché n. 진부한 표현, 상투적인 문구 attention n. 주의, 주목; 배려, 고려 disinteresting a. 재미없는 creative a. 창조적인; 독창적인; 창작적인; 건설적인 condescending a. 겸손한, 저자세의; 짐짓 겸손한 체 하는; 생색을 내는 outlandish a. 이국풍의; 이상스러운; 외진, 벽촌의 threadbare a. 입어서 떨어진; 초라한; 진부한, 케케묵은 halcyon a. 고요한, 평화로운

이미 여러 번 들은 적 있는 진부한 표현을 들으면, 사람들은 더 이상 당신에게 주의를 기울이지 않게 될 것이며, 대신에 다른 무언가에 주의를 기울이게 될 것이다. 진부한 표현을 지나치게 많이 사용하면 대화는 케케묵은 것이 되고 재미가 없어진다. 그들의 주의를 정말로 끌고자 한다면, 창의적인 말, 문구, 아이디어를 이용해야 한다.

14 ①

두 번째 문장에서, 주절의 내용과 양보의 접속사 Although가 이끄는 종속절의 내용은 대조를 이루어야 하는데, 주절과 종속절의 동사 표현 '더 이상 성행하지 않고 있다'와 '여전히 그러하다'가 이미 대조를 이루고 있는 상황이므로, 빈칸에는 주절의 주어와 같은 의미를 만드는 단어가 들어가면 된다. 따라서 자체에 physically의 의미를 가진 단어가 정답이 되며, ①이 이런 조건에 부합하는 단어이다.

approach n. 접근, 접근법; 연구법 inducement n. 유인책; 권유; 장려; 자극 spank n. 찰싹 때리기 sanction n. 시인, 찬성; 제재 vogue n. 유행, 인기 physically ad. 물리적으로; 물질적으로; 신체적으로 corporal a. 육체의, 신체의 refulgent a. 빛나는, 찬란한 colossal a. 거대한 pedagogic a. 교육학적인, 교육학상의; 교수법의; 현학적인

서방국가의 정부들은 가장 좋은 접근방법을 놓고 자기네들끼리 다투고 있다. 그들은 유인책이라는 사탕을 제공해야 할까 아니면 제재라는 채찍을 제공해야 할까? 서방국가 대부분에서 체벌은 더 이상 성행하고 있지 않지만, 북한을 물리적으로 응징하는 것은 여전히 세 번째 선택방안으로 남아 있다.

15 ④

총기 규제법에 대한 롬니의 견해가 두 번째 문장부터 이어지고 있다. 2004년에는 총기 소지에 강하게 반대하였다가, 나중에는 총기 협회의 종신회원이 되었고 그 단체를 지지했으므로, 결국 총기 규제에 대한 그의 견해는 확고하지 못하고 우유부단하다고 볼 수 있다.

assault n. 습격, 공격 endorse v. (공개적으로) 지지하다; 보증하다; 배서하다 lackadaisical a. 활기없는, 기력이 없는, 열의 없는 rule-of-reason a. 합리적인, 도리에 맞는 henpecked a. 공처가의 wishy-washy a. 미온적인, 확고하지 못한; 태도가 불분명한

총기 규제법에 대하여 롬니(Romney)는 매우 우유부단한 태도를 취해 왔다. 2004년에, 그는 매사추세츠 주(州)에서 공격용 총기를 금지하는 가장 엄격한 법안을 통과시켰다. 하지만 후에 롬니는 전미 총기 협회(NRA)에 종신회원이 되었으며 NRA를 공개적으로 지지하길 희망한다.

16 ④

두 번째 문장에서 '우리의 말을 심각하게 받아들이지 않을 것'이라고 했는데, 이는 곧 우리의 결의를 '가볍게' 여길 것이라는 뜻이다. 따라서 빈칸에는 seriously에 대해 반대 의미를 가진 단어가 필요하며, '경솔, 경박'이라는 의미의 ④가 정답이 된다.

sanction n. 인가, 시인; 제재 back up ~을 후원하다, 지지하다 renegade n. 배반자; 배교자; 반역자 resolution n. 결심, 결의; 결의안 request n. 요구, 의뢰; 수요 state-of-the-art a. 최첨단의, 최신식의, 최고급의 vessel n. 그릇; 배, 항공기 bare a. 벌거벗은, 가리지않은; 그저 ~뿐인 minimum n. 최소, 최소한도 mean business 진정이다, 진심이다 whimper n. 흐느낌; 탄원, 불평 verbiage n. 말이 많음, 용장(冗長) paroxysm n. (주기적인) 발작; 경련; (감정 등의) 격발 levity n. 경솔, 경박; 변덕

제재조치를 선언하고서 그 조치들을 뒷받침해 줄 군사력을 우리에게 제공하지 않는 것은 변절 국가들로 하여금 우리의 결의를 가볍게 여기도록 만들 뿐입니다. 그들은 우리의 말을 심각하게 받아들이지 않을 것입니다. 우리가 첨단 해군 선박 몇 척을 요구하는 것은 우리가 진심이라는 것을 그들에게 보여주기 위해 필요한 최소한의 것입니다.

17   ②

두 번째 문장은 '가정주부가 하는 일이 실제로는 상당히 많음'을 이야기하고 있다. 이와 같은 상황에서 첫 번째 문장에서 언급하고 있는 '가사일은 시간이 많이 걸리지도 않고, 공로도 없다'라는 말을 주부가 듣는다면, 불쾌한 기분을 나타내 보일 가능성이 크다. 따라서 빈칸에는 '노여움, 불쾌'라는 의미의 ②가 들어가는 것이 적절하다.

suggestion n. 암시, 연상; 제안 domestic a. 가정의, 가사의; 국내의; 국산의 responsibility n. 책임, 책무, 의무 time-consuming a. 시간이 걸리는, 시간을 낭비하는 merit n. 가치; 장점; 공적 bring home the bacon 생활비를 벌다; 성공하다 devote v. (노력·돈·시간 따위를) 바치다; 쏟다; 내맡기다 bashfulness n. 수줍어 함, 부끄러워 함 umbrage n. 불쾌, 분개, 노여움 sanctimony n. 신앙이 깊은 체 함 viand n. 식품; 음식

가사일이 시간이 많이 걸리지도 않고 공로도 없다는 말을 듣는 경우, 가정주부들은 분개할 지도 모른다. 어머니가 집에 있고, 아버지가 생활비를 벌어오는 경우, 어머니는 주당 53시간을 육아와 가사에 전념하는 데 반해, 일을 하는 아버지는 불과 2시간만을 할애한다.

18   ①

빈칸에 들어갈 단어를 다음 문장에서 '소리를 묘사하는 단어'로 표현하고 있다. 따라서 '의성어'라는 의미의 ①이 정답으로 적절하다.

auditory a. 청각의, 귀의 imagery n. 심상; 비유적 표현, 형상 buzz n. (윙윙) 울리는 소리, 소란스러운 소리 clap n. 찰싹, 짝짝, 쾅; 박수 소리, 천둥소리 meow n. 야옹; 고양이 울음소리 onomatopoeia n. 의성어 allonym n. 필명; 남의 이름으로 출판된 작품 synecdoche n. 제유, 일부로써 전체를 나타내는 표현법 litotes n. 곡언법, 완서법

때때로 시인은 당신이 무언가를 듣고 있다고 생각하도록 만들고 싶을 것이다. 이것은 청각적 심상이라 불리는 개념의 일부이다. 청각적 심상을 일으키는 일반적인 방법 가운데 하나는 의성어를 사용하는 것이다. 소리를 묘사하는 단어들 – 웅웅, 짝짝, 야옹과 같은 단어들에 대해 생각해 보라. 그 단어들을 큰 소리로 말하는 경우, 그것이 묘사하고 있는 것과 유사한 소리가 난다. 예를 들어, buzz라는 단어의 "zz"는 벌이 내는 소리와 유사한 소리가 난다.

19   ②

빈칸 뒤에 위치한 관계사절의 내용을 통해 정답을 찾아야 한다. '마술처럼 고효율, 고성능의 엔진으로 만들어준다'라는 말은 '어떤 경우에든 상황을 갑작스럽게 개선시킨다'라는 의미이므로, '특효약, 만병통치약'이라는 의미의 ②가 자연스럽게 호응한다.

vehicle n. 수송수단, 탈것; 매개물 additive n. 부가물, 첨가제 emission n. 배출, 발산; 배기가스 efficient a. 능률적인, 효과적인; 유능한 octane n. 옥탄(석유 중의 무색 액체 탄화수소) rating n. 등급, 급수 opus n. 저작; 작품 elixir n. 만병통치약, 특효약 nebbish n. 무기력한 사람, 박력이 없는 사람, 쓸모없는 사람 placebo n. 위약(僞藥); 위안

일반적으로, 만약 당신의 차(車)가 상태가 나쁘지 않다면, 성능, 배기가스, 연료 절약 등의 개선을 위해 첨가제가 필요하지는 않다. 마술처럼 엔진을 보다 효율적이면서도 강력하게 만들어주는 만병통치약은 존재하지 않는다. 당신의 차가 요구하고 있는 올바른 옥탄가의 연료를 사용하고 있지 않은 경우에는 아마도 이러한 첨가제들이 효과를 볼 수도 있을 것이다.

20   ①

Procrustean Bed가 이 문제를 풀 수 있는 키워드이다. 이 용어는 "획일적으로 자신의 생각에 맞추어 남을 바꾸려 강요하고 재단하는 것"을 뜻한다. 따라서 학습률이 떨어지는 아이의 경우 프로크로스테란 침대의 기준에 맞추려고 아이들을 무리하게 대할 것이다. 이와 반대로 성적이 뛰어난 아이의 경우 그 기준에 맞추어 제재를 할 것인데 발을 잘라내지는 않지만 학습을 방해한다고 했으므로 아이는 제대로 공부를 하지 못할 것이다. 이 문장에서는 다리를 비유적으로 언급했으므로 '절뚝거리다'는 뜻의 hobble이 두 번째 빈칸에 적절하다.

fall short 모자라다; 미치지 못하다 Procrustean Bed 무리하게 따르도록 하는 체제[방침, 주의], (지나치게) 획일화된 제도 hew v. 자르다 stretch v. 펴다, 잡아당기다 hobble v. 절뚝거리게 하다, 난처하게 하다 deter v. 제지하다, 단념시키다 sprain v. (발목, 손목 따위를) 삐다 chastise v. 응징하다; 질책하다 praise v. 칭찬하다 stomp v. 짓밟다 reinforce v. 강화하다, 보강하다

아이는 표준 시험으로 측정되는 일반적인 핵심 교육 과정의 기준에 얼마나 잘 맞는지 학문적으로 평가받는다. (이에) 미치지 못하는 아이들은 획일화된 제도에 그들을 맞추기 위해 때때로 가혹할 정도로 무리하게 대한다. 기준을 초과하는 아이들은 그들의 다리가 잘리지는 않는다. 대신에 그 아이들은 그들의 학습에 도움이 되는 두 다리를 완전히 사용하지 못하고 종종 절름발이가 된다. 이것은 어느 집단의 아이들에게도 공평하지 못하거나 유익하지 않다.

21   ②

첫 번째 빈칸의 경우, 바로 앞에서 '깨끗한 석탄'이라는 표현이 석탄이 가진 나쁜 이미지를 희석시키기 위한 것이라고 했는데, 석탄이 환경오염을 일으킬 수 있는 점을 감안하면, '실제로는 환경에 좋지 않음에도 해를 끼치지 않는 것처럼 포장한다'라는 의미를 내포한 단어가 필요함을 알 수 있다. greenwash, double-faced, sugar-coated가 가능하다. 한편, 마지막 문장도 '깨끗한 석탄'을 비판하는 내용이어야겠는데, 두 번째 문장에서 이 표현을 contradiction으로 설명하고 있으므로, 이와 유사한 의미를 가진 단어가 들어갈 수 있다. incongruity 또는 oxymoron이 가능하다. 상기 두 조건을 모두 만족시키는 ②가 정답이다.

kid oneself (사실은 그렇지 않은데) 좋은 쪽을 취하려 하다; 착각하다, 자만하다 president-elect n. 대통령 당선인 in terms 명확하게 contradiction n. 부인, 부정; 모순 industry n. 공업, 산업; 근면 buzzword n. 현학적인 전문용어, 유행어 insidious a. 음험한, 교활한; 잠행성(潛行性)의 eco-friendly a. 환경 친화적인, 친환경적인 incongruity n. 부조화, 부적합 greenwash a. 녹색분칠을 한, 실제로는 환경에 유해한 활동을 하면서 마치 친환경적인 것처럼 광고하는 oxymoron n. 모순어법 double-faced a. 두 마음이 있는, 위선의 tautology n. 동어반복,

불필요한 말의 반복 sugar-coated a. (사람들을 속이도록) 보기 좋게 꾸민, 사탕발림을 한 metonymy n. 환유법

오늘 아침에 스타킹에 묻은 석탄을 발견했다면, 대충 넘어가려 해선 안 된다. 그것은 결코 깨끗하지 않다. 대통령 당선인이 무엇을 생각하더라도, "깨끗한 석탄"은 분명히 모순되는 말이다. 그린피스(Greenpeace)는 '깨끗한 석탄'은 자신의 더러운 이미지를 깨끗하게 하기 위한 업계의 노력 - 친환경을 내세우기 위해 업계에서 쓰는 용어라고 말하고 있다. 워싱턴 포스트는 "깨끗한 석탄, 이 말보다 국민의 건강에 있어 더 우리를 함정에 빠뜨리거나 더 위험한 모순되는 말은 일찍이 없었다."라고 쓰고 있다.

22 ②

첫 번째 빈칸은 순접의 접속사 and를 통해 esoteric metaphor와 연결되어 있으므로 이것과 문맥상 유사한 의미를 가진 단어가 들어가야 한다. anagrams 또는 enigmas가 가능하다. 한편, 두 번째 빈칸 뒤의 prophecies는 결국 노스트라다무스의 시에 담긴 속뜻을 가리킨다고 보아야 하겠는데, 바로 앞에서 당국에서 그것을 알게 되는 것을 두려워했다고 했으므로 아무나 예언의 내용을 알 수 없도록 해놓았을 것이라 짐작할 수 있다. 따라서 두 번째 빈칸에는 '비밀스럽다'라는 의미를 가진 occult 또는 cryptic이 적절하다. 상기 두 조건을 모두 만족시키는 정답은 ②가 된다.

quatrain n. 4행시 esoteric a. 비밀의; 내밀한; 비법의 metaphor n. 은유 specific a. 독특한; 특정한; 구체적인 geographical a. 지리학의, 지리적인 reference n. 문의, 조회; 참고; 언급 arrange v. 배열하다, 정리하다; 조정하다 chronological a. 연대순의; 연대학의 preface n. 서문, 머리말 verse n. 운문, 시 authority n. 권위, 권력; 권위자; (pl.) 당국 prediction n. 예언, 예보 prophecy n. 예언 enlightened a. 식견 있는; 문명화된 anthem n. 찬송가; 축가 occult a. 신비로운, 불가사의의; 비밀의; 초자연적인 anagram n. 글자 수수께끼 cryptic a. 숨은; 비밀의 grumble n. 불만, 불평, 푸념 forlorn a. 버려진, 버림받은; 고독한 enigma n. 수수께끼; 불가해한 사물 antediluvian a. 대홍수 이전의; 낡은, 고풍의

노스트라다무스(Nostradamus)가 쓴 각각의 4행시는 비밀스런 은유와 수수께끼 같은 글자들로 가득 차 있다. 그 4행시들에는 날짜나 지리에 대한 구체적인 언급이 거의 없으며, 시간 순서대로 배열되어 있지도 않다. 서문에 따르면, 그 시들에는 이해하지 못하도록 하는 의도가 숨어 있었다. 노스트라다무스는 그가 살고 있던 시대의 당국에서 그의 예언을 완전히 알게 되는 경우 그의 작품이 폐기되고 말 것을 두려워했다고 말했다. 그는 그의 비밀스런 예언을 미래의 보다 식견 있는 사람들이 더 잘 이해할 것으로 보았다.

23 ②

빈칸이 포함된 문장과 마지막 문장 사이를 논리적으로 연결하려면 '광고와 소비 사이의 연관성이 미약함에도 불구하고 광고는 효과적이다'라는 의미가 되어야 한다. '불분명한', '희박한, 미약한' 정도의 의미가 들어가는 것이 적절하다.

shed light on ~을 비추다, ~을 밝히다 self-esteem n. 자부심 relieve v. 경감하다, 덜다 thirst n. 갈증, 목마름 interactive a. 쌍방향의, 상호 작용하는 tenuous a. 희박한, 미약한 in direct proportion 정비례 관계인 compelling a. 강력한

심리학 이론들은 또한 사람들이 가끔 예측 불가능한 방식으로, 심지어 겉으로 보기에 불합리한 방식으로 소비하는 이유를 설명해 줄 수 있다. 차량에서부터 잡지에 이르기까지 모든 것을 팔기 위해 성(性)이 이용된다는 것이나, 청량음료 광고는 갈증을 해소하겠다는 욕망보다는 소속감이나 자부심을 위한 욕망에 더 많이 호소한다는 것은 공공연한 사실이다. 사람들은 광고 캠페인과 그들이 그 제품을 구매함으로써 실제로 얻게 되는 것 사이의 연관성이 기껏해야 미약하다는 것을 의식적인 수준에서 알고 있다. 그러나 그렇다고 해서 광고 캠페인이 성공하지 못하는 것은 아니다.

24 ④

글 전체에서 이메일의 무분별한 범람에 대해 이야기하고 있음에 주목한다. 너무나도 많은 정보를 얻게 되는 상황에서는 그 정보 중에서 가치 있는 것과 그렇지 않은 것을 가려내는 일이 중요한 일로 대두하게 될 것이다.

estimated a. 평가상의, 견적의 figure n. 숫자; 합계; 모양; 인물 confine v. 제한하다; 감금하다 advent n. 도래(到來), 출현 longing n. 동경, 갈망, 열망 scarce a. 부족한, 적은; 희박한 resource n. 자원, 물자; 수단 readily ad. 즉시, 쉽사리; 기꺼이 available a. 이용할 수 있는, 쓸모 있는; 입수할 수 있는 make do with 임시변통하다, 때우다 take up time 시간이 들다, 시간이 소요되다 ask for the moon 무리한 요구를 하다 sift the wheat from the chaff 체질을 하여 왕겨에서 밀을 가려내다; 가치 있는 것과 없는 것을 가려내다

이것은 세계적인 문제이다. 2010년에 매일 2940억 통의 이메일이 발송된 것으로 추정되고 있으며, 그 수치는 계속해서 늘어나고 있다. 기술이 발전함에 따라, 그것에서 벗어나기가 점점 어려워졌다. 이메일을 보내는 것은 더 이상 사무실의 데스크탑 컴퓨터에 한정돼 있지 않다. 스마트폰이 출현하면서 사람들은 어디서든 자신의 이메일을 확인할 수 있게 되었다. 정보가 희귀한 자원이어서 밖으로 나가서 찾아다녀야 했던 시절이 다시금 그리워질 지경이다. 지금은 너무나도 많은 정보를 너무나도 손쉽게 얻을 수 있어서, 가치 있는 것과 없는 것을 가려내는 일이 어려운 일이 되었다.

25 ②

아리스토텔레스가 우리의 지각 능력과 인식 능력을 신뢰했다는 진술로부터 정답을 추론할 수 있다.

subject v. 종속시키다 searing a. 타는 듯한; 혹독한 perceptual a. 지각의 dally v. 희롱하다; 빈둥빈둥 지내다; 낭비하다 substantive a. 실질적인 throw up 토하다, 던지다 affirmative a. 단언적인; 긍정의; 승낙의 sceptical a. 의심 많은, 회의적인 neutral a. 중립의, 불편부당의 unbiased a. 편견이 없는, 공평한

아리스토텔레스의 철학에 대한 기본적인 접근법은 처음에 대조를 통해서 가장 잘 이해된다. 데카르트가 모든 지식주장들을 혹독한 방법론적인 회의에 종속시키는 것에 의해서 철학과 과학을 확고한 기반 위에 세워놓는 것을 추구한 반면, 아리스토텔레스는 우리의 지각과 인식 능력이 기본적으로 신뢰할 만하고, 실질적인 철학에 참여하기 전에 회의적인 자세를 갖고 시간을 낭

비할 필요가 없다는 확신을 가지고 철학을 시작한다. 따라서 그는 현대의 자연과학자와 같은 방식으로 탐구의 모든 영역 속으로 나아간다. 그가 철학적 탐구를 할 때, 아리스토텔레스는 이 세계의 모습들이 제기한 수수께끼에 대해 사유하고, 지금까지 그 수수께끼에 대해 논의되어진 것을 재검토하면서 이 세계가 어떻게 생겼는지를 고려하는 것에 의해서 철학을 시작한다.

TEST 26

01 ①	**02** ①	**03** ④	**04** ②	**05** ①	**06** ②	**07** ②	**08** ①	**09** ④	**10** ④
11 ①	**12** ②	**13** ④	**14** ①	**15** ①	**16** ③	**17** ③	**18** ①	**19** ④	**20** ③
21 ③	**22** ③	**23** ③	**24** ②	**25** ③					

01 ①

Because가 이끄는 종속절과 주절의 내용은 인과관계를 이뤄야 한다. monstrosity는 Because절에서 언급한 두 가지 가운데 was in a state of anarchy를 나타내고 있으므로, 빈칸에는 lacked a leader의 의미를 나타낼 수 있는 단어가 들어가야 한다. 따라서 '지도자가 없다'라는 의미의 ①이 정답이 된다.

anarchy n. 무정부; 무정부 상태 consecutive a. 연속적인, 잇따른; 시종일관된 monstrosity n. 기형(奇形), 기괴함; 괴물 acephalous a. 머리가 없는; 지도자가 없는 grandiose a. 웅장한, 숭고한, 장엄한 disheveled a. 흩어진, 헝클어진 well-heeled a. 부유한, 넉넉한

잇따른 전쟁 후에 무정부상태에 있었고 지도자가 없었기 때문에, 그 나라는 머리가 없는 괴물로 묘사되었다.

02 ①

shudder는 공포나 혐오감을 나타내므로 '혹평 받은'이라는 뜻의 ①이 정답으로 적절하다.

shudder v. 몸서리치다, 진저리치다 intermingling n. 혼합 shoot back 말로 되받아치다 hammer v. 헐뜯다, 혹평하다 reclaim v. 교정하다; 개간하다 condone v. 용서하다 ballyhoo v. 요란스럽게 선전하다

그의 가장 인기 있는 앨범인 1973년에 나온 블랙 버드는 비평가들의 혹평을 받았는데, 그들은 그 앨범이 재즈와 팝을 혼합한 것에 몸서리쳤다. 그는 "나는 창의적이지, 연예 오락적이지 않다. 나는 다른 모든 사람이 하는 것을 따라하지 않는다."라고 되받아쳤다.

03 ④

세 가지 선택안이 모두 적법절차를 따르지 않은 자의적 처분이므로, '자경주의'라는 의미의 ④가 정답으로 적절하다.

suspected a. 의심되는 detain v. 구금하다 out ad. 없어져, 유행이 지나 in ad. 들어와, 유행하여 appalling a. 경악스런, 섬뜩한 diachronism n. 통시적(通時的) 연구 paternalism n. 온정주의 evangelism n. 복음주의 vigilantism n. 자경주의: 사적인 처벌행위

테러 용의자를 발견할 때 그들은 세 가지 중 하나를 선택한다. 죽이거나, 현장에 그대로 내버려두거나, 지방 정부와 협조하여 구금한다. 인권은 없어지고 자경주의가 횡행하는 것 같다. 이것은 슬픈 일 이상으로 경악스런 일이다.

04 ②

평소에 관리를 잘 하는 운전자들을 가리켜야 하므로 빈칸에는 '세심히', '꼼꼼하게'라는 의미를 가진 ②가 정답으로 적절하다.

monitor v. 감시하다 mechanic n. 기계 수리공 tread n. 접지면 antifreeze n. 부동액 withstand v. 견디다 wear and tear 소모, 마멸 fitfully ad. 변덕스럽게 fastidiously ad. 세심하게, 꼼꼼하게 perfunctorily a. 피상적으로 unwittingly ad. 모르는 사이에

꼼꼼하게 연료 수준을 관리하고 타이어 공기압을 점검하는 운전자조차도 차가 또 한 차례 겨울의 마모를 견딜 수 있게 하려면 정비공에게 맡겨 배터리 충전 상태와 타이어 접지면의 상태와 부동액 수준을 점검해야 한다.

05 ①

중국 관광객들을 거만하고 정치적으로 옳지 않다고 생각하여 투숙까지 거부할 정도였다면, 여관 주인은 무척 화가 나 있었을 것으로 볼 수 있다. 그러므로 ①이 정답으로 적절하다.

influx n. 유입 arrogant a. 거만한 politically incorrect 정치적으로 옳지 않은 (소수집단에 대한 부정적인 편견을 가진) host v. 접대하다 apoplectic a. 몹시 흥분한, 화가 난 self-possessed a. 침착한, 냉정한 perky a. 의기양양한, 쾌활한 blithesome a. 즐거운, 유쾌한

여관 주인은 본토인들, 즉 중국 관광객들의 새로운 유입에 대해 몹시 화가 나 있었는데, 그는 그들이 거만하고 정치적으로 옳지 않은 것을 알게 되었던 것이다. 그는 비록 장사를 망쳐도 그들을 투숙시키기를 거부했다. 그는 중국인들이 골치라고 말했다.

06 ②

'재능'을 목적어로 취하여서 긍정적인 의미가 되기에는 '연마하다'라는 의미의 ②가 적절하다.

dame n. 부인, 여사 portray v. (역을) 연기하다 grill v. 굽다, 엄하게 신문하다 hone v. 연마하다 pop v. (폭죽을) 펑펑 터뜨리다 smear v. 더럽히다

나이가 많고 크게 성공했음에도 불구하고 주디 덴치 여사는 도전적인 역을 맡아 연기하고 계속 자신의 재능을 연마하기를 두려워하지 않는다. 그녀는 오늘날 젊은 여배우들에게 좋은 본이 됨이 분명하다.

---

07 ②

마지막 부분의 archaic(고풍스런)과 같은 의미인 ②가 빈칸에 들어가기에 가장 적절하다.

obvious a. 명백한, 이해하기 쉬운, 눈에 잘 띄는 restless a. 들떠있는, 끊임없는 unabashed a. 뻔뻔스런, 태연한 Georgian a. 조지 왕조 시대(1714-1830) 예술양식의 waver v. 망설이다 quaint a. 기묘한; 예스러운 멋이 있는 anemic a. 빈혈의; 활기 없는 latent a. 숨어 있는, 잠재적인

"예스런 멋이 있는"은 혁명과 끊임없는 팽창과 태연한 수익 추구 위에 세워진 국가인 미국에 대해 사용하기에 눈에 잘 띄는 단어가 아니다. 그러나 아름답게 복원된 식민지시대 윌리엄스버그의 조지왕조 양식의 거리는 놀라우리만치 고풍스러워 보인다.

---

08 ①

조화로운 음악표현들이 당시에는 모험적으로 여겨졌고 오늘날에는 전혀 괴상하게 여겨지지 않았다는 단서로부터 grotesque와 같은 의미의 표현을 찾으면 됨을 알 수 있다.

grotesque a. 기괴한; 이상한 freakish a. 변덕스러운; 기형적인, 기이한, 기괴한 bromidic a. 진부한 stiff-necked a. 완고한, 고집센 verboten a. (법률·당국에 의해) 금지된

종종 우리는 베토벤의 조화로운 표현들이 당시의 청중에게는 모험적이고 심지어 기괴하게 여겨졌음을 안다. 지금 완전히 익숙해진 그의 작품들은 결코 기이하게 보이지 않는다.

---

09 ④

첫 문장에서 '그'에 대해 부정적인 평가를 내리고 있으므로 첫 번째 빈칸에는 frustrates(좌절케 하다)나 baffles(당황케 하다)가 적절하고, 두 번째 빈칸에는 cheesy(저질스런)와 같이 부정적인 의미를 가진 harassing(괴롭히는)이나 patronizing(선심 쓰는 척하는)이 적절하다. 따라서 ④가 정답이 된다.

take the liberty to V 마음대로(멋대로) ~하다 cheesy a. 저질스런 gratify v. 만족시키다 discerning a. 식별력 있는 regale v. 즐겁게 하다 harassing a. 괴롭히는 frustrate v. 좌절시키다 approving a. 찬성하는 baffle v. 당황케 하다 patronizing a. 선심 쓰는 척하는

그와 같은 유명한 작가가 사람들을 제인 오스틴에 반대하는 것으로 자기 마음대로 일반화한 것은 알고 보면 슬픈 일이다. 그의 저질스런 농담이나 오스틴 독자들에게 선심 쓰는 척하는 그의 태도 이상으로 나를 당황케 하는 것은 그가 오스틴의 책들이 씌어진 시대를 이해하지 못하는 것 같다는 것이다.

---

10 ④

순접의 접속사 and로 연결돼 있는 tiring(지루한)과 어울리는 표현이 빈칸에 들어가야 할 것이므로, '성가신'이라는 의미의 ④가 정답으로 적절하다.

go through 겪다, 경험하다 tiring a. 지루한 point out 지적하다 winsome a. 매력 있는; 쾌활한 gruesome a. 무시무시한 cuddlesome a. 귀여운 cumbersome a. 성가신

"무엇이 실재인가?"라는 질문에 답을 하려면 "실재하는"이라는 단어가 의미하는 다양한 것들을 그 특정한 상황에서 실재한다고 여겨지지 않는 것과 대조하여 지적해내는 성가시고 지루한 일을 겪어야 한다.

---

11 ①

간단한 사건은 치명적인 위험 곧 시련과 대비되는 평범한 일상적인 사건인데, 이런 평범한 사건에서 시련을 이겨내는 데 도움이 되는 인생의 진실을 순간적으로 깨닫게 되었다는 말이므로 빈칸에는 '직관적 진실 자각'이라는 의미의 ①이 적절하다.

recall v. 생각해내다, 상기하다 ordeal n. 시련 crust n. 빵 껍질, 빵 한 조각 epiphany n. 직관적 진실자각; 본질적 의미의 돌연한 현현 increment n. 증대, 증식 paroxysm n. 발작 anathema n. 저주; 파문(破門)

거의 치명적인 신체적 위험을 헤치며 살아온 사람들은 시련 가운데서도 그들이 숲속의 새 소리를 듣는 것이나 어려운 일을 완수하는 것이나 빵 한 조각을 친구와 나누어 먹는 것과 같은 간단한 사건에 반응하여 특별히 풍부한 진실자각을 경험했음을 종종 상기한다.

---

12 ②

아이들이 감기에 걸렸을 때 바로 감기약을 사는 행동에 대해 두 번째 문장에서 굳이 그럴 필요가 없다고 말하고 있는데, 이것은 감기약이 아이들에게 효과가 별로 없기 때문일 것이다. 따라서 빈칸에는 '빈약한, 적은'이라는 의미를 가진 ②가 들어가는 것이 적절하다.

come down with (병에) 걸리다 medicine n. 약, 약물; 의학, 의술; 의사직 repeatedly ad. 되풀이하여, 몇 번이고, 여러 차례 benefit n. 이익, 이득; 은혜 unflinching a. 굽히지 않는, 위축되지 않는; 단호한 exiguous a. 근소한, 적은, 빈약한, 작은, 소규모의 stupendous a. 엄청난, 굉장한 nifty a. 익살맞은, 재치 있는, 멋들어진

아이들이 감기에 걸리면, 많은 부모들은 어린이용 감기약을 사러 곧장 약국으로 향한다. 굳이 그럴 필요가 없다. 감기약이 6세 이하의 아이들에게는 효과가 거의 없으며, 6세 이상 12세 미만의 어린이들에게는 적은 효과만을 나타낸다는 사실이 연구를 통해 계속해서 드러나고 있다.

대학생들은 해외취업 준비의 필요성을 비롯한 많은 이유로 외국에서 공부한다. 전 세계적으로, 학사모를 쓰게 되는 이주자의 수가 2000년 이후 두 배 이상 늘었다. 그리고 미국 대학의 외국인 학생 수는 지난 10년 사이에 40% 증가했다.

---

13   ④

첫 문장의 '서튼 판사의 현란한 말솜씨에 속지 마라'는 단서로부터, 합리적으로 들리는 동성애자에 대한 존중이 거짓과 '위선'임을 추론할 수 있다.

rhetoric 미사여구; 수사법 gloss n. 광; 광택제; 허울; 겉치레 odious a. 끔찍한, 혐오스러운 rump n. 엉덩이; 나머지, 잔여물 apoplectic a. 졸도할 지경으로 화가 나는 philia n. 병적인 애호, 그러한 경향 insecurity n. 불안정, 불안전 phobia n. (특정 사물·활동·상황에 대한) 병적 공포[혐오], 공포증 gloss n. 광; 광택제; 허울; 겉치레

서튼 판사의 현란한 말솜씨에 속지 마라. 동성애자들의 품위를 존중해주는 것처럼 그럴듯하게 들리는 겉만 번지르르한 그의 말 뒤에 도사리고 있는 것은 우리가 지금까지 줄곧 들어왔던 (동성애자에 대한) 역겨운 차별인데, 그 역겨운 차별은 두 남자 혹은 두 여자가 결혼할 수 있다는 사실에 대해 여전히 분노하는 급진적인 우파 잔당들에게서 들어온 말이다.

---

14   ①

여성의 능력을 인정한다는 사실과 여성이 실제로 할 수 있는 일을 허용한다는 것 사이의 불일치라는 단서로부터 빈칸에서 discrepancy와 유사한 개념의 표현이 와야 함을 추론할 수 있다.

discrepancy n. 불일치; 어긋남, 모순 lingering a. 오래 끄는 competence n. 적성, 자격, 능력 dissonance n. 부조화, 불협화음, 불화 redundancy n. 여분, 과잉, 중복 vantage n. 우세, 유리, 우월 validity n. 유효함, 정당함

여성들이 할 수 있는 것들에 대해 우리가 인정하는 것과 여성이 하는 일에 대해 우리가 허용하는 것 사이에 존재하는 불일치는 — 여성들은 여전히 하원의석의 19%와 포춘지가 선정한 500대 기업인들 가운데 5%만을 차지하고 있다. — 오랫동안 지속되어온 불화를 보여준다. 여성들은 그들의 유능함을 보여주기 위해서 남성들에게 적용되는 기준을 넘어서야 한다. 그러기 위해서 여성들은 더 열심히 노력해야 한다.

---

15   ①

공부하러 외국으로 나가거나 외국에서 들어오는 학생들에 대한 내용이므로, '학사모'라는 의미의 ①이 정답으로 적절하다.

global career 글로벌 커리어(국제무대(외국)에서 하는 직장생활) migrant n. 이주자, 이주 노동자 mortar boards 학사모 green cards 영주권 카드 walking papers 해고 통지서 red carpets 극진한 환영

---

16   ③

첫 번째 빈칸은 Corbyn이 전임자들이 포기한 공식을 제공하고 있을 뿐이라는 진술로부터 추론할 수 있고, 두 번째 빈칸은 exhausted로부터 유추할 수 있다.

benefit n. (pl.) 복리 후생 self-employed a. 자영업의 compromise v. 타협[절충]하여 처리하다, 화해하다; (명예·평판·신용 따위를) 더럽히다, 손상하다 salient a. 현저한; 돌출하는; 주목할 만한, 눈에 띄는 denounce v. 공공연히 비난하다 refined a. 세련된 stuck a. (불쾌한 상황·장소에) 갇힌[빠져나갈 수가 없는]; (특정 상황에서) 무엇을 할지 모르는 hollow a. 텅 빈, 공허한 revamp v. 가죽을 대다, 수선하다; 혁신하다 conducive a. 도움이 되는

오늘날 논쟁은 여러 쟁점으로 옮겨가며 진행되었다. — 새로운 기술과 지구화의 부작용인 점증하는 불평등에서, 자영업 노동자들로 구성된 우버화된(개인기사 서비스) 노동시장에서 고용, 연금, 복리후생의 본질을 거쳐, 효율적인 정부와 복지제도에 대한 필요성에 이르기까지. 이 모든 문제들에 대한 새로운 생각은 환영할만한 것이다. — 사실상 이러한 문제는 진보적인 좌파가 다루어야 할 자연스러운 영역임에 틀림없다. 그러나 Mr Corbyn(영국 노동당의 새로 선출된 당수)은 과거에 사로잡혀 있다. 그가 내세우고 있는 '새로운 정치'는 그의 전임자들이 포기했던 고갈되고 공허한 공식들 이외에 아무런 것도 제시하지 않고 있다.

---

17   ③

로버트 보일의 특징을 수식할 수 있는 형용사가 첫 번째 빈칸에 필요한데, 그는 기술적인 의사소통을 하는 데 간결함이 아니라 상세한 설명이 요구된다고 주장했으므로 brevity와 반대되는 의미를 가진 verbose, garrulous가 첫 번째 빈칸에 적절하다. 두 번째 빈칸에는 Twitter의 특징을 설명하는 표현이 적절한데, 트위터의 사용자들은 140자 이내의 단문으로 대화를 한다고 했으므로 두 번째 빈칸에는 abbreviated가 적절하다.

brevity n. 간결 converse v. 서로 이야기하다 contemplative a. 명상적인, 사색하는 affirmative a. 긍정의, 승낙의 strenuous a. 정력적인, 열심인 emphatic a. 어조가 강한; 힘준, 강조한 verbose a. 말이 많은, 다변의, 장황한 abbreviated a. 단축[생략]된, 짧게 한 garrulous a. 수다스러운, 말 많은 proliferative a. 증식[번식]하는; 급증하는

로버트 보일(Robert Boyle)은 인정하지 않았을 것이다. 잘 알려진 것처럼 장황하게 말이 많던 17세기의 자연 철학자이자 과학 방법론의 창시자였던 그는 기술적인 의사소통을 하는 데는 간결함이 아니라 상세한 설명이 요구된다고 주장했다. 그러나 사용자들이 '트윗'이라고 하는 140자 이내의 단문으로 대화하는 사회 관계망인 트위터의 영역 안에서는 보일과 같이 장황한 말을 할 수 없다. 연구원들은 현재 저널 클럽에 있는 논문을 토론하고 실시간으로 자료를 공유하는 데 그 사이트의 단문 메시지를 이용하고 있다.

18   ①

첫 번째 빈칸 앞에서 저자의 본성을 글의 본질적인 특성으로 읽는다고 했고 without regard to가 있으므로 첫 번째 빈칸에는 글의 본질적인 부분이 아닌 글의 화려한 꾸밈을 의미하는 flourishes가 적절하고, 두 번째 빈칸에는 마지막 문장의 동사인 determines와 같은 의미의 taxed가 적절하다.

probation n. 시험, 수습 curvet n. 도약 net result 최종결과 desultory a. 산만한, 단편적인 indifferent a. 무관심한, 냉담한 flourish n. 화려한 꾸밈 tax v. (보상금 등을) 사정(査定)하다, 평가하다(=assess) majesty n. 위엄 harry v. 괴롭히다 virtue n. 미덕 belittle v. 경시하다 stretch v. 펴다, 과장하다

작문에는 요행으로 되어가는 것이 없다. 작문은 속임수를 전혀 허용하지 않는다. 당신이 쓸 수 있는 가장 좋은 글은 최상의 당신 자신일 것이다. 모든 문장은 오랜 수습(연습)의 결과이다. 책 제목이 있는 지면에서 마지막 지면까지 저자의 본성이 읽힌다. 우리는 저자의 본성을, 글의 화려한 수식과는 무관하게, 육필로 쓴 글의 본질적 특성으로 읽는다. 그리고 작문 이외 다른 나머지 행동들의 경우도 마찬가지이다. 사람의 본성이 그 모든 행동들 사이를, 아무리 많은 도약이 생긴다 해도, 자로 그은 선처럼 똑바르게 관류한다. 우리의 전체 인생은 가장 사소한 일을 잘하는 것으로 평가된다. 그것이 인생의 최종결과이다. 우리가 냉담한 지금 이 시대에 지켜보는 이도 없고 흥미진진한 일도 없는 가운데 어떻게 먹고 마시고 잠자고 단편적인 시간을 사용하는가가 미래의 우리의 권위와 능력을 결정짓는다.

19   ④

항문암과 같이 특정한 암에 걸려 고통스러워하는 환자들에게 사회적인 편견이 따라붙는 것은 새로운 것이 아니라고 한 다음, 유방암과 고환암의 예를 들고 있다. 따라서 현재 유방암에 대한 사회적인 편견은 없지만 과거에는 편견이 따라붙었을 것이므로, 과거에는 쉬쉬하며 이야기되었을 것이다.

stigma n. 치욕, 오명, 낙인 anal cancer 항문암 revolutionary a. 혁명의; 혁명적인 mastectomy n. 유방 절제술 testicular a. 고환의 conventional a. 전통적인; 재래식의 detect n. 발견하다; 간파하다 self-diagnosis n. 자기 진단 hushed a. 작은 소리의, 비밀의

항문암에는 다른 암에 없는 실질적인 낙인이 따라붙는다. 특정한 암에 걸려 고통스러워하는 환자들에게 사회적 낙인이 따라붙는 것은 새로운 것이 아니다. 현재 핑크색의 온갖 것들로 소란스럽게 기려지는 유방암이 이전에는 쉬쉬하며 이야기되었다. 1974년에 당시 영부인이었던 베티 포드(Betty Ford)가 그녀의 유방암 진단과 근치적 유방절제술을 받았다는 것을 공개적으로 이야기했을 때 그것은 혁명적인 일로 간주되었다. 랜스 암스트롱(Lance Armstrong)이 고환암 투병을 공개하기 전까지 고환암 환자들도 이와 비슷한 사회적 편견을 받았다

20   ③

뮌하우젠 증후군은 치명적인 질병에 걸렸다고 반복적으로 꾀병을 부리는 일종의 정신질환인데, 첫 번째 빈칸 앞에 쓰인 which는 serious illness를 선행사로 하는 관계대명사로, 뮌하우젠 증후군 환자들의 경우 실제 존재하지 않거나 일부러 꾸민 증상으로 치료를 받는 사람들이라고 볼 수 있다. 따라서 첫 번째 빈칸에는 deliberately가 적절하다. 그리고 뮌하우젠 증후군의 바른 철자법은 H가 두 개 들어간 Munchhausen인데, 사람들이 일반적으로 H를 하나 생략해서 사용한다고 했으므로, 전문가들도 Munchhausen을 잘못된 철자로 여길 것이라고 볼 수 있다. 따라서 두 번째 빈칸에는 '오타'를 뜻하는 typo가 적절하다.

recurrent a. 재발[재현]하는; 정기적으로 되풀이되는 catastrophic a. 파멸의, 비극적인 disorder n. 장애, 질환 recurrently ad. 재발하여, 반복적으로 spell v. (낱말을 ~라고) 철자하다 involuntarily ad. 본의 아니게 jargon n. 특수용어 capriciously ad. 변덕스럽게 tactic n. 방책, 전법 deliberately ad. 고의로 typo n. 오타 judiciously ad. 분별력 있게 criterion n. (비판, 판단의) 표준, 기준 chivalrously ad. 예의 바르게 congruity n. 조화; 적합, 일치

뮌하우젠 증후군은 치명적인 병에 걸렸다고 반복적으로 속이는 꾀병이다. 이 증후군은 정신 질환인데 이 병에 걸린 사람은 존재하지 않거나 고의로 의도한 급성 그리고 종종 심각한 질병의 치료를 위해 계속해서 병원을 찾아온다. 즉, 환자들은 반복적으로 그들이 심각한 질병이 있어서 치료가 필요한 척 행동한다. 뮌하우젠 증후군은 Munchhausen의 경우(에서)와 같이 'H'가 철자에 두 번 들어가야 한다. 그러나 'H'를 단 한번만 쓴 잘못된 철자가 너무 흔히 사용되어 이것이 더 이상 철자 오류로 여겨지지 않으며, 상당한 수의 전문 의료진을 포함하여 아마도 많은 사람들은 심지어 정확한 철자법을 철자 오류로 여길지도 모른다.

21   ③

베토벤이 양극성 장애를 앓았다고 했으므로 우울증과 흥분한(행복한) 상태가 반복되었다고 볼 수 있다. 첫 번째 빈칸에는 우울증과 관련되어 나타날 수 있는 부정적인 뜻의 형용사인 suicidal과 languid가 적절하며, 두 번째 빈칸은 hypomanic(조증)을 부연 설명하므로 조증과 관련된 정신 상태인 felicity와 euphoria가 적절하다.

severe depression 심한 우울증 trigger v. 촉발시키다 consistent a. 일치하는, 조화된 bipolar disorder 조울증, 양극성 장애 hypomanic a. 조증의 languid a. 무감동한; 활기 없는 equilibrium n. 평형상태; 평정 prodigal a. 낭비하는 felicity n. 더없는 행복 suicidal a. 자살 충동에 쫓기는; 자멸적인 euphoria n. 행복감 clairvoyant a. 날카로운 통찰력을 가진 contentment n. 만족

베토벤은 심각한 우울증에 시달렸던 것으로 추정된다. 이 병이 아마도 그가 술에 의존하게끔 했을지도 모른다. 잘 알려지지 않은 사실은 그의 놀라운 창의성이 우울증보다는 양극성 장애로 고생하는 사람들에게서 보이는 충동과 에너지에서 비롯됐다는 것이다. 가끔 그는 자살 충동으로 고통을 받았지만, 또 다른 때에는 조증을 앓았는데, 이로 인해 행복감이 충만한 상태에서 그는 서로 다른 여러 가지 작품을 동시에 작곡할 수 있었다.

22   ③

문명이 부정적인 결과를 낳을 때 인문학자들과 과학자들이 서로에게 책임을 전가하는 내용의 글이다. 빈칸 다음의 for절이 빈칸의 이유를 나타내는데, mandarin은 문예(인문학)의 대가를 말하고 폭탄이나 공업은 과학의 산물이므로 빈칸에는 과학계에 책임을 돌리는 의미의 ③이 적절하다.

take flight 도망하다 fail v. 기대를 어기다, 실망시키다 the humanities 인문학 mandarin n. 보수적인 관리; (문예세계의) 거물 wash one's hands of ~에서 손을 떼다, 모면하다, 관계를 끊다 direct v. 지도하다, 관리하다 opposite n. 정반대의 사람[사물] decline n. 퇴보, 몰락

다른 사람들이 자신을 실망시켰다고 항변함으로써 문명의 각 구성원이 문명의 (부정적인) 결과에서 달아나는(책임 회피하는) 일이 더 일반적이다. 교육과 어쩌면 취향으로 인해 인문학만을 연구하게 된 사람들(인문학자들)은 문예의 거물들(인문학의 대가들)이 폭탄이나 공업을 만들지 않은 것이 분명하니까 과학자들만이 책임이 있다고 항변한다. 그러면 과학자들도 똑같이 경멸적으로 이렇게 말한다. 그리스 학자들과 진지한 동굴벽화 탐구자들은 책임을 회피하는 것이 좋겠지만, 사실 오류로부터 보다 무위로부터 더 자주 병폐가 자라나는 이 사회를 지도하는 데 도움을 주기 위해 그들은 무엇을 하고 있는가라고.

23   ③

과거 수세기 동안 종교는 우리 인간을 동물과 구분되게 하며, 높은 정신적인 수준으로 고양시켜 주어왔다고 했다. 그러나 오늘날에는 특정한 종교의 근본주의자들만이 아니라 종교 그 자체가 전 세계 흉악한 범죄의 진원지로 부상하고 있다고 했으므로, 특정 종교의 근본주의자들만이 교리를 악용하고 왜곡하고 있다는 주장은 '점점 공허하게 들린다(ring increasingly hollow)'고 해야 적절하다.

no more than 단지 ~에 지나지 않다, ~일 뿐 egotistic a. 이기적인, 독선적인 elevate v. 들어 올리다, 고상하게 하다 wellspring n. 샘, (용기 등의) 원천 assurance n. 확신, 주장 fundamentalist n. 근본주의자 pervert v. 악용하다, 곡해하다 creed n. 교리, 신조 atheism n. 무신론 gain momentum 탄력을 받다, 추진력을 발휘하다 be independent of ~와 관계없는 fiasco n. 큰 실수, 대실패 hollow a. 무의미한, 공허한 put the wire on ~을 중상모략하다, 비방하다 atheist n. 무신론자

수 세기 동안, 종교가 없다면 우리는 우리 몫만을 챙기려는 이기적인 동물에 지나지 않으며, 우리의 유일한 도덕수준은 한 떼의 이리가 갖고 있는 도덕수준에 지나지 않는다는 말을 우리는 들어왔다. 그래서 오직 종교만이 우리를 보다 높은 정신적인 수준으로 고양시킬 수 있다는 말을 들어왔다. (그러나) 오늘날에는 종교가 전 세계 흉악한 범죄의 진원지로 부상해서, 오직 기독교, 이슬람교, 또는 힌두교의 근본주의자들만이 그들의 교리가 제공하는 고상한 영적인 메시지를 악용하고 왜곡하고 있다는 주장들은 점점 공허하게 들린다. (이제) 유럽의 위대한 유산들 중 하나이자 평화를 얻을 수 있는 유일한 기회인 무신론을 복원해보는 것이 어떨까?

24   ②

음악치료가 개인들의 많은 요구를 처리한다는 단서로부터 정답을 추론할 수 있다.

veteran n. 노병; 퇴역 군인; 어떤 분야에서 경험이 풍부한 사람 medical practice 의료행위 ruin v. 파괴하다, 파멸시키다 tailor v. <방법·계획·각본 등을> (용도·목적에) 맞추다, (남에게) 맞게 하다 amuse v. 즐겁게 하다

치료 목적을 위한 수단으로 음악을 사용한다는 개념은 아주 오래된 것으로서 실제로 최소한 플라톤과 그의 제자인 아리스토텔레스가 쓴 저작까지 그 기원이 거슬러 올라갈 수 있다. 음악치료는 병원에서 활약한 지역 음악가들의 활동이 신체적, 정신적 트라우마로 고통받고 있던 제대군인들에게 긍정적으로 영향을 미친다는 사실이 알려진 두 차례에 걸친 세계대전 이후에 공식적인 직업으로 등장했다. 이러한 의료행위 속에서, 음악의 치료적 사용은 개인들의 많은 요구를 처리하는 데 이용되게 된다. 이와 같은 치료법은 개개인의 요구에 맞게 맞춤형으로 행해질 때 가장 효과가 큰데, 자격을 갖춘 음악치료사는 작곡, 노래, 율동, 음악 감상 등을 포괄하는 요법을 제공한다.

25   ③

기존의 질서를 전복하기 위해 필요한 것은 99%의 '단합된' 힘이다.

upturn n. 상승, 호전; 전복; (사회의) 격동 aberration n. 정도에서 벗어남, 변형 business share 사업 지분 pool v. 가입하다; 연합하다; 공동으로 출자하다 dispersed a. 흩어진, 분산된 salient a. 현저한; 돌출하는; 주목할 만한 cohesive a. 점착력이 있는, 결합력 있는, 밀착하는 reticent a. 말이 없는, 과묵한; 조심하는 garrulous a. 수다스러운, 말많은

2011년에 있었던 월가 점령 운동은 다음과 같은 아이디어와 슬로건에 기반해서 진행되었다: "우리는 1%의 탐욕과 부패를 더 이상 참을 수 없는 99%다." 이 운동이 일어나기 바로 전에 행해졌던 연구는 경기 상승을 통해 창출된 거의 대부분의 이윤이 미국의 가장 부유한 상위 1%에게 간다는 사실을 보여주었다. 이런 현상은 역사적 일탈이나 국가적 예외가 아니었다. 거의 모든 곳에서 유사한 결과가 정부 정책에 의해서 집요하게 유도되고 있다. 프랑스의 경우, 마크롱 대통령의 세금 정책을 통해서 주된 이익을 얻는 사람들은 '재산의 대부분을 금융투자나 사업 지분 형태로 보유하고 있는 가장 부유한 28만 가구'다. 그것이 (1%를 제외한) 다른 모든 사람들은 공통점이 너무나 많아 그들의 에너지를 한데 모아 기존의 절서를 전복할 수 있다는 것을 의미하는가? 나는 그럴 수 없다고 생각한다. 1%의 사람들이 전 세계의 부의 대부분을 차지하고 있다는 것이 곧 99%의 사람들이 비등점에 이른 정치 세력이거나 결속력이 있는 사회적 집단이라는 것을 의미하는 것은 아니기 때문이다.

T E S T **27**

01 ③	02 ①	03 ④	04 ①	05 ①	06 ②	07 ②	08 ④	09 ④	10 ①
11 ⑤	12 ④	13 ①	14 ④	15 ③	16 ③	17 ④	18 ④	19 ④	20 ①
21 ②	22 ①	23 ④	24 ②	25 ④					

01 ③

시민봉기 단계에서는 시리아 내의 여러 종파들을 강대국들이 후원하여 그 종파들이 강대국 대신에 전쟁을 치르는 양상이었는데 이제는 강대국들이 그들 대신 직접 나서서 싸우다 보니 국제전쟁의 양상을 띠게 되었다는 것이다. 따라서 빈칸에는 여러 종파에 해당하면서 patron states의 상대인 ③이 적절하다.

uprising n. 반란, 폭동, 봉기 patron n. 후원자 patron state 후견국가 wirepuller n. 뒤에서 조종하는 사람 antagonist n. 적대자 proxy n. 대리인 magnate n. 실력자, 거물

시민봉기로 시작된 시리아에서의 전쟁이 지금은 후견 국가들이 그들을 대리해온 세력들을 대신하고 있는 국제 전쟁에 더 가까워 보인다.

02 ①

세미콜론 이하에서 개인이 제도들을 좌지우지하지 못하고 교섭력이 없었다고 한 것은 그들이 중요하지 않은 존재였다는 의미이므로 빈칸에는 ①이 적절하다.

pluralist a. 다원적인 peasant n. 소작농민 bargaining power 교섭력 expendable a. 소모용의, 희생시켜도 좋은 wayward a. 변덕스러운; 제멋대로 하는 indispensable a. 없어서는 안 될, 필수적인 dominant a. 지배적인

초기 다원주의 사회에서는 개인이 소모용이었다. 제도들이 그들에 달려있지 않았고 소작농민이든 노동자이든 간에 개인은 아무런 교섭력도 갖고 있지 않았다.

03 ④

학습에 대해 스트레스를 받지 않으면 느긋한 마음으로 공부할 수 있을 것이므로 빈칸에는 ④가 적절하다.

sake n. 이익; 목적, 원인 headlong a. 무모한 down-to-earth a. 현실적인 bare-faced a. 뻔뻔스러운 laid-back a. 느긋한

그들은 학업성취도 평가를 받지 않을 것이기 때문에 학습과정에 대해 대체로 스트레스를 받지 않는다. 이것은 종종 그들이 공부에 대해 보다 느긋한 접근법을 취하고 순전히 학습을 위한 학습을 할 수 있음을 의미한다.

04 ①

간호사가 불러서 멋진 왕자님이라고 알려주는 것에서 fathers가 출산을 기다리는 곧 아버지가 될 사람들을 의미함을 알 수 있다. 따라서 빈칸에는 ①이 적절하다.

beckon v. 손짓으로 부르다 announce v. 알리다, 공표하다, 전하다 What's the idea? 대체 어떻게 할 거야(불만을 나타냄) expectant a. 기다리고 있는; 출산을 앞두고 있는 gifted a. 재능 있는 intolerant a. 불관용적인 auspicious a. 상서로운

병원에서 출산을 기다리던 한 무리의 아버지들 중 하나를 간호사가 손짓으로 부르고 "멋진 왕자님이세요."라고 알려주었다. 그러자 또 다른 남자가 즉시 달려오며 불평했다. "아니 어떻게 이럴 수가, 저 사람보다 내가 먼저 왔단 말이요!"

05 ①

'honorable한(명예로운) 경력에도 불구하고'라 했으므로 첫 번째 빈칸에는 부정적인 obloquy(악평)나 vituperation(질책)이 적절하고, 두 번째 빈칸에는 misfortunes(불행)의 원인으로 부정적인 bigotry(고집불통)나 rancor(깊은 원한)가 적절하다.

honorable a. 명예로운 incur v. (위해를) 당하다; (분노, 비난 등을) 초래하다 obloquy n. 악담, 비방 bigotry n. 편협, 고집불통 vituperation n. 질책, 혹평 acumen n. 총명함 accolade n. 칭찬 rancor n. 깊은 원한 plaudit n. 박수, 갈채 perspicacity n. 총명함, 통찰력

그는 오랜 명예로운 경력에도 불구하고, 노인들의 고집불통으로 인해 젊은 이들이 당하는 불행으로부터 젊은이들을 구하기를 바란 유일한 범죄 때문에 악평을 받았다.

06 ②

추운 기후와 더운 열대 기후의 효과는 상반될 것이므로 빈칸에는 stimulatory(자극적인)와 반대되는 '억제적인'이라는 의미의 ②가 적절하다.

genetic a. 유전의, 유전학적인 disparity n. 불균형, 불일치, 차이 invoke v. 호소하다 stimulatory a. 자극적인 humid a. 습기 있는, 다습한 tropical a. 열대의 marginal a. 주변의; 미미한 inhibitory a. 금지하는, 억제적인 provocative a. 도발적인 aggregate a. 총계의

유전학적 설명이 발달의 지역차에 대한 가능한 유일한 설명은 아니다. 또 다른 설명은 인간의 창의성과 활동력에 추운 기후가 미칠 것으로 생각되는 자극적 효과와 고온다습한 열대기후가 미치는 억제적인 효과에 호소하는 설명이다.

07 ②

분배 문제에 대한 해결책이란 불평등을 해소하는 방책을 말하는데, 풍요의 약속을 믿고 이주했지만 풍요해지지 못했으므로, 결국 오클라호마 황진지대의 가난(불평등)이 이주에 의해 캘리포니아로 옮겨진 셈이다. 따라서 빈칸에는 ②가 적절하다.

bring to mind 생각나게 하다 parable n. 우화, 비유이야기 dust bowl 황진지대(1930년대 모래강풍이 몰아닥친 지역) cautionary a. 경고의, 주의의 inherit v. 상속하다 transplant v. 옮겨 심다, 이식하다 disguise v. 위장하다, 변장하다 stigmatize v. 낙인찍다

대체로 분배의 문제인 것에 대해서는 이주가 해결책이라는 주장은 존 스타인백의 "분노의 포도"에 나오는 우화를 생각나게 한다. 조드 가족이 오클라호마의 더스트볼(황진)지대에서 캘리포니아로 풍요의 약속을 믿고 이주해가지만 그 약속이 실현되지 못한 것은 이식된(옮겨 심어진) 불평등에 대한 경고의 이야기이다.

08 ④

'this web of 빈칸'이 앞의 so much misrepresentation and slander를 의미하므로 빈칸에는 ④가 적절하다. slander 다음은 'so ~ that 절'에서 that이 생략되고 대신 콤마로 처리되었다.

sensational a. 세상을 놀라게 하는, 선정적인 misrepresentation n. 그릇된 설명 slander n. 비방 break through 돌파하다, 헤치고 나오다 malign v. 비방하다, 헐뜯다 manifest oneself 나타나다 plaudit n. 박수; 칭찬 decorum n. 예의바름 fracas n. 싸움, 소동 calumny n. 비방

선정적인 언론이 그녀를 둘러싸고 너무나 많은 잘못된 설명과 비방을 쏟아내었다 보니, 이런 온 사방에서의 비방에도 불구하고 진실이 드러나고 이 많은 비방을 받은 이상주의자에 대한 더 나은 평가가 나타나기 시작한다는 것은 거의 기적으로 여겨질 것이다.

09 ④

'신념이 위기를 겪었으며, 그것에 대해 아버지가 매우 유감스럽게 느꼈다'고 한 것에서 아버지가 가르친 사상에 대해 밀이 '심각한 회의' 혹은 '불신'을 느꼈음을 추론할 수 있다.

pivotal a. 중추적인, 중요한 immerse v. ~에 몰두하게 하다 creed n. 교리, 신념, 신조 utilitarianism n. 공리주의 chagrin n. 유감, 원통함, 분함 euphoriant a. 병적인 희열을 일으키는 a priori 선험적인 feasible a. 실행 가능한 chimerical a. 공상적인, 터무니없는, 허무맹랑한

그 전기에서 중요한 순간은 밀(Mill)이 20살 무렵 겪었던 신념의 위기이다. 그의 아버지의 공리주의 신조에 흠뻑 젖었던 청소년기를 지난 뒤, 밀은 그의 아버지에게는 매우 유감스럽게도 행복에 대한 공리주의의 약속이 허무맹랑한 것임을 깨달았다. 낭만주의 시인들의 영향 하에 그는 계산(이해타산)에 기초한 삶에서 돌아섰다.

10 ①

'정부, 왕, 여왕의 자리가 따로 없고 겸손이 선호되었다'는 진술에서 '호화스럽고, 과시하는 듯한' 궁전은 없었음을 추론할 수 있다.

monument n. 기념물, 기념비 modesty n. 겸손; 중용 pottery n. 도자기 standardize v. 규격화하다 seal n. 봉인 ostentatious a. 대단히 호사스러운; 허세를 부리는 callous a. 냉담한 exuberant a. 열광적인, 열의가 넘치는 wistful a. 동경하는

그 도시는 호사스러운 궁전, 사원 또는 기념물들이 거의 없다. 정부의 뚜렷한 자리도 없고 왕이나 여왕의 자리가 있었다는 증거도 없다. 겸손, 질서, 청결이 선호되었던 것이 분명하다. 도자기와 구리 및 석재로 만든 도구들은 규격화되어 있었다. 봉인과 중량은 매매를 철저히 관리하는 시스템이 있었음을 보여준다.

11 ⑤

앞에 창작의 '자유'라는 말이 주어져 있으므로, 빈칸에도 그와 유사한 의미의 표현이 필요하다.

edify v. 교화하다 agenda n. 의무, 과제 impose v. 부과하다, 강요하다 for the sake of ~을 위해서 zeitgeist n. 시대정신 naturalization n. 귀화 distraction n. 방심; 오락 pillar n. 기둥 autonomy n. 자율성

오늘날 저자의 위대함을 측정하는 척도는 그 사람이 얼마나 가르쳐주고 우리를 자유롭게 해주느냐이다. 이렇게 저자가 세상을 해석해주어야 한다는 과제는 예전 저자들에게 강요되었을 때는 문제가 되던 것이었다. 창작의 자유와 지적 성실성을 위해서 학자뿐 아니라 작가도 당대의 시대정신으로부터 좀 더 많은 자율성을 누려 마땅하다.

12 ④

주심이 첼시 팀에게 불리하게 판정을 했다고 했으므로, 첼시 팬으로서는 화가 날 수밖에 없었을 것이다.

manage to V 간신히 ~하다 squeeze out 짜내다 stamp n. 짓밟기 committed a. 헌신적인, 전념하는 aloof a. 무관심한, 초연한 disinterested a. 사욕이 없는, 청렴한 ballistic a. 탄도의, 비행물체의; 울컥 화를 낸 go ballistic 분통을 터뜨리다 disoriented a. 방향을 잃은, 혼란된

첼시는 노리치를 상대로 간신히 3대 2로 승리해, 프랭크 람파드 감독 체제에서 첫 승을 거두었다. 하지만 주심 덕분은 아니었다. 마틴 앳킨슨 주심은 정말 이상한 판정으로 평판을 잃었다. 그는 우리에게는 오프사이드를 엄격하게 적용했고, 벤 갓프리가 우리 팀 선수의 발을 밟은 것은 못 본 척했다. 당연하게도, 팬들은 소셜 미디어에서 분통을 터뜨렸다.

13 ①

시각을 잃으면 오히려 감각이 예민해진다고 했으므로, 시각은 우리의 지각을 '방해하는' 것이라 할 수 있다.

gift n. 재능 prehensile a. 잡을 수 있는 sensuous a. 감각적인 flicking a. 빨리 움직이는 distract v. 빗나가게 하다, 혼란하게 하다 encapsulate v. 요약하다 crystallize v. 결정화하다 calculate v. 계산하다, 추산하다

그는 "맹인은 미각과 촉각이 뛰어나다"라고 썼다. 그리고 이를 "맹인의 축복"이라고 말했다. 뤼세랑이 생각하기에 이 모든 것들은 합쳐져 하나의 근본적인 감각, 깊은 주의력이 된다. 그것은 속도가 빠르지 않지만, 거의 손에 잡힐 듯한 주의력이고, 시각이 빠르고 순식간이고 손쉬운 특성으로 인해 우리로 하여금 끊임없이 보지 못하게 만드는 그 세상과 감각적으로 친밀하게 하나로 일치된 상태이다.

14 ④

첫 문장에서 이들이 처한 상태가 자신이 인도 국민이라는 것을 서류로 입증하지 못하면 인도 국민이 아니게 될 즉 인도 국민에서 '제외'가 될 처지라는 것을 알 수 있으므로 빈칸에는 ④가 적절하다.

orphan n. 고아 authentic a. 진짜의, 인증된 document n. 문서, 서류 step in 개입하다 aggrieved a. 괴롭혀진, 학대받은, 권리를 침해당한 deception n. 사기, 기만 corruption n. 부패 treason n. 반역 exclusion n. 제외

자신의 고국에서 고아가 될 위험에 처한 보통 사람들이 자신이 인도인이라는 것을 인증된 서류로 증명하려고 애쓰고 있다. 나렌드라 모디 수상은 국가 시민권등록제를 도입한 것으로 찬사를 받지만, 그것은 그가 그의 국민을 위해 할 수 있는 가장 끔찍스런 일 중 하나이다. 이제 국제 사회가 개입하여, (국민이 아니라고) 제외되는 상태에 직면해 있는 이 고통 받는 사람들의 삶을 구해야 할 때이다.

15 ③

앞에서 백혈구가 효소를 방출해 침입자(세균)를 죽여 세균감염을 막는다고 했고 이 효소에 들어있는 철분 때문에 탁한 색의 콧물이 되는 것이므로 빈칸에는 ③이 적절하다.

nasal discharge 콧물 mucus n. 점액 nasal mucus 콧물 tinted a. 색을 띤 by-product n. 부산물 infection n. 세균감염 enzyme n. 효소 cloudy a. 탁한 imply v. 함축하다, 암시하다 immune system 면역 체계 signify v. 의미하다, 뜻하다 guarantee v. 보장하다, ~을 확실히 하다

많은 의사들이 콧물 색이 누렇거나 녹색을 띠었으면 그것이 박테리아가 있다는 의미라고 아직도 믿는다. 그러나 과학은 이것이 항상 사실인 것은 아니라는 것을 보여주었다. 색깔 있는 콧물은 치유 과정의 정상적인 부산물이다. 세균감염을 막기 위해 백혈구는 효소를 방출하여 침입자를 죽인다. 일부 효소에는 철분이 포함되어 있는데 철분의 색이 녹색이다. 따라서 탁한 색의 콧물이 자동적으로 세균감염을 의미하지는 않는다.

16 ③

기존의 것이 새것으로 인해 이름이 다시 붙여지는(renamed) 현상, 즉 거꾸로(retro-) 이름(-nym)이 만들어지는 언어 현상을 설명하고 있다.

clarification n. 설명 coinage n. 신조어 acoustic a. 전자장치를 사용하지 않은 악기의 etymology n. 어원학 semantics n. 의미론 retronym n. 신 복합어 acronym n. 두문자어

신 복합어는 기존의 형태나 버전을 좀 더 최근의 것과 구별하기 위해 기존의 것에 새로운 이름을 붙인 것이다. 따라서 그것은 앞서 (두 가지 유형이 있기 전에는) 설명이 필요치 않았던 두 유형을 구별하기 위해 만들어진 어휘인 것이다. 기술적 발전이 종종 이들을 새로이 조어하게 된 원인이다. 예를 들어, "어쿠스틱 기타"라는 말은 전자 기타가 등장하면서 신조어로 만들어졌고, 아날로그 시계는 디지털 시계가 발명되자 그것과 구별하기 위해 이름이 다시 붙여진 것이다.

17 ④

빈칸 다음에서 예술의 향유가 예술창작과 소비자에게 필수적인 것이라 했는데, 필수적인 것이라는 말은 꼭 있어야 하는 것으로 있어도 그만 없어도 그만인 부차적인 것이나 어쩌다가 있게 된 우연적인 것이 아니라는 말이므로 빈칸에는 ④가 적절하다.

private property 사유재산 contradiction n. 부인, 부정; 모순 exclusive a. 독점적인 profound a. 뜻깊은 effective a. 효과적인, 실제의, 실전적인 rewarding a. 득이 되는, 할 보람이 있는, (…할 만한) 가치가 있는 prosaic a. 평범한 jocund a. 즐거운 ethereal a. 공기 같은, 천상의, 하늘의; 이 세상 것이 아닌 fortuitous a. 우연한

사유재산의 원칙은 예술의 사회적 기능과 모순되는데, 예술은 예술가와 대중 사이의 광범위한 상호관계에, 즉, 미학적 향유가 더 이상 소수의 배타적 재산(독점물)일 수 없고 오히려 점점 더 심원하고 인간 보편적인 향유가 될

수 있는 실제적인 가능성에, 기초해야 한다. 이런 (예술의) 향유는 우연한 것이 아니다. 예술적 창작이 그 향유 속에서 실현되는 것인 한은 이 향유는 예술적 창작에 필수적인 것이며, 예술이 예술가만이 아니라 온 인류가 그들의 인간성을 심화시키기 위해 갖고 있는 가장 가치 있는 수단 중 하나인 한, 이 향유는 소비자에게 필수적인 것이다.

---

18 ④

빈칸 앞에서 설명한 의심과 증오와 분열에 불을 지핀 '반동적 민족주의'는 '국가, 교회, 지역사회에 대한 소속이 사람들을 단결시키고 그들을 공동의 이익을 위해 행동하도록 하는 동기를 부여한다'는 보수적 통찰과는 '정반대'이므로 ④가 빈칸에 적절하다.

exult v. 크게 기뻐하다, 의기양양하다 exclude v. 배척하다, 제외하다 discriminate v. 판별하다; 식별하다 hark back to ~의 기억을 되살리다 Reconquista n. 국토 회복 전쟁, 레콘키스타(8~15세기에 이베리아반도에서 있었던 싸움으로, 가톨릭교도가 이슬람교도를 축출하고 영토를 다시 정복하기 위해 일어남) reactionary a. 반동적인 kindle v. 불붙이다 conservative a. 보수적인 insight n. 통찰력 orthodoxy n. 정설 reinforcement n. 보강, 강화 antithesis n. 반대, 대조 integration n. 통합 harbinger n. 선구자; 전조(前兆)

우파는 소속의 의미를 바꾸고 있다. 헝가리와 폴란드에서 우파는 배제와 차별을 앞세우는 혈연과 지연의 민족주의 안에서 의기양양하다. 스페인의 새로운 세력인 복스(Vox)는 기독교인들이 이슬람교도들을 쫓아냈던 '국토회복전쟁' 시절을 떠오르게 한다. 분노한 반동적 민족주의는 의심과 증오와 분열에 불을 지핀다. 이것은 국가와 교회, 지역사회에 대한 소속이 사람들을 단결시키고 그들이 공동의 이익을 위해 행동하도록 동기를 부여할 수 있다는 보수적 통찰의 정반대에 해당한다.

---

19 ④

첫 문장에서 종교 특유의 가치를 부정하고 보편적 가치를 긍정하는데 ④에서 regardless of faith가 종교 특유의 가치를 부정하는 것이고 some principle accessible to all people이 보편적 가치를 의미하는 것이므로 빈칸에는 ④가 적절하다. ①도 종교 특유의 가치를 부정하고 보편적 가치를 긍정하는 것이지만 낙태가 여성 인권의 문제라고 하는 것은 낙태 찬성론자들의 주장이므로 저자(I)가 낙태를 반대함에 비추어 부적절하다.

deliberative a. 신중한, 토의의 pluralistic a. 다원론의 translate v. 해석하다, 환언하다 religion-specific a. 종교 특유의 amenable a. 순종하는 amenable to reason 도리에 따르는, 이치에 맞는 invoke v. (권위 있게 하거나 정당화하기 위해) 예로 인용하다 carry the day 승리를 거두다 precept n. 가르침, 교훈 supremacy n. 우위, 우월 accessible a. 접근하기 쉬운, 이용할 수 있는, 이해하기 쉬운 decriminalize v. 기소[처벌] 대상에서 제외하다, 합법화하다 medical procedure 수술

우리의 신중하고 다원적인 민주주의가 요구하는 바는 종교적 동기로 행동하는 사람들이 그들의 관심사를 특정한 종교만의 가치가 아니라 보편적인 가치로 해석하는 것이다. 그러려면 그들의 제안은 논쟁을 거쳐야 하고 이치에 맞아야 한다. 만일 내가 종교적인 이유로 낙태를 반대하고 낙태를 금지하는

법을 통과시키려고 한다면, 교회의 가르침을 지적한다거나 하나님의 뜻을 내세우는 것만으로는 그 논쟁에서 승리하기를 기대할 수 없다. 만일 내가 다른 사람들이 내 말에 귀 기울이기를 바란다면 나는 왜 낙태가 신앙을 막론하고 모든 사람이 이해할 수 있는 어떤 원칙을 위반하는지 설명해야 한다.

---

20 ①

첫 번째 빈칸은 badass가 dude(허세꾼)를 묘사하는 단어임에서 성품을 나타내는 부정적 의미의 표현이 요구됨을 추론할 수 있다. 두 번째 빈칸은 모든 것에 자부심이 있는 dude라는 내용으로부터 추론 가능하다.

badass a. (사람이) 거친, 공격적인 n. 거칠고 공격적인 사람 dude n. 멋쟁이, 젠체하는 사람, 친구, 동부의 도회지 사람 epitome n. 완벽한 (본)보기, 전형 radiate v. 빛나다; 발산하다, 빛을 발하다 confidence n. 신뢰; 자신, 확신 a set of wheels 자동차 swagger v. 으스대다, 허풍을 떨다 exemplify v. ~의 모범이 되다, ~을 내세우다 scheme v. 계획을 세우다 highbrow v. 지식인인 체하다 democratize v. 민주화하다

'badass'라는 단어 — 명사이자 형용사이고 명백히 거의 우아하지 않은 의미를 가지고 있는 합성어 — 는 전통적으로 멋쟁이들을 묘사하기 위해 사용되어 왔다. badass는 '미국 남성의 척도'로서, 그것이 '술을 주문하는 것이든, 자동차를 사는 것이든, 여성들을 상대하는 것이든, 그가 하는 모든 것에서 자부심으로 빛나는' 사람을 나타내는 말이다. 그는 '좀처럼 화를 내지 않지만' '일단 화가 나면 잔인하게 효율적으로' 반격을 가하는, 본질적으로 Dirty Harry나 Chuck Norris 같은 남자다. badass가 되기 위해서 그는 문자 그대로이건 아니건, 멋지게 허세를 떨어야 한다.

---

21 ②

첫 번째 빈칸 뒤의 "by slowing growth at home and a backlash to its assertive ways overseas"라는 내용에서 부정적인 중국의 미래를 추론 가능하다. 두 번째 빈칸은 바로 앞의 겸손함이 가질 수 있는 태도는 중국을 무시하지 않고 대등하게 여기는 것임을 추론할 수 있다.

overreach v. (지나치게 욕심을 내다가) 도를 넘다 stumble v. 비틀[휘청]거리다 backlash n. 역회전, 반동; 반발 assertive a. 단언적인, 단정적인 provoke v. (감정 따위를) 일으키다, 일으키게 하다; 유발시키다 delude v. 속이다, 착각하게 하다 exhort v. 권하다, 촉구하다 chasten v. 징벌하다, 훈계하다 extricate v. 벗어나다 glorify v. 찬미하다, 찬송하다

어떻게 중국과의 엄청난 패권 경쟁이 끝날지에 대해 미국인 전문가들에게 물어보라. 그러면 그들이 상정하고 있는 최선의 시나리오는 놀라울 정도로 유사하다. 그들은 중국이 무리를 하다가 휘청거리게 되는 가까운 미래를 묘사하고 있다. 그들은 국내에서의 둔화된 성장과 해외에서의 확신에 찬 방식에 대한 역효과에 의해서 잘못을 깨닫게 되는 중국을 상상한다. 그들은 중국이 국제 질서를 다시 만들기보다, 국제 질서를 다시 바라보고 그 안에서 주도적인 역할을 추구하기를 희망한다. 중국인 전문가들 또한 그들 자신에 관한 최선의 시나리오를 설명할 때 (중국의 입장에 서서) 비슷한 견해를 피력한다. 거칠게 말해, 미국은 잘난 척하지 말아야 한다. 더 점잖게 말해서 중국의 목소리는 10여 년 안에 미국이 중국을 대등한 상대로 받아들일 겸손함과 아시아의 뒷마당에서 중국을 자극하는 것을 피하는 지혜를 배우기를 희망하고 있다.

22   ①

"그렐린은 배고픔을 자극하며 렙틴은 뇌에 포만감을 전달하여 식욕을 억제한다."라고 했으므로, 결국 부족한 수면 시간은 배고픔을 자극하는 그렐린의 수치를 증가시키고 식욕을 억제하는 렙틴의 수치를 감소시킬 것이다. 따라서 ①이 빈칸에 적절하다.

snooze v. 잠깐 자다[눈을 붙이다] appetite n. 식욕; 욕구 obesity n. 비만 satiety n. 포만(감) have nothing to do with ~와 아무런 관련이 없다 stimulate v. 자극하다, 북돋우다 significant a. 중대한, 중요한; 상당한

체중과 관련해서 당신이 잠을 자면, 체중이 감소하게 될지도 모른다. 수면 부족은 배고픔과 식욕의 증가, 그리고 아마도 비만과 관련된 것처럼 보인다. 하루에 6시간 미만 잠을 자는 사람들은 7시간에서 9시간 잠을 자는 사람들보다 비만이 될 확률이 거의 30%나 높았다. 최근 연구는 수면과 식욕을 조절하는 펩티드 사이의 관계에 대해 초점이 맞춰졌다. "그렐린은 배고픔을 자극하며 렙틴은 뇌에 포만감을 전달하여 식욕을 억제합니다. 부족한 수면 시간은 렙틴의 감소와 그렐린의 증가와 연관되어 있습니다."라고 사이번(Siebern)은 말한다.

23   ④

무신론자와 가장 가까운 개념을 고른다. secular의 사전적 의미는 '종교와 무관한(have no connection with religion)'이다.

atheist n. 무신론자 beleaguer v. 에워싸다 stack up 계속 쌓이다 numerically ad. 숫자상으로 massive a. 육중한; 당당한 lion's share 제일 큰 몫(알짜) convincingly ad. 납득이 가도록 outnumber v. ~보다 숫자가 많다 nihilistic a. 허무주의의 esoteric a. 비밀스러운 pantheistic a. 범신론적인 secular a. 세속적인, 종교와 관련 없는

나탈리 앤기어(Natalie Angier)가 "뉴요커(New Yorker)"지에 다소 슬픈 글을 기고하면서 무신론자로서 살아가는 것이 얼마나 외로운지 토로했다. 그녀는 궁지에 몰린 소수자처럼 느끼는 것이 분명하다. 그러나 사실상 미국의 무신론자들의 숫자는 어떻게 늘어나고 있는가? 가장 최근 조사 결과는 놀라울 만큼 고무적으로 읽힌다. 그리스도교도가 물론 거의 1억6천만 명으로서, 전체 인구에서 가장 많은 몫을 차지한다. 그러나 2백8십만 명의 유대교도, 1백십만 명의 이슬람교도, 그리고 힌두교도, 불교도 및 여타 종교인들을 다 합친 것보다 많은 2위 그룹이 무엇이라고 생각하는가? 거의 3천만 명에 달하는 그 2위 그룹은 흔히 종교와 무관한 이들로 묘사된다.

24   ②

본문에 따르면, 자산을 소유주의 동의 없이 가져가는 것은 '절도죄', 자산의 소유자로부터 점유권을 합법적으로 위탁받은 뒤에 '그 자산을 마음대로 유용하는(misappropriate)' 것은 '횡령죄'라고 구별하고 있다.

embezzlement n. 횡령 withholding n. 주지 않음, 구금 entrust v. 맡기다 offense n. 범죄 subsequently ad. 그 후에 larceny n. 절도죄 consent n. 동의 augment v. 늘리다, 증대시키다 misappropriate v. (특히 자기에게 맡겨진 남의 돈·재산을) 유용하다 instigate v. 선동하다 aggravate v. 악화시키다

횡령 범죄는 하인, 대리인 또는 자산을 갖고 있도록 신탁되어진 다른 어떤 사람에 의해 자산이 절도되거나 되돌려 주어지지 않는 것으로 일반적으로 정의된다. 이 범죄에는 단일하거나 명료한 정의가 존재하지 않는다. 일반적으로 횡령은 어떤 사람이 합법적으로 점유하지만 그 후에 그 자산을 유용할 때 일어난다. 이러한 측면에서, 횡령은 다른 사람이 소유하고 있는 자산을 그의 동의 없이 가져가는 절도죄와 대조된다.

25   ④

첫 번째 빈칸 앞에서 '이러한 차별로 인해 수니파는 경제적 부의 상당 부분을 차지하고 있는 반면, 시아파는 경제적으로 빈곤하고 만성적으로 실업 상태에 있다'고 하였으므로 시아파가 경제적 '박탈'을 당하고 있다고 보는 것이 타당할 것이다. 다음으로, 수니파 정권은 가난한 시아파를 신경 쓰기보다는 차라리 외국에서 들어오는 수니파에게 시민권을 부여하고 있는데, 이는 그 정부의 기반을 '강화하기' 위한 정책이라고 추론할 수 있다.

chronically ad. 만성적으로 resentment n. 분노 spur v. 박차를 가하다 diversify v. 다변화하다 regime n. 정권 monarchy n. 군주국 ally n. 동맹 anoint v. ~에게 기름을 바르다; 지명하다 upheaval n. 격변 entrench v. 확립하다 impasse n. 교착 상태, 난국 promulgate v. 반포하다 recession n. 불황 dismantle v. 해체하다 disenfranchisement n. 참정권 박탈 bolster v. 강화하다

사회의 거의 모든 면에서 수니파 아랍인들, 특히 지배 부족인 알 칼리파(Al Khalifa) 부족 일원들은 더 큰 경제적 기회와 정치적 권리를 가지고 있다. 이러한 차별로 인해 수니파는 경제적 부의 상당 부분을 차지하고 있는 반면, 시아파는 경제적으로 빈곤하고 만성적으로 실업 상태에 있다. 경제적 박탈은 시아파 공동체 내부에 좌절과 분노를 증가시켜 2011년 시위에 박차를 가하는 데 일조했다. 나아가 바레인 경제가 다변화와 성장을 위해 고군분투하고 있는 상황에서 경제적 불평등은 정권을 계속 훼손할 것으로 예상해야 한다. 그 나라에는 군주제의 동맹들과 가난한 시아파들을 만족시킬 만한 충분한 부가 없다. 권력 기반을 강화하기 위해, 정부는 다양한 수니파 이주자들에게 시민권을 제공했다. 바레인과 깊은 관계가 없음에도 불구하고, 새로 시민으로 지정된 이 사람들이 시아파보다 더 많은 경제적, 정치적 권리를 누린다.

01 ②	02 ③	03 ①	04 ①	05 ④	06 ①	07 ④	08 ⑤	09 ①	10 ①
11 ②	12 ①	13 ⑤	14 ②	15 ①	16 ④	17 ③	18 ①	19 ②	20 ②
21 ④	22 ⑤	23 ④	24 ③	25 ④					

01   ②

언젠가 사용될 것으로 기대한다는 것은 당장 사용하지 않고 저장해둔 다는 말이므로 빈칸에는 ②가 적절하다.

wolf v. 게걸스럽게 먹다, 탐내다 squirrel v. 저장하다, 숨겨두다 dog v. 개로 추적하다, 미행하다 butterfly v. 팔랑팔랑 날아다니다, 나비꼴로 펴다

다양한 물건들이 언젠가 사용될 것을 기대하며 오랫동안 저장되어 왔다.

02   ③

and 이하에서 좌익 반군들이 국경을 들키지 않고 넘나들고 있다고 했으므로, 두 나라 사이에 있는 국경에는 많은 빈틈이 있음을 알 수 있다. 따라서 구멍투성이, 즉 허점이 많다는 의미의 ③이 빈칸에 적절하다.

left-wing a. 좌파[좌익]의 rebel n. 반대자[저항 세력] impregnable a. 난공불락의, 견고한 militarized a. 무장의, 무력의 porous a. 작은 구멍이 많은, 다공성의, 구멍투성이의 fortified a. 방어를 견고히 한

두 나라 사이의 국경은 구멍이 많아(허술해서) 좌익 반군들이 정기적으로 들키지 않고 국경을 가로질러 이동한다.

03   ①

빈칸 다음에서 더 많은 침이 입에서 뿌려져 나온다고 했는데, 이는 말을 강하게 할 경우에 해당하므로 ①이 빈칸에 들어가기에 적절하다.

spittle n. 침 spew v. 뿜어져 나오다, 분출되다 emphatic a. 어조가 강한, (표현상의) 힘이 있는 tedious a. 지루한; 장황한 impromptu a. 즉석의 contrite a. 죄를 깊이 뉘우치고 있는 deducible a. 추론할 수 있는

말을 할 때마다 침이 입에서 뿜어져 나오는데, 말을 더 강하게 할수록 더 많은 침이 입에서 뿌려져 나온다.

04   ①

빈칸 바로 뒤의 성장소설이라는 말로부터 정답을 추론할 수 있다. 따라서 '교양소설'이라는 의미의 ①이 정답이 되며, 교양소설은 '내면적으로 형성해 나가는 과정을 묘사한 소설'을 의미한다.

coming-of-age novel n. 성장소설 self-worth n. 자부심 bildungsroman n. 교양소설 epic n. 서사시, 서사시적 작품 saga n. 전설, 영웅적인 모험 이야기 novella n. 중편소설

어떤 독자들은 이 소설을 교양 소설 혹은 성장 소설로 여긴다. 왜냐하면 소설 말미에서 Sethe가 Paul D(이 소설의 남자 주인공)의 도움을 받아 마침내 자신의 가치를 발견하기 시작하기 때문이다.

05   ④

'외부인들은 이해하기가 어려운 자신들만의 언어를 그들끼리 사용한다.'라는 진술로부터 정답을 추론할 수 있다.

caliber n. 구경(口徑), 직경; 품질; 중요성 detriment n. 상해(傷害), 손해, 손실 accolade n. 명예, 표창 jargon n. (특정 분야의 전문·특수) 용어

모든 전문 직종은 각기 자신만의 전문어를 가지고 있다. 예를 들어, 의사들과 변호사들과 경제 분석가들은 모두 외부인들이 이해하기가 어려운 언어를 그들끼리 사용한다.

06   ①

더 많은 정보를 이용할 수 있는데도 더 모르고 확신할 수 없게 된다는 것은 의도하지 않은 부정적인 결과이므로 빈칸에는 ①이 들어가는 것이 적절하다.

perverse a. 사악한, 잘못된 chimerical a. 공상적인 salubrious a. 건강에 좋은, 유익한 connotative a. 함축적인

이용할 수 있는 엄청나게 많은 정보가 있지만, 그 모든 자료는 우리로 하여금 무엇을 믿어야 할지 혹은 누구를 신뢰해야 할지 더 모르고 확신이 없다고 느끼게 만드는 잘못된 결과를 낳을 수 있다.

07 ④

앞에서 마음의 상태가 끊임없이 동요(see-saw)했다고 했으므로 빈칸에는 이와 호응하는 의미를 가진 ④가 정답으로 적절하다.

see-saw n. 동요, 변동 wonder v. 의아하게 여기다, 의심하다 deceive v. 속이다 discern v. 분별하다 bridge v. 간격을 메우다 oscillate v. 동요하다, 갈팡질팡하다, 갈피를 못 잡다 coordinate v. 조화시키다

마음의 상태가 끊임없이 동요하는 가운데 그녀는 그가 자신에 대해 그녀에게 해준 이야기를 믿고 싶어 하는 것과 그가 자신의 인생의 근본적인 한 부분에 대해 그녀를 속이지 않았나 의심하는 것 사이에서 갈피를 못 잡았다.

08 ⑤

빈칸 이하의 술부 내용이 자국의 이익만 추구하고 불편한 사실에 대해서는 모르는 게 약이라고 생각하는 듯이 애써 모른 체하는 행태를 나타내므로 빈칸에는 ⑤가 적절하다.

ruling elite 지배엘리트, 소수 지배계급 vote for ~에 찬성표를 던지다 turn a blind eye to 못 본 체하다 humane anxiety 인도적인 걱정 silent abhorrence 침묵의 혐오 unlimited emergency 무한한 위급 consistent discomfort 일관된 불편함 blissful ignorance 행복한 무지

"행복한 무지"의 상태에 있는 미국의 소수 지배계급은 첨단 무기를 우크라이나에 공급하는 것에 찬성하고 그 나라 안에서의 무법과 이념적 극단주의와 정치적 암살에 대해서는 못 본 체한다.

09 ①

출세를 위해 권모술수를 부리면서 부유한 집안 여인들의 애정을 이용하려 한다면 '교묘히 그들의 환심을 사야' 할 것으로 추론할 수 있다.

Mme. n. 마님, 부인(madame) denounce v. 비난하다 social climber 출세주의자 schemer n. 책략가, 모사꾼 insinuate oneself into 교묘히 ~의 환심을 사다 play on ~을 이용하다 affection n. 애정 insinuate v. (몸을 서서히) 밀어 넣다; (사상 등을) 은근히 심어주다 insinuate oneself 서서히[넌지시] 환심을 사다, 교묘하게 들어가다 approbate v. 승인하다 engulf v. 사로잡다 enervate v. 기력을 떨어뜨리다

그는 레나 부인으로부터 중상하는 편지를 받는다. (그 편지에서는) 줄리앙을 자신의 이익을 위해 부유한 가문들의 환심을 사고 여인들의 애정을 농락하는 출세주의자이자 권모술수에 능한 사람이라고 비난한다.

10 ①

빈칸 다음의 delusions of grandeur(과대망상)과 가장 잘 어울리면서 radical과 상반되는 '생각이 분명치 않은 이상주의자'라는 의미의 ①이 빈칸에 적절하다.

social work 사회사업 radical a. 기본적인; 급진적인, 과격한 left-wing a. 좌익의 delusions of grandeur 과대망상 woolly-minded a. 생각이 모호한 capitalist n. 자본주의자, 자본가 self-deprecating a. 자기 비하하는 moralist n. 도덕가 altruist n. 이타주의자

일부 사람들의 생각에는, 사회사업이 급진적이고 좌익적인 정치와 연관되어 있고, 또 다른 사람들은 사회사업가를 아동학대를 방지하는 것과 사람들의 문제를 해결해주는 것과 일반적으로 도움과 배려에 있어 직업적인 전문가가 되는 것 등에 대해 과대망상을 가진, 생각이 분명치 않은 이상주의자로 생각한다.

11 ②

빈칸 다음의 조언과 단합활동이 보이스카우트라는 조직이 갖고 있는 장점에 해당하므로 보이스카우트는 이것들을 적극적으로 선전할 것이다. 따라서 빈칸에는 ②가 적절하다.

membership n. 회원자격, 회원 수 enroll v. 등록시키다 mentorship n. 조언 calibrate v. 구경을 측정하다; 조정하다 tout v. 끈덕지게 권하다; 극구 선전[칭찬]하다 delimit v. 한계를 정하다 nurture v. 양육하다 surpass v. 능가하다

보이스카우트는 1972년 절정에 달했을 때 회원 수가 6백만 명을 넘었다. 전국의 가족들은 노인들의 조언과 캠핑여행을 포함한 다른 소년들과의 단합 활동을 적극적으로 선전하는 그 조직에 아들을 등록시키기를 열렬히 원했다.

12 ①

일종의 whether A or B구문이고, 이 구문에서 A와 B는 반대이므로 의미상 benevolent의 반대가 되는 '아주 나쁜, 끔찍한' 정도의 의미인 ①이 적절하다.

in regard to ~와 관련하여 head for ~를 향해가다 recession n. 경기침체 subsequent a. 뒤따르는; 다음의 execrable a. 형편없는, 고약한 antiseptic a. 방부제의 sanguine a. 낙관적인 choleric a. 성마른

경제 체제와 관련해서 거의 모든 사람들이 반복적으로 묻는 첫 질문은 우리가 경기 침체로 나가고 있는가, 아니면 더 이상 그렇지 않은가이다. 두 번째 질문은 이어서 올 경기 침체가 끔찍한 것인가, 아니면 상대적으로 참고 견딜만한 것인가이다.

13 ⑤

medical condition이 '질병'이라는 의미이므로 질병과 어울리는 표현을 선택하면 된다.

affect v. 영향을 미치다, 악영향을 끼치다 steer v. 조종하다 contextual a. 문맥상의, 전후관계의 invigorate v. 기운 나게 하다 snap v. 부러지다 debilitate v. 쇠약하게 만들다

명예의 전당에 헌액된 쿼터백 존 얼웨이는 16년에 걸친 프로 선수 경력 중 다섯 번 슈퍼볼에 진출했었고, 지금은 덴버 브롱코스의 단장으로 일하고 있

다. 하지만 경기장 밖에서는 그의 손에 악영향을 미치는 쇠약하게 만드는 질병과 오랫동안 싸우고 있었다.

14 ②

빈칸 앞의 '균질화(homogenizing)'와 대립·대조적 관계에 있으면서 '차이(difference)'와 동일한 의미를 가진 표현을 고른다.

proliferation n. 급증, 증식, 확산 extinguish v. (불을) 끄다; 소멸시키다 homogenize v. 균질화하다 clapped-out a. (기계가) 낡은, 덜거덕거리는 disparate a. (본질적으로) 다른, 이질적인 waning a. 줄어드는, 쇠퇴하는 amicable a. 우호적인, 원만한

세계화에 관한 주된 불만 중의 하나는 서구 스타일과 제품, 취향이 확대됨에 따라 차이가 소멸된다는 것이다. 이런 견지에서 보면, 세계화란 단순히 이질적인 문화와 정체성들을 균질화하는 것을 나타낸다.

15 ①

마지막 문장에서 'are mocked by(무시당하다, 허사로 되다)'라 했으므로 빈칸에는 advances(진보)와 반대되는 ①이 적절하다.

abuse n. 학대 spouse n. 배우자 pose v. (문제를) 제기하다 pluralistic a. 다원적인 mock v. 조롱하다, 무시하다, 헛수고시키다 stasis n. 정체 상태 quirk n. 엉뚱한 행동, 기발함 plethora n. 과다, 과잉 boost n. 증가

아동학대와 배우자학대가 정신보건당국에 큰 문제가 되고 있다. 편견과 차별과 인종차별이 다원적인 우리 사회를 계속 분열시킨다. 그러나 이러한 인간관계 문제와 사회 문제를 이해하고 해결하는 우리의 능력이 정체 상태에 있음으로 인해, 우리 시대의 과학 진보는 허사가 되어버린다.

16 ④

자신에 대한 이야기로 협상을 시작한 집단의 성공률이 더 높았다고 했으므로 빈칸에는 '잡담이 성공적이다'라는 의미의 ④가 들어가는 것이 적절하다.

negotiation n. 협상 chatty a. 수다스런, 잡담의 beat about the bush 변죽을 울리다, 요점을 말하지 않고 둘러말하다 have a big mouth 큰소리치다 follow in ~'s step ~의 전철을 밟다 superior n. 윗사람, 상관 small talk 잡담 go a long way 성공하다, 유용하다(= be successful, be useful)

잡담이 성공한다. 연구자들은 이메일을 기반으로 한 협상에 참여한 사람들을 추적 조사해보았다. 한 집단은 곧장 협상업무로 들어갔고 두 번째 집단의 사람들은 상대편 사람들에게 자신에 대한 이야기를 해주면서 협상을 시작했다. 잡담으로 시작한 협상가들은 합의 성공률이 59%에 이른 반면에 업무 중심의 참여자들은 성공률이 39%에 그쳤다.

17 ③

우리는 한 친구가 나쁜 짓으로 우리를 실망시켜도 다른 여러 친구가 또 있기 때문에 그 친구와의 우정을 끊어버리지 않고 계속 지속하게 된다는 내용이므로 빈칸에는 ③이 적절하다.

split n. 헤어짐, 갈라섬, 사이가 틀어짐 monogamous a. 일부일처의 buddy n. 친구 drag down 타락시키다, (신체, 정신을) 쇠약하게 하다, 낙심시키다, 우울하게 하다 inertia n. 관성, 타성 get away with ~하고도 벌 받지 않고 지나가다

헤어지기가 왜 그렇게도 힘든가? 많은 이유가 있다. 친구관계는 일부일처의 관계가 아니어서 특정한 한 사람(친구)이 당신을 낙심시킬 때도 다른 친구들과의 관계를 즐기기가 쉽다. 그것은 뭔가 행동을 해야 한다는 압박감이 더 적다는 의미이다. 오랜 우정관계의 공이 굴러가고 있을 때 그것은 멈추기 어렵다. 그것은 우리 일상생활 리듬의 일부이며 그 관성은 막강하다. 이렇기 때문에 우리는 또한 우리의 친구들이 나쁜 짓을 저지르고도 그냥 지나가게 놔두는 경향이 있다.

18 ①

첫 문장에서 언급된 몇 가지 개념을 구별 짓는 것의 예로 흄과 그의 동료들이 낭만주의와 고전주의의 특성을 구별 지은 것이 두 번째 문장에 언급되고 있다. 구별된다는 것은 서로 상반된다는 말이므로 damp(눈물어린, 감상적인)와 dry(눈물 없는, 무미건조한, 꾸밈없는)가 상반되듯이 빈칸에는 hard(견실한, 믿을 수 있는, 현실적인)와 상반되는 의미를 가진 ①이 적절하다.

urge v. 추진하다 revisit v. 다시 고려하고 논의하다 polemical a. 논쟁의 review n. 재검토, 논평 manifesto n. 포고문, 선언문 Imagism n. 이미지즘, 사상주의 dismiss v. 무시하다, 멀리하다, 일축하다 gaseous a. 실속 없는, 믿을 수 없는, 공허한 sleek a. 매끄러운, 단정한 feasible a. 실행 가능한 grandiose a. 웅장한 corporeal a. 육체의, 유형의

1827년에 칼라일이 대논쟁이라고 부른 고전주의자들과 낭만주의자들 사이에 너무나 뜨겁게 진행된 논쟁은 여러 세대가 지난 후 종종 다시 고려되고 논의되었는데, 그것은 논쟁의 논평들과 선언들에서 몇 가지를 구별해야 할 필요가 있을 때였다. 예를 들어, 20세기 초에 T. E. 흄과 그의 이미지즘 서클이 빅토르 위고와 후기 빅토리아 시대 사람들의 감상적이고 공허한 낭만주의를 일축해버렸을 때 그들은 꾸밈없고 견실한 고전주의 양식을 위해서 그렇게 했던 것이다.

19 ②

미국이 다양한 나라의 사람들에 의해 세워진 다채로운 조합의 문화와 역사를 가지고 있다고 했으므로 미국 문화의 특징은 다양할 것이다. 따라서 첫 번째 빈칸에는 kaleidoscope, melting pot이 적절하며, 두 번째 문장은 이런 다양한 문화에 대한 예로 미국 음식 문화가 가진 독특한 특징을 언급하고 있으므로 두 번째 빈칸에는 culinary가 적절하다.

assemblage n. 집합(체), 모임 coalesce v. 융화하다, 서로 섞이다 melting pot n. (많은 사람·사상 등을 함께 뒤섞는) 용광로, 도가니 bucolic a. 목가적인; 전원생활의 kaleidoscope n. 변화무쌍한 것[모양, 상황, 장면 등] culinary a. 요리[음식]의 homogeneity n. 동종; 동질성 didactic n. 교훈적[설교적]인 lineage n. 혈통, 계통 eclectic a. 절충하는

미국은 변화무쌍한 문화, 즉 미국에 사는 다양한 나라의 사람들에 의해 세워진 다채로운 조합의 문화와 역사를 가진 나라로 종종 묘사된다. (하지만) 어떤 것도 미국의 음식과 같이 명확하게 이것을 보여주는 것은 없다. 미국에서 전 세계의 음식에 대한 지식과 기술은 잘 융화되어 어느 음식과도 다른 요리 환경을 만들어 낸다.

20 ②

나에게 삶은 이러이러한 것이지 저러저러한 것이 아니라고 한 것은 만일 내가 저러저러한 처지에 있게 되면 그것은 삶이 아니니 삶을 끝내고 싶다는 말이다. 즉 필자는 첫 문장의 질문에 긍정으로 답하고 있다. 따라서 빈칸에는 ②가 적절하다.

slump v. 털썩 주저앉다, 구부정한 자세를 취하다 institution n. 시설, 요양시설 chronic a. 만성적인 overworked a. 과로에 지친 dispensable a. 없어도 되는 available a. 이용할 수 있는 changeable a. 변할 수 있는 inevitable a. 불가피한

우리는 자신의 삶을 언제 끝낼지에 대한 선택권을 가져야 하는가? 그것은 각자가 삶에 대한 정의를 어떻게 내리느냐에 따라 달라진다. 나에게, 삶은 한 잔의 포도주를 마시며 일몰을 지켜보는 것, 친구들과 함께 식사를 하는 것, 예술을 즐기는 것 등등이지, 요양원에서 몸도 제대로 못 가눈 채 의자에 앉아 있는 것이나, 어쩌면 만성적인 통증을 갖고 살아가는 것이나, 과로에 지친 요양원 직원에게 나의 기본 욕구가 소홀히 여김을 당하는 것이 아니다. 간단히 말해, 나는 그 선택권이 내가 이용할 수 있는 것이면 좋겠다.

21 ④

'서로를 돌봐주는 잡담', '더 자연스럽고 인간적인 사회 소통 패턴', '사회적 생명줄' 등의 표현을 고려할 때 필자는 모바일 가십이 현대 생활의 소외와 고립을 극복할 수 있는 '해독제(또는 해결책)'라고 보고 있다고 할 수 있다.

space-age a. 우주 시대의; 초현대적인 humane a. 인간적인 grooming n. 털 손질 integrate v. 통합하다 gossip n. 수다, 한담 alienation n. 소외 fragmented a. 분열된, 파편화된 immunosuppressant n. 면역억제제 placebo n. 위약(僞藥) stimulant n. 흥분제 antidote n. 해독제; 해결 수단 narcotic n. 마약; 진정제

휴대 전화의 초현대적인 기술 덕분에 우리는 작고 안정된 공동체에서 살면서 긴밀히 통합된 사회 연결망을 통해 자주 '서로를 돌봐주는 잡담'을 즐겼던, 지금보다는 더 자연스럽고 또 인간적인 산업화 이전의 사회 소통 패턴으로 되돌아갈 수 있게 되었다. 빠르게 진행되는 현대 세계에서, 우리는 소셜 네트워크를 통한 의사소통의 양과 질 모두 심각한 제약을 받고 있었다. 모바일 가십은 우리의 연결감과 공동체 의식을 회복시키고, 현대 생활의 압박과 소외에 해독제를 제공한다. 모바일은 분열되고 고립된 세계에서 '사회적 생명줄'이다.

22 ⑤

산업도, 문화도 없고, 폭력적인 죽음은 만연해 있으며, 인간의 생은 외롭게 단명한다'면 그것은 '세상의 종말'이라고 보기에 부족함이 없을 것이다.

treatise n. 논문 obedience n. 복종 hereof ad. 이것의 commodity n. 물품 commodious a. 널찍한 solitary a. 고독한 nasty a. 심술궂은 brutish a. 잔인한 Dadaistic a. 전위주의적인 misanthropic a. 사람을 싫어하는, 염세적인 grotesque a. 기이한, 터무니없는 anarchistic a. 무정부주의의 apocalyptic a. 종말론적인

1651년에 출판된 정치적 복종에 관한 논문인 『리바이어던(Leviathan)』에서, 토마스 홉스(Thomas Hobbes)는 "이것의 결실은 불확실하므로 산업을 위한 자리는 이제 없다. 결과적으로 지구의 문화도, 항해도, 그리고 바다를 통해 수입될 수 있는 물품들의 용처도 없고, 널찍한 건물도 없고 … 예술도 없고, 문학도 없고, 사회도 없다. 그리고 최악인 것은, 계속되는 폭력적인 죽음의 위험과 공포, 그리고 인간의 생은 고독하고, 가난하고, 심술궂고 잔인하며 짧다는 것이다." 홉스가 이런 글을 썼던 프랑스에서 많은 사람들은 그의 종말론적 비전을 공유했다.

23 ④

이 글은 20세기 초부터 이어지고 있는 물리학계 내의 '조만간 모든 것이 설명될 수 있다는 자신감', '궁극적인 자연의 법칙에 대한 탐구가 거의 막바지에 이르렀을지도 모른다는 희망'에 대한 것이다. 필자는 그러한 물리학자들의 희망과 기대가 새로운 발견들로 깨지고 좌절되었던 역사적 사실을 말하기는 했지만(Having said this), 그럼에도 불구하고 필자는 여전히(still) '조심스러운 낙관론의 근거는 있다'고 믿는다.

property n. 특성 elasticity n. 탄성, 탄력성 conduction n. 전도 emphatic a. 단호한, 확실한 then again (앞 문장을 받아서) 그렇지 않고, 반대로 physicist n. 물리학자 equation n. 방정식 electron n. 전자 proton n. 양성자 neutron n. 중성자 knock ~ on the head ~을 좌절시키다 fundamental a. 근본적인, 주요한 optimism n. 낙천주의, 낙관론

20세기 초에는 모든 것이 탄력과 열전도 등 연속적인 물질의 성질로 설명될 수 있다고 생각되었다. 원자 구조의 발견과 불확실성의 원리는 이런 믿음을 단호하게 종식시켰다. 반대로 1928년 물리학자 겸 노벨상 수상자인 맥스 본(Max Born)은 괴팅겐 대학의 방문객들에게 "우리가 알고 있는 바와 같은 물리학은 6개월 안에 끝날 것이다"라고 말했다. 그의 자신감은 디락(Dirac)에 의한 전자를 지배하는 방정식의 최신 발견에 바탕을 두고 있었다. 그 당시 알려진 유일한 다른 입자인 양성자도 유사한 방정식이 지배할 것으로 생각되었고, 그것은 곧 이론물리학의 종언을 고하는 바였다. 그러나 중성자와 핵력의 발견은 그것 역시 좌절시켜버렸다. 이렇게 말했지만, 나는 여전히 우리가 이제 궁극적인 자연의 법칙에 대한 탐구가 거의 막바지에 이르렀을지도 모른다는 조심스러운 낙관론의 근거가 있다고 믿는다.

24 ③

마지막 문장은 대조의 접속사 while로 연결되어 있는데, 많은 팔레스타인 단체가 중동에서 경멸을 받는 이란과 동맹을 맺고 있다고 했으므로이스라엘과 과거에 적대적이었던 다른 아랍 국가들은 이를 막기 위해이스라엘의 영향력이 전략적으로 중동에 유리하다고 생각할 것이다.따라서 빈칸에는 ③이 적절하다.

ally with ~와 동맹을 맺다   neutral n. 중립적 위치에 있는 사람[국가]topsy-turvy a. 뒤죽박죽인, 엉망진창인 hostile a. 적대적인 monarchy n.군주국 theocratic a. 신정(주의)의 appendage n. 수행원, 종자 despiseda. 경멸 받는 provoke v. (감정 따위를) 일으키다; 유발시키다 antipathy n. 반감,혐오 masquerade v. 가장하다, 변장하다 expedient a. 도움이 되는, 유리한,합당한; 편의(주의)적인 geopolitical a. 지정학의

이스라엘은 특별한 전략적 목표를 공유할 때마다 동료 국가, 중립국, 이전의적이었던 국가들과 동맹을 맺는다. 혼란 속에 있는 중동에서 이스라엘은 현재 때때로 이집트, 요르단, 사우디아라비아, 그리고 다른 걸프지역의 군주국에 있는 이전에 적대적이었던 정권들과 전략적 동반자가 되기도 한다. 이 국가들은 모두 신정주의 이란과 레바논, 시리아, 예멘에 있는 이란의 테러리스트 분자들에 대한 더 큰 두려움을 공유하고 있다. 분명히 대부분의 아랍 세계는 더 이상 이스라엘을 멸망시키려는 팔레스타인의 바람에 예전과 같은관심을 가지고 있지 않다. 많은 팔레스타인 단체는 경멸받는 이란과 동맹을맺고 있는 반면, 많은 아랍 국가들은 이스라엘의 영향력이 때로는 전략적으로 유리하다고 생각한다.

25 ④

'이 바이러스는 사람을 가리지 않는다(무차별적이다)', '부자와 가난한사람들이 이 바이러스에 공통적으로 노출되어 있다'는 취지를 고려하면 빈칸에는 '이 바이러스 앞에서는 계층적 경계(또는 지역사회의 경계)가 무의미하다'는 의미의 진술이 들어가는 것이 적절하다.

indiscriminate a. 무차별적인 inclusive a. 포함하는 comprehensive a. 포괄적인 vulnerable a. 취약한 banish v. 추방하다 prioritize v. 우선시하다affluent a. 부유한 prowl v. 배회하다 transient a. 임시의 strengthen v.강화하다 barrier n. 장벽; 장애

싱가포르는 이 무차별적인 바이러스에 대해서는 어떠한 대응도 포함되어야한다는 것을 보여준다. 집에서 일할 수 없고 종합건강보험이 부족한 저소득층 미국인들은, 요양원에 갇힌 노인들만큼 특히 취약하다는 것이 분명해졌다. 그러나 이 바이러스는 젊고 부유한 사람들을 우선시함으로써 사회에서추방될 수 없다. 미국과 마찬가지로 싱가포르에서는 부자와 가난한 사람들이 같은 대중교통을 이용하고, 같은 승차 공유 앱을 이용하고, 같은 쇼핑몰을 돌아다닌다. 싱가포르의 비정부기구인 Transient Workers Count Too의 크리스틴 펠리 집행위원은 "바이러스는 지역사회의 장벽을 존중하지 않는다. 우리는 저임금 노동자들로부터 혜택을 많이 받는다. 그들의 안녕을 좀더 면밀하게 보살펴야 한다."라고 말한다.

01 ④	02 ③	03 ②	04 ①	05 ①	06 ①	07 ③	08 ③	09 ④	10 ②
11 ②	12 ④	13 ④	14 ③	15 ③	16 ①	17 ④	18 ①	19 ③	20 ③
21 ③	22 ①	23 ④	24 ③	25 ①					

01　④

단순해 보였다고 한 다음에 역접이 접속사 but이 왔으므로, 빈칸에는 이와 상반되는 의미를 가진 ④가 들어가야 한다.

inspection n. 검사, 조사 contumelious a. 오만한 sassy a. 뻔뻔스러운 primitive a. 태고의, 고대의 daedalian a. 다이달로스의 솜씨 같은, 정교한; 복잡한

규칙들은 단순해 보였다. 그러나 자세히 보면 정확하고 복잡했다. 대부분의 규칙들은 본질적으로 신사다웠고 모든 것들이 선수들에 의해서 존중되었다.

02　③

that big world와 the travel scene은 같은 것이고 끝의 it은 이것을 가리키고 있다. but 앞뒤가 역접관계에 있는데, 뒤에서 love it이라 했으므로 빈칸에는 싫어할 만한 의미인 ③이 적절하다.

settle v. 자리 잡다 superb a. 훌륭한, 멋진 facile a. 손쉬운, 용이한; 간편한 daunting a. 기를 꺾는, 힘겨운 propitious a. 순조로운; 상서로운

그 큰 세상에 첫 발을 들여놓을 때 약간 힘겨울 수 있지만, 시간이 지나면서 세상에 자리 잡음에 따라 곧 세상을 좋아하게 된다.

03　②

신과 자연이 하나라는 진술로부터 정답을 추론할 수 있다.

underlying a. 밑에 있는, 근원적인; 잠재적인 pluralistic a. 다원론의 monistic a. 일원론의 idealistic a. 이상주의적인; 공상적인, 비현실적인 materialistic a. 유물론의

스피노자의 형이상학적 견해는 본질적으로 일원론적이었다. 그는 신과 자연이 동일한 단 하나의 근원적인 실재에 대한 두 가지 이름에 지나지 않는다는 견해를 가지고 있었다.

04　①

졸음을 오게 하는 피로는 심신의 활동성을 떨어뜨리는 것인데, 이것을 방지하기 위해 아데노신을 차단하므로 아데노신은 심신의 활동성을 떨어뜨리는, 즉 마음을 가라앉히는 것이다. 따라서 ①이 정답으로 적절하다.

combat v. 싸우다 drowsiness n. 졸음 trick v. 속여서 ~하게 하다 alert a. 정신을 바짝 차린 sedate v. 진정시키다 fascinating a. 매혹적인 arouse v. 깨우다; 각성시키다 resuscitate v. 소생시키다

카페인은 뇌를 속여 정신이 바짝 들게 함으로써 졸음과 싸운다. 그것은 자연적으로 마음을 진정시키는 뇌 화학물질인 아데노신을 일시적으로 차단하여 피로를 방지한다.

05　①

두 번째 문장에서 '심한 고지대들과 저지대들이 있다'고 했으므로 빈칸에는 이러한 환경을 설명해주는 ①이 들어가는 것이 적절하다.

sense v. 지각하다, 알아채다 an intensity of 격렬한, 심한 precipitous a. 가파른 kaleidoscopic a. 변화무쌍한, 끊임없이 변화하는 enterprising a. 진취적인, 모험적인 accessible a. 접근하기 쉬운

로버트 루이스 스티븐슨은 한때 그의 고향 에든버러를 지형이 가파른 도시라고 불렀으며 그의 말은 전적으로 옳았다. 누구든 와보면 에든버러에는 심한 고지대들과 저지대들이 있다는 것을 알게 된다.

06　①

pro-life가 '낙태를 반대하는'의 뜻임을 감안하면, 빈칸에는 ①이 적절하다.

pope n. 교황 papacy n. 교황의 지위(임기) pro-life a. 낙태에 반대하는 abortion n. 유산, 낙태; (계획 등의) 실패 calamity n. 재난, 참화, 재해 warfare n. 전쟁 persecution n. 박해

프랜시스 교황은 서울에서 남동쪽으로 약 190킬로미터 떨어진 한 상징적인 "낙태 희생자 묘지"에서 조용히 기도하러 잠시 멈추었을 때 임기 중 가장 강력한 낙태 반대의 언급을 했다.

07 ③

the tail end of this year(올해의 끝)라 했으므로 빈칸에는 '마무리하다'라는 의미의 ③이 들어가는 것이 자연스럽다.

tail end 말단, 최종단계 feature v. 두드러지게 다루다, 대서특필하다, 특집으로 다루다 embodiment n. 구현, 구체적 표현 catch phrase 경구, 표어 cut away 베어내다 square up to 맞붙다 round out 마무리하다 usher in 도착을 알리다

이제 올해도 끝나게 되었다는 것이 믿기 어렵다. 한해를 마무리하기 위해 우리는 "특별한 일을 하는 보통 사람"이라는 표어를 구현한 사람이라고 생각되는 사람을 특집기사로 다루기로 했다.

08 ③

소설이 가장 완벽하게 인생을 반영하는 가장 대표적인 예술형식이라는 because절의 내용을 통해, 소설이 속해 있는 예술의 역사가 소설 속에서 재구성되고 요약된다는 것을 추론할 수 있다.

multiplicity n. 다수, 다양성 zest n. 열정, 풍미, 묘미 bewilder v. 당황하게 하다 gainsay v. 부정하다, 반박하다 recapitulate v. 요약하다, 결론짓다 vaticinate v. 예언하다

소설은 소설이 속한 예술의 역사를 요약한다. 왜냐하면 소설은 예술 형식들 중에서 삶의 다양성, 풍요로움 그리고 그 묘미를 포착하는 것에 가장 가까이 다가선, 가장 완벽하고 가장 민주적인 예술 장르이기 때문이다.

09 ④

앞에서 collector라 했으므로 진공청소기로 먼지를 빨아들이듯이 '흡수하다'는 뜻의 ④가 빈칸에 적절하다.

stake out (말뚝을 박아) 경계를 정하다, 잡아매다, (한곳에) 잠복 감시하다 squelch v. 억누르다, 억박지르다 jettison v. 버리다 immolate v. 산 제물로 바치다 hoover v. 흡수하다

사진작가(가 하는 일)는 단 한 순간에 관한 것이 아니다. 오히려 그는 장소를 고정시키고 단 한 곳에 대한 이야기를 할 수 있을 정도로 충분히 많은 순간들을 흡수하기까지 순간들을 모으는 사람이다.

10 ②

'우리 인간이 야생동물이나 식물을 우리에게 속해 있고 우리를 위해 봉사하는 것쯤으로 여기고 있다'는 내용으로부터 정답을 추론할 수 있다.

stock n. 저장, 축적; 주식; 재고; 줄기 disastrously ad. 끔찍하게 reinstate v. 이전 상태로 복위시키다, 복권시키다, 복직시키다 epitomize v. 전형이다; 요약하다 denunciate v. 비난하다 mitigate v. 완화하다; 누그러뜨리다, 가라앉히다; 경감하다

야생동물과 식물들은 마치 그들이 우리에게 속해 있고 그들의 역할이 우리를 위해 봉사하는 것인 양, '자원'이나 '재고'의 전형쯤으로 취급받는다. 그리고 이와 같은 개념은 '생태 서비스'라는 용어에 의해서 끔찍할 정도로 확대된다.

11 ②

뒤에 나온 litter라는 표현과 어울리려면 '지저분하고, 산만하다'는 의미를 가진 단어가 필요하다. 따라서 ②가 정답으로 적절하다.

revenue n. 수입 ticky-tacky a. 싸구려의 litter v. 어수선하게 만들다 amiable a. 호의적인 desultory a. 산만한, 일관성이 없는 knotty a. 매듭이 많은 amorous a. 요염한 cruise v. 순항하다

현재 페이스북은 82퍼센트의 수입을 광고로 얻고 있다. 그 광고 대부분은 사람들의 페이스북 프로필 오른쪽에 지저분하게 늘어서 있는 산만한 싸구려 광고들이다.

12 ④

빈칸에 해당하는 말은 주절의 heated tone인데, 열띤 어조는 그를 반대하는 사람들에게는 '자극적'이고 '선동적'인 것처럼 보일 것이므로 빈칸에는 ④가 적절하다.

oftentimes ad. 자주, 종종, 가끔 dependability n. 신뢰[의지]할 수 있음 awry a. (계획 등이) 빗나간, 엉망이 된 nonchalant a. 차분한, 태연한 phlegmatic a. 차분한, 침착한 incendiary a. 자극적인, 선동적인 oblique a. 간접의, 에두른, 완곡한

그 대통령 후보자는 종종 자극적인 연설과 논평으로 비판에 직면했지만, 그의 많은 지지자들은 그의 열띤 어조를 수십 년간의 공직 생활을 통해 얻은 진정성과 신뢰성의 표시로 보고 있다.

13 ④

Vladimir Putin이 the Russian President이고 the envoy가 Rex Tillerson인데, 첫 번째 문장에서 만나기로 동의했다고 했고 빈칸 앞에 부정어가 있으므로 빈칸에는 ④가 적절하다.

envoy n. 외교사절, 특사(特使) recrimination n. 되비난, 맞고소 drudge v. 꾸준히 열심히 일하다 hail v. 환호하여 맞이하다, 환영하다 charter v. 특허를 주다; (비행기, 버스 등을) 전세 내다 snub v. 냉대하다, 무시하다

결국 블라디미르 푸틴은 트럼프 행정부가 보낸 특사를 만나기로 동의했다. 시리아 내전을 둘러싼 상호 비난이 1주일 계속된 끝에 러시아 대통령은 모스크바를 처음으로 공식 방문한 미 국무장관 렉스 틸러슨을 냉대하지 않았다.

14 ③

and when 이하에서 일부 사람들이 행운의 눈짓을 외면하는 행동을 설명했으므로 빈칸에는 '마음이 뚱하고 무뚝뚝한'이라는 의미의 ③이 적절하다.

Lady Luck 행운(의인화한 표현) fancy v. 생각하다 come-hither n. 사람을 끄는 것, 유혹하는 것 grabby a. 욕심 많은 jovial a. 명랑한 dour a. 뚱한, 음침한 sapient a. 영리한

행운은 나를 좋게 대해주었다. 나는 행운이 많은 사람들을 좋게 대해주었다고 생각한다. 일부 사람들만 뚱해서 행운이 유혹하는 것과 같은 눈짓을 보낼 때 눈길을 내리깔고 몸을 돌려버린다. 그러나 나는 행운에게 윙크를 보내고 행운과 함께 간다.

15 ③

코로나바이러스 위기 속에 발견한 새로운 업무 방식들 중 일부는 위기가 지나간 후에도 계속 이용될 것이라는 말이므로, 빈칸에는 '~보다 오래 지속되다'라는 뜻의 ③이 적절하다.

no doubt 분명 search for 찾다 outdate v. 시대에 뒤지게 하다 outfit v. 공급하다 outlast v. ~보다 오래 지속되다 outrage v. 격분시키다

우리는 지금 일하는 새로운 방식들을 발견하고 있는데 그 중 몇몇 방식은 분명 이번 코로나바이러스 위기가 끝난 후에도 계속될 것이며, 우리는 또한 일과 가족과 신체 및 정신 건강의 필요를 충족시킬 새로운 방법을 찾고 있다.

16 ①

빈칸 앞에 역접의 접속사 but이 있으므로, 문맥상 gorgeous와 반의어 관계에 있는 표현이 들어가는 것이 적절하다.

illustration n. 실례, 보기 gorgeous a. 아주 멋진 undulating a. 물결모양의 quilt n. 누비이불 cereal n. 곡물 birch n. 자작나무 grove n. 숲 unromantically ad. 멋없이 down-at-heel a. 누추한, 초라한 heel-and-toe a. 경보하듯 걷는 hairy-heeled a. 버릇없는 well-heeled a. 부유한

예를 들어, 바르샤바에서 북쪽으로 운전해서 마조프셰로 들어가십시오. 이 지역은 마치 쇼팽의 협주곡처럼, 곡물 밭과 자작나무 숲으로 이루어진 물결 무늬 퀼트 모양의 아주 멋진 곳이지만, 1990년대만 하더라도 이곳 마을들의 모습은 멋없이 초라했습니다.

17 ④

poised to explode(곧 폭발을 일으킬)가 후치 수식하므로 첫 번째 빈칸에는 tinderbox(불씨)가 적절하다. 한편, 정치꾼들의 기회주의가 꺼져가는 불(잿불), 즉 분쟁의 불씨를 살려내는 것이므로 두 번째 빈칸에는 flared(확 타올라지다)나 fanned(부채로 부쳐지다)가 적절하다.

fanaticism n. 광신, 열광 assassination n. 암살 poised to V ~할 태세를 갖춘, 곧 ~할 수 있는 ember n. 타다 남은 것, 깜부기불, 잿불 opportunism n. 기회주의 polarize v. 양극화시키다, 대립시키다 windfall n. 횡재 asphyxiate v. 질식시키다 fireplug n. 소화전(消火栓) flare v. 확 타오르게 하다 quicksand n. 유사(流砂); 방심할 수 없는 위험한 상태[사태] quench v. (불 따위를) 끄다; (갈증 따위를) 풀다 tinderbox n. 불씨, 타기 쉬운 물건 fan v. 부채로 부치다

암살 이면의 종교적 광신이 전국적으로 폭발을 일으킬 수 있는 불씨다. 사회를 극심하게 양극화시켜서 국내 정치에서의 유리한 입지를 차지하려 하는 사람들의 기회주의가 타다 남은 잿불에 부채질을 한다.

18 ①

마지막 문장의 they는 잉카인들에게 정복당한 사람들을 가리키는데, 앞에서 잉카의 정복이 잔인하지 않았다고 했으므로 빈칸에는 ①이 적절하다.

conquest n. 정복 pay homage to ~에게 경의를 표하다; 신하의 예를 다하다 renounce v. 포기하다, 단념하다 venerate v. 존경하다; 공경하다 placate v. 달래다 embrace v. 포옹하다, 포용하다

잉카족의 정복은 대체로 대부분의 정복 국가들의 정복만큼 잔인하지 않았던 것으로 믿어진다. 잉카인들은 그들이 정복한 사람들에게 태양인 "인티"를 그들의 주신(主神)으로 받아들이고 잉카의 지도자들에게 경의를 표해야 한다고 주장했다. 그러나 그들은 그들 자신의 신들을 포기하도록 강요받지는 않았다.

19 ③

인생과 현실에 대해 배워야 할 것이 책에 더 많이 있다고 했으므로 책이 아니라 전자기기 화면을 오래 보면 인생과 현실에 대해 제대로 알지 못해 올바른 삶을 살지 못하고 표류하게 될 것이다. 따라서 빈칸에는 ③이 적절하다.

virtual reality 가상현실 headset n. 헤드셋(머리에 착용하는 시청각장치) ogle v. 추파를 던지다 pixel n. 픽셀, 화소 byte n. 바이트(정보단위) far-sighted a. 미래를 내다볼 줄 아는, 선견지명이 있는; 원시(遠視)의 Arcadia n. 아르카디아(옛 그리스 산속의 이상향) adrift a. 물에 떠돌아다니는, 표류하여; (정처 없이) 헤매어 rein n. 고삐; [pl.] 지배권 isolated a. 고립된, 격리된

가상현실이 미래의 모습일지 모르지만, 인생과 현실에 대해 배워야 할 것은 헤드셋보다 책에 훨씬 더 많이 있다. 픽셀과 바이트의 화면을 오래 볼수록 우리는 그만큼 더 멀리 표류하게 될 것이다.

20 ③

Those와 그다음의 명사가 합쳐서 interactions among disparate peoples를 가리키므로 crashes, collisions, encounters가 적절하고, 빈칸 이하에서 have still not died down이라 했으므로 created나 triggered가 적절하며, 혼란된 지역에서 계속되고 있다고 했으므로 breakthroughs와 innovations는 아니고 aftermaths나 reverberations가 적절하다. 따라서 ③이 정답이 된다.

disparate a. 서로 다른 epidemic n. 역병 genocide n. 대량학살 die down 조용해지다, 그치다 troubled a. 거친, 혼란된 disaster n. 재해, 재난, 참사 tone down 누그러뜨리다 aftermath n. 여파 crash n. 충돌 block off 차단하다 breakthrough n. 획기적 발전 collision n. 충돌 reverberation n. 반향 encounter n. 조우, 만남 trigger v. 촉발하다

여러 민족들 사이의 상호작용의 역사는 정복과 역병과 대량학살을 통해 현대 세계를 형성한 것이다. 그 충돌들은 반향을 일으켰는데 그 반향은 여러 세기가 지난 지금도 그치지 않았고 오늘날 세계에서 가장 혼란된 일부 지역에서 활발히 계속되고 있다.

21 ③

온라인 데이트 상대방이 대화를 시작하기도 전에 '변덕'을 부리며 '사라져버리고', 자신을 '대체 가능한' 존재로 여긴다면 '짜증스러울' 것이라고 추론할 수 있다.

fickleness n. 변덕스러움 peer n. 또래 initiate v. 시작하다, 개시하다 stoke v. 부추기다 ecstatic a. 황홀한 uproarious a. 시끌벅적한 vexing a. 짜증나게 하는, 애태우는 lachrymose a. 애절한

데이트 앱 사용자들은 상대 사용자들의 변덕스러움에 대해 불평했다. 많은 사람들이 그들의 짝과 대화를 시작하는 데 실패했다. 대화를 시작하면, 상대방은 곧 사라졌다. 사용자 연결의 용이함은 그들에게 (대화) 상대를 "대체 가능한" 듯이 대하도록 부추겼다. 이것이 좌절감을 유발했다. 지난 10월 미국 사용자들 중 45%가 온라인 데이트가 짜증 나는 경험이라고 우리에게 말했다.

22 ①

'상업적 세력은 대중들을 상대로 경제적 이득을 취하려 하므로 대중음악을 이용해 대중들을 '달래려는' 혹은 '회유하려는' 것임을 추론할 수 있다.

sophisticated a. 정교한 manipulate v. 조종하다 placate v. 달래다, 회유하다 flabbergast v. 깜짝 놀라게 하다 enlighten v. (설명하여) 이해시키다, 깨우치다 overbear v. 억압하다 encumber v. 지장을 주다

테오도르 아도르노(Theodor Adorno)는 20세기 대중음악의 본질에 대해 영향력 있고 철학적으로 정교한 설명을 제공한다. 그는 대중음악은 단순하고, 반복적이며, 지루한데 대중음악에 수동적으로 반응하는 대중들을 회유하고 조종하기 위해 상업적 세력이 대중음악을 조작하기 때문에, 대중음악은 계속해서 그런 식으로 머무를 것이라는 견해의 가장 뛰어난 원천이다.

23 ④

사실 주인은 손님을 당황하게 만들지 않으려고 예의상 양의 눈을 먹은 것이지만, 주인도 먹는 것을 본 영국 손님은 아랍에서는 양의 눈이 즐겨 먹는 맛있는 음식이라고 생각했을 것이므로 첫 번째 빈칸에는 dainty나 delicacy가 적절하고, and 다음에서 손님인 영국인을 당황하게 한다는 말이 이어지므로 두 번째 빈칸에는 양의 눈은 먹는 것이 아니라고 밝혀 잘못을 교정한다는 의미가 되도록 rectify나 correct가 적절하다.

tribal a. 부족의, 종족의 sheik n. (아랍의) 가장, 족장, 촌장 prize v. 소중히 여기다 treat n. 한턱, 대접 courteous a. 예의바른, 정중한 amulet n. 부적 rectify v. 교정하다, 고치다 dainty a. 고상한, 미려한; 맛좋은 postulate v. (자명한 일로서) …을 가정하다; (논리 전개를 위해) …을 전제로 하다 emblem n. 상징, 표상 revise v. 개정하다, 교정하다 delicacy n. 섬세, 미묘; 허약 correct v. 바로잡다, 고치다, 정정하다 anathema n. 저주, 저주받은 것 shun v. 피하다, 비키다

아랍의 에티켓에 대한 서구의 재미있는 오해가 있다. 양(羊)의 눈이 아랍에서 전형적으로 맛있는 음식이라는 것은 사실이 아니다. 이런 믿음의 기원은 한 족장에 의해 만찬에 초대된 영국 외교관이라는 말이 있다. 그 족장은 음식으로 내놓을 양고기가 신선하다는 것을 손님에게 알려주려고 양의 눈을 손님에게 보여주었다. 정말로 귀한 대접을 받고 있다는 생각에 그 외교관은 양의 눈을 예의상 먹었다. 예의바른 족장은 잘못을 바로잡아 그 영국인을 당황하게 만들기를 원치 않았고 그래서 다른 한쪽 눈은 자신이 먹어버렸다.

24 ③

'입술로만 신의 존재를 단언하고, 삶에서 행실로서는 신의 존재를 보여주지 못한다'면, 그런 사람들은 '교조(교리)적으로는 과잉, 즉 고혈압이요, 행실(실천)로는 과소, 즉 빈혈증'에 해당한다고 추론할 수 있다.

theoretical a. 이론적인 practical a. 실천적인 atheism n. 무신론 affirm v. 확언하다 creed n. 교리, 신념 dogmatism n. 독단주의, 교조주의 materialistic a. 유물론의 diabetes n. 당뇨병 anemia n. 빈혈 deed n. 행위, 행동 ideological a. 관념학의; 이데올로기의 metabolic syndrome 대사증후군 empirical a. 경험의, 경험적인

무신론에는 두 종류가 있다는 이론입니다. 자, 한 종류는 이론적인 종류인데, 누군가 앉아서 그것에 대해 생각하기 시작하면서, 신이 없다는 결론에 도달하는 겁니다. 다른 종류는 실천적인 무신론인데, 그런 종류는 마치 신이 없는 것처럼 사는 것에서 비롯되는 종류의 무신론입니다. 그리고 여러분이 잘 알듯이 세상에는 입술로 신의 존재를 단언하는 사람들이 많습니다. 그런데 그들은 그들의 삶에서 신의 존재를 부정합니다. 교조적으로는 고혈압이요, 행실로는 빈혈증인 이런 사람들을 여러분은 보셨을 겁니다.

25 ①

첫 번째 빈칸에는 노예의 도덕은 '외부의 것을 먼저 말하고, 이어서 자신에 대해 초점을 맞춘다'고 하였으므로 '외부의 것과 자신을 비교하다'

는 의미가 들어가는 것이 적절하다. 두 번째 빈칸에는 '행동하기 위해서는 외부의 자극이 먼저 있어야 한다'고 하였으므로 노예의 도덕은 능동적으로 먼저 행동(action)하는 것이 아니라, 어떤 자극이 먼저 있은 다음에야 그것에 대해 '반응(reaction)'하는 것이라고 추론할 수 있다.

ressentiment n. 르상티망, 원한, 패배주의적인 토라진 태도, (자기보다 잘 사는 사람에 대한) 노여운 마음 resentment n. 적개심 sentiment n. 정서, 감정 orientation n. 지향, 방향 afterthought n. 나중에 덧붙이는 생각 come about 생기다, 일어나다 opposing a. 대립되는 stimulus n. 자극 comparison n. 비교, 대조 reaction n. 반응, 반작용 aversion n. 혐오, 반감 impetus n. 힘, 추진력 contraposition n. 대치, 대위 instigation n. 선동, 부추김 incompatibility n. 양립하지 않음, 상반(相反) deterrent n. 억지력 detachment n. 초연 disillusionment n. 환멸

노예의 도덕은 르상티망(원한), 즉 힘없는 자가 강한 자에 대해 품는 적개심과 증오를 특징으로 한다. 니체(Nietzsche)는 르상티망을 완전히 부정적인 감정, 즉 다른 것에 대해, 자신의 '밖'에 있는 것, 또는 '타자'에 대해 '아니오'라고 말하면서 삶을 긍정하는 것에 대해 부정하는 태도라고 본다. 자기에 초점이 있는 고귀한 도덕의 지향과 달리, 르상티망은 외부에 대한 지향을 갖는 것이 특징이다. 주인은 '나는 선하다'라고 말하고, 그 뒤에 '따라서 그는 나쁘다'라고 덧붙이는 반면, 노예는 반대로 말한다. '그(주인이)는 나쁘고, 따라서 나는 선하다.' 따라서 가치 체계는 외부, 타자, 다른 것에 대한 비교나 반대에서 비롯된다. 니체는 "노예의 도덕이 나타나기 위해서는 먼저 대립하는 외부 세계를 가져야 한다. 심리적으로 말하면, 행동하기 위해서는 외부의 자극이 필요한 것이다. 즉, 그 작용은 기본적으로 하나의 반응(반작용)이다."라고 말한다.

01 ④	02 ②	03 ①	04 ②	05 ③	06 ①	07 ④	08 ②	09 ④	10 ②
11 ③	12 ③	13 ②	14 ③	15 ③	16 ③	17 ②	18 ④	19 ①	20 ②
21 ④	22 ⑤	23 ③	24 ②	25 ②					

01 ④

in other words 이하의 '우리의 욕망을 만족시키는 데'라는 표현과 '교환'이라는 단어에 주목해야 한다. '우리'라는 표현 안에는 보편적인 사람이란 뜻이 내포되어 있고, 교환이란 행위는 궁극적으로 타인을 필요로 한다. 그러므로 어떤 상품이 비록 희소하더라도, 나와 다른 사람의 욕망을 만족시키는 데 이바지하지 못한다면 교환은 이루어지지 못할 것이다. 나와 마찬가지로 타인에게도 별다른 필요가 없기 때문이다. 결국, 빈칸에는 '결여'의 의미를 가진 단어가 들어가야 하며, 정답은 ④가 된다.

commodity n. 일용품, 필수품, 물자; 상품 contribute v. 기부하다; 기여하다, 공헌하다 gratification n. 만족, 희열; 만족감을 주는 것 exchangeable a. 교환할 수 있는 scarce a. 부족한; 희귀한, 드문 feasible a. 실행할 수 있는; 가능한; 그럴 듯한, 있음직한 ecumenical a. 보편적인, 전반적인, 세계적인 pertinent a. 타당한, 적절한 destitute a. 빈곤한; (~이) 없는

만일 어떤 상품이 조금도 쓸모가 없다면, 바꿔 말해, 만일 그것이 우리의 욕망을 만족시키는 데 전혀 공헌할 수 없다면, 그 상품이 아무리 희소한 것일지라도 교환 가치가 없을 것이다.

02 ②

보호통로(protective corridors)라 했으므로 이와 관련 있는 ②가 빈칸에 들어가기에 적절하다.

corridor n. 복도, 통로 mobile a. 이동성이 강한 vault n. 둥근 천장, 지하 저장실 sanctuary n. 은신처, 보호구역 abyss n. 심연(深淵), 나락 maze n. 미로

이동하는 야생동물을 보호하는 가장 좋은 방법은 보호통로를 만드는 것이다. 그런 통로가 전체 이동 경로에 도움을 주지는 못하겠지만 몇몇 이동성이 대단히 강한 동물들을 위한 임시 보호소 역할은 할 것이다.

03 ①

tough enough 이하 전체는 rules를 수식하는 관계사절이다. 접속사로 쓰인 yet에 역접의 의미가 있으므로, 빈칸에는 앞의 tough에 대해 문맥상 반대 의미를 가진 단어가 필요함을 알 수 있다. '융통성 있는'이라는 의미의 ①이 들어가야만 tough와 대조를 이루고, 빈칸 뒤의 '은행을 질식시키지는 않는다'라는 내용과 자연스럽게 호응한다.

tighten v. 강화하다, 엄하게 하다 regulation n. 규칙, 규정, 법규 construct v. 조립하다, 세우다; 꾸미다, 구성하다 tough a. 질긴, 단단한; 완고한; 강인한 crisis n. 위기, 중대국면 strangle v. 교살하다, 질식시키다; 억압하다, 묵살하다 flexible a. 구부리기 쉬운; 유연성이 있는, 융통성 있는 ancillary a. 보조의, 부수적인, 종속적인 quenchable a. (갈증을) 풀 수 있는, 소멸시킬 수 있는 morose a. 까다로운, 뚱한, 기분이 언짢은; 침울한

금융 규제를 강화하기 위한 논의가 작년에 시작되었을 때, 중앙 은행가들과 은행 감독기구들은 또 다른 금융위기를 예방할 수 있을 정도로 강경하지만, 은행을 질식시키지는 않을 만큼 유연한 그런 규정들을 만들어야 했다.

04 ②

첫 번째 빈칸에는 or 앞의 didactic과 유사한 의미의 studious(면학적인)나 homiletic(설교적인)이 적절하고, 일상회화로도 예술(문학) 작품에도 사용되지 않았으면 발달되지 못했을 것이므로 두 번째 빈칸에는 arrested(정지된)나 delimited(한계가 정해진)가 적절하다.

colloquial a. 일상회화의 didactic a. 교훈적인, 설교적인 consequently ad. 결과적으로 studious a. 면학적인 prompted a. 촉진된 homiletic a. 설교적인 arrested a. 정지된 sleazy a. 허울[겉모양]만의; 싸구려의; 하찮은; 단정하지 못한 accelerated a. 가속화된 priggish a. 까다로운 delimited a. 한계가 정해진

히브리어는 적어도 천 년 동안 일상회화적인 의미로 말해진 적이 없었고, 교훈적이거나 설교적인 노력이 아니라 순수하게 예술적(문학적)인 노력으로 사용된 적도 없었으므로, 그 결과, 히브리어의 발달은 정지되었다.

05 ③

세 번째 문장의 '많은 훈련과 경험을 갖춘 사람들'은 대중적 이미지인 '팔방미인'과는 반대되는 '전문가'를 나타내고, 두 번째 문장의 주어와 세 번째 문장의 주어가 동일한 현대사회를 의미하므로 첫 번째 빈칸에는 부정적인 cloud(모호하게 하다)나 belie(거짓임을 나타내다)가 적절하고, 두 번째 빈칸에는 긍정적인 vies(경쟁하다)나 clamors(극성스럽게 요구하다)가 적절하다.

favor v. 닮다 roam v. 돌아다니다 jack-of-all-trades n. 팔방미인, 무엇이든 대충은 할 줄 아는 사람 fortify v. 강화하다 vie v. 경쟁하다 cloud v. 모호하게 하다 tremble v. 떨다, 전율하다; 몹시 belie v. 거짓임을 나타내다 clamor v. 외치다; 극성스럽게 요구하다 spawn v. 낳다; 야기하다 cater v. 부응하다

대중들이 생각하는 성공한 사람의 이미지(모습)는 자유로이 돌아다니는 팔방미인을 닮은 것 같다. 우리 문명의 현실은 이런 대중적 이미지가 사실과 다름을 보여준다. 우리의 산업 사회는 점점 더 많은 훈련과 경험을 갖춘 사람들을 극성스럽게 요구한다.

예술에서 새로운 운동이 어느 정도 유행에 이르렀을 때, 그 지지자들이 무엇을 목적으로 하고 있는지 알아보는 것이 좋다. 왜냐하면 오늘날에는 그들의 교의가 아무리 억지스럽고 불합리하다 해도, 장래에 아주 정상적인 것으로 간주될 수도 있기 때문이다.

---

06 ①

문학이 사회를 있는 그대로 단순하게 반영하는 것이 아니라 복잡하고 창의적으로 재구성한다는 내용의 글이다. 여기서 '단순한 반영'이라는 것은 어떤 대상을 조금의 변화도 없이 그대로 드러낸다는 뜻이므로, 그 대상과 반영된 결과물이 일대일 대응의 관계에 있다는 의미로 볼 수 있다. 따라서 ①이 정답이 된다.

mirror v. 비추다, 반영하다, 반사하다 proposition n. 제안, 건의; 명제; 주장 complex a. 복잡한; 어려운 correspondence n. 대응; 일치, 조화 allusion n. 암시; 언급 antithesis n. 대조, 정반대 dialectic n. 변증법; 논리학

문학이 사회를 반영한다는 사실은 널리 알려져 있으며 일반적으로 받아들여지고 있는 명제다. 그러나 그것은 단순한 반영 즉, 일대일 대응은 결코 아니다. 왜냐하면 훌륭한 문학작품은 사진과 같은 사실주의의 예가 아니기 때문이다. 문학은 살고 있는 현실을 다소 복잡하고, 창의적으로 재구성한 것이다.

---

07 ④

접속사 for 이하의 절은 'too ~ to …' 구문을 이루고 있다. 이러한 구문에 부정의 의미가 내포되어 있음에 유의하면, '다음 시대의 요구와 조건에 적응할 수 없는' 이유가 되기에 적절한 의미의 단어를 찾는 문제라 할 수 있다. 대체로 이전 시대의 것들에 빠져 있거나 동화되었을 경우에 새로운 것에 적응할 수 없는 경향이 있으므로, 정답은 ④가 된다.

ideology n. 이데올로기, 관념 adapt v. 적응시키다; 개작하다 demand n. 요구, 청구; 수요 plague v. (병에) 걸리게 하다; 괴롭히다, 애태우다 unfetter v. 차꼬를 풀다; 석방하다, 자유롭게 하다 confound v. 당황하게 하다 imbue v. 고취하다, 물들이다

문명의 발달에서 한 시대에 주도적인 역할을 하는 집단이 다음 시대에도 유사한 역할을 할 가능성은 많지 않다. 왜냐하면 그 집단은 이전 시대의 전통, 관심사, 이념 등에 너무 물든 나머지 다음 시대의 요구와 조건에 적응할 수 없기 때문이다.

---

08 ②

양보구문의 역접성을 고려하여 normal의 반대 개념을 추론하면 정답을 찾을 수 있다.

vogue n. 대유행, 인기 advisable a. 바람직한; 타당한 tenet n. 주의 prodigious a. 거대한, 막대한 far-fetched a. 믿기지 않는, 설득력 없는 stale a. 신선미가 없는, 진부한, 김이 빠진 rational a. 이성적인, 합리적인 innate a. 타고난, 본성의

---

09 ④

빈칸 앞에서 '매우 다양한 직업이 있기 때문에 그것의 선택이 결코 가볍지 않은 문제임'을 이미 언급했다. no matter 이하는 여기에 부연하는 내용이므로 '직업 선택을 신중하게 해야 한다'라는 맥락으로 이어져야 하는데, 빈칸 앞에 부정어 no가 있으므로 '즉석에서, 아무렇게나'라는 의미의 ④가 들어가는 것이 자연스럽다.

occupation n. 직업; 점유, 점령 bewilder v. 당황하게 하다, 어리둥절하게 하다 avenue n. 가로수길; 수단, 방법 pensively ad. 생각에 잠겨; 구슬프게 gratis ad. 무료로, 거저 resplendently ad. 눈부시게, 찬란하게 off-hand ad. 즉석에서, 되는 대로, 아무렇게나

오늘날 학교를 졸업하는 학생들은 예전보다 선택할 수 있는 직업의 폭이 훨씬 넓다. 학부모나 아이들 모두 들어갈 수 있는 길이 너무 많아서 어리둥절할 때가 종종 있다. 그러한 경우, 직업의 선택은 쉬운 일이 아니며, 아무렇게나 결정할 문제가 결코 아니다.

---

10 ②

첫 문장에 쓰인 sense와 feeling은 동의어이므로, feeling 이하의 that절은 빈칸에 들어갈 표현의 재진술이라 할 수 있다. 그러므로 빈칸에는 이 that절의 핵심 내용인 there is nothing of importance that the individual can do의 의미를 함축할 수 있는 단어가 들어가야 한다. '개인이 할 수 있는 중요한 일이란 아무 것도 없다'라는 느낌은 '무력감'이라 할 수 있으므로, ②가 정답이 된다.

oppress v. 압박하다, 억압하다, 학대하다 vastness n. 광대함, 거대함; 막대함 breadth n. 폭; 넓이 endurance n. 인내, 인내력 solstice n. 최고점, 극점, 전환점 impotence n. 무력, 무기력, 허약, 노쇠 reverie n. 공상, 환상, 몽상 cosmopolitanism n. 세계주의, 사해동포주의

나는 오늘날 많은 사람들이 거대한 현대 사회 속에서 무력감, 다시 말해 개인이 할 수 있는 중요한 것은 전혀 없다는 기분에 억눌려 있음을 발견한다. 이것은 잘못이다. 인류에 대한 사랑, 드넓은 비전, 용기, 인내력으로 충만해 있다면, 개인도 많은 것을 할 수 있다.

---

11 ③

'구글' 검색엔진이 널리 대중화되고 지배하게 된 결과라 했으므로 '구글하다'라는 단어의 사용도 '널리, 어디서나, 많이' 늘어났을 것이다. 따라서 첫 번째 빈칸에는 pervasively(널리)나 ubiquitously (어디서나)나 meteorically(급속히)가 적절하다. 한편, 구글 검색엔진이라는 발명품에서 '구글하다'라는 단어가 새로 만들어진 것이므로 두 번째 빈칸에는 '신조어'라는 뜻의 neologism이나 coinage가 적절하다.

popularity n. 인기, 대중성 dominance n. 우세, 지배 World Wide Web 월드 와이드 웹(인터넷에 연결된 컴퓨터를 통해 정보를 공유할 수 있는 전 세계적인 정보 공간) pervasively ad. 널리 syllogism n. 삼단논법 tenuously ad. 미약하게 abracadabra n. 헛소리; 주문(呪文) ubiquitously ad. 어디서나 neologism n. 신조어, 신어구 meteorically ad. 급속하게; 잠시 반짝이다가 misnomer n. 틀린 이름 spasmodically ad. 돌발적으로 coinage n. 화폐 주조; 신조어

구글 검색엔진이 날로 더 대중화되고 지배하게 된 결과, "구글하다"라는 타동사의 사용이 어디서나 늘어났다. 이 신조어는 일반적으로 어느 검색엔진이 사용되는지와 무관하게 월드 와이드 웹(인터넷)을 통해 정보를 찾는 것을 가리킨다.

12 ③

"당신의 스웨터가 마음에 듭니다"라는 말은 찬사(compliments)로서 의례적인 인사치레의 말인데, 정색을 하고 나타내 보이는 세 가지 서툰 반응은 사회적(사교적)으로 부적절함(ineptitude)을 보여준다.

clumsy a. 서툰, 어색한 intrusive a. 참견하는 itchy a. 가려운 repartee n. 재치 있는 즉답 gimmick n. 비밀장치, 트릭 interlocution n. 대화, 문답 stratum n. 계층 compliment n. 경의, 칭찬 ineptitude n. 부적절, 부적당, 부조리 salutation n. 인사 disruption n. 분열, 붕괴

칭찬의 말이 폭넓은 사회적 부적절을 보여줄 수 있다. 한 연구에서 "당신의 스웨터가 마음에 듭니다."라는 말에 대한 서툰 반응에는 칭찬 업그레이드("예, 이 스웨터 덕분에 제 눈의 푸른색이 정말로 돋보입니다.")와 주제넘게 참견하는 질문(정말로 그렇게 생각하세요? 빌려가고 싶으세요?)과 의견 불일치(옷이 가려워서 싫어요) 등이 포함되어 있었다.

13 ②

과거의 군주는 백성 위에 군림하면서 백성과 독립된(independent) 존재로 있었으나 민주적 통치자는 피통치자인 국민들 중에서 선출되어 국민이 부여한 권한을 행사하는 것이므로 국민에 대해 의존적이라 할 수 있다. 또한 국민은 그들의 통치자에게 부여한 권한을 취소할 수 있는(revocable) 것이다. 따라서 ②가 정답으로 적절하다.

human affair 인간사 magistrate n. 행정장관 tenant n. 임차인 delegate n. 대리인 at one's pleasure ~하고 싶은 대로 absolute a. 절대적인 executable a. 집행할 수 있는; 처형할 수 있는 independent a. 독립된 revocable a. 철회할 수 있는 alienable a. 양도할 수 있는 empowered a. 권한이 부여된 inherited a. 상속받은 detained a. 구금된

인간사의 발전에 있어 사람들이 그들의 통치자가 이해관계에 있어 그들과 반대되는 독립적인 권력이라는 것이 자연의 필연이라고는 더 이상 생각하지 않는 때가 도래했다. 그들이 보기에는 국가의 다양한 행정관들이 그들 마음대로 취소할 수 있는 임차인이나 대리인인 것이 훨씬 더 나아 보였다.

14 ③

앞에서 아프리카의 역사가 부정적으로 진술되었으므로 첫 번째 빈칸에는 부정적인 의미의 slipperier(더욱 미끄러운, 불안정한)나 bumpier (더욱 울퉁불퉁한, 험난한)가 적절하고, 직장 없는 청년이 많으면 일자리를 더욱 많이 만드는 것이 정부가 해야 할 일일 것이므로 두 번째 빈칸에는 imperative(필수적 임무)나 desideratum (절실한 요구)이 적절하다.

detached a. 분리된, 초연한 looming a. 어렴풋이 떠오르는 mitigate v. 완화하다, 가라앉히다 turbulence n. 소란, 소요 slippery a. 미끄러운; 불안정한 proscription n. 추방; 금지 vast a. 광대한, 거대한 corollary n. 당연한 결과 bumpy a. 울퉁불퉁한; 험난한 imperative n. 명령; 의무, 책임 flat a. 평평함 desideratum n. 바라는 것; 절실한 요구

사회지도층이 국민과 분리되었고 부패가 만연하고 목표를 달성하기 위해 폭력을 사용해온 역사로 인해 아프리카에서는 번영의 길이 아마 더욱 험난할 것이다. 여기에 청년 실업자의 수가 3억 명에 이를 것이라는 전망을 더하면 사회적 소요를 가라앉히기를 바라는 모든 아프리카 정부가 반드시 해야 할 임무는 분명해진다. 다음에 아프리카가 발전시켜야 할 부분은 고용이다.

15 ③

노동은 일 그 자체와 부를 축적하는 데 오는 정신적 이익, 사회적 지위의 추구, 상류계급 생활방식에 걸 맞는 많은 값비싼 풍요로운 것들을 구입할 수 있는 능력 등 여러 가지 것들이 복합적으로 구성된 것이므로, 빈칸에는 이 점을 비유적으로 나타내주는 '복합명사'라는 표현이 와야 한다. 문자적으로 볼 때 work라는 단어는 복합명사가 아니지만, 여기서는 비유적으로 그렇게 표현하여 표현의 역설적 묘미를 더하고 있다.

psychic a. 정신적인, 심적인, 심리적인 enrichment n. 풍부하게 함, 부유하게 함, 향상, 질을 높이기 bliss n. 지복, 더 없는 기쁨 compound noun 복합명사 cure n. 치료; 치료법; 구제책 inequality n. 불평등, 불공평

부유하고 야심이 있는 미국인들은 이미 그들을 성취로 이끄는 것에 더 많은 시간을 사용하고 있다. 그러나 그것은 일(노동)로 드러났다. 이러한 결론에서 노동은 복합명사로서, 일 그 자체와 부를 축적하는 데서 오는 정신적 이익, 사회적 지위의 추구, 상류계급 생활방식에 걸 맞는 많은 값비싼 풍요로운 것들을 구입할 수 있는 능력 등으로 구성된 복합명사이다.

16 ③

탈레반 지도자들의 캠프 데이비드 초대가 마지막에 철회됨으로 인해 그동안 정책상 충돌을 빚던 볼턴이 퇴장했으므로, 앞으로 트럼프의 행동은 자유로워질 것임을 추론할 수 있다.

transactional a. 거래의 catechism n. 교리문답(서) palpably ad. 명백하게; 감지할 수 있게 revocation n. 폐지, 철회 proximate a. 가장 가까운, 바로 다음의 creed n. 신조, 신념 crisis n. 위기; 난국 foundation n. 기초, 토대

대부분의 증언은 볼턴의 퇴장을 트럼프의 거래 중심적인 세계관과 볼턴의 매파 교리 문답 주의 간의 정책 추진을 둘러싼 충돌로 묘사하고 있는데, 이는 이제 트럼프가 그처럼 명백히 갈망해 온 북한, 이란, 그리고 아프가니스탄의 탈레반 지도자들 — 지난주에 있었던 캠프 데이비드 초대(탈레반 지도자들에 대한)와 마지막 순간의 철회가 볼턴 퇴장의 가장 직접적인 원인처럼 보인다. — 과 같은 전 세계 악당들과의 거래를 자유롭게 할 것이라는 것을 의미한다.

17 ②

벽에 세워둔 사다리 밑을 지나가면 불운이 따른다는 미신을 설명한 글인데, 성스러운 삼위일체를 깨뜨리는 것은 '성스러운, 거룩한'의 반대인 '불경한' 행동으로 여겨질 것이므로 빈칸에는 ②가 적절하다.

ladder n. 사다리 the Holy Trinity 삼위일체 the Holy Ghost 성령 sacred a. 성스러운 halcyon a. 평화로운, 행복한 blasphemous a. 불경한 iconoclastic a. 인습타파의 calamitous a. 재난의, 비참한

사다리와 불운에 대한 한 가지 설명은 종교에 뿌리를 두고 있다. 많은 기독교인들은 성부, 성자, 성령의 삼위일체를 믿는다. 이 믿음이 초기 기독교 시대에 3이라는 수를, 그리고 3과 함께 삼각형을, 성스러운 것으로 만들었다. 사다리를 벽에 기대어 세우면 삼각형 모양이 형성되고, 그 삼각형 공간을 걸어서 통과하는 것은 삼위일체를 "깨뜨리는" 것으로 간주되곤 했는데, 이것은 악마를 불러들일 수 있는 것으로 뿐 아니라 불경한 것으로도 간주되는 범죄였다.

18 ④

주민회의에서 여성과 유색인종, 재산이 없는 백인들이 배제되었다고 했으므로, (영국의) 식민지 시절 뉴잉글랜드 마을 주민회의가 자유롭고 민주적이고 문명화됐다는 인상을 가지는 것은 그 당시 상황을 지나치게 단순화시켜 보는 것이다.

impression n. 인상, 감명 selectman n. (미) (New England 각주의) 도시 행정위원 abandon v. 버리다; 단념하다, 그만두다 establish v. 설립하다, 창립하다 rational a. 이성적인 far from 결코 ~이 아닌 groundless a. 근거 없는, 사실무근한

(영국의) 식민지 시절 뉴잉글랜드 마을 주민회의가 자유롭고 민주적이고 문명화됐다는 인상을 가지는 것은 그 당시 상황을 지나치게 단순화하는 것이다. 첫 번째로 여성과 흑인과 아메리칸 인디언과 재산이 없던 백인 등에게는 투표를 할 수 있는 권리가 주어지지 않았다. 17세기에 마을 주민회의를 운영한 사람들은 "인민"들이 아니라 마을 행정위원이었다. 그러나 매사추세츠주에 있는 Dedham이라는 초기 식민지에서는 마을사람들이 마을 주민회의에 참여해서 마을의 중요한 결정들을 직접 행하기도 했다. 이 위대하고 고귀한 실험은 3년 동안 지속된 후 1639년 마을이 설립되었을 때 폐기되었다.

19 ①

첫 번째 빈칸은 음악이 만들어 내는 시간이 우리가 경험하는 일상적인 시간과 다르다는 사실로부터 추론할 수 있고, 두 번째 빈칸은 두 빈칸에 음악이 만들어 낸 시간이 와야 한다는 사실로부터 유추할 수 있다.

discrete a. 분리된, 개별적인, 따로따로의, 불연속적인 temporal unit 시간의 단위 semblance n. 유사, 외형 align with 동조하다; 보조를 맞추다 circulative a. 순환을 촉진하는, 순환성의 object to ~에 반대하다

지난해 「Nautilus」 잡지를 통해서 작곡가 Jonathan Berger는 음악이 할 수 있다고 Prince가 말한 바로 그것을 — 시간을 멈추는 것 — 어떻게 사운드(음악)가 수행하는 지에 대해서 설명했다. 음악은 분리된 시간 단위를 만들어 낸다. 그러나 음악이 만들어 낸 분리된 시간의 단위는 일반적으로 우리가 (일상에서) 측정하는 시간의 분리된 단위와 일치하지 않는다. 오히려 음악은 '시계로 측정되는 시간'을 왜곡하고 부정할 수 있는, 분리되고, 유사 독립적인 시간의 개념을 구현한다. (음악이 만들어 낸) 이 다른 시간은 우리가 우리 자신을 잃어버리거나 혹은 최소한 객관적인 시간 비슷한 것은 모두 잃어버리기 쉬운 병행하는 시간의 세계를 만들어 낸다.

20 ②

'과거를 현재보다 더 긍정적으로 보다', '향수를 느끼다' 등의 표현을 통해 과거를 '회상하다'는 표현이 들어가는 것이 적절함을 추론할 수 있다.

positively ad. 적극적으로; 긍정적으로 skeptical a. 회의적인 nostalgic a. 향수를 느끼는 integrate v. 통합되다 deviate v. 벗어나다 hark back to ~을 회상[상기]하다 allay v. 누그러뜨리다 berate v. 질책하다 relish v. 즐기다

유럽인의 2/3가 과거를 현재보다 더 긍정적으로 보고 있으며, 이민과 유럽연합 가입에 회의적이라는 것을 한 조사 결과가 보여준다. 조사 결과, 67%의 사람들이 향수를 느끼는 것으로 나타났다. 옛 시절을 회상하는 사람들 중 78%는 이민자들이 사회에 통합되기를 원하지 않는다고 느끼는 반면, 향수를 느끼지 않는 사람들은 63%가 그러한 의견을 갖고 있었다.

21 ④

십대들의 대마초 사용을 금지하는 광고가 '부메랑 효과'를 일으켜 본래의 광고 의도와는 달리 십대들의 대마초 사용을 증가시켰다고 소개하고 있다. 빈칸이 속한 문장은 이유의 since절로, "십대들이 마리화나 금지 광고에 나온 메시지에 대해 반발했다."라고 했으므로 광고가 십대들이 본래 알고 있던 마리화나에 대한 지식과 상반되기 때문이라고 볼 수 있다. 따라서 빈칸에는 '반대의'라는 의미의 ④가 적절하다.

explicit a. 분명한, 명쾌한 implicit a. 암시된, 내포된 counter a. 반대의, 거꾸로의 boomerang effect 부메랑 효과(어떤 행위가 의도한 목적을 벗어나 불리한 결과로 돌아오는 것을 일컫는 효과) rebel against ~에 대해 저항하다, 거역하다 stated a. 분명히 진술된, 사실로서 표현된 infallible a. 틀림없는, 절대 확실한 susceptible a. 민감한 empirical a. 경험적인 counter a. 반대의, 역(易)의 germane a. 밀접한 관계가 있는; 적절한

'대마초 금지와 금연 TV 광고의 명시적, 암시적 효과'라는 제목의 '중독 행동'에 대한 가장 최근의 연구는 과장된 공포에 기초하고 부정확한 광고가 '부메랑 효과'를 일으킨다고 결론을 내렸다. 십대 시청자들이 광고에서 권하는 태도를 취하는 대신 이 '부메랑 효과'는 십대들이 광고에 나온 메시지에 대해 반발하게 했는데 이것은 십대들이 대마초에 대해 이미 갖고 있던 지식에 반하는 것이었기 때문이다. 대마초 금지 광고의 노출은 그 약물에 대해 젊은 시청자들의 행동을 긍정적으로 변화시킬 뿐만 아니라, 대마초 사용의 위험을 직접적으로 증가시킬지도 모른다.

22

⑤

고국을 떠나 해외에서 살 때 심리적 고통을 겪게 된다는 것은 보편화된 상식처럼 되어 있지만, 해외 생활을 청산하고 고국으로 귀국하는 사람들도 심리적 고통을 겪는다는 것은 '보편화된 상식이 아니고', '전혀 준비되어 있지 못한' 그러한 상태인 것이다. 따라서 '고국에 돌아올 때 어려움을 예상해야 한다'는 것은 '직관적으로 이해가 되지 않는' 상황이라고 말할 수 있을 것이다.

proximal a. 가까운 repatriation n. 본국 송환, 귀환 distress n. 걱정; 고통 mediate v. 중재하다, 조정하다 mediating variable 매개 변수 intensify v. 강화하다, 심화시키다 unexpectedness n. 뜻밖임, 의외임 expatriate n. 고국을 떠나 해외로 이주한 사람 cognitive a. 인지적인 disconcerting a. 불안을 느끼게 만드는 spontaneous a. 자발적인; 자동적인 wearisome a. 피곤하게 하는; 싫증나는 disagreeable a. 불유쾌한 profound a. 심오한, 뜻깊은 counterintuitive a. 직관에 어긋나는

아들러(Adler, 1981), 마틴(Martin, 1984) 그리고 서스만(Sussman, 1986)은 귀국 고통의 가까운 원인 혹은 적어도 귀국 고통을 심화시키는 중요 매개 변수는 그것의 의외성이라고 주장하였다. 고국에 돌아올 때 어려움을 예상한다는 것은 직관적으로 이해가 되지 않는다. 해외에서의 삶에 인지적, 행동적으로 적응하는 것은 때때로 좌절과 불안, 그리고 스트레스를 야기하는 심리적 과정이라는 고국을 떠난 사람들에게 이제는 보편화된 상식과는 달리, 귀국하는 사람들은 고국에 돌아올 때 수반되는 심리적 고통과 불안에 대해 전혀 준비되어 있지 않은 것처럼 보인다.

23

③

what 관계절 안의 otherwise는 '위협이 아니라면'의 뜻인데, 위협이 아닌 다른 방법은 곧 실제적인 폭력행사를 의미하므로 빈칸에는 '공공연한, 명백한, 행동으로 나타난'의 뜻인 ③이 적절하다.

teller n. 은행 출납원 hostage n. 인질 armed robbery 무장 강도 lump v. 한 덩어리로 만들다 mugging n. 폭력강도 assault n. 폭행 bruise n. 찰과상 loot n. 약탈물, 전리품 degrade v. 격하시키다, 품위를 손상시키다 ulterior a. (표면에) 나타나지 않은, 숨은 reticent a. 과묵한 overt a. 공공연한, 명백한, 행동으로 나타난 domestic a. 가정의; 국내의

강도가 권총을 들고 은행에 들어와 은행원에게 총을 쏘겠다고 위협하고 그리고 돈이나 인질 혹은 둘 모두를 갖고 은행을 걸어 나간다고 가정해보라. 이것은 무장 강도 사건인데, 비록 모든 사람이 이 범죄 상황에서 아무런 찰과상도 부상도 입지 않는다 해도 우리는 온당하게도 이 사건을 도덕적으로

법적으로 말해 폭력강도 및 폭행 사건과 같은 부류에 넣는다. 그 이유는 거기에는 명백한 위협이 있으며 위협이 아닌 공공연한 폭력으로 성취할 수 있는 것을 이 위협에 의해 대단히 자주 성취하기 때문이다. 이 사건에서 강도범은 그만큼(공공연한 폭력을 행사한 경우만큼) 많은 약탈물을 차지할 뿐 아니라 그가 다루고 있는 사람들(범죄행위 대상자들)의 명예를 손상시키는 것과 관련해서도 (공공연한 폭력의 경우와) 같은 것을 성취한다.

24

②

미국이 1898년에 스페인으로부터 푸에르토리코를 획득했을 때 그것은 제국들이 식민지를 삼키던 제국주의적인 영토 탈취 행위였다. 푸에르토리코의 자치권을 다시 빼앗은 작년 미국 의회의 조치가 그런 행위는 아니었다는 뜻이므로 빈칸에는 '제국의 폭식'이라는 의미의 ②가 적절하다.

self-rule n. 자치 in effect 사실상 revoke v. 철회(폐지, 취소)하다 autonomy n. 자치권, 자율성 control board 통제 위원회 veto v. 거부하다 reversal n. 반전, 역전 stagnant a. 정체된, 부진한 sustain v. 지속하다, 참고 견디다 bankruptcy code 파산법 insolvent a. 지급불능의, 파산한 spectre n. 유령, 망령 default n. 채무불이행 financial bailout 재정적 구제(구제금융) imperial gluttony 제국의 폭식 economic stratagem 경제적 책략 public involvement 대중의 참여

1952년에 미국은 스페인으로부터 1898년에 획득했던 카리브 해의 푸에르토리코 섬에 자치를 허용했다. 작년에 미국 의회는 푸에르토리코 예산의 모든 항목을 거부할 수 있는 통제 위원회를 창설함으로써 그 자치권을 사실상 취소했다. 그러한 사태의 반전은 제국의 폭식 행위는 거의 아니었다. 푸에르토리코 섬은 700억 달러의 부채를 발생시켰는데, 이는 그 섬의 정체된 경제가 감당하기를 바랄 수 있는 수준을 훨씬 넘는 것이었다. 그러나 푸에르토리코는 (미국의) 주가 아니기 때문에 푸에르토리코의 공개기업들은 디트로이트 같은 지급불능 차용자들이 이용한 파산법을 이용할 수 없었다. 그것은 혼란스런 채무불이행의 망령을 떠올렸다.

25

②

parallel이 '어떤 두 사건이 동시에 발생하는'이라는 의미를 지닌다. 필자는 '동시적으로(simultaneously)', '즉각적으로(immediately)'와 같은 표현을 사용하여 의사결정 과정이 순차적이 아니라 '하나의 생각과 그것과 다른 대안적인 생각이 동시에 발생하는', 즉 '병행하는' 과정이라고 설명하는 내용을 소개하고 있다.

et al (특히 이름들 뒤에 써서) ~외, ~들, ~등 sequential a. 순차적인 consecutive a. 연속의 empirical a. 경험적인 material n. 논거, 자료 succession n. 연속 linear a. 선의, 선형적인 parallel a. 병행하는, 동시에 발생하는; 유사한 asymmetrical a. 비대칭적인, 불균형의 hierarchial a. 계급서열의 circular a. 순환적인, 원형의

듀이(Dewey), 사이먼(Simon), 그리고 브림(Brim) 등의 제안은 결정과정을 항상 동일한 절차 혹은 순서로 오는 부분들로 나눈다는 점에서 모두 순차적이다. 몇몇 학자들, 특히 위테(Witte)는 일반적 형태의 결정과정이 연속적인 단계로 구별된다는 생각을 비판하였다. 그의 경험론적인 논거들은 그 "단계

들"이 순차적이라기보다는 병행적으로 수행된다는 것을 보여준다. "인간은 어떤 방식으로 동시적으로 대안들을 개발하지 않은 채 정보를 취합할 수는 없다고 우리는 생각한다. 우리는 이러한 대안들을 즉각적으로 평가하지 않을 수 없으며, 그렇게 하면서 결정을 내릴 수밖에 없게 된다. 이것은 여러 활동들의 꾸러미이며, 시간이 흐르면서 이러한 꾸러미들이 연속됨으로써 전체적인 의사결정 과정이 구성된다."

01 ②	**02** ③	**03** ③	**04** ④	**05** ⑤	**06** ①	**07** ③	**08** ④	**09** ④	**10** ④
11 ④	**12** ③	**13** ②	**14** ①	**15** ②	**16** ①	**17** ②	**18** ④	**19** ④	**20** ③
21 ③	**22** ①	**23** ②	**24** ④	**25** ⑤					

01 ②

지루하지 않은 밤이라는 단서와 익살스럽고 재치 있다(facetious and witty)는 단서로부터 정답을 추론할 수 있다.

facetious a. 우스운, 익살맞은 valetudinarian n. 병약자; 건강을 지나치게 염려하는 사람 wag n. (머리·꼬리 등을) 흔들기; 익살꾸러기, 까불이 vocalist n. (특히 팝·재즈 밴드의) 보컬리스트[가수] bard n. 음유시인

피터가 대단한 익살꾼이었기 때문에 저녁 시간은 지루하지 않았다. 나는 그처럼 익살맞고 재치 있는 사람을 이전에 독일에서는 만나본 적이 없었다. 그는 나쁜 농담과 좋은 농담을 가리지 않고 쉴 새 없이 연발했다.

02 ③

항생제의 주된 기능은 질병을 '막는' 것이라 할 수 있으므로 빈칸에는 ③이 적절하다.

antibiotic n. 항생제 feed supplement 사료 보충제(첨가물) embolden v. 대담하게 하다, 용기를 돋우어 주다 excoriate v. 심하게[격렬히] 비난하다; 피부를 벗기다; <가죽을> 벗기다 forestall v. 방해하다, 좌절시키다; 저지하다; 기선을 제압하다 eulogize v. 찬양하다, 칭송하다

로이터 통신의 탐사보도에 의하면, 미국의 치킨 회사들은 질병을 예방하고 성장을 촉진시키기 위해서 광범위한 종류의 항생제를 일상적인 사료 보충제로 사용한다.

03 ③

두 번째 문장의 주어 It(약자의 착취)은 '약자의 노예화'와 같은 것이며 이것이 파시즘을 번성하게 한다고 했는데, 그러려면 파시즘 자체가 그것을 지지하는 것이어야 하므로 빈칸에는 ③이 적절하다.

exploitation n. 착취 venture n. 모험 fertile a. 비옥한 enslavement n. 노예화 eschew v. 회피하다, 삼가다 spurn v. 경멸하다; 퇴짜놓다 laud v. 칭찬하다, 찬양하다 proscribe v. 금지하다

적법한 자본주의적 활동으로서 약자를 착취하는 것은 언제나 위험한 모험이었다. 그것은 파시즘(독재적 국가주의)이 번성할 비옥한 풍토를 조성하는데, 파시즘 자체가 약자의 노예화를 찬양하는 정치철학이기 때문이다.

04 ④

'그 소수의 신중하게 세척된(정제된) 단어들'은 모래를 다 제거한 후에 남는 '몇 개의 순수한 금 알갱이'처럼 문체의 간결성을 나타내므로 빈칸에는 ④가 적절하다.

kinship n. 친척관계, 유사성 mineralogist n. 광물학자 assay n. 시금(試金), 분석 put A in mind of B A에게 B를 생각나게 하다 prospector n. 탐광자, 광맥 찾는 사람 sluice v. 물을 끼얹어 씻다 grit n. 잔모래, 자갈 speck n. 잔 알갱이, 작은 조각 pedantic a. 현학적인 cryptic a. 신비한; 숨은, 비밀의 sardonic a. 풍자적인 laconic a. 간결한; 말수가 적은

베이컨의 간결한 문체는 "essay(수필)"라는 단어와 광물학자의 "assay(시금)"라는 단어 사이의 유사성을 암시한다. 왜냐하면 베이컨의 수필에 나오는 그 소수의 신중하게 세척된(정제된) 단어들은 잔모래를 물로 씻어 흘러 보내어 마침내 냄비 바닥에 몇 개의 순수한 금 알갱이가 남게 하는 사금 캐는 사람을 생각나게 하기 때문이다.

05 ⑤

미국이 논란이 되고 있는 영공으로 장거리 폭격기를 출격시킨 것은 미국의 경고로 보인다고 했으므로, 역내 영공에 대한 지배권을 확대하려는 중국의 시도는 미국이 볼 때 '도발적(provocative)'이거나 '문제를 일으키는(troublesome)' 시도로 여겨질 수 있을 것이다. 따라서 ①, ②, ④는 빈칸에 들어갈 수 없으며, 이런 중국의 시도에 대해 미국은 경고 신호를 보내는 것이므로 첫 번째 빈칸에는 '정면으로 반대하다(defy)'가 적절하다. 따라서 두 빈칸에 모두 적절한 ⑤가 정답이다.

bomber n. 폭격기 contest v. 논쟁하다, 겨루다, 다투다, 싸우다 impede v. 방해하다, 지체시키다 capitalist a. 자본주의적인 accommodate v. 수용하다 dovish a. 비둘기파의, 온건파의 hail v. 환영하다, ~을 열렬히 지지하다 troublesome a. 문제를 일으키는, 성가신 besiege v. 포위하다 placate v. 달래다; 화해시키다 defy v. ~에 대해 공공연하게[정면으로] 반대하다 provocative a. 도발적인, 자극적인

미국이 두 대의 B-52 장거리 폭격기를 논란이 되고 있는 영공으로 출격시켰는데, 이번 조치는 역내 영공의 지배권을 확대하려는 중국의 도발적인 시도를 정면으로 미국이 반대한다는 경고로 보인다.

06 ①

however라는 역접의 연결사와 자신의 이익만을 생각한다는 진술로부터 빈칸에 부정적인 표현이 들어가야 함을 알 수 있다.

merchant n. 상인 peculiarly ad. 특별히; 기묘하게 attend to 처리하다, 돌보다, 정성을 들이다 grievous a. 괴롭게 하는, 한탄하게 하는; 슬픈 beneficial a. 유익한, 이익을 가져오는 compassionate a. 연민어린, 동정하는, 온정적인 empathetic a. 공감하는

아담 스미스는 자신이 살던 시대에 정책의 '주요 입안자들'인 '상인들과 제조업자들'이 영국 국민을 포함해 다른 사람들에게 미치는 영향이 아무리 '통탄할 만한' 것이라도 해도 자신들의 이익이 가장 특별한 배려를 받게 한다고 생각했다.

07 ③

유연하고 상황에 맞게 성향을 선택해야 한다는 진술로부터 정답을 추론할 수 있다.

introversion n. 내향성 extraversion n. 외향성 concurrently ad. 동시에 rigid a. 굳은, 엄격한, 고정된 asymmetry n. 불균형, 부조화 analogy n. 유추; 유사 balance n. 균형, 평형 anachronism n. 시대착오, 시대에 뒤떨어진 사람[사물]

어떤 때에는 내향성이 더 적절하다. 그리고 다른 때는 외향성이 더 적합하다. 이 두 가지 성향은 상호배타적이다. 내향적인 태도와 외향적인 태도를 동시에 취할 수는 없다. 그리고 이 두 가지 성향 중 하나의 성향이 더 우월한 것도 아니다. 이상적인 것은 유연하게 접근하여 주어진 상황에서 더 적합한 태도를 선택하는 것이다. 그리고 더 나아가서 이 세계에 대해 반응하는 고정되고 엄격한 방식을 개발하지 말고, 두 성향 사이의 역동적인 균형이라는 관점에서 행동하는 것이다.

08 ④

learning the truth가 satisfaction과 관련된 것이므로 빈칸에는 curious, inquisitive, prying 등과 가까운 의미인 ④가 들어가는 것이 적절하다.

popularize v. 대중화[통속화]하다, 보급시키다 frenemy n. 친구이자 적 (friend+enemy) gist n. 요점, 요지 feline n. 고양이 literally ad. 글자 그대로 worry oneself sick 너무 걱정하여 병이 나다 rejoinder n. 대답, 답변 publish v. 발표하다 bring back 되돌리다 avid a. 탐욕스러운; 열심인 discontented a. 불만스러운, 불평스러운 obtuse a. 우둔한, 둔감한 nosy a. 다른 사람의 일에 관심 갖고 알아내고 싶어 하는, 참견하기를 좋아하는

벤 존슨이 쓰고 그의 친구이자 적인 윌리엄 셰익스피어가 대중화한 "호기심(curiosity)이 고양이를 죽였다"는 표현의 알려진 최초의 버전은 "근심(care)이 고양이를 죽였다"이다. '근심(care)'이 여기서는 '걱정(worry)'이라는 의미로 사용되고 있어서, 이 표현이 예로부터 말하고자 하는 요지는 걱정하는 사람(혹은 고양이)은 말 그대로 너무 걱정하여 병이 날 수 있다는 것이다. 1800년대 후반에 어떻게 '근심'이 '호기심'으로 되었는지는 불분명하지만, 분명한 것은 오늘날 사람들은 1905년에 처음으로 나왔던 말인 "호기심이 고양이를 죽였다 .... 그러나 (호기심으로 알아낸 후의) 만족감이 고양이를 되살렸다"라는 말을 거의 언제나 잊고 있다는 것이다. 달리 말하자면, 관심을 갖고 알아내고 싶어 하는 것이 당신을 어려움에 빠뜨릴지도 모르지만, 진실을 아는 것은 종종 그 어려움을 겪게 될 위험을 무릅쓸만한 가치가 있는 것이다.

09 ④

공유지라는 미명하에 공해가 착취되고 있는 상황을 기술하고 있는 글이다. 온갖 국제협약과 국제법들이 짜깁기되어 있어도 결국은 명확한 관할 주체가 없으므로 공해의 어자원을 '아껴 쓰고, 절약하기'보다는 착취, 남용하는 것이 일반적이라고 말하고 있다.

governance n. 통치, 관리 subject to ~의 대상이다 patchwork n. 임시변통으로 그러모은 것, 잡동사니 enforcement n. 집행 incentive n. 장려, 자극, 동기; 장려금, 보상책(보상물) misaligned a. 어긋난, 정렬이 안 된 jurisdiction n. 사법권, 관할권 high seas 공해(公海) common n. 공유지 invested a. 투하된, 투자된 upkeep n. 유지; 양육 exploit v. 이용하다, 착취하다 win out over ~을 누르고 이기다 tricky a. 까다로운 quota n. 할당량 haul v. 끌다 catch n. 어획량, 포획량 with impunity 벌을 받지 않고, 활개 치며 capitalize v. 자본화하다; 이용하다 deploy v. 배치하다; 효율적으로 사용하다 prodigalize v. 낭비하다, 함부로 마구 쓰다 husband v. 절약하다 gobble v. 게걸스럽게 먹다

또 하나의 문제는 관리다. 바다는 법률들과 협정들의 적용을 받아야 한다. 법의 집행은 어렵고 보상책들은 종종 어긋나버린다. 국가의 관할권을 넘어선 수역들, 즉 공해(公海)는 세계의 공유지다. 명확한 재산권이나 공해 관리를 전담하는 공동체가 없으므로, 공해를 착취하는 개별 행위자들의 이해관계가 공해를 아껴 쓰는 것에 대한 집단적 이해관계를 압도해버린다. 물고기는 계속 움직이므로 특히나 까다롭다. 이웃 국가가 활개치며 마구 잡아가는데 할당량을 준수해야 할 이유가 어디 있겠는가?

10 ④

'자신들만의 고유한 환경을 창조한다', '미술작품 속에 개인적 세상을 창조한다', '스스로 선택한다', '스스로를 판단하지 말고 자신의 작품이 흘러나오도록 허용하라' 등의 진술을 통해 미술치료에서 강조되는 것은 '자기표현(self-expression)'임을 추론할 수 있다.

therapy n. 치료, 치료법 artwork n. 미술작품 material n. 소재 geometry n. 기하학 aestheticism n. 심미주의, 유미주의, 예술지상주의 verisimilitude n. 박진성, 핍진성(정말 진실같음) self-expression n. 자기표현

미술치료는 사람들에게 창조적인 방식으로 자신의 강점에 주목할 기회를 제공한다. 그들은 자신들만의 고유한 환경을 창조하고 자신들의 미술작품 속에 개인적 세상을 창조한다. 그 예술가는 자신이 창조한 우주의 주인으로서 자기만의 주제, 색깔, 모양, 소재, 이미지들을 선택한다. 미술치료사는 사람들에게 스스로를 판단하지 말고 자신의 작품이 흘러나오도록 허용하라고 북돋워준다. 참가자들은 자기표현이 창조적 작업에서 가장 중요한 측면임을 배우게 된다.

11 ④

빈칸 이하의 인용문이 앞의 "warts and all"보다 덜 어떠하냐고 묻는 문제이다. '있는 그대로' 그려달라고 말하지 않고 더 장황하게 말했으므로, 빈칸에는 '간결한'이라는 의미의 ④가 적절하다.

warts and all 있는 그대로 flatter v. 아첨하다; (그림이) 실물 이상으로 잘 묘사되다, 돋보이게 하다 roughness n. 거칠거칠함 pimple n. 여드름 wrinkle n. 주름살 a farthing 1파딩(= 1/4페니); (부정문에서) 조금도 ~아니다 gabby a. 수다스러운 wary a. 경계하는, 용의주도한 naggy a. 잔소리가 심한 pithy a. 간결한; 함축성 있는

자신의 모습을 "있는 그대로" 묘사하는 초상화를 그려달라고 요청한 것으로 말해지는 사람은 바로 올리버 크롬웰이다. 그러나 크롬웰이 죽고 1세기가 지난 후 글을 쓴 호레이스 월폴에 따르면, 그가 실제로 한 말은 다음과 같이 약간 덜 간결했다. "렐리 씨, 나는 당신이 당신의 모든 기량을 발휘해 정말로 나 같은 그림을 그려서, 절대로 나를 돋보이게 하지 말고 피부의 거칠거칠함, 여드름, 주름살 등, 당신 눈에 보이는 이 모든 것을 나타내주기를 바랍니다. 그렇지 않으면 그림 값을 한 푼도 주지 않겠소."

12 ③

두 번째 문장의 표지판의 내용으로 미루어 첫 번째 빈칸에는 '책임지기를 거부한다는 내용의 성명서'를 의미하는 disclaimers가 적절하고, 이것은 주차장 직원들에게 주차 차량에 대해 마음껏 범죄를 저지르게 허용할 것이므로 두 번째 빈칸에는 permission이 적절하다.

sign n. 표지판 liability n. 책임 theft n. 절도 sneer v. 비웃다; 냉소하다 billboard n. 광고판, 광고게시판 prohibition n. 금지 ultimatum n. 최후통첩 admonition n. 훈계, 권고, 충고 disclaimer n. 격식(책임·연루 등에 대한) 부인; 권리 포기 각서 permission n. 허가; 허용 declaration n. 선언, 포고, 공표 persuasion n. 설득; 확신

아시아에서는 사람들이 책임거부성명서를 무기로 사용한다. 홍콩의 한 주차장에는 벽에 다음과 같은 표지판이 걸려 있다. "본 주차장 주인측은 그 어떤 절도나 피해, 혹은 귀하의 차량에 대해 우리에 의해 직간접적으로 일어나는 또 다른 그 어떤 불상사에 대해서도 전혀 책임을 지지 않습니다." 이것은 주차장 직원들에게 당신의 차에 침입해 들어가 당신의 스테레오를 훔치고 당신의 음악적 취향을 비웃는 쪽지를 남길 수 있게 완전히 허용한다.

13 ②

빈칸을 제외한 전체 글이 털의 중요한 역할을 설명하고 있으므로, 빈칸에는 털의 기능을 설명한 ②가 적절하다. 앞에서 언급한 the bumpy air를 that turbulence로 받고 있다.

bump n. 융기 bumpy a. 덜컹덜컹하는; 난기류의 collision n. 충돌 depilate v. 털을 뽑다 altitude n. 고도 normality n. 정상 상태 destination n. 목적지, 행선지 detect v. 발견하다, 간파하다 turbulence n. 소란, 동란; (대기의) 난류(亂流) convey v. 나르다, 운반하다 magnetic a. 자석의, 자기의 contract v. (병에) 걸리다; (근육 등을) 수축시키다; 죄다; 축소하다 impact n. 충돌, 쇼크; 영향

박쥐가 날 때 공기가 날개를 따라 나있는 촉각 수용체 융기에서 자라는 작은 털을 지나서 흘러간다. 만일 박쥐의 날개가 나는 동안 어떤 방향으로 구부러지지 않으면 공기가 불규칙한 난기류가 된다. 털이 그 난기류를 감지하여 뇌에 정보를 전달한다. 그러면 심지어 완전히 어두운 가운데서도 박쥐는 날아가는 행로를 교정하여 충돌을 피할 수 있다. 오하이오 대학 신경과학 교수인 존 주크는 최근에 박쥐 날개에 탈모 크림을 발라서 이것을 시험해보았다. 털이 뽑힌 박쥐는 직선으로는 날아갈 수 있었지만, 급격한 방향전환을 시도했을 때 갑자기 고도가 낮아지거나 높아지곤 했다. 털이 다시 자랐을 때 박쥐는 다시 방향전환을 정상적으로 할 수 있었다.

14 ①

글의 흐름상 빈칸에는 네 번째 문장에 나온 not formal과 같은 의미의 표현이 필요하므로, '격식을 차리지 않는'이라는 의미의 ①이 정답으로 적절하다.

title n. 직함, 호칭 profession n. 직업 honor v. 존경하다 formal a. 격식을 차리는 nickname n. 별명 casual a. 격식을 차리지 않는 tactical a. 책략적인, 책략에 능한 practical a. 실제적인, 실용적인 conventional a. 관례적인

일부 문화권에서는 가족식구나 친구가 아닌 사람들과 이야기할 때 호칭을 사용하는 것이 일반적이다. 때때로 이 호칭들은 사람의 직업을 보여주거나, 아니면 그 사람이 나이가 많아 존경받아야 한다는 것을 우리에게 말해준다. 일반적으로 북미 사람들은 그다지 격식을 차리지 않는다. 그것은 호칭에 있어서도 그렇다. 일상생활에서 호칭은 의사를 위한 닥터(Dr.)와 때때로 대학 교수를 위한 프로페서(Prof.)를 제외하고는 사용되지 않는다. 당연히, 미스터 앤드 미시즈, 미스, 그리고 더 최근에 쓰이는 호칭인 미즈(미즈라고 발음되며 기·미혼의 모든 여성에게 사용된다)가 때때로 사용된다. 그러나 미국이나 캐나다 사람들은 오늘날 너무나 격식을 차리지 않다 보니 그들은 종종 처음 만난 후 곧바로 성을 빼고 이름만 사용한다. 사실, 직장 상사나 노인조차도 성을 뺀 이름이나 심지어 별명을 사용해달라고 당신에게 요청할 때가 많을 것이다.

15 ②

발견물들은 마구 쏟아져 들어오는데 박물관에서는 뒤처지고 있다고 했으므로, 박물관은 이 발견물들을 빨리 처리해야 할 것이다. 따라서 빈칸에는 ②가 적절하다.

unprecedented a. 전례 없는 archaeological a. 고고학의 find n. 발견물 keep up (일에 있어 뒤처지지 않고) 따라가다 fall behind 뒤처지다 spokesman n. 대변인 crucifix n. 십자가 bracelet n. 팔찌 rune stone 룬 돌(룬 문자가 새겨진 돌) retrieve v. 만회하다, 회수하다; 보상[변충]하다 process v. 처리하다; 가공처리하다 seize v. 붙잡다; 빼앗다 procure v. 획득하다

덴마크에서 아마추어 고고학자들의 발견물들이 전례 없을 정도로 쏟아져 들어온 후 덴마크 국립박물관은 더 이상 따라갈 수 없다고 선언했다. "우리는 뒤처져 있고 지금 현재도 점점 더 뒤처지고 있어요."라고 박물관 대변인은 말했다. 박물관이 처리해야 할 최근의 발견물에는 아직도 날카로운 3000년 된 청동기 시대의 칼과 1100년 된 금 십자가와 이제껏 덴마크에서 발견된 것 중 가장 큰 바이킹 금 발견물인 바이킹 시대의 팔찌 일곱 개와 어느 농가 뒷마당에서 발견된 1000년 된 룬 돌이 포함된다.

16 ①

그다음 문장에서 '자신이 동물과 만난 경험'을 이용한다고 했으므로 빈칸에는 '실제 사건이나 경험에 관한 이야기'인 ①이 적절하다. ②는 비유의 이야기이므로 정답이 될 수 없다.

ecologist n. 생태학자 intriguing a. 흥미로운 draw on ~을 이용하다 encounter n. 만남, 조우 deceive v. 속이다 grieve v. 슬퍼하다 shame n. 수치심 roller coaster 급변하는 사건(행동, 경험), (시세 등의) 심한 기복 empty v. 비우다 gratitude n. 감사, 고마움 insightful a. 통찰력 있는 convincing a. 설득력 있는 entertaining a. 재미있는 anecdote n. 일화 parable n. 우화, 비유 theorem n. 증명할 수 있는 일반원칙, 법칙 calamity n. 재난, 참화, 재해

독일 생태학자 피터 볼레벤이 인간은 감정을 느끼고 표현할 수 있는 유일한 종이라는 오랫동안 지속되어온 과학적 신념을 검증하는 일에 착수했을 때, 그는 이미 그의 견해를 의심하는 사람들에게 이의를 제기할 필생의 일화(실제 경험담)들을 갖고 있었다. 동물 감정에 대한 그의 흥미로운 보고서에서 볼레벤은 자신이 동물과 만난 경험을 이용하여 자신의 주장이 정당함을 밝힌다. 우리가 알게 되는 바로는, 수탉이 암탉을 속일 수 있으며 어미 사슴이 새끼의 죽음을 슬퍼한다. 심지어 말은 수치심을 경험할 수 있다. 새끼 새가 둥지를 비우고 떠날 때 어미 새가 느끼는 감정의 극심한 기복에서부터 과거에 집이 없던 유기견이 새 주인에게 표현하는 고마움에 이르기까지 이 통찰력 있는 과학적 증거들은 설득력 있고 재미있다.

17 ②

긍정을 100퍼센트 긍정하는 것이 아니라 겸손하게 좀 덜 긍정하여 긍정을 보완하는 것은 conservatively(조심스럽게, 신중하게)에 해당하고, 우리의 목적도 추구하면서 다른 사람들의 견해도 존중하는 조화를 이루는 것은 reconcilingly(절충적으로)와 flexibly(유연하게)에 해당하는데 빈칸 앞에 not이 있으므로 빈칸에는 ②가 적절하다.

do justice to ~를 공정하게 다루다 imponderable a. 평가[계량]할 수 없는, 헤아릴 수 없는 unique a. 고유한, 특유한 complement v. 보완하다, 보충하다 affirmation n. 긍정 humility n. 겸손 sensibility n. 감수성 light n. 견해, 관점 reconcilingly ad. 절충적으로 absolutely ad. 절대적으로, 무조건적으로 conservatively ad. 조심스럽게, 신중하게 flexibly ad. 유연하게, 융통성 있게

겉으로 드러나지 않은 것과 계측할 수 없는 것과 알려지지 않은 것을 공정하게 다루는 문제는 물론 유독 정치만의 문제가 아니다. 그것은 과학에서도 항상 우리에게 주어져 있는 문제이고, 가장 사소한 개인적 일상사에서도 그러하며, 저술과 모든 예술 형식의 큰 문제 중 하나이다. 그 문제를 해결하는 수단은 때때로 스타일이라고 불린다. 긍정을 제한되고 겸손하게 보완하는 것이 바로 스타일이며, 절대적으로가 아니라 효과적으로 행동하는 것을 가능하게 해주는 것이 스타일이며, 대외정책 영역에서 우리로 하여금 우리에게 가장 중요한 목적의 추구와 그 문제를 다른 관점에서 볼지도 모르는 사람들의 견해와 감수성과 열망에 대한 존중 사이에 조화를 찾을 수 있게 해주는 것도 스타일이다.

18 ④

죄책감을 느끼는 이유를 곰곰이 생각해보아서 실제로 그럴만한 일을 저질러서 죄책감을 느끼는 것인지 아닌지를 알아내야 한다고 했으므로 빈칸에는 그런 상황에서 실제로 일어나고 있는 일의 내막을 묻는 의문문인 ④가 적절하다.

disappoint v. 실망시키다, 낙담시키다 let down 낙담시키다 get rid of ~을 제거하다 guilt n. 죄책감

직장 심리학자 제니퍼 뉴먼은 업무 중 실수를 한 것에 대해 사원들이 죄책감을 느끼는 사례를 많이 보았다고 말한다. 따져보지 않은 무턱 댄 죄책감은 나쁜 결정을 내리도록 만들 수 있지만 이런 죄책감에 몸부림치고 있는 이유에 대해 곰곰이 생각해보는 것이 문제를 해결하는 데 도움을 줄 수 있다고 뉴먼은 말한다. "사람들을 실망시키거나 낙담시키고 있다는 느낌이 들 때, 그것이 사실인지 알아내야 합니다."라고 뉴먼은 말한다. 그래서 무언가에 대해 죄책감을 느끼면 "정말이지 지금 무슨 일이 일어나고 있는 거야(무엇이 문제인 거야)?"라는 질문을 던져야 한다고 그녀는 말한다. 사랑하는 사람과, 상사와, 심지어 자신과도 대화를 하고 나면 죄책감을 없애는 법을 배울 수 있다.

19 ④

뒤의 as 절에서 '그 어떤 경험적 정보도 구별지어주지 않으므로'라고 했으므로 첫 번째 빈칸에는 '경험적인'과 반대되는 metaphysical(형이상학적인, 추상적인)이 적절하고, 뒤의 which 관계절에서 한 개인을 다수의 유익을 위해 이용한다고 했으므로 두 번째 빈칸에는 utilitarian(공리주의적인)이 적절하다.

distinction n. 구별 empirical a. 경험적인 differentiate v. 구별 짓다 morality n. 도덕 immoral a. 비도덕적인 interpretation n. 해석 allow for 고려하다 materialistic a. 유물론적인 positivistic a. 실증주의적인 feasible a. 실행할 수 있는, 가능한 sectarian a. 당파적인; 편협한 tentative a. 시험적인, 임시의 pluralistic a. 다원주의적인 metaphysical a. 형이상학적인, 추상적인 utilitarian a. 공리주의적인, 실리적인

철학에서 '목적을 위한 수단'이라는 용어는 오직 다른 어떤 것(목적)만을 위해 실행되는 모든 행동(수단)을 가리킨다. 그 어떤 경험적 정보도 목적을 위한 수단인 행동을 그렇지 않은 행동, 즉 "그 자체로 목적"인 행동과 구별지어주지 않으므로 그것은 형이상학적 구별이라고 생각될 수 있다. 임마누엘 칸트의 도덕 이론은 다른 사람을 단지 목적을 위한 수단으로 이용하는 것은 비도덕적이며 어떤 경우에도 사람은 그 자체가 목적인 것으로 다루어져야 한다고 말한다. 이것은 개개인을 다수를 위한 수단으로 이용하는 것을 고려하는 공리주의적 시각의 일부 해석들과 대조된다.

20 ③

인간이 컴퓨터를 설계하는 것이 아니라 인간보다 더 똑똑한 컴퓨터가 컴퓨터 자신을 설계한다면 인간은 필요하지 않게 될 것이므로 빈칸에는 ③이 적절하다.

breed n. 종류 mimic v. 모방하다 neural network 신경망 singularity n. 특이점, 기술적 특이점(인공지능의 발전이 가속화되어 모든 인류의 지성을 합친 것보다 더 뛰어난 초인공지능이 출현하는 시점) popularize v. 대중화하다 design v. 설계하다 facilitate v. 손쉽게 하다; (행위 따위를) 촉진하다 species n. 종류, 종(種) mortal n. 인간, 죽음을 면할 수 없는 것

인간 뇌의 신경망을 모방하는 신종 컴퓨터 프로세서가 나왔다는 것은 몇 년 혹은 몇 십 년 더 지나면 인간처럼 학습하고 사고하는 것 같은 기계가 있게 될지도 모른다는 것을 의미한다. 이러한 가장 최근의 발전은 어쩌면 심지어 특이점에 이를 수도 있을 것인데, 이것은 컴퓨터 선구자 존 폰 노이만이 만들고 미래학자 레이 커츠와일과 공상과학 작가 버너 빈지가 대중화시킨 용어로, 컴퓨터가 인간보다 더 스마트할 뿐 아니라 훨씬 더 슈퍼스마트해지도록 자신을 설계할 수 있어서 더 이상 우리 인간이 필요하지 않을 시점을 말한다.

우리는 많은 것을 알아야 하고 또 실제로 많이 알고 있다. 그러나 지식의 가치와 진리성에 대한 확신은 정말이지 누구도 잘 갖지 못한다. 이것은 역사적 지식의 경우에 특히 그러하다. 예를 들어, 과거에는 대부분의 미국인들이 자신들의 유산의 일부로 인정한 단 하나의 국가 역사 이야기가 있었다. 지금은 민족적, 인종적, 성별(性別)적 경험의 다양성을 날로 더 강조하고 미국의 성취 이야기에 소수특권층의 권력을 은폐하는 자축(自祝)의 이야기 외에 다른 그 무엇이라도 더 있는지에 대해 깊이 의심하고 있다.

21 ③

두 번째 문장은 첫 문장에서 언급한 사실과 관련하여 구체적인 설명을 더하므로 첫 번째 빈칸에는 Indeed나 Moreover가 적절하고, 비현실적이고 이상적인 것이 낭만주의의 특징이므로 두 번째 빈칸에는 quixotic이나 utopian이 적절하며, 마지막 문장에서 변화를 언급하므로 세 번째 빈칸에는 cataclysmic이 적절하다.

inspire v. 영감을 주다, 고무하다, 자극하다 alignment n. 배열, 조절, 제휴, 연대 quixotic a. 공상적인, 비실제적인 ravishing a. 매혹적인 methodical a. 질서 있는, 체계적인 internecine a. 서로 죽이는, 치명적인 utopian a. 유토피아 같은, 이상향의 cataclysmic a. 대격변의 canonical a. 표준적인 apocalyptic a. 종말론적인

유럽의 낭만주의자들은 미국 식민지(13개 주)가 독립 전쟁에서 성공을 거두었으면 하는 마음이었다. 사실, 콜리지와 사우디 같은 영국의 낭만주의 시인들은 미국 서스쿼해나 강기슭으로 이민 가서 이상향적인 농장을 시작할 계획이었다. 그러나 1789년에 젊은이들의 상상력을 사로잡은 것은 물론 프랑스 혁명이었는데, 이 혁명은 부분적으로 미국에서의 사건(독립전쟁)에 고무되었지만 그보다 훨씬 더 큰 격변을 가져다주는 것이었다. 프랑스 혁명은 유럽에서의 여론과 정치구조와 정당 연대와 꿈과 악몽을 영구적으로 변화시켰다.

22 ①

마지막 문장에 단서가 있다. 미국인이라고 해도 실제로는 다양한 민족, 인종, 성별의 사람들이고 미국이 이룬 성취의 이야기라 해도 다양한 일반대중이 제외된 소수 백인들만의 이야기라면 그 이야기의 어떤 내용에 대한 지식이 전체 미국인들에게 가치 있는 진정한 미국의 역사적 사실에 대한 지식이라고 확신하기 어려울 것이다. 따라서 빈칸에는 '정말이지 모두에게 잘 포착되지 않는다'라는 의미의 ①이 적절하다.

confidence n. 확신 narrative n. 이야기 heritage n. 유산 ethnic a. 민족의, 인종의 skepticism n. 회의, 의심 comprise v. 포함하다, ~로 구성되다 self-congratulatory a. 자축(自祝)하는, 혼자 좋아하는 mask v. 숨기다, 감추다 elite n. 소수특권층 elude v. 교묘히 피하다, 벗어나다, 잘 잡히지 않다 just about 정말이지 underlie v. ~의 밑에 있다, ~의 근거에 있다 accrue v. 생기다, 불어나다 debunk v. 가면을 벗기다, 폭로하다 power elite 소수권력집단

23 ②

첫 번째 빈칸에는 필자와 반대되는 입장에 있는 이들로서, 빅 데이터를 활용한 연구의 장점을 열정적으로 옹호하는 이들, 즉 '광(狂), 마니아, 애호가' 등의 의미가 들어가는 것이 적절하다. 두 번째 빈칸과 관련해서 필자는 빅 데이터만으로는 과학 연구가 실패할 수 있으므로, '근간이 되는 시스템의 구조적 특성에 대한 모델링', '신뢰할 수 있는 예측 모델과 개념 지식' 즉 '가설 또는 이론(theory)'의 필요성을 주장하고 있다고 추론할 수 있다.

sophistication n. 정교함 data-driven a. (프로그램이) 데이터에 따라 처리하는 vital a. 필수적인 analysis n. 분석, 분해 aficionado n. 광(狂), 마니아 antithesis n. 정반대, 대조 abominator n. 혐오하는 사람, 혐오자 hypothesis n. 가설, 가정 connoisseur n. (미술품 등의) 감식가; (그 방면의) 통달자, 전문가

인공신경망과 같은 데이터 중심적 방법들의 '깊이'와 정교함에도 불구하고, 결국 그들은 기존 데이터에 따라 곡선을 조정할 뿐이다. 이러한 방법들이 통계적으로 신뢰할 수 있는 결과를 도출하기 위해서는, 언제나 빅 데이터 마니아들이 예상하는 것보다 훨씬 많은 양의 데이터를 필요로 할 뿐만 아니라, 근간이 되는 시스템의 구조적 특성을 모델링하도록 설계되지 않았기 때문에 그 방법들을 습득하는 데 사용되는 데이터의 범위를 벗어난 상황에서는 실패할 수 있다. 우리는 데이터 수집의 효율성을 극대화하기 위한 실험 설계의 지침으로 이론을 사용하고, 신뢰할 수 있는 예측 모델과 개념 지식을 생산하는 것이 필수적이라고 주장한다.

24 ④

첫 번째 빈칸 뒤에서 '과거에는 인간성의 구조에 암호화되어있는 것으로 추정되었던 사회적 행위'라고 한 것은 과거에는 사회적 행위를 인간 본성에서 비롯되는 것으로 보았다는 말인데, 앞에서 '고정된 범주에 의문을 제기했다'고 했으므로 이제는 사회적 행위를 그렇게 보지 않고 개별 인간의 특성과 사회와의 관계에서 비롯되는 것으로 보았을 것이므로 첫 번째 빈칸에는 denaturalized(본질을 바꾸었다, 변질시켰다)가 적절하다. 한편, 두 번째 빈칸 다음의 인용문은 모두 인간이나 과학에 관한 보편적인 기술들이므로 두 번째 빈칸에는 universality가 적절하다.

absolutism n. 절대론, 절대성 dethrone v. 권좌에서 몰아내다, 권위를 잃게 하다 endorse v. 승인하다 presume v. 추정하다 encode v. 암호화하다 humanness n. 인간성 routinely ad. 일상적으로 challenge n. 도전, 항의, 이의 제기 discompose v. 불안케 하다 rationality n. 합리성; 합리적 행동 detribalize v. (다른 문화와의 접촉에 의해) 부족 고유의 의식을 잃게 하다 generalization n.

일반화, 보편화 disintegrate v. 분해시키다 humanism n. 인도주의, 인문주의 denaturalize v. 본질을 바꾸다, 변질시키다 universality n. 보편성

2차 세계대전 후 수십 년 사이에 옛날에 지적으로 절대적이었던 과학, 과학적 역사, 국가주의에 이바지하는 역사 등이 권위를 잃어버렸다. 그 대신에, 전후(戰後)세대는 지식의 사회학, 다양한 종족의 기록, 집단 정체성과 성 정체성에 기초한 역사 등을 구축했다. 그리고 전후세대는 예전에는 모든 생각 깊은 사람들이 합리적인 것이라고 승인해주었던 고정된 범주들에 의문을 제기했으며, 과거에는 인간성의 구조에 암호화되어있는 것으로 추정되었던 사회적 행위의 본질을 바꾸어놓았다. 전후세대의 구성원으로서 우리는 일상적으로, 심지어 화를 내며, 누구의 역사인가? 누구의 과학인가? 그 사상들과 이야기들은 누구의 이익에 이바지하는가? 라는 질문을 던진다. 이러한 이의 제기는 "인간이란 ...."과 "당연히 과학이 말하는 바로는 ...."과 "우리 모두가 알고 있듯이 ...."와 같은 구절에 표현된 보편성에 대한 모든 주장에 대해 행해지는 것이다.

---

25 ⑤

until 절이 '~할 시기가 마침내 무르익을 때까지'인데 앞 절에서는 정치 자금 기부자들을 돌보고 도움을 준다고 했으므로 빈칸에는 부패한 정치인들이 기부자들을 돌보다가 마침내 할 행동으로 금전적 이득을 취하는 행동인 ⑤가 적절하다.

derivative a. 파생적인 A is all about B A의 내용/내막/영문은 전적으로 B이다(I don't know what this is all about. 난 이게 어찌된 영문인지 모르겠다.) outright a. 솔직한, 명백한 bribery n. 뇌물수수 fancy a. 엄청난, 대단히 좋은 junket n. 향연, 관비여행 honorarium n. 보수, 사례금 commonplace a. 흔해빠진 bidder n. 입찰자 rank a. 지독한, 썩은 dumb a. 벙어리의, 우둔한 contributor n. 기부자 feather their beds = featherbed them 그들을 보호하다, 도움을 주다 convince v. ~에게 납득시키다, 깨닫게 하다 support v. 지지하다; 편들다, 찬성하다 oppose v. 반대하다; 적대하다 extort v. 억지로 빼앗다, 강탈하다 enforce v. 실시하다, 집행하다; 강요하다 discrimination n. 구별, 식별;차별 oppression n. 압박, 억압 objectively ad. 객관적으로 lucrative a. 유리한, 수지 맞는 on behalf of ~을 대신하여, ~을 대표하여 regulate v. 조절하다, 규제하다

정치의 다른 대부분의 죄들은 이 더 큰 죄, 즉 이기고 싶은 욕구 뿐 아니라 지지 않고 싶은 욕구에서 파생된 것들이다. 분명 돈의 추구란 전적으로 그러한 것이다.(다른 여러 죄를 파생시키는 죄이다.) 돈이 노골적인 뇌물수수를 통해 정치를 결정짓던 때가 있었다. 그때는 정치인이 자신의 선거운동자금을 개인적인 은행계좌로 취급할 수 있었고 융숭한 향응을 받을 수도 있었으며, 영향력 행사를 구하는 사람들로부터 거액의 사례금을 받는 일이 흔히 있었으며, 제정되는 법률의 형태도 최고 입찰자(최고액의 뇌물공여자)의 몫이 되었다. 최근의 뉴스보도가 정확하다면, 이러한 더욱 지독한 형태의 부패가 지금 완전히 사라진 것은 아니다. 분명 아직도 워싱턴 정가에는 정치를 치부(致富) 수단으로 생각하는 사람들이 있는데, 이들은 일반적으로 소액의 돈 자루를 받을 정도로 우둔하지는 않지만, 한때 그들의 규제 대상자였던 사람들을 위해 로비활동을 하고 이득을 취하는 일에 뛰어들 시기가 마침내 무르익을 때까지 정치자금 기부자들을 돌보고 적절히 보호해줄 만반의 준비가 되어 있는 사람들이다.

01 ④	02 ②	03 ②	04 ④	05 ③	06 ④	07 ③	08 ②	09 ②	10 ①
11 ④	12 ①	13 ①	14 ④	15 ④	16 ②	17 ④	18 ②	19 ①	20 ①
21 ③	22 ①	23 ②	24 ③	25 ③					

01   ④

original subjects는 있는 그대로의 자연물인 반면에 그것을 찍은 사진이나 카메라는 제조된 사물인데 작품창작에서 이것에 의존한다는 것은 현대생활이 자연보다는 제조된 인공물에 더 의존함을 암시하므로 빈칸에는 ④가 적절하다.

subject n. 제재(題材), 화제(畵題), 피사체 shape v. 결정하다 obliquely ad. 비스듬히, 간접적으로, 완곡하게 contemporary a. 동시대의; 현대적인 artificial a. 인공의, 인위적인 genuine a. 진짜의; 거짓 없는 counterfeit a. 모조의; 가짜의 primitive a. 원시의; 원시적인 sophisticated a. 정교한; 고도로 세련된 manufactured a. 제조된, 생산된

포토리얼리즘(사진사실주의)은 원래의 제재(題材: 그리는 대상물)가 아니라 곧장 사진을 바탕으로 하여 작업을 하는 예술 형식이다. 그것은 사실성에 대한 우리의 이해를 결정하는 데 있어 카메라가 하는 역할을 인정하며, 현대생활이 종종 자연물보다는 제조된 물건들을 중심으로 하여 더 많이 이루어지고 있음을 완곡하게 암시한다.

02   ②

첫 번째 빈칸에는 hateful과 적절하게 호응하는 ethnocentric이나 xenophobic이 적절하고, 두 번째 빈칸의 경우 as long as 이하가 부정적인 내용이므로 elusive가 적절하다.

condone v. 용서하다, 눈감아주다 turn a blind eye to 못 본 체하다 mind-set n. 사고방식, 태도 belligerent a. 호전적인 n. 교전국, 전투원 ethnocentric a. 자기민족중심적인 feasible a. 실행 가능한 xenophobic a. 외국인 혐오의 elusive a. (뜻·성격 등이) 파악하기 어려운, 알기 어려운; (사람·동물 등이) 교묘히 잘 빠지는 anarchistic a. 무정부주의의 promising a. 전도유망한, 가망 있는 philanthropic a. 박애주의의, 인정 많은 visionary a. 환상의; 몽상적인

이스라엘을 지지하는 사람들은 이스라엘 주민들과 군대가 팔레스타인인들에게 행하는 불의를 더 이상 무시하거나 심지어 눈감아주지 말아야 한다. 마찬가지로, 팔레스타인을 지지하는 사람들도 하마스 같은 단체들이 만들어내는 증오에 찬 외국인 혐오적인 선전을 못 본 체하지 말아야 한다. 관련 교전국들의 태도에 종교가 계속 영향을 미치는 한 평화는 계속 잡히지 않을(달성되지 않을) 것이다.

03   ②

첫 문장 but 앞 절에서 전자 댄스 음악의 약물의존 경향을 말했으므로 첫 번째 빈칸에는 '약효가 강한'이라는 뜻인 potent가 적절하고, 마지막 인용문의 fans는 그 앞 문장의 a massive audience에 해당하고 이것을 대명사 it으로 가리키므로, 두 번째 빈칸에는 '무시하다'는 뜻의 tuning it out이 되도록 tuning이 적절하다.

fuel v. 연료를 공급하다, 동력원이 되다 ecstasy n. 황홀경, 마약의 일종 be into ~에 열중(몰두)하다 at heart 마음속으로, 내심, 실제로는 effusive a. 심정을 토로하는, 감정이 넘쳐나는 nerd n. 바보, 얼간이, 촌뜨기 eke out 보충하다 potent a. 세력 있는, 유력한 tune out 무시하다 innocent a. 순진한; 무해한 sort out 골라내다 invalid a. 병약한, 허약한 churn out 생산하다

전자 댄스 음악은 엑스터시 같은 약물의 힘으로 행해질지도 모르지만, 로빈슨은 자신은 약효가 카페인 이상으로 강한 것에는 전혀 빠져들지 않는다고 말한다. 실제로 그는 감정을 주체하지 못하는 촌놈으로 일본 문화와 자신의 텀블러 페이지에 빠져 있다. 그에게 많은 관객이 생겼지만 그는 그것을 무시해버린다. "팬만 생각하다가는 진지한 음악을 쓸 수 없잖아요"라고 그는 말한다.

04   ④

대학생들의 행태가 이 도시에 대해 심히 부정적이고 시공무원들이 자축해왔다고 했으므로 첫 번째 빈칸에는 뒤에 'A of B'를 취하여 'A에서 B를 제거하다'는 뜻이 되는 clearing이나 ridding이 적절하고, 두 번째 빈칸에는 '싸움과 기물 파손과 경찰에 반항하는 것과 같은 취지로 mayhem(무차별 폭력)이 적절하다.

congratulate v. 축하하다 destination n. 목적지 spring break party 봄 방학 파티 property n. 재산, 소유물 defy v. 반항하다, 무시하다 lift v. 들어 올리다; 일소하다, 제거하다 washout n. (폭우 따위로 토사·암석의) 유실; 대실패, 기대의 어긋남 clear v. 제거하다 felicity n. 더없는 행복 reform v. 개혁하다 arcana n. 비밀, 신비한 것들 rid v. 제거하다 mayhem n. 신체 상해, 무차별 폭력

수년 동안 시 공무원들은 그들의 도시를 난폭하고 파괴적인 봄 방학 파티의 목적지로 선택하곤 했던 미친 대학생들을 그들의 해변도시에서 없애버린 것을 자축해왔는데, 그런 파티에서 대학생들은 싸움을 벌이고 기물을 파손하고 경찰에 대항하고 무차별 폭력을 저질렀던 것이다.

05   ③

교과과정상 분리될 수 있다는 단서로부터 첫 번째 빈칸은 구분되어질 수 있다는 의미의 보기를 추론하는 것이 가능하고, granted의 역접성에 따라서 실제 교실에서의 학습과정에서는 구분의 모호함이, 즉 연속된 점차적 이행이 있음을 추론 가능하다.

language acquisition 언어 습득 contemplative a. 심사숙고하는, 묵상하는 persistence n. 끈기, 인내, 불굴, 집요 distinct a. 별개의; 뚜렷한, 다른 gradation n. 점차적(단계적) 변화, 점차적 이행 coterminous a. 공통경계의, 동일연장의 liberal arts 교양 과목

아이들의 언어습득에서의 학습곡선이 교과과정의 단계에 따라서 명백하게 구별되는 국면들로 분리될 수 있다는 것을 받아들인다고 할지라도, 우리가 실제 교실 환경에서 발견하는 것은 학습과정에서 점차적인 이행, 그 자체일 뿐이다.

06   ④

reduce(환원하다)는 복잡한 것을 간결하게 단순화하는 것이며, 그 다음 문장에서 mottoes and proverbs(금언과 격언)가 언급되었으므로 빈칸에는 '경구적 간결성'이라는 의미의 ④가 들어가는 것이 적절하다.

brood over 곰곰이 생각하다 reduce v. 단순화하다, 바꾸다, 환원하다 motto n. 표어, 금언 proverb n. 속담, 격언 liken v. 비유하다 ill-natured a. 심술궂은 thorn n. 가시 briar n. 찔레 덤불 prick v. 찌르다 scratch v. 할퀴다, 긁다 arcane a. 비밀의; 불가해한 legal a. 법적인; 합법의, 적법한 clarity n. 명료, 명확 aphoristic a. 격언의, 격언체의, 경구적인 brevity n. 간결

베이컨은 사회 관습이나 행동의 어떤 주제에 대해 곰곰이 생각한 후 마침내 그것에 대한 자신의 결론을 단순화하여 거의 경구에 가까울 정도로 간결하게 나타낼 수 있었다. 그래서 그의 글은 너무나 자주 일련의 금언이나 격언처럼 읽힌다. 예를 들어 그는 심술궂은 사람을 "달리 아무 것도 할 수 없어서 찌르거나 할퀴기만 하는 가시나 덤불"에 비유한다.

07   ③

빈칸 앞의 similar가 단서가 된다. 마지막 문장은 이전 문장에서 언급한 내용과 유사한 일이 그 이전에도 일어난 적이 있음을 언급해야 한다. 앞 문장에서는 '여러 종류의 인간이 지구상에 있었음'을 말하고 있는데, 이것은 결국 '다양성'과 관련된 것이므로 정답은 ③이 된다.

odd a. 홀수의; 기묘한, 이상한 hominid n. 사람과 비슷한 동물; 원인(原人) subterfuge n. 구실, 핑계, 속임수 sleight n. 능숙한 솜씨, 재빠르고 재치 있는 솜씨; 술책 multifariousness n. 다양성, 다채로움 physiognomy n. 골상학, 관상학; 인상

호모 사피엔스에 관해 가장 이상한 점 가운데 하나는 그가 혼자라는 것이다. 이야기꾼들은 인간과 비슷하게 생긴 상상의 동물들로 세상을 가득 채웠지만, 그것의 실제 흔적이 발견된 것은 없었다. 그러나 과거에는 그렇지 않았

다. 지금으로부터 4만 년 전에, 세 가지 서로 다른 종(種)의 인간이 지구에 있었다. 유럽의 네안데르탈인, 인도네시아의 '호빗족', 중앙아시아에 살고 있었던 데니소반인이 그들이다. 유사한 다양성이 보다 이른 시기, 즉 2백만 년 전에 아프리카에서도 있었다는 증거가 지금 나타나고 있다.

08   ②

두 번째 문장부터 소피스트들이 정의나 진리가 아닌 것을 가르칠 수도 있었고 자신의 주장을 관철하기 위해 기만도 마다하지 않도록 가르쳤음을 설명하므로 빈칸에는 '부정직함을 퍼뜨리는 사람들'이란 의미의 ②가 적절하다.

sophist n. 소피스트(옛 그리스의 철학, 수사학, 웅변술 교사), 궤변가 win one's point 자신의 주장을 남에게 납득시키다, 주장을 세우다 deceptive a. 기만적인, 속이는 sundry a. 여러 가지의, 잡다한 skeptic n. 회의론자, 무신론자 to the bone 뼛속까지; 철두철미한 purveyor n. (식료품) 조달자; (정보 등을) 퍼뜨리는 사람 dishonesty n. 부정직 apostle n. 사도; 주장자 preach v. 전도하다; 설교하다 peddler n. 행상인 sundry a. 갖가지의, 잡다한

소피스트들의 가르침의 목적은 공직에 당선되는 것이든 법정에서 승소하는 것이든 각자의 노력에서 성공을 거두는 것이었다. 그러나 대부분의 아테네인들이 분명히 깨달았듯이, 성공하는 법을 가르치는 것이 반드시 공명정대하도록, 혹은 진리를 알거나 말하도록 가르치는 것을 의미하지는 않았다. 비록 그렇게 하기 위해 남을 속여야 하더라도 자신의 주장을 남에게 납득시키는 방법이 소피스트들이 가르친 것이었다. 놀랍지 않게도, 많은 아테네인들은 그들을 부정직함을 퍼뜨리는 사람들에 거의 지나지 않는 것으로 간주했다.

09   ②

종교적인 관점에서 보면 감리교 목사가 동성애자인 아들의 결혼식을 주례하는 것이 잘못된 것으로 보일 것이다. 첫 번째 빈칸 뒤에 earned him a suspension이라고 했으므로 빈칸에는 그의 잘못된 행동과 관련된 말이 적절하므로 신성모독을 뜻하는 sacrilege가 적절하다. 그리고 세 번째 문장에서 프랭크 쉐퍼가 파면당했다고 했는데 그 다음 문장이 But으로 연결되었고 마지막 문장에서 그를 파면한 결정이 현명하지 않았다고 했으므로 결국 그는 복직되었다고 볼 수 있다. 두 번째 빈칸에는 reinstated가 적절하다.

methodist a. 감리교도[교파]의 preacher n. 설교자, 전도사 officiate v. (예배·미사를) 집전하다 defrock v. ~의 성직을 박탈하다 purification n. 정화; 재계(齋戒) exonerate v. 결백을[무죄를] 증명하다 sacrilege n. 신성한 것을 더럽힘; (신성) 모독 reinstate v. 복위[복직, 복권]시키다 allegiance n. 충성, 충절 dismiss v. (고려할 가치가 없다고) 묵살[일축]하다 baptism n. 세례, 침례 console v. 위로하다 consecration n. 신성화 reprimand v. 견책[징계]하다

펜실베이니아주의 감리교 목사인 프랭크 쉐퍼(Frank Shaefer)는 2007년 동성애자 자신의 아들의 결혼식을 주례했다. 이런 신성모독 행위로 그는 직무정지를 당했다. 그가 또 다른 동성 커플의 주례를 다시는 보지 않겠다는 약속을 하지 않자 미국 감리 교회는 작년에 그의 성직을 박탈하기로 결정했다. 하지만 6월 교회는 사건을 진척시켜 다시 성직에 복직시켰다. 심사위원

들을 그가 아직 하지 않은 어떤 일에 대해 그 목사를 처벌하는 것은 현명하지 않다고 결정했다.

10
①

대중음악 팬들은 새로운 종류의 음악이 나오면 예전에 좋아했던 음악을 금세 잊어버린다고 했으므로 이 예로 나온 조나스 브라더스가 대중의 관심으로부터 잊혀졌다고 볼 수 있다. 따라서 첫 번째 빈칸에는 oblivion이 적절하며, 두 번째 빈칸 다음에 human beings를 수식하는 관계대명사절에서 인간의 기분이 계속해서 바뀐다고 했으므로 이는 '변덕스러움'을 나타내는 것이다. 따라서 capricious의 동의어에 해당하는 mercurial이 두 번째 빈칸에 적절하다.

capricious a. 변덕스러운, (마음이) 변하기 쉬운 favorite n. 마음에 드는 것 optimistic a. 낙관적인, 낙천적인 inattention n. 부주의, 태만, 무관심 oblivion n. 망각; 잊혀짐 mercurial a. 변덕스러운 contempt n. 경멸, 모욕; 치욕 emphatic a. 단호한, 강조하는 snare n. 올가미, 덫, 유혹 gregarious a. 군생하는; 사교적인 egoism n. 이기주의 glitch n. 작은 문제; 결함 exoteric a. 개방적인, 공개적인, 통속적인

대중음악 팬들은 변덕스럽다. 새로운 종류의 음악이 나온 지 얼마 되지 않아 바로 그 동일한 십대들은 그들이 예전에 좋아했던 음악을 다 잊어버리는 것으로 보였다. 현재 그룹 조나스 브라더스는 세상에서 잊혀졌다. 최근 인터뷰에서 그 그룹의 대변인은 조나스 브라더스가 다시 인기를 회복하는 것에 대해 긍정적으로 생각하며 그들에 대한 사람들의 무관심은 그룹의 공연 때문이 아니라 오히려 기분이 계속 바뀌는 인간의 변덕스러운 본성 때문이라고 말했다.

11
④

영화에 대한 비판하는 어조가 중심이다. 허세(bravado)와 어울리는 것은 pageantry(허식, 겉치레)이다. 중세시대에 carnage(대학살)가 잦았다면, 그것과 어울리는 표현은 melee(난투, 아수라장)이다.

adapt v. 개작하다, 각색하다 bravado n. 허세, 객기 nationalistic a. 국수주의적인 undertone n. 숨은 뜻, 색채 understate v. 축소해서 말하다 tame a. 길들여진; 재미없는 carnage n. 대학살 clad a. ~을 입은 radiant a. 빛나는, 환한 omit v. 빠뜨리다, 누락시키다 artistry n. 예술성 triptych n. 3장 연속된 것, 세 폭짜리 그림[조각] bravery n. 용기, 용맹 chasm n. 갈라진 틈, 균열 senescence n. 노화, 노쇠 undulation n. 파동, 굽이침 pageantry n. 화려한 행사; 허식, 겉치레 melee n. 난투, 혼전; 아수라장

셰익스피어의 연극이 어떤 영화로 각색되었다. 그 영화를 비평하는 이들을 그 영화의 허식과 허세, 국수주의적 색채를 지적해 왔다. 영화 속 전투 장면은 축소되고 재미없으며 중세시대의 아수라장과도 같았던 학살 장면은 거의 없다. 멋진 날씨에 촬영되었고 배우들은 환한 색상의 의상을 입고 있다. 헨리(Henry)에 의한 가혹한 재판 장면도 빠져있다.

12
①

첫 번째 문장이 주제문이며, 두 번째 문장은 시인인 예이츠의 시를 소개하며 그가 매우 선견지명이 있음을 밝히고 있다. 예전에 쓰인 작품이 현대에도 공감을 주는 예로 시와 이슬람국의 파괴행위에 대해 언급을 하고 있으므로 첫 번째 빈칸에는 pertinent가 적절하고, 두 번째 빈칸에는 prescient의 유의어인 prophetic이 적절하다.

prescient a. 선견지명[예지력]이 있는 meditation n. 묵상; 명상; (pl.) 명상록 ingenious a. 교묘한, 독창적인; 발명의 재능이 풍부한, 창의력이 풍부한 pertinent a. 딱 들어맞는, 적절한 prophetic a. 예언의, 예언적인 immune a. (공격·병독 등을) 면한, 면역성의 spurious a. 가짜의, 위조의 subordinate a. 부수[종속]하는 mellow a. 부드럽고 풍부한, 그윽한 patriotic a. 애국적인

W. B. 예이츠(W. B. Yeats)가 살아 있는 느낌이 드는 이유는 그의 많은 시구가 매우 선경지명이 있는 것처럼 보이며 그가 살던 시대뿐만 아니라 우리 시대에도 관련이 있기 때문이다. 시리아에 있는 고대도시 팔미라의 이슬람 국가에 의한 임박한 파괴행위에 대한 대응으로 나는 예이츠의 가장 어두운 분위기의 명상록 중 하나인 『1919』에서의 예언적인 구문을 회상했다. 『1919』가 쓰여진 시기는 아일랜드의 분열이 치닫던 시기였다: "독창적으로 아름다운 많은 것들이 사라진다. 대중들에게 순전히 기적으로 보였던 것들이."

13
①

첫 번째 빈칸 앞에서 데미안 라이언의 연출이 감탄스러울 정도로 놀랍다고 했으며, "공통점이 없는 많은 아이디어들을 데미안 라이언이 감쪽같이 결합시켰다"라고 했으므로, 첫 번째 빈칸에는 하나의 '응집력 있는 (cohesive)'이나 '흠잡을 데 없는(impeccable)'이 적절하다. 그리고 데미안 라이언이 연출한 『헨리5세』라는 연극은 감탄스러울 정도로 놀라워서 '진부한' 표현으로는 거의 다룰 수 없는 수준이라고 하였으므로, 데미안 라이언이 하나의 완전체로 만든 연극은 상상을 '불가능하게 한다(beggar)'가 문맥상 적절하다. 따라서 두 빈칸 모두에 적절한 ①이 정답이다.

have an acquaintance with ~을 알고 있다, ~에 대한 지식을 지니다 passing a. 대충의 hackneyed a. 진부한, 평범한 touch on ~을 간단히 언급하다[다루다] pull together ~을 뭉치게 하다, 합치다 disparate a. 공통점이 없는, 다른 whole n. 완전체, 전체 cohesive a. 응집력이 있는, 결합시키는 beggar v. (표현·비교 등을) 불가능하게 하다 viscous a. 끈적거리는, 점성이 있는 dwarf v. 왜소해 보이게 만들다 impeccable a. 흠잡을 데 없는, 완벽한 orphan v. (아이를) 고아로 만들다 sexist a. 성차별주의자의 cook v. 요리하다; (특히 당황하여) 꾸며대다 hump v. 새우등이 되게 하다; 짜증나게 하다 crown v. 왕위에 앉히다; 완벽하게 하다

『헨리5세』는 자주 연출되는 연극이어서 20세기에 고등학교를 나온 대부분의 사람들은 『헨리5세』라는 연극을 대충 알고 있다. 『헨리5세』를 연출하기 위해 새롭고 다른 방법을 찾는 것은 아주 어려운 일이다. 『헨리5세』를 연출하는데 있어서 데미안 라이언(Damien Ryan)이 도전장을 내밀었다. 그러나 '새롭고 다른'과 같이 진부한 형용사들은 이 감탄스러울 정도로 놀라운 『헨리5세』 연출의 본질을 거의 다루지 못한다. 공통점이 없는 많은 아이디어들을 데미안 라이언이 감쪽같이 결합시켜서 하나의 응집력 있는 완전체로 표현하는 방식은 상상을 불가능하게 만든다.

14
④

조지 오웰은 소설 『1984』에서 모든 것을 알고 있고 만물을 꿰뚫어 보는 전체주의국가에 대해 경고 했는데 이것이 실제로 에드워드 스노든에서 밝혀졌으므로 그의 소설이 '통찰력/선견지명'이 있었음을 알 수 있다. 따라서 첫 번째 빈칸에는 clairvoyant와 prescient가 적절하다. 그리고 스노든이 뉴스를 장악한 후 아마존닷컴에서 『1984』의 판매부수가 급증했다고 했으므로 미국 독자들은 『1984』와 스노든의 사건이 유사함을 알게 되었다고 볼 수 있다. 따라서 두 번째 빈칸에는 parallels가 적절하다.

leaker n. 누설자 clot v. 움직일 수 없게 하다 pundit n. 학자, 박식한 사람 dystopian a. 반(反)이상향의 totalitarian a. 전체주의의 clairvoyant a. 통찰력이 있는 bluff n. 허세, 으름장 elusive a. 알기 어려운 discrepancy n. 불일치; 어긋남, 모순 apathetic a. 냉담한; 무관심한 controversy n. 논쟁, 논의; 말다툼 prescient a. 선견지명[예지력]이 있는 parallel n. 유사점 absurd a. 불합리한; 부조리한 modification n. 수정, 변경

누설자인 에드워드 스노든이 국가정보국(NSA)이 운영하는 대규모 국내 감시프로그램의 존재를 폭로한 후에 학자들과 정치인들이 본인들이 피상적으로만 알고 있는 것 같은 한 남자를 떠올리는 일로 방송은 넘쳐났다. 반이상향의 고전인 『1984』의 작가인 조지 오웰은 모든 것을 알고, 만물을 꿰뚫어 보는 전체주의국가에 대해 경고했다. 우리는 이제 이 책이 선견지명이 있었다는 것을 알고 있다. 미국 독자들 또한 유사점을 발견했다. 스노든의 폭로가 뉴스를 장악하면서 『1984』의 판매부수는 아마존닷컴에서 하루만에 6,021% 증가했다.

15
④

첫 번째 빈칸의 정답은 '당신이 이 모든 것을 해볼 수 있게 될 것이다.'라는 단서로부터 추론할 수 있고, 두 번째 빈칸의 정답은 '우리가 가상현실을 믿지 않을 만큼 진화된 존재가 아니다'라는 진술로부터 유추할 수 있다.

reptilian a. 파충류 같은; 비열한 scary a. 무서운, 두려운 conform v. (사회의 규범·관습 따위에) 적합[순응]시키다; 따르게 하다 glamorize v. 매력적으로 만들다 rat on 약속 등을 어기다 magnify v. 확대하다; 과장하다 juggle with 왜곡하다 resurface v. (수면 아래나 보이지 않게 잠재되어 있던 것이) 다시 떠오르다[드러나다] live up to 기대치에 부응하다 fool v. 놀리다, 우롱하다; 속이다

당신은 십중팔구 화성에 가보지 못할 것이고, 돌고래와 더불어 춤을 추어보지도 못할 것이고, 원더걸스와 같은 무대에서 노래를 부를 수도 없을 것이다. 그러나 만일 가상현실이 내건 약속에 가상현실이 부합하게 된다면 당신은 이 모든 것들을 ― 그리고 더 많은 것들을 ― 집을 떠나지 않고서도 해볼 수 있을 것이다. 우리가 이와 같이 반응하는 것은 전문가들에 따르면 우리가 화면으로 보는 것이 우리의 머릿속에서 일어나는 움직임을 잘 따라갈 때 우리의 뇌가 쉽게 속기 때문이라고 한다. "우리는 마치 그것을 실제라고 느끼는 파충류처럼 미개한 본능을 가지고 있습니다. 저 절벽을 향해 행진을 개시해서는 안 돼; 이 전투는 무시무시해."라고 (우리의 뇌가 느낀다고) 스탠포드 대학의 Virtual Human Interaction Lab의 창립 책임자인 Jeremy Bailenson은 내게 말했다. "우리의 뇌는 이것(가상현실)이 실제가 아니라고 당신에게 말해줄 만큼 진화되지 못했습니다."

16
②

첫 번째 빈칸은 'morally courageous and fiercely independent'라는 단서로부터 추론할 수 있고, 두 번째 빈칸은 '역경'과 '존경 받는다'라는 진술로부터 유추할 수 있다.

defiantly ad. 반항적으로 mercurial a. 변덕스러운; 재치 넘치는 Byronic a. 바이런식의(비장하면서도 낭만적임) disconsolate a. 서글픈, 우울한; 절망적인 surrender to ~에 굴복[항복]하다 virtuous a. 도덕적인, 고결한 overcome v. 극복하다, 이겨내다 punctilious a. 지나치게 꼼꼼한 eschew v. 피하다, 삼가다 fragile a. 망가지기 쉬운; 무른; 허약한 survive v. ~의 후까지 생존하다[살아남다]

반항적으로 고결하고, 도덕적으로 용기 있고, 그리고 맹렬하게 독립적인 새로운 종류의 여주인공과 더불어, 샤를로트 브론테는 역경을 극복하는 그녀의 능력으로 존경받는, 인습에 얽매이지 않는 여성을 제시하면서 당대 소설의 양식에 변화를 가져왔다. 잔인한 이모의 돌봄 아래서 고아로 비천하게 삶을 시작한 가정교사 제인 에어는 재기 넘치면서도 변덕스러운 그녀의 고용주인, 비장하면서도 낭만적인 Edward Rochester와 사랑에 빠진다. 그러나 그의 저택인 Thornfield Hall의 어두운 비밀은 그녀가 열심히 노력해서 성취한 모든 것을 파괴해버리고자 위협한다.

17
④

앞에서 '마룻바닥에 뚫고 깔개로 덮어놓은 구멍'이라 했고 that절의 내용이 꼼짝 못하는 상황을 말하므로 첫 번째 빈칸에는 함정을 의미하는 bear trap이 적절하고, 앞 문장의 내용이 '행복을 정의내리고 거기에 맞게 삶을 조정하여 행복을 얻는 방책'을 의미하는데 이것의 효과가 부분적인 효과에 그친다고 부정적으로 진술하므로 두 번째 빈칸에는 Still(그래도)이 적절하다.

Whole Foods 홀 푸드 마켓(미국의 대형 슈퍼마켓 체인) rug n. 깔개, 양탄자 implication n. (의미의) 내포, 함축, 암시 specific a. 구체적인 blueprint n. 청사진, 설계도 align v. 일직선으로 맞추다 recipe n. 요리법, 비결, 방책 fiddle with 만지작거리다 red tape 관료적 형식주의 silver bullet 묘책 tall talk 허풍 bear trap 함정

아이들은 단지 행복해지기를 원한다. 강아지들도 마찬가지이다. 행복은 건강하고 정상적인 욕망인 것 같다. 신선한 공기를 마시고 싶다거나 홀 푸드(유기농으로 재배된 건강에 좋은 식품) 마켓에서만 물건을 사고 싶다는 것과 같은 것이다. 그러나 "단지 행복해지고 싶다"는 것은 마룻바닥에 뚫고 깔개로 덮어놓은 구멍이다. 일단 그런 말을 하고나면 그 말이 은연중에 당신이 행복하지 않다는 것을 의미하기 때문이다. "단지 행복해지고 싶다"는 것이 감추고 있는 곰 덫(무서운 함정)은 행복이 정확히 무엇인지를 정확히 정의하기까지는 결코 행복을 느끼지 못한다는 것이다. 행복하다는 것이 당신에게 무엇을 의미하든 그것은 구체적이어야 하고 또한 가능해야 한다. 행복을 위한 청사진(설계도)을 갖고 있다면 그것을 당신의 삶 위로 덮어씌우고 청사진의 이미지와 삶의 이미지가 더욱 일치하도록 하려면 무엇을 바꾸어야 하는지 알아보라. 그래도, 행복을 정의내리고 당신의 삶을 조정하여 행복을 얻는 이러한 방책은 일부 사람들에게는 효과가 있을 것이지만 다른 사람들에게는 그렇지 못할 것이다. 나는 그 다른 사람들 가운데 하나이다.

18   ②

지식의 전달 과정은 일방적으로 주기만 하는 것이 아니라 가르치는 자도 그만큼 배운다고 하였다. 따라서, 한쪽의 이익은 다른 한쪽의 손해를 의미하는 '제로섬 게임'이 아니라고 진술하는 것이 타당하다.

group performance 집단 작업 at the expense of ~을 희생시키면서 tutor v. 개인 교수하다 reinforce v. 강화하다 sophisticated a. 정교한, 세련된 cliché n. 상투적인 말 arrangement n. 방식, 배열 a rat race (대도시 삶의) 극심한 생존 경쟁[무한 경쟁], 치열한 경쟁, 과당 경쟁(=very hectic activity) zero-sum a. 제로섬의, 한쪽의 득점이 다른 쪽에는 같은 수의 실점이 되는 win-win a. 상황이 (관련된) 모두에게 유리한[모두가 득을 보는], 윈윈의 norm-referenced test 규준 참조 검사(規準參照檢査)

문제 해결에 있어서 집단 작업이 심지어 가장 숙련된 집단 구성원들의 개별 작업보다 낫기 때문에 학생들이 협력할 때 더 잘 배운다는 것은 놀라운 일이 아닐 것이다. 하지만 학생들이 서로 돕게 하는 방법은 능력 수준이 더 높은 학생들을 희생시키면서 능력 수준이 낮은 학생들이 도움을 받고 있는 것은 아닌지라는 의문을 제기한다. 이것이 사실일까? 다행히 지식은 제로섬 게임의 산물이 아니다. 가르치거나 개인 지도를 해 본 사람은 누구나 그렇게 하는 것이 자신의 지식을 강화시킬 뿐만 아니라 그 자료에 대해 보다 더 정교한 이해로 자신을 이끄는 경우가 흔하다는 것을 알고 있다. 학생만큼 교사도 배운다는 것에 관한 상투적인 말은 아주 사실이고 협동적인 교실에서 일어나는 지도는 경쟁적이거나 혼자서 공부하는 방식보다 사실 도와주는 사람과 도움을 받는 사람 모두를 이롭게 한다.

19   ①

첫 번째 빈칸은 그녀의 자살로 그녀가 불멸이 되었다는 진술로부터 추론할 수 있고, 두 번째 빈칸은 Marilyn Monroe의 archetypal과의 비교로부터 유추할 수 있다.

speculation n. 추측, 억측; 사색; 심사숙고; 투기 prurience n. 호색, 색욕; 열망 flatten v. 평평해지다; 무미건조해지다 maniac n. 열광자, 마니아; 미치광이 bloom v. 개화하다; 번영하다 prototype n. 원형(原型); 표준, 모범 wither v. 시들다, 말라 죽다 maniac n. 미치광이, 애호가 alleviate v. 경감하다, 완화하다 protocol n. 의전, 의례(외교) ratify v. 비준하다, 재가하다 iconoclast n. 우상 파괴자

50년 전 Sylvia Plath는 자살을 해서 불멸을 얻었다. 자살은 썩은 음식에 이끌리는 파리들과 같은 억측과 열망을 불러일으킨다. 자살을 한 대부분의 작가들 ― 예를 들어, Ernest Hemingway, David Foster Wallace, Spalding Gray 그리고 Virginia Woolf 같은 작가들 ― 은 죽기 전에 이미 작가로서의 그들의 입지를 다졌다. Plath의 (문학적) 명성은 그녀의 죽음의 구름 아래에서 피어났다. 그 어떤 작가의 삶도 Plath의 삶처럼 그들의 작품에 짙은 그림자를 드리운 적은 없다. Plath의 삶은 그녀의 작품에 더 어두운 그림자를 드리울 뿐이다. 마치 Marilyn Monroe가 지금 비극적인 할리우드 금발 여배우의 전형처럼 보이는 것처럼, Plath는 정신적으로 고통 받은 시인, 배반당한 여자, 비극적인 문학계의 금발 여주인공의 전형으로 무미건조해진 존재가 되었다. (그녀의 자살의 후광 때문에 그녀의 문학에 대한 진지한 평가가 사라졌다는 의미)

20   ①

자유를 위해 싸웠던 계급이 투쟁에 승리하고 나면 자신들이 스스로 자유의 억압자 편에 서게 된다는 것이 글의 요지이다. 첫 번째 빈칸에는 특권을 가진 '자들에 맞서(against those)' 투쟁하다는 의미가 적절하다. 두 번째 빈칸에는 승리가 획득되고 그들이 '새로운 특권을 가지게 되었을 때' 또는 '새로운 특권이 지켜져야 할 때(new privileges were to be defended)'라는 의미가 들어가는 것이 적절하다.

center around(in, on) ~을 중심으로 하다 shackle n. 구속 bind v. 묶다, 구속하다 the oppressed 억압받은 사람들 class n. 사회 계급 liberation n. 자유 domination n. 지배 as such 그러한 것으로서, 보통 말하는[엄밀한 의미의] 그런 longing n. 갈망 virtually ad. 사실상 at one stage 한 단계에서, 한때에서 side with ~ 편을 들다 privilege n. 특권 withdraw v. 철회하다; 취소하다 approval n. 승인, 찬성 revolutionary a. 혁명적인 sentiment n. 감정, 정서

근대 유럽과 미국의 역사는 그들을 속박하였던 정치적, 경제적, 정신적 속박으로부터 자유를 얻으려는 노력을 중심으로 전개된다. 자유를 위한 투쟁은 지켜야 할 특권을 가진 자들에 맞서 억압받는 자들에 의해, 새로운 자유를 원하는 이들에 의해 전개되었다. 어떤 계급이 지배로부터 자신의 해방을 위해 투쟁할 때, 그 계급은 자신이 보통 말하는 인간의 자유를 위해 투쟁하고 있다고 믿었다. 그래서 어떤 이상에 호소 할 수 있었고, 억압받는 모든 이들 속에 뿌리박한 자유에 대한 갈망에 호소할 수 있었다. 그러나, 길고 사실상 지속적이었던 자유를 위한 투쟁에서 어떤 단계에서 억압에 맞서 싸웠던 계급들이, 승리가 획득되고 새로운 특권이 지켜져야 할 때, 자유의 적들 편에 서게 되었다.

21   ③

문장의 주어인 tensile strength(인장강도: 잡아 늘이는 데 견디는 힘)가 유연성(resilience)을 의미하고 유연성은 곧 극단으로 치우치지 않고 다시 균형을 잡을 수 있는 힘을 의미하므로 첫 번째 빈칸에는 equipoise(균형)가 적절하고, 두 번째 빈칸에는 앞뒤의 triviality와 cynicism처럼 부정적인 의미의 dilettantism(아마추어 예술, 수박 겉핥기의 지식)이 적절하다.

playfulness n. 쾌활함, 장난스러움 piety n. 경건 note n. 특징, 분위기, 어조 predominantly ad. 뛰어나게, 현저히 pious a. 경건한 qualify v. 제한하다 tensile strength 인장강도 fanaticism n. 광신주의 messianism n. 메시아 신앙, 절대적 지지(신념) magnificent a. 훌륭한 mean a. 비열한 intellectualism n. 지성주의 be of the essence of ~에 꼭 있어야 하다 rapport n. (친밀한·공감적인) 관계, 조화 egalitarianism n. 평등주의 linkage n. 결합, 연계 integrity n. 성실, 정직, 고결 equipoise n. 평형; 균형 dilettantism n. 아마추어 예술, 수박 겉핥기의 지식 antagonism n. 적대, 대립 majesty n. 위엄; 장엄

당신은 지성인의 두 가지 특성인 장난스러움과 경건함 사이에 모순이 있지 않는지 의문을 분명 가질 것이다. 당신이 아는 지성인들을 생각해보면, 생각나는 지성인들 중에 일부는 장난스런 분위기가 더 강한 것 같은 사람들이고 또 다른 지성인들은 대단히 경건한 축에 속하는 사람들이다. 그러나 지성인으로서 안정성을 가진 모든 지성인들에게 있어 이 두 가지 특징 각각은 다른 나머지 한 가지 특징에 의해 어느 정도 제한된다. 아마도 지성인의 인장 강

도는 자신의 이 두 가지 측면 사이에 적절한 균형을 유지할 수 있는 능력에 의해 측정될 수 있을 것이다. 저울의 한쪽 끝에서 장난스러움이 지나치면 그것은 시시함을 낳고, 얄팍한 지식을 낳고 냉소주의를 낳고 모든 지속적인 창의적 노력의 좌절을 낳는다. 저울의 다른 쪽 끝에서 경건함이 지나치면 그것은 광신주의를 낳고 절대적 신념을 낳고 도덕적으로 훌륭할 수도 비열할 수도 있지만 어느 쪽이든 지성주의의 방식은 전혀 아닌 그런 생활방식들을 낳는다. 균형을 취하는 것은 지성인에게 꼭 있어야 하는 것이다.

22　　　　　　　　　　　①

"나의 주중은 20세기 기자들보다 더 주말 같은 느낌을 준다(나의 주말은 더 주중 같은 느낌을 준다.)"라는 단서로부터 기자로서 글쓴이에게 주말과 주중이 따로 없다는 사실을 추론할 수 있다. 즉 주중(일)과 주말(여가) 사이에 구멍이 숭숭 뚫려 있어서 구별하기가 어렵다는 사실을 추론할 수 있다.

snugly ad. 아늑하게, 포근하게, 편안하게; 아담하게 leaky a. 새는, 새는 구멍이 있는; 물이 새는 golden nugget 금괴 lede n. (신조어) (신문 등) 해당 페이지에서 가장 먼저 눈에 띄는 곳에 배치한 주요 소식 downtime n. 휴지 시간, 중단 시간 theoretically ad. 이론적으로, 이론상 surface v. 표면에 나타나다; 나타나다 porous a. 구멍이 있는, 구멍이 많은

나의 직업은 이러한 범주에 꼭 들어맞는다. 글쓰기는 새기 쉬운 일이다. 글쓰기 일과 여가의 경계 사이에는 항상 구멍이 숭숭 뚫려 있는 새는 구멍이 있다. 내가 트위터에 접속할 때 혹은 일요일 아침에 뉴스를 볼 때, 나는 통찰력이라는 금괴를 빛내는 일을 계획하고 있는 것일까, 아니면 정신 건강을 위한 휴식을 취하고 있는 것일까, 혹은 그사이 어딘가에 있는 것일까? 이것은 말하기 어려운 것이고, 때때로 나는 심지어 (그것에 대해) 알지도 못한다. 내가 읽은 소설이 기사의 주요 부분이 될 수 있다. 내 책상 위에 역사책이 (신문)칼럼에 영감을 불어넣어 줄 수 있다. 논픽션 저널리즘의 범위는 무한하기 때문에 내 휴식시간의 매 순간에 이론적으로는 이야기가 될 수 있는 생각이나 두서없는 논평을 떠올릴 수 있다. 그 결과, 나의 주중은 20세기 기자들보다 더 주말 같은 느낌을 준다.(나의 주말은 더 주중 같은 느낌을 준다.)

23　　　　　　　　　　　②

난민처리 문제를 놓고 주교와 정치가 사이에 이견이 있다는 진술로부터 정답을 추론할 수 있다.

parish n. 교구 prelate n. 고위성직자 accommodate v. ~에 편의를 도모하다; 수용하다 refugee n. 피난자, 난민 spar v. 말다툼하다 bishop n. 주교 barbed a. 가시 있는; 신랄한 xenophobic a. 외국인 혐오증의 hawk v. 행상하다; 팔러 다니다 cantankerous a. 성미가 고약한; 잘 싸우는 reconciliation n. 조정; 화해 conflicting a. 충돌하는, 일치하지 않는

최근 들어 교황은 유럽의 모든 교구와 종교 공동체를 향해 난민 가족을 수용해줄 것을 촉구하고 있다. 그러나 이탈리아의 모든 가톨릭 교인들과 그들의 정치적 대표가 될 사람들이 교황의 말에 동의하는 것은 아니다. 지난 몇 주 동안 선임 고위 성직자와 우파의 떠오르는 정치인 사이에 다툼에 가까운 고약한 종류의 공개적인 의견교환이 있었다. the Northern League party의 지도자이자 새롭게 떠오르고 있는 이탈리아 민족주의의 옹호자인 Matteo

Salvini는 이탈리아 주교회의 비서인 Nunzio Galantino를 상대로 언쟁을 벌였다. 반(反)이민 고정관념을 신랄하게 논박하면서 Galantino주교는 외국인 혐오적인 감정을 이용하는 정치가들 스스로가 가치 없는 장신구들을 팔러 다니는 거리의 행상이나 돌아다니는 영업사원이라고 말했다. 이에 대해 Salvini씨는 평범하고 오류에 빠지기 쉬운 가톨릭 신도로서 자신에게 최소한 공산주의인 주교만큼 자신도 솔직하게 말할 자격이 있다고 말했다. 그는 이어서 교회 안에 많은 사람들이 이탈리아인의 이익을 가장 우선시하는 그의 감정에 공감하고 있다는 사실도 알고 있다고 말했다.

24　　　　　　　　　　　③

끝에서 네 번째 문장에서 시는 추상하지 않는다고 했는데 첫 문장에서 우리는 추상의 세계에서 자랐다고 했으므로 그런 우리에게는 시가 이해되지 않는 괴상한 개념일 것이다. 따라서 첫 번째 빈칸에는 fanciful(괴상한)이 적절하다. 마지막 문장에서 우리가 알 수 있는 세계는 논리적으로 분석하는(analyzing) 지성이 추상하는 세계라 했으므로 두 번째 빈칸에는 analyzing에 반대되며 시와 예술에 적절한 지성을 나타내는 imaginative가 적절하다.

abstraction n. 추상 abstract v. 추상하다 dissolve v. 용해시키다 analyze v. 분석하다, 분해하다 intellect n. 지성, 지능 humdrum a. 평범한, 단조로운, 지루한 plausible a. (이유·구실 따위가) 그럴 듯한, 정말 같은 unbiased a. 편견 없는

과학이 우리를 위해 준비해놓은 추상의 세계에서 그리고 그 세계가 만들어내는 종류의 학교, 즉 거의 모든 가르침이 추상의 가르침인 학교에서 자라난 우리들 대부분에게는 지식으로서의 시, 지식으로서의 예술이라는 개념은 괴상한 개념이다. 추상에 의한 지식을 우리는 이해한다. 과학은 사과에서 사과에 대한 개념들을 추상할 수 있다. 그것은 그런 개념들을 조직하여 사과에 대한 지식으로 만들어낼 수 있다. 그러고 나서 그것은 그 지식을 우리 머리에 집어넣을 수 있다. 어쩌면 우리 머리도 추상이니까. 그러나 우리가 알기로 시는 추상하지 않는다. 시는 사물을 사물대로 보여준다. 그리고 사물을 있는 그대로 아는 것, 사과를 사과로 아는 것이 가능해야 한다는 것 이것을 우리는 이해하지 못한다. 우리가 알 수 있는 전부란 분석하는 지성이 용해시켜 추상화하는 세계이지, 상상력 풍부한 지성이 세계 그 자체로 구성해내는 세계가 아니다.

25　　　　　　　　　　　③

소설을 각색한 영화가 많은 비평을 받고 있지만, 대중들에게 원작에 대한 새롭고 재미있는 기회를 준다고 했다. 그리고 빈칸 앞에서 아주 형편이 없는 영화라고 할지라도 원작을 대중의 의식 속에 넣을 수 있는 특징을 갖고 있다고 했다. 결국 원작을 각색한 영화는 그 자체로 의미가 있으므로 비평을 하는 것이 타당하지 않다는 ③이 빈칸에 적절하다.

canonical a. (성경이) 정본에 속하는; (문학 작품이) 고전으로 여겨지는 high horse 거만한 태도 foot on ~에 발을 딛다[발을 들여놓다] glossy a. (겉보기에) 화려한, 윤이 나는 shoehorn v. 좁은 장소로 밀어넣다[쑤셔넣다] adaptation n. 적응; 순응; 개작(改作) depraved a. 타락한, 부패한 critical reception 비평 irrelevant a. 무관한

감동적인 소설을 접해보는 것만큼이나 개인적인 예술적 경험은 거의 없다. 그래서 인기가 많은 책을 대중 시장을 위한 영화로 각색하는 것에 대해 배신감을 느끼는 것은 이해하기 쉬운 일이다. 이로 인해 생기게 되는 비판은 고전 문학작품의 경우에 대체로 정당화된다. 그러나 우리는 원작에 대한 경험의 진실성을 강화하려는 (솔직히 이기적인) 필요 이외에 고려해야 할 것들이 더 있다. 귀중한 문학작품을 발견할 수 있는 새롭고 재밌을 수도 있는 기회가 사람들에게 주어지며 이것은 우리의 지적 오만함에 대한 우리의 입장보다 훨씬 더 중요한 가능성이다. 레오 톨스토이(Leo Tolstoi)가 윙크하는 이미지가 담긴 번쩍거리는 표지로 사람들의 이목을 끌 수 있다면 그렇게 인쇄를 하는 것이 좋다. 심지어 아주 형편없이 각색된 영화라고 할지라도 원작을 대중의 의식 속에 넣을 수 있는 독특한 특징이 있기 때문이다. 그런 기회의 진정한 가치를 모르는 것이 훨씬 더 반(反)지성적 행위이다. 여기서 영화 자체에 대한 비평은 타당하지 않다.

MEMO

MEMO

MEMO

MEMO

MEMO